PATERNOSTER BIBLICAL MONOGRAPHS

Word-Order Variation in Biblical Hebrew Poetry

Differentiating Pragmatics and Poetics

PATERNOSTER BIBLICAL MONOGRAPHS

*A complete listing of all titles in this series
appears at the close of this book*

PATERNOSTER BIBLICAL MONOGRAPHS

Word-Order Variation in Biblical Hebrew Poetry

Differentiating Pragmatics and Poetics

Nicholas P. Lunn

Foreword by Jean-Marc Heimerdinger

Eugene, Oregon

Wipf and Stock Publishers
199 W 8th Ave, Suite 3
Eugene, OR 97401

Word-Order Variation in Biblical Hebrew Poetry
Differentiating Progmatics and Poetics
By Lunn, Nicholas P.
Copyright©2006 Paternoster
ISBN 13: 978-1-59752-959-4
ISBN: 1-59752-959-1
Publication date 10/18/2006
Previously published by Paternoster, 2006

This Edition reprinted by Wipf and Stock Publishers
by arrangement with Paternoster

PATERNOSTER BIBLICAL MONOGRAPHS

Series Preface

One of the major objectives of Paternoster is to serve biblical scholarship by providing a channel for the publication of theses and other monographs of high quality at affordable prices. Paternoster stands within the broad evangelical tradition of Christianity. Our authors would describe themselves as Christians who recognise the authority of the Bible, maintain the centrality of the gospel message and assent to the classical credal statements of Christian belief. There is diversity within this constituency; advances in scholarship are possible only if there is freedom for frank debate on controversial issues and for the publication of new and sometimes provocative proposals. What is offered in this series is the best of writing by committed Christians who are concerned to develop well-founded biblical scholarship in a spirit of loyalty to the historic faith.

Series Editors

I. Howard Marshall, Honorary Research Professor of New Testament, University of Aberdeen, Scotland, UK

Richard J. Bauckham, Professor of New Testament Studies and Bishop Wardlaw Professor, University of St Andrews, Scotland, UK

Craig Blomberg, Distinguished Professor of New Testament, Denver Seminary, Colorado, USA

Robert P. Gordon, Regius Professor of Hebrew, University of Cambridge, UK

Tremper Longman III, Robert H. Gundry Professor and Chair of the Department of Biblical Studies, Westmont College, Santa Barbara, California, USA

*This book is dedicated to translators
of the Bible throughout the world*

Contents

Foreword		xv
Preface		xvii
Abbreviations		xix
Linguistic Notation		xxi

Chapter 1
The Problem of Word Order in Biblical Hebrew Poetry — 1
1.1 Differences between Biblical Hebrew Poetry and Prose — 1
1.2 Constituent Order in Biblical Hebrew — 4
1.3 The Nature of the Problem — 5
1.4 The Extent of the Problem — 6
1.5 A Linguistic Approach to a Solution — 9
1.6 The Organisation of the Book — 9
1.7 The Corpus of Selected Data — 10

Chapter 2
A Description of the Basic Units of Hebrew Poetry — 11
2.1 The Colon — 11
2.1.1 *Terminology* — 11
2.1.2 *The Poetic Colon in Relation to the Grammatical Clause* — 12
2.1.3 *The Relative Frequency of Colon Structures* — 13
2.2 Parallelism in Biblical Hebrew Poetry — 14
2.2.1 *The Character of Parallelism* — 14
2.2.2 *Additional Features of Parallelism* — 18
    (a) GAPPING — 18
    (b) EMBEDDING — 19
    (c) EXTENDING — 20

2.2.3	The Rhetorical Function of Parallelism	20
2.3	Intercolon Relations	21
2.4	Summary	26

Chapter 3
Pragmatic Factors Influencing Word Order in Biblical Hebrew 27

3.1	Previous Considerations of Word Order in Biblical Hebrew	27
3.2	The Theory of Information Structure	29
3.3	Lambrecht's *Information Structure and Sentence Form*	32
3.3.1	*Topic and Activation State*	33
3.3.2	*Focus, Assertion and Presupposition*	35
3.3.3	*The Three Focus Structures*	36
	(a) PREDICATE FOCUS	37
	(b) ARGUMENT FOCUS	38
	(c) SENTENCE FOCUS	39
3.4	Information Structure and Biblical Hebrew	41
3.4.1	*The Three Focus Structures in Hebrew Narrative*	41
	(a) PREDICATE FOCUS	41
	(b) ARGUMENT FOCUS	44
	(c) SENTENCE FOCUS	45
3.4.2	*Focus Particles and Focus Categories*	47
	(a) CONTRASTING FOCUS	48
	(b) PARALLEL FOCUS	48
	(c) REPLACING FOCUS	50
	(d) RESTRICTING FOCUS	50
	(e) EXPANDING FOCUS	52
	(f) SELECTING FOCUS	53
	(g) SPECIFYING FOCUS	53
3.4.3	*Extraposition*	54
3.5	Unmarked Sentence-Initial Phrases of Setting	55
3.6	Summary	59

Chapter 4
Pragmatic Markedness in Poetic Cola: (1) Non-Parallel Lines 61

4.1	Quotation of Marked Clauses from Prose within Poetry	61
4.2	Similarity of Marked Structures in Prose and Poetry	63
4.2.1	*Marked Clauses with Focus Particles*	64
	(a) EXPANDING FOCUS WITH גַּם	64
	(b) EXPANDING FOCUS WITH אַף	67

	(c) RESTRICTING FOCUS WITH רַק	69
	(d) RESTRICTING FOCUS WITH אַךְ	70
4.2.2	*Marked Clauses without Focus Particles*	71
	(a) SPECIFYING FOCUS	72
	(b) REPLACING FOCUS	73
	(c) CONTRASTING RELATIONSHIPS	75
4.2.3	*Sentence-Focus Clauses*	79
	(a) EVENT-REPORTING CLAUSES	79
	(b) PRESENTATIONAL CLAUSES	82
4.2.4	*Extraposed Constructions*	82
4.2.5	*Doubly Marked Clauses*	84
4.3	Implications of Allo-Clauses in Poetic Texts	86
4.4	The Use of Independent Pronouns	92
4.5	Summary	94

Chapter 5
Defamiliarised Word Order in Parallel Lines 95

5.1	The Order of Clause Constituents in Parallel B-Lines	95
5.2	Attempted Pragmatic Interpretations of Parallel B-Lines	97
5.2.1	*Buth on Psalm 51*	97
5.2.2	*Shimasaki on Parallel Constructions*	102
5.2.3	*Parallel Lines and Parallel Focus*	104
5.3	Poetically Defamiliarised Word Order	105
5.3.1	*Poetic Freedom in Parallel Lines*	105
5.3.2	*Parallel Lines in Other Languages*	107
5.3.3	*The Form of Reordering in Parallel Lines*	107
	(a) TWO-PART CHIASMUS	107
	(b) THREE-PART CHIASMUS	107
	(c) PARTIAL CHIASMUS	108
	(d) NON-CHIASTIC REORDERING	108
5.3.4	*The Notion of Symmetry*	109
5.3.5	*A Choice of Variables*	109
5.4	The Labelling of Colon-Types and the Description of Parallelisms	110
5.5	Pattern Formation Involving Defamiliar Cola	112
5.6	The Environment and Distribution of Defamiliar Cola	114
5.7	The Priority of the A-Line	115
5.7.1	*Dependence in Topical Reference*	116
5.7.2	*Dependence in Gapping*	116

5.7.3	*Dependence in Gender Parallelism*	117
5.7.4	*Dependence in Tense-Shifting*	117
5.7.5	*Pragmatic Dependence*	118
5.8	Summary	119

Chapter 6
Distinguishing Marked and Defamiliar Word Order   121

6.1	The Priority of Environment over Form	121
6.2	Resolving Complex Cases	122
6.3	Pitch Prominence in Distinguishing Marked from Defamiliar	124
6.4	Contrast and Chiasmus	127
6.5	Summary	129

Chapter 7
Pragmatic Markedness in Poetic Cola: (2) Parallel Lines   131

7.1	Constraint upon Pragmatic Marking in Parallelisms	131
7.2	Examples of Pragmatic Marking in Parallelisms	132
7.2.1	*Two Cola in Parallelism*	132
	(a) SV//SV	132
	(b) OV//OV	133
	(c) MV//MV	134
7.2.2	*Two Bicola in Parallelism*	135
7.2.3	*Two Preverbal Elements in Parallelism*	136
7.2.4	*Parallelism with Focus Particles*	138
7.2.5	*Parallelism with Extraposition*	140
7.2.6	*Parallelism with Gapping*	141
7.2.7	*Extended Parallelism*	144
	(a) IDENTICAL ORDERING	144
	(b) MEDIAL VARIATION	145
	(c) FINAL VARIATION	148
7.3	The Co-Occurrence of Pragmatic Marking and Poetic Defamiliarisation	150
7.4	Exceptions to the Constraint	151
7.4.1	*Phrases of Setting*	151
	(a) TEMPORAL	151
	(b) SPATIAL	152
7.4.2	*Pronominal Forms*	152
	(a) INDEPENDENT PRONOMINAL SUBJECT	153
	(b) INDEPENDENT PRONOMINAL OBJECT	153

		(c) Pronominal Prepositional Phrase	154
7.5		Reason for the Constraints	155
7.6		Summary	156

Chapter 8
Discourse Functions of Unusual Colon Arrangements — 159

8.1		Introduction: Reversal of the Norm	159
8.2		Rare Parallel Constructions in Specific Distribution	159
8.2.1		*DEF-Initial Parallelisms*	160
		(a) DEF//CAN	160
		(b) DEF//DEF	176
		(c) DEF//Gap	180
		(d) DEF//Nom	182
8.2.2		*MKD-Initial Parallelisms*	182
		(a) MKD//CAN	182
		(b) MKD//DEF	184
		(c) MKD//Gap	187
8.2.3		*Gap-Initial Parallelisms*	188
		(a) Gap//DEF	188
		(b) Gap//MKD	189
		(c) Gap//CAN	189
8.3		Defamiliar Cola in Non-Parallelisms	190
8.4		The Noetic Effect of Unusual Patterns	192
8.5		Summary	193

Chapter 9
Application: Standard and Difficult Texts — 195

9.1	Standard Texts	195
9.1.1	*Psalm 1*	195
9.1.2	*Psalm 103*	200
9.1.3	*Job 12*	208
9.1.4	*Song of Songs 1*	218
9.1.5	*Numbers 23:7–10*	225
9.1.6	*Conclusions*	229
9.2	Potential Difficulties	231
9.2.1	*Incorrect Verse Division*	231
9.2.2	*Incorrect Syntactic Analysis*	232
9.2.3	*Implicit Relativizer*	233
9.2.4	*Unrecognised Embedded Parallelism*	234

9.2.5	*Unrecognised Extended Parallelism*	235
9.2.6	*Textual Variant*	238
9.3	Difficult Texts	239
9.3.1	*Psalm 44:2–9*	239
9.3.2	*Isaiah 42:1–4*	246
9.3.3	*Isaiah 60:1–3*	250
9.4	Summary	254

Chapter 10
Alternative Approaches: Rosenbaum and Gross — 255

10.1	General Observations	255
10.2	Rosenbaum's *Word-Order Variation in Isaiah 40–55*	256
10.2.1	*Examples Relating to Pragmatic Factors*	257
10.2.2	*Examples Relating to Poetic Factors*	264
10.2.3	*Conclusions*	267
10.3	Gross' *Doppelt besetztes Vorfeld*	268
10.3.1	*Examples*	270
10.3.2	*Conclusions*	273
10.4	Summary	273

Chapter 11
Conclusions — 275

11.1	Summary of Findings	275
11.2	Relative Frequency of Colon-Types	276
11.3	For Further Study	279
11.4	Concluding Remarks	280

Bibliography — 281

Appendix 1: Statistical Comparison of Word Order in Biblical Hebrew Prose and Poetry — 291

Appendix 2: The Database — 293

Scripture Index — 365

Author Index — 371

FOREWORD

In the study of an ancient language such as Biblical Hebrew it is easy to identify and list grammatical units and constructions but far more complicated to discover and explain adequately the functions or communicative roles such patterns play. This book sets a standard in its balance between structural analysis and functional explanations. It is an illuminating study of word order in the verbal clause of Biblical Hebrew poetry.

Biblical Hebrew is a Verb-Subject-Object language, but the verbal clause may deviate from this default order, both in prose and poetry, and various pragmatic or syntactic explanations have been provided by scholars to explain such changes.

Lunn first observes that the departure from Verb-Subject-Object word order in poetic texts statistically occurs more than twice as much as in narrative. He goes on to explain that whereas some clauses can be elucidated pragmatically by using a theory of information structure, this turns out to be impossible with another set of clauses. In the case of these latter, their variable patterns have to be explained by a function that Lunn calls 'poetical defamiliarisation'. This is one of Lunn's many important insights. He makes a fundamental distinction, upon objective grounds, between linguistically motivated variation and variation resulting from poetic defamiliarisation, thus allowing a more precise definition at clause level of the linguistic building blocks that constitute the poetic line. He also establishes that behind the parallelisms of Biblical Hebrew poetry lies a clearly identifiable and coherent system of invariants and variables encoded in clauses through word order as well as a binary relation between two or more contiguous cola. The system of invariants and variables is such that the poet's selection in the second line of a parallelism may be constrained as a result of his selection in the first.

This description, based on a careful analysis of an extensive amount of data, not only enables us to understand how the writers of poetry could combine the clauses in the construction of parallelisms, but also how these clauses could be given specific discourse functions in a poem. Lunn's treatment of the topic of 'poetic function' is probably the most innovative and comprehensive today and this book will become an automatic point of reference in the continuing effort to understand ancient Hebrew poetry. It presents an entirely fresh perspective on the linguistic construction of the poetical line, and many of Lunn's conclusions will certainly necessitate and lead to a re-evaluation of a number of current conceptions and descriptions of Biblical poetry. Amongst others, it will have an important impact on the study of tense-shifting and our understanding of the temporal meaning of verbal forms in poetry.

This is a very important book whose stimulating insights probe into the heart of Biblical Hebrew poetry. It is sure to provoke lively interest and open up the subject to wider debate. It is a 'must-read' for the serious student of Biblical Hebrew poetry, the exegete, and the Bible translator.

Dr. Jean-Marc Heimerdinger
London School of Theology

Preface

One of my great joys is to read the poetic passages of the Old Testament in the original Hebrew. It was this love for the poetry of Scripture that led to me choosing the subject of the present work. This portion of the Bible has been the object of much theological and literary study, but as yet little of a truly linguistic nature has been done on it. The present work will perhaps stimulate more of the latter.

The substance of this book is my PhD thesis, completed at the London School of Theology in 2004. I was privileged to have as my supervisor Dr. Jean-Marc Heimerdinger, whose own work on topic and focus in Hebrew narrative gave impetus to the present study. His guidance and constructive criticism were invaluable in keeping my research on track and in my seeing it through to completion.

Throughout the time of my research there were many to whom I am indebted for their assistance. Among these are my colleagues in Wycliffe Bible Translators (SIL), Bible Translation & Literacy (Kenya), and Wycliffe Associates (UK). I am especially obliged to the latter for their help in bibliographical and technical matters. Those who I would like to particularly thank for their indispensable help are Nick Bailey, and Derek Cheeseman together with his team of helpers. Deserving of special mention is Katy Barnwell, who first pointed me in the direction of doctoral studies. I am also particularly grateful for the financial support provided by SIL, Dallas.

I wish to express my appreciation for the encouragement of friends at Kileleshwa Community Church (Nairobi) and Purley Baptist Church (UK) during the time of my research.

I would also like to acknowledge the help of my wife Amanda, Christine Gaish, and Andrew Coleman, in the final stages of preparing the text for publication.

A note of gratitude is due to Paternoster for their interest in this work, and for those members of the Paternoster team who provided me with the necessary advice and guidance in the process of transforming it from a thesis into book form.

Last, but certainly not least, I want to thank Amanda, Matthew, and Benjamin for their understanding and patience while my devotion to Hebrew poetry threatened to usurp my devotion as a husband and father.

It is my prayer that this book, under the blessing of God, will be a useful tool for those engaged in translating, teaching, and preaching the Word of God, and that it will glorify Him who inspired the exalted poetry of the Hebrew Scriptures.

> 'Not to us, O LORD, not to us but to your name be the glory,
> because of your love and faithfulness' (Ps. 115:1)

Nicholas Lunn
December 2005

Abbreviations

AB	Anchor Bible
AOTC	Apollos Old Testament Commentary
ASV	American Standard Version
AV	Authorised Version
BBR	*Bulletin for Biblical Research*
BHS	Biblia hebraica stuttgartensia
BT	*The Bible Translator*
CBQ	*Catholic Biblical Quarterly*
CEV	Contemporary English Version
DCH	*Dictionary of Classical Hebrew*
ESV	English Standard Version
fn	footnote
HALOT	*Hebrew and Aramaic Lexicon of the Old Testament*
HTR	*Harvard Theological Review*
HUCA	*Hebrew Union College Annual*
JANES	*Journal of the Ancient Near Eastern Society*
JBL	*Journal of Biblical Literature*
JNSL	*Journal of Northwest Semitic Languages*
JOTT	*Journal of Translation and Textlinguistics*
JQR	*Jewish Quarterly Review*
JSOT	*Journal for the Study of the Old Testament*
JSS	*Journal of Semitic Studies*
LXX	Septuagint
MSS	manuscripts
MT	Masoretic Text
NAC	New American Commentary
NASB	New American Standard Bible
NCB	New Century Bible
NCV	New Century Version
NICOT	New International Commentary on the Old Testament
NIDOTTE	*New International Dictionary of Old Testament Theology and Exegesis*
NIV	New International Version
NJB	New Jerusalem Bible

NJPS	New Jewish Publication Society Tanakh (The Holy Scriptures)
NKJV	New King James Version
NLT	New Living Translation
NRSV	New Revised Standard Version
OTL	Old Testament Library
OPTAT	*Occasional Papers in Translation and Textlinguistics* (SIL)
REB	Revised English Bible
SBL	Society of Biblical Literature
SIL	Summer Institute of Linguistics (Wycliffe Bible Translators)
SOAS	School of Oriental and African Studies
START	*Select Technical Articles Related to Translation* (SIL)
Syr	Syriac (Peshitta)
Targ	Targum
TEV	Today's English Versions (Good News Bible)
TOTC	Tyndale Old Testament Commentary
TWOT	*Theological Wordbook of the Old Testament*
UBS	United Bible Societies
VT	*Vetus Testamentum*
Vulg	Vulgate
WBC	Word Biblical Commentary
ZAH	*Zeitschrift für Althebraistik*
ZAW	*Zeitschrift für die alttestamentliche Wissenschaft*
[דָּבָר]	square brackets around Hebrew denote Ketib/Qere variant in MT

Linguistic Notation

Adj	adjective
Adv	adverb
Comp	complement
C	conjunction
DO	direct object
E	existential particle (יֵשׁ 'there is/are')
E^{Ng}	negative existential particle (אֵין 'there is/are not')
Exc	exclamative expression (e.g., אָח 'alas')
Ext	extraposed element
H	attention-getting particle (הֵן / הִנֵּה)
Impv	imperative
Inf	infinitive/infinitival clause
IO	indirect object
M	clause modifier (PP or Adv)
Ng	negative
NP	noun phrase
NP[Su]	subject noun phrase
NP[Ext]	extraposed noun phrase
NP[DO]	object noun phrase
NP[IO]	indirect object noun phrase
O	object
-o	object pronominal suffix
Pn	pronoun
Pn[Su]	independent subject pronoun
Pn[DO]	independent object pronoun
PP	prepositional phrase
P	particle
Ptcp	participial clause
Q	interrogative
R	relative pronoun
[R]	implicit relative pronoun
S	subject
-s	subject pronominal suffix
S^{Pn}	independent pronominal subject

S^{Pt}	participle functioning as subject
V	verb
V^{Ng}	negated verb
V^{Pt}	participial predicate (functioning as verb)
Voc	vocative
VP	verb phrase
w-	*wāw* (Hebrew copula)
/	a major pause in a poetic line
//	denotes the relationship of poetic parallelism

CHAPTER 1

The Problem of Word Order in Biblical Hebrew Poetry

1.1 Differences between Biblical Hebrew Poetry and Prose

Everyone acquainted with the Hebrew Bible will be aware how the language of its poetry has an altogether different character from that of its prose. In the area of grammar features such as the less frequent usage of the definite article ה, the object marker את, and the relative pronoun readily come to mind as being characteristic of the poetic genre. Other elements common to prose, such as the ubiquitous *wayyiqtol* verb-form at the beginning of the clause, rarely make an appearance. Regarding vocabulary there is likewise a notable difference – unfamiliar words and forms abound in poetry which are not to be found in prose. Sappan goes so far as to say that 'The language of Biblical Poetry has a sufficient number of distinctive features both in the grammar and the lexicon, to justify considering it as a special dialect of Biblical Hebrew, "Dialectus Poetica" ... as distinct from the ordinary ("standard") language of Biblical prose'.[1] Though this may be overstating the case, the difference between the two genres must be taken as a significant one,[2] and one of such a degree that the particular character of the poetic form is a potential cause of difficulty for the interpreter.[3]

Watson, in his classic work on Hebrew poetry, lists no less than nineteen characteristics, or 'indicators', as he terms them, of the poetic genre.[4] The major items he identifies are: established line-forms, ellipsis, unusual vocabulary, conciseness, unusual word-order, archaisms, metre and rhythm, regularity and symmetry, parallelism of various forms, word-pairs, chiastic

---

1   R. Sappan, *The Typical Features of the Syntax of Biblical Poetry in its Classical Period* (Jerusalem: Kiryat-Sefer, 1981), p. IV.
2   S. A. Geller says, 'all that is required of "poetry" to establish its independence as a concept for Biblical literature is that it be *perceived* to differ significantly from "prose"', 'Theory and Method in the Study of Biblical Poetry', *JQR 73.1* (1982), pp. 66–67.
3   A. Niccacci declares, 'That analysing Biblical Hebrew Poetry is not an easy task needs no proof', 'Analysing Biblical Hebrew Poetry', *JSOT 74* (1997), p. 77.
4   W. G. E. Watson, *Classical Hebrew Poetry* (Sheffield: Sheffield Academic Press, 1986), pp. 46–47.

patterns, repetition, rhyme and other sound patterns. Besides these, Watson observes, there is a noticeable scarcity of many elements typical of prose.

All these indicators appearing in the poetic text result in what linguists refer to as 'defamiliarisation' of the language, a concept first given expression by Victor Shklovsky of the Russian formalist school.[5] By the defamiliarisation of the language is meant the device of 'making it strange and the device of impeded form which augments the difficulty and duration of perception, since the process of perception in art is an end in itself, and is supposed to be prolonged'.[6] It is this distinctiveness that gives the poetic literature its particular impact. Its purpose is not simply to communicate information but to impress the reader/listener as an art form. This it does through the departure from those familiar forms and patterns that constitute the normal means of communication. A significant shift, therefore, occurs in poetry from the norms of the regular register of language to its own particular conventions. Some of these poetic conventions may from a cross-linguistic perspective be universal or commonplace, while others may be language specific. These elements, such as those listed by Watson for Hebrew, considered collectively, are a means of drawing attention to the special form of the text, that is, marking it as poetry.[7] Throughout this study the term 'defamiliarised' will be employed to denote these unusual elements of the poetic genre.[8]

The various defamiliarised features characteristic of Hebrew poetry can be classified according to the level of language that they affect. Certain of these elements relate to sound, some to words, some to the form of words, and others to the arrangement of words.[9] We are able, therefore, to posit a four-fold classification of poetic features on the basis of phonological, lexical, morphological, and syntactic considerations. We may also observe that lexical and morphological defamiliarisation involves substitution at a *paradigmatic* level, whereas syntactic defamiliarisation resorts to *syntagmatic*

---

5 L. Matejka and K. Pomorska, *Readings in Russian Poetics: Formalist and Structuralist Views* (Cambridge, Massachusetts: MIT Press, 1971), p. 12. Also known as 'foregrounding', see Van Peer, in R. E. Asher (ed.), *Encyclopedia of Language and Linguistics*, (Oxford: Pergaman Press, 1994), vol. 3, pp. 1272–75.

6 Matejka and Pomorska, *Readings in Russian Poetics*, quoting Shklovsky.

7 N. Fabb, *Linguistics and Literature: Language in the Verbal Arts of the World* (Oxford: Blackwell, 1997), p. 144. These features have what Roman Jakobson refers to as 'poetic function', *Language in Literature* (Cambridge, Massachusetts: Harvard University Press, 1987), pp. 69–70.

8 Since 'foregrounding' (see fn. 5 above) is also used in modern discourse analysis with a different meaning, this term is avoided in the present study.

9 The classification offered here differs from that of Watson (*Classical Hebrew Poetry*, p. 47. Watson's own classification is according to structure, sound, and a rather vague and general class which he terms 'broad', consisting of such diverse features as syntax, metre, vocabulary, and style.

variation. The former two concern the choice of one word over another or one form over another,[10] the latter with the organisation of words in a particular way. It is with this last category that this study will be concerned.

Irregular word order is a feature of Old Testament poetry noted by many. 'Unusual word-order' appears as number 5 on Watson's list of poetic indicators.[11] Sappan gives word order first in his list of syntactic features of Biblical Hebrew poetry,[12] and Harman too, in his introduction to the Psalms, places variation of the normal word order, or 'non-predictable word order', as he labels it, as the first item in his discussion of the major characteristics of the genre.[13] Other scholars affirm the prominence of this feature. Statements such as the following are typical: 'the regular order of main words ... is not always followed',[14] 'word order ... differs markedly from that in prose usage',[15] and 'the poet may ... invert the usual word order'.[16] Scholars of Hebrew poetry concur, therefore, that deviation from normal word order contributes significantly to giving this poetry its particular character.

Yet despite the fact that this feature of Hebrew poetry has often been noted in the various commentaries and introductions, the authors concerned generally do not themselves go to any great lengths to account for it. Invariably in such works it is parallelism and metre that receive most attention.[17] Perhaps it is assumed that the fact that one is dealing with poetry is itself a sufficient explanation for the irregularity of word order. If poetic licence can extend to the choice of vocabulary and the non-usage of various forms and particles featuring regularly in prose discourse, then perhaps poetic licence can also be extended to word order.[18] This assumption is only partially correct. An adequate account of word-order variation in Hebrew poetry, as shall be demonstrated, will require more than merely appealing to poetic licence.

---

10 For example, in Hebrew poetry, the verb הָבָה (Ps. 29:1) for נָתַן ('give'), or the poetic form לָמוֹ (Ps. 2:4) for the usual לָהֶם ('to/for them').
11 Watson, *Classical Hebrew Poetry*, p. 46.
12 Sappan, *Typical Features of the Syntax of Biblical Poetry*, p. IV.
13 A. Harman, *Psalms* (Fearn, Scotland: Christian Focus Publications, 1998), pp. 11–12.
14 E. R. Wendland, *Analyzing the Psalms*, (Dallas, Texas: SIL, 1998), p. 156.
15 E. S. Gerstenberger, *Forms of Old Testament Literature,* vol. 14, Psalms, Part 1 (Grand Rapids, Michigan: Eerdmans, 1988), p. 34.
16 W. D. Reyburn, *A Handbook on the Book of Job* (New York: UBS, 1992), p. 9.
17 As, for example, P. C. Craigie, *Psalms 1–50*, WBC (Waco, Texas: Word Books, 1983), pp. 36–38; and J. E. Hartley, *The Book of Job*, NICOT (Grand Rapids, Michigan: Eerdmans, 1988), pp. 33–35. E. Dhorme, *A Commentary on the Book of Job* (Nashville, Tennessee: Thomas Nelson, 1984), pp. clxxx–clxxxix, deals exclusively with metre, as does M. H. Pope in *The Song of Songs*, AB (New York: Doubleday, 1977), pp. 37–40.
18 Cf. the comments of L. Zogbo and E. R. Wendland, *Hebrew Poetry in the Bible: A Guide for Understanding and Translating* (New York: UBS, 2000), p. 95.

1.2 Constituent Order in Biblical Hebrew

Biblical Hebrew has been commonly classified as a VSO (Verb–Subject–Object) language.[19] This, to use the words of Muraoka, is the 'statistically dominant and unmarked word-order' of the verbal clause.[20] The term 'unmarked' is often used to describe the normal order of clause constituents in a language, any deviation from which may be called 'marked'.[21] Some linguists, however, prefer the positive term 'canonical'[22] to describe the predominant order of clause constituents, and it is this word that will be employed throughout the present work. We will reserve the description 'marked' to refer to those instances of deviant word order which can only be accounted for in strictly linguistic terms. Such markedness, as shall be explained, may have some particular function at that level of language linguists refer to as 'pragmatic',[23] or may have an important role at the level of the discourse.

While the constituent order found in the narrative sections of the Old Testament most frequently follows the VSO pattern, a significant proportion of clauses do not.[24] This shows that though VSO is canonical for Biblical Hebrew, it is by no means obligatory. Variations of the basic constituent order are syntactically permissible, resulting in a whole range

---

19 For example, R. J. Williams, *Hebrew Syntax: An Outline* (Toronto: University of Toronto Press, 1976), §572; B. K. Waltke and M. P. O'Connor, *An Introduction to Biblical Hebrew Syntax* (Winona Lake, Indiana: Eisenbrauns, 1990), p. 635; C. H. J. van der Merwe, J. A. Naudé, and J. H. Kroeze, *A Biblical Hebrew Reference Grammar* (Sheffield: Sheffield Academic Press, 1999), p. 336; cf. B. L. Bandstra, 'Word Order and Emphasis in Biblical Hebrew Narrative: Syntactic Observations on Genesis 22 from a Discourse Perspective', in W. R. Bodine (ed.), *Linguistics and Biblical Hebrew* (Winona Lake, Indiana: Eisenbrauns, 1992), p. 115, who says, 'Biblical Hebrew is a verb-first language. When an explicit subject is present, the expected and most frequent order of constituents in narrative verbal clauses is V–S–O'. R. E. Longacre, a linguist, characterises Biblical Hebrew as 'strongly VSO', 'Left Shifts in Strongly VSO Languages', in P. Downing and M. Noonan (eds.), *Word Order in Discourse* (Amsterdam/Philadelphia: John Benjamin's Publishing, 1995), p. 332.
20 P. Joüon and T. Muraoka, *A Grammar of Biblical Hebrew*, Part 3: Syntax (Rome: Biblical Institute Press, 1991), §155k.
21 S. A. Groom, *Linguistic Analysis of Biblical Hebrew* (Carlisle, Cumbria: Paternoster, 2003), p. 149.
22 For example, K. Lambrecht, *Information Structure and Sentence Form: Topic, focus and the mental representations of discourse referents* (Cambridge: Cambridge University Press, 1994), p. 16. The term 'canonical' has previously been applied with reference to Hebrew by the linguist J. Myhill, in 'Non-Emphatic Fronting in Biblical Hebrew', *Theoretical Linguistics 21* (1995), pp. 93, 97.
23 This term is defined in 3.3.
24 See section 1.4 below.

of different sequences even in narrative genre. SVO, OVS and MVS are not at all uncommon in the historical books. This inherent flexibility of constituent order that Hebrew exhibits in the normal register of language manifests itself more extensively in the even greater word-order variation seen in poetry. Obviously a defamiliarised ordering still has to remain within the limitations imposed by the syntactic constraints of the language. The word order of Hebrew poetry may often differ from the norm, but it cannot therefore be said to be ungrammatical.

1.3 The Nature of the Problem

The variation in word order that is present in Hebrew narrative texts raises an important issue that has a significant bearing on the variation that is seen in poetry. The predominant form of Biblical Hebrew (i.e., narrative) itself shows some departure from the canonical order. This cannot be accounted for in terms of defamiliarisation. The variation seen in narrative clauses, as is widely interpreted to be of a purely linguistic nature,[25] following conventions that are open to linguistic investigation. Such is not the case with defamiliarisation in poetry, where the variation is the product of more subjective concerns, whether stylistic, aesthetic, or prosodic.[26] Clearly, if the order of constituents is linguistically determined, this is of a fundamentally different nature to that variation of word order which we are attributing to defamiliarisation.

The question that this raises is the following – if linguistically motivated word-order variation is evident in Hebrew narrative, cannot the same exist in poetry? Or, to express it in other words, can we assume from the presence of marked word order in narrative, the presence of similar markedness in poetry? If this can in fact be established then it would mean that there are not one but two possible motivations for the word order occurring in poetry. It is a reasonable assumption that both linguistic mechanisms and defamiliarising processes are at work in the ordering of the poetic clause.

It will later be demonstrated[27] that marked word order of the same kind as that seen in narrative also appears in poetry, besides defamiliarised patterns. This being the case, then it naturally leads us to a second question, which is, whether or not there is any objective means of differentiating between these two factors affecting word order. In his 1999 article, 'Reading Hebrew Poetry – Linguistic Structure or Rhetorical Device?', Talstra observes the uncertainty among scholars as to whether a particular

---

25 By those scholars, for example, mentioned in chapter 3, fn. 6.
26 Cf. Wendland, *Analyzing the Psalms*, p. 231.
27 In chapter 4.

feature of Hebrew poetry is to be taken as literary or linguistic.[28] Talstra registers the problem, with respect to word order and other aspects of the language, and, although not attempting a solution himself, he reveals his optimism that the problem can be solved. He says, 'It is unlikely that within one text the linguistic system and literary devices should be in conflict'.[29] He assumes that the potential confusion between the two may be removed and issues a challenge for scholars to address this problem. The study of the relationship between the linguistic system of Hebrew and the architecture of its poetry, it is said, 'has barely begun'.[30] The present study explores this question with reference to word order, offering a solution for distinguishing a purely poetic arrangement of clause constituents from that which is dictated by definable linguistic principles.

This problem is seen to be an important one when it is recalled that approximately 40% of the whole Old Testament is written in poetic language.[31] A resolution to the matter is particularly needed to facilitate accurate exegesis and translation of this major portion of the Scriptures.

1.4 The Extent of the Problem

Before we attempt a solution to the problem we need an accurate appraisal of what it is that needs to be accounted for. To what degree exactly does the word order of Hebrew poetry differ from that of prose? This is to ask, what are the relative proportions of canonical and non-canonical clauses within the two genres? As we begin to look at the poetic material of the Hebrew Scriptures in order to answer this question, it is first necessary to clarify what is covered by the term 'canonical' within the present study. There are three things that are important to note:

(1) The following investigation concentrates solely upon the verbal clause.[32] It is only to clauses containing a finite verb that the terms canonical and non-canonical are here employed. This restriction is far from

---

28 E. Talstra, 'Reading Biblical Hebrew Poetry – Linguistic Structure or Rhetorical Device?', *JNSL* 25.2 (1999), p. 104.
29 *Ibid.*, p. 124.
30 *Ibid.*, p. 102 (quoting Lowery).
31 Cf. Craigie, *Psalms 1–50*, p. 36, 'between a third and a half of the OT is poetic in form'.
32 We shall not go over again the well-worn ground of whether a clause in which a noun is placed before the verb should be classed as a noun-clause, as in Classical Arabic, and as argued by Niccacci in his *Syntax of the Verb in Classical Hebrew Prose* (Sheffield: Sheffield Academic Press, 1990). This view, which goes against the definitions of modern linguistics, has been ably treated by W. Gross, in 'Is there Really a Compound Nominal Clause in Biblical Hebrew?' in C. L. Miller (ed.), *The Verbless Clause in Biblical Hebrew: Linguistic Approaches* (Winona Lake, Indiana: Eisebrauns, 1999), pp. 19–49.

narrow. In the selected poetic texts forming the basis of our analysis[33] more than 7,400 verbal clauses occur, as compared with only 2,190 noun-clauses[34] and 545 participial clauses. Also the factors governing the ordering of the latter two clause-types would seem to differ sufficiently from the case of verbal cases as to warrant separate studies of their own. The preference for a preverbal subject with participles,[35] therefore, cannot legitimately be classed alongside the proportionately much rarer preverbal subject with finite verbs.

(2) Certain elements in Biblical Hebrew necessarily occupy the initial position. These include interrogatives (מִי, לָמָּה, etc.), conjunctions (כִּי, עַתָּה, etc.), negatives (לֹא, אַל), the intensifying infinitive absolute,[36] and the copula וְ. Since these are as a rule placed first in the sentence, the occurrence of such items before the verb is not counted as rendering the clause non-canonical.

(3) Postverbal word order is not taken into account. In the following study canonical clauses are those in which the verb is placed first (apart from those elements just mentioned).[37] Again we note that this is not a severe limitation of the area of research. As a case in point, we observe that in the selected poetic texts the clause sequence VOS occurs only ten times, as compared with hundreds of instances of VSO and V-s O clauses. With regard to sequences with a postverbal M constituent,[38] VSM and VMS are both common, though the former appears twice as often as the latter. Concerning such postverbal word order rules have been proposed. Generally these have to do with matters of phrase length and the tendency to bring a pronominal form alongside its governing verb, rather than with pragmatic concerns,[39] though this would benefit from further investigation.

---

33 Introduced in section 1.7 below.
34 Traditionally termed 'nominal clause'; also sometimes described as 'verbless clause'. Cf. Miller, *The Verbless Clause in Biblical Hebrew*, p. 3.
35 Cf. R. Buth, 'Functional Grammar, Hebrew and Aramaic: An Integrated, Textlinguistic Approach to Syntax', in W. R. Bodine (ed.), *Discourse Analysis of Biblical Literature* (Atlanta, Georgia: Scholars Press, 1995), pp. 82–83.
36 As described in Van der Merwe (et al.), *Biblical Hebrew Reference Grammar*, p. 158; e.g., Ps. 118:18, יַסֹּר יִסְּרַנִּי יָּהּ (NASB, 'The LORD has disciplined me severely').
37 In his description of 'normal order' Muraoka includes both the sequences VOS and VAS (our VMS), that is, where objects or adverbs intervene between the verb and subject, *Emphatic Words and Structures in Biblical Hebrew* (Leiden: Brill, 1985), p. 30, fn. 67.
38 Throughout this thesis, 'M' refers to a 'modifier', which includes all prepositional phrases and adverbs. The same abbreviation was used by Collins (see fn. 44 below) and Bandstra ('Word Order and Emphasis in Biblical Hebrew Narrative').
39 See, for example, W. Gross, *Die Satzteilfolge im Verbalsatz alttestamentlicher Prosa: Untersucht an den Büchern Dtn, Ri und 2Kön.* (Tübingen: J. C. B. Mohr, 1996), pp. 261–64. A more pragmatic analysis is offered in the two articles by L. Lode,

In order to assess the extent of the difference between the word order of the two genres a comparison was made between a similar number of clauses taken from prose and from poetry. Approximately 1,200 verbal clauses were taken from selected narrative portions of the Old Testament and compared with a similar number of clauses from poetic texts.[40] The constituent order of each clause was examined and categorised as either canonical or non-canonical, this latter term covering all deviations from canonical word order. The results are as follows:

Genre	Total clauses	Canonical	Non-canonical
Prose	1,190	1,017 [85.5 %]	173 [14.5 %]
Poetry	1,243	821 [66.0 %]	422 [34.0 %]

These figures tell us two things: (1) that the word-order variation of poetic texts is more than twice as much as that of narrative; and (2) that even though poetry displays a larger degree of variation than narrative, the majority of verbal clauses still reflect the canonical word order. Although we would expect the language used by the Hebrew poets to be defamiliarised in its nature, the basic verb-initial constituent order still dominates. This fact reminds us that the variation of word order in itself is only one component out of many that all join together to contribute to the defamiliarisation of the poetic text. As is the case with the rare lexical items and unusual morphology, the defamiliarisation of word order is not total. Familiar words and forms exist alongside those that are only found in a poetic context, and likewise we observe the co-occurrence of both canonical and non-canonical order.

We can say then that approximately a third of all verbal clauses in poetic texts display a departure from canonical word order. The task in hand is to account for this greater proportion of non-canonical clauses in poetry with reference to the two potential motivating factors that have been identified, i.e., pragmatic and poetic.

'Postverbal Word Order in Biblical Hebrew: Structure and Function', *Semitics 9* (1984), pp. 113–64; and 'Postverbal Word Order in Biblical Hebrew: Structure and Function: Part Two', *Semitics 10* (1989), pp. 24–38. We note the significant cross-linguistic assessment of Steele, that languages in which VSO is the dominant order frequently also show VOS with no clear semantic distinction, S. Steele, 'Word Order Variation', in J. H. Greenberg (ed.), *Universals of Human Language*, vol. 4: Syntax (Stanford, California: Stanford University Press, 1978), pp. 596, 602. For VSO languages generally the most common variation is simply the inversion of the post-verbal elements, to VOS (Steele, 'Word Order Variation', p. 600).

40 For these texts, see Appendix 1.

1.5 A Linguistic Approach to a Solution

In her ground-breaking book on biblical parallelism Adele Berlin made the insightful comment that 'linguistics is fast becoming the prism through which poetry is viewed'.[41] The task of separating pragmatically marked constituent order from that which is simply poetic is essentially a linguistic one. It is also one, as Talstra declared, that has been little touched upon before.[42] Earlier linguistic approaches to Biblical Hebrew poetry were concerned with features of the genre other than variation in word order. Some, such as Geller[43] and Berlin, offer a linguistic description of parallelism, while others, O'Connor[44] and Collins,[45] analyse the constituents of Hebrew verse. O'Connor carries out his analysis on the basis of the number of constituents making up the poetic line, while Collins considers the particular constituents that compose the line. The latter does acknowledge the existence of word-order variation, but he sees this merely as the permutation of a basic line-type. He fails to explore to any degree the significance that these permutations might have.[46] Since it was not the intention of either of these authors to tackle the issue of word order per se, their work on poetry is not directly relevant to the question in hand.

Of much greater relevance are two more recent studies, Michael Rosenbaum's *Word-Order Variation in Isaiah 40–55* (1997), and the study of Walter Gross, entitled *Doppelt besetztes Vorfeld: Syntaktische, pragmatische und übersetzungs-technische Studien zum althebräischen Verbalsatz* (2001). These are the only published works of any length to date that relate directly to the issue of word order in Biblical Hebrew poetry. A whole chapter is later given over to the work of these two scholars in the light of the present study.

1.6 The Organisation of the Book

We begin with a description of the characteristics of the poetic colon and the way that cola are combined (ch. 2). This will introduce all the relevant

---

41 A. Berlin, *The Dynamics of Biblical Parallelism* (Bloomington, Indiana: Indiana University Press, 1985), p. 18.
42 Talstra, 'Reading Hebrew Poetry', p. 102.
43 S. A. Geller, *Parallelism in Early Biblical Poetry* (Missoula, Montana: Scholars Press, 1979).
44 M. O'Connor, *Hebrew Verse Structure* (Winona Lake, Indiana: Eisenbrauns, 1997).
45 T. Collins, *Line-Forms in Hebrew Poetry: A Grammatical Approach to the Stylistic Study of the Hebrew Prophets* (Rome: Biblical Institute Press, 1978).
46 For example, his treatment of Nahum 3:10 (Collins, *Line-Forms in Hebrew Poetry*, p. 28), classified as NP^1 V M, does not concern itself with matters of pragmatics. The method adopted by Collins ignores the presence of the focus particle גַּם and the possible influence this might have upon word order. Thus both SV-clauses and *gam*-SV clauses would be identically classified. Cf. J. Barr, 'Line-Forms in Hebrew Poetry' (review article), *JSS* 23 (1978), p. 234.

terminology and concepts from a poetic perspective. We then move on to look at how variations in word order have been accounted for in Hebrew narrative, that is, in terms of pragmatic functions (ch. 3). After this we directly consider those same pragmatic functions within the context of poetry (ch. 4). The following chapter examines the question of purely poetic, i.e., non-pragmatic, variation (ch. 5), which is followed by a consideration of the issue of distinguishing between the two kinds of variation (ch. 6). We next investigate the effect that pragmatics has upon the poetic feature of parallelism (ch. 7). The analysis of the latter, as shall be seen, raises certain matters regarding the pragmatic structuring of the parallel lines. A chapter is then devoted to those specially constructed cola that do not conform to the general pattern described in the foregoing chapters, and the reasons why they depart from the norm (ch. 8). To illustrate and confirm the solution that is proposed, it is applied to several longer passages of Hebrew poetry, some with a moderate degree of word-order variation, and others with more extensive variation, and then a range of potential difficulties are discussed (ch. 9). Two alternative approaches to the subject of poetic word order are treated (ch. 10). Finally, the findings are all summarised in a brief concluding chapter (ch. 11).

1.7 The Corpus of Selected Data

For the basis of this research an extensive database was chosen in order to achieve results that could be taken as applicable to Biblical Hebrew poetry in general. The data analysed consists of the whole book of Psalms, Isaiah 40–66,[47] Job 3–14, Proverbs 1–9, the Song of Solomon and, to represent poetry embedded within narrative, the Balaam oracles found in Numbers 23–24. The whole of this data, to be found with analysis in Appendix 2, amounts to more than 4,000 verses of Hebrew poetry.[48]

All the Hebrew data cited in this volume is obtained from that form of the Masoretic text represented by BHS.

---

47 That the language of Isaiah is to be classed as poetry is widely accepted. The assessment of Craigie in fn. 31 above must include material from the prophetic books. Linguistic studies such as those of Collins (*Line-Forms in Hebrew Poetry*) and M. Rosenbaum, *Word-Order Variation in Isaiah 40–55: A Functional Perspective* (Assen, The Netherlands: Van Gorcum, 1997), are founded upon this very fact. The same is assumed by many commentators. J. N. Oswalt, for example, is of the opinion that the latter half of the book contains 'some of the most glorious poetry in Hebrew literature', *The Book of Isaiah Chapters 40–66*, NICOT (Grand Rapids, Michigan: Eerdmans, 1998), p. 8.
48 These selected portions contain more than 10,000 clauses of the various kinds: verbal, participial, verbless, and infinitival.

CHAPTER 2

A Description of the Basic Units of Hebrew Poetry

This chapter offers a description of the basic units that are employed in the composition of Biblical Hebrew poetry, as much as is necessary to serve as a basis for the analysis of poetic texts which follows. Following a brief outline of the shape of the smallest poetic unit, the colon, we discuss those particular colon arrangements known as parallelisms, the various additional features that accompany them, and their rhetorical function. In the latter part of the chapter we will examine a method of depicting basic intercolon relations which will aid us in the application of the theory to be advanced in the following chapters.

2.1 The Colon

The introductory material that follows in this section is in broad agreement with material found in the standard textbooks on the subject.

2.1.1 Terminology

Kugel was surely right when he wrote, 'The clauses of parallelistic verse have been referred to by a bewildering variety of names: hemistichs, stichs, versicles, cola, bicola, half-verses'.[1] Even then he did not exhaust all the possibilities: 'half-line', 'line', 'line-pair', are also found in the literature.[2] Watson, in his treatment of Hebrew poetry, prefers the terms 'colon' and 'bicolon'.[3] As Watson's work is currently the standard introduction to the

---

1   J. L. Kugel, *The Idea of Biblical Poetry* (New Haven: Yale University Press, 1981), p. 2; cf. W. T. W. Cloete, 'Some Recent Research on Old Testament Verse: Progress, Problems and Possibilities', *JNSL* 17 (1991), p. 190, 'there prevails a terminological *confusion*'.
2   E.g., O'Connor, *Hebrew Verse Structure*, p. 52.
3   Watson, *Classical Hebrew Poetry*, p. 11. Watson does also use other terms, such as 'couplet', which, he explains, is only 'for the sake of variety'; cf. his discussion of terminology in 'Chiastic patterns in Biblical Hebrew poetry', in J. W. Welch (ed.), *Chiasmus in Antiquity* (Hildersheim: Gerstenberg, 1981), pp. 119–20. Wendland too prefers the terms 'colon', 'bicolon', 'tricolon' etc., *Analyzing the Psalms*, pp. 58–59. Yet we should note that these are not acceptable to all scholars of Hebrew poetry.

field we will follow his example. One advantage of this is that, as the colon is extended, it is simple to add quantifying prefixes to indicate the number of cola that have been joined together, producing the terms: 'bicolon', 'tricolon', 'tetracolon', and so forth. We therefore use 'bicolon' with the sense of 'couplet', 'tricolon' as an equivalent of 'tristich', and 'tetracolon' with the same meaning as 'quatrain'.

Regarding the larger sections of poetry the confusion in nomenclature continues. Many scholars use 'stanza', 'strophe', or other technical names to describe the segments of discourse into which a poem or song may be divided. In order to simplify things, in this study we will refer to larger segments of poetic text simply as 'sections' or 'units', and smaller segments as 'sub-sections' or 'sub-units'. Such descriptions are considered to be adequate for present purposes.

Certain traditional terms employed to describe relationships between parallel lines, such as synonymous and antithetical,[4] are held to be insufficient and the cause of potential confusion. These will be discussed, and modified or rejected, as we proceed with our description and analysis.

2.1.2 The Poetic Colon in Relation to the Grammatical Clause

The typical poetic unit consists of two cola with a medial pause[5] indicated by the Masoretic accent ˄ (ʾatnāḥ):

: _____ ˄ _____

The properties of the poetic colon are quite uncontroversial. We accept Wendland's assessment of the colon as 'the smallest intrinsic segment of discourse' in Hebrew poetry.[6] He further states that, 'A colon averages three rhythmic words or accent-units, each one containing a single major stress'.[7]

It needs to be emphasised at the outset that although it is poetry that forms the subject of our study, since our approach is linguistic rather than literary, it is the grammatical clause that is of primary interest to us rather

---

Alter rejects the term 'colon' in that it has 'misleading links with Greek versification ... also inadvertently calling up associations of intestinal organs or soft drinks', R. Alter, *The Art of Biblical Poetry* (Edinburgh: T. & T. Clark, 1990 [1985]), p. 9. Alter himself prefers to use 'verset'.

4 As outlined, for example, by D. Kidner, *Psalms 1–72*, TOTC (Leicester: Inter-Varsity Press, 1973), pp. 2–4.
5 In the denotation employed in the present work the pauses within the line are indicated by a single backslash /. For example, a bicolon might be composed of VSO/VS (as Ps. 122:6).
6 E. R. Wendland, *Discourse Perspectives on Hebrew Poetry of the Scriptures* (New York: UBS, 1994), p. 11.
7 *Ibid.*

than the colon as such. Our analysis will be of word order variation within the Hebrew poetic clause as a basic unit of meaning. It is fortuitous that on the vast majority of occasions clause structure in Hebrew poetry coincides with poetic division into cola.[8] Sometimes, however, a bicolon may contain a single grammatical clause (e.g., Ps. 79:10, where the NP[Su] alone occupies the whole B-line). Or sometimes a bicolon may contain two clauses not matching the colon structure of the verse, one clause extending beyond the confines of a single poetic colon (e.g., Ps. 15:5, where the ʾatnāḥ separates the NP[Su] from its predicate). Conversely, a single colon may contain more than one clause. It is not uncommon to find a colon consisting of two distinct verbal clauses (e.g., Ps. 6:11a, where a four-member colon is composed of V w-VMS). The tension between literary and grammatical division we see as only slight and no real obstacle to the kind of analysis that we are to undertake.

By and large the versification of the books of Psalms, Proverbs and Job follows the division of the Hebrew text into bicola.[9] This is not generally the case in the book of Isaiah where a single verse can contain two or even three bicola.

2.1.3 *The Relative Frequency of Colon Structures*

Biblical Hebrew verse is most commonly structured into pairs of cola, i.e., bicola. This is evident even from just a cursory glance at an English translation of the Psalms. Perhaps as much as 75% of the total number of poetic lines are organised in this way.[10] Most of the remainder are tricola, amounting to 20%, with monocola, tetracola, and larger formations accounting for only 5%. The distribution of these units of varying sizes is not always even. While the bicolon dominates overall, some individual psalms or poems may show a preference for the smaller or larger units.

The comparative rarity of both monocola and tricola (plus tetracola, etc.) means that such forms are frequently employed with specific functions within the poetic text. In a poem that predominantly consists of bicola the shorter and longer arrangements commonly function to mark special junctures in the discourse, these being textual boundaries such as aperture and closure, and also peak.[11] These are key requirements in poetry,

---

8 *Ibid.*
9 Cf. S. Segert, 'Phonological and Syntactic Structuring Principles in Northwest Semitic Verse Systems', in H. Jungraithmayr and W. W. Müller (eds.), *Proceedings of the Fourth International Hamito-Semitic Congress*, Current Issues in Linguistic Theory 44 (Amsterdam: John Benjamin, 1987), p. 552, 'The boundaries of syntactic units, clauses and sentences, as a rule correspond to the limits of poetic units, cola and verses'.
10 Figures are taken from Wendland, *Discourse Perspectives on Hebrew Poetry*, p. 11.
11 See Watson, *Classical Hebrew Poetry*, pp. 171–72, 183.

where the nature of the genre means that many of the usual indicators of boundary, as are found for example in narrative, are lacking. A portion of Hebrew narrative is typically readily divisible into its natural units, but we find that this is generally not so with poetry. The absence of linear progression and the presence of repetition makes text segmentation often less precise than in the case of narrative and expository material. Nevertheless, there did exist a range of means and devices available to the Hebrew poets by which they were able to demarcate the boundaries of the various sections within the larger text.[12]

2.2 Parallelism in Biblical Hebrew Poetry

The organisation of bicola into two related parallel lines has long been recognised as a characteristic feature of Hebrew verse.[13] Yet this phenomenon is certainly not limited to Biblical Hebrew. Parallelism is also evident in the great epic literature of Babylon[14] and Ugarit.[15] Indeed such parallelism is not even a particularly Semitic feature. In his discussion of poetry in general, Fabb tells us that 'Parallelism is widespread in the verbal arts of the world'.[16] It has been identified in Russian, Chinese, Turkic poetry, and in a number of other non-Semitic languages, ancient and modern.[17]

2.2.1 The Character of Parallelism

In poetry where parallelism is characteristic, it functions as a basic structuring principle, analogous to the way that rhyme or metre operates in the poetry of other languages.[18] In fact parallelism has been defined as a form of rhyme, existing at the level of meaning rather than of sound. It has been variously described as 'thought-rhyme'[19] or 'sense rhythm'.[20] As a basic principle of organisation Fabb states that parallelism 'divides the text

---

12 These will be discussed in 8.2.
13 Cf. Berlin, *Dynamics of Biblical Parallelism*, p. 5.
14 G. B. Gray, *The Forms of Hebrew Poetry* (New York: Ktav, 1972 [1915]), pp. 38–39.
15 M. C. A. Korpel and J. C. de Moor, 'Fundamentals of Ugaritic and Hebrew Poetry', in W. van der Meer and J. C. de Moor (eds.), *The Structural Analysis of Biblical and Canaanite Poetry*, JSOT Supplement Series 74 (Sheffield: Sheffield Academic Press, 1988), pp. 1 and 17.
16 Fabb, *Linguistics and Literature*, p. 159; cf. p. 144.
17 Jakobson, *Language in Literature*, p. 125; Berlin, *Dynamics of Biblical Parallelism*, p. 4.
18 Fabb, *Linguistics and Literature*, p. 159.
19 Kidner, *Psalms 1–72*, p. 2; cf. K. Seybold, *Introducing the Psalms* (T. & T. Clark: Edinburgh, 1990), p. 68.
20 G. Grogan, *Prayer, Praise and Prophecy* (Fearn, Scotland: Christian Focus Publications, 2001), pp. 55–56.

into sections (typically "line pairs") and then requires the second half of each section to resemble the first half'.[21] This is a fair definition of the function of parallelism, though the word 'resemble' requires further explanation.

The two lines of a poetic parallelism[22] may resemble each other in one or more different ways. Parallelism may exist at the level of semantics, syntax, morphology, lexis, phonology, or rhythm.[23] It may be total, with respect to all elements in both lines, or partial, only respecting some.[24] Principally parallelism is seen as a semantic relationship.[25] According to Fabb, 'Semantic parallelism holds between two sections of text when they can be interpreted to be the same in some component of their meaning'.[26] But parallelism of meaning is often accompanied by parallelism of form.[27] This is certainly the case with the bulk of parallelisms in Hebrew poetry. Where two lines are related in meaning there is usually also a relationship of syntax, though by no means necessarily so, as illustrated by:[28]

2 Samuel 22:29

For you are my light, O YHWH,　　　　　כִּי־אַתָּה נֵירִי יְהוָה
and YHWH lightens up my darkness.　　וַיהוָה יַגִּיהַּ חָשְׁכִּי׃

The two cola clearly correspond at the level of meaning. Both speak of God giving illumination to the psalmist. Yet syntactically the two lines differ considerably. The first is a noun-clause, the second a verbal clause. Together they produce a bicolon with the overall structure S Comp // SVO.[29] The A-line addresses God directly in the 2nd person, the B-line refers to him in the

---

21 Fabb, *Linguistics and Literature*, p. 142.
22 It should be noted that the two lines need not be immediately adjacent to each other to be classed as a parallelism. Wendland rightly distinguishes between 'connected parallelism', where the two lines are conjoined, and 'distant parallelism', where the two lines are separated by an intervening span of text (*Analyzing the Psalms*, p. 57 and p. 101). It is principally the word-order variation relating to the former kind of parallelism which relates to the subject matter of this study.
23 E. L. Greenstein, 'How Does Parallelism Mean?', in S. A. Geller, E. L. Greenstein, and A. Berlin, *A Sense of Text: The Art of Language in the Study of Biblical Literature*, JQRSupp (Winona Lake, Indiana: Eisenbrauns, 1982), p. 43.
24 P. D. Miller, 'Synonymous-Sequential Parallelism in the Psalms', *Biblica 61* (1980), p. 256, describes parallelism as a 'gradation'.
25 With respect to Hebrew psalmody, R. G. Boling, '"Synonymous" Parallelism in the Psalms', *JSS 5* (1960), p. 221, affirms that the majority of specimens of parallelism can be assigned to the 'synonymous class'.
26 Fabb, *Linguistics and Literature*, p. 137.
27 *Ibid.*, p. 138.
28 Quotations from BHS are made without any emendation. Unless stated otherwise, English translations are the author's.
29 Note that the double backslash // is employed throughout the present work to denote the relationship of parallelism.

3rd person. Semantically the complement of the noun-clause (נֵרִי) and the verb (יַגִּיהַּ) of the parallel colon both concern 'light', and the grammatical subject of both these elements refers to 'YHWH'. Despite the wide syntactic divergence the strong semantic overlap makes this an actual instance of parallelism,[30] and similar cases will be treated as such in the following analysis.[31] In addition to noun-clauses, we also find participial and infinitival clauses placed in parallelism with finite verbal clauses.[32]

More typically the similarity of meaning between the two cola is matched by a similarity of syntax:

Proverbs 6:8

| It [the ant] prepares its food in summer; | תָּכִין בַּקַּיִץ לַחְמָהּ |
| it gathers its provisions in harvest. | אָגְרָה בַקָּצִיר מַאֲכָלָהּ׃ |

Here there is an obvious semantic relationship. Moreover, besides the correspondence between the overall meaning of each line, each of the three sentence constituents of the A-line bears a relationship to the each of the three contained in the B-line. This time both lines are verbal clauses composed of the same three constituents forming an identical VMO syntactic pattern.[33]

Parallelism in Biblical Hebrew poetry, though predominantly existing at the semantic level, need not do so at all. Parallelism may apply, for example, solely with respect to the syntax. As Bratcher and Reyburn state, 'Two lines may be parallel syntactically without having much parallelism of meaning'.[34] The same holds true for the other forms of parallelism – grammatical, morphological, lexical, phonological, etc., – though typically these are found combined with a correspondence of meaning also. The manner in which parallelism operates at these other levels has been amply demonstrated by Berlin[35] and need not detain us long here. One example of each will be given by way of illustration. Morphological parallelism

---

30 It is worthy of note that the version of this song contained in the book of Psalms makes both lines verbal clauses: כִּי־אַתָּה תָּאִיר נֵרִי יְהוָה אֱלֹהַי יַגִּיהַּ חָשְׁכִּי, 'For you, YHWH, lighten my lamp, my God will lighten my darkness' (Ps. 18:29).

31 Cf. the comments and further examples given by Berlin, *Dynamics of Biblical Parallelism*, pp. 54–55.

32 Further on this, see 5.4.

33 This is a simple example. Often, however, there is complete semantic parallelism with only partial syntactic parallelism. E.g., S and O, though differing syntactically, may be parallel in meaning, as in: שַׁתּוּ בַשָּׁמַיִם פִּיהֶם וּלְשׁוֹנָם תִּהֲלַךְ בָּאָרֶץ, 'They set their *mouths* [DO] against heaven, and their *tongues* [Su] range over the earth', VMO//SVM (Ps. 73:9).

34 R. G. Bratcher and W. D. Reyburn, *Handbook to the Psalms* (New York: UBS, 1993), p. 5.

35 Berlin, *Dynamics of Biblical Parallelism* – morphological parallelism, pp. 32–53; lexical parallelism, pp. 65–72; phonological parallelism, pp. 103–121.

involves the matching of grammatical forms, gender, or number:

Isaiah 49:22cd

and they shall bring your sons in their breast,   וְהֵבִיאוּ בָנַיִךְ בְּחֹצֶן
and your daughters shall be carried   וּבְנֹתַיִךְ עַל־כָּתֵף תִּנָּשֶׂאנָה:
on their shoulders.

In this parallelism there is a pattern observable in the arrangement of the nouns.[36] The gender of the four nouns forms the pattern: masculine–masculine // feminine– feminine.

Lexical parallelism consists of a pair of words, being either synonyms, near-synonyms, two of the same class, or opposite extremes, one appearing in each line. The word may be a noun, verb, adverb, or adjective:

Psalm 114:4

The mountains skipped like rams,   הֶהָרִים רָקְדוּ כְאֵילִים
the hills like lambs.   גְּבָעוֹת כִּבְנֵי־צֹאן:

The word-pair גְּבָעוֹת/הָרִים ('mountains'/'hills') are commonly found together in parallel lines.[37]

To illustrate phonological parallelism, that is, the matching of sound, we may take the following example:

Job 4:11

A lion perishes without prey,   לַיִשׁ אֹבֵד מִבְּלִי־טָרֶף
and the lion cubs are scattered.   וּבְנֵי לָבִיא יִתְפָּרָדוּ:

In this case there is a correspondence between the consonants of the two cola: *mbly ṭrp* and *lbyʾ ytprdw* (both parts contain *l b y* and *t/ṭ p r*).[38] Phonological parallelism may also exist between vowel sounds (e.g., Prov. 9:5).

In the poetry of the Hebrew Scriptures it is uncommon for parallelism to exist merely at one of the several different levels. Typically two or more of the above will feature side by side in the same parallel structure. For example, Isaiah 66:8 (הֲיוּחַל אֶרֶץ בְּיוֹם אֶחָד אִם־יִוָּלֵד גּוֹי פַּעַם אֶחָת) besides lexical parallelism, also shows semantic and syntactic. When parallelism exists only on one level most usually it will be semantic, less so syntactic.

Finally in this section, it is to be observed that parallelism can exist on various scales. By this we mean that though the typical Hebrew parallelism consists of one colon in parallel with another, this is by no means always the case. On occasions the parallelism exists within the confines of a single colon, that is, a half-line. If the colon contains four or more

---

36 This example is discussed by Watson, *Classical Hebrew Poetry*, p. 123.
37 E.g., Psalm 72:3; Proverbs 8:25; Song 2:8; Isaiah 2:2; 41:15; 65:7.
38 Cited by Berlin, *Dynamics of Biblical Parallelism*, p. 117.

constituents it is possible for these to form two clauses in parallelism with each other. This is the case, for example, in Psalm 16:9ab, where the first colon itself consists of (C) V S // w-V S, forming a semantic and syntactic parallelism. Alternatively, the parallelism may exist on a larger scale, such as between one bicolon and another, as, for example, in Proverbs 6:27-28, Q-V S O M / w-S V // Q-V S M / w-S V.

2.2.2 Additional Features of Parallelism

Parallelism is a complex phenomenon. Besides the number of different levels of the language at which parallelism may adhere, there are certain other features commonly appearing in connection with this characteristic of Biblical Hebrew poetry. The principal of these are described here in brief.

(a) GAPPING

This feature, also known as 'ellipsis',[39] in essence could be described as 'incomplete parallelism'.[40] Where this takes place, one or more constituents that are present in the A-line have no corresponding element in the B-line where the parallelism creates the expectation that such would occur.[41] Examples abound in Hebrew poetry, for instance:

Proverbs 5:15

| Drink water from your own cistern, | שְׁתֵה־מַיִם מִבּוֹרֶךָ |
| and running water from your own well. | וְנֹזְלִים מִתּוֹךְ בְּאֵרֶךָ׃ |

Here the A-line exhibits the constituent structure VOM. The parallel B-line consists only of OM. In this particular instance the verb is the gapped element, which is most frequently the case, though gapping may occur with any category of sentence constituent.[42] Most commonly just one constituent is gapped, as in the example, but occasionally two constituents are omitted (e.g., Ps. 78:71).[43] The remaining ungapped elements are known as the

---

39 Watson, *Classical Hebrew Poetry*, pp. 303–04. O'Connor, *Hebrew Verse Structure*, p. 122, prefers the term 'gapping', as does L. A. Schökel, *A Manual of Hebrew Poetics* (Rome: Editrice Pontificio Istituto Biblico, 1988), p. 157. Wendland uses both, *Analyzing the Psalms*, pp. 65, 151. Fabb, in his cross-linguistic treatment of parallelism, also refers to this feature as 'gapping', *Linguistics and Literature*, pp. 146–47.
40 W. L. Holladay, 'Hebrew Verse Structure Revisited (I)', *JBL 118* (1999), p. 23.
41 Watson, *Classical Hebrew Poetry*, p. 304.
42 M. Dahood gives many examples of gapping involving various elements, *Psalms III, 101–150*, AB (New York: Doubleday, 1970), pp. 435–39.
43 There is some ambiguity in the description of those instances where not just one but two constituents are gapped in the B-line, as in Psalm 120:2, which reads: יְהוָה הַצִּילָה נַפְשִׁי מִשְּׂפַת־שֶׁקֶר מִלָּשׁוֹן רְמִיָּה ('O YHWH, deliver my soul from lying lips, from a deceitful tongue'). The constituent order is: [Voc] V O M // M. When the only element remaining in the B-line matches syntactically the final element of the B-

'sentence fragment'.[44]

It frequently happens that when gapping occurs in the B-line an accompanying lengthening of the remaining constituent(s) also takes place. This is known as 'ballast variant'.[45] A good example of this device is:

Psalm 47:6

| God has gone up with a shout, | עָלָה אֱלֹהִים בִּתְרוּעָה |
| YHWH with the sound of a trumpet. | יְהוָה בְּקוֹל שׁוֹפָר: |

The constituent structure of this verse is: VSM//SM. The verb has been gapped in the B-line of the parallelism. To compensate for this missing component the M element has been lengthened, from the single noun with preposition בִּתְרוּעָה to the construct chain בְּקוֹל שׁוֹפָר. The motivation for such an occurrence, Watson tells us, is that the 'two cola of a couplet in parallelism must balance'.[46] While this often does happen, it is not necessarily so. On occasion the gapped line may be left without a ballast variant (e.g., Prov. 6:4).

Finally on the subject of gapping, in a very small number of cases (e.g., Job 4:10) a component is missing from the A-line rather than the B. This is variously referred to as 'backwards gapping',[47] 'leftward gapping',[48] or 'retrospective ellipsis'.[49] This is extremely rare and shall be seen to have a specific discourse function.[50]

(b) EMBEDDING

A two-line parallelism may be placed, or embedded, within a larger unit. It is not uncommon for a tricolon to contain two parallel lines, while the third stands outside the parallel relationship. This third line might differ both semantically and syntactically from the lines forming the parallelism. For example:

Psalm 50:16

A	And God says to the wicked:	וְלָרָשָׁע אָמַר אֱלֹהִים
B	'What right have you to recite my statutes,	מַה־לְּךָ לְסַפֵּר חֻקָּי
C	and take my covenant upon your lips?'	וַתִּשָּׂא בְרִיתִי עֲלֵי־פִיךָ:

---

line, which is frequently the case, this may also be analysed as apposition rather than gapping. The existence of such an alternative analysis of these particular verse-types in no way affects the theory proposed in subsequent chapters.

44 See C. L. Miller, 'A Linguistic Approach to Ellipsis in Biblical Poetry', *BBR* 13.2 (2003), p. 253.
45 Watson, *Classical Hebrew Poetry*, p. 343.
46 *Ibid.*
47 O'Connor, *Hebrew Verse Structure*, p. 126.
48 *Ibid.*, p. 404.
49 Alter, *The Art of Biblical Poetry*, p. 23.
50 See 8.2.3.

Lines B and C are semantically parallel, concerning the mention by the wicked of God's holy laws and covenant. Line A is closely bound to these two cola, being the speech introduction for them, but obviously itself forms no part of the parallelism.

(c) EXTENDING

A parallelism can extend beyond the confines of the basic bicolon. Structures composed of three parallel cola are not uncommon (e.g., Ps. 17:1), nor are four (e.g., Job 4:3-4). Parallelisms containing five, six, or even seven cola are occasionally found (e.g., Prov. 9:1-2; Song 2:11-13). To illustrate the extended parallelism we give the following:

Job 10:10-11

Did you not pour me out like milk	הֲלֹא כֶחָלָב תַּתִּיכֵנִי
and curdle me like cheese,	וְכַגְּבִנָּה תַּקְפִּיאֵנִי:
clothe me with skin and flesh,	עוֹר וּבָשָׂר תַּלְבִּישֵׁנִי
and knit me together with bones and sinews?	וּבַעֲצָמוֹת וְגִידִים תְּסֹכְכֵנִי:

All four cola display an obvious similarity of meaning, relating to the manner in which God had fashioned Job (cf. v. 9). Syntactically also there is a close correspondence, each line consisting of a preverbal constituent followed by a verb. They are further united by the fact that all depend on the opening interrogative הֲלֹא. Morphologically the forms of the verbs match, each being a *yiqtol* with object suffix. There is, then, good reason to take these cola as forming a single unit, a tetracolon.

Lastly on the matter of additional features pertaining to parallelism, we note that there is nothing to prevent more than one of the three items mentioned above being applied at the same time. A single parallel structure may, for example, be both extended and contain gapping.

2.2.3 *The Rhetorical Function of Parallelism*

Before moving on to look at intercolon relations, a few brief remarks are necessary concerning the rhetorical function of parallelism. Several writers on Hebrew parallelism have commented on the rhetorical effect caused by the device.[51] Alter speaks of it in terms of 'heightening or intensification', or 'focusing, specification, concretization'.[52] Berlin claims that parallelism

---

51 For example, Alter, *The Art of Biblical Poetry*, pp. 3-26; Berlin, *Dynamics of Biblical Parallelism*, pp. 135-41; Kugel, *The Idea of Biblical Poetry*, pp. 51-52; Wendland, *Analyzing the Psalms*, p. 62.

52 Alter, *The Art of Biblical Poetry*, p. 19. Though in some cases Alter does acknowledge the existence of what he calls 'static' parallelism (p. 22), consisting of a simple repetition which lacks any intensifying effect (i.e., 'dynamic' parallelism).

'heightens the focus on the message'.[53] Kugel speaks of the emphatic 'seconding' character of the parallel line.[54] Wendland too is of the opinion that 'the B colon ... often contributes some form of *emphasis* to line A'.[55] All these descriptive terms are appropriate for the rhetorical effect that the various writers are considering. Our concern, however, in this treatment of Hebrew poetry is solely from the point of view of word order. One pragmatic function of word order variation in poetry as in narrative, is focus or prominence, which shall be discussed in detail in the next chapter. There are also other kinds of focusing or highlighting devices present within Hebrew poetry that operate on a different level from pragmatic markedness. A certain rhetorical highlighting effect may be produced by several means, such as repetition, various kinds of literary structures, the employment of poetic lexical items, and so forth. We may include parallelism among suchlike features of the genre. The study of these features of poetry does not directly relate to that manner of marking caused by the departure from canonical word order, and consequently does not fall within the scope of this present work. The presence of these elements, however, needs to be mentioned, chiefly in order to clarify the distinction between prominence at the rhetorical level and markedness at the pragmatic level such as is treated in this study. The impact caused by the presence of a parallel line and that caused by a departure from usual word order relate to different aspects of the language and should not be confused. The manner of 'focus' is different in each case, as shall become apparent when we shortly come to consider pragmatic focus.

2.3 Intercolon Relations

We have previously noted the predominance of the bicolon, or two-line unit, in Biblical Hebrew poetry, and how on occasion larger units might occur.[56] Now we come to consider the relationships that adhere between one colon and the other(s) with which it is joined. These relationships may pertain at a number of different levels, whether semantic, logical, or grammatical. The method of portraying these relationships that follows enables a clearer understanding of how one colon relates to another and so allows us to differentiate between one bicolon and another on the basis of how its two cola interrelate. Also this manner of depicting the relationships will assist in disambiguating the components of more complex verses.

At the simplest level bicola (and larger structures) consist of conjoining cola which relate to each other either as a parallelism or as a non-

---

53 Berlin, *Dynamics of Biblical Parallelism*, p. 141.
54 Kugel, *The Idea of Biblical Poetry*, p. 51.
55 Wendland, *Analyzing the Psalms*, p. 62.
56 2.1.3.

parallelism. We have previously considered the construction of parallel lines. These may be denoted as:

HEAD + Parallel

where 'HEAD' indicates the main proposition or base-line. While the B-line of the parallelism is invariably co-ordinate with and may be grammatically independent of this base-line, semantic dependence is shown where gapping occurs, in that the preceding line provides information necessary to the full understanding of the B-line.

The remainder of poetic bicola, those not exhibiting parallelism, are constructed in one the following possible ways:

(a) HEAD^1 + HEAD^2
(b) HEAD + Subordinate
(c) HEAD [Phrase^1 + Phrase^2 ...]

(a) HEAD^1 + HEAD^2 consists of a bicolon containing two grammatically independent clauses. They offer two semantically distinct, that is non-parallel, propositions which, while independent with respect to grammar, may relate to each other on a logico-semantic level as a sequence of time or thought, or as a co-ordination of two distinct propositions concerning the same sentence topic. The following illustrate this type:

Isaiah 50:9

Behold, it is the Lord YHWH who helps me.   הֵן אֲדֹנָי יְהוִה יַעֲזָר־לִי
Who is it that will condemn me?   מִי־הוּא יַרְשִׁיעֵנִי

Job 13:4

However, you smear me with lies;   וְאוּלָם אַתֶּם טֹפְלֵי־שָׁקֶר
you are worthless physicians, all of you!   רֹפְאֵי אֱלִל כֻּלְּכֶם׃

(b) HEAD + Subordinate. In this category are included all those B-lines that show either semantic or grammatical dependence upon the first line of the pair. This dependent clause may function as a temporal or circumstantial clause, a reason, purpose, result, condition, concession, comparison, etc., or show grammatical dependence as a relative, participial, complement[57] or infinitival clause. In some cases the appropriate Hebrew connector will be used (e.g., כִּי, לְמַעַן, כַּאֲשֶׁר, etc.), though in many cases the secondary clause is placed alongside in a simple paratactic relationship (i.e., without any connecting word). Not infrequently the sequence of cola appears as Subordinate + HEAD. In this case it is the B-line which comprises the main clause. Here are several examples of these types:

---

57 Including speech (that is, the A-line contains the speech margin and the B-line the speech itself).

Psalm 91:12 (Purpose clause)
On their hands they will bear you up,
so that you will not strike your foot against a stone?

עַל־כַּפַּיִם יִשָּׂאוּנְךָ
פֶּן־תִּגֹּף בָּאֶבֶן רַגְלֶךָ׃

Song 8:1 (Participial clause)
Oh that you were like a brother to me,
nursing at my mother's breast!

מִי יִתֶּנְךָ כְּאָח לִי
יוֹנֵק שְׁדֵי אִמִּי

Job 9:3 (Conditional clause)
If one wished to contend with him,
he could not answer him
one time out of a thousand.

אִם־יַחְפֹּץ לָרִיב עִמּוֹ
לֹא־יַעֲנֶנּוּ
אַחַת מִנִּי־אָלֶף׃

Isaiah 62:2 (Relative clause)
And you will be called by a new name
which the mouth of YHWH will designate.

וְקֹרָא לָךְ שֵׁם חָדָשׁ
אֲשֶׁר פִּי יְהוָה יִקֳּבֶנּוּ׃

Psalm 14:7 (Infinitival clause)
When YHWH restores the fortunes of his people,
let Jacob rejoice and Israel be glad!

בְּשׁוּב יְהוָה שְׁבוּת עַמּוֹ
יָגֵל יַעֲקֹב יִשְׂמַח יִשְׂרָאֵל׃

(c) HEAD [Phrase¹ + Phrase² ...]. Here each colon contains a phrase or phrases (NP, VP, PP, or Adv) which, when the two cola are taken together, form a complete sentence. Although the bicolon is divided poetically into two separate units in the same way as the above two types, grammatically it is one whole proposition. For example:

Psalm 48:10
We reflect on your steadfast love, O God,
in the midst of your temple.

דִּמִּינוּ אֱלֹהִים חַסְדֶּךָ
בְּקֶרֶב הֵיכָלֶךָ׃

This single sentence contains the syntactic components V [Voc] O / M, with the B-line containing the final modifying phrase.

Psalm 79:10
Let be known among the nations in our sight
the avenging of the shed blood of your servants.

יִוָּדַע בַּגּוֹיִם לְעֵינֵינוּ
נִקְמַת דַּם־עֲבָדֶיךָ הַשָּׁפוּךְ׃

The constituent order of this verse is V M M / S, where the subject phrase occupies the whole of the B-line of the colon.

Under this category we include those bicola whose B-line is an appositional phrase[58] dependent upon A, such as:

---

58 Apposition in general is discussed by Van der Merwe (et al.), *Biblical Hebrew Reference Grammar*, pp. 228–30, 353.

Isaiah 41:15

Behold, I will make you into a threshing-sledge,   הִנֵּה שַׂמְתִּיךְ לְמוֹרַג
sharp and new, with many teeth.   חָרוּץ חָדָשׁ בַּעַל פִּיפִיּוֹת

Where apposition exists, the appositional phrase cannot stand alone and is therefore not to be viewed as a separate HEAD but as one that is dependent upon the foregoing A-line.

Extended poetic units may be constructed out of a combination of any of the above types. The proposed categorisation will assist in the analysis of such complex structures. The following extended formations may be broken down according to different grammatical and logico-semantic relations between the various cola:

Psalm 66:12

A You let men ride over our heads;   הִרְכַּבְתָּ אֱנוֹשׁ לְרֹאשֵׁנוּ
B we went through fire and through water;   בָּאנוּ־בָאֵשׁ וּבַמַּיִם
C but you have brought us out to refreshing.   וַתּוֹצִיאֵנוּ לָרְוָיָה׃

This verse consists of three clauses forming a HEAD^1 + HEAD^2 + HEAD^3 tricolon.

Psalm 102:14

You will arise and have compassion on Zion;   אַתָּה תָקוּם תְּרַחֵם צִיּוֹן
for it is time to be gracious to her,   כִּי־עֵת לְחֶנְנָהּ
for the appointed time has come.   כִּי־בָא מוֹעֵד׃

Here the arrangement of the various cola is more complicated. A solely linear representation as HEAD + Subordinate^1 + Subordinate^2 would be misleading. This does not bring out the parallelism existing between B and C, nor does it convey the fact that colon C does not relate directly to B but to A. In such a situation a diagrammatic representation would more accurately depict the relations:[59]

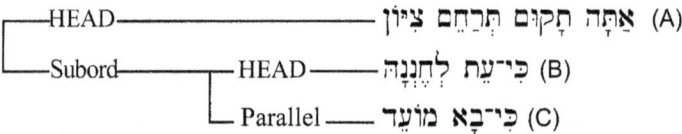

By this means it can be seen how cola B and C relate to each other and how both relate to A. This is an instance of an embedded parallelism functioning as a reason for the foregoing HEAD-line. Depicted this way the order of hierarchy is clearly observable, the primary units being to the left side of

---

59 Such diagramming is typical of the 'Semantic Structure Analysis' employed in textual study by SIL (Wycliffe Bible Translators). See J. Beekman and J. Callow, *Translating the Word of God* (Grand Rapids, Michigan: Zondervan, 1974), chs. 17–19.

the diagram. Line C forms a parallel to B, and both together are subordinated to clause A.

Here is another example of a complex tricolon with a different set of intercolon relations:

Job 8:6

If you are pure and upright,	אִם־זַךְ וְיָשָׁר אָתָּה	A
surely now he will rouse himself on your behalf,	כִּי־עַתָּה יָעִיר עָלֶיךָ	B
and restore you to your rightful place.	וְשִׁלַּם נְוַת צִדְקֶךָ׃	C

The arrangement of the verse is Subordinate + HEAD^1 + HEAD^2. Again the fact that the content of A, a condition, also relates to C, is not clearly indicated by this means. We may therefore display the tricolon in the following way:

```
┌─Subord──────────────── אִם־זַךְ וְיָשָׁר אָתָּה (A)
└─HEAD─────┬─HEAD¹──── כִּי־עַתָּה יָעִיר עָלֶיךָ (B)
           └─HEAD²──── וְשִׁלַּם נְוַת צִדְקֶךָ (C)
```

The various relationships between the individual cola are now evident. Lines B and C are two co-ordinate clauses which together relate to the A-line as the main proposition (or apodosis) that would result from the fulfilment of the condition.

In the chapters that follow resort will sometimes be made to the foregoing kind of diagramming of intercolon relations to facilitate our analysis.[60]

---

60 It is necessary to remark briefly upon the approach of Wendland to the analysis of poetic bicola. In his work on *Analyzing the Psalms* he offers an extremely comprehensive breakdown of the various possible semantic relations between conjoining lines (pp. 61–92). This breakdown is helpful in appreciating intercolon relations, yet Wendland is mistaken when he defines *all* of the bicola he analyses as 'parallelisms'. Not only is his 'base-similarity' (i.e., a synonymous parallelism, our HEAD + Parallel) categorised as a parallelism but also a whole range of other semantically related cola, such as: base-circumstance, reason-result, means-purpose, cause-effect, condition-result, base-manner, base-comparison, and a good many others. All of these he describes as 'semantic relations between parallel lines' (p. 91), and occur in a chapter entitled 'Connected Parallelism' (ch. 3). To include bicola having this wide range of semantic relations is inconsistent with his own definition of parallelism at the beginning of the same chapter. There Wendland states that 'Such a coupling of poetic lines is effected by formal as well as semantic repetition' (p. 58). Most of his various categories in fact lack entirely the component of 'semantic repetition'. Thus, according to Wendland, 'By the strength of your arm, preserve those condemned to die' (Ps. 79:11), is an instance of connected parallelism (p. 78), which is evidently not the case. Wendland's analysis would be on a sounder footing if he discarded the term 'parallelism' altogether for the majority of his descriptions of interlineal relations. Many of his examples in this chapter would come under the

2.4 Summary

In this chapter we have looked at the nature of the basic poetic unit, the colon, and how several of these may be constructed into larger units. We have discussed the various types of parallelism, how this is mainly semantic, though syntactic, morphological, lexical, and phonological parallelism also exist. In addition, further features that frequently accompany parallelism were reviewed, namely, gapping, embedding, and extending. A four-fold classification of basic relations between cola was proposed, these being HEAD + Parallel, $HEAD^1$ + $HEAD^2$, HEAD + Subordinate, and HEAD[$Phrase^1$ + $Phrase^2$]. A manner of clearly displaying these relations in more complex poetic structures was also demonstrated.

The description of the poetic line outlined in this chapter will provide a framework to which reference will be made in the subsequent chapters. Yet, before we can begin to explore to the problems relating to word order in poetry, we must first look in the next chapter at previous studies of word order in Biblical Hebrew, and how variation in its most common genre, i.e., narrative, is best accounted for.

---

categories that have been proposed of $HEAD^1$ + $HEAD^2$ and HEAD + Subordinate, both of which fall outside of the category of parallelism. (Note that in his analysis Wendland prefers to call the HEAD line the 'base'. This, we feel, is not as appropriate as HEAD, which can apply equally well to monocola and those bicola containing just a single grammatical sentence and therefore lacking any element to which the term 'base' could accurately apply).

CHAPTER 3

Pragmatic Factors Influencing Word Order in Biblical Hebrew

This chapter considers the previous neglect and the recent emergence of word order studies in Biblical Hebrew. The theory of information structure is outlined and the manner in which this has already been applied to Hebrew narrative is illustrated. The contents of this chapter thus provide the theoretical frame of reference for the analysis of poetry that follows.

3.1 Previous Considerations of Word Order in Biblical Hebrew

That Biblical Hebrew can vary its basic word order has long been recognised. The medieval rabbinic interpreters showed that they were aware of such variations in the biblical text, yet they commented little upon the feature. This was true even of those with a reputation for a stricter adherence to the grammatico-historical approach, such as Abraham ibn Ezra and David Kimhi.[1] Taking as an example a prominent chiasmus, such as הַשָּׁמַיִם מְסַפְּרִים כְּבוֹד־אֵל וּמַעֲשֵׂה יָדָיו מַגִּיד הָרָקִיעַ: (Ps. 19:2, 'The heavens declare the glory of God, the firmament proclaims the work of his hands'), although the parallelism of the two cola is noted by these commentators, the corresponding inversion of clause components (*abc//cba*) goes completely unremarked by both. In rabbinic exegesis when an interpretation of word order was offered it was often midrashic in nature,[2] rather than linguistic or stylistic.

Traditional Hebrew grammars, like those of Gesenius and Davidson, note the possibility of shifting a noun phrase to preverbal position, and refer

---

1   A look at ibn Ezra on Isaiah 40–66 and Kimhi on selected Psalms (1–24, 120–150) revealed scarcely any comments relating to the significance of word order.
2   That is, according to *derash* rather than the *peshat*, or plain sense; cf. D. W. Halivni, *Peshat and Derash: Plain and Applied Meaning in Rabbinic Exegesis* (New York: Oxford University Press, 1991), pp. 7–8. An example of such an interpretation is to be found in Job 1:1, where the word order אִיּוֹב שְׁמוֹ (Comp S: 'Job was his name') is said to signify the wickedness of the person named, while the reverse order, שְׁמוֹ אִיּוֹב (S Comp: 'his name was Job'), would indicate the character's righteousness! See M. Eisemann, *Job: A New Translation with a Commentary Anthologized from Talmudic, Midrashic, and Rabbinic Sources* (New York: Mesorah, 1994), p. 4.

to it simply as 'emphasis'. Gesenius tells us that 'a variation of the usual order of words frequently occurs when any member of the sentence is to be specially emphasized by priority of position'.[3] The notion of emphasis is left undefined.

More than a century later, despite the publication of Muraoka's pioneering *Emphatic Words and Structures in Biblical Hebrew*, a major work on Hebrew syntax by Waltke and O'Connor includes absolutely nothing concerning constituent order in the verbal clause per se.[4]

It was really in the wake of the popularisation of functional grammar in the mid 1980s that the first serious linguistic attempts to account for word order in the Hebrew verbal clause were conducted. This was a grammatical approach well suited, among other things, to the analysis of word order. The late 1980s and 1990s saw a steady stream of articles applying the functional perspective to Biblical Hebrew. It is not our intention to survey this literature. This has been done, not just once but several times.[5] Here it will suffice to list in a footnote those publications which paved the way for others to follow.[6]

---

3 W. Gesenius, *Gesenius' Hebrew Grammar*, translated by A. E. Cowley (Oxford: Clarendon Press, 1910), §142*f*; cf. J. D. Martin, *Davidson's Introductory Hebrew Grammar* (Edinburgh: T. & T. Clark, 1993), p. 38, 'The fact that the subject comes first ... may imply an emphasis on the subject'.

4 In Waltke and O'Connor's *Biblical Hebrew Syntax* the matter of word order is treated, but only in relation to the verbless clause (pp. 130–35). Emphasis is also discussed but only regarding the emphatic nature of pronouns (pp. 293–97), the infinitive absolute (pp. 584–88), and emphatic adverbs (pp. 668–73). A work published over twenty years earlier is far more helpful in its observations on word order and emphasis, i.e., Williams, *Hebrew Syntax*, §§573–74.

5 C. H. J. van der Merwe, 'Explaining Fronting in Biblical Hebrew', *JNSL* 25.2 (1999), pp. 174–79; J.-M. Heimerdinger, *Topic, Focus and Foreground in Ancient Hebrew Narratives*, JSOT Supplement Series (Sheffield: Sheffield Academic Press, 1999), pp. 15–26; K. Shimasaki, *Focus Structure in Biblical Hebrew* (Bethesda, Maryland: CDL Press, 2002), pp. 22–30.

6 S. H. Levinsohn, 'Unmarked and Marked Instances of Topicalisation in Hebrew' Work papers of the Summer Institute of Linguistics, University of North Dakota, vol. 34 (1990); Niccacci, *The Syntax of the Verb in Classical Hebrew Prose* (1990); G. Payne, 'Functional Sentence Perspective: Theme in Biblical Hebrew', *Scandinavian Journal of the Old Testament 1* (1991); C. H. J. van der Merwe, 'The Function of Word Order in Old Hebrew – with Special Reference to Cases where a Syntagmeme Precedes a Verb in Joshua', *JNSL 17* (1991); Bandstra, 'Word Order and Emphasis in Biblical Hebrew Narrative: Syntactic Observations on Genesis 22 from a Discourse Perspective' (1992); R. Buth, 'The Hebrew Verb in Current Discussions, *JOTT 5* (1992); W. Gross, 'Zur syntaktischen Struktur des Vorfelds im hebräishen Verbalsatz', *ZAH 7* (1994). From a more discourse-oriented perspective, but also dealing with word order, we may note R. E. Longacre, *Joseph: A Story of Divine Providence. A Text Theoretical and Textlinguistic Analysis of Genesis 37 and 39–48* (Winona Lake, Indiana: Eisenbrauns, 1989), and D. A. Dawson, *Text-*

Following these years of word order studies, the day has now come in which a Hebrew reference grammar has seen the light that gives significant place to the function of fronted constituents.[7] Yet despite this fact, the scholarly authors of Bible commentaries are still behind in these developments and generally choose either to ignore the marked ordering or put it down to the vague notion of emphasis, as did the earlier grammarians.[8]

There is a significant degree of overlap between the various functional approaches to word order in Biblical Hebrew. It is widely agreed among those Hebraists and linguists who have addressed the problem that preverbal clause components are marked either in order to highlight an element that is in focus, or to show a new topic that is entering the discourse. This agreement is only evident at the most general level. At the same time consensus has been lacking concerning the precise description of these marked constituents and their diverse functions.

The analytical method adopted here, that of information structure shortly to be explained, has the advantage over earlier functional approaches in that it relates all variations in surface form to the underlying pragmatic organisation of the utterance. The theory of information structure is able to provide the precise pragmatic description which functional grammar is unable to achieve. Once the pragmatic articulation of a clause has been determined, one is in a much better position to offer an explanation for its constituent order. The usefulness of this particular theory to the study of Biblical Hebrew has already been demonstrated by others, to be mentioned as we proceed, with respect to the narrative genre,[9] a fact which encourages its application to other genres.

3.2 The Theory of Information Structure

One important development from early functional grammar was the theory of functional sentence perspective. Functional linguists maintained that 'every sentence has two parts; the part that refers to what the addressee is presumed to already have in mind, and the part that adds some new information'.[10] In time this bipartite approach to the analysis of utterances received further refinement and was labelled by Halliday as the 'information

---

Linguistics and Biblical Hebrew, JSOT Supplement Series (Sheffield: Sheffield Academic Press, 1994). Several relevant papers were also published in Bodine (ed.), *Linguistics and Biblical Hebrew* (1994).

7 Van der Merwe (et al.), *Biblical Hebrew Reference Grammar*, chapter 7.
8 This fact will be made apparent in chapter 9.
9 See the references to Heimerdinger and Shimasaki in 3.4 below.
10 T. E. Payne, *Describing Morphosyntax* (Cambridge: Cambridge University Press, 1997), p. 267.

structure' of the sentence.[11] The mechanisms involved in information structure have been described by Van Valin and LaPolla as follows:

> Whenever a sentence is uttered or written, it is done so in a particular communicative context, and for the addressee to correctly interpret the communicative intent of the speaker/writer, the addressee must interpret the sentence in that same context. But as this context goes far beyond the immediate linguistic context to include assumptions of many different types, identification of the proper context by the addressee is not always possible, and so misunderstandings can take place. In order to decrease the chance of misunderstanding, the speaker, in creating the sentence, tailors the form of the sentence to allow the hearer to create the proper context for interpretation with minimal processing effort. For his part, the hearer assumes that the sentence will be tailored in just this way, and so takes the first proposition that comes to mind as the one the speaker intended to communicate, and the first associated set of contextual assumptions that come to his mind as the intended background assumptions. A crucial aspect of this tailoring is the distribution of information in the sentence, which we will call the 'information structure' of the sentence.[12]

Lambrecht's 1994 publication *Information Structure and Sentence Form*[13] presented the first systematic analysis of the various aspects of information structure theory. Though Lambrecht's own application of this theory was entirely to modern languages, this work was to provide further impetus to Biblical Hebrew studies. Two works on Hebrew have seen the light in recent years, which both make extensive use of Lambrecht's work. The first of these was Heimerdinger's *Topic, Focus and Foreground in Ancient Hebrew Narratives* (1999), summarised by one of its reviewers as an 'application of Lambrecht's work on information structure to ancient (Biblical) Hebrew narratives'.[14] The second work was Shimasaki's *Focus Structure in Biblical Hebrew* (2002), which the author presents likewise as 'an application of Lambrecht's "three focus-structure categories" to Biblical Hebrew'.[15] Both works originated as doctoral theses, apparently researched

---

11 R. D. Van Valin and R. J. LaPolla, *Syntax: Structure, Meaning and Function* (Cambridge: Cambridge University Press, 1997), p. 199; cf. K. Lambrecht, *Information Structure and Sentence Form: Topic, focus and the mental representations of discourse referents* (Cambridge: Cambridge University Press, 1994), p. 2.
12 Van Valin and LaPolla, *Syntax*, p. 199.
13 Published in the 'Cambridge Studies in Linguistics' series.
14 S. H. Levinsohn, 'Review of Jean-Marc Heimerdinger's *Topic, Focus and Foreground in Ancient Hebrew Narrative*', *JOTT 14* (2002), p. 126.
15 Shimasaki, *Focus Structure*, p. 30.

contemporaneously without knowledge of each other,[16] yet coming to broadly similar conclusions.

Each of the above two studies tends to concentrate upon the narrative form of the language, a justifiable place to begin since this is the most common form available to us. As the title of the volume by Heimerdinger openly declares, it was the author's express intention to focus upon Hebrew narrative.[17] In the case of Shimasaki it is not stated anywhere that the scope of his research is to be limited in any way, but in practice he also largely confines himself to non-poetic genres. His data consists of Deuteronomy 4:4–11:32, containing 476 clauses, 528 verbless clauses considered in Andersen's *Verbless Clause in the Pentateuch*, and the 296 verbal clauses showing inverted word order listed in the works of Gesenius, Muraoka, and Joüon.[18] Out of these 1,300 clauses all but 40 or so belong to the narrative and legal genres. The remainder are taken from poetic texts, of which only a handful are actually analysed in his work.

Since the labours of the two aforementioned scholars have borne fruit in applying Lambrecht's theory of information structure to Hebrew narrative, it is our aim in the present study to utilise the same basic linguistic framework with exclusive reference to Biblical Hebrew poetry. The object of study, therefore, is a largely untouched field of research. While this application of information structure to the poetic genre is a major aspect to our research, the study is taken further. Following the identification and description of various focus structures in poetic texts and their distinction from purely defamiliar forms, the question is also tackled as to how variation of word order influences the phenomenon of parallelism, one of the principal rhetorical features of Hebrew poetry. The diverse forms of this poetic parallelism are investigated and related to their focus structures. As a result of this, it is possible to describe a number of constraints that certain focus structures impose upon the formation of parallel lines.[19] The scope of study also covers the specific functions exercised by particular unusually constructed forms of parallelism. It can be seen, therefore, that the present study goes beyond a simple application of Lambrecht to poetry. However, it is with his description of information structure and sentence form that we must begin.

---

16 Suggested by the fact that neither writer makes reference to the other.
17 Heimerdinger (*Topic, Focus and Foreground*, p. 27) lists his data as: Genesis, Exodus 1–12, Numbers 20–23, Joshua, Judges, 1 and 2 Samuel, and 1 and 2 Kings. Heimerdinger does also give a number of examples falling outside of this data, a few of which are taken from poetic texts (e.g., Is. 1:3 on p. 171).
18 Shimasaki, *Focus Structure*, p. 34.
19 See chapter 7.

3.3 Lambrecht's *Information Structure and Sentence Form*

In this section an outline of the theory of information structure and the definitions of its essential components are presented in order to give the reader a working knowledge of what is involved in the theory.[20]

Lambrecht's work centres upon the principal pragmatic functions of language in general. By 'pragmatic' is meant that aspect of language which goes beyond sentence grammar, which takes into consideration both the context in which the utterance was spoken and the shared cultural and informational assumptions of the interlocutors.[21] So Lambrecht proposes a technical definition of information structure as:

> That component of sentence grammar in which propositions as conceptual representations of states of affairs are paired with lexicogrammatical structures in accordance with the mental states of interlocutors who use and interpret these structures as units of information in given discourse contexts.[22]

In short, the information structure of an utterance is the formal expression of its pragmatic organisation. When one speaks of the topic of a sentence, therefore, this is a pragmatic consideration, as also is the concept of focus. When the topic entity is related to its comment and the focus element to its presupposition, the manner in which these components are organised in context may be called the information structure of the sentence. In this matter of organisation, information structure is bound up with components of the language such as morphology, syntax, word order, and phonology.

From the perspective of information structure there are two ways that sentences may be pragmatically articulated, these being topic-comment and presupposition-focus. These two articulations will be illustrated below[23] and encountered again as we analyse diverse Hebrew texts.

---

20 For the subjects treated in this section the reader is especially referred to Heimerdinger, *Topic, Focus and Foreground*, pp. 13–15 (for information structure in general); pp. 128–33 (for topic), and pp. 162–70 (for focus structure); and Shimasaki, *Focus Structure*, pp. 84–101 (for topic), and pp. 50–55 (for focus structure).

21 Cf. Shimasaki, *Focus Structure*, pp. 114–15. It should be noted that linguists divide pragmatics into 'conversational pragmatics', which chiefly considers utterances in relation to their conversational settings, and 'discourse pragmatics', which concerns how the form of the sentence relates to its discourse context and the shape of the utterance in relation to the assumed state of knowledge in the mind of the addressee (cf. Lambrecht, *Information Structure*, pp. 4–5). It is with this latter that we are concerned.

22 Lambrecht, *Information Structure*, p. 5.

23 See 'The three focus structures', 3.3.3 below.

3.3.1 Topic and Activation State

In connection with the organisation of a proposition, the two key functions of topic and focus require definition. Our treatment of these concepts will restrict itself to their essential features.

Within the context of information structure 'topic' is not merely a structural position in the sentence, as some functional linguists would maintain.[24] Rather, Lambrecht defines topic in terms of its pragmatic function, which is naming 'the thing which the proposition expressed by the sentence is ABOUT'.[25] As a more formal definition he offers the following:

> TOPIC: A referent is interpreted as the topic of a proposition if in a given situation the proposition is construed as being about this referent, i.e., as expressing information which is relevant to and which increases the addressee's knowledge of this referent.[26]

'Referent' is that term used by Lambrecht to mean 'The entities and states of affairs designated by linguistic expressions in particular utterances'.[27] When the proposition presents information *about* this referent, says Lambrecht, then that referent has the status of topic in the proposition. In the English sentence 'John is sleeping' (where the consideration is 'What is John doing?'), 'John' is the topic.

Often the word or phrase indicating the topic will fulfil the role of grammatical subject in a sentence, but this is not necessarily so. Lambrecht spells out the fact that 'non-subjects may act as topics ... and subjects may act as non-topics'.[28] It might be the case that the topic expression occupies the position of direct object, indirect object, etc.[29] Moreover, not all sentences have topics. Strictly speaking, in the sense defined here, they are

---

24 Cf. Van Valin and LaPolla, *Syntax*, p. 203. Note that in this discussion 'topic' always signifies the sentence topic, not the discourse topic. The latter pertains more to text cohesion that to the structure of sentences. See T. A. van Dijk, *Macrostructures: An Interdisciplinary Study of Global Structures in Discourse, Interaction and Cognition* (Hillsdale, New Jersey: Lawrence Erlbaum Associates, 1980), pp. 94–98. Nor does this 'topic' relate to that element, sometimes referred to as 'topicalisation', whose function is to set the scene within which the following prediction holds. See 3.5 below and Lambrecht, *Information Structure*, p. 118.
25 *Ibid.*
26 *Ibid.*, p. 131.
27 *Ibid.*, p. 37.
28 *Ibid.* In argument focus, for example, the grammatical subject in focus does not have the function of sentence topic. In such a case the referent indicated by the subject phrase is being identified, not being commented upon, that is, it is not what the proposition is about. See 3.3.3(b) below.
29 Cf. Lambrecht's Spanish and German examples, *Information Structure*, p. 133.

only to be found in sentences of the topic-comment kind,[30] which is just one possible pragmatic articulation of a proposition.

To describe the different manifestations of topic expressions within discourse earlier functional grammar employed terms such as New Topic, Given Topic, Resumed Topic, and so forth.[31] The theory of information structure prefers to describe the topical relation in terms of the 'activation state' of the referent.[32] This designation signifies the level of consciousness a person possesses concerning the particular entity being referred to. The entity might be at the centre of the person's consciousness, on its periphery, or might not be present at all. This entails that a speaker will represent referents in different ways according to his assumptions of the hearer's knowledge of those referents at the time of communication. The less the knowledge that is assumed by the speaker, the greater the representation of the entity in question to the mind of the addressee.

Lambrecht, developing the ideas of Chafe before him, defines the three distinct activation states, that is, the levels at which an entity or concept may be active in a person's consciousness, as:[33]

1. Active:
   the referent is the current focus of the hearer's consciousness.
2. Accessible:
   the referent, though not the current focus of consciousness, may be inferred from the physical or linguistic context.
3. Inactive:
   the referent is in the hearer's long-term memory.

In each of the above cases the referent may be identified since the present mental focus of the addressee, the context in which the communication occurs, or the addressee's long-term memory, make the referent available. In such cases the referent is said to be 'identifiable'.[34] Yet it is also possible that none of the above factors will enable the hearer to make a correct identification of the referent. In the case of brand new referents nothing is assumed to exist in the current focus of consciousness, or context, or past memory, which the speaker can draw upon to allow an accurate identification of the referent he wishes to mention. Lambrecht

---

30 That is, 'predicate-focus' clauses. See 3.4.1 (a) below.
31 See S. C. Dik, *The Theory of Functional Grammar*, Part 1: The Structure of the Clause (Dordrecht: Foris Publications, 1989), p. 267; cf. the discussion of Rosenbaum in chapter 10 of this volume.
32 Lambrecht, *Information Structure*, p. 93.
33 *Ibid.*, pp. 93–95; cf. Van Valin and LaPolla, *Syntax*, p. 200.
34 Lambrecht, *Information Structure*, p. 106.

speaks of such referents as 'unidentifiable'.[35] When this situation pertains, then the speaker has to resort to other means in order to facilitate the representation of the referent to the mind of the hearer. One such means is 'anchoring', that is, a totally new referent may be introduced by connecting it with some more identifiable referent.[36] Typically this would be done by combining an indefinite phrase with one that is definite, such as, 'A friend of mine', but anchoring may take on other forms also. When such anchoring is not possible, then the brand-new topic can only be introduced by a special presentational device, for which languages have their own particular forms, such as a dummy subject or an existential verb. A common method of doing this in English would be to use 'There was a man ...'.

These various activation states have a correlation with the way in which the referent will be '[en]coded' in the language.[37] Active referents, for example, are generally encoded by means of an unaccented constituent.[38] Likewise, all pronominal forms necessarily have an active referent. In English an inactive but identifiable referent will typically be activated through a definite noun phrase bearing pitch prominence. Lambrecht observes, however, that those topics categorised as 'accessible' have no direct phonological or morphosyntactic correlates, but may be encoded in different ways depending on whether they are textually, situationally, or inferentially accessible.[39]

3.3.2 Focus, Assertion and Presupposition

Coming now to the term 'focus', this is defined by Lambrecht with reference to other important concepts which will also require explanation:

> FOCUS: The semantic component of a pragmatically structured proposition whereby the assertion differs from the presupposition.[40]

To understand what Lambrecht means by this we also need to know what is intended by the terms 'assertion' and 'presupposition'. The assertion, or more strictly speaking, the 'pragmatic assertion',[41] in the context of

---

35 *Ibid.*, p. 105.
36 *Ibid.*, p. 105; cf. Van Valin and LaPolla, *Syntax*, p. 200.
37 Lambrecht, *Information Structure*, p. 106, uses the term 'coded'. Heimerdinger prefers 'encoded', *Topic, Focus and Foreground*, p. 114.
38 Lambrecht says that 'Unaccented expressions are marked for the feature "active referent" but accented expressions are unmarked for this feature' (*Information Structure*, p. 106).
39 *Ibid.*, p. 107.
40 *Ibid.*, p. 213.
41 *Ibid.*, p. 52.

information structure, denotes that piece of information, expressed through a sentence, that the speaker expects the addressee to come to know as a result of hearing it.[42] In this proposition it is not new or focused information alone that makes it informative, but the relationship between this information and what is already assumed. This latter is referred to as the 'pragmatic presupposition'.[43] The other element of the assertion, that which is unknown or unpredictable, is described as the 'focus'. Together, therefore, both focus and presupposition constitute an assertion, as Lambrecht says, 'To make an assertion is to establish a RELATION between a presupposed set of propositions ... and a non-presupposed proposition, the latter being in some sense added to, or superimposed on, the former'.[44] By way of illustration,[45] the name 'John' standing alone is not informative. If, however, 'John' is taken as a focused noun phrase and combined with a presupposition that 'X hit me' (where X is some yet unidentified agent), then it becomes meaningful, such as in the sentence 'It was John who hit me', or in response to the question 'Who hit me?'. This combination now creates a fully formed assertion. We may simply depict this relationship as:

Assertion =
Presupposition + Focus

The following sub-section will illustrate how the components of presupposition and focus vary in the pragmatic organisation of different kinds of sentences.

3.3.3 The Three Focus Structures

At the heart of Lambrecht's theory of information structure are the three focus structures: predicate focus, argument focus, and sentence focus. All

---

42 *Ibid.*
43 *Ibid.* Cf. Van Valin and LaPolla, *Syntax*, p. 201. There it is explained that the assertion and presupposition may be described as 'pragmatic' because 'it is a pragmatically structured utterance, generally involving both "old" information, such as the topic and the presuppositions associated with the topic, and "new" information, such as the comment about the topic'.
44 *Ibid.*, pp. 57–58. We acknowledge Dryer's criticisms of Lambrecht's not wholly adequate understanding of pragmatic presupposition, in M. S. Dryer, 'Focus, Pragmatic Presupposition, and Activated Propositions', *Journal of Pragmatics 26* (1996), pp. 515–17. Dryer claims that a distinction should be maintained in the presupposition of things believed, and of things mentally represented, though not believed. Note that this distinction does not in any way effect the findings of the present study.
45 Adapted from Van Valin and LaPolla, *Syntax*, p. 202.

meaningful propositions exhibit one of these categories of focus structure.[46] It is this aspect of Lambrecht's writing that is prominent above all else in the application to Biblical Hebrew by Heimerdinger and Shimasaki, and to which frequent reference will be made in the ensuing chapters of the present work.

It has previously been stated[47] that all propositions may be pragmatically organised as either topic-comment or presupposition-focus. The former of these articulations has only one realisation. The latter, however, has three, distinguished by the extent of the focus domain, whether only one clause constituent, the entire predication, or the whole clause.

We illustrate the various focus structures briefly in turn with reference to the English sentence: 'The children went to school'.[48] This proposition could be expressed having each of the three focus structures, though with varying pragmatic import.

(a) PREDICATE FOCUS

The sentence could be uttered in response to a question as follows:

Q. What did the children do next?
A. The children went to school.

In this case 'the children' indicates an active topic. Either the previous conversation or the circumstances in which the proposition was uttered has activated this particular topic in the minds of the interlocutors. Being active the topic is available to comment upon. The question is posed as to what particular action the children performed. Here we detect the presupposition. Underlying the question is the pragmatic presupposition on the part of the speaker that 'the children did X', where X denotes some unknown activity. The information the speaker lacks is what that X might be. The answer provides that information in the form of the assertion that the topic(s) under discussion 'went to school'. This information is predicated to the subject phrase of the sentence. The articulation of the proposition, therefore, is of the topic-comment kind, and with respect to its focus structure has predicate focus. The various components which combine to create the information structure of this utterance may be tabulated as follows:[49]

---

46 By 'focus structure' Lambrecht (*Information Structure*, p. 222) means 'the conventional association of a focus meaning with a sentence form'. For example, the sentence pragmatically articulated as topic-comment correlates with a particular focus structure identifiable in the lexical, grammatical or phonological features of the language.
47 See 3.3 above.
48 Based upon the examples in Lambrecht, *Information Structure*, p. 121.
49 This manner of representing the information structure is that employed by Lambrecht, e.g., *Information Structure*, p. 226.

Sentence:	'The children went to school'
Presupposition:	'Children are available as a topic for comment X'
Assertion:	'X = went to school'
Focus:	'went to school'
Focus domain:	VP (i.e., predicate)

In English the pragmatic implications of the utterance would be conveyed by prosodic means. This prosodic marking Lambrecht represents as: 'The children WENT TO SCHOOL', where the upper case letters represent prominent pitch. Respecting such topic-comment articulations English would place low pitch upon the topic item and high pitch upon the close of the focus domain, here the verb phrase.

Lambrecht adds the important observation that sentences of this type, whose function is simply to comment, are 'syntactically and prosodically UNMARKED with respect to their information structure'.[50] This would mean that in a language permitting word-order variation[51] like Biblical Hebrew, such topic-comment propositions would employ the basic VSO constituent order.

(b) ARGUMENT FOCUS

Alternatively, the utterance might be in answer to a differently framed question, such as the following:

Q. Who went to school?
A. The children went to school.

In this instance the speaker does not offer a statement about the children, as in the previous example. Rather, Lambrecht informs us, 'its communicative function is to provide the referent solicited by the word *who* in the preceding question'.[52] In this sentence the presupposition is that someone, X, did in fact go to school. The whole of the information contained in the predicate, therefore, is known. The inquirer wishes to learn who that X was. In response the person questioned asserts that this X is 'the children'. Hence the function of this sentence is that of identification,[53] since it serves to identify the missing referent, which is an argument forming part of the proposition. The information may be schematically shown as:

---

50 *Ibid.*, p. 122; cf. p. 228, 'the predicate-focus structure is the UNMARKED pragmatic articulation'.
51 That is typically where the placement of a constituent in a particular position is not necessary to signify its grammatical role within the clause.
52 *Ibid.*, p. 122.
53 Lambrecht refers to such argument-focus clauses as 'identificational', *ibid*, pp. 122-23.

Sentence:	'The children went to school'
Presupposition:	'X went to school'
Assertion:	'X = the children'
Focus:	'children'
Focus domain:	NP[Su] (i.e., argument)

Regarding the pragmatic marking in English, Lambrecht defines the prosodic pattern as: 'The CHILDREN went to school'. It is the focused element, here the grammatical subject, that carries the prominent pitch pattern.

In contrast to the previous sentence-focus type, we note that 'the children' here is not the topic, since the sentence articulation is not that of the topic-comment. Rather the NP[Su] is the focus expression of the proposition, and is not making itself available for comment. In English this distinction is clearly observable through the prosodic marking of the NP[Su] (as focus) in the case of argument focus, but the non-marking of the NP[Su] (as topic) in predicate focus.[54]

(c) SENTENCE FOCUS

A third possibility is that the question to which the proposition forms a response is:

Q. What happened?
A. The children went to school.

The major difference between this and the foregoing two sentence types is the absence of any pragmatic presuppositions whatsoever.[55] It is not assumed by the speaker either that there is an active topic who did something, as in (a), or that somebody went to school, as in (b). It is merely presupposed that something happened. The purpose of the sentence, says Lambrecht, is not primarily to convey information about the children, but 'to inform the addressee of an EVENT involving the children as participants'.[56] In such cases the focus covers the whole proposition. Everything that is presented is in effect new, both the

---

54 In later sections of his book Lambrecht goes on to show that other languages might indicate the distinction by other means, whether phonological, morphological, lexical, syntactic, or by variation in word order.
55 Cf. Lambrecht, *Information Structure*, p. 233. This need not mean that there exist no presuppositions at all on the part of the speaker, but that there are no pragmatic presuppositions. Obviously, it is presupposed that events occur and that one may have just happened. But presuppositions of this kind have no bearing on the information structure of the sentence.
56 *Ibid.*, p. 124.

participant, 'children' not currently being an active topic, and the action in which they are involved. For this reason, Lambrecht refers to it as an 'out of the blue' utterance. More formally he describes clauses of this type as 'event-reporting', since that is their main function. In such cases the pragmatic structure of the proposition can be seen to be non-binary, in contrast with the other two structures, since assertion and focus coincide.[57] The information structure of this sentence-focus example may be represented in the following way:

Sentence:	'The children went to school'
Presupposition:	Ø
Assertion:	'The children went to school'
Focus:	'The children went to school'
Focus domain:	Clause (i.e., sentence)

With respect to the prosodic marking Lambrecht shows the pitch pattern to be: 'The CHILDREN went to SCHOOL', in which the sentence is uttered with two prosodic peaks.[58] The focus marking in English, therefore, would differ with respect to all three sentence types.

One other function of the sentence-focus structure is that which Lambrecht refers to as 'presentational'.[59] By this is meant sentences that 'serve to introduce not-yet activated referents into a discourse'.[60] This particular focus structure is, therefore, multifunctional, i.e., event-reporting and presentational.[61]

In the foregoing texts we have exemplified the three basic forms of information structure that Lambrecht identifies. The form, designation, and function of each may be summarised by means of the following table:

Sentence form	Focus structure	Pragmatic function
The children WENT TO SCHOOL	Predicate focus	Commenting
The CHILDREN went to school	Argument focus	Identification
The CHILDREN went to SCHOOL	Sentence focus	Event-reporting

---

57 *Ibid.*, p. 234.
58 *Ibid.*, p. 121.
59 *Ibid.*, pp. 143-44, 222.
60 *Ibid.*, p. 143.
61 The similarity between these two is discussed by Lambrecht, *ibid.*, pp. 143-44.

Finally, it is important to note that each of the three English sentences above consists of the same essential semantic content. In each case NP[Su], V, and NP[DO] are identical. Yet as regards the pragmatic structuring each clause is unique. In English each one would be differentiated by its own particular pitch pattern. In his work Lambrecht uses the term 'allosentences' to describe clauses which are 'semantically equivalent but formally and pragmatically divergent'.[62] That is to say, they differ, like our three examples, only with respect to their pragmatic structuring. These English allosentences all have the same syntactic structure. In other languages this need not be the case. Where the focus structure is marked by means other than prosodic, the allosentences might all differ in form. This would be the case, for example, where the language expressed its focus structure through word order, as in Biblical Hebrew.

3.4 Information Structure and Biblical Hebrew

We come now to consider the application of Lambrecht's theory of information structure to the narrative language of the Old Testament, that is, the language that predominates in the historical books.

3.4.1 The Three Focus Structures in Hebrew Narrative

First the three focus structures, predicate-focus, argument-focus, and sentence-focus structure, are illustrated with reference to Hebrew narrative texts. Since both Heimerdinger and Shimasaki treat each of these categories in some depth, reference will often be made to their works. At this stage we restrict ourselves to a demonstration of how different kinds of Hebrew sentence may be analysed in terms of their information structure. Later more detailed discussion will be presented in the context of the analysis of specific poetic texts.

(a) PREDICATE FOCUS

Sentences having predicate-focus structure, as seen above, place the focus upon the information contained in the predicate rather than on the entity to which that information is predicated. Their function is to comment[63] upon a topic that is active, or at least accessible. In Biblical Hebrew the basic form of the verbal clause with this information structure is VSO.[64] The majority of *wayyiqtol* narrative clauses fall into this category. Several examples are given by way of illustration.

---

62 *Ibid*, p. 6 (adopting terminology proposed by Daneš); cf. p. 120. Shimasaki prefers to use the term 'allo-clauses', which shall also be employed in the present work.
63 Shimasaki, *Focus Structure*, pp. 84, 86.
64 Where both an explicit subject phrase and object phrase are optional.

(1) *Exodus 2:15*

Moses fled from Pharaoh
and he settled in the land of Midian.

וַיִּבְרַח מֹשֶׁה מִפְּנֵי פַרְעֹה
וַיֵּשֶׁב בְּאֶרֶץ־מִדְיָן

Both verbal clauses given here are pragmatically constructed after the manner of predicate focus. Each clause is verb-initial, and in each clause the topic commented upon is Moses. In the first clause (VSM) Moses is encoded as a NP, מֹשֶׁה. Even though he is the major participant in the discourse, this explicit reference to Moses is necessary to avoid ambiguity, since the previous sentence mentions both Pharaoh and Moses. The second clause (VM), however, continues the same topic as the first and so the referent is simply encoded in the form of the verbal affix. Both clauses, therefore, have the function of commenting upon an active referent.[65]

(2) *Exodus 2:4*

His sister stood at a distance,
to find out what would happen to him.

וַתֵּתַצַּב אֲחֹתוֹ מֵרָחֹק
לְדֵעָה מַה־יֵּעָשֶׂה לוֹ׃

In this example the sister of Moses cannot be said to be an active topic. She has not been mentioned before in the book of Exodus up to this point. Yet the previous three verses of Exodus 2 do relate the affairs of Moses' family, making explicit reference to his father, his mother and his birth. To introduce a sister in verse 4, therefore, is to present a topic that, although not active, may be readily inferred in the light of the context.[66] The narrator is speaking of the family of Moses, and it is not unreasonable to suppose that he had siblings. For this reason, his sister can enter the narrative without any special presentational clause.[67] We note that she is linked, or 'anchored',[68] to Moses by means of the possessive suffix 'his sister', a common device with respect to such accessible referents. The sister immediately begins to participate in the action, and so she occupies the place of a topic in this predicate-focus clause.

---

65 It is to be noted that in the first clause of this example the predicate domain is split into two. The verb precedes the subject while the modifying phrase follows it. On this feature Givón comments, 'One must first note that a VSO language is "pragmatically schizophrenic," since the *new information* portion of the sentence is scattered on both sides of the topic/subject' ('The Drift from VSO to SVO in Biblical Hebrew', p. 241), quoted in Shimasaki, *Focus Structure*, p. 105.
66 This is a case of what Lambrecht would describe as 'inferentially accessible' (*Information Structure*, p. 100). Cf. Shimasaki, *Focus Structure*, p. 39. From the comments of Heimerdinger, *Topic, Focus and Foreground*, p. 138, we could say that the mention of Moses' mother and father has created what he terms 'a "family" frame' and that, as Heimerdinger states, 'the referents included in this frame are considered as identifiable'.
67 Such as those described below under sentence focus.
68 Cf. 3.3.1 above.

(3) *Genesis 14:21*
Give me the people,
but take the goods for yourself.

תֶּן־לִי הַנֶּפֶשׁ
וְהָרְכֻשׁ קַח־לָךְ׃

This verse introduces us to the concept of the 'dominant focal element' within a predicate-focus sentence. Following Lambrecht, we observe that, 'The syntactic domain in a sentence which expresses the focus component of the pragmatically structured proposition will be called the FOCUS DOMAIN'.[69] With regard to predicate-focus clauses the focus domain could contain a verb phrase comprising both verb and direct object, indirect object, or some prepositional or adverbial phrase. We may say, therefore, that in this particular category of clause type there is a 'broad' focus in that it extends over more than one constituent.[70] This is in contrast with the 'narrow' focus that pertains in argument-focus, where the focus falls upon a single constituent only. However, as Heimerdinger points out, within the broad focus domain pertaining in predicate-focus clauses, there can be one element that is more important that the other(s).[71] This Heimerdinger refers to as the DFE, or 'dominant focal element'. It is that constituent which is the 'informationally pivotal element of the assertion'.[72] This explains why it is that sometimes within a predicate-focus clause a normally postverbal constituent is shifted to the clause-initial position before its governing verb. In such cases it is this fronted constituent that is more prominent within the broader focus domain. Genesis 14:21 cited above contains a clear example of this phenomenon. Here the king of Sodom is addressing Abram following his recovery of the captives and goods taken from the cities of the plain. The two clauses both have predicate focus. Abram is evidently an active topic[73] and is referred to simply through the 2nd person forms of the imperative. Yet the issue concerns the two NP[DO]s within these predicates, i.e., the people and the plunder. Due to Abram's efforts the king makes him the generous offer of all the goods, while the king receives back only his own people. These two NPs, therefore, are seen to be in a contrastive relationship.[74] Contrast is one of the several specific categories of focus to be mentioned below.

---

69 Lambrecht, *Information Structure*, p. 214.
70 Cf. Van Valin and LaPolla, *Syntax*, p. 206; cf. Heimerdinger, *Topic, Focus and Foreground*, p. 165.
71 *Ibid.*, pp. 167–68. This is regarded by one of his reviewers as a significant element in Heimerdinger's work. See Levinsohn, 'Review of Jean-Marc Heimerdinger's *Topic, Focus and Foreground in Ancient Hebrew Narrative*', p. 136.
72 Heimerdinger, *Topic, Focus and Foreground*, p. 168.
73 Being the sentence topic in verse 20c.
74 Hence NRSV ESV TEV NLT make the connector between the two clauses 'but'. Cf. Heimerdinger's own rendering, *Topic, Focus and Foreground*, p. 172.

(b) ARGUMENT FOCUS

In this second type of focus structure, the focused element of the proposition consists solely of one constituent. In Biblical Hebrew this constituent will generally be placed in the preverbal position. All else in the clause that follows the fronted element is presuppositional information. The reasons for the markedness of the particular constituent are manifold. These will all be investigated in due course. For the present, two examples suffice.

(1) *Judges 1:1–2*

The Israelites inquired of YHWH, saying,	וַיִּשְׁאֲלוּ בְּנֵי יִשְׂרָאֵל בַּיהוָה לֵאמֹר
'Who shall go up first for us	מִי יַעֲלֶה־לָּנוּ אֶל־הַכְּנַעֲנִי בַּתְּחִלָּה
to fight against the Canaanites?'.	לְהִלָּחֶם בּוֹ׃
YHWH said, 'Judah shall go up'.	וַיֹּאמֶר יְהוָה יְהוּדָה יַעֲלֶה

When asked which of the twelve tribes was to lead the others in their assault upon the occupants of Canaan, the Lord answers by means of an SV-clause, יְהוּדָה יַעֲלֶה. The answer could simply have been the single NP יְהוּדָה,[75] since obviously the content of the verb would have been implicitly understood. But in this case the verb יַעֲלֶה is repeated from the question. We see, therefore, that the NP[Su] expresses the newly asserted information,[76] while the information of the verb phrase is entirely presuppositional. This example illustrates the role of identification which is the primary function of argument-focus clauses.[77]

(2) *1 Samuel 8:7*

YHWH said to Samuel,	וַיֹּאמֶר יְהוָה אֶל־שְׁמוּאֵל
'Obey the voice of the people	שְׁמַע בְּקוֹל הָעָם
in all they say to you;	לְכֹל אֲשֶׁר־יֹאמְרוּ אֵלֶיךָ
for they have not rejected you,	כִּי לֹא אֹתְךָ מָאָסוּ
but they have rejected me	כִּי־אֹתִי מָאֲסוּ
from reigning over them'.	מִמְּלֹךְ עֲלֵיהֶם׃

In the previous example the fronted argument was a NP[Su]. Here it is a Pn[DO] that appears preverbally in two clauses. Both Heimerdinger and Shimasaki concur in taking the proposition 'they rejected X' as presupposed

---

75 On clause fragments as legitimate answers to questions, cf. S. C. Dik, *Theory of Functional Grammar*, Part 2: Complex and Derived Constructions (Berlin: Mouton de Gruyter, 1997), p. 379.

76 And therefore would probably have been the sole bearer of prominent pitch in the clause. Cf. Shimasaki, *Focus Structure*, p. 144, where the argument-focus SV-clause of Judges 1:2 (יְהוּדָה יַעֲלֶה) is contrasted with the sentence-focus SV-clause of Joshua 18:5 (יְהוּדָה יַעֲמֹד).

77 *Ibid.*, pp. 142, 241; cf. 3.3.3 (b) above.

information.⁷⁸ This is evident from the background to the conversation (vv. 4–6). The two direct objects provide the identity of the two possible candidates whom Israel had rejected. In Samuel's mind it was himself, but through their request for a king it was in fact God whom they had rejected. The context and use of the Hebrew construction ... כִּי לֹא ... כִּי suggests that manner of focus usually designated 'replacing'.⁷⁹ Again in this example the function of identification is evident.

Additional examples of argument focus could be adduced in which the fronted constituent is an indirect object, a prepositional phrase, adverb, or an infinitival phrase.⁸⁰

(c) SENTENCE FOCUS

In Biblical Hebrew, according to both Heimerdinger and Shimasaki, sentence-focus verbal constructions consist of a NP + V clause.⁸¹ Here the whole clause, both argument and predicate, is in focus. It will be observed that, as regards the surface form of the Hebrew, this resembles the argument-focus clause treated above. However, there is a clear distinction between the contexts in which each type of focus structure operates, and Shimasaki proposes an original difference in pitch between the two clause types. While argument-focus clauses invariably show a definite dependence on the immediately preceding text, which provides the rationale for the focused constituent, sentence focus is independent – sequentially, logically, or temporally⁸² – of the preceding context. Regarding the pitch, Shimasaki argues that in sentence-focus clauses both argument and predicate would have been phonologically marked by high pitch, whereas in clauses having argument focus this would have been true of the former component only.⁸³

In order to illustrate the form and function of sentence-focus clauses in Hebrew narrative we present two examples. The first is typical of the event-reporting kind of proposition. The second demonstrates how the

---

78 Heimerdinger, *Topic, Focus and Foreground*, p. 183; Shimasaki, *Focus Structure*, p. 137.
79 See below in 3.3.2 (c), and later poetic examples in 4.2.2 (b).
80 Examples with various arguments may be found in Heimerdinger, *Topic, Focus and Foreground*, pp. 180–81; Shimasaki, *Focus Structure*, pp. 135–38.
81 Heimerdinger, *Topic, Focus and Foreground*, pp. 146–48, 214–18; Shimasaki, *Focus Structure*, pp. 143–84. It should be noted that while Heimerdinger follows Lambrecht's terminology in calling this sentence type 'sentence-focus', Shimasaki prefers to refer to it as 'clause-focus'.
82 Shimasaki, *Focus Structure*, p. 148.
83 *Ibid.*, pp. 144–45. This reasoning is supported by cross-linguistic evidence. Lambrecht discusses the question of what he terms 'prosodic marking' at some length. In that discussion he states that it is usual for the verb phrase (i.e., the predicate) in argument-focus structures to be unaccented (*Information Structure*, p. 307).

sentence-focus structure may also be used in Biblical Hebrew to present new topics into the discourse.

(1) *Genesis 29:9* [SV]

While he was still speaking with them,   עוֹדֶנּוּ מְדַבֵּר עִמָּם

Rachel came with her father's sheep.   וְרָחֵל בָּאָה עִם־הַצֹּאן אֲשֶׁר לְאָבִיהָ

Here the SV-clause functions as an event-reporting utterance. Both Heimerdinger and Shimasaki follow Lambrecht closely here in describing this as the kind of event which comes 'out-of-the-blue'.[84] In Heimerdinger's discussion of the above example[85] he comments that the clause 'reports the event of Rachel's arrival at the well'. However, he continues, 'it does not establish the referent *Rachel* as a topical participant of the chunk of discourse which immediately follows. Rachel's presence at the well having been made known, she fades into the background'. This is one of the distinctive characteristics of clauses of the event-reporting type, that it brings into the discourse an event in isolation, the referent contained in the clause not being maintained as a topic in the following discourse.[86] In this respect it differs from the presentational type of sentence-focus clause illustrated below.

We note in this connection, that the event in question may be either one that occurs as an isolated event within the same temporal framework as the surrounding discourse, as in the above example, or the event may be one that is anterior in time, that it, a flashback to a previous event (e.g., Gen. 31:19).[87] Though both of these are identical with respect to their pragmatic structuring, in the latter case the verb has to be inferred as being temporally pluperfect.[88]

(2) *1 Kings 20:35* [SV]

A certain man of the sons of the prophets said   וְאִישׁ אֶחָד מִבְּנֵי הַנְּבִיאִים אָמַר

to his friend at the command of YHWH ...   אֶל־רֵעֵהוּ בִּדְבַר יְהוָה ...

In this particular example the function of the clause with sentence focus is to present a brand-new referent into the discourse.[89] Unlike the previous event-reporting clause, here the participant is being presented in order to

---

84 Heimerdinger, *Topic, Focus and Foreground*, p. 216; Shimasaki, *Focus Structure*, p. 150; cf. Lambrecht, *Information Structure*, p. 124.
85 Heimerdinger, *Topic, Focus and Foreground*, p. 217.
86 *Ibid.*, p. 216.
87 Cf. Heimerdinger, *Topic, Focus and Foreground*, pp. 217–18; Shimasaki, *Focus Structure*, p. 156. Many instances of this clause type are to be found in Z. Zevit, *The Anterior Construction in Classical Hebrew*, SBL Monograph Series (Atlanta, Georgia: SBL, 1998), pp. 15–32.
88 Heimerdinger, *Topic, Focus and Foreground*, p. 218.
89 Discussed in Heimerdinger, *Topic, Focus and Foreground*, p. 146.

become an active topic in the ensuing discourse.[90] Typically clauses of this presentational kind serve to introduce new episodes or sub-units within the narrative.[91] Shimasaki describes this particular function as 'initiation'.[92]

3.4.2 Focus Particles and Focus Categories

While the constituent order and a consideration of the matters of the focus and presuppositions inherent in a clause determine its information structure, it is the context which allows us to classify the particular pragmatic implications of the focus structure in question. Traditional functional grammar has identified a range of common focus categories, shortly to be described and illustrated. Before doing so, it should be remarked that languages commonly possess a number of focus particles which assist in identifying the particular manner of focus present in a marked structure. This is true of Biblical Hebrew. Its chief focus particles are: רַק, אַךְ, גַּם, אַף, and כִּי אִם.[93] Such words are usually classed as adverbs.[94] Their function is to place a specific manner of focus on the sentence constituent that follows them, or on the whole clause they introduce. Where no such particle occurs, the connotation of the focused component can only be derived from the context.[95]

There follows an overview of the diverse categories of focus, or focus sub-types, that are commonly found.[96] Certain of these are also applicable with respect to marked topics.

---

90 *Ibid.*, p. 215.
91 Cf. Shimasaki, *ibid.* pp. 148–49, 163–64.
92 *Ibid.*, p. 164. The term 'initiation', it should be said, has connotations of a function at the level of discourse rather than at the level of pragmatics.
93 Cf. Heimerdinger, *Topic, Focus and Foreground*, p. 170. אַף is not included, probably since it mostly appears in poetry, whereas Heimerdinger's concern is with narrative.
94 Van der Merwe (et al.), *Biblical Hebrew Reference Grammar*, p. 311; cf. E. König, *The Meaning of Focus Particles: A Comparative Perspective* (London: Routledge, 1991), p. 10. In the present dissertation, however, since these adverbs fall into a category of their own, they are identified by the abbreviation 'P' for 'particle'.
95 As in the case of contrast, for example. See Shimasaki, *Focus Structure*, p. 64.
96 The material that follows draws upon several different works: S. C. Dik, *Functional Grammar* (Dordrecht: Foris Publications, 1981), pp. 69–73; A. Bolkestein, M., C. de Groot and J. L. Mackenzie (eds.), *Syntax and Pragmatics in Functional Grammar* (Dordrecht: Foris Publications, 1985), pp. 44–45; A. Sierwierska, *Functional Grammar* (London: Routledge, 1991), pp. 176–80; Payne, *Describing Morphosyntax*, pp. 268–70; and specifically with reference to Biblical Hebrew: N. Winther-Nielsen, *A Functional Discourse Grammar of Joshua: A Computer-Assisted Rhetorical Structure Analysis*, Coniectanea Biblica, Old Testament Series (Stockholm: Almqvist and Wiksell International, 1995), pp. 67–68; Rosenbaum, *Word-Order Variation in Isaiah 40–55*, pp. 67–70; Shimasaki, *Focus Structure*, pp. 44, 63–70, 137, 187–90.

(a) Contrasting Focus

1 Samuel 18:12

Saul was afraid of David,	וַיִּרָא שָׁאוּל מִלִּפְנֵי דָוִד
because YHWH was with him	כִּי־הָיָה יְהוָה עִמּוֹ
but had departed from Saul.	וּמֵעִם שָׁאוּל סָר:

Contrasting (or 'contrastive') constructions may indicate either 'X did A, but did not do B', or 'X did A, but Y did B'. The difference between the two is in the number of participants involved. In the former case, as in the above example, there is only one, while in the latter there are two. The verse from 1 Samuel 18 tells us that God was with David but had departed from (i.e., was not with) Saul. In the second clause the constituent (PP), relating to Saul, is positioned before the verb in that it is the dominant focal element in the broader domain of predicate focus.

Examples where two separate topical participants perform contrasting actions are also to be found, as in:

1 Samuel 4:1

| They encamped at Ebenezer, | וַיַּחֲנוּ עַל־הָאֶבֶן הָעֵזֶר |
| but the Philistines encamped at Aphek. | וּפְלִשְׁתִּים חָנוּ בַאֲפֵק: |

Here one action is carried out by the Israelites (the referents of 'they'), who camped at Ebenezer, while the Philistines camped in a different place, Aphek. In this instance, therefore, there is a contrast with regard to both the sentence topics and the sentence foci.[97] Respecting the former it is the topic that is marked in the second clause, from which the contrast with the previous clause is to be inferred, while the latter remain in the clause-final position. When there is a contrast between topics as well as foci, it is possible for the topical elements of both members of the contrasting clauses to occupy the clause-initial position (e.g., 1 Sam. 16:7).[98]

(b) Parallel Focus

Genesis 45:14

Then he fell upon his brother Benjamin's neck	וַיִּפֹּל עַל־צַוְּארֵי בִנְיָמִן־אָחִיו
and wept,	וַיֵּבְךְּ
while Benjamin wept upon his neck.	וּבִנְיָמִן בָּכָה עַל־צַוָּארָיו:

---

97 This text is discussed in Heimerdinger, *Topic, Focus and Foreground*, pp. 207–08. On the distinction between contrastive foci and contrastive topics, see Lambrecht, *Information Structure*, pp. 286–96.

98 This is especially the case when the two clauses are in the form of an antithetical proverb or saying (X ... // but Y ...). See 4.2.2 (c).

The 'parallel' pragmatic relationship[99] has been variously defined in functional grammar. Some see it as a type of contrast.[100] Others take it as a form of comparison.[101] In this present work the term will be used to describe that category of focus or topic whereby two participants carry out two similar or (as in the present example) identical actions, possibly but not necessarily simultaneous, with no contrast being inferred.[102] The pattern, therefore, may be described as 'X did A, [while] Y did A' '.

Some difference of opinion exists as to how the focus structure is to be analysed in the two SV-clauses, וּפְלִשְׁתִּים חָנוּ בָאֵפֶק and וּבִנְיָמִן בָּכָה עַל־צַוָּארָיו, in the two foregoing examples. In this instance the SV sequence would be considered by Shimasaki to indicate sentence focus.[103] More probably the focus structure is that of predicate focus, as Heimerdinger would maintain.[104] This is suggested by the fact that both participants, the Israelites and Philistines in the former case, Joseph and Benjamin in the latter, are active topics in the discourse. The fronting of the second NP[Su]s shows that the topics are focused elements for which the contrasting or parallel relationship between them and the preceding topics may be contextually inferred. This is the particular analysis of such contrastive and parallel focus clauses that shall be adopted in the present study. This category of pragmatic relationship, we note, is reasonably common elsewhere in the Hebrew Scriptures, as in:

יְהוָה יִלָּחֵם לָכֶם וְאַתֶּם תַּחֲרִישׁוּן: (Ex. 14:4)
The Lord will fight for you, and you will be still. [SV/SV]

הִתְיַצֵּב כֹּה עַל־עֹלָתֶךָ וְאָנֹכִי אִקָּרֶה כֹּה:[105] (Num. 23:15)
Stand here by your burnt offering, and I will meet the Lord over there. [VM/SVM]

וִהְיִיתֶם לִי לְעָם וְאָנֹכִי אֶהְיֶה לָכֶם לֵאלֹהִים: (Ezek. 36:28)
And you will be my people, and I will be your God. [VMM/SVMM]

All the above examples exhibit marked S^{Pn} V word order in the second clause.

---

99 Not to be confused with the rhetorical parallelism so prevalent in Hebrew poetry. See 2.2.
100 E.g., Dik, *The Theory of Functional Grammar*, Pt. 1, pp. 282–83.
101 E.g., Rosenbaum, *Word-Order Variation in Isaiah 40–55*, p. 70.
102 Cf. Bolkestein (et al.), *Syntax and Pragmatics in Functional Grammar*, pp. 44–45.
103 Shimasaki, *Focus Structure* ch. 8.3. He comes to this conclusion in that he interprets the second parallel clause as 'a fresh, new start' (p. 186), which to his mind can only be sentence focus. This is one area in the application of Lambrecht to Biblical Hebrew where Shimasaki and Heimerdinger do not agree.
104 Cf. the discussion in Heimerdinger, *Topic, Focus and Foreground*, pp. 206–7.
105 The repetition of כֹּה reinforces the parallel nature of the two clauses.

(c) REPLACING FOCUS

Judges 7:2

The men who are with you are too many	רַב הָעָם אֲשֶׁר אִתָּךְ
for me to give the Midianites into their hand,	מִתִּתִּי אֶת־מִדְיָן בְּיָדָם
lest Israel take the credit away from me,[106]	פֶּן־יִתְפָּאֵר עָלַי יִשְׂרָאֵל
saying, 'My own hand has delivered me'.	לֵאמֹר יָדִי הוֹשִׁיעָה לִּי׃

Replacing (or 'replacive') focus is a particular kind of contrast expressing the idea of 'Not X but Y'. The words recorded in this example concern the potential danger that the Israelite victory over the Midianites might be ascribed to their own efforts. God, therefore, drastically reduces the number of men with Gideon so that it is abundantly clear that it was he who gave the victory, and not themselves. In the final clause, יָדִי הוֹשִׁיעָה לִּי, the fronted NP[Su] is the focused argument, while the following verb phrase contains information that is presuppositional. That the Israelites would in fact be delivered from their enemy is assumed in these words that God speaks to Gideon.

It is often the case that the item replacing that which is replaced is adjoined to כִּי אִם, as in the following example:

Numbers 10:30

He said to him, 'I will not go,	וַיֹּאמֶר אֵלָיו לֹא אֵלֵךְ
but I will go to my own land	כִּי אִם־אֶל־אַרְצִי
and to my kindred'.	וְאֶל־מוֹלַדְתִּי אֵלֵךְ׃

The context is that of Moses inviting Hobab the Midianite to journey to Canaan with the Israelites. In reply Hobab says, 'I will not go', the information 'to the place you have mentioned' being implicit. Instead he would rather return to his own land. Thus the first-mentioned place (Canaan) is replaced by the latter (Hobab's own land), which appears in the clause-initial position with כִּי אִם. The following verb אֵלֵךְ ('I will go') is presuppositional, the idea of going being present in Moses' question (v. 29), as well as in the opening response of Hobab (לֹא אֵלֵךְ). Instances of replacing focus are also sometimes found where כִּי alone is used before the marked constituent (e.g., Gen. 19:2).

(d) RESTRICTING FOCUS

i. *Joshua 8:27* [רַק]

| Only the livestock and the spoil of that city | רַק הַבְּהֵמָה וּשְׁלַל הָעִיר הַהִיא |
| Israel took as their plunder. | בָּזְזוּ לָהֶם יִשְׂרָאֵל |

---

106 Although the general sense is clear, this clause is not easily translated into good English. For the third line NJB more idiomatically renders: 'Israel might claim the credit for themselves at my expense'.

ii. *1 Kings 22:44* [אַךְ]
Only they did not remove the high places.   אַךְ הַבָּמוֹת לֹא־סָרוּ

Restricting (or 'restrictive') focus is of the form 'Only/Except X'. The Hebrew particles רַק and אַךְ may both be used in these contexts. Overtly there appears to be no difference between the two, but there may be a subtle distinction relating to the recontextualisation of the restricted items,[107] a matter which falls outside the scope of the present study. In the first text the background is the capture and destruction of Ai at the hands of Joshua and the Israelites. The previous verse tells us that Joshua utterly destroyed all the inhabitants of the city. Verse 27 then informs us that the animals and spoil of the city were not included in that destruction. The fronted NPs contain the excluded items and form the dominant focal element in a predicate-focus structure. The second example forms part of the narrator's summing up of the reign of Jehoshaphat. He was one of those kings of Judah who 'did what was right in the eyes of YHWH' (v. 43), with the exception, that is, of the issue of the high places where the people continued to offer sacrifices and incense. Again the clause has predicate-focus structure with a preverbally placed dominant focal element.

There is an extended sense in which the above two particles may be employed. Besides restriction they may also be found expressing *certainty* or *correctness*,[108] as in:

1 Samuel 25:21
Surely it was in vain that I protected   אַךְ לַשֶּׁקֶר שָׁמַרְתִּי
all that this man has in the wilderness.   אֶת־כָּל־אֲשֶׁר לָזֶה בַּמִּדְבָּר

David is here speaking of the flocks of Nabal, over which his men had been watching in the wilderness. When David expected some favour in return, none was forthcoming (vv. 10–11), hence his declaration that his kindness in protecting Nabal's flocks was לַשֶּׁקֶר, 'in vain' (NRSV NASB) or 'a waste of time' (REB NJB). In this utterance the PP is fronted with the particle אַךְ. The following verb, NP[DO] and locative PP all contain presuppositional material, that is, things stated explicitly earlier in the chapter. The clause is therefore one having argument focus. By means of this structure David is asserting the fact that his (known) efforts were surely all for nothing.

---

107 As proposed in an unpublished paper by C. M. Follingstad, 'Additive Strengthening and Restrictive Elimination in Identical and Parallel Contexts: a Relevance-Theory Account of the Two "Alsos" and the Two "Onlys" in Biblical Hebrew' (A paper presented at a Biblical Hebrew discourse workshop, held by SIL, at Horsleys Green, UK, November 2002).
108 Van der Merwe (et al.), *Biblical Hebrew Reference Grammar*, pp. 309, 311.

(e) EXPANDING FOCUS

i. *Numbers 13:28* [גַּם]
And we also saw the descendants of Anak there.

וְגַם־יְלִדֵי הָעֲנָק רָאִינוּ שָׁם׃

ii. *Deuteronomy 15:17* [אַף]
You shall do the same also to your female slave.

וְאַף לַאֲמָתְךָ תַּעֲשֶׂה־כֵּן׃

This category of focus, also known as 'additive',[109] indicates 'also Y (besides X)'. As with restrictive focus two particles exist, and a similar distinction has been suggested as with the former.[110] The first example deals with the report of the spies upon their return from Canaan. After describing the land, its fruit, its people, and their cities (vv. 27–28a), they then add the information that they also saw there these Anakim, probably giants. In this instance the clause has argument focus in that the final two elements, the verb and adverb, contain presupposed information, that is, that the spies 'saw' (רָאִינוּ) certain things in that place (שָׁם) which they had spied out. The second example[111] differs with respect to its particle, yet has the same information structure.

In the context of expanding focus we also need to include that manner of focus indicating something unexpected or, as it is generally known, contra-expectation,[112] as in the following text:

2 Samuel 19:31
Mephibosheth said to the king,
'Let him even take it all,
since my lord the king has come
to his house in safely'.

וַיֹּאמֶר מְפִיבֹשֶׁת אֶל־הַמֶּלֶךְ
גַּם אֶת־הַכֹּל יִקָּח
אַחֲרֵי אֲשֶׁר־בָּא אֲדֹנִי הַמֶּלֶךְ
בְּשָׁלוֹם אֶל־בֵּיתוֹ׃

Here the implication is 'even X', where X is something unexpected. Most probably, since the same focus particles are employed, this is to be seen as an extension of expanding focus, the only difference being the fact that the added item is one that was outside the parameters of reasonable expectation considering the context. 2 Samuel 19:25–28 relates the explanation of Mephibosheth as to why he did not flee Jerusalem with David at the time of

---

109 König, *The Meaning of Focus Particles*, p. 33.
110 See fn. 107 above. We also note that אַף is not as common in narrative as גַּם. Cf. 4.2.1 (b).
111 Strictly speaking this example is from a genre of a legal nature rather than pure narrative. Heimerdinger also occasionally mixes in examples taken from the law with those from narrative (e.g., *Topic, Focus and Foreground*, p. 182). Shimasaki, as we have observed, derives the largest proportion of his data from the book of Deuteronomy. Evidently these two genres display a much greater similarity with each other than with poetry.
112 Sometimes also referred to as 'counter-presuppositional focus', e.g., Payne *Describing Morphosyntax*, p. 269.

Absalom's rebellion. In response to this David commands that Mephibosheth's land should be divided, one half to Mephibosheth, and the other to Ziba, a former servant of the house of Saul (cf. 2 Sam. 9:2). To this Mephibosheth declares that Ziba should be given all the estate, since the former was content, he asserts, that David had returned triumphantly to Jerusalem. The clause גַּם אֶת־הַכֹּל יִקָּח expresses the idea that not just half but *all* the land ought to be given to Ziba.[113] Rather than accept the king's offer, which itself is not unreasonable, Mephibosheth proposes a division of the land that is quite contrary to expectation. The clause has argument focus, since the fact that Ziba would receive some of the land has already been proposed. Our translation here, 'Let him even take it all' follows NASB. Heimerdinger renders it more literally as, 'Even all of it, let him take (it)'.[114]

(f) SELECTING FOCUS

Judges 1:2

YHWH said, 'Judah shall go up'.   וַיֹּאמֶר יְהוָה יְהוּדָה יַעֲלֶה

In selecting (or 'selective') focus one item is selected out of a set of alternatives. This text from Judges was discussed above under argument-focus. When the question is asked, 'Who shall go up first for us against the Canaanites?', the choice is limited to the twelve tribes. From these Judah is identified as the one that shall lead the others.

(g) SPECIFYING FOCUS

Genesis 6:14, 16

Make for yourself an ark of gopher wood;	עֲשֵׂה לְךָ תֵּבַת עֲצֵי־גֹפֶר
make cabins in the ark ...	קִנִּים תַּעֲשֶׂה אֶת־הַתֵּבָה ...
Make a window for the ark,	צֹהַר תַּעֲשֶׂה לַתֵּבָה
and finish it to a cubit above;	וְאֶל־אַמָּה תְּכַלֶּנָּה מִלְמַעְלָה
and put the door of the ark in its side;	וּפֶתַח הַתֵּבָה בְּצִדָּהּ תָּשִׂים
make it with lower, second, and third decks.	תַּחְתִּיִּם שְׁנִיִּם וּשְׁלִשִׁים תַּעֲשֶׂהָ׃

This particular manner of focus, also called 'itemizing'[115] or 'listing',[116] invariably follows a proposition of a general character which, in the present case, is 'Make for yourself an ark of gopher wood'. Following this unmarked VO-clause, the various features to be incorporated in the vessel are then specified. In all these subsequent clauses, the detail of the ark in question is

---

113 This text is discussed by Heimerdinger, *Topic, Focus and Foreground*, pp. 181–82.
114 *Ibid.*, p. 181.
115 Shimasaki, *Focus Structure*, p. 187.
116 B. B. Harold, 'Subject-Verb Word Order and the Function of Early Position' in P. Downing and M. Noonan (eds.), *Word Order in Discourse* (Amsterdam/Philadelphia: John Benjamin, 1995), pp. 145–46.

placed in the clause-initial position, thus producing a series of NP/PP + V clauses. Seeing that the verbs in these clauses (תִּכָּלֶנָה, תֵּעָשֶׂה, and תָּשִׂים) all relate to construction, an activity presupposed in the general opening statement, it is to be understood that we are looking at a series of argument-focus structures specifying the various components that go to make up the general proposition.

All the above examples in which the several Hebrew focus particles are employed consist of either predicate-focus or argument-focus clauses. It is not impossible that one of these particles may be adjoined to a sentence-focus clause. In such cases the particular focal sense of the particle is to be applied to the whole proposition, not just to the initial constituent (e.g., Gen. 38:22).

3.4.3 Extraposition

To conclude our survey of topic and focus structures in Biblical Hebrew, some mention must be made of the particular syntactic construction known as *extraposition*.[117] Word-order variation and the use of focus particles are not the only surface realisations of the presence of marked focus. Extraposition may also serve to identify a focused constituent. As regards the form of this construction, an element stands outside of a clause, in Hebrew usually before it,[118] having no grammatical connection with it.[119] Within the clause itself there is usually some pronominal component having reference to the extraposed element and from which its grammatical relation to the clause may be ascertained.[120] This pronominal form is commonly known as the *resumptive pronoun*. Extraposition is not infrequent in Biblical Hebrew. Two examples from narrative are given here:

(1) *Genesis 3:3*

but from the fruit of the tree	וּמִפְּרִי הָעֵץ אֲשֶׁר בְּתוֹךְ־הַגָּן
which is in the middle of the garden,	אָמַר אֱלֹהִים
God has said, 'You shall not eat from it ...'	לֹא תֹאכְלוּ מִמֶּנּוּ ...

---

117 Sometimes also referred to as 'cleft sentence' or 'clefting', e.g., S. A. Geller, 'Cleft Sentences with Pleonastic Pronoun: A Syntactic Construction of Biblical Hebrew and Some of its Literary Uses', *JANES* 20 (1991), pp.13–33. More traditionally it was termed *casus pendens*.

118 In certain languages the extraposed element may also stand after the clause, in which case it is commonly known as 'tail', Dik, *Functional Grammar*, p. 130.

119 D. Payne differentiates marked word order from extraposition, termed 'left-dislocation', not on the basis of form only but also intonation. She states, 'a rule of thumb is that a left-dislocated phrase occurs under a separate intonation contour', 'Verb Initial Languages and Information Order', in Downing and Noonan (eds.), *Word Order in Discourse*, p. 455,

120 Cf. G. Khan, *Studies in Semitic Syntax* (Oxford: Oxford University Press, 1989), pp. 71–74.

These words come from the conversation between Eve and the serpent in Eden. The serpent had just suggested that God had said the man and woman were not to eat from any tree in the garden (v. 1). Eve corrects the serpent's allegation, by saying, 'We may eat of the fruit of the trees in the garden; but from the fruit of the tree which is in the middle of the garden, God has said, "You shall not eat from it ..."' (vv. 2b–3a). The extraposed element is the whole PP וּמִפְּרִי הָעֵץ אֲשֶׁר בְּתוֹךְ־הַגָּן, which is resumed by the coreferential PP מִמֶּנּוּ at the end of the main clause. The context clearly infers a contrast. God had in fact granted them permission to eat of the trees of the garden, but not from the one particular tree described as being 'in the middle of the garden'.

(2) 1 Kings 5:19

Your son whom I will set	בִּנְךָ אֲשֶׁר אֶתֵּן
on your throne in your place,	תַּחְתֶּיךָ עַל־כִּסְאֶךָ
he shall build the house for my name.	הוּא־יִבְנֶה הַבַּיִת לִשְׁמִי׃

Solomon here explains to Hiram king of Tyre his father David's inability to build the temple in Jerusalem. He says, 'David could not build a house for the name of YHWH his God because of the wars he fought on all sides' (v. 17).[121] In contrast to David, God had now given Solomon peace (v. 18), and for that reason Solomon could proceed with the temple. Solomon then quotes to Hiram in verse 19 the words God had earlier spoken to David concerning the proposed building. It was not to be David who would build a temple, God had told him, but his son. This is a clear instance of replacing focus ('not X but Y'). In this text it is בִּנְךָ אֲשֶׁר אֶתֵּן תַּחְתֶּיךָ עַל־כִּסְאֶךָ that is extraposed, and resumed by means of the Pn[Su] הוּא.

From these two examples we see that extraposition may be employed simply to indicate the same types of focus as marked word order. However, there may be functions other than at the level of focus, such as discourse-level, which the extraposed construction may perform.[122]

Extraposition will be encountered again during the course of our analysis of markedness in the context of Hebrew poetry.[123]

3.5 Unmarked Sentence-Initial Phrases of Setting

A number of key scholars who have researched in this area are in broad agreement that there is a difference between fronted elements which are genuinely marked (i.e., for topic or focus) and certain elements which are commonly found in the initial position merely in order to orient the

---

121 The Hebrew versification of this chapter differs from the English versions. Verse 19 in the MT is verse 5 in English.
122 E.g., what Khan describes as 'span closure' (*Studies in Semitic Syntax*, pp. 83–84).
123 See 4.2.4 and 7.2.5.

reader/listener, that is, to provide a framework within which the utterance that follows is to be located, usually with respect to time or place.

In the literature a whole range of different terms are employed to refer to these spatio-temporal orienters. Lambrecht calls them 'scene-setting', that is, they provide the scene for the matrix clause.[124] Several writers, following the Prague school linguist Beneš, describe them as 'points of departure'.[125] Van der Merwe prefers 'points of orientation'.[126] Still others use 'setting'.[127] Gross has his own German terms, 'Zeitangaben' (time-indicators) and 'Anknüpfung' (linkage).[128] In his study Shimasaki opts for 'contextualization'. When he defines this as 'information of a temporal or spatial framework',[129] it is evident that he is talking about the same feature as the previously mentioned scholars.

Despite the numerous ways of referring to such phrases, all the above named linguists and Hebraists are in agreement that they should not be accorded the same status as those clause-initial phrases marked for topic or focus. Lambrecht is of the view that these expressions should be regarded as 'pragmatically unmarked'.[130] Their function relates more to the organisation of the text than the marking of certain components within it.[131] The Joüon-Muraoka grammar explains that whereas certain adverbial modifiers may be 'placed at the beginning wherever there is some emphasis on them', it is also the case that 'many common adverbs or adverbial

---

124 Lambrecht, *Information Structure*, pp. 125–26. In the same context Lambrecht also refers to such expressions as 'background-establishing'.

125 E.g., Heimerdinger, *Topic, Focus and Foreground*, p. 122; S. H. Levinsohn, 'NP References to Active Participants and Story Development in Ancient Hebrew', Work papers of the Summer Institute of Linguistics, University of North Dakota, vol. 44 (2000), p. 8. The first usage of this term is found in Beneš, 'Die Verbstellung im Deutschen, von der Mitteilungs-perspektive herbetrachtet', *Philologia Pragensia 5* (1962), pp. 6–11.

126 Van der Merwe (et al.), *Biblical Hebrew Reference Grammar*, p. 339.

127 E.g., Rosenbaum, *Word-Order Variation in Isaiah 40–55*, p. 41, who is here following Buth.

128 W. Gross, *Doppelt besetztes Vorfeld: Syntaktische, pragmatische und übersetzungstechnische Studien zum althebräischen Verbalsatz* (Berlin: de Gruyter, 2001), pp. 310–11.

129 Shimasaki, *Focus Structure*, p. 173.

130 Lambrecht, *Information Structure*, p. 126.

131 Cf. Payne, 'Functional Sentence Perspective: Theme in Biblical Hebrew', p. 68. Regarding time phrases C. H. J. van der Merwe says that such adverbials 'anchor events on the time-line', 'Reconsidering Biblical Hebrew Temporal Expressions', *ZAH 10.1* (1997), p. 48. This agrees with the comment of W. L. Chafe that time phrases at the beginning of a sentence 'are dependent on the need to provide the addressee with an initial temporal orientation on whatever is to follow', 'Language and Memory', *Language 49* (1973), p. 280. The same could be said to apply with respect to spatial orientation.

expressions, especially those which are anaphorically linked to what immediately precedes occupy the initial slot' where no such emphasis is intended.[132] Here are included adverbs such as כֹּה, כֵּן, עַתָּה, and שָׁם, and also adverbial time phrases such as בָּעֵת הַהִיא, אַחֲרֵי־כֵן and so forth.[133]

The question arises, however, as to how these phrases are to be distinguished from genuinely marked fronted constituents. Levinsohn[134] offers several cross-linguistic means of distinguishing these 'points of departure' from elements fronted for reasons of focus: (1) In oral discourse the point of departure does not carry the primary accent, unlike the focus which is accented. (2) The information contained within the point of departure 'must either be already established in the text or be easily related to one that is already established'.[135] On the other hand, focal information has either 'NOT been established in the text or needs to be RE-established'. By this Levinsohn means that the point of departure functions to anchor the subsequent clause to an already existing temporal or spatial framework.[136] (3) Should the preposed (i.e., fronted) expression be grammatically definite or contain an anaphoric demonstrative, this usually shows that the information within it is established, and therefore more likely to be a point of departure. To these observations, which chiefly serve to differentiate points of departure from focus, we may add the comment of Rosenbaum to the effect that 'these phrases ... function to limit or frame the Topic within a certain temporal or spatial setting but they are not the Topic'.[137]

It is not hard to see that such phrases do not function to introduce the sentence topic. Thus in Genesis 22:4, 'On the third day' (בַּיּוֹם הַשְּׁלִישִׁי) Abraham looked up and saw the place far away', the PP clearly falls within the category of temporal setting. Although occurring sentence-initially, 'the third day' is obviously not the topic, which is Abraham. It is a definite phrase which, in keeping with Levinsohn's criterion, shows that there is a previously established framework to which the new event is being related. In this chapter of Genesis that framework is not difficult to discern. In the immediately preceding verse Abraham rose early in the morning to begin his journey to the mountain that God had shown him. The time phrase בַּיּוֹם הַשְּׁלִישִׁי connects Abraham's seeing the place with the commencement of the journey. We see, then, that though such points of departure are

---

132 P. Joüon and T. Muraoka, *A Grammar of Biblical Hebrew*, Part 3 (Rome: Biblical Institute Press, 1991), p. 584.
133 *Ibid.*
134 S. H. Levinsohn, 'Analysis of Narrative Texts' (SIL, 2003), {https://mail.jaars.org/~bt/narr.zip}, ch. 4.5.
135 Here Levinsohn is following Lambrecht, *Information Structure*, p. 164.
136 Cf. R. A. Dooley and S. H. Levinsohn, *Analyzing Discourse: A Manual of Basic Concepts* (Dallas, Texas: SIL, 2001), p. 68.
137 Rosenbaum, *Word-Order Variation in Isaiah 40–55*, p. 43.

placed initially, this is for an entirely different purpose, i.e., orientation, than in the case of marked topic and focus structures. So, as pertaining to the question of word order, there may sometimes be potential for confusion between pre-sentential phrases of setting and of topic or focus, yet when the function within the context is considered, the phrases may be rightly appraised.

It is not impossible, of course, that in certain circumstances these initial phrases *may* be pragmatically marked. When this is so, it is indicated either (a) by the presence of a focus particle, or (b) when its marked nature is contextually inferable from the presence of pragmatic presuppositions.[138] Generally speaking, however, the majority of the sentence-initial phrases in question are unmarked.

There are numerous examples of these time and space indicators in non-poetic texts. With respect to their form they may be constructed in a variety of ways (prepositional phrase, adverb, or infinitive, etc.), yet the setting function remains the same. We may cite the following by way of illustration:

Genesis 31:32 [Spatial PP]

Before our kinsfolk	נֶגֶד אַחֵינוּ
identify what I have that is yours,	הַכֶּר־לְךָ מָה עִמָּדִי
and take it.	וְקַח־לָךְ

Joshua 6:5 [Temporal Inf]

When you hear the sound of the trumpet,	[וּכְשָׁמְעֲכֶם] אֶת־קוֹל הַשּׁוֹפָר
let all the people give a loud shout.	יָרִיעוּ כָל־הָעָם תְּרוּעָה גְדוֹלָה

Likewise, in poetry similar sentence-initial spatial and temporal indicators may be found, as in:

Isaiah 40:9 [Spatial PP]

Go up to a high mountain, Zion,	עַל הַר־גָּבֹהַ עֲלִי־לָךְ
herald of good news ...	מְבַשֶּׂרֶת צִיּוֹן ...
say to the cities of Judah,	אִמְרִי לְעָרֵי יְהוּדָה
'Behold, your God!'	הִנֵּה אֱלֹהֵיכֶם

Rosenbaum includes this verse as one of his examples of 'setting'. He comments, 'In this series of instructions to the messenger/Zion [Topic], we would be mistaken to assume that the messenger's location "on a high mountain" [Setting] was the most important, salient information in this instruction just because it appears first, rather than the content of the message, "Behold, your God!"'.[139]

---

138 For example, contra-expectation in גַּם־שָׁם ('even there'), Psalm 139:10 (discussed further in 8.2.1), and by contrast, as in וּבְקִרְבָּם ('but in their hearts'), Psalm 62:5b.
139 Rosenbaum, *Word-Order Variation in Isaiah 40–55*, p. 44.

Psalm 4:2 [Temporal Inf]
When I call, answer me, O God of my righteousness.   בְּקָרְאִי עֲנֵנִי אֱלֹהֵי צִדְקִי

This colon begins with an adverbial infinitive, translated by the English versions as the temporal clause 'when I call/pray'. This is simply the setting within which the appeal, עֲנֵנִי, is made. Significantly, in translation the infinitival expression has been postponed (i.e., placed in sentence-final position) in virtually all the versions (NRSV NASB ESV NIV NKJV NJPS REB TEV NCV NLT). This is a clear indication that the translators recognised that it is the imperative, and not the infinitive, which carries the focus of the utterance.

In the study that follows, fronted phrases of spatial and temporal orientation will not be reckoned as rendering the sentence in which they occur as pragmatically marked. It needs to be stressed, however, that since the number of instances of this feature in the selected data is relatively small,[140] to consider them as marked or unmarked makes no major difference to the overall results. The most important characteristic of these phrases is that, if they do not exhibit the same markedness as those instances of marked topic and focus to be investigated, then these initial phrases of setting need not comply with the rules that shall later be established for marked word order in Hebrew poetry.[141]

3.6 Summary

This chapter has presented an outline of the work of Lambrecht on information structure. The various concepts involved were defined: topic (together with its activation states), focus, presupposition, and assertion. All meaningful propositions can be classified according to their information structure as either having: predicate focus, argument focus, or sentence focus. Predicate-focus clauses generally follow the unmarked constituent order and have a topic-comment articulation. Examples of the three focus structures were taken from Biblical Hebrew narrative. Both focus particles and context allow a sub-categorisation of focus. Extraposition is another form of markedness, the functions of which may overlap with fronting. Pre-sentential words or phrases of spatial and temporal orientation are not to be considered as being marked in the same way as fronted clause constituents.

---

140 The infrequent number of occurrences in the data is no doubt due to the fact that the poetic genre makes significantly less use of such orientation than narrative. In the latter the temporal or spatial framework is a much more prominent feature than in the former, where the framework is often more thematic in nature.
141 See especially 7.4.1 below.

CHAPTER 4

Pragmatic Markedness in Poetic Cola: (1) Non-Parallel Lines

We now set out to demonstrate that the same marked constituent order seen in Hebrew prose, as shown in the preceding chapter, is to be observed in poetry, and for the same pragmatic reasons. This chapter is essentially a comparison between marked forms in the two genres to prove that identical pragmatic motivations are at play in both types of discourse.

At present we do not venture into the area of markedness occurring within parallelisms. Parallelism of poetic cola is a relationship with special features with regard to pragmatics and the order of clause constituents. This will therefore be dealt with later in a separate chapter (ch. 7).

4.1 Quotation of Marked Clauses from Prose within Poetry

First, in order to show that pragmatically marked word order also appears in poetry in the same form as in prose, we consider quotations within poetry. In a small number of instances the marked word order of a clause appearing in a narrative context reappears with the same word order in a poetic text. In such cases the similarity between the two texts suggests that the poet is almost certainly citing, though perhaps not verbatim, the original prose form. For example:

Psalm 105:11

saying, 'To you I will give the land of Canaan
as the portion of your inheritance'.

לֵאמֹר לְךָ אֶתֵּן אֶת־אֶרֶץ־כְּנָעַן
חֶבֶל נַחֲלַתְכֶם:

There is no doubt from the context that the psalmist is here relating the ancient patriarchal promise. Verses 8–10 of the psalm declare,

> [8] He is mindful of his covenant forever,
> of the word that he commanded, for a thousand generations,
> [9] the covenant that he made with Abraham,
> his sworn promise to Isaac,
> [10] which he confirmed to Jacob as a statute,
> to Israel as an everlasting covenant ... (NRSV)

The quotation frame לֵאמֹר suggests that this is a citation.[1] In Genesis the promise of the land had been reiterated several times to Abraham, Isaac and Jacob:

קוּם הִתְהַלֵּךְ בָּאָרֶץ לְאָרְכָּהּ וּלְרָחְבָּהּ כִּי לְךָ אֶתְּנֶנָּה: (Gen. 13:17)
Rise and walk through the length and breadth of the land, for *to you* I will give it.

הָאָרֶץ אֲשֶׁר אַתָּה שֹׁכֵב עָלֶיהָ לְךָ אֶתְּנֶנָּה (Gen. 28:13)
The land that you dwell in, *to you* I will give it.

וְאֶת־הָאָרֶץ אֲשֶׁר נָתַתִּי לְאַבְרָהָם וּלְיִצְחָק לְךָ אֶתְּנֶנָּה (Gen. 35:12)
The land which I gave to Abraham and to Isaac, *to you* [Jacob] I will give it.

From the perspective of word order the significant feature in these verses from Genesis is that in each case the promise that God would give the land to Abraham and his descendants is expressed by means of a marked clause. Each fronts the indirect object לְךָ ('to you'), with the verb נָתַן ('give') following. The information structure in all the above quotations is predicate focus – God, the active topic, is speaking, saying that he will give the land to the patriarchs, who are being addressed. Thus the fronted constituent לְךָ must be taken as the dominant focal element[2] within the broader focal domain of the predicate. That the NP[IO] should be marked in this context seems appropriate, though the precise nature of the markedness in question is open to discussion. Most likely it is an instance of selective focus.[3] In this situation it is presupposed that someone would possess the land and, out of all the various possibilities, God had selected the offspring of Abraham for that privilege. What is of most relevance for the present purposes is that the same pragmatic marking as found in the patriarchal promises of Genesis has been preserved in the psalm. Therefore in this particular case the constituent order in Psalm 105:11 can be said to be an unquestionable instance of marked word order.

Another example similar to the above is this time in connection with God's promises to David concerning his descendants who would reign after him. In Psalm 89 the psalmist records God as declaring concerning David, 'I will establish his line for ever, his throne as long as the heavens endure' (v. 30). Then the psalmist continues with a clear reference back to the original promises given to David through Nathan the prophet in 2 Samuel 7. Both the psalm and 2 Samuel relate, in clearly dependant

---

1 Cf. C. L. Miller, 'Introducing Direct Discourse in Biblical Hebrew Narrative', in R. D. Bergen (ed.), *Biblical Hebrew and Discourse Linguistics* (Dallas, Texas: SIL, 1994), p. 209.
2 For 'dominant focal element', see 3.4.1 (a).
3 Described in 3.4.2 (f). It is conceivable, however, that the fronting of 'to you' might be indicative of the *certainty* of the act; cf. 3.4.2 (d).

language,[4] what would happen should David's descendants prove to stray from God's law:

> When he commits iniquity, I will punish him with a rod [שֵׁבֶט] of men,
> and with the scourges [נִגְעֵי] of the sons of men. (2 Sam. 7:14)

> If his children forsake my law and do not walk according to my ordinances,
> if they violate my statutes and do not keep my commandments,
> then I will punish their transgression with the rod [שֵׁבֶט]
> and their iniquity with scourges [נְגָעִים]. (Ps. 89:31-33)

The next clauses following these two passages show so close a correspondence with each other that it is hard to conceive that one is not quoting the other:

2 Samuel 7:15a
but my steadfast love will not depart from him.   וְחַסְדִּי לֹא־יָסוּר מִמֶּנּוּ

Psalm 89:34a
but my steadfast love I will not break off from him.   וְחַסְדִּי לֹא־אָפִיר מֵעִמּוֹ

If the variant reading of the verb in the psalm version, אָסִיר, is adopted,[5] then the resemblance is closer still. However, whether the verbs differ or not, the important point is that each clause has an identical focus structure. Both the clause from 2 Samuel and that from the psalm consist of OVM constituent order, with the same NP[DO] (חַסְדִּי) placed preverbally. The context here supplies an obvious cause for the fronting of this element. Versions and commentators agree that this is a contrast, and typically in such contrastive structures in Biblical Hebrew the focal element is placed in the clause-initial position.[6] So we see another instance where the marked word order of a clause occurring in a narrative context has been preserved unchanged when reappearing within a poetic text.

Such direct quotations from prose which adhere to the original marked word order demonstrate beyond doubt that Biblical Hebrew poetry allowed the use of marked clause structures identical to those found in prose.

4.2 Similarity of Marked Structures in Prose and Poetry

Next we come to look at a whole range of instances in which similar marked

---

4 For a detailed discussion of the relationship between these two passages, see M. E. Tate, *Psalms 51-100*, WBC (Dallas, Texas: Word Books, 1990), pp. 417-18. Harman, *Psalms*, p. 304, describes Psalm 89:30-34 as 'a paraphrase of 2 Samuel 7:14'.
5 This is the reading of a number of Masoretic MSS, followed by the Syriac, two different versions of the Targum, and Jerome in the *Psalterium iuxta Hebraeos*.
6 For markedness in contrasting relationships, see 3.4.2 (a); cf. 4.2.2 (c) below.

structures exist in poetry of the same form as those to be observed in prose. We consider, firstly, those marked clause types which are accompanied by a focus particle (4.2.1),[7] and secondly, those in which no such particle is employed (4.2.2).

4.2.1 Marked Clauses with Focus Particles

Here we present poetic clauses where the marked order of constituents is further identified as marked through the presence of a focus particle, (a) גַּם (b) אַף (c) רַק and (d) אַךְ. Each example follows a closely related structure from Hebrew narrative, which is placed alongside to show the essential similarity between the two. The examination of the ensuing particles and their uses is not intended to be exhaustive. Here we analyse a sufficient number of instances where major focus particles occur in order to satisfactorily demonstrate that identical marked constructions are to be found in poetry in an identical manner to prose.

(a) EXPANDING FOCUS WITH גַּם

Here גַּם is used as an additive particle, that is, indicating expanding focus.

Numbers 24:25

And Balaam got up and went	וַיָּקָם בִּלְעָם וַיֵּלֶךְ
and returned to his place,	וַיָּשָׁב לִמְקֹמוֹ
and Balak also went on his way.	וְגַם־בָּלָק הָלַךְ לְדַרְכּוֹ:

Psalm 83:9

| Assyria also has joined them; | גַּם־אַשּׁוּר נִלְוָה עִמָּם |
| they are the strong arm of the children of Lot. | הָיוּ זְרוֹעַ לִבְנֵי־לוֹט: |

In both instances we find the order *gam*–SV. In the narrative text the departure of the prophet Balak is added to that of Balaam the king. The verb וַיֵּלֶךְ in the first line has predicate-focus structure, being a comment relating to the active topic, Balaam. In the second clause the action of הָלַךְ is now presuppositional information, but a second topic, Balak, is seen to perform a similar action, in what is an argument-focus clause. The poetic example has identical information structure to the prose. Here Assyria is added to those nations hostile to Israel mentioned in the preceding verses (vv. 3–8). These enemies are said to 'consult together' (v. 4, וְיִתְיָעֲצוּ) and 'conspire with one accord' (v. 6, נוֹעֲצוּ לֵב יַחְדָּו). Now in verse 9 Assyria joins with them. The activity of hostile conspiracy in which they engage is in this verse a presupposition. Assyria, the new information, is added as another participant in that activity.

---

7 For focus particles, see 3.4.2.

Pragmatic Markedness: (1) Non-Parallel Lines

In the preceding example it is the grammatical subject that is fronted. Other examples could be adduced in which the O or M element is placed in the preverbal position with גַּם as an additive particle:

Judges 20:48

The Israelites turned back	וְאִישׁ יִשְׂרָאֵל שָׁבוּ
against the Benjaminites,	אֶל־בְּנֵי בִנְיָמִן
and put them to the sword – the city, the people,	וַיַּכּוּם לְפִי־חֶרֶב מֵעִיר מְתֹם
the animals, and all that was found.	עַד־בְּהֵמָה עַד כָּל־הַנִּמְצָא
Also all the towns that were found	גַּם כָּל־הֶעָרִים הַנִּמְצָאוֹת
they set on fire.	שִׁלְּחוּ בָאֵשׁ:

Psalm 78:20

Behold, he struck the rock so that water gushed out	הֵן הִכָּה־צוּר וַיָּזוּבוּ מַיִם
and streams overflowed,	וּנְחָלִים יִשְׁטֹפוּ
can he also give bread,	הֲגַם־לֶחֶם יוּכַל תֵּת
or provide meat for his people?	אִם־יָכִין שְׁאֵר לְעַמּוֹ:

In both the prose and poetic texts the order is *gam*–OV. In Judges 20:48 the catalogue of destruction in the first part of the verse is expanded to include the burning of certain other 'towns' in the final clause. In Psalm 78:20 the miracle of bringing forth water from the rock is recited, to which the question concerning the provision of food is then added. The basic overall sense here is 'If God could cause water to come forth from a rock, can he not also provide food for his people?' The reference is to the manna (vv. 24–25) which was to follow the miraculous provision of water. The basic information structure of the additive clauses in the two verses is the same. In the former case other entities which suffer destruction are added, and in the latter God makes an additional provision besides that already given for sustaining the Hebrews.

In the following two examples it is an M constituent (PP or Adv) which occupies the marked position:

2 Chronicles 19:8

In Jerusalem also Jehoshaphat appointed	וְגַם בִּירוּשָׁלַםִ הֶעֱמִיד יְהוֹשָׁפָט
certain Levites and priests	מִן־הַלְוִיִּם וְהַכֹּהֲנִים
and heads of families of Israel,	וּמֵרָאשֵׁי הָאָבוֹת לְיִשְׂרָאֵל
for the judgment of YHWH	לְמִשְׁפַּט יְהוָה
and to settle disputes.	וְלָרִיב

Isaiah 57:7

Upon a high and lofty mountain	עַל הַר־גָּבֹהַּ וְנִשָּׂא
you have placed your bed,	שַׂמְתְּ מִשְׁכָּבֵךְ

and there also you have gone up גַּם־שָׁ֥ם עָלִ֖ית
to offer sacrifice. לִזְבֹּ֥חַ זָֽבַח׃

Here the additive element has the structure *gam*–MV in both verses, where M possesses a locative sense. The context of the first is the appointment by king Jehoshaphat of certain officials throughout his kingdom. Verse 5 says, 'He appointed (וַיַּעֲמֵד) judges throughout the land in all the fortified cities of Judah", to which are added the instructions he gave them, that is, to judge for YHWH (vv. 6–7). Now in verse 8 the attention turns specifically to the capital Jerusalem. There also the king appointed judges. Although the persons appointed seem to be of a different class ('Levites, priests, and heads of families'), their charge is basically the same ('the judgment of YHWH'). The Isaiah text occurs in a passage relating the various abominable practices in which the Judeans themselves had engaged.[8] In verse 6 the prophet had just berated them for the offences committed in the valley, and now in verse 7 the scene moves to the mountain-tops. There the people, poetically portrayed under the figure of an adulterous woman, placed their beds, a figure of speech no doubt making reference to the ritual prostitution and fertility rites that transpired at such high places.[9] Then in the final clause of the verse the prophet mentions the offering of sacrifice, presumably to Canaanite gods, practised at those places. Here it should be noted how crucial it is to pay attention to the context to establish which information is presupposed and which is the focus of the utterance. According to the information structure of this final clause, having the syntactic composition *gam*–M V Inf O, it is not the verb with its accompanying telic infinitive construct that is marked, but the locative adverb שָׁם ('there'). From the perspective of information structure this is entirely in harmony with the context, since the fact that the Judeans were offering pagan sacrifices has already been declared in verses 5–6. So the new information relates to the *place* where this was being done, not to the *practice*. Through this clause the prophet is saying 'also there you have gone up to sacrifice'. In other words the same kind of abominations they were practising in the valley they were also doing on the mountain-tops. The prophet is in effect highlighting the fact that idolatrous worship was ubiquitous in Judah. The expanding focus structure adds one place to another where similar acts of paganism were being performed, not one practice to another. In other words, the focused information relates back to the place of verse 6 ('the valley'), and not to the action described in the earlier part of verse 7.[10]

---

8 J. N. Oswalt, *The Book of Isaiah 40–66*, p. 478.
9 J. D. W. Watts, *Isaiah 34–66*, WBC (Waco, Texas: Word Books, 1987), p. 258.
10 None of the standard commentaries (Motyer, Oswalt, Watts, Young) correctly discerns the function of the focus particle. Of the English versions, NRSV NIV TEV NLT NCV and CEV make no attempt to translate the additive connotations. REB and NJPS have the right sense in 'there too'.

Before moving on to look at other focus particles, we note the use of focused structures with גַּם to denote contra-expectation ('even').[11] The sense here differs from the additive use of the same particle ('also'). Again the same forms are to be noticed in poetry as found in prose:

2 Kings 16:3

He walked in the way of the kings of Israel;	וַיֵּלֶךְ בְּדֶרֶךְ מַלְכֵי יִשְׂרָאֵל
he even made his son pass through fire,	וְגַם אֶת־בְּנוֹ הֶעֱבִיר בָּאֵשׁ
according to the abominations of the nations.	כְּתֹעֲבוֹת הַגּוֹיִם

Psalm 41:10

Even my close friend in whom I trusted,	גַּם־אִישׁ שְׁלוֹמִי אֲשֶׁר־בָּטַחְתִּי בוֹ
who ate my bread,	אוֹכֵל לַחְמִי
has lifted his heel against me.	הִגְדִּיל עָלַי עָקֵב׃

The first verse is describing the deeds of Ahaz, king of Judah. The narrator tells us that he followed in the ways of the kings of Israel, that is, he was an idolater (cf. 1 Kgs. 16:32-33; 2 Kgs. 17:8-12; 23:19). Yet his assimilation to idolatrous practices even extended to that of the sacrifice of his own son, a fact clearly contrary to expectation. In Psalm 41 the psalmist bewails the fact that he had been betrayed by his own friend,[12] one with whom he had enjoyed close fellowship, again a fact that one would not suppose possible.[13]

In the foregoing examples the constituents S, O, and M appearing in the fronted position were all considered. The same could be done for all the following particles, however, due to limitations of space, only one example of each will be given.

(b) EXPANDING FOCUS WITH אַף

For pragmatic purposes the Hebrew particle אַף performs substantially the same functions as גַּם,[14] that is, expanding focus and contra-expectation.[15] The following are examples of אַף used in a marked expanding focus construction:

2 Chronicles 12:5

Thus says YHWH,	כֹּה־אָמַר יְהוָה
'You have abandoned me,	אַתֶּם עֲזַבְתֶּם אֹתִי

---

11 Cf. 3.4.2 (e).
12 Harman, *Psalms*, p. 178.
13 In both these verses the particle גַּם is translated 'even' by virtually all the major English versions.
14 In an unpublished paper (see chapter 3, fn. 107) Follingstad proposes that the two did not have entirely identical functions, the nature of the difference relating to the representation of information presented in the attached clause, not the information structure.
15 It is to be noted that אַף is much more common in poetry than in other genres.

I also have abandoned you	וְאַף־אֲנִי עָזַבְתִּי אֶתְכֶם
into the hands of Shishak'.	בְּיַד־שִׁישָׁק׃

Psalm 89:27–28

He shall call to me, 'You are my Father,	הוּא יִקְרָאֵנִי אָבִי אָתָּה
my God, and the Rock of my salvation!'	אֵלִי וְצוּר יְשׁוּעָתִי׃
I will also appoint him the firstborn,	אַף־אָנִי בְּכוֹר אֶתְּנֵהוּ
the highest of the kings of the earth.	עֶלְיוֹן לְמַלְכֵי־אָרֶץ׃

These two quotations make an interesting parallel in their focus structure. As is necessary for expanding focus, the clause containing אַף follows a preceding statement to which it adds certain information. In the prose example God declares that the Israelites had forsaken God, and so he too would forsake them. Here both the initial and the expanding clause are marked by the presence of the independent subject pronouns: '*You* have abandoned me, *I* also will abandon you'. The verbal activity of עָזַב ('abandon') is presuppositional information in the second clause, the new information being that God would treat his people in the same way they had treated him – *he also* would abandon them. The example from Psalm 89 also shows markedness in both clauses by the use of the pronoun. The first clause (v. 27) concerns the king calling out to God, declaring him to be his 'Father'. God's response to this, beginning as it does with the marked אַף־אָנִי, shows that it is in some way expanding upon the previous statement, just like the second clause of 2 Chronicles 12:5. Through the expanding focus structure God announces that 'I also will appoint him the firstborn (בְּכוֹר)'. In this case the nature of the presuppositional information is not as distinct as in the prose example, where the identical verb was used in both clauses, yet it is discernible nevertheless. The presupposition lies in the similarity between the verbal activities of קָרָא and נָתַן, the first meaning 'name', the second having in this context the sense of 'appoint'. The Davidic king in the psalm had named God as his 'Father', and in return[16] God also performs a comparable act – the appointing of the king as his 'firstborn'.[17] It is as if God were saying, 'Since he has chosen me for his father, I also will chose him for my firstborn son'. The underlying information structure, therefore, of both the prose and the poetic text, is virtually

---

16 This is how Delitzsch translates the clause, 'In return I will make him My first-born', in C. F. Keil and F. Delitzsch, *Commentary on the Old Testament*, vol. 5, 'Psalms' (Grand Rapids, Michigan: Eerdmans, 1986 [1877]), p. 31.

17 There is an obvious connection between this passage and that of Psalm 2:6–7, where God says 'I have set my king on Zion, my holy hill'. To this the king responds, 'I will tell of the decree of YHWH: He said to me, "You are my son (בְּנִי אַתָּה); today I have begotten you"'. The similarity between the two psalms is noted by Tate, *Psalms 51–100*, p. 424.

identical, as is the surface structure $'ap$–S^{Pn} V.[18]

The particle אַף, like גַּם, may also be employed with a fronted constituent in the context of contra-expectation (e.g., Ps. 16:7b; Job 14:3a).

(c) RESTRICTING FOCUS WITH רַק

Next in our discussion of marked structures with particles, we come to consider the restrictive particle רַק. This occurs much more frequently in narrative than in poetry,[19] where the alternate אַךְ is preferred. One of only two poetic instances of רַק in a verbal clause is given here:

Deuteronomy 10:15

On your fathers only did YHWH set his heart,   רַק בַּאֲבֹתֶיךָ חָשַׁק יְהוָה
to love them.   לְאַהֲבָה אוֹתָם

Psalm 91:8

You will only observe with your eyes   רַק בְּעֵינֶיךָ תַבִּיט
and see the punishment of the wicked.   וְשִׁלֻּמַת רְשָׁעִים תִּרְאֶה׃

The words attributed to Moses from Deuteronomy concern the divine choice of the patriarchs. In order to correctly interpret the marked element it is necessary to read the whole of verses 14–15: 'Indeed heaven and the highest heavens belong to the LORD your God, *also* the earth with all that *is* in it. The LORD delighted only in your fathers, to love them; and He chose their descendants after them, you above all peoples, as *it is* this day' (NKJV, italics included). McConville is correct in seeing in these verses 'two theological statements ... namely Yahweh's universal rule, and his election of one nation, Israel'.[20] The context speaks of God as sovereign over all creation and therefore over all nations. From all of this vast dominion he only elected the forefathers of the Hebrews. According to the information structure of verse 15 the fact is presupposed that God would elect some persons or nation. Moses is bringing to the attention of the Israelites that they out of all nations were the ones God had chosen, with which comes certain responsibilities, as the chapter goes on to relate. The verse from Psalm 91 has the same syntactic construction, *raq* MV, as Deuteronomy 10:15. Verses 7–8 of the psalm say: 'A thousand may fall at your side, ten

---

18 The fact that the second clause in the psalm has two fronted elements has not been overlooked. Those instances where two preverbal constituents occur will be dealt with below (4.2.5). In this particular case, we would just note that the information structure of בְּכוֹר אֲתָנֻהוּ matches that of the corresponding component in the previous verse, אָבִי אָתָּה, where the noun denoting the role into which each of the two participants is being placed occurs is a fronted position. It is evident that besides the two participants 'he' (הוּא) and 'I' (אֲנִי), the terms אָבִי and בְּכוֹר are also marked.
19 רַק is only found in the selected corpus of poetic texts at Psalms 32:6 and 91:8.
20 J. G. McConville, *Deuteronomy*, AOTC (Leicester: Inter-Varsity Press, 2002), p. 199.

thousand at your right hand, but it will not come near you. You will only look with your eyes and see the punishment of the wicked' (NRSV). For an explanation of these verses we quote Tate's commentary, 'The point is not that a thousand or ten thousand have fallen, but if they do, the cause of their destruction "will not come near you" (the addressee). If such dreadful events do transpire, the one who is under the protection of Yahweh will simply look on as punishment comes to the "wicked" (v. 8)'.[21]

If Tate is right, as we believe him to be, then the fronted PP makes good sense considering the overall context. Interpreted in the way suggested, verse 8a has to be taken together with 7c, 'it will not come near you'. What the psalmist is saying is that the one whom he addresses in these words would not be physically harmed, but the destruction spoken of in 7ab would be something that he would experience only through his eyes (רַק בְּעֵינֶיךָ). He would only behold it visually coming upon those around him, but not suffer physically himself – 'it will not come near you, only through your eyes will you look upon it'. Delitzsch shows a correct appreciation of this text when he explained the meaning as, 'Only a spectator shalt thou be ... being thyself inaccessible and left to survive'.[22] Just one of the major English versions consulted brings out this sense of the Hebrew focus structure.[23]

(d) RESTRICTING FOCUS WITH אַךְ

Hebrew poetry much more often employs אַךְ as a restrictive particle, yet it is not employed in narrative as frequently as רַק.[24] For examples we take the following:

Genesis 34:15

Only on this [condition] will we consent to you:	אַךְ־בְּזֹאת נֵאוֹת לָכֶם
that you will become as we are	אִם תִּהְיוּ כָמֹנוּ
by every male among you being circumcised.	לְהִמֹּל לָכֶם כָּל־זָכָר׃

Job 13:20

| Only two things do not do to me, | אַךְ־שְׁתַּיִם אַל־תַּעַשׂ עִמָּדִי |
| then I will not hide myself from your face: | אָז מִפָּנֶיךָ לֹא אֶסָּתֵר׃ |

In the narrative example the structure is *ʾak*–MV. The context concerns the proposed marriage of Dinah, daughter of Jacob, to Shechem son of Hamor.

---

21 Tate, *Psalms 51–100*, p. 456.
22 Delitzsch, 'Psalms', p. 64.
23 NCV, 'You will only watch what happens'. Several of the versions alter the sense completely, e.g., NJB, 'You have only to keep your eyes open to see how the wicked are repaid'. Others, such as REB and TEV, have 'with your own eyes', which again misses the point.
24 According to Waltke and O'Connor, *Biblical Hebrew Syntax*, p. 669, fn. 91, רַק is found in the Old Testament 109 times in total and אַךְ 161 times.

In request for the hand of their sister the sons of Jacob give the answer, deceitful though it is, that they could not give Dinah to wed one who was uncircumcised. They then impose upon Shechem and his father the one condition mentioned in verse 15, that of circumcision. Here the fronted element is cataphoric, referring to the single condition that is to be stated. The example from Job has the syntactic structure, ʾak̲–OV. The context of the following verse makes the content of Job's request apparent: 'withdraw your hand far from me, and do not let the dread of you terrify me' (v. 21). A slight obscurity is introduced by the fact that one request is grammatically positive and the other negative. This probably accounts for the negated volitional אַל־תְּעַשׂ.[25] Clines comments that the construction here is 'formally inconsistent' but that 'the sense is plain enough, for both halves of v 21 have in view essentially negative acts of God'.[26] By this he means that the verb 'withdraw' (הַרְחַק), though not grammatically negative, is logically negative in that certain activity is no longer performed. What Job is asking for is that he may continue his disputation with God having the assurance of his own safety, and not to be punished even further for daring to enter into dispute with God himself.[27] Once granted only these two things mentioned in verse 21, God and Job could then carry on with the lawsuit (v. 22). Like the Genesis example, the fronted constituent also refers cataphorically. We see, then, in the above two examples an essential similarity in the restrictive focus constructions in which the fronting of the clause constituent in both narrative and prose is due to pragmatic markedness, identifying the item(s) to which the restriction applies.

In total the data shows 35 instances of marked word order following the above focus particles (גַּם = 13, אַךְ = 11, אַךְ = 9, רַק = 2).

4.2.2 Marked Clauses without Focus Particles

We now come to give several examples where marked pragmatic structures are used without any particle to assist in identifying the nature of the focus. In such cases the markedness is evidenced by the particular order of constituents alone. Greater attention to context is necessary, therefore, in order to determine the focus function of the marked clause. Here we consider: (a) specifying focus, (b) replacing focus, and (c) contrasting relationships.

---

25 The negative particle does not appear in the LXX rendering: δυεῖν δέ μοι χρήσῃ.
26 D. J. A. Clines, *Job 1–20*, WBC (Dallas, Texas: Word Books, 1989), p. 316; Dhorme, who recognises the restrictive nature of the clause, translates as 'Spare me only in two matters', *Commentary on the Book of Job*, p. 189.
27 Cf. Clines, *Job 1–20*, p. 317.

(a) SPECIFYING FOCUS

First to be illustrated is that category of focus which was earlier designated 'specifying' or 'itemizing'.[28] Such a marked structure, we recall, invariably follows a general statement or account, and gives certain specific details pertaining to it.

Numbers 5:2–3

Command the Israelites	צַו אֶת־בְּנֵי יִשְׂרָאֵל	A
that they send away from the camp	וִישַׁלְּחוּ מִן־הַמַּחֲנֶה	B
everyone who is leprous, or has a discharge,	כָּל־צָרוּעַ וְכָל־זָב	C
or who is defiled by a corpse;	וְכֹל טָמֵא לָנָפֶשׁ:	D
both male and female you shall send away,	מִזָּכָר עַד־נְקֵבָה תְּשַׁלֵּחוּ	E
to outside the camp you shall send them.	אֶל־מִחוּץ לַמַּחֲנֶה תְּשַׁלְּחוּם	F

Isaiah 59:2–3

Rather your iniquities have made a separation between you and your God,	כִּי אִם־עֲוֺנֹתֵיכֶם הָיוּ מַבְדִּלִים בֵּינֵכֶם לְבֵין אֱלֹהֵיכֶם	A, B
and your sins have hidden his face from you so that he does not hear.	וְחַטֹּאותֵיכֶם הִסְתִּירוּ פָנִים מִכֶּם מִשְּׁמוֹעַ:	C, D
For your hands are defiled with blood,	כִּי כַפֵּיכֶם נְגֹאֲלוּ בַדָּם	E
and your fingers with iniquity;	וְאֶצְבְּעוֹתֵיכֶם בֶּעָוֺן	F
your lips have spoken lies,	שִׂפְתוֹתֵיכֶם דִּבְּרוּ־שֶׁקֶר	G
your tongue mutters wickedness.	לְשׁוֹנְכֶם עַוְלָה תֶהְגֶּה:	H

The general command of God in the first text was that anyone who was ritually unclean through the reasons given (CD) should be expelled from the camp of Israel, וִישַׁלְּחוּ מִן־הַמַּחֲנֶה (B). Following this, two specifics follow (EF), both in marked word order (MV–MV): (1) the commandment includes both male and female, and (2) when the unclean are sent out in this way it is to a place outside the camp. This latter clause F cannot be a mere restatement of the initial general command. In that first instance the Hebrew simply said מִן־הַמַּחֲנֶה, 'from the camp' (B). But then the Israelites are told more precisely that these individuals are not just to be sent away, which could be taken as implying indefinite distance,[29] but that they are only to go אֶל־מִחוּץ לַמַּחֲנֶה literally 'to outside of the camp'. It is evident from other occurrences of אֶל־מִחוּץ in the book of Numbers (e.g., 15:36; 19:3; 31:13) that this referred to the surrounding area outside the camp where certain cultic rituals and events are described as taking place, and therefore cannot

---

28 See 3.4.2 (g).
29 Or permanent expulsion; cf. Genesis 3:23, וַיְשַׁלְּחֵהוּ יְהוָה אֱלֹהִים מִגַּן־עֵדֶן ('and God drove him [Adam] out of the Garden of Eden').

be understood as being far.³⁰ So by means of these marked clauses the opening general statement is further defined. The example from Isaiah, although a poetic text, shares the same essential characteristics. In verse 1 of the chapter the prophet had declared to the people, 'Behold, the hand of YHWH is not too short to save, nor his ear too dull to hear'. This may have been the thought in the minds of many Judeans in view of the downtrodden condition in which they found themselves. But the prophet counters this when he continues, 'Rather your iniquities have made a separation between you and your God, and your sins have hidden his face from you so that he does not hear' (v. 2). These four cola create a marked parallelism (AB//CD).³¹ Each half of the parallelism itself shows markedness through a preverbal NP[Su] since the relationship in which it stands with respect to the preceding verse (v. 1) has definite pragmatic implications. There the idea that God was incapable of taking action in order to deliver the Israelites was rejected. This was not the reason for their particular predicament. Rather, says the prophet, it was owing to their own sins (v. 3). This is another good example of replacing focus (following כִּי אִם). The parallel lines of verse 2 (A–D) state the nature of the problem, the two NP[Su]s being the generic terms עֲוֹנֹתֵיכֶם ('your iniquities') and חַטֹּאותֵיכֶם ('your sins'). Cola E–H present more detail concerning the sins of the people.³² Each of the four clauses concerns one body part and a particular sin associated with it. In each clause the body part appears in the initial position. The particular function of this focused structure in its context is that of indicating specification. Having stressed the presupposed fact of the peoples' sin as being the cause of their separation from God, the prophet now lists specific offences they had committed. So once again we see that the word order of the Hebrew is far from arbitrary in a poetic text, but shows markedness in a pragmatic context similar to its prose counterpart.

(b) REPLACING FOCUS

This particular category of focus may be formed by means of כִּי or כִּי אִם,³³ but not necessarily so. The following texts exemplify the similarity between marked replacing structures in both prose and poetry without the use of any particles:

---

30 Cf. the translation of T. R. Ashley, 'To the outside of the camp', *The Book of Numbers*, NICOT (Grand Rapids, Michigan: Eerdmans, 1993), p. 109. P. J. Budd, *Numbers*, WBC (Waco, Texas: Word Books, 1984), claims that 'the combination of prepositions here [אֶל־מִחוּץ] has each retaining its full force – "out in front of"', p. 53.
31 Pragmatic marking in parallelism is to be examined in a subsequent chapter (ch. 7).
32 It is noteworthy that Watts, *Isaiah 34–66*, p. 281 observes the 'general' and 'specific' distinction between verse 2 and verse 3. Cf. Oswalt, *The Book of Isaiah 40–66*, p. 514.
33 Examples appear in 3.4.2 (c) and 9.1.1.

Numbers 12:6–8

When there is a prophet of YHWH among you,	אִם־יִהְיֶה נְבִיאֲכֶם יְהוָה	A
I make myself known to them in visions;	בַּמַּרְאָה אֵלָיו אֶתְוַדָּע	B
I speak to them in dreams.	בַּחֲלוֹם אֲדַבֶּר־בּוֹ׃	C
Not so with my servant Moses;	לֹא־כֵן עַבְדִּי מֹשֶׁה	D
he is faithful in all my house.	בְּכָל־בֵּיתִי נֶאֱמָן הוּא׃	E
With him I speak face to face,	פֶּה אֶל־פֶּה אֲדַבֶּר־בּוֹ	F
clearly, not in riddles;	וּמַרְאֶה וְלֹא בְחִידֹת	G
and he beholds the form of YHWH.	וּתְמֻנַת יְהוָה יַבִּיט	H

Isaiah 45:18

For thus says YHWH,	כִּי כֹה אָמַר־יְהוָה	A
who created the heavens,	בּוֹרֵא הַשָּׁמַיִם	B
he is God,	הוּא הָאֱלֹהִים	C
who formed the earth and made it,	יֹצֵר הָאָרֶץ וְעֹשָׂהּ	D
it is he who established it,	הוּא כוֹנְנָהּ	E
he did not create it as a empty waste,	לֹא־תֹהוּ בְרָאָהּ	F
but he formed it as a place to be inhabited.	לָשֶׁבֶת יְצָרָהּ	G

In the first example the context is that of Aaron and Miriam questioning the role of Moses as the sole spokesman for God. 'Has YHWH spoken through [דִּבֶּר בְּ] Moses only?' they ask (v. 2). God then intervenes with the words of the above text. First he explains that in the case of other prophets he reveals his will to them through visions and dreams. But this is not the case with Moses. He has a unique position over the people, and the way in which God speaks with him is also unique. This communication is not through visions and dreams, but פֶּה אֶל־פֶּה אֲדַבֶּר־בּוֹ (lit., 'mouth to mouth'), which is further explained by the adjoining phrase וּמַרְאֶה וְלֹא בְחִידֹת, indicating openness and clarity. Without doubt the whole concept of divine communication is central to this passage – reflected in the verbs דִּבֶּר ('speak') and אֶתְוַדָּע ('I will make myself known'). In the focus construction of line F (MV) the verb דִּבֶּר is presuppositional. We note that אֲדַבֶּר־בּוֹ in this line is simply a verbatim repetition from line C. The focus in F is on the argument פֶּה אֶל־פֶּה, the fact that God did actually speak to Moses being presupposed. The marked information פֶּה אֶל־פֶּה is replacing the בַּמַּרְאָה and בַּחֲלוֹם of the earlier statements (BC). In the Isaiah text the same basic structure is exhibited, though this time the feature of replacing construction is even more apparent in that the two relevant clauses are adjacent rather than separated as in the previous example. God as Creator is the principal theme of the passage,[34] seemingly being contrasted to useless

---

34 Cf. J. A. Motyer, *The Prophecy of Isaiah* (Leicester: Inter-Varsity Press, 1993), p. 364.

idols (cf. v. 16 and v. 20). The verse first states the fact that God created the heavens and earth, and then his primary intention in so doing. There are clear echoes here of the creation narrative in Genesis (בָּרָא, יָצַר, עָשָׂה, תֹהוּ, הָאָרֶץ, הַשָּׁמַיִם). The marked word order that concerns us is found in lines F and G, לֹא־תֹהוּ בְרָאָהּ לָשֶׁבֶת יְצָרָהּ, having the constituent order M V-o / Inf V-o. It is the fronted element in each clause which stands in the replacing relationship. Each clause has a verb relating to the act of creation (בָּרָא and יָצַר). In this context no obvious distinction is being drawn between them but they function as synonyms.[35] So the argument-focus structure is apparent. That God created the earth is presupposed, it is his intention in so doing that remains to be decided. Was it to leave it void and desolate, or to populate it? Through these words the former is rejected (לֹא־תֹהוּ בְרָאָהּ), and the latter (לָשֶׁבֶת יְצָרָהּ) accepted as the divine end in bringing the earth into existence.[36] Thus again we see the pragmatic significance of the particular word order in this poetic text and how it matches that found in prose where the same function is in evidence.

(c) CONTRASTING RELATIONSHIPS

In this section we examine the pragmatic relationship of contrast, whether it pertains to the pragmatic function of topic or of focus. Since both of these exhibit the same structure as regards word order, they may be analysed together.

As is well-known, Biblical Hebrew typically employs *wāw* for 'but', as well as for 'and',[37] though the use of *wāw* is by no means obligatory. It is primarily the context that indicates whether or not the relationship of contrast is present.[38] Invariably in such a relationship the contrasted element in the second clause is marked by placing it in the preverbal position. As the presence of contrast in the following examples is evident, we shall here limit the analysis and give more space to the range of forms that are associated with contrast in both prose and poetry. The following two instances exemplify the typical structure where one NP[Su] stands in contrastive relationship with another:

1 Samuel 14:26–27

| When the people came into the forest, | וַיָּבֹא הָעָם אֶל־הַיַּעַר | A |
| there was honey dripping out; | וְהִנֵּה הֵלֶךְ דְּבָשׁ | B |

---

35 As elsewhere in this part of Isaiah (43:1, 7).
36 REB translates accurately: 'who created it not as a formless waste but as a place to be lived in'. Cf. E. J. Young, *Isaiah* (Grand Rapids, Michigan: Eerdmans, 2000 [1969]), vol. 3, p. 211.
37 Cf. Waltke and O'Connor, *Biblical Hebrew Syntax*, p. 651, who make the distinction between the 'Conjunctive' and 'Disjunctive' use of *wāw*.
38 Cf. Shimasaki, *Focus Structure*, p. 64, 'Contrast is the product of context'.

yet nobody put their hands to their mouths,	וְאֵין־מַשִּׂיג יָדוֹ אֶל־פִּיו	C
for they feared the oath.	כִּי־יָרֵא הָעָם אֶת־הַשְּׁבֻעָה׃	D
But Jonathan had not heard his father make the	וְיוֹנָתָן לֹא־שָׁמַע	E
people take the oath.	בְּהַשְׁבִּיעַ אָבִיו אֶת־הָעָם	F

Isaiah 45:16–17

They are all put to shame and disgrace,	בּוֹשׁוּ וְגַם־נִכְלְמוּ כֻּלָּם	A
together the makers of images	יַחְדָּו הָלְכוּ בַכְּלִמָּה	B
go in disgrace.	חָרָשֵׁי צִירִים׃	C
But Israel is saved by YHWH	יִשְׂרָאֵל נוֹשַׁע בַּיהוָה	D
with eternal salvation;	תְּשׁוּעַת עוֹלָמִים	E
you shall not be put to shame or confounded	לֹא־תֵבֹשׁוּ וְלֹא־תִכָּלְמוּ	F
to all eternity.	עַד־עוֹלְמֵי עַד׃	G

In the text from 1 Samuel the activity of Jonathan is contrasted with that of the people of Israel. The contrast is between the fact that הָעָם ('the people', AD), having heard Saul's oath, feared the consequences of eating the honey, and יוֹנָתָן, who had not heard, and so proceeded to eat. This latter clause has a preverbal subject phrase (E). Isaiah 45 resembles the pragmatic organisation of the first text, especially as regards constituent order in the second member of the contrast. The text opens with a canonically ordered V w-V S colon (A). Here the pronominal referent of its grammatical subject, כֻּלָּם, is to be identified as the חָרָשֵׁי צִירִים ('makers of images', C).[39] Predicated to these idolaters is the presupposed experience of shame and confusion (בּוֹשׁ and כָּלַם). Verse 17 begins with a clause (D) containing a preverbal NP[Su], here יִשְׂרָאֵל. To Israel is predicated not shame but salvation (נוֹשַׁע). Thus here also the construction consists of two contrasting elements, the idolaters and Israel, the second appearing in the preverbal position with a contrasting predicate, just as in the contrastive clause of the prose text.

In the above examples the contrast is between two participants encoded by means of a noun phrase. It is frequently the case where two active participants in a given discourse do not share the same number or gender that the second, placed preverbally in the second clause, will be encoded as a pronoun. In such cases no ambiguity occurs. In both the following examples the participant indicated by the pronoun, referring to the second contrasted member, is also the direct object of the first clause:

---

39 For reasons of length BC has been written on two lines, although combined they form a single parallel line with A. It is of note that the NIV places 'makers of idols' as the grammatical subject of the first line, with an anaphoric pronoun following, 'All the makers of idols will be put to shame and disgraced; they will go off into disgrace together'.

Genesis 42:8
Joseph recognised his brothers, וַיַּכֵּר יוֹסֵף אֶת־אֶחָיו
but they did not recognise him. וְהֵם לֹא הִכִּרֻהוּ׃

Psalm 106:43
Many times he delivered them, פְּעָמִים רַבּוֹת יַצִּילֵם
but they were rebellious in their designs, וְהֵמָּה יַמְרוּ בַעֲצָתָם
and were brought low in their iniquity. וַיָּמֹכּוּ בַּעֲוֺנָם׃

In certain situations where there is no possibility of ambiguity, i.e., where the topics are activated, both topical participants will be expressed by means of independent pronouns, as in:

Deuteronomy 28:44
He will lend to you, הוּא יַלְוְךָ
but you will not lend to him. וְאַתָּה לֹא תַלְוֶנּוּ

Psalm 20:9
They will stumble and fall, הֵמָּה כָּרְעוּ וְנָפָלוּ
but we shall rise and stand firm. וַאֲנַחְנוּ קַּמְנוּ וַנִּתְעוֹדָד׃

In the text from Deuteronomy Moses is telling the Israelites of the curses that shall come upon them should they turn away from the divine law. Verses 43–44 relate how the alien residing in Israel will gain the ascendancy over the impoverished Hebrews. The stranger will be in a financial position to lend to his Israelite neighbours, but the reverse will not be true.[40] The second example contains a direct polar contrast between topical participants – those who put their confidence in military might and those who place their trust in the Lord (v. 8).

We observe in the above two texts that both pronouns are fronted. It is often the case in polar contrasts such as the previous examples that both topical subjects appear in the clause-initial position, even when they are represented by a full noun phrase:

1 Samuel 16:7
For man looks on the outward appearance, כִּי הָאָדָם יִרְאֶה לַעֵינַיִם
but YHWH looks at the heart. וַיהוָה יִרְאֶה לַלֵּבָב׃

Psalm 37:22
Those blessed by him [God] will possess the land, כִּי מְבֹרָכָיו יִירְשׁוּ אָרֶץ
but those cursed by him will be cut off. וּמְקֻלָּלָיו יִכָּרֵתוּ׃

---

40 Cf. E. H. Merrill, *Deuteronomy*, NAC (Nashville, Tennessee: Broadman & Holman, 1994), p. 364.

Such SV/SV contrasts are common in sayings and proverbs.[41] Perhaps this is because of the balance between the two parts, or, as Shimasaki argues,[42] due to the fact that such sayings may stand independently of their context. This is the most prevalent form for antithetical bicola in the book of Proverbs.[43]

Similar contrastive structures to the foregoing are found where the object phrase or adverbial constituent stands in the contrastive relationship. Again, as the following examples will show, there is no discernible distinction with respect to word order between instances found in prose and those in poetry:

1 Samuel 15:15 [V O / O V]

The people spared the best of	חָמַל הָעָם עַל־מֵיטַב
the sheep and oxen …	הַצֹּאן וְהַבָּקָר…
but the rest we have utterly destroyed.	וְאֶת־הַיּוֹתֵר הֶחֱרַמְנוּ׃

Proverbs 10:32 [V O / O V]

| YHWH does not let the righteous go hungry, | לֹא־יַרְעִיב יְהוָה נֶפֶשׁ צַדִּיק |
| but he thwarts the craving of the wicked. | וְהַוַּת רְשָׁעִים יֶהְדֹּף׃ |

Judges 19:24 [V M / M V]

Do to them whatever you want;	וַעֲשׂוּ לָהֶם הַטּוֹב בְּעֵינֵיכֶם
but against this man do not do	וְלָאִישׁ הַזֶּה לֹא תַעֲשׂוּ
such a vile thing.	דְּבַר הַנְּבָלָה הַזֹּאת׃

Proverbs 3:5 [V M / M V]

| Trust in YHWH with all your heart, | בְּטַח אֶל־יְהוָה בְּכָל־לִבֶּךָ |
| do not lean upon your own understanding.[44] | וְאֶל־בִּינָתְךָ אַל־תִּשָּׁעֵן׃ |

Also two fronted O or M elements may be found in polar contrasts, as, for example, in Psalm 119:113 (O V / O V), and Isaiah 60:10 (M V / M V).

---

41 Craigie uses the term 'proverb' to describe Psalm 37:22, *Psalms 1–50*, p. 298.
42 Shimasaki, *Focus Structure*, pp. 193–94.
43 Proverbs 10:8, 21, 27, 31; 11:3, 27; 12:24, 25; 13:6, 9, 11, 16, 20; 14:1, 11, 15, 17; 15:1, 2, 5, 14, 18, 28; 16:9; 17:22; 18:14; 19:4; 21:28; 27:12; 28:4, 5, 13, 18, 25; 29:3, 4, 8, 10, 25. In these examples each line contains a full verbal clause. Not included are those proverbs where gapping takes place in the B-line (e.g., 12:17, S V O / w-S O), where a finite verb is paralleled by a participle (e.g., 15:20, S V O / w-S V[Pt] O), or where the B-line consists of a noun-clause (e.g., 10:1, S V O / w-S Comp), each of which may be seen to have the same information structure as S V / S V contrasts.
44 Though English versions do not use 'but' in their translation, a contrast is clearly present. Cf. R. E. Murphy, *Proverbs*, WBC (Nashville, Tennessee: Nelson, 1998), p. 21, who sees here 'The contrast between … trust [in the Lord] and one's own intelligence or insight'.

4.2.3 Sentence-Focus Clauses

Since all the examples so far examined have illustrated either argument focus or predicate focus with a marked dominant focal element, it is necessary to devote a sub-section to the sentence-focus clause (SV) in particular. This differs from the fomer two focus structures in that it is not as dependent upon preceding information,[45] a fact that will be seen in the following examples.

Shimasaki lists a whole range of diverse functions which may be performed by the sentence-focus clause.[46] Yet these may all be reduced to the two basic functions discussed in chapter 3 of event-reporting and presentation. Several examples of these functions will serve to illustrate the essential identity between the sentence-focus structure in Hebrew narrative and in poetry with respect both to form and function.

(a) EVENT-REPORTING CLAUSES

As noted earlier,[47] in a clause having sentence-focus there is no one particular component of the clause which is in focus, but rather the focus is upon the entire proposition. As Heimerdinger states,[48] the proposition is uttered in answer to the implicit question *What happened?* In Biblical Hebrew narrative such clauses commonly occur in certain specific contexts. Shimasaki helpfully sub-categorises these into explanation, cause, anteriority, parenthesis, and so on,[49] but for the purpose of illustrating the essential sameness between sentence-focus in prose and poetry, all the various sub-types of event-reporting clauses will not be elaborated upon here.

Genesis 3:13

And the woman said,	וַתֹּאמֶר הָאִשָּׁה
'The serpent deceived me	הַנָּחָשׁ הִשִּׁיאַנִי
and I ate'.	וָאֹכֵל׃

Psalm 71:11

... saying,	לֵאמֹר
'God has forsaken him;	אֱלֹהִים עֲזָבוֹ
pursue and seize him'.	רִדְפוּ וְתִפְשׂוּהוּ

There is an obvious correlation between the use of the sentence-focus clause in the text from Genesis and the psalm. In both cases the SV-clause

---

45 On the independence of the sentence-focus clause, see Shimasaki, *Focus Structure*, pp. 147-48.
46 Shimasaki, *Focus Structure*, p. 143.
47 3.3.3 (c).
48 Heimerdinger, *Topic, Focus and Foreground*, pp. 131, 157.
49 Shimasaki, *Focus Structure*, pp. 156-60.

initiates a sequence of direct speech. The context of the first quotation is that of Adam and Eve being interrogated by God upon being found hidden in the garden. God asks Eve, 'What is this you have done?', to which she gives the words of the above text by way of reply. Although the question posed by God, probably to be interpreted as rhetorical,[50] is framed in the 2nd person singular, that is, predicate focus, with Eve as active topic, her answer initially adopts a totally different information structure. Before speaking of the fact of her eating the fruit, which would be to answer the question directly, she states הַנָּחָשׁ הִשִּׁיאַנִי (SV), 'The serpent deceived me'. This is not a comment about her own action (*What did you do?*), but a clause in which both subject and predicate share equal focus (*What happened?*). Eve is describing to God an event that had occurred, performed by another agent (3rd person singular), which in its context, according to Eve, accounts for the fact that she had eaten the fruit of the tree. In other words, she is saying that an event had transpired (the serpent had deceived her) which she reports to God as an explanation for the fact that she had eaten what God had forbidden. This utterance of Eve is her attempt to transfer the responsibility of her sin from herself to the serpent.[51] The context of the passage from the psalm concerns opposition against the psalmist – 'my enemies speak concerning me, and those who watch for my life take counsel together' (v. 10). Verse 11 contains the direct speech of the adversaries. Their intention is to pursue him and seize him. This is the counsel they had taken together. But preceding this, the SV-clause gives the grounds for their particular course of action. אֱלֹהִים עֲזָבוֹ stands as an independent event performed by a participant other than the one that is the centre of their concern. The intentions of these enemies towards the psalmist would not be possible had not they first concluded that God had abandoned him. This fact is reported as an isolated clause in which the topic (God) and the action (forsake the psalmist) have an equal status with respect to the focus of the utterance. It is this event which led to their decision to pursue him, just as in the case of Eve the event that she reported led to her transgression. In both verses the independent event reported forms the logical basis (whether explanation or grounds) for the remainder of the speech that follows.

Another use of sentences of the event-reporting kind is that which, according to Shimasaki, expresses a 'solemn proclamation' or 'emotional outburst'.[52] Typically such clauses are extremely short and to the point, as would be expected of an exclamation or proclamation which was to capture attention and impress itself upon the mind of the listener. Invariably they

---

50 Cf. G. J. Wenham, *Genesis 1–15*, WBC (Waco, Texas: Word Books, 1987), p. 78.
51 A virtually identical parallel use of the sentence-focus structure is to be found in 2 Samuel 19:27 (עֲבָדִּי רִמָּנִי), also in the context of placing the blame on another.
52 Shimasaki, *Focus Structure*, p. 150.

concern God, the king, or other important personages. A good narrative example of this particular function of the sentence-focus clause appears in 1 Kings 14:11, 'Dogs will eat those belonging to Jeroboam who die in the city, and the birds of the air will feed on those who die in the country. The LORD has spoken!' (NIV). It is only the final declaration which interests us here. 'The LORD has spoken!' translates an original יְהוָה דִּבֶּר (SV). From poetic texts we include in this category the repeated SV-clause יְהוָה מָלָךְ in certain of the kingship psalms in that group of 93–100 (93:1; 96:10; 97:1; 99:1; cf. 1 Chr. 16:31).

Psalm 96:10

Say among the nations, 'YHWH reigns!'	אִמְרוּ בַגּוֹיִם יְהוָה מָלָךְ
The world is firmly established;	אַף־תִּכּוֹן תֵּבֵל
it shall never be moved.	בַּל־תִּמּוֹט
He will judge the peoples with equity.	יָדִין עַמִּים בְּמֵישָׁרִים:

Psalm 97:1

YHWH reigns!	יְהוָה מָלָךְ
Let the earth rejoice;	תָּגֵל הָאָרֶץ
let the many coastlands be glad!	יִשְׂמְחוּ אִיִּים רַבִּים:

Three of the aforementioned psalms begin with this marked utterance, yet a comparison with the fourth (96:10), and with the occurrence of the same phrase in the psalm of 1 Chronicles 16 (both following the verb אָמַר, 'say') suggests that its function is not simply the presentation of a new topic[53] but a proclamation that is to be broadcast. In Psalm 96:10 the line אִמְרוּ בַגּוֹיִם יְהוָה מָלָךְ clearly places the sentence-focus clause in the category of solemn declaration.[54] Those English versions are surely right which place the translation of יְהוָה מָלָךְ in 96:10 in quotation marks (as NIV NJB) or close it with an exclamation mark (as NRSV TEV). It is noteworthy that CEV renders the speech introduction in this verse as 'Announce to the nations', and NJPS, 'Declare among the nations'. If the SV-clause functions in this proclamatory sense in one of the psalm passages, then it arguably has the same connotation in the other closely related psalms. Commenting on Psalm 97:1 Harman describes the opening יְהוָה מָלָךְ as a 'declaration';[55] while Kidner attributes to the same words in 93:1 'the ring of a proclamation'.[56]

---

53 See the next example.
54 The significance of the *qatal* verb-form as distinct from *yiqtol* is another question, which does not directly relate to word order. For a discussion, see Tate, *Psalms 51–100*, p. 472; cf. Delitzsch, 'Psalms', pp. 73–74.
55 Harman, *Psalms*, p. 324.
56 D. Kidner, *Psalms 73–150*, TOTC (Leicester: Inter-Varsity Press, 1975), p. 338.

(b) PRESENTATIONAL CLAUSES

Instances of this presentational function abound in Hebrew narrative and, although much less common in poetry, are observable there also. We give one example:

2 Samuel 12:1

| And he [Nathan] said to him [David], | וַיֹּאמֶר לוֹ |
| 'There were two men in the same city ...' | שְׁנֵי אֲנָשִׁים הָיוּ בְּעִיר אֶחָת |

Song 8:11

There was a vineyard of Solomon	כֶּרֶם הָיָה לִשְׁלֹמֹה
at Baal-Hamon;	בְּבַעַל הָמוֹן
he gave the vineyard to keepers ...	נָתַן אֶת־הַכֶּרֶם לַנֹּטְרִים...

Both texts begin new sections of discourse. The first, the opening of Nathan's parable of reproof to King David, is unquestionably so. Regarding Song 8:11 Murphy says that verses 11-12 'seem to comprise a separate unit, in which the topic is vineyards'.[57] Verse 11 is therefore taken as opening a new section in TEV and a new paragraph in ESV NJPS NJB NLT. The information structure of the two opening clauses is basically the same. A SV-clause initiates the text segment presenting the participant that is to become the topic of the immediately following discourse. It is evident that the same strategy of presentation, through the marked order of constituents, appears in both genres.

4.2.4 Extraposed Constructions

The nature of extraposition in Biblical Hebrew, and how it comprises a structural variation on the basic marked form of simple word-order variation, was outlined in 3.4.3. There examples from prose texts were presented. Here we demonstrate briefly that the same forms of extraposition occur within poetic texts in contexts where pragmatic markedness is in evidence:

Genesis 17:15

Sarai your wife, you shall not call	שָׂרַי אִשְׁתְּךָ לֹא־תִקְרָא
her name Sarai,	אֶת־שְׁמָהּ שָׂרָי
but Sarah shall be her name.	כִּי שָׂרָה שְׁמָהּ׃

Job 3:6

That night, let thick darkness seize it!	הַלַּיְלָה הַהוּא יִקָּחֵהוּ אֹפֶל
Let it not be counted among the days of the year;	אַל־יִחַדְּ בִּימֵי שָׁנָה
let it not come into the number of the months.	בְּמִסְפַּר יְרָחִים אַל־יָבֹא׃

---

57 R. E. Murphy, *Song of Solomon*, Hermeneia (Minneapolis, Indiana: Fortress Press, 1990), p. 193. T. Longman III concurs that 8:11–12 form a separate unit, *Song of Songs*, NICOT (Grand Rapids, Michigan: Eerdmans, 2001), pp. 218–20.

Putting aside the question ambiguity of the verb in the Job text,[58] it is evident that in each of the above the author makes use of an extraposed nominal phrase in order to indicate a change in topic. The position of each text within the discourse is similar in that they appear medially within the larger text. By this we mean that the discourse is already under way and at the point in the discourse where these two texts occur the speaker changes from one topic to another. In the first instance, Genesis 17, God had been addressing Abraham concerning the covenant of circumcision. At verse 14 this particular subject matter is concluded, but God continues to speak to Abraham of another issue – his wife and the birth of her child. At this point in the discourse the NP[Ext] שָׂרַי אִשְׁתְּךָ in verse 15, resumed in the following clause through the suffix of שְׁמָהּ ('her name') signals the shift to a new topic. Exactly the same function may be attributed to the extraposed הַלַּיְלָה הַהוּא in Job 3:6. Following the severe blows that he has suffered (chs. 1–2) Job begins (ch. 3) to lament the day of his birth. Job announces his theme at the onset of the speech, 'Let the day [יוֹם] perish in which I was born, and the night [הַלַּיְלָה] that said, "A man-child is conceived"' (3:3 NRSV). He then proceeds by first cursing the 'day', יוֹם, of his birth (vv. 4–5). From the day he then turns to the 'night' (vv. 6–10). The Hebrew marks this shift through placing the NP[Ext] הַלַּיְלָה הַהוּא, resumed through the object suffix on the verb יִקָּחֵהוּ, at the very beginning of the new unit. As Khan observes, this boundary-marking function of extraposition is widespread in Biblical Hebrew.[59] The point to be stressed is that it takes on precisely the same form in both prose and poetic texts. The ordering of the various syntactic components of this construction is not altered by the fact of its appearing in a poetic literary environment. One further example of extraposition will suffice:

Deuteronomy 1:37-38

You also shall not enter there,	גַּם־אַתָּה לֹא־תָבֹא שָׁם:
but Joshua son of Nun, who attends you,	יְהוֹשֻׁעַ בִּן־נוּן הָעֹמֵד לְפָנֶיךָ
he shall enter there.	הוּא יָבֹא שָׁמָּה

---

58 In the translation offered יָחַד is taken as meaning 'be joined/united', being derived from the root יחד (*DCH*, vol. 4, p. 195), as in Targ Vulg Syr NIV NJPS REB TEV NCV NLT. This sense offers a much better parallelism to the following line than to take the verb as 'rejoice' (cf. NRSV NASB NKJV) from חדה.

59 Khan, *Studies in Semitic Syntax*, p. 78. For the function of extraposition marking change of topic, see pp. 79–81. In his treatment of this construction Khan reminds us of the fact that extraposition is a particular type of markedness which, although varying in form from straightforward fronting, often overlaps with fronting in the pragmatic functions that it performs. In the case of topic-shift, for example, a simple SV-clause would have served the same purpose, pp. 95–96.

Psalm 37:9

For the wicked shall be cut off,	כִּי־מְרֵעִים יִכָּרֵתוּן
but those who wait for the YHWH	וְקֹוֵי יְהוָה
they shall inherit the land.	הֵמָּה יִירְשׁוּ־אָרֶץ:

In both the prose and the poetic texts the NP[Ext] stands in a contrastive relationship to a NP in the preceding clause.[60] In the first instance, Moses is reporting to Israel the words of God that he would not enter Canaan. The first clause is itself marked for expanding focus in that mention has just been made of the 'evil generation' who shall not see the land (v. 35). The fact that neither they nor Moses would enter the land is therefore presupposed when we come to the clause הוּא יָבֹא שָׁמָּה. The NP[Ext] is the proper name יְהוֹשֻׁעַ בִּן־נוּן, with accompanying descriptive phrase, resumed by the preverbal Pn[Su] הוּא. The example from the psalm is essentially identical. The extraposed element is וְקֹוֵי יְהוָה, which is contrasted with the foregoing NP[Su] מְרֵעִים. As in the narrative example the NP[Ext] is resumed by means of a preverbal Pn[Su], הֵמָּה. Again we see that, despite the difference in genre, the same construction is found in both texts.[61]

4.2.5 Doubly Marked Clauses

The possibility exists that in a verbal clause not just one but two marked constituents may be placed before the verb. We note with agreement the comment of Buth that when two preverbal elements exist, the usual sequence is topic followed by focus.[62] It is here demonstrated that this feature is not peculiar to poetry, but that identical constructions are attested in narrative also. The following two pairs of examples illustrate this:

Genesis 14:10

Now the Valley of Siddim	וְעֵמֶק הַשִּׂדִּים	A
was full of bitumen pits;	בֶּאֱרֹת בֶּאֱרֹת חֵמָר	B
and the kings of Sodom and Gomorrah fled,	וַיָּנֻסוּ מֶלֶךְ־סְדֹם וַעֲמֹרָה	C
and they fell into them,[63]	וַיִּפְּלוּ־שָׁמָּה	D
but those who remained fled to the hill country.	וְהַנִּשְׁאָרִים הֶרָה נָּסוּ:	E

---

60 For extraposition in contrast, cf. Khan, *Studies in Semitic Syntax*, pp. 93–95.
61 This use of extraposition in contexts of contrast is common in Hebrew Proverbs (e.g., Prov. 12:2).
62 R. Buth, 'Topic and Focus in Hebrew Poetry: Psalm 51', in J. J. Hwang Shin and W. R. Merrifield (eds.), *Language in Contest: Essays for Robert E. Longacre* (Arlington, Texas: SIL and The University of Texas, 1992), p. 88.
63 Wenham interprets this as a general comment concerning the troops of the kings of Sodom and Gomorrah, since the king of Sodom evidently survived the battle (v. 17), *Genesis 1–15*, p. 312.

Pragmatic Markedness: (1) Non-Parallel Lines

Psalm 9:7–8a

The enemy has been ruined for ever,	הָאוֹיֵב תַּמּוּ חֳרָבוֹת לָנֶצַח	A
you have overthrown their cities;	וְעָרִים נָתַשְׁתָּ	B
the very memory of them has perished,	אָבַד זִכְרָם הֵמָּה׃	C
but YHWH sits enthroned forever ...	וַיהוָה לְעוֹלָם יֵשֵׁב ...	D

Genesis 14 records the defeat of the kings who fought against Chedorlaomer king of Elam and his allies. In the final clause (E) of this prose text we are confronted with two preverbal constituents: SMV. In both lines C and E the verb is נוס ('flee'). Those referred to in B fled to the valley where the bitumen pits were, and there they fell (D). Yet others, mentioned in line E, managed to escape to the hills. This is clearly a contrastive construction. The NP[Su] וְהַנִּשְׁאָרִים contrasts as the clause topic with the preceding topic encoded in the compound NP[Su] מֶלֶךְ־סְדֹם וַעֲמֹרָה and the 3rd person plural pronominal affixes on the verbs וַיָּנֻסוּ and וַיִּפְּלוּ. The second element in E, the locative form הָרָה,[64] stands in contrast to the place of bitumen pits in line A and the coreferential adverbial שָׁמָּה in D. We therefore see that both contrasting elements in E, the topical constituent and the locative adverb, are fronted.[65] The pragmatic situation is very similar in Psalm 9:7–8. There line A speaks of הָאוֹיֵב, 'the enemy', a collective noun in this context.[66] The verbal clauses of lines A–C all describe the overthrow of this enemy. Lines A and C especially express a certain finality to their destruction, both by the verb תַּמּוּ with its durative adverbial לָנֶצַח, and the phrase אָבַד זִכְרָם. Line D comes as a stark contrast to the fate of the enemy. Here the topical NP[Su] וַיהוָה contrasts with הָאוֹיֵב, and the adverbial לְעוֹלָם in connection with God's rule stands in direct opposition to the synonymous לָנֶצַח in line A concerning the destruction of the enemy. The latter is destroyed for ever, whereas the Lord reigns for ever. These two examples show how closely the information structure of the SMV clause in the narrative text matches that of a similarly ordered clause in the poetic text. It can hardly be doubted that the motivation is one and the same, i.e., pragmatic, in both cases.

One more pair of examples containing double fronting will be considered:

Judges 21:25

In those days there was no king in Israel;	בַּיָּמִים הָהֵם אֵין מֶלֶךְ בְּיִשְׂרָאֵל
each man did what was right in his own eyes.	אִישׁ הַיָּשָׁר בְּעֵינָיו יַעֲשֶׂה

---

64 Where the locative ה is added to the noun to indicate movement towards a place; cf. Van der Merwe (et al.), *Biblical Hebrew Reference Grammar*, pp. 227–28.

65 In a recent article L. J. de Regt also detects contrast with respect to both preverbal elements in this clause, 'Hebrew Syntactical Inversions and their Literary Equivalence in Robert Alter's Translation of Genesis', *BT 54.1* (2003), p. 115.

66 Cf. Craigie, *Psalms, 1–50*, p. 115.

Isaiah 9:19

He devoured on the right, but was still hungry,	וַיִּגְזֹר עַל־יָמִין וְרָעֵב
he ate on the left, but was not satisfied;	וַיֹּאכַל עַל־שְׂמֹאול וְלֹא שָׂבֵעוּ
each eats the flesh of his own kindred.	אִישׁ בְּשַׂר־זְרֹעוֹ יֹאכֵלוּ׃

These texts both display SOV word order, where the subject is the noun אִישׁ. The prevalence of the use of אִישׁ in the clause-initial position, indicating an indefinite topic, is noted by Muraoka.⁶⁷ In both of the above texts the verbal action is seen to be presuppositional within its context. The verb יַעֲשֶׂה in the Judges example contributes little to the utterance in that it can be assumed that people 'did' (habitual aspect) something. Clearly the focus, in the absence of any king to govern, is upon the object phrase הַיָּשָׁר בְּעֵינָיו. The implication is that should there have been a king in Israel, each man would have acted according to the rule of the king. But that not being so, it was 'what was right in his own eyes' that determined a man's conduct. In the Isaiah example, אִישׁ בְּשַׂר־זְרֹעוֹ יֹאכֵלוּ,⁶⁸ the verbal action of eating is also presupposed since the idea is strongly present in the preceding clauses. So again it must be that the focus falls the object phrase, בְּשַׂר־זְרֹעוֹ. This is evidently the main point of the proposition. In this time when the people experience the wrath of God (v. 18), they shall look for food but not be filled. In a last desperate attempt to satisfy their hunger they will consume their own offspring (literally 'their arm').⁶⁹ Undoubtedly the extreme nature of eating one's own kin makes this information the most salient in the prophet's utterance. So again we have two closely corresponding texts from both poetry and prose, with the greater complexity of not one but two constituents (first topic, then focus) being positioned before the verb.

4.3 Implications of Allo-Clauses in Poetic Texts

We now come to consider the existence of and difference between pairs of phrases consisting of Verb + NP/PP that are distinguished only with regard to word order. Here, for example, we are thinking of how בָּטַחְתִּי בוֹ ('I trust in him') might differ from בּוֹ בָטַחְתִּי ('In him I trust'). We have seen that when such pairs are identical in all other respects excepting their

---

67 In Joüon and Muraoka, *Grammar of Biblical Hebrew*, §155nf, 'The word אִישׁ ... used in indefinite sense ... fairly frequently occupies the initial slot in the clause'; cf. Muraoka, *Emphatic Words and Structures in Biblical Hebrew*, pp. 34–35.
68 Though examples with אִישׁ as the first of two fronted elements may have been drawn from within the selected portion of poetic texts (e.g., Is. 47:15), this particular text from outside the data was chosen in that it provides a better parallel with the prose example.
69 Cf. Motyer, *The Prophecy of Isaiah*, p. 110; Young, *Isaiah*, vol. 1, p. 354.

information structure, the technical term by which they are known is 'allo-sentences',[70] also referred to here as 'allo-clauses'. On the purely semantic level allo-clauses have equivalent meaning, and at the syntactic level they are constructed from the same components. It is solely at the pragmatic level that the two clauses are distinct from each other. In the light of the fact that marked clauses appear in Hebrew poetry in the same form as in prose, we should view the difference between allo-clauses in poetic texts as significant, with implications for both accurate exegesis and translation.

We have already noted (4.1) that לְךָ אֶתֵּן in Psalm 105:11 is marked in poetry in precisely the same way as it is in prose. This means that pragmatically it is distinct from its allo-clause, אֶתֵּן לְךָ. Though this allo-clause does not exist in this exact form (1st person singular verb + 2nd person singular pronominal suffix) in the poetic texts available, we find occasions where the indirect object follows the verb 'give' and other occasions when it precedes. If what we are arguing in this present study is correct, then these alternate forms display the difference between markedness and canonicity. We now demonstrate this by investigating a number of exact allo-clauses, or very similar clauses, which differ primarily in their constituent order. In those cases where some element is placed preverbally, we attempt to identify the pragmatic factors that are operating in order to account for its marked position.

Psalm 41:5

O YHWH, be gracious to me; heal me,   יְהוָה חָנֵּנִי רְפָאָה נַפְשִׁי
for I have sinned against you.   כִּי־חָטָאתִי לָךְ׃

Psalm 51:6

Against you alone have I sinned,   לְךָ לְבַדְּךָ חָטָאתִי
and done what is evil in your sight.   וְהָרַע בְּעֵינֶיךָ עָשִׂיתִי

The first text has the canonical VM order, חָטָאתִי לָךְ.[71] This clause has predicate focus, being a comment upon an active topic ('I'). The psalmist appeals for grace in view of the fact that he had sinned against God. Here the whole of חָטָאתִי לָךְ constitutes the predicate domain, and nothing in this domain is being especially marked for focus. In the second example,[72] however, לְךָ is put into prominence by being positioned before the verb חָטָאתִי. There can be no doubt that in this second instance the order MV is indicative of pragmatic marking. Regarding the semantic content of his utterance the psalmist is expressing essentially the same information: 'I

---

70 See 3.3.3.
71 לָךְ being in pausal form.
72 Verse 6 in MT is numbered as verse 4 in English Bibles.

have sinned against God', but in this case there are pragmatic implications – his sin was *only* against God, an implication not present in the first example. חָטָאתִי ... לְךָ undoubtedly displays restrictive focus. This is confirmed by the co-occurrence of לְבַדְּךָ, 'you alone', alongside לְךָ. The fact that the psalmist has sinned is evidently presuppositional, being mentioned in both verse 4 and 5 of the psalm ('Wash me thoroughly from my *iniquity*, and cleanse me from my *sin*. For I know my *transgressions*, and my *sin* is ever before me', NRSV, italics added). Now in verse 6 he presents the new information that his sin was against God only. Tate points out that 'other OT passages make it clear that from an early time in Israel sins against persons were believed to be sins against God ... see 2 Sam. 12:9, 10, 13; Gen. 39:9; Prov. 14:31; 17:5'.[73] Harman offers the helpful comment 'no matter how much he [the psalmist] has sinned against others ... the reality of the situation is that his sin was primarily against God'.[74] Harman then shows his awareness of the markedness of the original text, albeit not expressed in linguistic terms, when he adds, 'The NIV[75] translation brings out well the force of the Hebrew word order here. The primary focus of sin is against God'.[76] Psalm 51:6, as compared with 41:5, provides a good illustration of the clear distinction between canonical and marked constituent order, and how the Hebrew poets, even within their own particular literary genre, were attentive to such distinctions.

Another instance of differentiation, with a different category of focus, is to be seen in the following pair of verses:

Psalm 86:9

All the nations you have made will come	כָּל־גּוֹיִם אֲשֶׁר עָשִׂיתָ יָבוֹאוּ
and bow down before you, O YHWH,	וְיִשְׁתַּחֲווּ לְפָנֶיךָ אֲדֹנָי
and they will glorify your name.	וִיכַבְּדוּ לִשְׁמֶךָ:

Psalm 115:1

Not to us, O YHWH, not to us,	לֹא לָנוּ יְהוָה לֹא לָנוּ
but to your name give glory,	כִּי־לְשִׁמְךָ תֵּן כָּבוֹד
for your steadfast love and your faithfulness.	עַל־חַסְדְּךָ עַל־אֲמִתֶּךָ:

The first text has the canonical verbal clause וִיכַבְּדוּ לִשְׁמֶךָ, having predicate focus. From the viewpoint of information structure this is a comment on the active topic, כָּל־גּוֹיִם, 'all the nations'. In the second verse the verbal clause has as its nucleus תֵּן כָּבוֹד לְשִׁמְךָ, 'give glory to your name', with an equivalent semantic value to וִיכַבְּדוּ לִשְׁמֶךָ in the

---

73 Tate, *Psalms 51–100*, p. 17.
74 Harman, *Psalms*, p. 202.
75 'Against you, you only, have I sinned'.
76 Harman, *Psalms*, p. 202.

first text. Yet in Psalm 115:1 the element לְשִׁמְךָ occupies the preverbal position. This shift from canonical constituent order is highly significant, and the reason may be precisely defined from the immediate context. The preceding לֹא לָנוּ ('not to us') points to a replacing focus construction.[77] In fact this present verse may be said to be a classic representation of that particular focus category, having the basic form לֹא ... כִּי ... (cf. Gen. 45:8; Deut. 5:3; 1 Sam. 8:7, etc.). Through these words the psalmist denies for himself and Israel the glory that is due to their God.[78] Again we notice here the importance of discerning the pragmatic implications of word order changes in poetry. The non-canonical positioning of לְשִׁמְךָ is not merely a matter of poetic freedom due to the genre, but a deliberate marked focus structure.

The following pair of texts illustrate the pragmatic distinction between אֶל– הִתְפַּלֵּל and הִתְפַּלֵּל אֶל–:

Isaiah 44:17

The rest of it he makes into a god, his idol,	וּשְׁאֵרִיתוֹ לְאֵל עָשָׂה לְפִסְלוֹ	A
bows down to it and worships it;	יִסְגָּד־[לוֹ] וְיִשְׁתָּחוּ	B
and he prays to it and says,	וְיִתְפַּלֵּל אֵלָיו וְיֹאמַר	C
'Deliver me, for you are my god!'	הַצִּילֵנִי כִּי אֵלִי אָתָּה:	D

Isaiah 45:14

Thus says YHWH,	כֹּה אָמַר יְהוָה	A
'The wealth of Egypt and the merchandise of Cush,	יְגִיעַ מִצְרַיִם וּסְחַר־כּוּשׁ	B
and the Sabeans, tall of stature,	וּסְבָאִים אַנְשֵׁי מִדָּה	C
shall come over to you and be yours,	עָלַיִךְ יַעֲבֹרוּ וְלָךְ יִהְיוּ	D
they shall follow you;	אַחֲרַיִךְ יֵלֵכוּ	E
they shall come over in chains	בַּזִּקִּים יַעֲבֹרוּ	F
and bow down to you.	וְאֵלַיִךְ יִשְׁתַּחֲווּ	G
They will make supplication to you, [saying],	אֵלַיִךְ יִתְפַּלָּלוּ	H
"God is among you alone,	אַךְ בָּךְ אֵל	I
and there is no other; there is no god besides him"'.	וְאֵין עוֹד אֶפֶס אֱלֹהִים:	J

Isaiah 44:12–20 concerns the futility of idolatry. The prophet points out the absurdity of using part of a piece of wood for kindling a fire and baking bread or roasting meat (vv. 15–16), and then fashioning an object of worship with the remainder of the same piece of wood. Once the idol is completed the man who made it then renders his obeisance in the manner described in verse 17. הִתְפַּלֵּל אֶל– occurs as one of a series of acts that the worshipper performs before his idol, יִסְגָּד־[לוֹ] וְיִשְׁתַּחוּ וְיִתְפַּלֵּל אֵלָיו (BC).

---

77 See 3.4.2 (c); 4.2.2 (b).
78 Cf. Harman, *Psalms*, p. 370.

There is nothing remarkable about the word order of these verbal clauses. All exhibit predicate-focus structure. In Isaiah 45, verse 14 relates the future status of restored Israel (addressed in the 2nd person feminine singular) among the nations. Fronting is a prominent feature in this text. Note the sequence of marked clauses (DEGH):

עָלַיִךְ יַעֲבֹרוּ וְלָךְ יִהְיוּ אַחֲרַיִךְ יֵלֵכוּ ... וְאֵלַיִךְ יִשְׁתַּחֲווּ אֵלַיִךְ יִתְפַּלָּלוּ

Here the response of the Gentile nations towards the new Israel is described.[79] From the point of view of pragmatic functions certain clause constituents are repeatedly fronted in this series of clauses. In each a preverbal PP is present, making reference to 'you', that is, Israel. This striking feature of the word order is observed by Motyer. He remarks, 'All the pronouns in this verse (*e.g, to you*) hold emphatic positions'.[80] No attempt is made, however, to define the character of the emphasis. In this particular instance the precise nature of the markedness is not so readily defined. Yet the fact that the author was consciously using marked word order cannot be doubted. We note the obvious pragmatic marking of the noun-clause following the series of marked verbal clauses, beginning as it does with אַךְ בָּךְ (I).[81] Again it is the PP with 2nd person singular affix that is in the clause-initial position. Such a consistent use of fronting in a consecutive series of several clauses is surely indicative of the prominence of 'you' (Israel) in this text rather than due to factors of a merely poetic nature. Why the phrases 'to you' and 'after you' should be marked in this way is probably due to an implicit replacing focus. וְלָךְ יִהְיוּ, 'they shall belong *to you*', suggests that the nations had once belonged elsewhere. In אַחֲרַיִךְ יֵלֵכוּ, 'they shall follow *you*', is implicit the assumption that they had formerly followed another/others. So too in וְאֵלַיִךְ יִשְׁתַּחֲווּ אֵלַיִךְ יִתְפַּלָּלוּ it is presupposed that the Gentile nations had formerly made obeisance and supplication to others. It is at this point that we note that here in 45:17 are found verbs identical to those of 44:17. That earlier verse, speaking of the idolater, said וְיִשְׁתַּחוּ וְיִתְפַּלֵּל אֵלָיו.('he worships [it] and prays to it', BC). And now it is said of the Gentiles, וְאֵלַיִךְ יִשְׁתַּחֲווּ אֵלַיִךְ יִתְפַּלָּלוּ ('and they will worship *you* and make supplication *to you*', GH). This close similarity between the two texts strongly suggests that the prophet had the former in mind when expressing the latter. If this is the case then the replacing focus,

---

79 Cf. Young, *Isaiah*, vol. 3, p. 207.
80 Motyer, *The Prophecy of Isaiah*, p. 364. Two other commentaries consulted showed awareness of the word order. Oswalt, in a brief footnote, comments, 'The preposition ʾēlayik̠, "to you", is in an emphatic position, which makes Jerusalem even more prominent as the recipient of the homage', *The Book of Isaiah 40–66*, p. 215, fn. 63. Also Young mentions in passing, 'Emphasis is given by placing *unto thee* before the verb', *Isaiah*, vol. 3, p. 207.
81 On the sense of 'only', see Watts, *Isaiah 34–66*, p. 160.

in the case of these two verbs at least, becomes more explicit. The prophet is saying that these pagan nations would no longer bow down to and supplicate their carved images, but from henceforth they would come and bow down before God's people and make supplication to them. This, as the commentators note, is not to be taken as an act of divine worship but one of submission owing to the truth the nations had come to apprehend, that 'God is with you alone, and there is no other; there is no god besides him' (end of v. 17).[82] By means of this pragmatic marking the prophet is declaring that the Gentiles will come and prostrate themselves before Israel, and not their idols which they had served formerly. To attribute the MV word order to merely stylistic influences would be to overlook these important nuances in the prophet's message.

As a final illustration of the distinction between allo-clauses in terms of pragmatic information, we take the pair בָּטַח אֶל– and אֶל– בָּטַח:

Psalm 4:6

Offer right sacrifices, and trust in YHWH.   זִבְחוּ זִבְחֵי־צֶדֶק וּבִטְחוּ אֶל־יְהוָה׃

Psalm 31:7

You(?) hate those who regard worthless idols,   שָׂנֵאתִי הַשֹּׁמְרִים הַבְלֵי־שָׁוְא
but I trust in YHWH.   וַאֲנִי אֶל־יְהוָה בָּטָחְתִּי׃

The first text contains two commands of a general nature. The reader/listener is being addressed and told to engage in proper modes of sacrifice and to have a right attitude towards God. Both clauses, VO and VM, have predicate focus. Before we can analyse the second verse there is a textual variant to be noticed. The MT has the 1st person singular verb שָׂנֵאתִי ('I hate'), apparently referring to the psalmist. On the other hand, one Hebrew MS, LXX, Syr, Vulg, and the Arabic version all read 2nd person singular, 'you hate'.[83] This latter reading has been adopted by NRSV NJB and TEV.[84] Since the textual variant does not effect the information structure of the verse, we choose here the 2nd person form as the basis for our analysis. The first clause of 31:7, whether the grammatical subject be 1st or 2nd person, has predicate focus, the active topic being either God, as we shall understand it, or the psalmist. The second clause has two fronted

---

82 Young, *Isaiah*, vol. 3, p. 208, 'He [the prophet] does not mean that they will worship Israel, but that in bowing down they are acknowledging that only in Israel is the true God to be found. Likewise the prayer to Israel is not worship but the confession that in Israel God is truly present'. Delitzsch makes the comment that 'In the prophet's view, Jehovah and His church are inseparably one', in Keil and Delitzsch, *Commentary on the Old Testament*, vol. 7, 'Isaiah', p. 225.

83 The Hebrew MS is De-Rossi, IV. 23 (cf. Craigie, *Psalms 1–51*, p. 258). By Vulg here we mean Jerome's translation of the psalter *iuxta Hebraeos*.

84 Also ESV footnote.

elements, w-S^Pn M V. The first of these, וַאֲנִי, expresses a contrasting topic.[85] We need look no further than the previous clause to identify those with whom the psalmist contrasts himself,[86] הַשֹּׁמְרִים הַבְלֵי־שָׁוְא ('those who regard worthless idols').[87] The construct noun phrase here, according to Harman, 'refers to false gods which disappoint their worshippers'.[88] The way the Hebrew is expressed (lit., 'empty things of vanity') suggests that it is vain to place one's trust in such non-entities. In contrast with persons like these, the psalmist has put his trust elsewhere, אֶל־יְהוָה. He is saying, in effect, 'But as for me, *it is in YHWH* that I will trust'. It can be seen, therefore, that both of the preverbal elements in the second clause stand in a contrasting relationship to the preceding. וַאֲנִי contrasts with the vain worshippers, while אֶל־יְהוָה contrasts with the objects of their worship. The sequence is Contrasting Topic + Contrasting Focus + Verb.[89] Thus we see from these examples how בָּטַח אֶל־יְהוָה and אֶל־יְהוָה בָּטַח, though semantically and syntactically identical, differ with respect to their pragmatic implications. In the former allo-clause אֶל־יְהוָה forms one part of the predicate domain, and is unmarked. In the latter אֶל־יְהוָה is marked to identify it as information that contrasts with an entity in the preceding context.

Other fruitful comparisons of such pairs include אֶזְבְּחָה־לָּךְ (Ps. 54:8) with לְךָ־אֶזְבָּח (Ps. 116:17), יְחַלְנוּ לָךְ (Ps. 33:2, in pause) with לְךָ הוֹחָלְתִּי (Ps. 38:16), and קִרְאוּ בִשְׁמוֹ (Ps. 105:1) with בְשִׁמְךָ נִקְרָא (Ps. 80:19). In each of these cases the surrounding context of the marked form will provide satisfactory pragmatic reasons for the particular word order that the author has chosen.

The foregoing texts demonstrate how the Hebrew poets, like their prose counterparts, show a sensitivity towards word-order variation of a pragmatic nature. Often their choices are of significance and not to be interpreted as merely arbitrary.

4.4 The Use of Independent Pronouns

Lastly in this chapter some comment is necessary regarding the use of pronouns. In several of the examples analysed earlier in this chapter the marked constituent took the form of an independent pronoun. This is

---

85 Virtually all the major English versions translate by 'but' (NRSV ESV NASB NKJV NJPS NJB TEV CEV).
86 Delitzsch rightly states, 'אֲנִי is not an antithesis to the preceding clause, but to the member of that clause which immediately precedes it', that is, the direct object phrase הַשֹּׁמְרִים הַבְלֵי־שָׁוְא, 'Psalms', p. 385.
87 Cf. the similar phrase in Jonah 2:9, מְשַׁמְּרִים הַבְלֵי־שָׁוְא.
88 Harman, *Psalms*, p. 142.
89 Cf. 4.2.5.

typically the case where there is no ambiguity regarding the referent of the pronoun. However, a number of instances are to be observed in the data where the pronoun, although redundant from the point of view of referentiality,[90] does not seem to express markedness of the pragmatic kind considered elsewhere in this study. Significantly, this is often the case with the common verbs יָדַע ('know') and אָמַר ('say') and possibly one or two others.[91] Examples with יָדַע include Psalms 40:10; 51:5; 69:6; 139:2; 141:4; Job 11:11, and with אָמַר, Psalms 41:5; 82:6; 116:11. This phenomenon is not exclusively poetic since the same is also observable in prose (e.g., Ruth 4:4; 1 Sam. 17:28). If this particular use of the pronoun is not due to matters of topic and focus, then how is it to be accounted for? This is a matter for further research. The answer, however, may possibly be sought in one of two areas. Either the reason for the occurrence of the pronoun is to be found in the notion of 'semantic primitives',[92] of which the verbs 'know' and 'say' are prime examples. These semantic primitives are universals, occurring in all languages. Because such verbs are so basic to thought and communication, they are frequently irregular. This irregularity may manifest itself in the retention of archaic forms (as in English, know: knew, say: said), or possibly in some other way, of which the irregular use of the pronoun with these verbs may be a reflection. Alternatively, and perhaps more plausibly, the pronouns juxtaposed to these verbs may function as 'evidentials'.[93] An evidential indicates the evidence upon which a statement is being made. Both knowing and, to some extent, saying, are based upon some sort of evidence. A person knows something because of some evidential basis. When a person says something it is directly related to his state of knowledge. (In Biblical Hebrew we recall that אָמַר is also commonly used for acts of thinking). So it might possibly be that the inclusion of the independent pronoun with these verbs signals the fact that the item of knowledge or the content of the speech is based upon the personal evidence of the speaker. This would distinguish, 'I know [אֲנִי יָדַעְתִּי] because I saw/experienced it', from a simple, 'I know [יָדַעְתִּי] because it was reported to me'. This agrees with the fact that in the data the majority of these pronouns are referring to God, who more than any other would know from experience rather than mere report the truth of a matter. To determine satisfactorily which of these two explanations, or some other, accurately explains this particular use of the Hebrew pronoun falls outside the scope of the present work.

---

90 Since the same referent is encoded by means of the verbal affix.
91 The verb עָשָׂה ('do') may perhaps be included.
92 A. Wierzbicka, 'Semantic Primitives' in W. Bright (ed.), *International Encyclopedia of Linguistics* (New York: Oxford University Press, 1992), vol. 3, pp. 402-3.
93 A. Wierzbicka, *Semantics, Primes and Universals* (Oxford: Oxford University Press, 1996), ch. 15, 'The Semantics of Evidentials'.

4.5 Summary

In this chapter numerous examples of diverse kinds of marked word order have been considered in poetry and compared with similar variation of word order in prose. From the comparisons between texts of both genres it has been established that marked constituent order of the same form appears in poetry just as in prose. In one sense, this conclusion is what we would expect – it would be unreasonable to suppose that pragmatically marked order should vanish entirely from the poetic genre. It would be hard to conceive of a reason why forms reflecting pragmatic connotations should have been denied to the composers of song and poem, when freely employed by the narrator.

One consequence arising out of this is that attention needs to be given by the reader of Hebrew poetry to such variations. The study of allo-clauses revealed that it is frequently the case that the choice of word order by the poet is pragmatically significant.

So far we have distinguished those poetic cola exhibiting canonical constituent order, which may be labelled CAN, and those non-canonical cola, henceforth designated MKD or marked. To be investigated next is the question whether it is every departure from canonical order, or only some, which can be assigned to the motivation of pragmatic marking.

CHAPTER 5

Defamiliarised Word Order in Parallel Lines

Having shown that pragmatically marked word order operates in Hebrew poetry in precisely the same manner as in prose, it is now necessary to consider if this pragmatic factor alone is able to account for all word-order variations in poetry. We noted in the introduction (1.4) that in the prose genre there is a 14.5% departure from canonical order, while in poetry the percentage is significantly higher, 34%. Can every instance of non-canonical order in these poetic clauses be attributed to pragmatic considerations, or is a certain proportion due to factors of a purely poetic nature? And if there is in addition to pragmatic influences a poetic motivation for varying word order, which is an altogether separate dynamic from the former, how can these two be distinguished? These are the two questions explored in the present and the following chapters.

5.1 The Order of Clause Constituents in Parallel B-Lines

The comparisons of marked structures in prose and poetry revealed no difference between their forms and functions in the two genres. There are, however, certain instances of departure from the canonical base which have no parallel in narrative.[1] When presented with extended portions of poetic text the reader/listener soon registers the fact that variation in word order figures prominently within the context of parallelisms.[2] It is frequently the case that a canonical A-line is followed by a parallel B-line which, while differing little semantically, varies the sequence of constituents from what is found in A, such as in Isaiah 40:12 (QVMO//OMV):

Who has measured the waters in the hollow of his hand	מִי־מָדַד בְּשָׁעֳלוֹ מַיִם
and marked off the heavens with a span?	וְשָׁמַיִם בַּזֶּרֶת תִּכֵּן

This phenomenon is to be observed in the data on numerous occasions –

---

1 This, of course, does not include those poems and songs found embedded within narrative. These will be seen to follow the principles laid down in this work for Hebrew poetry in general. Cf. the analysis of the first Baalam oracle (Num. 23:7–10) in 9.1.5.
2 On the character of Hebrew parallelism, see 2.2.

330 times in all. While frequently occurring in isolated instances, it is most striking in those sections of poetry where several CAN//non-CAN parallelisms are strung together consecutively. The following three passages exemplify this (the B-lines are indented from the left to highlight the prominence of this feature):

Psalm 20:4–6b

A	יִזְכֹּר כָּל־מִנְחֹתֶךָ May he remember all your offerings,	V O	CAN
B	וְעוֹלָתְךָ יְדַשְּׁנֶה סֶלָה׃ and may he accept your burnt sacrifices.	w-O V	Non-CAN
A	יִתֶּן־לְךָ כִלְבָבֶךָ May he give you your heart's desire,	V-IO M	CAN
B	וְכָל־עֲצָתְךָ יְמַלֵּא׃ and may he fulfil all your plans.	w-O V	Non-CAN
A	נְרַנְּנָה בִּישׁוּעָתֶךָ We will sing for joy for your salvation,	V M	CAN
B	וּבְשֵׁם־אֱלֹהֵינוּ נִדְגֹּל and in the name of our God will raise a banner.	w-M V	Non-CAN

Isaiah 42:15–16b

A	אַחֲרִיב הָרִים וּגְבָעוֹת I will lay waste the mountains and hills,	V O w-O	CAN
B	וְכָל־עֶשְׂבָּם אוֹבִישׁ and I will dry up all their grass.	w-O V	Non-CAN
A	וְשַׂמְתִּי נְהָרוֹת לָאִיִּים And I will turn the rivers to islands,	w-V O M	CAN
B	וַאֲגַמִּים אוֹבִישׁ׃ and I will dry up the pools.	w-O V	Non-CAN
A	וְהוֹלַכְתִּי עִוְרִים בְּדֶרֶךְ לֹא יָדָעוּ And I will lead the blind by a road they do not know,	w-V O M	CAN
B	בִּנְתִיבוֹת לֹא־יָדְעוּ אַדְרִיכֵם and in paths they do not know I will guide them.	M V-o	Non-CAN

Proverbs 5:12–13

A	וְאָמַרְתָּ אֵיךְ שָׂנֵאתִי מוּסָר And you said, 'How I hated discipline,	w-V C V O	CAN
B	וְתוֹכַחַת נָאַץ לִבִּי׃ and my heart despised reproof.	w-O V S	Non-CAN
A	וְלֹא־שָׁמַעְתִּי בְּקוֹל מוֹרָי And I did not listen to the voice of my teachers.	w-V M	CAN
B	וְלִמְלַמְּדַי לֹא־הִטִּיתִי אָזְנִי׃ or incline my ear to my instructors'.	w-M V^{Ng} O	Non-CAN

This readily recognisable feature of variation in parallel lines accounts for over 20% of all non-canonical clauses in the selected poetic material.

5.2 Attempted Pragmatic Interpretations of Parallel B-Lines

How is this deviation from canonical word order in parallelisms to be interpreted? Some are of the view that such variations in order are to be understood in the same way as if the text were simply prose. Although this is not a subject which has received detailed scholarly treatment, there are those whose work has touched upon it at least in part. Two Hebrew scholars, Buth and Shimasaki, would assign these variations exhibited by parallel B-lines to pragmatic causes.

5.2.1 *Buth on Psalm 51*

In a 1992 article Randall Buth presented an analysis of Psalm 51.[3] In this article Buth attempts to account for every instance of non-canonical word order in the psalm as being due to pragmatic marking, that is, relating to questions of either topicality or focality within the text. Verses 3 and 4 are a case in point:

Be gracious to me, O God,	חָנֵּנִי אֱלֹהִים כְּחַסְדֶּךָ
according to your steadfast love,	כְּרֹב רַחֲמֶיךָ מְחֵה פְשָׁעָי׃
according to your great compassion	[הֶרֶב] כַּבְּסֵנִי מֵעֲוֹנִי
blot out my transgressions.	וּמֵחַטָּאתִי טַהֲרֵנִי׃
Wash me thoroughly from my iniquity,	
and cleanse me from my sin.	

---

3   Buth, 'Topic and Focus in Hebrew Poetry – Psalm 51'.

We note that these two verses closely resemble the passages quoted in the preceding section (5.1), i.e., they contain a sequence of canonical and non-canonical cola in parallelism. Their basic structure is V-o M // M V O, V-o M // M V-o, creating an *ab//ba, ab//ba* pattern. Buth explains this in the following way:

> parallel repetition is used as a kind of linking topicalization. For example, verses 3b, 4b ... [etc.] all use a preverb phrase to repeat salient information from the previous colon. Because such repetitive clauses bring a pause to any chronological or logical movement in the text, they typically use topic structures in narrative. We may be inclined to label these as topics here in poetry, too. There is, however, a natural prominence or highlighting effect when one colon parallels or repeats a previous colon. When we consider that the fronted phrase repeats the salient information of the previous clause we recognize that this is part of the 'and-what's-more', to borrow Kugel's words. Such a marked salient phrase can rightly be taken as focus. In fact, more of these examples may reflect both topic marking and focus marking on the same phrase in the underlying grammar.[4]

Here, in order to understand the non-canonical ordering of constituents, Buth appeals to both the pragmatic functions of topicalisation and focus. It is unnecessary to enter into a discussion of his definitions of these terms presented in the article, but clearly he sees the word-order variation as significant in not just one but in two respects. Firstly, the marked order of the B-line creates a disjuncture or 'pause' in the text, that is, it breaks the sequential development of the discourse. For Buth, such a feature is indicated in Hebrew narrative by means of a marked clause structure,[5] and he proceeds to apply the same to poetry,[6] proposing that the fronted constituent be interpreted in terms of topic. Secondly, he makes the claim that this initial element of the B-line underlines the most prominent information of the previous line, which he describes as focus. Buth adopts the same approach with respect to all parallel lines in the psalm (verses 6b, 8b, 11b, 12b, 15b, 18b, 19b).[7]

---

4 *Ibid.*, p. 90.
5 Cf. his discussion of Genesis 37:2-3, *ibid.*, p. 87.
6 Buth comments, *ibid.*, p. 85, 'I assume that a writer or reader of a poem uses the normal grammatical devices of a language to find the meaning in a text. Any structure used *will be* interpreted by the audience. Until the audience has learned a special grammar for poetry, it perceives the normal functions and relationships of those structures. We can, therefore, begin our analysis from what is known about the language in general in order to determine how the system applies to a poem'. By 'normal grammatical devices', Buth means those employed in prose texts.
7 *Ibid.*, p. 90.

In this matter of word order in parallel B-lines, we take issue with Buth. An analysis in terms of pragmatic markedness is questionable in several respects:

(1) It fails to account for the fact that numerous similar parallelisms occur elsewhere in biblical poetry showing the symmetrical patterns V O // V O or V M // V M, where both cola contain canonical clauses (e.g., Ps. 132:2–3; Prov. 1:23–24). The CAN//CAN form of parallelism is in fact the most common of the various parallel combinations.[8] In such cases we allow, with Buth, that the 'repetitive clauses bring a pause to any chronological or logical movement in the text', yet the word order of the parallel line is not marked in any way. The presence of a parallel colon *in itself* causes lack of movement, regardless of the order of its syntactic components. It is not 'topicalisation', as Buth terms it, but the repetition that produces this effect.

(2) Is it in fact true to say that in the parallel line 'the fronted phrase repeats the salient information of the previous clause'? Buth fails to back up this statement with evidence. To say that כְּחַסְדְּךָ ('according to you steadfast love') in Psalm 51:3a is the most prominent information of the colon, and that therefore כְּרֹב רַחֲמֶיךָ ('according to your great compassion') is placed first in v. 3b seems to be an unfounded assumption. What is there, either linguistically or contextually, demanding that כְּחַסְדְּךָ be taken as the salient information? One would have thought that the chief thing in David's[9] mind was, in view of the grievous sin he had committed, to be shown grace (חָנֵּנִי) and for his transgression to be blotted out (מְחֵה פְשָׁעָי). The logic of Buth's reasoning breaks down when other similar examples are considered. In Psalm 58:4 we find the following parallel lines:

| The wicked go astray from the womb, | זֹרוּ רְשָׁעִים מֵרָחֶם |
| those who speak lies err from their birth. | תָּעוּ מִבֶּטֶן דֹּבְרֵי כָזָב׃ |

These two clauses have the constituent order V S M // V M S. On the analogy of Buth's argument regarding Psalm 51:3 the element מֵרָחֶם (occupying the same position as כְּחַסְדְּךָ) would be taken as the salient information of the A-line.[10] Yet the corresponding element in the B-line, מִבֶּטֶן, is not fronted, as one would expect if Buth's analysis of 51:3 were correct, but in fact occupies the medial position in the clause. Similarly Psalm 149:2:

| Let Israel be glad in his Maker, | יִשְׂמַח יִשְׂרָאֵל בְּעֹשָׂיו |
| let the children of Zion rejoice in their King. | בְּנֵי־צִיּוֹן יָגִילוּ בְמַלְכָּם׃ |

Following Buth's reasoning, the coreferential NP[Su]s, the postverbal יִשְׂרָאֵל ('Israel') in line A and the clause-initial בְּנֵי־צִיּוֹן ('sons of Zion') in

---

8 Approximately 360 CAN//CAN parallelisms appear in the data (Appendix 2).
9 Assuming Davidic authorship of the psalm.
10 And arguably from the context this is the case.

B, should be considered prominent above the other constituent, since the latter occurs first in the B-line. How the clause-medial יִשְׂרָאֵל, to which בְּנֵי־צִיּוֹן corresponds, can be taken as most prominent in the A-line is far from obvious. Numerous other like instances could be adduced where the fronted element of the B-line can hardly be considered focused, all of which would cast serious doubts upon Buth's assertion that the initial element in the parallel line serves to highlight the most salient information of the previous line.

(3) It is sometimes to be observed that semantically similar parallelisms are found having one form, i.e., canonical in both lines, in one instance, and the other form, i.e., non-canonical in the B-line, elsewhere. Note the resemblance between the following two verses:

Psalm 150:3

| Praise him with the sounding of the trumpet, | הַלְלוּהוּ בְּתֵקַע שׁוֹפָר |
| praise him with melody with harp and lyre. | הַלְלוּהוּ בְּנֵבֶל וְכִנּוֹר: |

Psalm 33:2

| Praise YHWH with the lyre, | הוֹדוּ לַיהוָה בְּכִנּוֹר |
| make melody to him on the ten-stringed harp. | בְּנֵבֶל עָשׂוֹר זַמְּרוּ־לוֹ: |

The first example has the same canonical V-o M // V-o M order in both lines, while the second has inverted word order in the parallel colon, V IO M // M V IO. Why matters of focus, as proposed by Buth, should result in the particular musical instruments being fronted in one case but not the other is not apparent. Again in Isaiah 43 we find both of the following constructions in the parallel B-line:

Isaiah 43:19

| I will even make a way in the wilderness, | אַף אָשִׂים בַּמִּדְבָּר דֶּרֶךְ |
| and rivers in the desert. | בִּישִׁמוֹן נְהָרוֹת |

Isaiah 43:20

| because I give waters in the wilderness, | כִּי־נָתַתִּי בַמִּדְבָּר מַיִם |
| and rivers in the desert. | נְהָרוֹת בִּישִׁימֹן |

The verb has been gapped in the parallel lines, but the order of the identical nominal constituents in the remaining sentence fragment[11] has been reversed. Can a plausible case be put forward to prove that pragmatic influences are operative in determining this variation in word order? There is nothing observable from the context that would require the fronting of one element in the first case and the other element in the second.

---

11 For this term, see 2.2.2 (a).

(4) There is also the fact that where variation exists in the parallel line, it is not always simply a matter of the fronting of one particular element, as is most frequently the case with pragmatic markedness. This may appear to be the case only because the majority of poetic cola consist of just two syntactic components. Yet where more than two exist, the parallel line may have two elements preceding the verb (e.g., OMV in Is. 46:6b), and occasionally even three (e.g., SMMV in Ps. 102:20b). Although from the perspective of pragmatic functions the presence of two fronted elements is not an impossibility,[12] it does make the task of a consistent reading of the constituent order in terms of pragmatic influences even more challenging, and in the case of three preverbal elements a virtual impossibility. Such multiple-fronting is markedly more commonplace in poetry than in prose, a fact which should make us wary of interpreting this feature in the same way in both genres, as Buth attempts.

(5) Furthermore, when all the existing patterns of the sequential arrangement of the B-line are considered, one would be hard pressed to convincingly explain each of these instances of deviant word order in the B-line with reference to topic or focus. Taking a parallel bicolon of three constituents in each colon as a basic model, we find in the selected corpus of data every permutation possible, as exemplified by the following:

1	Ps. 109:11	יְנַקֵּשׁ נוֹשֶׁה לְכָל־אֲשֶׁר־לוֹ וְיָבֹזּוּ זָרִים יְגִיעוֹ׃	VSO//VSO
2	Ps. 58:4	זֹרוּ רְשָׁעִים מֵרָחֶם תָּעוּ מִבֶּטֶן דֹּבְרֵי כָזָב׃	VSM//VMS
3	Ps. 69:22	וַיִּתְּנוּ בְּבָרוּתִי רֹאשׁ וְלִצְמָאִי יַשְׁקוּנִי חֹמֶץ׃	VMO//MVO
4	Ps. 6:10	שָׁמַע יְהוָה תְּחִנָּתִי יְהוָה תְּפִלָּתִי יִקָּח׃	VSO//SOV
5	Ps. 9:16	טָבְעוּ גוֹיִם בְּשַׁחַת עָשׂוּ בְּרֶשֶׁת־זוּ טָמָנוּ נִלְכְּדָה רַגְלָם׃	VSM//MVS
6	Ps. 142:3	אֶשְׁפֹּךְ לְפָנָיו שִׂיחִי צָרָתִי לְפָנָיו אַגִּיד׃	VMO//OMV

The total of six possible permutations are:

| 1 | *abc*
abc | 2 | *abc*
acb | 3 | *abc*
bac | 4 | *abc*
bca | 5 | *abc*
cab | 6 | *abc*
cba |

---

12 As shown in 4.2.5.

Why the corresponding element to a postverbal subject of the A-line should in one case appear in the same medial position in the B-line (e.g., Ps. 109:11), in another case the clause-initial position (e.g., Ps. 6:10), and yet in another be placed clause-finally (e.g., Ps. 58:4), is a question to which pragmatic markedness cannot offer a reasonable solution.

(6) Finally, if the ordering of syntactic components in parallel lines were in fact the result of pragmatic influences, then taken to its logical conclusion we would be required to completely disallow any poetically motivated word order in Hebrew poetry.[13] It is apparent from Buth's analysis of Psalm 51 that he makes no room for any other variation other than that which signifies the marking of topic and focus. He is aware that there are those who resort to poetic influences in an attempt to explain the variation,[14] but this is dismissed in favour of what may be described as a 'pan-pragmatic' approach.[15]

5.2.2 Shimasaki on Parallel Constructions

Shimasaki's work on focus structure in Biblical Hebrew, as stated earlier,[16] concentrates primarily upon narrative and legal texts. He does, however, offer some discussion of poetic parallelism and chiasmus. We have no disagreement with Shimasaki's analysis of synonymous parallelism where the cola in parallel relationship contain two clauses having predicate focus, both showing canonical word order (CAN//CAN). Such is the case, for example, in his treatment of Isaiah 19:12 (VS//VS).[17] Yet where he deals with inverted B-lines, we would question his particular way of understanding its form. One of the poetic texts that Shimasaki analyses is the following:[18]

Isaiah 3:17

The Lord will put sores on the heads
of the daughters of Zion,
and YHWH will lay bare their secret parts.

וְשִׂפַּח אֲדֹנָי קָדְקֹד בְּנוֹת צִיּוֹן
וַיהוָה פָּתְהֵן יְעָרֶה:

---

13 This will become apparent as we proceed, since it is precisely in parallel lines that most freedom of word order is permissible on the part of the Hebrew poets.
14 Buth, 'Topic and Focus in Hebrew Poetry – Psalm 51', p. 85.
15 As this book was in the final stages of preparation before printing, a newly published journal article tackling word order in poetry came to the author's attention: S. J. Floor, 'Poetic Fronting in a Wisdom Poetry Text: The Information Structure of Proverbs 7', *JNSL 31.1* (2005), pp. 23–58. Although Floor seeks to apply the information structure theory of Lambrecht, he follows the same path as Buth in endeavouring to impose pragmatic markedness in every instance of non-canonical word order. Like Buth he allows no place for purely poetic variation
16 See 3.2.
17 Shimasaki, *Focus Structure*, p. 185.
18 *Ibid.*, p. 163 and p. 234.

This parallelism has the basic structure VSO//SOV. To the B-line Shimasaki assigns sentence focus, even though it includes not just one but two preverbal elements, a feature not agreeing with the typical (SV) sentence-focus clause.[19] Yet, insisting the clause to have this particular focus structure, he proposes alternatives to account for this phenomenon.[20] First, the second line might have one of the actual functions which he claims for sentence-focus structure. This could be, he suggests, either 'closure' to the whole parallel unit,[21] or what he describes as a 'paraphrasing or explaining' of the foregoing line.[22] Another possibility is that the information structure of the parallel line is deliberately ill-formed. Shimasaki himself prefers this latter alternative since many places where sentence-focus clauses occur in such chiastic constructions show no signs of closure or paraphrase/explanation. In support of this he observes that 'Smooth information flow does not always exist in conversation', an example of which is offered from English.[23] Then, regarding the construction in Hebrew, he adds, 'In poetry unexpected grammar or an ill-formed information structure may be a device to produce a special literary effect or function. Some clauses with chiastic construction are not operating independently from the information structure, but are deliberately overriding it for literary effect'.[24] By 'overriding it' Shimasaki means that the clause does not in fact possess the sentence-focus structure that its form suggests to him.

Casting doubt on Shimasaki's interpretation is the fact that, firstly, he offers no explanation why the sequence SOV should be counted as sentence focus, since this is not its usual form. He makes no attempt to account for the fronting of both the NP[Su] and NP[DO]. Nor, secondly, does he make any comment on the fact that both inverted and non-inverted B-lines are common in such parallelisms. Why should one B-line of a canonical A-line display sentence focus and another predicate focus?[25]

Shimasaki, we recall, had earlier rightly assigned the basic function of 'independence' to sentence-focus clauses.[26] Yet parallel lines in poetry show quite the opposite characteristic. Colon B often depends on A with respect to topicality, deixis, tense and aspect, as much as it does in connection with the more obvious phenomenon of gapping. Why the sentence-focus clause in particular, if that indeed is what it is, should be

---

19 See 3.4.1 (c).
20 Shimasaki, *Focus Structure*, pp. 233–34.
21 *Ibid.*, pp. 179–80.
22 *Ibid.*, p. 158.
23 *Ibid.*, p. 234.
24 *Ibid.*
25 As the previously mentioned Isaiah 19:12.
26 Shimasaki, *Focus Structure*, p. 147; cf. 3.4.1 (c) above.

selected for constructing parallel lines Shimasaki has not, we contend, convincingly explained.

In order to account for the order of such parallel clauses in poetry both Buth and Shimasaki operate within the confines of a pragmatic approach. Buth endeavours to account for all preverbal constituents in terms of topic and focus, while Shimasaki feels obliged to assign such clauses to one of Lambrecht's three focus structures, even though neither the precise form nor the function point in that direction. Each of these attempted explanations, we have shown, is unsatisfactory.

5.2.3 Parallel Lines and Parallel Focus

In the context of interpreting word-order variation in parallel lines pragmatically, it is necessary to remark that the category earlier described as 'parallel'[27] topic or focus also fails to account for the facts. The designation *parallel* might lead one to suspect that such pragmatic marking with respect to either topic or focus might provide the solution to the form of parallel lines. This, however, is not the case. These marked parallel constructions, as shall be seen from the following texts, do not share the same components as poetic parallelism.

1 Samuel 26:25

| So David went on his way, | וַיֵּלֶךְ דָּוִד לְדַרְכּוֹ |
| and Saul returned to his place. | וְשָׁאוּל שָׁב לִמְקוֹמוֹ: |

Psalm 149:2

| Let Israel be glad in his Maker, | יִשְׂמַח יִשְׂרָאֵל בְּעֹשָׂיו |
| let the children of Zion rejoice in their King. | בְּנֵי־צִיּוֹן יָגִילוּ בְמַלְכָּם: |

Here the constituent order is VSM–SVM in the prose example, and VSO//SVO in the poetic. The only syntactic difference between these two is the nature of the phrase following the verb, though this is of no consequence for the present consideration. The essential point to note is that both texts consist of a canonical clause followed by one that is SV, i.e., non-canonical. 1 Samuel 26:25, a typical example of parallel topic structure, has two subject phrases which, unlike the poetic parallelism, are not coreferential, and indeed, in this particular focus construction they could never be so. Two independent participants are required in order to act in parallel. This contrasts with the psalm text where the subject phrases, יִשְׂרָאֵל and בְּנֵי־צִיּוֹן, are virtually synonymous, and certainly coreferential. Moreover, the predications in each example are of quite a different character. In the prose text the predicates of the two clauses signify differing actions – David went in one direction and Saul another. In the

---

27 See 3.4.2 (b).

parallelism, on the other hand, the predicates indicate two semantically similar actions, יִשְׂמַח and יָגִילוּ. ('be glad' and 'rejoice'). We see, therefore, that although the two texts are formally constructed in a similar fashion, semantically the two clauses in each relate together in quite a different manner. The parallel topic construction consists of two distinct participants performing two different actions, while parallelism concerns what is basically a single entity and a single action, heightened rhetorically by means of its restatement through varying lexis. The similarity that exists between the above prose and poetic examples, we conclude, is therefore purely coincidental. We are made certain of this when we consider that other parallelisms could have been adduced in which the subject constituent in the second line occupies the second or third position, as referred to earlier in this chapter, thus destroying the formal correspondence with the prose parallel structure.

In the light of the foregoing, we can conclude as a general rule in Biblical Hebrew poetry that the ordering of clause constituents in B-lines of parallel cola is not something governed by linguistic rules relating to pragmatic functions.

5.3 Poetically Defamiliarised Word Order

If pragmatics fails to account for the variation exhibited by parallel lines, then what is the motivating factor that produces such a feature? We would maintain that the characteristics of non-canonical B-lines in parallelisms point us in the direction of a purely poetic manner of word-order variation.

5.3.1 Poetic Freedom in Parallel Lines

The chief indicators that suggest the strictly poetic nature of the variation observed are the following:

(1) The optionality of the variation. We have seen in the preceding section that poetic parallelisms may be either of the form CAN//CAN or CAN//non-CAN.

(2) The frequency of the variation. The not too disproportionate figures of 360 CAN//CAN compared with 330 CAN//non-CAN parallelisms does not suggest some special markedness in the case of the latter.

(3) The degree of the variation. Parallel B-lines can be found, as noted, with one, two, or even three preverbal constituents.

(4) The diversity of the variation. In parallel B-lines all possible permutations of word order are to be found in the data. Any constituent may appear in any position.

Over against these four factors relating to poetic cola there is the noticeably different character of pragmatic marking within prose. The same optionality between marked and unmarked forms is not at all in evidence, nor do we observe the same degree or diversity of variation. Pragmatic marking mostly consists of a single fronted element, much less often two, and not all patterns are present in prose.[28]

In view of these facts we hold the view, contrary to Buth and Shimasaki, that the variation manifested by such parallel cola is more suitably explained in terms of poetics, that is, the artistic creativity allowable in the poetic genre. This latter factor is quite distinct from that of pragmatic marking in producing word-order variation. The lack of any inner logic or consistency among the aforementioned characteristics of parallel lines serves to highlight the freedom of the phenomenon. It would suggest that in the context of parallel B-lines the Hebrew poet had complete licence with respect to the arrangement of words.

This posited freedom need not mean that the choices made by the poet regarding word order were completely random. Artistic factors may have been operative, involving sound, rhythm and balance.[29] But these were for the most part matters of personal style on the part of the individual author rather than being precisely linguistically determined.

It could also be argued from the prevalence of variation in parallel lines that the reader/listener would have been sufficiently familiar with the compositional conventions and forms of Hebrew poetry so as to appreciate the strictly poetic nature of such variation and not to interpret all non-canonical clauses in such contexts as being marked in some way.[30] We disagree, therefore, with Buth's view that the original readers of Hebrew poetic texts would employ the 'normal grammatical devices'[31] to interpret the meaning. Buth seems to reject the idea of what he refers to as 'a special grammar for poetry',[32] yet the existence of certain grammatical peculiarities within the poetic genre is widely acknowledged.[33] It is simply not true to say that the same rules governing Hebrew prose are applicable to poetry regarding the use of the definite article, the object marker (אֶת/־אֶת), and the

---

28 Cf. Gesenius, *Hebrew Grammar*, §142 *f*, where the lack of narrative examples with two preverbal elements is noticeable. Gesenius only lists one in a finite verbal clause, from 2 Kings 5:13. This however may not be a genuine case of OSV. LXX, Syr and Vulg reflect a possible OVS original, or ellipsis of a relative pronoun may have taken place.

29 Cf. Wendland, *Analyzing the Psalms*, p. 156, who mentions rhythm and euphony as possible influencing factors.

30 Note the claim of Fokkelman that, 'Competent readers know how to handle the conventions and techniques employed in the text', J. P. Fokkelman, *Reading Biblical Poetry* (Louisville, Kentucky: Westminster John Knox Press, 2001), p. 50.

31 Buth, 'Topic and Focus in Hebrew Poetry – Psalm 51', p. 85. Cited in fn. 6 earlier in the chapter.

32 *Ibid.*

33 In 1.1 we noted Sappan's comment to the effect that the language of Hebrew poetry be considered 'a special dialect of Biblical Hebrew'.

relative pronoun. If the reader needs to adjust his knowledge of grammar with respect to these features to allow for the specialised genre of poetry, then arguably the same could apply to the matter of word order.

5.3.2 Parallel Lines in Other Languages

Support is given to the above interpretation by cross-linguistic studies. Previous mention has been made of the fact that parallelism is not uncommon in the poetry of world languages.[34] Further to this, linguists have observed with respect to the second line of parallelisms the possibility of deviation from the unmarked order of clause constituents. Fabb refers to this potential for variation as 'reordering'.[35] This especially pertains to those languages having the required freedom of word order.[36] Biblical Hebrew is one such language. Though having a basic unmarked, or canonical, word order, Hebrew is not dependent upon that order for identifying the grammatical roles of the various constituents in the clause. So the reordering of syntactic components making up parallel B-lines is seen to be an allowable feature of the Hebrew poetic genre, as shall next be demonstrated.

5.3.3 The Form of Reordering in Parallel Lines

Cross-linguistically, according to Fabb, the most frequently found form of such reordering is *chiasmus*, 'where the components are the same in both parts of the line but in mirror-image order'.[37]

(a) Two-Part Chiasmus

In Hebrew poetry the feature of chiasmus is extremely common where each of the cola forming the parallelism contains two constituents. For example:

Isaiah 61:4

| They shall build up the ancient ruins, | וּבָנוּ חָרְבוֹת עוֹלָם |
| they shall raise up the places long devastated. | שֹׁמְמוֹת רִאשֹׁנִים יְקוֹמֵמוּ |

The constituent order of the A-line, V O, has been inverted in the B-line to O V, making the chiastic pattern: *ab//ba*.

(b) Three-Part Chiasmus

Where a colon possesses just two constituents, if reordering occurs, it can only take one form, that of chiastic inversion. Where there are three (or

---

34 See 2.2.1.
35 Fabb, *Linguistics and Literature*, p. 146.
36 *Ibid*.
37 *Ibid*.

more) constituents, there exists not just one but several options for reordering. Again the three members may be reordered to create a chiastic pattern, as in:

Psalm 7:17

His mischief will return upon his own head, יָשׁוּב עֲמָלוֹ בְרֹאשׁוֹ
and his violence will descend upon his own crown. וְעַל קָדְקֳדוֹ חֲמָסוֹ יֵרֵד׃

The constituent order of this bicolon is VSM//MSV, forming a three-member chiastic arrangement: *abc//cba*.[38]

Such three-part inversions, the selected data informs us, do not occur in Hebrew poetry as often as is commonly supposed.[39] Much more frequently, as will be shown next, the reordering that occurs in the B-line does not result in a precise chiasmus at all.

(c) PARTIAL CHIASMUS

Another option for the order of constituents in the B-line of a three-member parallelism is to create a chiasmus with respect to two elements only, while the third remains in the same position. Watson describes this as 'partial chiasmus'.[40] This may be illustrated by:

Psalm 65:14ab

The meadows clothe themselves with flocks, לָבְשׁוּ כָרִים הַצֹּאן
the valleys deck themselves with grain. וַעֲמָקִים יַעַטְפוּ־בָר

The constituent order VSO//SVO results in a pattern of the type *abc//bac*. The alternate partially chiastic pattern has the form *abc//acb*, which is also found (e.g., Ps. 58:4), though this would be a CAN//CAN parallelism, since both clauses are verb-initial.

(d) NON-CHIASTIC REORDERING

Despite the presence of chiastically arranged parallelisms, it cannot be said that it was the primary intention of the Hebrew poets to create such chiastic patterns when reordering the constituents in the B-lines. In many instances the elements of the parallel are simply reordered with no chiastic or even partially chiastic effect, as in:

---

38 Occasionally the central (*c*) element of the chiasmus only occurs once, *abcba* (e.g., Ps. 5:2).
39 In the data only 14 instances of the *abc//cba* chiasmus were found in verbal clauses (Pss. 7:6cd, 17; 88:4; 102:4; 142:3; Is. 40:12ab, 27cd; 42:12; 58:8ab; 59:14ab; 62:1cd; 64:5cd; Prov. 3:10; 7:4). Parallelisms composed of participle and noun-clauses may also be organised chiastically.
40 Watson, *Classical Hebrew Poetry*, p. 203.

Proverbs 2:10

For wisdom will come into your heart,   כִּי־תָבוֹא חָכְמָה בְלִבֶּךָ
and knowledge will be pleasant to your soul.   וְדַעַת לְנַפְשְׁךָ יִנְעָם:

Here the constituent order is (C-)VSO//SOV. The order of the B-line could equally have been OVS (e.g., Prov. 5:12b).

5.3.4 The Notion of Symmetry

Treatments of Biblical Hebrew poetry often resort to the notion of symmetry to describe the relationship between parallel lines. Referring back to the various permutations listed in 5.2.1 (5) above, we regard the term 'symmetrical' as most suitably employed for parallelisms of the first kind (no. 1), that is, *abc//abc*, where the B-line consists of a straightforward repetition of the same syntactic components in identical sequence as the A-line.[41] Example 6 in the list of permutations shows the chiastic order in the B-line. For this we will use the term 'asymmetrical'. The intervening examples (nos. 2–5) display no strict symmetry at all, and these may be described as 'non-symmetrical'. In these definitions the concept of *a*symmetry means the form of symmetry that gives the reverse order of the original, that is, inverted symmetry.[42] On the other hand, '*non*-symmetry' indicates the total absence of any manner of symmetry, whether of the same order or chiastic inversion.

It should be stressed at this point that the terms relating to symmetry proposed here reflect solely the ordering of constituents in the line, and offer a description completely independent of the syntactic composition or semantic contents of the verse. Two parallel cola may be both semantically and syntactically equivalent, and yet be symmetrical, asymmetrical, or non-symmetrical. The former are terms relating to the form of parallelism, the latter to relationship of word order.

5.3.5 A Choice of Variables

From the foregoing discussion we see that when it came to the B-line of parallelisms the Hebrew poet had several choices available to him from a

---

41 Note that the terms used here differ from those proposed by Watson in his discussion of parallelism (*Classical Hebrew Poetry*, pp. 114–19). For Watson the term 'symmetry' means the same as chiasmus, or $a_1\ a_2\ a_3\ //\ a_3\ a_2\ a_1$ in his notation.

42 To the present writer this makes more sense than say Watson's use of the term 'symmetry'. The idea of **a**-symmetry implies the absence of something. Yet it does not seem appropriate to use this term to describe two parallel lines having the same order: *abc//abc*. There is nothing absent from the B-line that is not present in A. Yet a parallelism with the inverted order *abc//cba* has departed from the original pattern, and it is therefore felt to be more suitable to use the negatively prefixed term **a**-symmetry with reference to this changed pattern and symmetry for the unchanged pattern.

number of variables. The options were: to repeat the original order (symmetry), to invert it (chiasmus), to mix these two (i.e., partial chiasmus), or simply to rearrange the order without pattern.[43] Moreover, in addition to this already highly flexible dynamic, gapping could occur with any of the elements in the B-line, presenting the poet with another set of choices. We are reminded of the words of Jakobson, 'Any form of parallelism is an apportionment of invariants and variables'.[44] We are thus confirmed in the view that Hebrew poetry permitted complete freedom in the sequential organisation of the parallel line, the ordering of the words being one of the variables of parallelism.[45] This variability of word order in parallel lines is to be classed as one particular manifestation of the previously mentioned 'defamiliarisation' of language[46] characteristic of Biblical Hebrew poetry.

5.4 The Labelling of Colon-Types and the Description of Parallelisms

We have already made use of the label CAN//CAN to denote parallelisms where the canonical word order of the A-line has been preserved in B, that is, it forms an unmarked symmetrical parallelism. The remaining asymmetrical and non-symmetrical patterns, i.e., nos. 2–6 in 5.2.1 (5), each have B-lines exhibiting poetically defamiliarised constituent order and, regardless of the particular sequence in which the parallel line is reordered, will be labelled CAN//DEF. This denotes a canonical A-line followed by a defamiliar, that is, poetically reordered, B-line. So, by way of illustration, the sequence of cola quoted from Psalm 20:4–6 earlier in this chapter (5.1) would be described as CAN//DEF, CAN//DEF, CAN//DEF. Where an extended parallelism occurs the labels are simply multiplied. For example, the parallel tetracolon of Psalm

---

43 Fundamentally the basic choice was to repeat or vary, a fact discernible in other forms of parallelism, such as morphological parallelism: sing–plur // sing–plur, or sing–plur // plur–sing, that is *ab*//*ab* or *ab*//*ba*, (Berlin, *Dynamics of Biblical Parallelism*, pp. 47–48); or gender parallelism: masc–fem // masc–fem, or masc–fem // fem–masc (Watson, *Classical Hebrew Poetry*, pp. 123–25). The only difference is that the number of constituents in a verbal clause allows a greater degree of variety than a simple binary choice of same or different.

44 Jakobson, *Language in Literature*, p. 173.

45 Note that such reordering also occurs in the case of vocatives appearing in a parallel line. A whole range of differing patterns are found: V [Voc] // V [Voc] (Ps. 4:8); V [Voc] // [Voc] V (Ps. 38:22); [Voc] V // [Voc] V (Is. 42:18); [Voc] V // V [Voc] (Ps. 84:9); V [Voc] O // [Voc] V O (Prov. 8:5); V [Voc] O // V O [Voc] (Ps. 147:12), etc. Since the vocative is an extra-clausal constituent (cf. Dik, *Theory of Functional Grammar*, Pt. 1, p. 264), its placement in such various positions cannot have anything to do with the question of the topical or focal features of the clause. This high degree of variation of position shows all the indications of being simply another manifestation of the freedom available to the Hebrew poet in parallel lines.

46 See 1.1.

18:5-6 has the constituent order V S // S V // S V // V S, and will therefore be labelled in the following manner: CAN//DEF//DEF//CAN. Only the B and C-lines of the four-line parallelism have undergone the reordering of their syntactic components, while the D-line returns to the canonical order of A.

With reference to word order, therefore, on the basis of the findings of chapter 4 and of the present chapter, we identify three colon-types among verbal clauses in Biblical Hebrew poetry: CAN, DEF, and MKD. The latter two may both be included under the broader descriptive term 'non-canonical', or non-CAN, but the labels DEF and MKD specify the motivating factors underlying their departure from the canonical order. This may be depicted thus:

CAN =		Colon with a canonically ordered verbal clause
non-CAN =	MKD	Colon with pragmatically marked verbal clause
non-CAN =	DEF	Colon with poetically defamiliar verbal clause

Other colon-types that do not fall directly within the scope of this study include: Nom (a noun-clause), Ptcp (participial clause), and Inf (infinitival clause). These are the labels employed in the data listed in Appendix 2. Lower case letters are used to distinguish them from the main types which form the principal object of our analysis.

Parallelisms in Hebrew poetry may be formed through a variety of possible combinations of the different colon-types. The three most frequently employed arrangements by far are the symmetrical CAN//CAN, the asymmetrical or non-symmetrical CAN//DEF, and the usually symmetrical MKD//MKD. The latter arrangement will be treated in detail in a later chapter, when the issue of pragmatic marking in parallel lines is considered.[47] Other common parallel forms are Nom//Nom and Ptcp//Ptcp. Inf//Inf may also be found, but less often. It is sometimes the case that a parallelism may occur in which the correspondence between the two lines exists chiefly at the level of meaning rather than form or syntax. Parallel configurations such as Nom//CAN, CAN//Nom, CAN//Ptcp, Ptcp//CAN, CAN//Inf, and Inf//CAN are also found. Another arrangement is for a Ptcp A-line to be paralleled by a reordered B-line containing a finite verbal clause, that is, Ptcp//DEF,[48] much less frequent is Inf//DEF. Forms containing one marked verbal clause in combination with a verbless clause, that is, MKD//Nom or Nom//MKD, and MKD//Ptcp or Ptcp//MKD are also occasionally found, and several examples of these will be discussed in due course.

---

47 Chapter 7.
48 Examples of this will be encountered in the analysis of extended texts in chapter 9.

Besides the aforementioned arrangements some parallelisms occur involving an unusual combination of colon-types, such as DEF//CAN or DEF//DEF, where either it is the A-line or both lines which display a defamiliar ordering of constituents. These rarer formations have specific discourse-level functions, the topic of a later chapter.[49]

5.5 Pattern Formation Involving Defamiliar Cola

There is one notable feature relating to defamiliar B-lines worthy of remark in the context of the question discussed earlier, concerning whether the non-canonical order exhibited by such lines is to be seen as pragmatic marking or otherwise.

In support of the essential freeness exhibited by DEF cola in parallel lines is the fact that such DEF clauses may alternate with CAN cola in the formation of rhetorical patterns typical of Biblical Hebrew poetry. Four examples serve to illustrate (DEF cola are indented):

(1) *Psalm 26:4–5*

I do not sit with deceitful men,	לֹא־יָשַׁבְתִּי עִם־מְתֵי־שָׁוְא	A
nor will I go with pretenders.	וְעִם נַעֲלָמִים לֹא אָבוֹא׃	B
I hate the assembly of evildoers,	שָׂנֵאתִי קְהַל מְרֵעִים	A
and I will not sit with the wicked.	וְעִם־רְשָׁעִים לֹא אֵשֵׁב׃	B

The verses clearly contain an extended parallelism,[50] that is, four lines showing a close semantic and syntactic relationship, though the order of syntactic components has been inverted in the second and fourth cola. The basic structure is V M // M V // V O // M V, that is, cola of the types CAN//DEF//CAN//DEF. We observe that the extended parallelism alternates CAN and DEF cola to create an ABAB pattern.[51]

(2) *Psalm 21:10*

You will make them like a fiery furnace at the time of your appearing.	תְּשִׁיתֵמוֹ כְּתַנּוּר אֵשׁ לְעֵת פָּנֶיךָ	A
YHWH will consume them in his wrath,	יְהוָה בְּאַפּוֹ יְבַלְּעֵם	B
and fire will devour them.	וְתֹאכְלֵם אֵשׁ׃	A

---

49 Chapter 8.
50 See 2.2.2 (c).
51 Since this is an extended parallelism this structure is not the same as those sequences of CAN//DEF cola cited at the beginning of the chapter (4.1). Those passages contained instances of individual parallelisms in sequence, that is, CAN//DEF, CAN//DEF, etc. Here in Psalm 26 all four cola occur within one larger parallel structure, CAN//DEF//DEF//CAN, in which the DEF colon-types have been strategically placed.

The order of syntactic components is V-o M M // S M V-o // V-o S. Again there are clear affinities of thought between the three lines. The first and last cola are expressed in canonical word order, each making reference to אֵשׁ ('fire'). The second colon, though relating closely to the meaning of the surrounding lines, is quite different in form, containing a non-canonical clause with two preverbal elements. The overall colon arrangement is CAN//DEF//CAN, forming an ABA pattern.

(3) *Psalm 18:5–6*

The cords of death encompassed me,	אֲפָפוּנִי חֶבְלֵי־מָוֶת	A
the torrents of perdition overwhelmed me,	וְנַחֲלֵי בְלִיַּעַל יְבַעֲתוּנִי׃	B
the cords of Sheol entangled me,	חֶבְלֵי שְׁאוֹל סְבָבוּנִי	B
the snares of death confronted me.	קִדְּמוּנִי מוֹקְשֵׁי מָוֶת׃	A

These two verses form a four-part synonymous and syntactic parallelism, having the order V-o S // S V-o // S V-o // V-o S. Here the first and last lines are symmetrical with one another, each displaying canonical constituent order, while the middle two lines show asymmetrical rearranging. The formation may therefore be labelled: CAN//DEF//DEF//CAN, producing an ABBA pattern.

(4) *Isaiah 43:23–24*

You did not bring me sheep for your burnt offerings,	לֹא־הֵבֵיאתָ לִּי שֵׂה עֹלֹתֶיךָ	A
	וּזְבָחֶיךָ לֹא כִבַּדְתָּנִי	B
nor did you honour me with your sacrifices.	לֹא הֶעֱבַדְתִּיךָ בְּמִנְחָה	A
	וְלֹא הוֹגַעְתִּיךָ בִּלְבוֹנָה׃	A
I did not cause you to worship with grain offerings,	לֹא־קָנִיתָ לִּי בַכֶּסֶף קָנֶה	A
nor weary you with incense.	וְחֵלֶב זְבָחֶיךָ לֹא הִרְוִיתָנִי	B
You bought me no sweet cane with silver,		
nor did you satisfy me with the fat of your sacrifices.		

In this series of cola there exists a more complex structure of a six-part extended parallelism. Each line consists of a negated verbal clause making reference to some aspect of the cultic offerings.[52] Two of the six clauses show inversion. At first sight these two non-canonical clauses may appear to be randomly placed within the overall structure, but further examination shows that the whole has been artfully constructed and the placing of the DEF clauses not merely arbitrary. First we observe the perfectly even distribution of the *wāw*. It is interposed between the first and second cola, the third and fourth, and the fifth and sixth, grouping the six cola into three

---

52 Cf. Oswalt, *The Book of Isaiah 40–66*, p. 159.

pairs. It is the first and third pair which have the CAN//DEF arrangement, while the central pair is CAN//CAN. We also observe that this central bicolon has 1st person verbs, in contrast to the four 2nd person verb forms of the two outer bicola. Thus the whole six-part structure, CAN//DEF//CAN//CAN//CAN//DEF, can be seen to create an AB|AA|AB pattern. At a larger level this may be analysed as an ABA pattern produced by alternate asymmetrical and symmetrical parallelisms. From the perspective of pragmatic marking the variation in the B-lines of the first and third bicola yet not in the second would be difficult to explain. If markedness was required in these two, why not in the remaining one? Clearly the poet is simply using the freedom of word order available to him to create rhetorical patterning, such as is done with many other features of the language.[53]

In the above examples the Hebrew poet has artistically used the reordered line to produce patterns in extended parallelisms. While this is frequently done, the aim is not always to produce a balanced pattern. Sequences such as CAN//DEF//DEF//DEF are also found (e.g., Ps. 89:31–32; Job 4:3–4), with each of the secondary lines having the defamiliar word order. Here too there is further evidence against a possible pragmatic interpretation. The fact that the third line of the parallelism is DEF and not CAN as in example (1) above, forming an ABAB pattern, or that the final line is DEF and not CAN as in (3), forming an ABBA pattern, again points to the essential freeness of the variation. Evidently any of these alternatives was possible, and the determining factor is thus more plausibly poetic than pragmatic.

5.6 The Environment and Distribution of Defamiliar Cola

It is helpful at this point to introduce the concepts of *environment* and *distribution* as additional factors that will enable us to define the criteria for establishing what is defamiliar word order and what is not.

By 'environment' we mean the position of one colon relative to its corresponding colon within a parallelism. Here we are thinking of whether the colon in question is the primary line of the parallelism, i.e., the A-line, or the secondary line, the B-line.[54] All the defamiliar clauses we have considered so far have been within the environment of the B-line paralleling a canonical A-line, this being the typical place where such defamiliarisation occurs (i.e., CAN//DEF). The B-line of such parallelisms may therefore be designated the *common* environment within which defam-

---

53 As, for instance, the patterns produced by number parallelism: sing–plur // sing–plur, or sing–plur // plur–sing, that is *ab–ab* or *ab–ba*, (Berlin, *Dynamics of Biblical Parallelism*, pp. 47–48); or gender parallelism: masc–fem // masc–fem, or masc–fem // fem–masc (Watson, *Classical Hebrew Poetry*, pp. 123–25), etc.
54 Here what holds true for the B-line is also applicable to any further parallel lines (C, D, etc.) if the parallelism is extended.

iliarisation of word order may occur. However, as shall presently be seen,[55] on a limited number of occasions it is the A-line of the parallelism which contains the defamiliar word order, while the B-line remains canonical. Such a case, which would be labelled DEF//CAN, is not the norm, and the so the A-line of this type of parallel construction would be called the *limited* environment within which defamiliarisation can occur.

The term 'distribution' refers to the positions in which a parallelism may occur within the larger text. Most parallel formations can be placed at any point within the whole poem, whether text-initial, medial or final. We describe this as *universal* distribution, meaning that such parallelisms are not limited in the extent of their use. Other combinations of parallel lines, for instance, the DEF//CAN mentioned in the previous paragraph, are only found in certain significant points in the poetic discourse, that is, they appear in *specific* distribution. Those parallelisms of universal distribution may appear at those junctures of the text where those of specific distribution may also be found, but the converse is obviously not the case.

The relevance of the above distinctions will become apparent as we proceed. A consideration of both the environment within which a colon appears and the distribution of a particular form of parallelism within the larger poetic discourse will enable us to establish objective grounds on which to base decisions relating to the significance of non-canonical constituent order.

5.7 The Priority of the A-Line

Comment is necessary concerning the priority of the A-line in the typical Hebrew poetic parallelism. It was stated in the previous section that the most common environment in which the defamiliarisation of constituent order takes place is the B-line of the parallelism. Defamiliarisation outside of this environment is comparatively rare. Although individual DEF//CAN bicola are sometimes found, it is of note that extended sequences of DEF//CAN parallelisms, such as noted for CAN//DEF in 5.1, are strikingly absent from the poetic corpus. For example, series of cola having the order S V // V S, S V // V S or O V // V O, O V // V O are unattested in the entire Hebrew Bible. This is a highly significant observation. It suggests that when DEF//CAN parallelisms do occur, they stand alone, a fact which points to their special function, which we shall explore further in due course.

Generally speaking, the facts regarding the environment in which the DEF colon-type may occur demonstrate that the word order of the A-line of the parallelism cannot be defamiliarised under normal circumstances. The reason for this is probably to be attributed to the fact that it is the A-line that carries the essential linguistic information for the whole of the parallelism.

---

55 In chapter 8.

By this we mean that the A-line is primary, not just sequentially, in that it precedes the B-line, but also with respect to the grammar, syntax, semantics, deixis, and reference of the whole parallel unit. For these elements the B-line invariably shows dependence upon its A-line, which as stated earlier, functions as its Head.[56] We see that the B-line may vary the order, as well as other components, of the A-line, since everything needed for correctly processing the grammatical, syntactic, semantic and pragmatic import has already been laid out in A.

This dependence of the B-line is illustrated with reference to several aspects: topical reference, gapping, gender parallelism, and tense-shifting.

5.7.1 Dependence in Topical Reference

Dependence of the parallel line upon its Head is quite obvious with respect to topic, as shown by the following text.

Isaiah 49:13cd

| For YHWH has comforted his people, | כִּי־נִחַם יְהוָה עַמּוֹ |
| and he has had compassion on his afflicted ones. | וַעֲנִיָּו יְרַחֵם: |

In the B-lines it is often the case that a synonymous or coreferential NP[Su] will appear in each colon (as in Ps. 149:2 quoted earlier, where both יִשְׂרָאֵל and בְּנֵי־צִיּוֹן are found). Yet it frequently also happens that the topic of the B-line is simply encoded by means of verbal affixation, as is the case with יְרַחֵם in the above example. The predicate contained in B-line, although semantically overlapping that of the A-line, has no identifiable topic. It is the A-line that provides the information that is lacking, here יְהוָה.

5.7.2 Dependence in Gapping

The common occurrence of gapping in parallelism has already been noted.[57] Here also the need for line A to enable understanding of B is apparent.

Proverbs 5:15

| Drink water from your own cistern, | שְׁתֵה־מַיִם מִבּוֹרֶךָ |
| flowing water from your own well. | וְנֹזְלִים מִתּוֹךְ בְּאֵרֶךָ: |

In this synonymous parallelism, consisting of VOM//w-OM, both lines express in figurative terms the satisfaction that a man is to derive from his own wife.[58] The verb has been elided from the second colon and so, taken in isolation, the meaning of this line would be uncertain. Yet the reader/listener of the proverb is able to supply the missing component from the parallel

---

56 See 2.3.
57 See 2.2.2 (a).
58 Cf. Murphy, *Proverbs*, p. 32.

relationship that holds between this line and its preceding A-line. This clearly shows a dependence of the B-line upon the A-line for full comprehension.

5.7.3 Dependence in Gender Parallelism

The same dependence upon the A-line can be seen to exist with regard to poetic variables. By this we mean those diverse forms of parallelism, involving variation in such grammatical features as gender, number, morphology, and so forth. Where such parallelism occurs, it may be observed that the form appearing in the A-line is that which is most suitable to the context, while the B-line simply contains the variant form. This can be illustrated by reference to gender parallelism:[59]

Isaiah 11:12

and he will assemble the outcasts of Israel, וְאָסַף נִדְחֵי יִשְׂרָאֵל
and gather the dispersed of Judah. וּנְפֻצוֹת יְהוּדָה יְקַבֵּץ

Here the first colon has the masculine plural construct form נִדְחֵי, and the second colon feminine plural construct נְפֻצוֹת. Although certain of the earlier commentators argued that the actual gender of the nouns should be taken literally as indicating groups of males and females respectively,[60] it is generally considered by modern scholars and translators that the variation is simply a poetic device.[61] The B-line has the alternate form to what appears in A. In this case we note that the A-line contains the expected masculine form, which is invariably used in Biblical Hebrew for referring to a group of mixed gender.[62] Therefore the grammatical gender of the A-line determines the same for the B also. Although formally the noun is feminine, it is evidently to be taken as denoting mixed gender.

5.7.4 Dependence in Tense-Shifting

For one further example we mention that kind of grammatical parallelism

---

59 On gender parallelism, see Berlin, *Dynamics of Biblical Parallelism*, pp. 41–44.
60 Cf. Alexander, *The Prophecies of Isaiah*, p. 258, citing Gesenius and Ewald. Note that such an interpretation, if pressed, makes little sense. The first NP is in a construct relationship with 'Israel', and the second NP in a similar relationship with 'Judah'. If the gender were taken literally, then it would be only the men of Israel and the women of Judah who would be gathered, which the prophet obviously did not intend to say.
61 Motyer, *The Prophecy of Isaiah*, p. 126, describes the terms as 'synonymous'. None of the modern versions (NRSV ESV NIV NASB NKJV NJPS REB TEV NJB NLT NCV CEV) differentiates between the gender of the two nouns.
62 Cf. Van der Merwe (et al.), *Biblical Hebrew Reference Grammar*, p. 181. We note that the masculine form only of the same noun וְהַנִּדָּחִים is employed in Isaiah 16:4; 27:12; and 56:8 (cf. Ps. 147:2).

usually referred to as 'tense-shifting'.[63] The following verse offers a typical example of this phenomenon:

Proverbs 3:13

| Happy is the man who finds wisdom, | אַשְׁרֵי אָדָם מָצָא חָכְמָה |
| and the man who gains understanding. | וְאָדָם יָפִיק תְּבוּנָה: |

The verb in the A-line is *qatal* in form, while the B-line has a *yiqtol* form. When one considers the overall meaning of the parallelism it is hard to accept that the author really intended to assign both verbs their own inherent tense and aspect independent of each other. The English versions and the translation offered by Murphy[64] in his commentary do not distinguish between the two. Most versions render both verbs as a general present tense, which is the usual way of translating the Hebrew 'gnomic' perfect, here מָצָא, into English.[65] We consider therefore that both verbs are to be understood as having identical aspectual and temporal reference, even though they differ in form. In this matter we endorse Buth's treatment of tense-shifting in which he describes the phenomenon taking place here as the 'alternation of verb forms for purely poetic reasons ...'.[66] He is surely right to identify this as 'a poetic device' and not a semantic distinction.[67]

Concerning these instances of tense-shifting Buth makes the important observation that 'the first verb of such units is more appropriate'.[68] The verb form of the B-line is simply a variation on that appearing in the A. The first verb has established the temporal and aspectual components of meaning, and so the B-line is free to exploit poetic variation. This phenomenon is therefore simply another manifestation of defamiliar language characteristic of the poetic genre.

5.7.5 Pragmatic Dependence

The situation in the foregoing instances is, we submit, closely analogous to variation in word order where a similar dependence holds. If the change in the form of the verb or the gender of the noun in the B-line is non-semantic, as the examples have demonstrated, then by analogy the change in order of the words may be taken as non-pragmatic. In such instances the usual prose

---

63 Berlin deals with this under the heading 'Contrast in Tense', *Dynamics of Biblical Parallelism*, pp. 35–40.
64 Murphy, *Proverbs*, p. 18.
65 On the gnomic perfect, see Van der Merwe (et al.), *Biblical Hebrew Reference Grammar*, p. 359.
66 R. Buth, 'The Taxonomy and Function of Hebrew Tense-Shifting in the Psalms', *START 15* (1986), p. 26.
67 *Ibid.*, p. 28.
68 *Ibid.*

form has been 'violated', to quote Buth,[69] in favour of poetic considerations. The B-line in such cases contains the poetic variant or alternation, which, when analysed in the context of the parallelism, no longer possesses its strictly semantic, grammatical or, we contend, pragmatic value. It is the A-line, containing the canonical or expected form, which determines these for its parallel line and enables the processing of the whole. We conclude therefore regarding word order that the first line adheres to the norm, and then the following line, if the poet so wishes, departs from that norm as an expression of the defamiliarisation characteristic of the genre.

The foregoing discussion offers a reasonable explanation as to why defamiliarisation generally does not take place within the A-line of poetic parallelisms. Since this is the line that maintains a control over the meaning and grammar of the entire parallelism, we see that there is no room for free variation to occur.[70]

5.8 Summary

In this chapter we have noted the frequency with which the reordering of clause constituents is found in the B-lines of parallelisms based upon a canonical A-line. Though there are advocates of a purely pragmatic interpretation of this reordering, it was concluded that the degree of variety and its apparent freeness and optionality do not easily allow an interpretation in terms of pragmatic markedness. It is much more in accord with the character of such reordering to take it is as one area in which poetic defamiliarisation is found in the poetry of the Hebrew Bible.

Labels were proposed for the different colon-types, those with which we are chiefly concerned being CAN, DEF, and MKD. It was also observed how the Hebrew poets produced rhetorically structured patterns using alternating CAN and DEF cola, another fact pointing to the nature of DEF cola as essentially that of a poetic variant. The various combinations and frequency of the different colon-types in parallel lines were discussed.

The notions of environment and distribution were presented as an aid in determining where DEF clauses may occur. The B-line of the parallelism was identified as the common environment for defamiliar constituent order in universal distribution. Conversely, the A-line of the parallel was identified as the limited environment in which defamiliar ordering may

---

69 R. Buth, 'Hebrew Tenses and the Magnificat', *JSNT 21* (1984), p. 70
70 To put the DEF line first in a parallelism, and the CAN line second, would result in a significant increase in cognitive effort to correctly understanding the meaning of the whole unit. As chapter 8 will demonstrate, such a thing does occur and for deliberate reasons. Such parallelisms have a function in the poetic text which is entirely appropriate to the effect that such a reversed colon arrangement would have upon the reader/listener.

occur in specific distribution. This latter is something that remains to be treated in a subsequent chapter.

Finally, the fundamental priority of the A-line was considered. In the matter of variation within parallel lines it is the initial line which generally contains the linguistically expected form (e.g., of verb or gender), while the ensuing line(s) may show the variant or alternate form. The fact that poetic variation in other aspects of the language occurs in the B-line is an argument in favour of a purely poetic reordering of clause components in the same environment.

CHAPTER 6

Distinguishing Marked and Defamiliar Word Order

The main purpose of this brief chapter is to highlight the importance of paying attention to environment, and to analyse several examples in which failure to do so might result in mistaking a MKD colon for one that is DEF, and vice versa. Other means by which MKD and DEF clauses were originally differentiated in Biblical Hebrew poetry are also discussed. Lastly, in the light of the marked/defamiliar distinction, the traditional category of antithetical parallelism is reassessed.

6.1 The Priority of Environment over Form

In the previous chapter it was shown how defamiliar word order is permissible in Hebrew poetry within the confines of certain definable environments. In reading poetic texts, therefore, non-canonical clauses, being either MKD or DEF, must be carefully distinguished from each other on the basis of the context in which they occur, not by the particular form which they take. Both may exhibit identical surface form. For instance, Proverbs 1:5b, וְנָבוֹן תַּחְבֻּלוֹת יִקְנֶה ('the discerning acquire wise counsel') and Proverbs 6:26b, וְאֵשֶׁת אִישׁ נֶפֶשׁ יְקָרָה תָצוּד ('the wife of another man hunts for a precious life'), each having SOV word order, are formally indistinguishable. Moreover, both appear in the B-line of a bicolon. Yet in the first text that bicolon creates a synonymous parallelism, and the sequence of 1:5b is, therefore, the product of that poetic reordering admissible in such environments. 6:26b, on the other hand, is a semantically independent clause, not a parallel line, and there are clear contextual implications of a contrast.[1] Its constituent order is therefore the product of pragmatic considerations.

Conversely, we should add, difference of form does not necessarily entail a pragmatic distinction. Whether or not related pairs like לְזַמֵּר לְשִׁמְךָ

---

1 NRSV ESV REB NJB TEV CEV and Murphy (*Proverbs*, p. 35) join 26b to 26a with 'but'. On the latter part of this verse Estes comments, 'though resorting to a prostitute may reduce a man to minimal means, sexual entanglement with another man's wife brings total financial and personal ruin', D. J. Estes, *Hear, My Son: Teaching and Learning in Proverbs 1–9*, New Studies in Biblical Theology 4 (London: Apollos, 1997), p. 56.

(Ps. 92:2b, 'to sing to your name') and the non-canonical לְשִׁמְךָ אֲזַמֵּרָה (Ps. 18:50b, 'to your name I will sing') have different pragmatic import depends again on the environment in which they occur. Both are in fact located within the B-lines of synonymous parallelisms. In such cases, we contend, the difference between them is of no pragmatic significance, the variation in form being a defamiliar aspect of the poetic genre.

6.2 Resolving Complex Cases

Generally speaking, it is easy to establish, on semantic grounds, whether or not a B-line forms part of a parallelism. On occasion, however, especially in those structures larger than a bicolon, it can be less obvious. In such instances the manner of laying out the text as proposed in chapter 2 can be helpful,[2] as in the following examples.

Psalm 146:9

YHWH watches over the stranger;	יְהוָה שֹׁמֵר אֶת־גֵּרִים	A
he supports the orphan and the widow,	יָתוֹם וְאַלְמָנָה יְעוֹדֵד	B
but the way of the wicked he brings to ruin.	וְדֶרֶךְ רְשָׁעִים יְעַוֵּת:	C

This three-line structure consists first of a participle-clause A, with the order S V^{Pt} O. Then B is a verbal clause in which the verb appears in the clause-final position. It is clear that this line forms a parallelism with A, both concerning God's care for vulnerable members of society. The Ow-OV order of the parallel B-line we therefore identify as defamiliar. As noted previously,[3] it is not uncommon for participial A-lines to be paralleled by defamiliar verbal clauses in the B-line. In line C, however, the context demands a relationship of contrast between how God deals with the 'wicked' mentioned there and the way he upholds the 'stranger', 'orphan' and 'widow' of the first two cola. Here then, the OV constituent order of C is due to pragmatic marking, as is typical in such contrastive structures. It is also to be observed that this is a case of embedded parallelism.[4] The first two lines form a parallel bicolon, while the third line relates to the whole. These interrelations may be depicted as:

```
┌─ HEAD¹ ──────── HEAD ──── יְהוָה שֹׁמֵר אֶת־גֵּרִים   (Ptcp)
│                └── Parallel ── יָתוֹם וְאַלְמָנָה יְעוֹדֵד   (DEF)
└─ HEAD² ─────────────────── וְדֶרֶךְ רְשָׁעִים יְעַוֵּת   (MKD)
```

This verse is labelled: Ptcp//DEF/MKD.

---

2 2.3.
3 5.4.
4 2.2.2 (b).

Psalm 138:6

For YHWH is exalted,	כִּי־רָם יְהוָה	A
yet he regards the lowly,	וְשָׁפָל יִרְאֶה	B
but the haughty he knows from afar.	וְגָבֹהַּ מִמֶּרְחָק יְיֵדָע:	C

We observe here an interesting double case of markedness. The verse begins with the proposition A, 'YHWH is exalted', having the form C-V^Pt S. This is immediately followed by a contrast B, literally 'but the lowly he regards', having the constituent order w-OV. The adjective שָׁפָל signifies one who is 'low', and it therefore forms a striking contrast with the fact that God is רָם, 'high'. Nevertheless, despite God's exaltedness, the psalmist tells us, he is not so remote that he does not favourably look upon the humble.[5] Having declared this fact, the verse continues with yet a further contrast C: 'but the haughty he knows from afar'. In Hebrew the term גָּבֹהַּ, 'haughty', has connotations of highness.[6] This adjective therefore stands in an obvious polar contrast to the preceding שָׁפָל. Line C consists of a clause having two preverbal elements, OMV. Frequently such a deviant constituent order in a secondary line indicates defamiliarisation, but this is not so here. The colon in question is not a parallel line, and the definite pragmatic marking of the initial NP[DO] element would lead us to suspect similar markedness with respect to the following PP, מִמֶּרְחָק ('from afar'). The context provides a suitable explanation for the preverbal position of this element. The accompanying verb יְיֵדָע evidently contains presuppositional information, being semantically related to the verb יִרְאֶה in B. God, in his omniscience, has knowledge of all men. Through the marked order the psalmist is indicating that the verb 'he knows' is not the assertion of the utterance, but rather מִמֶּרְחָק forms the focus. God does know these people, just as he knows all human beings, but these haughty ones he knows *from afar*. He views them distantly, not having a close relationship with them. This last clause, therefore, we take as displaying both marked (contrastive) topic (גָּבֹהַּ) and marked focus (מִמֶּרְחָק). We conclude, therefore, that in this verse every instance of departure from canonical word order has definable pragmatic implications. The text may be displayed as:

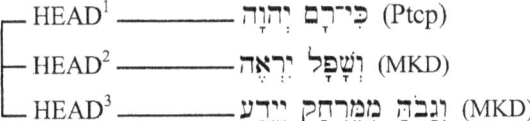

Psalm 138:6 can be designated: Ptcp/MKD/MKD.

---

5 Cf. Harman, *Psalms*, p. 430, 'The God of glory stoops to look with favour on the lowly'.
6 *TWOT*, vol. 1, p. 306.

Psalm 16:9

Therefore my heart is glad,	לָכֵן שָׂמַח לִבִּי	A
and my soul rejoices;	וַיָּגֶל כְּבוֹדִי	B
my body also dwells secure.	אַף־בְּשָׂרִי יִשְׁכֹּן לָבֶטַח:	C

The verse begins with a synonymous parallelism (A//B) consisting of canonical V S // w-V S order. The two verbs are virtual synonyms and the NP[Su] in both clauses refers to the inner being of the speaker.[7] The final clause (C) continues in a similar vein, though is sufficiently removed from the previous two lines semantically, lexically and syntactically so as not to be considered a third line in the parallelism. The NP[Su] now relates to the outer body rather than inner. The verbal idea is no longer that of rejoicing but of dwelling securely, and the third verb is *yiqtol* in form as distinct from the parallel *qatal* and *wayyiqtol* of the first two lines. Moreover, the focus particle אַף appears, accompanied by a fronted subject constituent, a structure denoting pragmatic markedness.[8] This final line, therefore, has all the indications of being an adjoining colon standing outside of the parallelism, containing an expanding focus structure, adding information (rather than parallel) to the foregoing. What the psalmist is expressing through this marked clause is in effect: 'My heart and soul rejoices, and not only this, my body will dwell securely'. The third colon is adding to his joy his confidence in the fact that his future would not merely be physical decay, as the next verse makes clear, 'because you will not give me up to Sheol, nor will you let your faithful one see the pit' (v. 10). Having set God before him (v. 8), the psalmist already experiences present joy, and now through verse 9c he adds the conviction he has of also being granted future security. The focused information is, therefore, the assured continuation of physical life. The verse may be portrayed diagrammatically as follows:

```
┌─HEAD¹ ──┬── HEAD ──── לָכֵן שָׂמַח לִבִּי (CAN)
│         └── Parallel ── וַיָּגֶל כְּבוֹדִי (CAN)
└─HEAD² ─────────────── אַף־בְּשָׂרִי יִשְׁכֹּן לָבֶטַח (MKD)
```

This tricolon is of the structure: CAN//CAN/MKD.

6.3 Pitch Prominence in Distinguishing Marked from Defamiliar

Now that we have argued for the division of non-canonical poetic clauses into defamiliar and marked, some comment ought to be made regarding the

---

7 כְּבוֹדִי, literally 'my glory', is rendered as 'soul' by NRSV and NJB and 'spirit' by REB. The word may originally have been 'liver' (cf. כָּבֵד, *DCH*, vol. 4, p. 353) approximating to the sense of 'heart'; cf. Kidner, *Psalms 1–72*, p. 85, fn. 2; p. 129, fn. 1.
8 3.4.2 (e) and 4.2.1 (b).

question of pitch. Lambrecht informs us that focus structure is indicated by diverse mechanisms in different languages.[9] He also demonstrates that in a single language the marking of the focus structure may be present in more than one dimension. It could be signalled at the level of one or more of the following: syntax, word order, lexis, morphology, or phonology (whether tone or prosody). English, for example, chiefly indicates the focus structure by prosodic means, i.e., the pitch of the voice,[10] yet special syntactic constructions, such as cleft-sentences,[11] also exist. It is possible that with respect to pragmatic marking in Biblical Hebrew the word-order shift was accompanied by a prominence in pitch. Although this is strictly unverifiable since we are not dealing with a living form of the language, it is at least a plausible deduction in the light of cross-linguistic evidence. Discussing this very question with respect to Biblical Hebrew, Buth argues that 'we can assume from language universals that certain pitch contours fit certain clause types and communication situations ... Similarly ... we can assume that special contours for focal information existed'.[12] Throughout his work on focus Shimasaki repeatedly contends for the existence of phonological factors in the marking of information structure. Informational prominence in Hebrew, he argues, would be matched by pitch prominence.[13]

In his treatment Shimasaki resorts to matters of phonology in order to differentiate between two of the focus structures which may display the same surface structure, that is, sentence focus and argument focus. Each of these may be realised syntactically by a clause consisting of S V. Yet in each case the information structure is clearly distinct. In the former the whole proposition is in focus, while in the latter it is only the preverbal element. Shimasaki proposes that Biblical Hebrew would mark this difference through the use of prominent pitch. In a sentence-focus clause both S and V would bear high pitch, and in an argument-focus clause only S, leaving the V with low pitch in that it makes reference only to presuppositional information.[14]

Here we take up Shimasaki's proposition regarding the use of pitch prominence, but give it a different application. If distinguishing between

---

9   Lambrecht, *Information Structure*, pp. 221; 223; cf. G. Brown and G. Yule, *Discourse Analysis* (Cambridge: Cambridge University Press, 1983), pp. 164–69.
10 E.g., 'JOHN did it'.
11 E.g., 'It was JOHN who did it'.
12 R. Buth, 'Word Order in the Verbless Clause', in C. Miller (ed.), *The Verbless Clause in Biblical Hebrew: Linguistic Approaches* (Winona Lake, Indiana: Eisenbrauns, 1999), p. 83, fn. 10. There Buth also makes the significant observation that for non-tonal languages, among which Biblical Hebrew would be classed, 'the existence of Focal contours ... is the default situation, whose nonexistence would be quite surprising and need justification'.
13 E.g., Shimasaki, *Focus Structure*, p. 68, where he speaks of focused constituents as 'fronted and high-pitched'.
14 *Ibid.*, pp. 144–45.

certain focus structures with similar forms was a question of phonology, then the same could hold true for distinguishing between focused (marked) and non-focused (defamiliar) structures. To illustrate this we note the similarity and dissimilarity between the following verses:

Job 35:11

... who teaches[15] us by the animals of the earth, מַלְפֵנוּ מִבַּהֲמוֹת אָרֶץ
and makes us wise by the birds of the sky? וּמֵעוֹף הַשָּׁמַיִם יְחַכְּמֵנוּ׃

Psalm 115:16

The heavens belong to YHWH, הַשָּׁמַיִם שָׁמַיִם לַיהוָה
but the earth he has given to the sons of men. וְהָאָרֶץ נָתַן לִבְנֵי־אָדָם׃

These texts are similar in that both contain the lexical pair שָׁמַיִם and אָרֶץ ('heavens' and 'earth'),[16] and in each case the second line has a fronted constituent. They differ significantly, however, in the fact that the two lines of the first bicolon form a synonymous parallelism, while the second contains two lines relating as a contrast. The V^{Pt}-o M // M V-o arrangement of the former is a poetic inversion (*ab*//*ba*), that is, the B-line is DEF. In the latter text, however, the OV order of the B-line is owing to focus on the direct object, that is, it is a MKD colon. Clearly in Job 35:11 the point the author wishes to make through the two PPs (מִבַּהֲמוֹת אָרֶץ and וּמֵעוֹף הַשָּׁמַיִם) is one and the same, that God instructs man by means of the animal creation. This is true of the animals of the 'earth' as much as of the birds of the 'sky'. In Psalm 115:16 a very different relationship exists between שָׁמַיִם and אָרֶץ. Heaven is God's sole domain, the psalmist tells us, while he has freely disposed of the earth as he has seen fit, as Delitzsch comments, 'He [God] has reserved the heavens to Himself, but given the earth to men'.[17] The context of contrast triggers the marked word order.[18] In the light of Shimasaki's comments regarding the possible function of pitch prominence in Biblical Hebrew it is not unreasonable to suppose that in the above two cases the B-lines would each carry a different stress pattern. In the first text the clause-initial element וּמֵעוֹף הַשָּׁמַיִם, being merely a parallel phrase to מִבַּהֲמוֹת אָרֶץ, would not involve any special prosodic prominence, whereas the clause-initial וְהָאָרֶץ in the second text, standing as it does in contrast to

---

15 The form מַלְפֵנוּ is probably to be taken as a verb derived from the root אלף, cf. Hartley, *The Book of Job*, p. 464, fn. 7. The preposition 'by' in the above translation follows Dhorme, *Commentary on the Book of Job*, p. 534, who makes the valid comment that were the text simply saying that man was wiser than the animals, 'Such an observation is surely too commonplace. It is precisely his understanding which makes man superior to the animals'.

16 Cf. Watson, *Classical Hebrew Poetry*, p. 132.

17 Keil and Delitzsch, *Commentary on the Old Testament*, vol. 5, 'Psalms', p. 213.

18 For contrastive marked structures, see 4.2.2 (c).

הַשָּׁמַיִם in the A-line, would bear the pitch appropriate to a constituent having contrastive connotation, most probably high.[19]

Consider how a variation in pitch would facilitate the differentiation of marked and defamiliar sequences in the following three-line structure:

Isaiah 29:13

because these people draw near with their mouth,	יַעַן כִּי נִגַּשׁ הָעָם הַזֶּה בְּפִיו
and honour me with their lips,	וּבִשְׂפָתָיו כִּבְּדוּנִי
but their heart is far from me.	וְלִבּוֹ רִחַק מִמֶּנִּי

A synonymous parallelism occurs in the first two lines, C V S M // w-M V-o, forming a CAN//DEF arrangement. Adjoining this is a clause consisting of w-SVM, indicating a contrast, that is, between outward worship and the inner state of the heart. The overall colon arrangement is therefore CAN//DEF/MKD. Assuming the correctness of the foregoing comments regarding pitch, then the switch from DEF to MKD, where both clauses begin with a *wāw* plus preverbal constituent, would be marked by a corresponding change in pitch. וּבִשְׂפָתָיו would carry regular pitch and וְלִבּוֹ high pitch, so making what was not discernible to the eye, detectable to the ear.

Admittedly there is much uncertainty surrounding the function of pitch in Biblical Hebrew and the above argument remains only a supposition. Yet if it were to be substantiated, then this would be an additional way in which the original speakers and hearers of Hebrew poetry would have been able to differentiate between potentially confusing ordering of constituents. Together with the particular environment in which the non-canonical word order appeared, the presence of prosodic clues would have greatly assisted in creating a distinction between that which was pragmatically marked and that which was poetically defamiliarised.

6.4 Contrast and Chiasmus

In the context of differentiating between marked structures and those which are purely defamiliar, some comment is in order concerning the relationship between contrast and chiasmus. There are a number of scholars who hold to the opinion that there is an inseparable connection between the two. One of these is Watson himself, who claims that 'antithesis or contrast' is a function of chiasmus.[20] Wenham, a notable Old Testament scholar, assumes

---

19 Cf. Shimasaki, *Focus Structure*, p. 68. A more detailed discussion of pitch in contrastive contexts is presented by K. van Deemter, 'Contrastive Stress, Contrariety, and Focus', in P. Bosch and R. van der Sandt (eds.), *Focus: Linguistic, Cognitive and Computational Perspectives* (Cambridge: Cambridge University Press, 1999), pp. 3-17.

20 W. G. E. Watson, 'Chiastic Patterns in Biblical Hebrew Poetry', in J. W. Welch (ed.), *Chiasmus in Antiquity* (Hildersheim: Gerstenberg, 1981), p. 129, where one of

the same. In his volume on Genesis 1–15 he invariably refers to the inversions of word order in contrastive contexts as 'chiasmus' or 'chiastic'.[21] Niccacci, too, follows in the same vein.[22] In the light of the evidence the view of such scholars is surely mistaken. Two basic facts that have been so far observed undermine the supposed relationship:

(1) It has been demonstrated by several examples, that SV/SV, i.e., a symmetrical, non-chiastic arrangement, also often occurs with contrastive implications.[23]

(2) It has also been demonstrated that the chiastically ordered VS//SV is frequently found in synonymous parallelism, where contrast is completely excluded.[24]

These facts suggest that the presence of chiasmus alone need not have contrastive implications, and conversely, that where contrast is present chiasmus need not take place at all. Although in certain cases there may be a resemblance between the two, no intrinsic link exists. As a matter of fact, there is a fundamental difference between the two, as they exist on two totally essentially unrelated levels of language. Chiasmus is a rhetorical pattern, contrast is a semantic relationship. It cannot be said, therefore, that contrast is a function of chiasmus.

The confusion no doubt arises from the similarity of appearance that sometimes exists between chiasmus and marked word order. This is so when each clause involved in the contrast has only two elements. In a situation where the first clause consists solely of VO, and the second has the contrasting NP[DO] in the marked position, then the appearance is that of a chiasmus, where VO is followed by OV (cf. Ps. 145:20). However, when there are three or more clause constituents, the nature of the pragmatic fronting is readily distinguishable from the chiastically ordered pattern. Rhetorical chiasmus would produce an *abc–cba* arrangement,[25] as Psalm 142:3, yet pragmatic marking would only require the shift of the contrasting element to the focal clause-initial position, that is, *abc–bac*. So, for example, in the contrast of Ruth 1:14 the constituent order of the two clauses is VSM–SVM.[26] It would not have been difficult to create a total chiasmus, but in prose such a thing is never found in three-member clauses

---

the functions of chiasmus listed is to express 'antithesis'; cf. Watson, *Classical Hebrew Poetry*, p. 206.

21 Wenham, *Genesis 1–15*, pp. 3, 4, 19, 33, 94, etc.
22 Niccacci, *The Syntax of the Verb in Classical Hebrew Prose*, p. 31.
23 See 4.2.2 (c), especially fn. 43.
24 5.3.
25 See 5.3.3 (b).
26 Even though he employs the term 'chiastic', the majority of instances to which Wenham refers are actually not strictly so, but of the same structure as Ruth 1:14 (e.g., Genesis 4:2, V S Comp – S V Comp). This highlights the unsuitability of his description.

within the context of contrast. In poetry it is significant that the chiastic *abc–cba* sequence exists predominantly not in contrastive relationships but synonymous.[27] This fact alone rules out the essential connection between the two.

One important corollary of the foregoing is that the traditional literary category of 'antithetical parallelism', as advanced by Bishop Lowth in the eighteenth century,[28] needs to undergo reassessment. In the light of the relationship between word-order variation and pragmatic functions it must be doubted whether we may define antithetical bicola as any manner of parallelism at all.[29] The motivating factor determining the form of the B-line is strictly pragmatic and, as observed, no difference exists between the construction of contrastive sentences in poetry from those in prose. To use the term 'parallelism' in such circumstances would therefore be as inaccurate and unsuitable in the former genre as it would in the latter. What we are dealing with here is not a literary form, which is what parallelism is, but one that is linguistically structured and describable strictly in terms of pragmatic markedness.[30]

6.5 Summary

This chapter has shown that environment is a crucial factor in determining whether a poetic clause is marked or defamiliar. Form alone is insufficient. It was also suggested that in the original pronunciation of Biblical Hebrew poetry pragmatically marked forms, unlike defamiliar ones, would have been accompanied by an equally distinct pitch pattern. Finally, it was argued that chiasmus and contrast exist independently at different levels of the language, one rhetorical, the other pragmatic. It was proposed that the

---

27 In verbal clauses a wholly chiastic *abc–cba* pattern in a contrast is almost non-existent. None at all occurs within the data selected for this study, and outside of this the only instances known to the present writer take the form of proverbs (e.g., Prov. 10:12; 18:23). Most of the examples listed by Watson (*Classical Hebrew Poetry*, p. 206) are two-part chiastic patterns, not three.
28 Cf. Kidner, *Psalms 1–72*, pp. 2–3.
29 In contrast there must of course be a certain correspondence of the elements involved, otherwise no contrast would be possible. A sentence such as 'The President flew to Washington, but the cat was sleeping in front of the fire', while syntactically unobjectionable, is nonsensical. We would expect some relationship like 'President/the President's wife', 'flew/drove', or 'Washington/New York', in order to make the contrasting statement meaningful. Cf. the comment of Fokkelman, 'Only when X and Y have something in common is it possible and meaningful to speak of an antithesis between them', *Reading Biblical Poetry*, p.27.
30 All antithetical parallelisms, therefore, are here analysed as CAN/MKD (or MKD/MKD in those instances where a fronted element also occurs before the verb in the first clause), and not CAN//MKD.

rhetorical constructions traditionally designated antithetical parallelism be redefined in terms of pragmatics, since the word-order variation exhibited by such is of a strictly pragmatic nature.

CHAPTER 7

Pragmatic Markedness in Poetic Cola: (2) Parallel Lines

In chapter 4 the question of pragmatic marking in poetry was investigated. The texts included in that chapter were analysed independently of the common poetic feature of parallelism. We now inquire into the question how pragmatic markedness effects the construction of parallel lines. As shall become apparent, when a parallelism has a marked rather than canonical base-line, there are certain consequences regarding the pragmatic organisation of the B-line.

7.1 Constraint upon Pragmatic Marking in Parallelisms

With respect to parallelisms in which the base-line, i.e., the A-line, shows canonical constituent order, we observed that there was complete freedom in how the B-line might be ordered.[1] Parallelisms of this type, we saw, could either be CAN//CAN, where the order of syntactic components is reproduced, or CAN//DEF, where the elements of the A-line are reordered in B, sometimes creating a chiastic pattern, but most often not.

When we come to parallelisms in which the A-line is MKD, the situation is very different from that of CAN A-lines. A consistent pattern emerges from the data. What we observe is that when the A-line of a parallelism occurring in general distribution[2] is marked, the only option for the B-line is that it exhibits the same marked order of constituents. What this means is that a marked A-line will typically produce a symmetrical parallelism of the arrangement MKD//MKD.[3] There are very few exceptions to this, which shall be considered later in this chapter and in the next. It is simply the case that parallelisms of the type MKD//CAN and MKD//DEF do not generally occur. On the few occasions when such sequences are found, the verse in

---

1 5.3.
2 This is a crucial factor which should not be overlooked, see 5.6.
3 This of course does not mean that obligatory sentence-initial elements, such as conjunctive phrases, interrogatives, negatives, etc., will have corresponding components in the parallel line. See 1.4 (2).

question is clearly specially constructed and positioned within the discourse, that is, of what we have termed specific distribution, as shall be demonstrated in due course. So we posit the following general constraint: *A parallelism with a marked A-line will also have an equally marked B-line.*

7.2 Examples of Pragmatic Marking in Parallelisms

Instances of MKD//MKD parallelisms abound in the data. This section presents texts containing SV-, OV-, and MV-clauses, where the context has obvious pragmatic connotations and where the initial marked colon is followed by one that is a synonymous parallel.

7.2.1 Two Cola in Parallelism

(a) SV//SV

First we give an instance in which the marked constituent order is due to the presence of sentence-focus structure, that is, where there is no pragmatic presupposition.

Psalm 37:30

| The mouths of the righteous talk of wisdom, | פִּי־צַדִּיק יֶהְגֶּה חָכְמָה |
| and their tongues speak justice. | וּלְשׁוֹנוֹ תְּדַבֵּר מִשְׁפָּט: |

As previously observed,[4] the SV(O) sentence-focus clause is commonly found in independent sayings. This parallel bicolon, SVO//SVO, has all the appearances of such a saying. This is supported by the fact that the psalm is an acrostic, and each letter (here פ) begins a new unit not connected to the foregoing. In his introduction to this psalm Harman observes that 'Many of the statements are in the form of proverbs, which are general assertions of a truth ...',[5] while Craigie identifies this verse itself as a 'proverb'.[6] Both these commentators note the close parallel between 30a and the proverbial פִּי־צַדִּיק יָנוּב חָכְמָה ('The mouth of the righteous brings forth wisdom', Prov. 10:31), having the same information structure in the A-line as the present example. We note that the SVO//SVO parallelism is commonplace in the book of Proverbs.[7]

The following example also contains two SV-clauses in parallel, though this time the pragmatic marking is due to the presence of a replacing focus construction:

---

4   See 3.4.1 (c).
5   Harman, *Psalms*, p. 161.
6   Craigie, *Psalms 1–50*, p. 299.
7   For example, Proverbs 15:30; 16:28; 17:20; 18:15; 19:5, 15, 28; 23:33; 26:28; 27:18, 20; 30:33; (and with gapping of verb in the B-line: 20:30; 21:14; 25:23; 26:14).

Isaiah 62:9

but those who harvest it shall eat it	כִּי מְאַסְפָיו יֹאכְלֻהוּ
and praise YHWH,	וְהִלְלוּ אֶת־יְהוָה
and those who gather it shall drink it	וּמְקַבְּצָיו יִשְׁתֻּהוּ
in my holy courts.	בְּחַצְרוֹת קָדְשִׁי׃

This parallelism has a preverbal subject, in the form of a nominal participle (מְאַסְפָיו and וּמְקַבְּצָיו) in each half. A close relationship with the previous verse is apparent: 'I will not again give your grain to be food for your enemies, and foreigners shall not drink the wine for which you have laboured' (v. 8). It will not be the enemy who eats the produce of Israel, the prophet says, but those Israelites who harvest the crop will themselves eat it. Each member of the replacing construction (i.e., v. 8 and v. 9) takes on the form of a parallel bicolon. In such cases it is the second half of the structure that typically shows markedness in both lines A and B, as here.

Other examples of SV//SV parallelisms in the data include Psalms 2:4; 37:15; 83:3; 109:24; Isaiah 41:20; 54:10; 60:7; Proverbs 2:11; and Job 13:11.

(b) OV//OV

Psalm 145:11

They shall speak of the glory of your kingdom,	כְּבוֹד מַלְכוּתְךָ יֹאמֵרוּ
and they shall tell of your might.	וּגְבוּרָתְךָ יְדַבֵּרוּ׃

These parallel lines consist of OV//OV. In this case the reason for the pragmatic marking is perhaps not so readily detected, though one can be discerned nevertheless. Once more the context is vital in determining the character of the focus that is present. It is helpful to quote the whole of verses 10–12:

> [10] All your works shall give thanks to you, O YHWH,
> and all your faithful ones shall bless you.
> [11] They shall speak of the glory of your kingdom,
> and they shall tell of your might,
> [12] to make known to all people your mighty deeds,
> and the glorious splendour of your kingdom.

Verse 10 contains a general statement to the effect that all God's works and all his people shall praise him. The grammatical object in both clauses is a 2nd person pronominal suffix having reference to God. Now in verse 11 the two clauses are formed around two *verba dicendi* with fronted objects denoting the content of the speech of those mentioned in verse 10. The grammatical subject remains the same, i.e., the works and people of God.

Again the grammatical object makes reference to God, though this time by means of the possessive suffix ךָ–, 'your'. It is the matching noun phrases, מַלְכוּתְךָ and וּגְבוּרָתְךָ, that now comprise the salient information of this bicolon. Having declared the fact of the praise of God by all his works and people in verse 10, the psalmist now focuses upon these two particular aspects of their praise in verse 11, thus intimating a general-specific relationship between the two verses. That the elements מַלְכוּתְךָ and וּגְבוּרָתְךָ are in focus is confirmed by verse 12. Together verses 11 and 12 form a chiastic pattern with respect to the object phrases:

11a	כְּבוֹד מַלְכוּתְךָ	'the glory of your kingdom'	A
11b	וּגְבוּרָתְךָ	'your might'	B
12a	גְּבוּרֹתָיו	'your mighty deeds'	B'
12b	וּכְבוֹד הֲדַר מַלְכוּתוֹ	'the glorious splendour of your kingdom'	A'

The repetition of similar phrases in verse 12 suggests that these were indeed the focal elements in verse 11.[8]

Examples of O V // O V parallelisms found elsewhere include Psalms 7:13; 21:3; 90:17; Isaiah 45:2; 59:5; 60:6; and Job 13:25.

(c) M V // M V

Job 4:9

By the breath of God they perish,   מִנִּשְׁמַת אֱלוֹהַּ יֹאבֵדוּ
and by the blast of his anger they are consumed.   וּמֵרוּחַ אַפּוֹ יִכְלוּ׃

In this parallel bicolon, M V // M V, each line begins with a prepositional phrase with בְּ–. Both phrases relate to the breath of God. The adjoining verbs are virtually synonymous in this context, both having to do with perishing. In this part (4:7–11) of the speech of Eliphaz he is considering the question, raised in verse 7, 'Call to mind now, who that was innocent ever perished? Or where were the upright cut off?', likewise containing two parallel verbs of perishing. His assumption in these rhetorical questions is that the righteous will not altogether perish, and so Job, if innocent, need not fear such an end.[9] It is only 'those who plough iniquity' (v. 8) who will experience this fate.[10] Consequently, from the point of view of presuppositional information, by the time we reach verse 9, the fact that the wicked 'perish' has already been established in the discourse, implicitly in verse 7, and explicitly in verse 8. This accounts for the word order of this verse,

---

8 Kidner, *Psalms 73–150*, p. 481, notes 'the stress on the word *kingdom* (four times: 11, 12, 13, 13)' in this passage.
9 Cf. F. I. Andersen, *Job*, TOTC (Leicester: Inter-Varsity Press, 1976), p. 112.
10 Cf. Clines, *Job 1–20*, p. 125.

consisting of argument-focus clauses. The presupposition follows the focal component, which is expressed in the two PPs. According to Eliphaz the wicked perish 'By the breath of God'. The focus is upon the divine agency, as Hartley remarks, 'The final end of wicked is administered by God ... God participates in executing judgment so that the sinner will receive a full and proper reward'.[11] In other words, to quote Clines, God is 'consciously their executor'. The reference to God's 'breath', Clines proposes, 'betokens his personal involvement in retribution'.[12] So, by means of these marked clause constituents, it is not the mere fact of the end of the wicked that is in view, but the manner in which God himself acts for their destruction.

Among the many other instances of M V // M V parallelisms in the data are Psalms 5:4; 18:30; 82:7; 104:7; Isaiah 40:11; 48:9; 66:12; Proverbs 2:3; 4:20; and Numbers 23:9.

In the following sub-sections are presented a series of examples in which the parallelism of MKD clauses does not take the basic S V // S V, O V // OV, or M V // M V form.

7.2.2 Two Bicola in Parallelism

It has been remarked previously that not all parallelisms are between one colon and another.[13] On occasion the parallel relationship adheres between one bicolon and the following. In such cases the markedness of the initial colon of the parallelism will be reproduced, not in the colon immediately following, but in the third. This may be illustrated by the following two texts:

Psalm 127:1

Unless YHWH builds the house,	אִם־יְהוָה לֹא־יִבְנֶה בַיִת	A
those who build it labour in vain.	שָׁוְא עָמְלוּ בוֹנָיו בּוֹ	B
Unless YHWH guards the city,	אִם־יְהוָה לֹא־יִשְׁמָר־עִיר	C
the guard watches in vain.	שָׁוְא שָׁקַד שׁוֹמֵר׃	D

It is evident that the first (A) and third (C) of these four lines parallel each other, both semantically and syntactically, and since A is marked C also has a corresponding markedness, both clauses having a preverbal subject. In each of these two cola the NP[Su] is יְהוָה. The reason for this, as Allen affirms, is to emphasise that 'all comes from Yahweh'.[14] Pragmatically, the constituent order of the clauses is probably due to the fact that the building

---

11 Hartley, *The Book of Job*, p. 108; cf. Clines, *Job 1–20*, p. 127, 'God is the agent of humans' annihilation when it occurs before the due time'.
12 *Ibid.*
13 See 2.2.1.
14 L. C. Allen, *Psalms 101–150*, WBC (Waco, Texas: Word Books, 1983), p. 178.

of a house and the guarding of the city are assumed, i.e., presupposed, activities. The markedness of יְהוָה seems to have the function of identifying the Lord as the one who ultimately fulfils these tasks. Similarly, lines B and D form a parallelism. Again the first of these is marked (MV), and that markedness reappears in the latter. The motivating factor for the word order can be taken as the same as that for lines A and C, that is, the actions indicated by the verbs, 'labouring' and 'watching', are presuppositional information in argument-focus clauses. This must be so in B and D in that A and C have already mentioned the ideas of building and guarding, which in turn presuppose labouring and watching. The preverbal element, שָׁוְא, serves to highlight the vanity of the activities of these people unless the Lord himself is also engaged. The overall form of the unit may therefore be designated as MKD/MKD//MKD/MKD, where the parallelism exists between each bicolon.

Isaiah 65:13

Behold, my servants shall eat,	הִנֵּה עֲבָדַי יֹאכֵלוּ	A
but you shall be hungry;	וְאַתֶּם תִּרְעָבוּ	B
Behold, my servants shall drink,	הִנֵּה עֲבָדַי יִשְׁתּוּ	C
but you shall be thirsty.	וְאַתֶּם תִּצְמָאוּ	D

Here again the parallelism is obviously between lines A and C (both HSV) and then B and D (both S^{Pn} V).[15] This example happens to aptly illustrate the distinction between pragmatic and non-pragmatic colon relationships. Line A relates to B pragmatically as a contrast, while to C rhetorically as a poetic parallel.

7.2.3 Two Preverbal Elements in Parallelism

This following example shows how an A-line with two preverbal elements will be paralleled by a line placing the two corresponding syntactic components in the same positions.

Isaiah 60:4cd

| Your sons shall come from far away, | בָּנַיִךְ מֵרָחוֹק יָבֹאוּ |
| and your daughters shall be carried in the arms. | וּבְנֹתַיִךְ עַל־צַד תֵּאָמַנָה׃ |

This bicolon has the syntactic composition SMV//SMV. In order to appreciate its information structure the preceding clauses also have to be considered. The prophet has just declared (v. 4ab), שְׂאִי־סָבִיב עֵינַיִךְ וּרְאִי כֻּלָּם נִקְבְּצוּ בָאוּ־לָךְ ('Lift up your eyes and see; they all gather, they come

---

15 This example is actually the first part of an extended parallelism stretching over two verses. Certain distinctive features of extended parallelisms are discussed below (7.2.7).

to you'). The addressee, 'you', is Jerusalem, here personified as a mother,[16] and the subject the prophet is talking about is simply 'they all' (כֻּלָּם). It is not immediately apparent from this first half of the verse who the prophet is speaking of. Not until the third and fourth cola (v. 4cd) are these referents identified. כֻּלָּם is now understood to refer to the 'sons' and 'daughters' of Zion. We may therefore account for the initial NP[Su]s in terms of specification. Those vaguely introduced in 4b are now actually specified, that is, both male and female offspring. Following the clause-initial subject phrases, the reason for the second preverbal element, the PP, is not difficult to discern. Already in 4b the verb בָּאוּ has been employed. Consequently, it is presupposed information that these sons and daughters 'will come'. Hence, in the parallelism under consideration, the verbs of motion יָבֹאוּ ('will come') and תֵּאָמַנָה ('will be carried') are placed later in the clause, as being presuppositional. What the prophet is focusing upon in 4cd in these argument-focus clauses is not the previously stated fact of their coming, but on certain details relating to the manner of their coming. The newly presented information is that they will come 'from afar' and that those coming will be carried (literally) 'on the side' (עַל־צַד).[17] Motyer describes this as a 'great homeward march in which distance is no barrier (*from afar*) and frailty (*carried*/"nursed"), no hindrance'.[18]

It is enlightening to contrast the foregoing parallelism with a similar one in Isaiah 49:22de, וְהֵבִיאוּ בָנַיִךְ בְּחֹצֶן וּבְנֹתַיִךְ עַל־כָּתֵף תִּנָּשֶׂאנָה ('they will bring your sons in their bosom, and your daughters will be carried on their shoulders'). In this case the word order of וְהֵבִיאוּ בָנַיִךְ בְּחֹצֶן is unmarked (VOM), seeing that the pragmatic presuppositions are different from 60:4. The above words follow on from the divine declaration, 'I will soon lift up my hand to the nations, and raise my signal to the peoples' (v. 29bc). Unlike 60:4 no statement has yet been made regarding the bringing home of the sons and daughters, so such information is not presuppositional. Rather this text concerns the divine instigation of the event in stirring up the agents who will perform it. Verse 22de is a parallel bicolon of the type CAN//DEF, the canonical A-line allowing the opportunity to reorder the constituents of the B-line to SMV. The information structure is predicate focus, the referents of the verbal affixes being the 'nations' and 'peoples' of the

---

16 Cf. Young, *Isaiah*, vol. 3, p. 446.
17 Some translate as 'on the hip', e.g., Watts, *Isaiah 34–66*, p. 290. Watts explains this expression with reference to the assistance given to the returning exiles by the Persian authorities, *ibid.*, p. 295. Oswalt, *The Book of Isaiah 40–66*, p. 533, fn. 8, offers the explanation that 'supported on the side' was 'evidently the common practice in some cultures of carrying the infant straddled on the hip and supported with one hand'.
18 Motyer, *The Prophecy of Isaiah*, pp. 494–95.

earlier part of the verse. From the comparison of these two texts, 49:22 and 60:4, dealing with similar events, the importance of the word-order variation in poetry is clearly exemplified.

Occurrences of parallelisms with two preverbal elements are relatively rare, but we note that the subject-initial patterns SMV//SMV and SOV//SOV are much more common than other variations, e.g., Psalms 38:12; 72:10; Isaiah 51:4; and Job 14:22.

7.2.4 Parallelism with Focus Particles

Where a marked construction occurs together with a focus particle,[19] it is typically the case that the particle itself will only appear in the A-line of the parallelism, while the marked constituent remains fronted in both lines:

Isaiah 49:25bc

| Even the captives of the mighty shall be taken, | גַּם־שְׁבִי גִבּוֹר יֻקָּח |
| and the prey of the tyrant be delivered. | וּמַלְקוֹחַ עָרִיץ יִמָּלֵט |

This verse occurs in a passage concerning the restoration of exiled Israel. In the course of this prophecy the imaginary objection is interposed:[20] 'Can the prey be taken from the mighty, or the captives of a tyrant be delivered?' (v. 24). This rhetorical question anticipates a negative response. Under normal circumstances rescue from the hands of the גִבּוֹר and the עָרִיץ would not be anticipated. But the divine answer (v. 25bc) repeats the contents of the question, though this time framed as a positive declaration. Here the particle גַּם is employed, having the sense of something unexpected – '*Even* the captives of the mighty ...' would be delivered. It is to be observed that the question of verse 24 shows no pragmatic marking, having the form CAN// DEF (VMS//w-SV), while the answer in verse 25, is MKD//MKD (*gam*–SV// w-SV), where the pragmatic connotation of contra-expectation is present.[21]

Job 14:3

| On such a one do you fix your eyes, | אַף־עַל־זֶה פָּקַחְתָּ עֵינֶךָ |
| and bring me[22] into judgment with yourself? | וְאֹתִי תָבִיא בְמִשְׁפָּט עִמָּךְ: |

This parallelism has the structure *ʾap*–M V O // O V M M. Although the two initial elements differ grammatically (a PP and Pn[DO]), they match in that

---

19 Examples of focus particles in non-parallelisms were discussed in 4.2.1.
20 Oswalt, *The Book of Isaiah 40–66*, p. 313, suggests that here 'the prophet plays devil's advocate'. The ability of God to deliver from such extreme circumstances is thrown into doubt only that he might be shown all the more able to deliver. Cf. also Young, *Isaiah*, vol. 3, p. 292.
21 For גַּם signifying contra-expectation, see 3.4.2 (e) and 4.2.1 (a).
22 LXX, Vulg, Syr, read a 3rd person pronoun at this point.

they have identical reference, that is, to Job himself. After pointing out the frailty and fleetingness of human nature, Job here questions God. The basic import of the question is 'Why should God judge such a defenceless creature?'.²³ Several commentators, though invariably employing linguistically imprecise terminology, note the focus function of the particle אַף. More than one sense is possible for phrases containing this particle. Dhorme and Reyburn both interpret Job's expression as one of surprise.²⁴ This makes אַף have the force of contra-expectation, which is one of its possible uses,²⁵ as seen previously. Clines, describing this as an 'intensive clause', assigns a different sense to the particle, that of 'surely, indeed', which again is a proper use of the particle.²⁶ He comments, 'Such human frailty and impermanence is contrasted with the divine inquisition, which is of course thorough and long extended. The amazing disproportion is highlighted by the introductory particle'. Either of these two interpretations is suitable to the context. The essential thing for our purposes is that the markedness present in the A-line of the bicolon is carried over into B, producing the equally marked sequence וְאֹתִי תָבִיא, in which the fronted pronoun is coreferential with the pronominal form זֶה in the A-line. In both lines the verb phrases, we note, contain information which is contextually presupposed, i.e., that God is judging Job.

Repetition of the focus particle is rare but not unknown, as in the following example:

Psalm 39:6

| Surely every man walks about like a shadow; | אַךְ־בְּצֶלֶם יִתְהַלֶּךְ־אִישׁ |
| surely they bustle about for nothing. | אַךְ־הֶבֶל יֶהֱמָיוּן |

This synonymous parallelism is composed of ʾak–M V S // ʾak–M V. The particle אַךְ, though undoubtedly focal, may be understood in two different ways. Most versions take it as affirmative, 'surely' or 'indeed' (e.g., NASB NRSV NKJV), but a restrictive sense, 'only' or 'merely', is also a possibility

---

23 Cf. R. Zuck, *Job* (Chicago: Moody Press, 1978), p. 64.
24 Dhorme, *Commentary on the Book of Job*, p. 196, '"אַף־עַל־זֶה even on such a one!" ... is an exclamation of surprise. It [*sic*.] spite of the misery of this creature, whose condition I have just described, Thou openest Thy eye to judge him!'; Reyburn, *Handbook on the Book of Job*, p. 143, 'Job expresses surprise that God should examine anything as unimportant as a human being'.
25 See 4.2.1 (b). Van der Merwe (et al), *Hebrew Reference Grammar*, pp. 312–13, includes Job 14:3 as an example of what is termed *extreme case*, noting that in such contexts is usually translated as 'even'.
26 Clines, *Job 1–20*, p. 325, citing Genesius, *Hebrew Grammar*, §153, for intensive clauses. In his translation Hartley, *The Book of Job*, p. 229, also gives אַף the sense 'Indeed'.

(e.g., NIV NJB).[27] Either way the information structure of each clause is the same. In this context the psalmist presupposes the fact that man 'goes about' (יִתְהַלֶּךְ) and 'bustles about' (יֶהֱמָיוּן). The focal information he intends to impart is the vain or transitory nature of these activities,[28] expressed through the two fronted PPs.

Other instances of MKD//MKD parallelisms involving focus particles include: Psalms 58:3; 84:4; 85:13; 139:12; and Isaiah 48:13.

7.2.5 Parallelism with Extraposition

The not infrequent employment of extraposition to indicate markedness was discussed in general in 3.4.3 and with respect to Hebrew poetry in 4.2.4. Since the functions of this construction with respect to pragmatic marking largely coincide with those of straightforward fronting, it is not surprising to find that a colon with an extraposed NP, PP, or Adv is sometimes placed in parallelism with a colon containing a clause marked simply through word order, as in:

Psalm 50:23

He who offers a thank-offering honours me;   זֹבֵחַ תּוֹדָה יְכַבְּדָנְנִי
and he who orders his way I will show him   וְשָׂם דֶּרֶךְ אַרְאֶנּוּ בְּיֵשַׁע אֱלֹהִים׃
the salvation of God.

In this example the A-line displays the marked constituent order SV-o, while the B-line consists of w-NP[Ext] V-o M, where the extraposed NP is followed by a resumptive object clitic-pronoun affixed to the verb. The initial elements of each line, זֹבֵחַ תּוֹדָה and וְשָׂם דֶּרֶךְ, relate semantically in that both relate to the true worshipper, and both are composed of participles governing an object.[29] Pragmatically the motivation for the marked construction has to be sought in the larger context. If one goes back to verse 16 of the psalm we notice that this final section (vv. 16–23) is addressed to 'the wicked'. In the verse preceding our example it is 'those who forget God' to whom the words are directed (v. 22). Yet these wicked retain an outward form of religion in that they continue to recite God's laws (v. 16b). In the light of the overall context the markedness evident in verse 23 is best interpreted as replacing focus: 'It is not those X who honour God but those Y'. It is not the aforementioned persons who have God's law in their mouths yet not in their lives who honour God, but these who render to him

---

27 Cf. Delitzsch, 'Psalms', p. 29 (in Keil and Delitzsch, *Commentary on the Old Testament*, vol. 5).
28 Kidner, *Psalms 1–72*, p. 156 says that the term הֶבֶל here, as in Ecclesiastes, exposes 'the fatal insufficiency of all that is earthbound'; cf. Harman, *Psalms*, p. 171.
29 Cf. Craigie, *Psalms 1–50*, p. 363.

sincere thank-offerings and who adhere to his way. Delitzsch's remarks lend support to this interpretation.[30]

Only rarely do both lines of MKD//MKD parallelisms contain matching extraposed phrases:

Psalm 101:5

He who slanders a neighbour in secret,	[מְלָשְׁנִי] בַסֵּתֶר רֵעֵהוּ
him I will destroy;	אוֹתוֹ אַצְמִית
He who is proud and arrogant,	גְּבַהּ־עֵינַיִם וּרְחַב לֵבָב אֹתוֹ
him I will not endure.	לֹא אוּכָל:

This synonymous and syntactic parallelism is composed of closely matching elements: NP[Ext] Pn[DO] V // NP[Ext] Pn[DO] V. In the two verses before this the psalmist affirms, 'I will not set before my eyes anything that is base. I hate the work of those who fall away; it shall not cling to me. Perverseness of heart shall be far from me; I will know nothing of evil' (vv. 3–4 NRSV). Significantly, three of these preceding clauses contain marked word order: (v. 3b) לֵבָב עִקֵּשׁ יָסוּר מִמֶּנִּי שָׂנֵאתִי (OV), (v. 4a) עֹשֵׂה־סֵטִים (SV), (v. 4b) רָע לֹא אֵדָע (OV). It seems most plausible to understand these marked elements in terms of specification. In verse 3a the psalmist had stated his general rule, 'I will not set before my eyes anything that is base [דְּבַר־בְּלִיָּעַל]'. These ensuing clauses may then be thought of as listing diverse categories of baseness. Those referred to in the extraposed phrases of verse 5, the slanderer and the proud, are also included among the base.[31]

7.2.6 Parallelism with Gapping

Gapping of elements in parallel lines was discussed in our general introduction to Hebrew poetry in chapter 2.[32] In a situation where the A-line of the parallelism is canonical the B-line may gap any element whatsoever, a fact in keeping with the large degree of freedom evident in such parallel lines.

---

30 Delitzsch says that, 'Under the name שֹׁכְחֵי אֱלוֹהַּ are comprehended the decent or honourable whose sanctity relies upon outward works, and those who know better but give way to licentiousness ... In dead works God delighteth not, but whoso offereth thanksgiving ... he praises him' (in Keil and Delitzsch, *Commentary on the Old Testament*, vol. 5, p. 131).

31 Why these last two participants only of the several listed should be encoded through exposition is a question worth considering. Perhaps the *length* of the NP is a relevant factor in determining whether or not it is placed in extraposition or simply fronted. If it is long (i.e., three or more components), then it is extraposed, with a resumptive pronoun. Note that an identical extraposed construction occurs at the end of verse 6 of the same psalm: הֹלֵךְ בְּדֶרֶךְ תָּמִים הוּא יְשָׁרְתֵנִי.

32 See 2.2.2 (a).

Most frequently the gapping is of the verb, the initial constituent of the unmarked A-line (e.g., Prov. 5:15), but it could be of a postverbal nominal phrase or adverb (e.g., Ps. 102:15), or even of two elements (e.g., Ps. 9:10, where both V and NP[Su] are gapped). However, with respect to parallelisms having marked A-lines such freedom is not to be found. A constraint is placed upon which constituent may be elided. According to the data, in general distribution[33] gapping may only occur in the B-line with elements that do not occupy the fronted position in the A-line. In other words, if a clause constituent in the base-line of the parallelism occupies the focal, i.e., clause-initial, position, it cannot be gapped in the B-line. This is illustrated in the following examples containing fronted NP[Su]s, NP[DO]s, and PPs:

Psalm 84:4

| Even the sparrow finds a home, | גַּם־צִפּוֹר מָצְאָה בַיִת |
| and the swallow a nest for herself. | וּדְרוֹר קֵן לָהּ |

This bicolon shows the constituent order *gam*–SVO//SO. The subject phrase occupies the clause-initial position in both cola, while the second constituent, the verb, has been gapped in the parallel line. Here the intended sense of the focus construction is evidently that of contra-expectation, as the majority of commentators and translations agree. God's house, which the context of the verse concerns, is a sanctuary not only for his worshippers, but *even* for the birds.

Psalm 135:4

| For YHWH has chosen Jacob for himself, | כִּי־יַעֲקֹב בָּחַר לוֹ יָהּ |
| Israel for His own possession. | יִשְׂרָאֵל לִסְגֻלָּתוֹ׃ |

In this example, consisting of OVS//OM, it is an object phrase that is fronted in each line. In the B-line the verb is gapped but the focal element remains in its clause-initial position. The focus here is upon the people of Israel as the object of the divine election which is presupposed. Israel of all nations were the only ones whom God had so chosen. Kidner acknowledges the names יַעֲקֹב and יִשְׂרָאֵל to be 'emphatic', and offers the translation, 'For it was Jacob that the Lord chose ...',[34] which we believe well conveys the sense. Furthermore, Kidner makes the important observation that this verse looks back to Deuteronomy 7:6. There both the verb בָּחַר and the noun סְגֻלָּה are likewise to be found in the context of election, and the marked word order, בְּךָ בָּחַר יהוה ('it was you YHWH chose') is significantly also employed. In both cases the focus structure can be attributed to the nature

---

33 See fn. 2 above.
34 Kidner, *Psalms 73–150*, p. 455. Cf. Allen's own emphatic rendering, *Psalms 101–150*, p. 221, 'because Jacob it was whom Yah(weh) chose as his own'. Most modern English translations, however, overlook the focus structure of this verse.

of the divine choice, i.e., selective focus.³⁵ Out of all the options available to him, it was the people of Israel whom God chose.

Psalm 19:5

| Their line has gone forth in all the earth, | בְּכָל־הָאָרֶץ יָצָא קַוָּם |
| their words to the ends of the world. | וּבִקְצֵה תֵבֵל מִלֵּיהֶם |

Here the constituent structure of the parallelism is MVS//MS. Again we observe that the element corresponding to the fronted PP of the A-line holds the same position in B. The theme of these opening verses of the psalm is the witness of the natural creation to the glory of God.³⁶ After declaring in the first verse (v. 2 in MT) that 'The heavens tell the glory of God; and the firmament proclaims his handiwork', the psalmist then adds, יוֹם לְיוֹם יַבִּיעַ אֹמֶר וְלַיְלָה לְּלַיְלָה יְחַוֶּה־דָּעַת (v. 3, 'Day to day pours forth speech, and night to night declares knowledge'). This bicolon itself shows marked word order, MVO // w-MVO. Here the two initial adverbial phrases relate to time, as Craigie explains, 'By day, the sky is characterized by sun and light, and by night its darkness is punctuated by the light of moon and stars; both these dimensions combine to recount God's glory'.³⁷ Through these opening verses the fact that God's universe communicates the message of his glory provides the presupposition for verse 5 which we are considering. The bicolon of verse 5, like verse 3, has two fronted phrases, but this time locative, rather than temporal, signifying throughout all the earth/world.³⁸ The information structure is the same as verse 4, though the syntax 5b displays the additional feature of gapping. Having stated the fact of the revelation of God in the universe (v. 2), the psalmist then expands upon this through these two bicola giving salience firstly to the time (day and night, v. 3) and then place (everywhere, v. 5) where this revelation is discernible. The initial M constituent in each instance is therefore made the dominant focal element.³⁹

Where the A-line of a parallelism contains two preverbal elements, both of these fronted phrases, since they are in marked positions, will be preserved in the B-line. Only the third constituent, the verb, may be found gapped. This is seen in the following:

Psalm 33:11

| [But] the counsel of YHWH stands forever, | עֲצַת יְהוָה לְעוֹלָם תַּעֲמֹד |
| the thoughts of his heart to all generations. | מַחְשְׁבוֹת לִבּוֹ לְדֹר וָדֹר: |

---

35 See 3.4.2 (f).
36 Kidner speaks of 'the wordless revelation of the universe', *Psalms 1–72*, p. 97.
37 Craigie, *Psalms 1–50*, p. 180.
38 Cf. Harman, *Psalms*, p. 113, 'Nowhere in the world is isolated from this message, for it penetrates everywhere... The voice of creation is a universal messenger'.
39 For this term, see 3.4.1 (a), example (3).

This bicolon stands in a contrastive relationship with the previous verse,[40] 'YHWH brings the counsel of the nations to nothing; he frustrates the plans of the peoples' (v. 10). The plans of the nations are thwarted, but God's own plans stand for ever. The A-line consists of Contrasting Topic + Contrasting Focus + Verb,[41] while the B-line just retains the two marked elements, the third being elided.

These above texts have illustrated the constraint imposed upon Hebrew poetry concerning gapping, that *a marked constituent in the A-line cannot be gapped in the parallel B-line*. At the close of this chapter the reason for both this and the first constraint will be discussed.

7.2.7 Extended Parallelism

The next topic of inquiry is how pragmatic marking influences not just the B-line of a parallelism but further parallel lines extending beyond the basic bicolon. Three patterns are observable: (a) where the same essential markedness is found throughout all lines of the parallel structure, (b) where there is some variation visible in the medial line or lines, and (c) where there is some variation visible in the final line.

(a) IDENTICAL ORDERING

Here each colon in a whole series of parallel cola shows the same marked constituent order. This may be seen in three-line extended parallelisms, four-line, and larger:

Psalm 89:16b–17 (Basic structure: M V // M V // M V)

O YHWH, in the light of your countenance they walk;	יְהוָה בְּאוֹר־פָּנֶיךָ יְהַלֵּכוּן:	A
in your name they exult all day long,	בְּשִׁמְךָ יְגִילוּן כָּל־הַיּוֹם	B
and in your righteousness they exult.	וּבְצִדְקָתְךָ יָרוּמוּ:	C

Psalm 145:6–7 (Basic structure: O V // O V // O V // O V)

They shall proclaim the might of your awesome deeds,	וֶעֱזוּז נוֹרְאֹתֶיךָ יֹאמֵרוּ	A
and I will relate your greatness.	[וּגְדוּלָּתְךָ] אֲסַפְּרֶנָּה:	B
They shall celebrate the remembrance of your abundant goodness,	זֵכֶר רַב־טוּבְךָ יַבִּיעוּ	C
And they shall sing aloud of your righteousness.	וְצִדְקָתְךָ יְרַנֵּנוּ	D

---

40 Craigie speaks of verses 10 and 11 as 'contrasting', *Psalms 1–50*, p. 273. NIV REB NJB NLT TEV NCV CEV all connect the two verses with 'but'.

41 Identical to the information structure of Psalms 9:7–8 (4.2.5) and 31:7 (4.3).

Song 2:10b–13 (Basic structure: S V // S V // S V // S V // S V // S V // S V)

Arise, my love, my fair one,	קוּמִי לָךְ רַעְיָתִי יָפָתִי	
and come away;	וּלְכִי־לָךְ:	
for see the winter is past,	כִּי־הִנֵּה [הַסְּתָיו] עָבָר	A
the rain is over and gone.	הַגֶּשֶׁם חָלַף הָלַךְ לוֹ:	B
The flowers appear on the earth;	הַנִּצָּנִים נִרְאוּ בָאָרֶץ	C
the time of singing has come,	עֵת הַזָּמִיר הִגִּיעַ	D
and the voice of the dove is heard in our land.	וְקוֹל הַתּוֹר נִשְׁמַע בְּאַרְצֵנוּ:	E
The fig tree puts forth its figs,	הַתְּאֵנָה חָנְטָה פַגֶּיהָ	F
and the vines in blossom give fragrance.	וְהַגְּפָנִים סְמָדַר נָתְנוּ רֵיחַ	G
Arise, my love, my fair one,	קוּמִי [לָךְ] רַעְיָתִי יָפָתִי	
and come away.	וּלְכִי־לָךְ:	

Isaiah 51:6cde (Basic structure: S M V // S M V // S M V)

for the heavens will vanish like smoke,	כִּי־שָׁמַיִם כֶּעָשָׁן נִמְלָחוּ	A
the earth will wear out like a garment,	וְהָאָרֶץ כַּבֶּגֶד תִּבְלֶה	B
and those who live on it will die like flies.[42]	וְיֹשְׁבֶיהָ כְּמוֹ־כֵן יְמוּתוּן	C

Our discussion of extended MKD parallelisms will centre upon a consideration of the form rather than the pragmatic function of the markedness. A sufficiently diverse number of examples of the latter have been dealt with earlier in this chapter. In the above texts the marked elements of the two passages from the psalms are to be taken as specifying focus in both cases. The parallelism from the Song 2:10–13 is the lengthiest example of its kind appearing in the data. It is composed of a series of no less than seven SV-clauses. The content of these lines points to their being event-reporting clauses of the sentence-focus type. We further observe, in passing, the inclusio[43] (v. 10b, v. 13c), repeated verbatim at the beginning and end, neatly framing the whole parallel structure.[44] The final example, from Isaiah 51, serves to illustrate how, similar to the case of two-line parallelisms, those extended parallelisms showing two fronted elements in the A-line, position the same two elements preverbally in the second and following lines also.

(b) MEDIAL VARIATION

An alternative way of constructing parallelisms with a marked base-line is

---

42 כְּמוֹ־כֵן may also be interpreted as meaning 'in like manner' (LXX NASB NKJV).
43 Cf. Wendland, *Analyzing the Psalms*, pp. 101–02.
44 This passage is treated at length by Watson (*Classical Hebrew Poetry*, pp. 368–71). He makes apposite remarks regarding its balanced structure, certain phonological features, various poetic devices, and the use of rare vocabulary, but overlooks entirely the significance of the SV word order.

not to reproduce the same basic sequence in all lines, but to vary the pattern in the medial colon/cola of the structure and then return to the form of the base-line in the final colon. This variation of the medial line(s) could be done in a variety of ways: through gapping, through a clause displaying a different form of markedness, or even through a clause that is to all appearances canonical in form:

Isaiah 50:6 (Basic structure: O V M // O M // O V M)

A	גֵּוִי נָתַתִּי לְמַכִּים	I gave my back to those who struck me,
B	וּלְחָיַי לְמֹרְטִים	and my cheeks to those who pulled out my beard,
C	פָּנַי לֹא הִסְתַּרְתִּי מִכְּלִמּוֹת וָרֹק:	I did not hide my face from shame and spitting.

Here lines A and C both consist of OV-clauses. In the medial colon B the verb has been gapped,[45] yet the initial constituent in the B-line remains that which corresponds to the fronted elements in A and C. Each of these marked object phrases relates to part of the speaker's body (his 'back', 'cheek', and 'face') which had suffered abuse. This verse presents instances of specifying focus in the NPs. Another example of a slightly different kind is:

Psalm 40:7 (Basic structure: O O V // O V M // O O V)

A	זֶבַח וּמִנְחָה לֹא־חָפַצְתָּ	Sacrifice and offering you do not desire,
B	אָזְנַיִם כָּרִיתָ לִּי	you have given me an open ear.
C	עוֹלָה וַחֲטָאָה לֹא שָׁאָלְתָּ׃	Burnt offering and sin offering you have not required.

Again the B-line differs from A and C. Here it is further to be observed that the medial line does not correspond so closely semantically as do the outer two lines, which resemble each other in both meaning and syntax. All lines contain a fronted object phrase but, while A and C consist of negated clauses regarding the non-desirability of sacrifice, B states positively the desirability of personal commitment and obedience to God.[46]

The medial line in the following example shows a more radical departure from the order of the marked A-line:

Psalm 46:10bcd (Basic structure: O V // V O // O V)

A	קֶשֶׁת יְשַׁבֵּר	He breaks the bow,
B	וְקִצֵּץ חֲנִית	and shatters the spear;
C	עֲגָלוֹת יִשְׂרֹף בָּאֵשׁ׃	he burns the chariots[47] with fire.

---

45 See 7.2.6 above.
46 Cf. Harman, *Psalms*, p. 174; Kidner, *Psalms 1–72*, p. 159.
47 Some understand עֲגָלוֹת to mean 'shields' (cf. NRSV NIV NJB NLT).

These lines provide specific details after the general proposition (v. 10a), 'He [God] makes wars cease to the end of the earth' (מַשְׁבִּית מִלְחָמוֹת עַד־קְצֵה הָאָרֶץ). Following this now presupposed information, verse 10bcd sandwiches a seemingly canonical clause (B) between two that are marked (AC). Semantically and syntactically all three lines have similar components, that is, a piece of military equipment ('bow', 'spear', 'chariot') as the direct object of a verb of destruction ('break', 'shatter', 'burn'). In this case we argue that the VO-clause in the B-line is not actually but only apparently canonical. Since the usual constraint in MKD parallel cola is that the markedness of the A-line will reappear in B, if this verse were composed of only two lines the same OV order would be expected in B, as in 7.2.1 (b) above. However, as this parallelism extends beyond two lines to three, it is in colon C that the marked form of A reappears and the constraint enforced. In the situation of such extended parallelism, we argue, the medial line, being merely transitionary, may deviate from the marked order found in A. The motivation for this word-order in the medial line, it is suggested, is that of defamiliarisation. Although the VO-clause of colon B is canonical in form, the A-line, together with C, has established the fact that we are looking at pragmatic marking in the object phrases. This markedness is doubtless to be accepted as true of the whole parallelism, even though the medial line does not show it in its surface form. The particular ordering of the B-line in this case, we suggest, is not due to matters of pragmatics, but rather is simply a variation from the order of A, which in this context is allowable in that the marked order of A is restored in C, following the temporary departure from it in B. So taking all things into consideration, it is more accurate in such contexts as these to label the medial clause as DEF rather than CAN, since its form is a manifestation of poetic defamiliarisation (i.e., departure from the norm[48]) rather than a question of pragmatic non-markedness. Psalm 46:10 we therefore interpret as MKD//DEF//MKD.[49]

Psalm 89:34–35 (Basic structure: O V^{Ng} // V^{Ng} M // V^{Ng} M // O V^{Ng})

[But] I will not remove from him	וְחַסְדִּי לֹא־אָפִיר מֵעִמּוֹ	A
my steadfast love,	וְלֹא־אֲשַׁקֵּר בֶּאֱמוּנָתִי׃	B

---

48 The 'norm', or established pattern, in this context is marked.
49 In effect, the same dynamics are operative in the medial colon of such marked parallelisms as in unmarked. Just as the medial colon in a CAN//DEF//CAN parallelism (such as Ps. 94:23) is not of itself pragmatically significant, neither is the medial colon in a marked parallelism. In both instances the pragmatic component of the medial line is determined by its base-line (A). The only difference is that in the case of a marked parallelism, following the medial deviation there must be a return to the markedness of the A-line, this being the effect of the constraint, while in an unmarked parallelism it is optional whether the ensuing line is CAN or DEF.

or be false to my faithfulness.	לֹא־אֲחַלֵּל בְּרִיתִי	C
I will not violate my covenant,	וּמוֹצָא שְׂפָתַי לֹא אֲשַׁנֶּה׃	D
or alter the word that went forth from my lips.		

This four-line example, presenting a contrast, resembles the foregoing in that it departs from the marked order to what is formally a canonically ordered clause, though in this case two medial lines, B and C, occur before reverting to the same marked order in D as in A. This confirms the idea that the particular ordering of the medial lines is merely a temporary deviation before the original order is restored. The above parallelism could not be left hanging as a MKD//CAN//CAN arrangement. Such a pattern, like the two-line MKD//CAN, is never found in general distribution in the data. In view of the discussion on the previous verse this parallel tetracolon is labelled MKD//DEF//DEF//MKD.

(c) FINAL VARIATION

It is not infrequently the case that these extended synonymous structures consist of a series of parallel lines which are brought to a closure with a clause that is distinct in some way from those preceding, as seen in the following two passages:

Psalm 132:15–16 (Basic structure: O V // O V // O V // S V)

I will abundantly bless its provisions;	צֵידָהּ בָּרֵךְ אֲבָרֵךְ	A
I will satisfy its poor with bread.	אֶבְיוֹנֶיהָ אַשְׂבִּיעַ לָחֶם׃	B
Its priests I will clothe with salvation,	וְכֹהֲנֶיהָ אַלְבִּישׁ יֶשַׁע	C
and its faithful will shout for joy.	וַחֲסִידֶיהָ רַנֵּן יְרַנֵּנוּ	D

Isaiah 44:5 (Basic structure: $S^{Pn} V ... // S^{Pn} V ... // S^{Pn} V ... // M V$)

This one will say, 'I belong to YHWH',	זֶה יֹאמַר לַיהוָה אָנִי	A
this one will be called by the name of Jacob,	וְזֶה יִקְרָא בְשֵׁם־יַעֲקֹב	B
this one will write on his hand,	וְזֶה יִכְתֹּב יָדוֹ לַיהוָה	C
'Belonging to YHWH',	וּבְשֵׁם יִשְׂרָאֵל יְכַנֶּה׃	D
and will surname himself by the name of Israel.		

In the first example there is a change of grammatical role in the fronted constituent. The first three lines all place the NP[DO] in the initial position, while the concluding colon D has a NP[Su]. In the second example the $S^{Pn} V$ of lines A–C switches to M V in the final colon. What is observed in these extended parallelisms is a common poetic device for closure, that is, to vary the structure in the final element to signal that the unit has come to an end.[50]

---

50 Cf. Wendland, *Discourse Perspectives on Hebrew Poetry*, p. 13.

In the lengthy example given above from Song 2 it was the presence of inclusio that performed the same function.

In this connection we note that five instances exist in the data where the closing colon of a marked extended parallelism is canonical in appearance. This feature should occasion no surprise in that the situation parallels that of medial cola previously discussed. In such medial lines it was observed above that they could depart from the form of the base-line in a number of ways, among which were the use of a different marked order, or even a switch to an apparently canonical form. In the same way, the signalling of closure following a series of marked parallel lines might be performed either by a variation in the marked sequence, as seen in the foregoing two examples, or by a colon containing a seemingly canonical clause in which the expected markedness is absent. This latter can be seen in the following text:

Psalm 55:5-6 (Basic structure: S V // S V // S V // V S)

My heart is in anguish within me,	לִבִּי יָחִיל בְּקִרְבִּי	A
the terrors of death have fallen upon me.	וְאֵימוֹת מָוֶת נָפְלוּ עָלָי:	B
Fear and trembling come upon me,	יִרְאָה וָרַעַד יָבֹא בִי	C
and horror overwhelms me.	וַתְּכַסֵּנִי פַּלָּצוּת:	D

Here lines A–C contain a series of SV-clauses, while D, the final line, rounds off the unit with a VS-clause. The other places in the data where parallelisms with similar closure occur are Psalm 40:11 (tricolon), Psalm 143:11-12 (tetracolon), Isaiah 57:5-6 (hexacolon), and Job 14:18-19 (tetracolon). In each of these five cases, it is significant that *all* of the preceding lines display marked word order. It is only the final line that differs. It is precisely this difference that gives the colon its concluding effect. Though CAN in form it is in fact defamiliar in that it departs from the expected order, which is MKD in the context in which it appears. This colon-type no longer has the pragmatic function of indicating information structure, which has been repeatedly set forth in the preceding cola of the parallelism, but the discourse function of unit-closure. Since to fulfil this function it must of necessity depart from the norm it is interpreted in this context as a DEF colon.

To conclude our analysis of extended MKD parallelisms we may state the following:

(1) The parallel arrangements found in the data are: MKD//MKD//MKD, MKD//DEF//MKD, and MKD//MKD//DEF. In the latter two cases it is the return to the marked form in the final colon, or the fact that all the cola prior to the closing DEF are MKD, which are sufficient to establish the pragmatic organisation of the whole.

(2) Neither MKD//DEF//DEF nor MKD//DEF//MKD//DEF sequences ever

occur in the data.[51]

(3) In extended marked parallelisms DEF colon-types, in order to differ from the marked form, may take on the appearance of CAN cola. Contextually, however, since they deviate from the anticipated form, they are to be regarded as defamiliar.

(4) These patterns do not fundamentally contradict the constraint that a MKD colon must be paralleled by one that is equally MKD. In fact the consistent return to the marked order following a medial deviation from it confirms the force of the constraint.

7.3 The Co-Occurrence of Pragmatic Marking and Poetic Defamiliarisation

On a small number of occasions the word order of a parallelism manifests both pragmatic marking and defamiliarised reordering *in the same clause*. In such instances the constraint regarding marked word order is still upheld, it only being *after* the focal elements that the defamiliarisation takes place. This is illustrated in the following text:

Isaiah 65:25ab

The wolf and the lamb will graze together,   זְאֵב וְטָלֶה יִרְעוּ כְאֶחָד
the lion will eat straw like the ox.   וְאַרְיֵה כַּבָּקָר יֹאכַל־תֶּבֶן

This parallelism has the basic order SVM//SMVO. In its context it forms part of a prophecy relating to the new heavens and new earth (v. 17). The oracle describes the transformed conditions of life that will exist at that time. Verse 25ab is composed of two SV-clauses. The reason for this focus structure may be due to the fact that they are reporting future events or, alternatively, the contents of this verse may be framed in the form of a proverb, and proverbial parallelisms, we recall,[52] are commonly structured as SV//SV. Watts' remark that 'wolf' and 'lamb' are 'proverbial opposites'[53] lends support to this latter view.[54] In either case the focus structure would

---

51 That is, in general distribution. See the discussion of the specially constructed Isaiah 45:12–13 (MKD//DEF//MKD//DEF) in 8.2.2 (b).
52 Cf. 7.2.1 (a) above.
53 Watts, *Isaiah 34–66*, p. 355.
54 It is not without interest that the very similar verse of Isaiah 11:7 ('The cow and the bear shall graze, their young shall lie down together; and the lion shall eat straw like the ox', NRSV) has a closely related structure to 65:25. In the former we find a tricolon of the basic pattern SVM//VS//SMVO, that is, with a medial colon which departs from the markedness of the other two lines, creating a MKD//DEF//MKD arrangement. We note that there also in lines A and C (line C being identical to 65:25b) the switch from VM to MV occurs following the same positioning of the subject constituent at the beginning of the clause.

be sentence focus. In this parallelism both clauses place the subject phrase in the initial position, while the M element, which in each line takes the form of a PP with -בְּ, is placed postverbally in the A-line but preverbally in B. That this difference in position is significant from a pragmatic perspective cannot easily be maintained. Arguably this is simple poetic variation in the B-line. The A-line places the M constituent in its proper unmarked place, and B makes a variation as an expression of defamiliarisation seen elsewhere in parallel lines. But it is a notable fact that this occurs only after the marked subject phrase has been placed in the same position as in the A-line. In other words, the focus structure is given priority, and only once this is done can defamiliarisation occur with the remaining unfocused constituents.

It is perhaps not merely coincidental that, with one exception (Ps. 44:9), all of the verses discovered in the selected data containing parallelisms of the type described above are located in the book of Isaiah (44:16; 61:11; 64:9; 65:25; 66:3–4). Evidently this more involved form of marked parallelism was particular to the style of this author.

7.4 Exceptions to the Constraint

There are certain words and phrases which do not conform to the principle established in this chapter, that a pragmatically marked element will have a corresponding marked element in a parallel B-line. These exceptions fall into two basic kinds: *settings* and *pronominal forms*.

7.4.1 Phrases of Setting

At the close of chapter 3 mention was made of those pre-sentential elements which most scholars in the field do not reckon as belonging to the same category as marked focal and topical constituents.[55] There it was seen how these opening phrases simply have the function of orientation or providing the setting in which the following utterance is to be framed. As stated in that earlier chapter, setting is not as common in poetry as it is in narrative. Yet when it does occur in a poetic parallelism, the important thing to note is that since it is not to be considered as marked, it is not repeated in the parallel line(s).

(a) TEMPORAL

Psalm 18:7ab

When in anguish I called upon YHWH; בַּצַּר־לִי אֶקְרָא יְהוָה
to my God I cried for help. וְאֶל־אֱלֹהַי אֲשַׁוֵּעַ

---

55 See 3.5.

The opening בְּצַר־לִי is given to indicate the time or occasion in which the psalmist called upon the Lord. It does not function to introduce a topic, nor is it in this context a focal element. It is noteworthy that in the Masoretic punctuation, this sentence-initial phrase is separated from what follows by the disjunctive accent *məhuppāk̲ ləg̲armēh*:

בַּצַּר־לִ֨י ׀ אֶקְרָ֣א יְהוָה֮ וְאֶל־אֱלֹהַ֪י אֲשַׁ֫וֵּ֥עַ

Accompanying this accent is the vertical stroke *pāsēq* (|), which serves to highlight further the separation of the phrase from what follows.[56] What does follow can then be seen to be a typical asymmetrical parallelism consisting of VM//MV, based upon a canonical A-line. This text has, therefore, been entered in the data as CAN//DEF.

(b) SPATIAL

Psalm 137:3

| For there our captors asked us for songs, | כִּ֤י שָׁ֨ם שְֽׁאֵל֪וּנוּ שׁוֹבֵ֡ינוּ דִּבְרֵי־שִׁ֗יר |
| and our tormentors asked for mirth. | וְתוֹלָלֵ֥ינוּ שִׂמְחָ֑ה |

This text contains another example of the same setting function, this time spatial. The initial locative adverb, or an equivalent, is not reproduced in the B-line. In his treatment of fronted elements in Hebrew poetry, Gross takes pains to point out that שָׁם merely functions as a deictic particle to establish a link ('Anknüpfung') between what follows with what precedes.[57] He excludes the adverb from being marked.[58] Gross offers indirect support to our observations on the non-compliance of שָׁם with the constraint established concerning the repetition of marked constituents in parallelisms. Since it is not pragmatically marked there need be no matching element in the B-line.[59] Following the opening שָׁם we find a typical parallelism of the form VSO//SO, showing a canonical A-line and the gapping of the verb in B.

7.4.2 Pronominal Forms

Besides these sentence orienters there are certain other clausal components which do not follow the rule by having a matching element reappear in the

---

56 Though no sure guide in itself, the Masoretic accents do lend support to the view that such temporal and spatial orienters are in some way distinct from the rest of the sentence.
57 See Gross, *Doppelt besetztes Vorfeld*, pp. 189–90, 311.
58 Though it is possible that context or the use of focus particle may demand putting a marked construction upon שָׁם. See the discussion of Psalm 139:10 in 8.2.1.
59 There is perhaps some significance in the fact that for several occurrences of sentence-initial שָׁם the Masoretic separator *pāsēq* is also employed, as in Psalm 18:7 above, to demarcate it from the main clause. See Psalms 14:5; 53:6; 122:5; 133:3.

parallel line. These are all proforms of various kinds, whether independent or affixed to prepositions.

(a) INDEPENDENT PRONOMINAL SUBJECT

The most prevalent exception to the constraint is when the preverbal element in the A-line takes the form of Pn[Su]. Where this occurs it is typical, though by no means universal,[60] that the pronoun will not be repeated in the parallel line(s). There are numerous instances of this. For example:

Psalm 9:9
He it is who will judge the world with justice;   וְהוּא יִשְׁפֹּט־תֵּבֵל בְּצֶדֶק
he will judge the peoples with equity.   יָדִין לְאֻמִּים בְּמֵישָׁרִים:

Psalm 71:22
I also will praise you with the harp   גַּם־אֲנִי אוֹדְךָ בִכְלִי־נֶבֶל
For your faithfulness, O my God;   אֲמִתְּךָ אֱלֹהָי
I will sing praises to you with the lyre,   אֲזַמְּרָה לְךָ בְכִנּוֹר
O Holy One of Israel.   קְדוֹשׁ יִשְׂרָאֵל:

Psalm 24:2
For it was he who founded it on the seas   כִּי־הוּא עַל־יַמִּים יְסָדָהּ
and established it on the waters.   וְעַל־נְהָרוֹת יְכוֹנְנֶהָ:

The first text has the structure S^{Pn} VOM//VOM. With the exception of the initial Pn[Su] the two cola are virtually identical in meaning and syntax. The second text has the focus particle and pronoun, גַּם־אֲנִי, in the A-line but neither in B. In the third text two preverbal elements are present in the A-line, S^{Pn}MV. The pronoun is not repeated in the B-line but the second marked element remains in the fronted position, MV-o. In both Psalm 9:9 and 24:2 we follow the REB in its rendering of the focal pronoun הוּא, 'He it is who' and 'it was he who'.[61] Psalm 71:22 has definite additive connotations.[62]

(b) INDEPENDENT PRONOMINAL OBJECT

Much less frequently it is a fronted Pn[DO] that occurs only in the A-line of a parallelism, as in:

Isaiah 57:11a–d
A   Whom did you dread and fear   וְאֶת־מִי דָּאַגְתְּ וַתִּירְאִי
B   that you have been false?   כִּי תְכַזֵּבִי

---

60 E.g., Psalm 33:9, where הוּא is repeated.
61 The NJB is the only other English version consulted that also attempts to bring out the force of the focus structure in both verses.
62 For additive or expanding focus, see 3.4.2 (e) and 4.2.1 (a) – (b).

C	וְאוֹתִי לֹא זָכַרְתְּ
D	לֹא־שַׂמְתְּ עַל־לִבֵּךְ

And me you did not remember
nor give a thought?

Here lines CD form a parallelism, yet only the base-line (C) has the preverbal object pronoun אוֹתִי. This is clearly pragmatically marked. In this verse God, through his prophet, is rebuking Israel for fearing others more than himself,[63] resulting in their infidelity to him. Implicit in these four lines is the idea that the Israelites had stood in dread of others, but not of God, whom they ought to have feared above all. This contrast is made explicit in the NJPS rendering, 'But you gave no thought to Me'. Although in the parallel line (D) the 1st person object 'me', referring to God, is clearly intended, the pronoun is not repeated in the Hebrew.[64]

(c) PRONOMINAL PREPOSITIONAL PHRASE

On several occasions a sentence-initial PP with a pronominal suffix occurs only at the beginning of the A-line of the parallelism. For instance:

Psalm 69:8

It is for your sake that I have borne reproach,	כִּי־עָלֶיךָ נָשָׂאתִי חֶרְפָּה
that shame has covered my face.	כִּסְּתָה כְלִמָּה פָנָי:

Isaiah 57:6cd

... even to them you have poured out a drink offering,	גַּם־לָהֶם שָׁפַכְתְּ נֶסֶךְ
you have brought a grain offering.	הֶעֱלִית מִנְחָה

Both the above examples consist of close semantic and syntactic parallels, excepting the initial PP. In the first text the fact that the speaker had borne reproach is presuppositional information, as is evident from the preceding verses of the psalm (especially v. 5). The focus of the sentence is that it was for God's sake that he experienced this. In the Isaiah text the pronominal 'them' refers to the stones of the valley in 6ab, which are worshipped as 'idols' (NIV CEV).[65] The prophet says 'even to them' (NASB NKJV),[66] that is, the stones, the Israelites offered libations and grain-offerings. This is the use of גַּם with a connotation of contra-expectation.[67]

---

63 Cf. Watts, *Isaiah 34–66*, p. 259, 'Here apparently a greater *dread* has replaced it [the fear of Yahweh] and made apostasy possible'.
64 The translators of Isaiah in the LXX do in fact repeat the pronoun: οὐδὲ ἔλαβές με εἰς τὴν διάνοιαν. It is also added in several English versions (e.g., NRSV NASB REB).
65 Or 'gods' (TEV); cf. Ibn Ezra,'והטעם שיבקשו אבנים חלקים לציירם להיות פסילי ('The sense is that they seek smooth stones to shape them into idols'), M. Friedländer, *The Commentary of Ibn Ezra on Isaiah* (New York: Philipp Feldheim, 1873), p. 98 (Hebrew section).
66 Cf. Oswalt, *The Book of Isaiah 40–66*, p. 473.
67 This agrees with the sense of the phrase גַּם־שָׁם in verse 7 of the chapter.

From the foregoing examples it would be hard to deny that, unlike phrases of setting, these pronominal expressions are genuinely pragmatically marked. For what reason then is the constraint regarding markedness not enforced in such cases? If one were to venture an answer to this question, it might lie in the tendency of Hebrew poetry to avoid exact repetition in parallel lines. Since a pronoun is simply a deictic particle, i.e., it refers to a participant, there is no possibility of varying this in the B-line. Repetition of the identical proform is the only option. The same holds true for those PPs with pronominal affix. It would be difficult to imagine how the author could provide poetically parallel phrases for כִּי־עָלֶיךָ and גַּם־לָהֶם. This situation, we suggest, is similar to the avoidance of the repetition of the focus particles themselves, as noted above.[68] These, unlike verbs, nouns, and adjectives, all belong to a closed set of lexical items. We note in passing that other sentence-initial bound forms, such as conjunctions and interrogatives, are not reproduced in parallelisms. So it would appear that since in the cases mentioned the only option for the B-line would be a verbatim repetition, it is preferable that the whole phrase is dropped.

It should be emphasised before concluding this section that apart from the non-repetition of the independent subject pronoun, which is reasonably common, the other two exceptions are only of minor consequence in that each occurs an amount of times (less than ten) that is incomparable to the total number of instances where the constraints for markedness are applied.

7.5 Reason for the Constraints

In our earlier investigation of parallelisms having a canonical base-line (chapter 5) the issue of constraints was wholly absent. There the opposite feature of freedom was a major characteristic of the B-line. This was true with respect to both two-line and extended parallel structures. The present chapter has demonstrated that the same freedom does not exist when the parallelism is founded upon a marked base-line. Where such a circumstance applies, the Hebrew poet was much more limited in the options available to him. Marked constituent order in the A-line had extensive implications with regard to the construction of parallel lines. Two results of our investigation are that defamiliarised word order may only be located in medial or final cola of extended parallelisms or, in the case of a very small number of texts, following the placement of a parallel marked element clause-initially in the B-line. Both of these are noticeably restricted in comparison with the defamiliarisation observable in canonically based parallelisms.

---

68 7.2.4.

The question arises as to why it is that markedness produces these constraints upon the formation of parallelisms. The answer obviously is closely bound up with the nature of markedness. In a canonical line there is nothing of special pragmatic significance to which attention is drawn. Pragmatically speaking, the word order is not marking anything as being salient or focused. Where a parallel line is subjoined to this manner of base-line, there is no pragmatic component of the A-line the markedness of which the B-line needs to reinforce. Seeing the A-line lacks marked word order, the B-line itself need not be concerned with matters of markedness. Whereas, if the base-line is marked, the parallel line has a role to play. The repetition of the same marked order in the B-line indicates that the word order of the A-line is unusual in some way. Reproducing the same essential markedness draws attention to the special pragmatic import of the A-line. Further, if marked word order were accompanied by distinctive pitch prominence, as Shimasaki claims,[69] then there would be a cogent prosodic justification for preserving the same word order and thus the same pitch pattern in the parallel line.

The foregoing also has obvious relevance to the non-gapping of marked elements from the B-line. These fronted constituents, as prominent indicators of the information structure, could not possibly be elided,[70] and, assuming the correctness of Shimasaki's claims, they would be required as bearers of the prominent pitch.

We see then that the constraints imposed upon marked parallelisms are to be perceived as functional. They serve to highlight the special pragmatic implications inherent in the base-line, which would not be present if that line were canonical. Hence in the former case repetition is the operative principle, and in the latter the option of non-repetition, that is, freedom either to repeat or to reorder.

7.6 Summary

In this treatment of marked parallelisms the two principal conclusions reached were: (1) The B-line will be ordered according to the markedness of the A-line. (2) In the event of gapping only elements not occupying the marked position may be omitted from the B-line. These conclusions were formulated into the two following constraints:

---

69 See the discussion in 6.3.
70 In the context we draw attention to the words of Lambrecht (*Information Structure*, p. 224) 'A constituent in focus can by definition not be omitted without depriving the utterance of some or all of its information value'.

1. A parallelism with a marked A-line will also have an equally marked B-line.

2. A marked constituent in the A-line cannot be gapped in a parallel B-line.

In addition, the data showed that extended parallelisms may depart from the opening marked line, either medially, in a transitional line, before returning to the original marked form, or finally, employing the deviation from the norm as a rhetorical signalling of closure. In both cases apparently canonical clauses may be found, though in the context of a marked parallelism these are more appropriately reckoned as defamiliar since they are not the form expected.

A number of exceptions to the constraints were considered. Besides the non-repetition of temporal and spatial settings, the chief of these is the single occurrence of the independent subject pronoun in the base-line only, and the same to a lesser degree with respect to other pronominal forms.

Finally, a justification for the two constraints was proposed. In the context of a marked base-line, the same order in the parallel line serves to underline the special word order. This means preserving focused constituents in their marked position.

CHAPTER 8

Discourse Functions of Unusual Colon Arrangements

There is a small proportion of the data that does agree with certain of the conclusions reached in the preceding chapters. This present chapter examines those colon patterns that do not behave according to what has previously been prescribed, and seeks to provide an explanation for these forms.

8.1 Introduction: Reversal of the Norm

It has been stated with respect to parallelisms that a DEF colon can only follow one that is CAN, and that a MKD A-line will be followed by a B-line that is equally MKD. This is to say, that poetic defamiliarisation only occurs where the base-line of the parallelism is canonical, while a marked base-line will retain the same markedness of word order in its parallel line. These conclusions hold true for the overwhelming majority of poetic parallelisms. In certain places, however, the various established patterns disappear and the constraints no longer apply. These, as shall shortly be demonstrated, do not disprove the theories advanced concerning word order in parallelisms. What has been argued so far, as has been stressed on several occasions, has reference to those parallelisms occurring in 'universal distribution',[1] that is, those structures that are found in any point within the poetic text. The divergent structures we now consider are seen to have a noticeably different distribution. This is what was earlier termed 'specific distribution',[2] the precise meaning of which will become apparent as we proceed. Such parallel constructions, we shall discover, possess special functions at a higher level of discourse.

In addition to unusually formed parallelisms we shall also examine the even smaller number of DEF cola which occur outside of parallelisms. These latter, it shall be shown, perform similar functions to the former.

8.2 Rare Parallel Constructions in Specific Distribution

We shall examine the occurrences of each of the following unusual forms of parallelism:

---

1 See 5.6.
2 *Ibid.*

1. DEF-initial parallelisms: DEF//CAN, DEF//DEF, DEF//Gap, and DEF//Nom.
2. MKD-initial parallelisms: MKD//CAN, MKD//DEF and MKD//Gap.
3. Gap-initial parallelisms: Gap//DEF, Gap//MKD, and Gap//CAN.

Each of these arrangements departs from those common patterns, CAN//CAN, CAN//DEF, and MKD//MKD, described in the foregoing chapters.

8.2.1 DEF-Initial Parallelisms

In these parallelisms the A-line may be labelled DEF (rather than MKD) for one or both of the following reasons: (1) the absence of any presuppositions derivable from the context requiring the fronted element(s) to be taken as marking a pragmatic function; (2) the particular character of the word-order variation involved. By this latter we mean that the first line of a parallelism is more probably to be interpreted as DEF if it has the form OSV, MSV, OMV, or MOV, sequences which are rare in pragmatically marked contexts in Hebrew narrative.[3] SOV or SMV, on the other hand, are much more common in narrative texts and therefore when occurring in poetry could be either DEF or MKD with equal probability. The contextual factor, i.e., whether there are pragmatic implications or not, is of greater importance in such cases for determining the colon-type. Generally speaking, the above two considerations are sufficient to remove any ambiguity. As far as we are concerned in this present chapter, however, the difference is only of minor practical significance since DEF//CAN and MKD//CAN both share the basic out-of-the-ordinary non-CAN//CAN sequence, and, as shall be seen, both possess identical discourse functions.

(a) DEF//CAN

The data reveals that on a limited number of occasions parallel bicola appear having the form DEF//CAN. This is the reverse of the usual manner of defamiliarisation in parallelisms. In effect the typical A//B parallelism has become B//A.

Just 40 instances of DEF//CAN are attested out of over 1,300 verbal-clause parallelisms in the data.[4] This is the most common of the DEF-initial arrangements, the other such forms, discussed subsequently, occurring far

---

3   Reading through the historical books from Joshua to 2 Kings, we find that these clausal forms are virtually non-existent. Marked clauses with two preverbal constituents, when they do occur, are generally SMV or SOV. Cf. Gesenius, *Hebrew Grammar*, §142 *f*, where all the SOV examples are from poetry, and OSV is listed as 'very rarely', with only one example from narrative (2 Kgs. 5:13).
4   This figure includes parallelisms of all forms involving verbal clauses, whether between two verbal clauses, or between a verbal clause and a non-verbal, such as a participial or noun-clause. This figure of 40 has to be compared with 330 CAN//DEF parallelisms.

less often. The departure from the commonly found patterns of parallelism alerts us to the fact that these constructions are significant in some way. This significance can be ascertained by an examination of the surrounding context in which these verses occur. We discover that the irregular form in which these parallelisms are cast has a specific function at the discourse-level, and not at the inter-clausal level as is typically the case with pragmatically marked constituents. In the majority of cases, the DEF//CAN parallelism coincides with a textual boundary, whether the opening of a new unit, which we call *aperture*, or the end of a unit, generally termed *closure*:

Ref.	Form	Function	Versions & Commentaries
Ps. 5:2	OV[Voc]//VO	Aperture [Chiasm]	First verse in psalm
Ps. 5:8	[S^{Pn}]MVO//VMM	Aperture	NRSV NIV NKJV ESV REB NJPS TEV NLT NCV CEV Terrien Craigie Kraus Anderson Kidner Delitzsch
Ps. 29:10	SMV//VSM	Aperture	NRSV NIV NASB NKJV ESV TEV NCV CEV Terrien Craigie Anderson Kidner Delitzsch
Ps. 37:14	OVS//VO	Aperture [Chiasm]	NRSV NIV ESV REB NJB TEV NLT Terrien Craigie
Ps. 38:3	CSVM//VMS	Closure[5]	NRSV NKJV ESV TEV NLT CEV Delitzsch
Ps. 38:11	SV//VS//Nom	Closure [Tricolon]	NKJV NASB NJB CEV Terrien Kraus Harman Delitzsch
Ps. 68:23	MV//VM	Aperture	Onset of direct speech
Ps. 73:27	CHSV//VO	Aperture	NRSV NIV NKJV ESV NJB TEV NLT NCV CEV Terrien Tate Kraus Kidner Delitzsch

---

5   S. Terrien, *The Psalms: Strophic Structure and Theological Commentary* (Grand Rapids, Michigan: Eerdmans, 2003), p. 323, H.-J. Kraus, *Psalms 1–59* (Minneapolis: Augsburg, 1988), p. 411, A. A. Anderson, *The Book of Psalms*, NCB (London: Oliphants, 1972), vol. 1, p. 302, and Craigie, *Psalms 1–50*, p. 303, all take this as aperture.

Ps. 84:10	OV[Voc]//VO	Closure	NRSV NIV NKJV ESV NJPS NJB TEV NCV CEV Terrien Kraus Anderson Harman
Ps. 89:5	MVO//VMO *Selah*	Closure	NRSV NIV NASB ESV NKJV NJPS NJB TEV NLT NCV CEV Terrien Tate Kraus Kidner Harman Delitzsch
Ps. 90:2	CSV//VSS/MSComp	Closure [Tricolon]	NRSV NIV NASB ESV NKJV NJPS REB TEV NLT NCV CEV Terrien Tate Kraus Anderson Kidner Harman
Ps. 90:9	CSVM//VOM	Aperture[6]	NRSV ESV NJB TEV CEV Terrien Delitzsch
Ps. 91:13	MV//VM	Closure	NRSV NIV NKJV ESV NJPS NJB REB TEV NLT NCV CEV Tate Kraus Anderson Kidner Harman Delitzsch
Ps. 91:16	MV//VM	Closure	Last verse in psalm
Ps. 111:9	OVM//VMO/CompS	Closure[7] [Tricolon]	NIV NCV CEV Kraus Harman
Is. 40:3	MVO//VMOM	Aperture	Opens direct speech
Is. 43:9	SVM//VS	Aperture	NJPS
Is. 48:21	OMVM//VOVS	Closure	NRSV NIV NKJV ESV NJPS REB TEV NLT NCV Motyer
Is. 49:18	CSMV//VM	Closure[8]	NRSV NIV NKJV ESV TEV NLT NCV CEV
Is. 51:11	SSV//VSS	Closure [Chiasm]	MT[ס] All English versions Oswalt Watts Motyer Young
Is. 66:2ab	OSV//VS	Closure נְאֻם־יְהוָה	NIV NJPS REB NLT NCV CEV Watts

---

6 NLT agrees it is a boundary, but a closure (and possibly Tate also, *Psalms 51–100*, p. 442).
7 This tricolon is made an opening boundary by NJB and Terrien (*Psalms*, p. 755).
8 Motyer, *The Prophecy of Isaiah*, p. 394, also considers verse 18 to mark a boundary, though he understands this to be the opening of a new section (as NJB).

Job 3:24	CMSV//VMS	Aperture	REB NJPS NJB
			Clines Gordis Alden
Job 4:12	MSV//VSOM[9]	Aperture	NRSV NIV NASB ESV NKJV NJPS REB TEV NLT NCV CEV
			Clines Hartley Pope Andersen Habel Alden Rowley
Prov. 2:19	SV//VO	Closure	NRSV NIV NKJV ESV NJPS REB NJB NLT NCV CEV
			Murphy Fox McKane Garrett Waltke
Prov. 2:22	[S]MV//[S]VM	Closure	Last verse in chapter
Prov. 3:11	O[Voc]V//VO	Aperture MT[ס]	NRSV NIV NKJV ESV NJB TEV NLT NCV CEV
			Murphy Fox Whybray Kidner
Prov. 3:19	[S]MVO//VOM	Aperture	NRSV NIV NKJV ESV NJPS NJB NLT NCV CEV
			Murphy Fox Whybray Garrett
Prov. 4:11	MV//VM	Aperture?	
			Fox
Prov. 4:14	MV//VM	Aperture	NKJV NLT
			Fox McKane Whybray Kidner Waltke
Prov. 4:25	[S]MV//[S]VM	Aperture?	NLT
			McKane

The above chart lists all 30 instances in the data where DEF//CAN is located at a textual boundary. In the right hand column is given supporting evidence for the presence of a division in the text according to the major English versions and commentators. At these points the translators and scholars recognise a thematic or logical break in the flow of the text. Where the versions are unanimous in their witness, 'All English versions' is written in the column, otherwise each version is listed separately. From the absence of a particular commentator it should not necessarily be inferred that he argues against the boundary at the point in question, but possibly he makes no comment upon it at all, or is unclear on this particular issue. Where the verse is the first or last verse in a psalm or chapter, or marks the onset of direct speech, this fact is noted without reference to the versions

---

9   The parallelism of this verse, though not recognised by some English translations, is effectively brought out by NJB: 'I have received a secret revelation, a whisper has come to my ears'.

and commentaries. The square brackets around a clause constituent, such as [S], denote a pragmatically marked element after which poetic defamiliarisation occurs.[10]

It is noteworthy that the DEF//CAN sequence, along with those similar rare colon patterns to be discussed below, often accompany other well established boundary-marking devices.[11] Scholars of Biblical Hebrew poetry have identified a whole range of devices employed by the psalmists and poets to divide their texts into shorter units. These include the vocative, the tricolon, chiasmus, the unit-initial independent pronoun (indicating a shift in topic), the quotation frame נְאֻם־יְהוָה and the occurrence of the psalmodic term סֶלָה (*selah*).[12] To these we may add the later manuscript abbreviations ס (סְתוּמָא, 'closed') and פ (פְּתוּחָא, 'opened'), which often coincide with recognised textual boundaries. These unusual parallelisms, we should stress, like all these other features, are not an obligatory marker of boundary, but optional. They are just one means among several available to the Hebrew poet to segment the song or poem.

For the most part the information contained in the chart speaks for itself. It is reasonable to suppose the presence of a textual boundary in almost every case. These unusual parallelisms occur text-initially and text-finally, and also text-medially, i.e., at the opening or close of a medial strophe in the psalm or poem, as illustrated in the following:

Job 4:11–13 [v. 12 Text-medial aperture]

The strong lion perishes for lack of prey,	Ptcp//DEF	לַיִשׁ אֹבֵד מִבְּלִי־טָרֶף
and the whelps of the lioness are scattered.		וּבְנֵי לָבִיא יִתְפָּרָדוּ׃
Now a word came stealing to me,	DEF//CAN	וְאֵלַי דָּבָר יְגֻנָּב
my ear received the whisper of it.		וַתִּקַּח אָזְנִי שֵׁמֶץ מֶנְהוּ׃
Amid thoughts from visions of the night,	Nom//Inf	בִּשְׂעִפִּים מֵחֶזְיֹנוֹת לָיְלָה
when deep sleep falls upon men ...		בִּנְפֹל תַּרְדֵּמָה עַל־אֲנָשִׁים׃

Here Eliphaz completes what, in his opinion, is a description of the doctrine of retribution (vv. 7–11), before launching into a report of the vision he claims to have received (vv. 12–21).[13] The DEF//CAN parallelism functions

---

10 On the co-occurrence of pragmatic and defamiliar factors, see 7.3.
11 For a comprehensive treatment of the various boundary-marking devices of Hebrew poetry, see Wendland, *The Discourse Analysis of Hebrew Prophetic Literature*, pp. 30–61; cf. Watson, *Classical Hebrew Poetry*, pp. 164, 183.
12 Cf. Craigie, *Psalms 1–50*, p. 76, '*Selah* ... is used sometimes at the end of sections which may be equivalent to strophes or stanzas ... sometimes at the end of a psalm'. Harman, *Psalms*, p. 76, claims that *Selah* 'always comes at the end of a section'. Watson, *Classical Hebrew Poetry*, p. 373, does not specify whether *selah* marks aperture or closure but simply states that it 'probably marks a major division'.
13 Here in 4:12 R. L. Alden describes Eliphaz as trying 'a new tack', *Job*, NAC (Nashville, Tennessee: Broadman & Holman, 1993), p.86.

to mark the commencement of a new unit within the larger discourse. While most of the texts in the above list are, like Job 4:12, self-evident cases of boundary, there are a few which warrant some explanatory comment.

Isaiah 40:3

A voice cries: קוֹל קוֹרֵא

'In the wilderness prepare a way for YHWH, בַּמִּדְבָּר פַּנּוּ דֶּרֶךְ יְהוָה

make straight in the desert a highway for our God'. יַשְּׁרוּ בָּעֲרָבָה מְסִלָּה לֵאלֹהֵינוּ׃

There are alternative ways of dividing the syntactic components of this verse. The Masoretic accentuation[14] and the majority of English versions understand it as translated above. The NKJV (following AV), however, makes בַּמִּדְבָּר part of the speech introduction: 'The voice of one crying in the wilderness'. The LXX, Vulg, and Syr all seem to understand it similarly. Such an analysis is possible, but unlikely. To construe the syntax in this way, although resulting in two verb-initial clauses (i.e., CAN//CAN), would destroy the obvious parallelism between the PPs בַּמִּדְבָּר ('in the wilderness') and בָּעֲרָבָה ('in the desert'), since the former would then be part of the speech introduction rather than the direct speech itself. These two phrases contain a common poetic word-pair. מִדְבָּר and עֲרָבָה are found elsewhere in parallel in the book of Isaiah in 35:1, 6; 41:19; 51:3, each time with מִדְבָּר in the first colon, and עֲרָבָה in the second. It is most probable, therefore, that בַּמִּדְבָּר is the opening word of the direct speech, forming a bicolon consisting of M V O // V M O M. This would be a DEF//CAN parallelism, having the function of marking a new beginning, here speech-onset.

Isaiah 43:9ab

Let all the nations gather together, כָּל־הַגּוֹיִם נִקְבְּצוּ יַחְדָּו

and let the peoples assemble. וְיֵאָסְפוּ לְאֻמִּים

Although for the most part the English versions do not place a boundary at this juncture, the NJPS does not make this an aperture without good cause. Verse 8 consists of a 2nd person singular command for God's people, i.e., Israel, to be brought forth. It is not until verse 10 that God actually addresses them (his words being introduced by the speech formula נְאֻם־יְהוָה). Between these two verse 9 clearly stands out as an independent unit, addressing in the 3rd person plural, not Israel, but the nations. It is the DEF//CAN parallelism of 9ab that marks the beginning of this separate six-line unit.

Proverbs 2:21–22

For the upright will dwell in the land, כִּי־יְשָׁרִים יִשְׁכְּנוּ־אָרֶץ A

and the blameless will remain in it; וּתְמִימִים יִוָּתְרוּ בָהּ׃ B

---

14 See Young, *Isaiah*, vol. 3, p. 27.

C	וּרְשָׁעִים מֵאֶרֶץ יִכָּרֵתוּ	but the wicked will be cut off from the land,
D	וּבוֹגְדִים יִסְּחוּ מִמֶּנָּה:	and the treacherous will be rooted out of it.

These two verses contain two parallelisms in a contrastive relationship. The basic constituent order consists of SVO//SVM/SMV//SVM. The first parallel bicolon comprises two SV-clauses concerning the upright. These latter, the author tells us, shall continue to live in the land. Not so with the wicked. These shall be removed from the land. The parallelism of verse 22 (CD) also places the contrasting topics, רְשָׁעִים and בּוֹגְדִים, in the fronted position, as is usual for such constructions. Yet there is one further difference. Like 21a (A), 22a (C) also makes mention of the 'land', and as in 21b (B), 22b (D) refers back to the 'land' of the A-line by means of a pronominal suffix attached to a preposition (מִמֶּנָּה). But the position of מֵאֶרֶץ in line D does not match the final position of the corresponding elements in the surrounding lines. The syntactic structure is SMV//SVM. What we observe here is, in fact, a rarity in Hebrew poetry. It is a parallelism that contains word-order variation due to both pragmatic marking *and* poetic defamiliarisation. Both factors are at play, though on separate clause constituents. The clause-initial position of the NP[Su]s in verse 22 is to be attributed to the contrastive connotations as described, but following these subject phrases 22a (C) inverts the expected VM sequence (from SVM to SMV). This is deliberate, rather than coincidental. The author creates a DEF//CAN parallelism with the remaining constituents following the pragmatically motivated placement of the marked elements. Its purpose is to signal a boundary, here closure, since verse 22 is the final verse of the chapter.[15] This structure of markedness followed by defamiliarisation in the A-line is extremely unusual. The only other occurrences in the data of this particular configuration are Psalm 44:6 and Proverbs 4:25, both of which have special discourse functions, as shall presently be shown.[16]

The following two verses from Proverbs 4 are both MV//VM. Besides this sameness of colon arrangement, there is also an obvious relationship of content between them:

Proverbs 4:11

I have taught you the way of wisdom,	בְּדֶרֶךְ חָכְמָה הֹרֵתִיךָ
I have led you in the paths of uprightness.	הִדְרַכְתִּיךָ בְּמַעְגְּלֵי־יֹשֶׁר:

Proverbs 4:14

Do not enter the path of the wicked,	בְּאֹרַח רְשָׁעִים אַל־תָּבֹא
and do not walk in the way of evil men.	וְאַל־תְּאַשֵּׁר בְּדֶרֶךְ רָעִים:

---

15 Proverbs 3:1, having its own boundary devices, clearly indicates the commencement of a new section.

16 For Proverbs 4:25, see later in this chapter. Psalm 44:6 will be analysed in chapter 9.

Discourse Functions of Unusual Colon Arrangements   167

Verse 11 concerns 'the way of wisdom', verse 14 'the path of the wicked'. The former contains the parallel pair דֶּרֶךְ and מַעְגָּל, the latter אֹרַח and דֶּרֶךְ, all being virtual synonyms ('way' or 'path'). Viewed in context, it appears that each of these DEF//CAN verses heads a new sub-section within the larger discourse unit. Murphy, in agreement with many versions (e.g., NIV REB TEV), delineates the larger unit as verses 10–19,[17] consisting of the instructions of a father to a son. Murphy does not offer a further breakdown of this unit, but Fox presents a more detailed analysis of the structure as an 'Exordium' (v. 10), followed by the lessons 'Choose the way of wisdom' (vv. 11–13) and 'Shun the way of evil' (vv. 14–17), concluded by a section dealing with 'The two paths' (vv. 18–19).[18] We agree with Fox's analysis, and would claim that the DEF//CAN structure of verses 11 and 14 functions suitably within this framework. To show the structure of verses 10–19 more clearly the text (here NRSV) may be displayed as follows:

10	Hear, my child, and accept my words,	Call to attention
	that the years of your life may be many.	
11-13	I have taught you **the way of wisdom**;	Way of wisdom
	I have led you in the paths of uprightness.	
	When you walk, your step will not be hampered;	
	and if you run, you will not stumble.	
	Keep hold of instruction; do not let go;	
	guard her, for she is your life.	
14-17	Do not enter **the path of the wicked**,	Path of the wicked
	and do not walk in the way of evildoers.	
	Avoid it; do not go on it;	
	turn away from it and pass on.	
	For they cannot sleep unless they have done wrong;	
	they are robbed of sleep unless they have made someone stumble.	
	For they eat the bread of wickedness	
	and drink the wine of violence.	
18	But **the path of the righteous** is like the light of dawn,	Path of the righteous
	which shines brighter and brighter until full day.	
19	**The way of the wicked** is like deep darkness;	Way of the wicked
	they do not know what they stumble over.	

17 Murphy, *Proverbs*, p. 27.
18 M.V. Fox, *Proverbs 1–9*, AB (New York: Doubleday, 2000), pp. 178–79.

The passage concludes with two noun-clauses (vv. 18–19) in which the key words אֹרַח and דֶּרֶךְ are also present. Similarly, these two verbless clauses place the phrase 'The path/way of X' in the initial position, as do the verbal clauses 11a and 14a. The marking of these phrases in bold above highlights their discourse function. We observe a well-defined structure to the overall passage, which contrasts two 'ways',[19] a common motif in the book of Proverbs.[20] It is apparent that the two DEF//CAN parallelisms begin each of the major sub-sections within the unit. As noted in the foregoing chart, some English versions recognise verse 14 as the beginning of a new section, though not verse 11.

Job 3:24

For my sighing comes before I eat,[21]   כִּי־לִפְנֵי לַחְמִי אַנְחָתִי תָבֹא

and my groanings pour out like water.   וַיִּתְּכוּ כַמַּיִם שַׁאֲגֹתָי׃

Three English versions (REB NJPS NJB), together with the commentaries of Clines and Gordis, make this verse the opening of a new section. In support of such a segmentation of the text is the change in person from verse 23 to 24. The contents of the preceding verses (20–23) are expressed in the 3rd person plural, having general reference to those overwhelmed by the troubles of life. In verse 24 Job reverts to the 1st person singular. A shift in person is, according to Wendland, one of the chief signs of aperture in poetic discourse.[22] It is not unreasonable to suppose, therefore, the presence of a boundary at this point in the text.

There remain ten instances of DEF//CAN which have not yet been analysed. These do not fall within the category of boundary-marking units, though the function that most of these have is related to that just discussed. We draw attention to the fact that, in the standard textbooks on Biblical Hebrew poetry, those devices which are commonly considered to indicate a textual boundary frequently have another discourse function, that of marking *peak*. Wendland informs us that those various literary features employed for signalling a textual boundary 'may also be utilized by the poet to highlight distinct points of prominence within the text'.[23] Watson

---

19 Cf. D. Kidner, *Proverbs*, TOTC (London: Inter-Varsity Press, 1964), p. 67, 'Two paths are set before us. Verses 10–13 describe *the way of wisdom* (11) and verses 14–17 *the path* (or *way*) *of the wicked* (14, 19). In verses 18, 19 the two paths are compared'.
20 Murphy, *Proverbs*, pp. 16, 27.
21 This translation of לִפְנֵי לַחְמִי follows ASV NJKV and LXX. The root לחם also appears as a verb (*NIDOTTE*, vol. 2, p. 789), as in Psalm 141:4; Proverbs 4:17; 23:1; and Obadiah 7.
22 Wendland, *The Discourse Analysis of Hebrew Prophetic Literature*, pp. 32, 38.
23 Wendland, *Discourse Perspectives on Hebrew Poetry*, p. 15. Also Wendland, *Analyzing the Psalms*, p. 112, 'the same devices may appear in a closure as in an aperture. They may even occur at a point of thematic emphasis ("peak")'.

would no doubt concur with this. With noticeable frequency in his volume on Hebrew poetry, for one and the same feature he lists 'climax marker' or 'dramatic effect' alongside the functions of opening and closing sections of discourse.[24] We should not be surprised, therefore, if the DEF//CAN parallelism also appears at the climactic point of the unit in which it occurs. The places where this peak-marking function is a possible explanation of this particular form are Psalms 38:19; 44:3, 6; 83:4; 85:6; 139:10; Isaiah 59:7, and Job 12:18. These shall now be briefly considered. The final two instances of DEF//CAN, Proverbs 1:16 and 4:25, shall then be treated separately.

Firstly, regarding the two verses from Psalm 44, these shall be dealt with in detail in the analysis of verses 2–9 of that psalm in chapter 9. As shall be seen, there is a contextual reason to support the existence of a textual peak in both. The same applies to Job 12:18. The whole of this chapter is also discussed in chapter 9. Of the remaining instances, a reasonable case can be made for the presence of peak in the following four verses.

Psalm 85:6

Will you be angry with us forever?   הַלְעוֹלָם תֶּאֱנַף־בָּנוּ

Will you prolong your anger to all generations?   תִּמְשֹׁךְ אַפְּךָ לְדֹר וָדֹר:

That God was currently angry with his people is a prominent idea in the first half of this psalm. This wrath contrasts starkly with the favour they had previously experienced (vv. 2–4). The psalmist pleads with God for restoration to his favour and a cessation of his displeasure (v. 5). Surely then, verse 6 comes as a cry of the heart from the faithful in Israel. The fact that this verse consists of two rhetorical questions in parallel supports its climactic character. Two leading scholars in the field, Watson and Wendland, both agree that the rhetorical question is also a common peak-marking device in Biblical Hebrew poetry.[25]

Psalm 139:10

even there your hand shall lead me,   גַּם־שָׁם יָדְךָ תַנְחֵנִי

and your right hand shall hold me.   וְתֹאחֲזֵנִי יְמִינֶךָ:

---

24 E.g., for the tricolon, and for the pivot-pattern (Watson, *Classical Hebrew Poetry*, p. 183, and pp. 219–20).

25 Watson, *Classical Hebrew Poetry*, p. 341, says: 'In general, the rhetorical question is used for *dramatic effect*: it involves the audience directly, if they are addressed, or it creates tension which then requires resolution'. Wendland, *Analyzing the Psalms*, p. 147: 'A rhetorical question causes a pause in the flow of discourse. It is an open invitation to the listener to participate by responding to the question form. To this extent, it can be said to interrupt the progression of the argument, exposition, complaint, or conversation wherever it occurs ... normally in isolation it contributes to textual discontinuity'. Also p. 148, 'the highlighting function of an RQ [rhetorical question] is quite appropriate ... in this climactic location'.

This verse comes after a series of two conditional sentences (v. 8), and after not just one but two conditional protases (v. 9), which it completes as an apodosis. The apodosis in both 8a and 8b consists merely of a brief verbless clause (שָׁם אַתָּה and הִנֶּךָ). But the apodosis offered by verse 10 is lengthy, covering a whole parallel bicolon, and opens with the marked גַּם־שָׁם, 'even there', indicating something unexpected.[26] This focused prepositional phrase itself is followed by a preverbal subject. This unusual sequence PP S V is best taken as showing both pragmatic marking (in PP) and defamiliarisation (in SV). A plausible case can be made for interpreting the DEF//CAN structure of verse 10 as a climactic device. It should be noted that the following two verses (11–12) show a closely related pattern to verses 8–10, and lend some support to understanding verse 10 as a textual high point. Verse 11 again consists of two conditional protases, while verse 12 supplies the apodosis.[27] Again the apodosis is marked pragmatically (*gam*–SV) for contra-expectation ('even'), and though verse 12 is not a DEF//CAN parallelism, it does take the form of a tricolon, another frequently used marker of peak.[28]

Psalm 38:19

I will confess my iniquity;	כִּי־עֲוֹנִי אַגִּיד
I will be sorry for my sin.	אֶדְאַג מֵחַטָּאתִי׃

The climactic nature of this DEF//CAN bicolon is perhaps not immediately obvious. Yet when its context in the psalm as a whole is taken into account, a good case for peak can be made. The psalmist begins by begging God not to rebuke him in his anger (v. 2). Verses 3 and 4 then describe the disquieting effect of the divine wrath upon him. He then declares in verse 5, 'My iniquities [עֲוֹנֹתַי] have gone over my head; they weigh like a burden too heavy for me', such was the sense of his guilt. The psalm then continues in the same vein of despondency and spiritual oppression, predominantly using the *qatal* verb-form. Through a *yiqtol* verb תַעֲנֶה (v. 16) denoting future action[29] the psalmist expresses his hope for a divine response to his plight. It is significant that the verse under discussion also employs the *yiqtol* form.[30] This change is noticeable and cannot be arbitrary.[31] Here the

---

26 This is clearly not a fronted phrase of spatial orientation. See 3.5.
27 Significantly, Allen (*Psalms 101–150*, p. 251) terms verse 12 a 'rhetorical climax'.
28 Cf. fn. 24 above, and J. T. Willis, 'The Juxtaposition of Synonymous and Chiastic Parallelism in Tricola in Old Testament Hebrew Psalm Poetry', *VT* 29 (1979), p. 480.
29 Cf. Craigie, *Psalms 1–50*, p. 301, 'you will answer'.
30 The other *yiqtol* verb-forms appearing in this passage (v.14, וַאֲנִי כְחֵרֵשׁ לֹא אֶשְׁמָע וּכְאִלֵּם לֹא יִפְתַּח־פִּיו; v. 17 פֶּן־יִשְׂמְחוּ־לִי) could be explained as expressing either a specific mood or aspect (cf. Waltke and O'Connor, *Biblical Hebrew Syntax*, pp. 507 and 639–40). יַעֲמֹדוּ in verse 12 (in parallel with a *qatal* form) is anomalous, and is probably to be taken as a primitive *yaqtul* preterite (*ibid.*, pp. 497–98, especially note fn. 4), as LXX ἔστησαν.

psalmist announces his intention to confess his iniquities to God. No doubt this, he believes, will bring him relief – an interpretation supported by a comparison with the similar subject matter in Psalm 32:3–5. Verse 19 may therefore be taken as climactic in that it highlights the solution to the burden the psalmist has been bearing. In addition, it is possible that the particle כִּי with which the first line of the bicolon begins should be interpreted in this context as marking information of significance. In his in-depth analysis of this particle Follingstad states that כִּי may have the function of indicating 'the information salience of the semantic context of the clause which it marks'.[32] By 'information salience' we understand a prominent juncture in the text, that is, a peak or climax.[33]

Isaiah 59:7ab

| Their feet run to evil, | רַגְלֵיהֶם לָרַע יָרֻצוּ |
| and they hurry to shed innocent blood. | וִימַהֲרוּ לִשְׁפֹּךְ דָּם נָקִי |

This is another verse which, at first sight, does not seem to warrant being designated a peak in the discourse. However, a closer examination of the surrounding context will produce some justification for the DEF//CAN pattern at this particular point. In verses 5 to 8 the prophet describes the injustice of the people, speaking in the 3rd person.[34] The first half of this passage (vv. 5a–6b) contains an extended parallelism of six cola, having the structure MKD//MKD//MKD//MKD//MKD//DEF.[35] All these lines speak meta-phorically of the evil plans of the people in terms of snakes hatching eggs, or spiders weaving webs. In 6c the parallelism ends and there is a noticeable return to more literal language describing the wickedness of the people. Verses 6c to 7d contain the following (NRSV):

| 6c | Their works are works of iniquity, | Noun-clause |
| 6d | and deeds of violence are in their hands. | Noun-clause |

---

31 LXX notes the change and translates as future (ἀναγγελῶ, μεριμνήσω).
32 C. M. Follingstad, *Deictic Viewpoint in Biblical Hebrew Text: A Syntagmatic and Paradigmatic Analysis of the Particle* כִּי (Dallas, Texas: SIL, 2001), p. 51.
33 Waltke and O'Connor, *Biblical Hebrew Syntax*, p. 665, offer the translation 'indeed' for this emphatic use of כִּי. Craigie shows that he detects this same sense in Psalm 38:19 when he translates it as, 'Indeed, I will declare my wickedness', Craigie, *Psalms 1–50*, p. 301.
34 The preceding verses (2–4) address the people directly in the 2nd person plural. REB, NJPS, Motyer (*The Prophecy of Isaiah*, p. 485) and Young (*Isaiah*, vol. 3, p. 431–33) make verse 5 open a new sub-section. Verse 9, beginning as it does with עַל־כֵּן ('Therefore'), is commonly taken as marking the onset of a new section (e.g., NRSV NIV REB NJPS TEV).
35 On this type of extended parallelism made up of marked clauses, and closed with one that is apparently not marked, see 7.2.7 (c).

7a	Their feet run to evil,	Verbal clause
7b	and they rush to shed innocent blood.	Verbal clause
7c	Their thoughts are thoughts of iniquity,	Noun-clause
7d	desolation and destruction are in their highways.	Noun-clause

It is clear that 6cd and 7cd match one another closely. Syntactically the construction of each parallel unit is virtually identical:

(6cd) מַעֲשֵׂיהֶם מַעֲשֵׂי־אָוֶן // וּפֹעַל חָמָס בְּכַפֵּיהֶם:

(7cd) מַחְשְׁבוֹתֵיהֶם מַחְשְׁבוֹת אָוֶן // שֹׁד וָשֶׁבֶר בִּמְסִלּוֹתָם:

6c and 7c are both constructed of S Comp, where the subject phrase consists of a plural noun (each formed with the prefix מַ– and ending with the pronominal suffix –יהֶם). The nominal complement in both cases is a construct chain in which the governing noun is the same as the subject and the noun in the genitive relationship is אָוֶן. 6d and 7d again both consist of S Comp. A single noun with preposition (–בְּ) serves as a locative complement. In both complement phrases the attached noun is a plural form with the 3rd person plural masculine suffix.[36] For our purposes the important fact is that these two closely corresponding noun-clause parallelisms bracket the DEF//CAN parallelism in question, that is, 7ab forms the central piece in this ABA' rhetorical structure. The significance of this lies in the fact that it is typically the middle unit of such concentric patterns that forms the climactic point. Wendland informs us that the peak frequently occurs 'at the central core' of what he calls a 'chiastic introversion', as is present here (in the pattern ABA').[37] This central element, he continues, 'realizes the peak (thematic focus) or climax (emotive high) of a given segment'. Other scholars of the literary techniques of the Hebrew Bible have detected this same function.[38] In keeping with this, the text under discussion shows a discernible increase in intensity from A (6cd) to B (7ab), then back down to A' (7cd). The two outer elements simply contain descriptive statements regarding the people's deeds and thoughts. The central unit, however, concerns action, and it is heightened action. Their deeds are not just evil,

---

36 Considering the closeness of the correspondences, it is surprising that the relationship between these two units goes entirely unobserved in the standard commentaries.

37 Wendland, *Discourse Perspectives on Hebrew Poetry*, p. 15; cf. p. 13, 'an important topical element (key word[s], phrase, colon) is frequently located in the center of two or more pairs of corresponding enclosing units, thus highlighting the thematic peak, emotive climax'.

38 E.g., D. A. Dorsey, *The Literary Structure of the Old Testament* (Grand Rapids, Michigan: Baker Books, 1999), p. 41, 'in nonnarrative compositions with a symmetric structure, the central unit often presents the highlight, centerpiece, or most important point'.

nor do they simply do evil, but a step-up in thought is expressed through the verbs יָרֻצוּ and וַיְמַהֲרוּ, that is, they are *swift* to do these things. It speaks of their eagerness with respect to evil. Thus the verbal clauses of 7ab can be seen to be far more forceful and expressive than the static noun-clauses that frame it. We conclude, therefore, that the DEF//CAN pattern is appropriate as a further indicator of peak in this particular context.

There remain three further DEF//CAN parallelisms to consider which are of a more problematical nature. In these cases the peak-marking function of the unusually formed parallelism is admittedly not apparent.

Psalm 83:4

They devise crafty schemes against your people, עַל־עַמְּךָ יַעֲרִימוּ סוֹד
and conspire together against those you treasure. וְיִתְיָעֲצוּ עַל־צְפוּנֶיךָ׃

This DEF//CAN parallelism does not appear to be placed at a boundary.[39] Structurally this bicolon, as in the previous example, is located at the centre of a sub-unit, comprising the six-lines introduced by כִּי in verses 3–5:[40]

> ³ For behold, your enemies make an uproar,
> and those who hate you have lifted up their heads.
> ⁴ They devise crafty schemes against your people,
> and conspire together against those whom you treasure.
> ⁵ They say, 'Come, and let us wipe them out from being a nation,
> that the name of Israel be remembered no more'.

We further observe that the syntactic components of this middle bicolon produce the form of a chiasmus: PP V NP[DO] // V PP, creating an *abcba* pattern. Such a chiastic ordering, Wendland informs us, is an artistic way of 'emphasizing the content of the bicolon as a whole'.[41] Both with respect to structure and word order, therefore, the psalmist seems to be highlighting the contents of this particular verse. What is not so clear perhaps in this case is his reason for doing so. Verse 3 contains a general statement to the effect that God's enemies have risen up, without mentioning specifically against whom. Verse 4 fills out both the manner (crafty scheming) and object (Israel) of their activity. So an upward progression may be detected

---

39 NJB stands alone in making it an aperture.
40 Following this, according to several commentaries and versions, another sub-unit begins, also introduced by כִּי (v. 6). Terrien (*Psalms*, p. 592), Delitzsch (in Keil and Delitzsch, *Commentary on the Old Testament*, vol. 5, 'Psalms', p. 405), NIV NKJV NJB TEV CEV all place a boundary between verses 5 and 6.
41 Wendland, *Analyzing the Psalms*, p. 63; cf. J. Breck, *The Shape of Biblical Language: Chiasmus in the Scriptures and Beyond* (New York: St. Vladimir's Seminary Press, 1994), p. 59; A. R. Ceresko, 'The Function of Chiasmus in Hebrew Poetry', *CBQ 40* (1978), p. 6.

between these two verses, but how verse 4 stands out above the contents of verse 5 is not obvious. This latter gives expression in the form of direct speech to the schemes of verse 4, and so seems to be of equal prominence. We must recall, however, that any rhetorical highlighting given to a specific unit is according to the perceptions of the individual author. The reason may be in the fact that verses 3–5 provide the grounds for the preceding appeal (v. 2) for God not to remain inactive. It is possible that in the mind of the psalmist it is verse 4 that forms the essence of those grounds.

We next turn to Proverbs 1:16. Studying this verse in the context of its larger unit (vv. 10–19) we see no reason to ascribe to it a peak or boundary-marking function. Here the solution to this particular verse seems to lie elsewhere – in textual criticism. We notice two things concerning this verse. First, it is completely absent from the LXX, and secondly, it is almost verbatim the same as Isaiah 59:7 just discussed:

(Is. 59:7) רַגְלֵיהֶם לָרַע יָרֻצוּ וִימַהֲרוּ לִשְׁפֹּךְ דָּם נָקִי

(Prov. 1:16) כִּי רַגְלֵיהֶם לָרַע יָרוּצוּ וִימַהֲרוּ לִשְׁפָּךְ־דָּם

The only difference, apart from the conjunction (כִּי), is the adjective נָקִי qualifying the 'blood', though the fact that it was 'innocent' could in any case be assumed from the context. This virtual identity between the two verses rules out the similarity being merely coincidental. Obviously one is the source of the other. In view of the omission of this verse from the best Greek manuscripts of Proverbs, it would seem more likely that Isaiah gives the original, which at a later date was imported into a similar context in Proverbs. Murphy gives his support to such an explanation when he writes, 'This verse appears to be a gloss or insertion from Is. 59:7a'.[42] We have seen how the DEF//CAN arrangement of the verse is entirely in keeping with its climactic function in Isaiah 59, a further fact in favour of its originating in that location. When the verse was inserted into Proverbs 1, its form was kept unchanged and the DEF//CAN pattern therefore stands out as being inappropriate to its position in this new context.

The final verse to be considered is also from Proverbs. Of all the examples considered, the particular form of this one is the least obvious:

Proverbs 4:25

| Let your eyes look directly forward, | עֵינֶיךָ לְנֹכַח יַבִּיטוּ |
| and let your eyelids look straight before you. | וְעַפְעַפֶּיךָ יַיְשִׁרוּ נֶגְדֶּךָ׃ |

This parallel bicolon seems to show both markedness and defamiliarisation. Both cola open with semantically corresponding clause-initial NP[Su]s. Following this the A-line has MV, and the B-line VM. This rare SMV//SVM

---

42 Murphy, *Proverbs*, p. 10; cf. R. N. Whybray, *Proverbs*, NCB (London: Marshall Pickering, 1994), p. 41.

sequence is identical to that of Proverbs 2:22 discussed earlier in this section. There the pragmatic marking of the subject phrases was owing to its contrastive relationship with the previous verse, while the defamiliarised ordering of the remaining constituents we attributed to closure, in that it marked the end of a well-defined section in the discourse. The fact that 4:25 has the same structure and occurs in such close proximity to the earlier example would suggest that its form is deliberate and functional rather than merely arbitrary. What that function is in this instance is admittedly not at all apparent. NLT considers it to mark an aperture, and the commentary of McKane concurs with this,[43] but this is slender evidence. A fronted subject phrase may have any one of a range of different functions. In this context, we somewhat diffidently assign to it the same as that seen in 2:22, that is, contrast. Taken together with the preceding verse this is not an impossible pragmatic implication:

> [24] Put away from you crooked speech,
> and put devious talk far from you.
> [25] [But] let your eyes look directly forward,
> and your gaze be straight before you.

In verse 24 there appear two nouns (עִקְּשׁוּת and לְזוּת) descriptive of perverseness. The wise man advises his son to put away all crookedness of speech. And then (v. 25), in what could be seen as contrast with such perversity, come the two phrases לְנֹכַח and נֶגְדֶּךָ (with the verb יַיְשִׁרוּ), expressing the idea of 'straightness' or 'directness'. Murphy's comment here is that 'the perceptive person looks straight ahead at wisdom' (cf. Prov. 17:24).[44] So the forward-looking eyes (a positive attribute) could be taken as standing in a contrastive relationship with the deviating lips (a negative attribute). The reason for the departure from the expected word order following this initial marked constituent is also far from certain. As remarked in the discussion of Proverbs 2:22, it is exceedingly rare for this to occur within the A-line. Had it occurred in B, then there would be nothing left to explain. But the SMV sequence of the A-line shows defamiliar order after the clause-initial NP[Su] and, from what has been observed elsewhere, this would seem to indicate some significance at discourse level. One possibility is that verse 25, as in the case of Isaiah 59:7 treated above, occupies the central unit of an ABA pattern relating to different parts of the body: mouth/eyes/feet. The use of the jussive *yiqtol* in verse 25 does set it apart from the surrounding imperatives (24a, 24b, 26a),

---

43 W. McKane, *Proverbs*, OTL (London: SCM Press, 1970), pp. 310–11.
44 Murphy, *Proverbs*, p. 28.

but why the contents should be considered climactic is not evident. Future study will perhaps provide a more adequate answer.

Every instance of DEF//CAN has now been considered. In almost every case a satisfactory explanation, in terms of discourse-function (boundary or peak), has been found to account for the unusual form of the parallel structure.

(b) DEF//DEF

On fewer occasions, 19 in total, we find the colon arrangement DEF//DEF. This can also be seen to occur in specific distribution, having the same functions in the discourse (i.e., marking aperture, closure, and peak) as DEF//CAN parallelisms.

Ref.	Form	Function	Versions & Commentaries
Ps. 9:19	CMVS//SVM	Closure [Chiasm]	NRSV NIV NKJV ESV NJB TEV NLT NCV CEV Terrien Anderson Kidner Harman Delitzsch
Ps. 17:2	MSV//SVM	Closure	NRSV ESV NKJV NJB TEV NLT CEV Terrien Craigie Kraus Anderson Delitzsch
Ps. 29:11	SOMV//SVOM	Closure	Last verse in psalm
Ps. 37:23	MSV//OV	Aperture	NRSV NIV ESV NKJV NJB REB TEV NLT NCV CEV Terrien Kidner
Ps. 77:2	MM(w-)V//MM(w-)VM	Aperture	First verse in psalm
Ps. 89:2	OMV//MVOM	Aperture	First verse in psalm
Ps. 89:3	MSV//NVOM	Peak[45]	Separate unit of direct speech
Ps. 92:13	SMV//MV	Aperture	NRSV NIV ESV NJB TEV CEV Anderson Harman
Ps. 102:9	MVS//SMV	Closure	NASB NJB TEV Terrien Delitzsch
Ps. 103:19	SMVO//SMV	Aperture	NRSV NIV NKJV ESV NJB REB TEV NLT NCV CEV

---

45 Since this DEF//DEF parallelism stands alone its form might also be an indicator of boundary.

Discourse Functions of Unusual Colon Arrangements 177

			Tate Kraus Anderson Kidner Delitzsch
Ps. 104:12	MSV//MVO	Closure	REB NJB TEV
			Kraus
Ps. 142:2	MMV//MMV	Aperture	First verse in psalm
Ps. 145:4	SMVO//OV	Aperture	NRSV ESV NKJV NJB TEV
			NLT NCV CEV
			Terrien Allen Kraus Anderson
Is. 42:13ab	SMV//MVO	Aperture	NJPS
			Oswalt Watts Motyer
Is. 51:5	SOV//MSV//MV	Peak [Tricolon]	Motyer
Is. 54:3	SOV//OV	Closure	NRSV NIV ESV NKJV NJPS
			REB TEV NLT NCV CEV
			Oswalt Watts Motyer
Job 4:17	QSMV//CMVS	Aperture [Rhet Qu]	Begins direct speech
Job 12:11	QSOV//SOV	Peak [Rhet Qu]	(See discussion in chapter 9)
Prov. 3:20	MSV//SVO	Closure	NRSV NIV ESV NASB NKJV
			NJB REB TEV NLT NCV
			Murphy Fox Whybray
			McKane Garrett Waltke

The marking of peak in Job 12:11 will be discussed when the whole of Job 12 is analysed in the next chapter. Of the other verses some comment will be made on Psalm 77:2, Isaiah 42:13, 51:5, and Job 4:17.

Though the syntax of Psalm 77:2 would suggest it is simply a Nom-CAN//Nom-CAN parallelism, it seems right that this verse should in fact be counted as DEF//DEF. This is owing to its close resemblance to Psalm 142:2:

(Ps. 77:2) קוֹלִי אֶל־אֱלֹהִים וְאֶצְעָקָה קוֹלִי אֶל־אֱלֹהִים וְהַאֲזִין אֵלָי:

(Ps. 142:2) קוֹלִי אֶל־יְהוָה אֶזְעָק קוֹלִי אֶל־יְהוָה אֶתְחַנָּן:

The use of the *wāw* in 77:2 would suppose that קוֹלִי אֶל־אֱלֹהִים stands independently as a noun-clause. The sense intended, however, is identical to that of 142:2, as understood by the translations, ancient and modern. We note that the LXX, Vulg, and Syr ignore the presence of *wāw* in its first instance. In addition, that a *wāw* might be located within a verbal clause after such a fashion is not unknown in Biblical Hebrew syntax.[46] In view of

---

46 Cf. Waltke and O'Connor, *Biblical Hebrew Syntax*, p. 538.

this similarity, and the fact that both 77:2 and 142:2 mark the opening of a psalm, 77:2 is best placed in this DEF//DEF category alongside 142:2.

Isaiah 42:13ab

YHWH goes forth like a warrior,	יְהוָה כַּגִּבּוֹר יֵצֵא
like a soldier he stirs up his zeal.	כְּאִישׁ מִלְחָמוֹת יָעִיר קִנְאָה

The constituent order of this bicolon is SMV//MVO. As regards its form it could be either DEF//DEF or MKD//MKD. The latter would require the final position of the verb יֵצֵא to indicate its presuppositional status and the two preverbal phrases (SM) to be focused. Since the context lacks anything to support this, the former designation is to be preferred. Surprisingly, of all English translations only NJPS makes this bicolon a new juncture in the discourse. In view of the fact that three major commentaries see an aperture here, one would have thought that more of the versions would have followed suit. In his literary analysis Oswalt makes a sub-unit of verses 13–16, unified, he claims, by an 'emphasis on the sovereign activity of God that begins in v. 13 [and] is continued through v. 16'.[47] Watts identifies verses 13–25 as the first of five scenes making up the larger section of 42:13–43:21. He remarks that 'The usual division of verses at the beginning places v. 13 with the previous section ... But v. 12 contains the imperative calls to praise that usually close a hymn. V. 13 makes a fresh start ... It is an announcement, not an ascription, and belongs thematically with what follows'.[48] Motyer sees verses 10–12 as a summons to the world to sing, and verses 13–17 as the grounds of the song. According to Motyer's analysis verses 13–17 form a well-defined unit in which verses 13 and 17 bracket the 1st person speech by the Lord contained in verses 14–16.[49] Although their overall analysis varies, each commentator gives some justification for seeing a new beginning at verse 13.[50] This, we suggest, is further supported by other opening defamiliar SMV units with יְהוָה as subject that are to be found in Isaiah (40:10; 66:15).

Isaiah 51:5cde

and my arms will judge the peoples;	וּזְרֹעַי עַמִּים יִשְׁפֹּטוּ
the coastlands wait for me,	אֵלַי אִיִּים יְקַוּוּ
and for my arm they hope.	וְאֶל־זְרֹעִי יְיַחֵלוּן׃

---

47 Oswalt, *The Book of Isaiah 40–66*, pp. 122, 124.
48 Watts, *Isaiah 34–66*, pp. 128–29.
49 Motyer, *The Prophecy of Isaiah*, pp. 323–24.
50 It should be noted that K. Baltzer, *Deutero-Isaiah: A Commentary on Isaiah 40–55*, Hermeneia (Minneapolis, Indiana: Fortress Press, 2001), p. 141, describes verse 13 as a 'climax', another appropriate function for the unusual form of parallelism.

Discourse Functions of Unusual Colon Arrangements

It is widely accepted that verses 4–6 form a distinct unit (as in NRSV NIV NJB TEV NCV, etc.). The highly defamiliarised cola, SOV//MSV//MV, of 5cde, according to Motyer, form the central element of the larger unit. He affirms that 'the poem has a focal point',[51] which he represents diagrammatically in the following way:

    A¹ Summons to hear (4ab)
        B¹ Light for the peoples, salvation speeding (4c–5b)
            C The arm of the Lord (5c–e)
    A² Summons to look (6ab)
        B² The world's inhabitants transitory, salvation eternal (6c–f)

Moyter continues by saying that 'the central truth' of this section is that 'the "arm" of the Lord, the divine personal act ... will effectuate salvation'.[52] This literary analysis agrees with what was stated earlier in this chapter concerning the climactic nature of the central element in such rhetorical constructions.[53] Further support, moreover, comes from the presence of parallel pairs throughout verses 4–6, with the significant exception of 5cde. This feature has been noted by Baltzer.[54] The words in question are:

4ab	עַמִּי // וּלְאוּמִּי	my people // my people
4cd	תּוֹרָה // וּמִשְׁפָּטִי	my justice // law
5ab	צִדְקִי // יִשְׁעִי	my salvation // my righteousness
5cde	וּזְרֹעַי // אֵלַי // זְרֹעִי	my arm // to me // my arm
6ab	לַשָּׁמַיִם // אֶל־הָאָרֶץ	to the earth // to the heavens
6cd	שָׁמַיִם // וְהָאָרֶץ	and the earth // heaven
6ef	וִישׁוּעָתִי // וְצִדְקָתִי	and my righteousness // and my salvation

Viewing these pairs in such a way serves to highlight both the central position occupied by 5cde and its unique three-member composition in the larger unit of verses 4–6. The inclusio in 5cde produced by the noun זְרוֹעַ is also evident. Baltzer's comment on this arrangement is that the irregularity of verse 5 compared to the rest of the series functions as a 'special signal',[55] though he does not venture to define further what he means by that.

---

51 Motyer, *The Prophecy of Isaiah*, p. 404.
52 *Ibid.*, p. 405.
53 Cf. footnotes 37 and 38 above.
54 Baltzer, *Deutero-Isaiah*, p. 351.
55 *Ibid.*

Job 4:17
Can a mortal be righteous before[56] God?   הַאֱנוֹשׁ מֵאֱלוֹהַ יִצְדָּק
Can a man be pure before his Maker?   אִם מֵעֹשֵׂהוּ יִטְהַר־גָּבֶר׃

This parallelism, having the sequence QSMV//CMVS, is highly defamiliarised with respect to word order. Its special function within the overall discourse is apparent. Firstly, it clearly indicates aperture in that with these words Eliphaz begins his report of the mysterious revelation made known to him. But the peculiar DEF//DEF may at the same time mark a thematic highpoint. That this is a key verse in the speech cycle of the book of Job is demonstrated by the fact that similar verses, virtually quotations, are to be found in 9:2b and 25:4a (both וּמַה־יִּצְדַּק אֱנוֹשׁ עִם־אֵל). This proves the prominence of the contents of 4:17, how a man can be righteous before a holy God, in the on-going debate between Job and the three friends. Clines is surely correct when he describes this specific verse as 'the utterance that forms the climax' of this section.[57] Moreover, the fact that the parallelism is constructed in the form of two rhetorical questions[58] is entirely in keeping with its climactic character.[59]

(c) DEF//Gap

Ref.	Form	Function	Versions & Commentaries
Ps. 33:6	MSV//MS	Aperture	NRSV NIV NKJV ESV REB NJB TEV NLT NCV CEV Terrien Craigie Anderson Harman Delitzsch
Ps. 72:1	[Voc]OMV//OM	Aperture	First verse of psalm
Ps. 121:6	MSV//SM	Closure[60]	NRSV NIV NKJV ESV TEV CEV Terrien Harman Delitzsch
Num. 23:7	MVS//SM	Aperture	First verse of oracle

In these four instances where a defamiliar A-line is paralleled by a B-line in which the verb is gapped, no further explanation is required as to their

---

56 On the sense of the preposition מִ־ as 'before', rather than 'more than', see Reyburn, *Handbook on the Book of Job*, p. 101. Cf. וִהְיִיתֶם נְקִיִּים מֵיהוָה וּמִיִּשְׂרָאֵל, 'and you shall be innocent before the LORD and before Israel' (Num. 32:22).
57 Clines, *Job 1–20*, p. 132.
58 The rhetorical nature of the questions is noted by Reyburn, *Handbook on the Book of Job*, p. 101.
59 Cf. the comments on the rhetorical questions earlier in this chapter on Psalm 85:6.
60 Allen, *Psalms 101–150*, pp. 151, 153, takes this verse as an aperture.

function, which is evidently boundary-marking in all cases. There are matters of interest, however, respecting the third text.

Psalm 121:6

The sun shall not strike you by day,   יוֹמָם הַשֶּׁמֶשׁ לֹא־יַכֶּכָּה

nor the moon by night.   וְיָרֵחַ בַּלָּיְלָה׃

This parallel bicolon has the constituent structure M S V^{Ng} // w-S M. The A-line has two preverbal elements. In clause-initial position is the temporal adverb יוֹמָם, and the NP[Su] הַשֶּׁמֶשׁ in second position. The verb has been gapped from the B-line. Of the remaining two constituents the NP[Su] now occupies first position, and the adverbial בַּלָּיְלָה, corresponding to יוֹמָם in the A-line, the final position. This is a highly unusual order of clause constituents in a parallel structure. Although the above chart lists this verse as closure according to its position in a number of major English translations and commentaries, it is possible that the verse is also intended to indicate peak. What we see here is a well-constructed example of merismus. Krašovec defines this as 'the art of expressing a totality by mentioning the parts, usually the two extremes'.[61] Typical word-pairs involved in such constructions are 'heaven'/'earth', 'day'/'night', 'morning'/'evening', and 'sea'/'land'.[62] The use of this poetic device in Psalm 121:6 is acknowledged by Kidner, who makes the comment, 'The two lines of verse 6 are not only two poetic parallels ... but use a favourite Heb. way of expressing totality: naming a pair of opposites to include everything between'.[63] The presence of merismus does not always have implications regarding word order. Sometimes the two elements creating the effect are situated at the head of their clause (as Job 21:33), or both at the end (as Jer. 31:37). In the case of Psalm 121:6 the two temporal phrases have been strategically placed at the outer limits of the parallelism to highlight the two semantic opposites rhetorically by their positions in the bicolon. According to Watson merismus may serve to heighten the 'dramatic effect'.[64] In this particular case, therefore, the DEF//Gap may denote a climactic point in the psalm – the fact that the divine protection, says Kidner, 'avails against the known and the unknown; perils of day and night; the most overpowering forces and the most insidious'.[65]

---

61   J. Krašovec, 'Merism – Polar Expression in Biblical Hebrew', *Biblical 64* (1983), p. 232; cf. A. M. Honeyman, 'Merismus in Biblical Hebrew', *JBL 71* (1952); Watson, *Classical Hebrew Poetry*, pp. 321–24.
62   Cf. Berlin, *Dynamics of Biblical Parallelism*, p. 76.
63   Kidner, *Psalms 73–150*, p. 432, fn. 1.
64   Watson, *Classical Hebrew Poetry*, p. 324.
65   Kidner, *Psalms 73–150*, p. 432.

(d) DEF//Nom

Ref.	Form	Function	Versions & Commentaries
Ps. 10:7	MSVM// Comp S S	Aperture[66]	NRSV REB NJB NLT Terrien Craigie Harman
Ps. 56:6	MOV//S Comp	Aperture	NRSV NIV NKJV ESV NJB TEV NLT NCV CEV Terrien Tate Kraus Anderson Kidner Harman
Ps. 102:26	MOV// Comp S	Aperture	NRSV ESV NJB CEV Kraus Anderson Kidner
Is. 66:15	CHSMV// Comp S[67]	Aperture	ESV NJPS REB NJB TEV Oswalt Motyer Young
Prov. 8:4	M[Voc]V// S Comp	Aperture	Opens direct speech

In each of these five instances where a defamiliar verbal clause is paralleled by a noun-clause in the B-line, the presence of a textual-boundary is well attested.

Before leaving these various forms of DEF-initial parallelisms, it is of interest that they are not distributed evenly throughout the data. We observe that when one psalm or chapter uses such a boundary or peak-marking device, it often does so more than once. In the following texts the device is found twice: Psalms 5, 29, 37, 38, 73, 89, 90, 91, 92, 102; Proverbs 2 and 3, while in Proverbs 4 it is employed no less than three times. This fact leads us to the conclusion that this particular feature was popular with certain Hebrew poets and not at all with others. It was a question of an individual author's style.

8.2.2 MKD-Initial Parallelisms

(a) MKD//CAN

In chapter 7 the matter of parallelisms involving pragmatic marking was discussed. There it was concluded that in general distribution only parallelisms of the form MKD//MKD were admissible. That is, the markedness of the A-line was preserved in the B-line. Yet, in certain restricted contexts, the form MKD//CAN is found. These, like the DEF-initial

---

66 Some versions (NKJV TEV CEV) take verse 7 as a closure, which is still of course in keeping with the function of the unusual character of the parallelism.

67 This opening DEF line has interesting parallels in Deuteronomy 33:2 and Habakkuk 3:3, both marking an opening textual boundary, and both consisting of an initial SMV (DEF) clause with a semantic content similar to Isaiah 66:15.

patterns just described, only occur in what we have termed specific distribution. The pragmatic marking of the A-line is entirely appropriate to their context (e.g., presentation of topic, contrast, etc.), which sets them apart from the DEF-initial parallelisms considered in the first half of this chapter. Their irregularity arises from the fact that the markedness of the A-line is not reproduced in the parallel line.

The colon arrangement MKD//CAN occurs at the beginning of a new text-unit, where the MKD A-line presents a new topic by means of a sentence-focus clause. These, according to the terminology of Shimasaki, have the function of 'initiation'.[68] This is illustrated by the following texts:

Psalm 33:10

YHWH foils the counsel of the nations,   יְהוָה הֵפִיר עֲצַת־גּוֹיִם
he thwarts the plans of the peoples.   הֵנִיא מַחְשְׁבוֹת עַמִּים׃

Psalm 35:9

My soul shall rejoice in the YHWH,   וְנַפְשִׁי תָּגִיל בַּיהוָה
it shall delight in his salvation.   תָּשִׂישׂ בִּישׁוּעָתוֹ׃

Proverbs 9:1

Wisdom has built her house,   חָכְמוֹת בָּנְתָה בֵיתָהּ
she has hewn her seven pillars.   חָצְבָה עַמּוּדֶיהָ שִׁבְעָה׃

All these texts are definite cases of aperture. The first is taken as such by NRSV ESV NKJV REB NJB TEV NLT CEV, as well as the commentaries of Terrien, Craigie, Kidner and others.[69] The second marks the commencement of a new section in NRSV ESV NKJV REB NJB TEV NLT CEV, together with the commentaries of Craigie and Delitzsch.[70] The third example is the recognised opening of a new chapter. Strictly these texts are all parallelisms, having coreferential subjects and semantically related verb phrases. Yet in neither case is the fronted NP[Su] of the first clause matched in the B-line, as is typically the case in MKD//MKD parallelisms of general distribution. Rather the parallel lines simply indicate the same referent by means of verbal affixation. In such unit-initial sentence-focus clauses, the constraint is not enforced, giving them their distinctive character as opening verses.

In just one instance, Isaiah 57:13, a SVO//VO parallelism, of the same form as the foregoing, seems to mark closure.[71]

---

68 See 3.4.1 (c).
69 E.g., Terrien, *Psalms*, p. 295; Craigie, *Psalms 1–50*, p. 271; Kidner, *Psalms 1–72*, p. 135.
70 Craigie, *Psalms 1–50*, p. 285; Delitzsch, in Keil and Delitzsch, *Commentary on the Old Testament*, vol. 5, 'Psalms', p. 414.
71 As in Oswalt, *The Book of Isaiah 40–66*, p. 474; Watts, *Isaiah 34–66*, p. 256; Young, *Isaiah*, vol. 3, p. 406; plus NRSV NIV ESV NASB NKJV REB NJB TEV NCV CEV.

(b) MKD//DEF

On five occasions a NP or PP occupies the marked position with a focus particle, with no equivalent phrase in the B-line:

Ref.	Form	Function	Versions & Commentaries
Ps. 73:13	ʾak-MVO//VMO	Aperture	NIV NJPS REB NJB TEV NLT Terrien Tate Kraus Anderson
Ps. 73:18	ʾak MVO//V-oM	Aperture	NIV ESV NJPS REB TEV NLT NCV Terrien Tate
Ps. 78:20	Q-gam-OVInf//CVOM	Closure	NRSV ESV NKJV TEV NJB CEV Terrien Tate Harman
Ps. 140:14	ʾak SVM//VSM	Closure	Last verse in psalm
Job 6:27	ʾap̄-MV//VM	Closure	NRSV NIV ESV NCV Clines Dhorme Habel Alden Andersen

Each of these above verses deviates from the normal MKD//MKD sequence in order to alert the listener/reader to the fact that a new section of the poem is commencing or coming to a close. These are different from the previous MKD//CAN parallelisms in that the corresponding constituent to the marked (S, O or M) element of the A-line does actually appear in B, though not in the anticipated initial position. These B-lines, therefore, though canonical in appearance, are best described as DEF,[72] in that the order of the parallel line diverges from what is expected. These are also to be distinguished from DEF//CAN parallelisms, since a particular category of focus is definitely marked by the presence of a focus particle in each case. The particular focus constructions present in Psalms 73 and 140 (all with the particle אַךְ) express the idea of certainty,[73] Psalm 78:20 (with גַּם) shows expanding focus, and Job 6:27 (with אַף) contra-expectation.[74]

The following single instance of the MKD//DEF parallelism does not appear to be placed at a textual boundary. The sole commentator who supports its boundary-marking function is Gordis.[75] It may possibly be better explained with reference to peak.

---

72 As was used in the case of canonical clauses in extended MKD parallelisms. See 7.2.7.
73 See 3.4.2 (d).
74 See 3.4.2 (e).
75 R. Gordis, *The Book of Job: Commentary, New Translation and Special Studies* (New York: Jewish Theological Seminary of America, 1978), p. 132.

Job 14:10

But man dies, and is laid low, וְגֶ֣בֶר יָ֭מוּת וַֽיֶּחֱלָ֑שׁ
a human being expires, and where is he? וַיִּגְוַ֖ע אָדָ֣ם וְאַיּֽוֹ׃

The form of this MKD//DEF parallelism (SVV//VSQ) is unusual in that the clause-initial position of גֶּ֣בֶר ('man') is not paralleled by אָדָ֣ם ('human being') in the same position, as is invariably the case when the A-line is marked. The reason for the fronting of גֶּ֣בֶר lies in its contrastive relationship with the foregoing verses.[76] There Job says, 'For there is hope for a tree, if it is cut down, that it will sprout again, and that its shoots will not cease. Though its root grows old in the earth, and its stump dies in the ground, yet at the scent of water it will bud and put forth branches like a young plant' (vv. 7–9 NRSV). A tree at least, Job claims, has hope if it is cut down. Its stump may grow again.[77] But not so with man. He dies and is gone for good. The pragmatic marking of the A-line is entirely appropriate, therefore, to the contrastive implications present in the context. But the failure to comply with the constraint in the B-line sets this bicolon apart as fulfilling a specific function. There is little to suggest that this function is that of indicating the presence of a boundary.[78] Much more likely it signals a thematic highpoint – a fact further suggested by the use of the rhetorical question form, '… and where is he?'.[79] Job's words in this verse, we observe, concern the essential mortality of man and the finality of death. That this is a prominent idea in the mind of Job in this speech is demonstrated by the fact that it finds expression again just a few verses later in verse 14, also through a rhetorical question ('If a man dies, will he live again?').

Lastly in this section we include a number of places, nine in total, where an A-line marked by the presence of an independent Pn[Su] is paralleled by a defamiliar B-line. These differ from other MKD parallel cola in that the B-line typically does not repeat the pronoun. This, we recall,[80] is one of the common exceptions from the rule regarding the reduplication of marked components in parallel lines. It is only with respect to those elements subsequent to the pronominal subject that the reordering of constituents occurs. Six of these texts are clear instances of boundary. These are given below. Two of the examples, we note, although including an appositional noun phrase following the pronoun (Ps. 79:13; Prov. 8:12), are of the same basic structure and function:

---

76   Clines, *Job 1–20*, p. 328.
77   Cf. Zuck, *Job*, p. 65; Dhorme, *Commentary on the Book of Job*, p. 199.
78   Although it should be noted that TEV makes this verse a closure, and NLT an aperture.
79   Cf. fn. 25 above.
80   See 7.4.2 (a).

Ps. 69:6	S^{Pn}VM//SMV	Aperture[81]	NASB NKJV REB NLT NCV Terrien Tate Anderson Harman Delitzsch
Ps. 79:13	S^{Pn}S/VMM//MVO	Closure [Tricolon]	Last verse in psalm
Is. 41:16cd	S^{Pn}VM//MV	Closure	NRSV NIV NKJV ESV NJPS REB TEV NLT NCV CEV Oswalt Watts Motyer Young
Is. 65:14bc	S^{Pn}VM//MV	Closure	Marks the end of an extended parallelism
Prov. 5:23	S^{Pn}VM//MV	Closure	Last verse in chapter
Prov. 8:12	S^{Pn}SVO//OV	Aperture	NIV ESV NASB NKJV REB NJPS NJB NLT NCV CEV Murphy Fox Whybray Garrett Walkte

Since these six texts clearly perform the role of demarcating textual boundaries, it would be expected that the remaining three instances of this particular form also possess special discourse-level functions. In each of these, in fact, a plausible reason can be found for understanding their location in the text as indicating a climactic point.

Is. 45:12-13	S^{Pn}VO//SMV SVO//OV S^{Pn}VM//OV S^{Pn}VO//OV/Nom	Climactic	God as sovereign
Is. 66:3e-4b	gam-S^{Pn}VM//MSV gam-S^{Pn}VM//OVM	Climactic	Centre of unit
Job 8:5	CS^{Pn}VM//MV	Climactic	Seek God

In brief, we observe in the extended parallel construction of Isaiah 45:12–13 that God, speaking in the 1st person, identifies himself as both the Creator of heaven and earth and everything in them, and also as the one who raised up Cyrus to restore his people – both key themes in this portion of Isaiah. God, the prophet here teaches, is sovereign in both creation and history. Oswalt notes that the repeated use of independent pronouns in these verses gives it a 'special emphasis'.[82] A case could be made for taking these

---

81 NRSV NIV ESV NJB CEV, Kidner, *Psalms 1–72*, p. 246, and Kraus, *Psalms 60–150* (Minneapolis: Augsburg, 1989), p. 61, consider it a closure.
82 Oswalt, *The Book of Isaiah 40–66*, p. 210.

two verses as a separate logical sub-unit, as does Motyer.[83] The end of verse 13 certainly marks a closure (through the formula אָמַר יְהוָה צְבָאוֹת). Verse 12a marks the switch from 2nd person plural to 1st person singular, and from a question posed to an answer given.

The four-part parallelism from Isaiah 66 forms the centre-piece[84] of the unit contained in verses 3–4.[85] It can be seen that the material both preceding (a series of participial clauses describing acts of unacceptable worship) and following (a series of reasons regarding the people's refusal to listen) contains less prominent information.[86] Lines 3e–4b, the unusually formed parallelism, arguably contain the crux of the matter: 'These have chosen their own ways, and in their abominations they take delight; I also will choose to mock them, and bring upon them what they fear' (NRSV).

In the final text, Job 8:5, Bildad proposes that Job earnestly turn in supplication to God for relief from his trials. This recommendation is arguably the most salient point in the whole section of 8:2–7.[87] Hartley argues that the use of the pronoun here is deliberately to draw Job's attention to this particular statement.[88]

(c) MKD//Gap

There is just a single place where we find a possible occurrence[89] of an unusual MKD//Gap parallelism, having the order SVO//MO.

Psalm 35:28

Then my tongue shall tell of your righteousness　　וּלְשׁוֹנִי תֶּהְגֶּה צִדְקֶךָ
and of your praise all day long.　　כָּל־הַיּוֹם תְּהִלָּתֶךָ׃

The SV-clause here is probably to be taken as indicating the sentence-focus function of declaration or proclamation.[90] It is perhaps significant that TEV renders this verse as 'Then I will *proclaim* your righteousness' (italics

---

83　Motyer, *The Prophecy of Isaiah*, p. 362.
84　On the importance of this 'central core' of a rhetorical structure, see the comments earlier in this chapter on Isaiah 59:7.
85　We note the inclusio produced by the re-occurrence of the two principal verbs of the central piece, בָּחַר ('choose') and חָפֵץ ('delight'), in the concluding statement of verse 4f. This is observed by Motyer, *The Prophecy of Isaiah*, p. 534.
86　Further evidence that these two parallelisms (3ef, 4ab) were intended to stand out is provided by Watts (*Isaiah 34–66*, p. 350), who points out that both have the metrical pattern 3 + 3, in contrast to the surrounding cola, most of which are 2 + 2.
87　It is also to be noted that this is a reiteration of the same suggestion earlier on the part of Eliphaz (5:8).
88　Hartley, *The Book of Job*, p. 156.
89　We use the word 'possible' because an alternative analysis might be offered. Rather than a MKD//Gap parallelism, it might be taken as a MKD/Nom bicolon where the B-line simply contains nominal constituents in apposition to the A-line.
90　Cf. the discussion of Psalms 96:10; 97:1 etc., in 4.2.3 (a).

added). What makes this a rare form of parallelism is not the mere fact of gapping which, as stated earlier, does in fact happen with respect to non-focal elements in marked parallelisms.[91] The notable feature in this case is that it is the clause-initial subject phrase together with the verb that have been elided from the second line. Since this is the last verse of the psalm it is unquestionably an instance of closure.

8.2.3 Gap-Initial Parallelisms

In chapter 2 the phenomenon of gapping in parallelisms was described.[92] In that context the fact of retrograde or backward gapping was noted in passing. In such a case an element, invariably the verb, is absent from the first line, where it would be expected. It is not until one gets to the end of the second line that the verb is supplied. This is a much rarer feature of parallelism in Biblical Hebrew poetry. These gap-initial parallelisms fall into the same category as the other unusual colon arrangements examined in this chapter.[93] Only five occur in the data. These fall into three basic kinds according to the type of clause following the one which is gapped.

(a) Gap//DEF

Psalm 70:2

[Come quickly], O God, to save me,   אֱלֹהִים לְהַצִּילֵנִי
O YHWH, come quickly to help me.   יְהוָה לְעֶזְרָתִי חוּשָׁה׃

This is a good illustration of the phenomenon, having the order: [Voc] Inf // [Voc] Inf V. The imperative verb, חוּשָׁה, in the final position of the second clause, does duty for both lines. Since this is the opening verse of the psalm, the function of the peculiar Gap//DEF form is to signal aperture.

Song 4:8ab

With me from Lebanon, my bride,   אִתִּי מִלְּבָנוֹן כַּלָּה
with me from Lebanon come.   אִתִּי מִלְּבָנוֹן תָּבוֹאִי

This bicolon has the composition MM[Voc]//MMV. Following the lengthy description of the woman in verses 1–7, largely through verbless clauses, her lover invites her to come away with him. This is taken as the beginning of a new section by NIV REB NJB TEV and NLT, as well as in the commentaries of Longman III, Murphy, and Carr.[94]

---

91 See 7.2.6.
92 See 2.2.2 (a).
93 This feature is discussed by Z. Zevit, 'Roman Jakobsen, Psycholinguistics, and Biblical Poetry', *JBL 109* (1990), p. 395, who is in broad agreement with our conclusions on this kind of structure.
94 Longman III, *Song of Songs*, p. 148; Murphy, *The Song of Songs*, pp. 158–59; G. L. Carr, *The Song of Solomon*, TOTC (Leicester: Inter-Varsity Press, 1984), p. 113.

(b) Gap//MKD

Psalm 92:10

For behold your enemies, O YHWH,	כִּי הִנֵּה אֹיְבֶיךָ יְהוָה
for behold your enemies shall perish,	כִּי־הִנֵּה אֹיְבֶיךָ יֹאבֵדוּ
all evildoers shall be scattered.	יִתְפָּרְדוּ כָּל־פֹּעֲלֵי אָוֶן:

Here the verse structure is CHS[Voc]//CHSV/VS, lines A and B relating together as a parallelism. The repetition of the NP[Su] in both lines, combined with the particle הִנֵּה ('behold'), suggests that this constituent is in focus, being a new topic brought into the discourse. The gapping of the verb from the A-line is the opposite of what typically occurs.[95] The three cola create a tricolon,[96] another previously identified boundary-marking device.[97] Virtually all the English versions recognise a boundary here, though they are divided between aperture (NIV NJPS NJB TEV NCV), and closure (NRSV ESV NKJV NASB REB NLT CEV). Most commentators (e.g., Terrien, Kidner, Harman, Delitzsch) take it as closure. Whichever way it is taken, it is widely recognised as one of the limits of a sub-section of the psalm.

Psalm 94:3

How long shall the wicked, O YHWH,	עַד־מָתַי רְשָׁעִים יְהוָה
how long shall the wicked exult?	עַד־מָתַי רְשָׁעִים יַעֲלֹזוּ:

This verse consists of QS[Voc]//QSV. It is taken as marking the closure of the first section of the psalm in NRSV NIV NKJV CEV, and in the commentaries of Terrien, Kidner, Harman, and Delitzsch.[98]

(c) Gap//CAN

Psalm 94:1

O God of vengeance, YHWH,	אֵל־נְקָמוֹת יְהוָה
O God of vengeance, shine forth!	אֵל נְקָמוֹת הוֹפִיעַ:

This [Voc]//[Voc]V parallelism is the verse with which the psalm opens.

These five are the only unequivocal examples of this phenomenon[99] encountered in the entire data.[100]

---

95 Cf. 7.2.6.
96 Tate, *Psalms 51–100*, pp. 462, 467.
97 Cf. 8.2.1 (a) above.
98 Terrien, *Psalms*, p. 661; Kidner, *Psalms 73–150*, p. 340; Harman, *Psalms*, pp. 316–17; and Delitzsch, 'Psalms', p. 77. Kraus, *Psalms 60–150*, p. 240; and Anderson, *Psalms*, vol. 2, p. 671, both take it as aperture.
99 Holladay ('Hebrew Verse Structure Revisited II', p. 410) also proposes Job 4:10, שַׁאֲגַת אַרְיֵה וְקוֹל שָׁחַל וְשִׁנֵּי כְפִירִים נִתָּעוּ ('The roar of the lion, the voice of the fierce lion, and the teeth of the young lions are broken'). This is better taken, however, as a single clause with an extended subject phrase (S w-S/w-S V). There is

8.3 Defamiliar Cola in Non-Parallelisms

Up to now we have only considered infrequent forms of parallelisms. However, it is also to be observed that non-parallel structures may contain unusual sequences of word order. On occasions a DEF colon will appear in a non-parallelism. In such cases, the context does not lend support to construing the word order as pragmatically marked. The occurrence of each of these instances at an obvious textual boundary, strongly suggests that even an independent DEF colon may have the same function as irregularly formed parallelisms.

Ref.	Form	Function	Versions & Commentaries
Ps. 3:5	MMV/VM *Selah*	Closure	NRSV NIV NKJV ESV TEV NJB NLT NCV CEV Craigie Kidner Delitzsch Harman
Ps. 4:9	MMVV/CS[Voc]MMV	Closure	Last verse in psalm
Ps. 5:13	C-S^{Pn}VO[Voc]/MMV	Closure	Last verse in psalm
Ps. 7:8	SV-o/MMV	Closure	ESV NJB CEV Kraus
Ps. 7:14	MVO/OMV	Closure	NIV NKJV NLT NCV CEV Terrien Delitzsch
Ps. 9:13	C-SOV/VO	Closure	NRSV NIV NKJV ESV REB TEV NLT CEV Terrien Anderson Kidner Delitzsch Harman
Ps. 12:9	MSV/M	Closure	Last verse in psalm
Ps. 14:2	SMVM/InfQ-ES/V^{Pt}O	Aperture	NRSV NIV NKJV ESV NJB TEV NLT NCV CEV Terrien Kraus Kidner

nothing to suggest that this verse has any special discourse function. Rosenbaum's examples of verb gapping in the A-line are unconvincing (*Word-Order Variation in Isaiah 40–55*, pp. 161–63). In both of his examples (Is. 40:15; 46:4) the A-line can in fact be read without difficulty as a syntactically complete noun-clause.

100 The reader should also be aware that backwards gapping of an object noun phrase is also attested, though this in no way influences the markedness of the clauses involved. It is significant that the three examples encountered in the data, Psalms 93:3; 96:7 and Isaiah 45:8, are all well supported instances of boundary (aperture). Further, a single instance of Gap/MKD, i.e., in a non-parallel relation, was noted. This is Psalm 20:8, taken as aperture by several versions (e.g., NKJV NJB CEV) and commentators (e.g., Craigie, Harman, Delitzsch).

Ps. 25:1	M[Voc]OV	Aperture [Monocolon]	First verse in psalm
Ps. 30:13	CVSV/[Voc]MV	Closure	Last verse in psalm
Ps. 42:7	MSV/CVM/M	Aperture	NIV NKJV ESV NJPS REB TEV NLT CEV Terrien Craigie Kraus Anderson Kidner Harman
Ps. 75:11	OV/VS	Closure	Last verse in psalm
Ps. 80:9	OMV/VOV	Aperture	NRSV NIV NKJV ESV NJPS REB NJB TEV NCV CEV Terrien Tate Kraus Anderson Kidner Harman
Ps. 85:14	SMV/VMO	Closure	Last verse in psalm
Ps. 120:1	MMVV	Aperture [Monocolon]	First verse in psalm
Is. 40:10	HSMV/SV^{Pt}M	Aperture	NKJV NJB TEV Watts
Is. 42:1	OMV	Aperture [Monocolon]	(See discussion in chapter 9)
Is. 42:4	MSV	Closure [Monocolon]	NRSV NIV ESV NKJV NJPS REB TEV NLT NCV CEV Oswalt Watts Motyer Young
Is. 48:3	OMV/MVV-o	Aperture	NRSV ESV NKJV NJPS REB TEV CEV Watts Motyer
Is. 61:7	CMOV/SVM	Closure	NRSV NIV NKJV ESV TEV NLT CEV Oswalt Watts Motyer
Job 8:19	HS^{Pn}Comp/MSV	Closure	NRSV NIV ESV REB TEV NLT NCV CEV Hartley Clines Rowley Andersen Habel Alden Driver & Gray
Job 11:12	SV/SCompV	Closure	All English versions Hartley Clines Rowley Andersen Habel Alden Driver & Gray
Job 13:16	P-S^{Pn}MComp/M^{Ng}SV	Closure	NJPS NJB NLT Clines Habel

Prov. 1:7	SComp/OOSV	Closure MT [ס]	NRSV NIV ESV NKJV NASB NJPS REB NLT NCV CEV Murphy Fox McKane Whybray Garrett Waltke Kidner
Prov. 3:35	OSV/OV^PtS	Closure	Last verse in chapter

Significantly we observe a certain pattern in that when the function is aperture only the A-line is DEF, yet with closure either the A-line and/or subsequent lines may be DEF. Logically it would perhaps be expected that aperture would consistently employ a DEF A-line, as is the case.

Further comments are offered on two of the above texts, Psalm 75:11 and Isaiah 40:10. The two monocola from Isaiah 42 will be dealt with in the next chapter, in which the whole of 42:1–4 will be analysed.

Psalm 75:11

I will cut off all the horns of the wicked,   וְכָל־קַרְנֵי רְשָׁעִים אֲגַדֵּעַ
but the horns of the righteous shall be exalted.   תְּרוֹמַמְנָה קַרְנוֹת צַדִּיק׃

This verse is unique among all the entries in the data. The two cola, OV/VS, stand in a straightforward contrastive relationship between the 'horns of the wicked' and the 'horns of the righteous'. Yet the expected form is completely reversed. Invariably such a contrast would appear as CAN/MKD (that is, here VO/SV).[101] The remarkable sequence MKD/CAN, more appropriately labelled as DEF/CAN, functions as an indicator of a closure, since with this verse the psalm ends.

Isaiah 40:10

Behold, the Lord YHWH comes with might,   הִנֵּה אֲדֹנָי יְהוִה בְּחָזָק יָבוֹא
and his arm rules for him.   וּזְרֹעוֹ מֹשְׁלָה לוֹ

Among the various versions and commentators the boundary-marking function of this verse is not quite so strongly attested as others. Yet it does show obvious affinities with the unit-initial HSMV clause in Isaiah 66:15 (הִנֵּה יְהוָה בָּאֵשׁ יָבוֹא) and the SMV opening clause of Isaiah 42:13, both mentioned earlier in this chapter. The close resemblance between these lends support to the DEF clause of 40:10 also being a device to signal a new section in the discourse.

8.4 The Noetic Effect of Unusual Patterns

All the various patterns of parallel and non-parallel bicola, tricola and tetra-cola considered in this chapter have one thing in common – the unusualness

---

101 And on fewer occasions MKD/MKD. See 4.2.2 (c).

of their form. The bulk of parallelisms either have a canonical A-line followed by an equally canonical or defamiliar B-line, or a marked A-line paralleled by an identically marked B-line. Where this is not the case, a special signal is being sent to the listener/reader. When the regular pattern is broken, either by placing the defamiliar colon in the position of the base-line, i.e., line A, or by the B-line violating the constraint pertaining to markedness, it produces what may be described as 'a zone of turbulence'.[102] This has a certain 'noetic' effect[103] upon the recipient, that is, it impacts the manner of mental processing undertaken by the listener/reader. Since the normal patterns are not followed, greater effort is required to decode the linguistic information of the utterance so that the recipient can comprehend its communicative intent. In the case of initial DEF cola, it is not until the completion of the second line that the focus structure of the whole can be determined. In the case of initial MKD cola, the second line is not what the listener/reader is anticipating. The effect of each is to produce a discontinuity in the flow of the text. In both situations it happens that the larger degree of processing required causes a slowing down in the pace at which the information is apprehended. This slowing down is entirely in harmony with the specific contexts, i.e., those of boundary and peak, in which these unusual forms occur. The poetic author employs this device[104] to draw greater attention to particular verses, since these function at a level higher than the inter-clausal. These unusual forms may justifiably be termed 'marked', marked that is, not pragmatically with respect to word order, but with respect to colon arrangement, functioning at a level higher than that of pragmatics. By this means the author is alerting the listener/reader to significant junctures in the discourse.

8.5 Summary

In this chapter we have surveyed rare colon arrangements. These may be tabulated as:

PARALLELISMS		NON-PARALLELISMS	
DEF-initial	MKD-initial	Gap-initial	DEF/CAN
DEF//CAN	MKD//CAN	Gap//DEF	DEF/MKD
DEF//DEF	MKD//DEF		CAN/DEF
DEF//Gap	MKD//Gap		MKD/DEF
DEF//Nom			etc.[105]

---

102 Cf. the use of the term by R. E. Longacre, *The Grammar of Discourse* (New York: Plenum Press, 1983), p. 25.
103 Cf. Zevit, 'Roman Jakobsen, Psycholinguistics, and Biblical Poetry', p. 393.
104 Among those others noted during the course of this chapter.
105 It should be observed that there is no restriction upon form in the case of non-parallel sequences such as exists in the case of parallelisms.

These irregular formations, it was seen, are not randomly placed but only appear at specific junctures in the text. The unusual form of these poetic units creates an interruption in the information flow, thus serving to draw attention to the presence of a boundary, or a point of climax in the discourse.

CHAPTER 9

Application: Standard and Difficult Texts

Most of the texts studied up to now have been dealt with in relative isolation apart from their immediate contexts. So we now come to illustrate the outworking of the ideas put forward in the foregoing chapters by their application to extended passages from the selected corpus of data. First the analysis of several complete poetic sections from the Old Testament will be undertaken (9.1). These are Psalms 1 and 103, Job 12, Song of Songs 1, plus the first of the Balaam oracles in Numbers 23 to represent early biblical poetry. Study of these will serve to illustrate how the approach presented earlier helps in the understanding of word order in a variety of what may be described as fairly typical poetic texts. By 'typical' we mean that these passages display an average degree of word-order variation relative to other texts of Hebrew poetry, or that the departure from canonical word order which they manifest is readily accounted for. Secondly (9.2), a number of factors are listed which are the cause of potential difficulties, yet where, once all things are taken into consideration, the word order is capable of satisfactory explanation. We then finally (9.3) analyse certain texts which contain a much higher proportion of non-canonical clauses, and where some of these, at first sight, might be thought conflict with what has previously been proposed.

9.1 Standard Texts

9.1.1 Psalm 1

1a	אַשְׁרֵי־הָאִישׁ Happy is the man	Comp S
1b	אֲשֶׁר לֹא הָלַךְ בַּעֲצַת רְשָׁעִים who does not walk in the counsel of the wicked,	R V^{Ng} M
1c	וּבְדֶרֶךְ חַטָּאִים לֹא עָמָד and does not stand in the way of sinners,	w-M V^{Ng}
1d	וּבְמוֹשַׁב לֵצִים לֹא יָשָׁב׃ and does not sit in the seat of scoffers.	w-M V^{Ng}

2a	כִּי אִם בְּתוֹרַת יְהוָה חֶפְצוֹ But his delight is in the law of YHWH;	C Comp S
2b	וּבְתוֹרָתוֹ יֶהְגֶּה יוֹמָם וָלָיְלָה׃ and in his law he meditates day and night.	w-M V M w-M
3a	וְהָיָה כְּעֵץ שָׁתוּל עַל־פַּלְגֵי מָיִם He shall be like a tree planted by streams of water,	w-V Comp
3b	אֲשֶׁר פִּרְיוֹ יִתֵּן בְּעִתּוֹ which gives its fruit in season,	R O V M
3c	וְעָלֵהוּ לֹא־יִבּוֹל and whose leaves do not whither,	w-S V^{Ng}
3d	וְכֹל אֲשֶׁר־יַעֲשֶׂה יַצְלִיחַ׃ and everything he does prospers.	w-O(R V) V
4a	לֹא־כֵן הָרְשָׁעִים The wicked are not so;	Comp^{Ng} S
4b	כִּי אִם־כַּמֹּץ אֲשֶׁר־תִּדְּפֶנּוּ רוּחַ׃ but they are like the chaff that the wind drives away.	C-Comp R-V-o S
5a	עַל־כֵּן לֹא־יָקֻמוּ רְשָׁעִים בַּמִּשְׁפָּט Therefore the wicked will not stand in the judgment,	C V^{Ng} S M
5b	וְחַטָּאִים בַּעֲדַת צַדִּיקִים׃ nor sinners in the assembly of the righteous.	w-S M
6a	כִּי־יוֹדֵעַ יְהוָה דֶּרֶךְ צַדִּיקִים For YHWH knows the way of the righteous,	C-V^{Pt} S O
6b	וְדֶרֶךְ רְשָׁעִים תֹּאבֵד׃ but the way of the wicked shall perish.	w-S V

Verse 1. The first verbs of the psalm appear in what is grammatically a relative clause. The opening nominal construction, אַשְׁרֵי־הָאִישׁ אֲשֶׁר, 'Happy is the man who ...', introduces three negative verbal clauses. These are described by Craigie as three parallel lines which are 'poetically synonymous'.[1] The constituent composition of each of these clauses is identical – a negated verb with a modifying prepositional phrase. However, while the first clause adheres to canonical word order (V^{Ng} M), the following two have been inverted (M V^{Ng}) – *ab//ba//ba*. As has been demonstrated earlier,[2] this reordering of constituents in the secondary lines of parallelisms is a commonplace feature in the poetry of the Old Testament.

Verse 2. The compound כִּי אִם here functions as a connector between verses 1 and 2. It is followed by two clauses, first a noun-clause, then a

---

1 Craigie, *Psalms 1–50*, p. 60.
2 See 5.3.

verbal clause. The context demands some close connection between the content of this verse and the foregoing. The blessed man does not do those things described in verse 1, but what he does do is now given in the second verse. This connection is shown by the many English translations which render כִּי אִם as 'but' (e.g., NRSV NIV NASB NJB), suggesting a contrast. Yet what is involved is not a direct polar contrast, but rather an instance of replacing focus.[3] The two verses tell us that the righteous man does not do X but Y. The psalmist uses here the standard construction for this category of focus, taking the form ... לֹא ... כִּי אִם ... (appearing again in verse 4). As was observed in our discussion of replacing focus, fronting invariably takes place in the clause containing the information replacing that of the negated first clause. The first colon of verse 2 places בְּתוֹרַת יְהוָה in the clause-initial position. Though this is a noun-clause and its structure is not our primary concern, we may nevertheless say that the appearance of this PP in the initial position indicates that it is the most prominent idea in the author's mind.[4] We may identify the clause-final חֶפְצוֹ as the presupposition,[5] and the clause-initial בְּתוֹרַת יְהוָה as the focus. In harmony with this is the fact that the virtually identical PP וּבְתוֹרָתוֹ occurs in the first position in the verbal clause of the B-line. Thus the phrase 'in the/his law' heads both cola. Together they form a closely matching parallelism. We recall the constraint upon marked word order in parallelisms[6] that the markedness of the A-line will be repeated in the B. Though the parallelism here is between a noun-clause and a verbal clause the same constraint is seen to apply.

Verse 3. This is a four-line unit which will require greater space to elucidate. After a canonical A-line, lines B, C and D all display non-canonical word order in that each contains a sentence constituent occupying the preverbal position. The inter-relations between the various clauses of this verse might be analysed in a number of different ways. The analysis offered here attempts to account for each of the fronted elements in context. Beginning with the A-line we observe that on the semantic level its contents are of a general nature. It speaks simply of a 'tree' (עֵץ). In each of the following two cola there is a NP, פִּרְיוֹ and וְעָלֵהוּ, in a relative clause referring back to the tree. These NPs both refer to parts of the tree, and both nouns appear with the possessive suffix, 'its', referring to the tree itself as the possessor – 'its fruit' and 'its leaves'. It is these two NPs which are placed in the clause-initial position in lines B and C. What we have here in

---

3 See 3.4.2 (c) and 4.2.2 (b).
4 Cf. Buth, 'Word Order in the Verbless Clause', p. 99, who affirms the salience of the initial element in the noun-clause.
5 Assuming that the delight of the blessed man must be in something.
6 See 7.1.

these two clauses well fits the description of specifying focus.[7] Having mentioned the tree in the opening line of the verse (3a), we are then introduced to two particular components of the tree, and these are placed in the preverbal position. We conclude therefore that lines B and C show marked focus. In addition to this, we may describe these two MKD cola as an embedded parallelism within the larger unit. The two fronted NPs correspond, as we have seen, and though with respect to different parts of the tree, the overall meaning of each cola is nevertheless quite similar. Both concern the growth that the tree produces, its fruit and its foliage. The former is given at the time it is expected, the latter is permanent. This productivity of both elements comes as a result of what was stated in the A-line, that the tree was 'planted by streams of water' (3a). If taken as a parallelism then the constraint concerning markedness in parallelisms is also seen to apply. The marked focus construction of the head-line (3b) reoccurs in the parallel-line (3c). Finally, line D rounds off the verse with another clause departing from canonical word order. From the point of view of the semantic content it cannot be said that D follows on as a third parallel line from B and C. The colon does not concern part of the tree but rather, like line A, is a statement of a more general nature. Moreover, the clause contains no proforms (such as 'its' in lines B and C) referring back to the tree, and grammatically it is not contained within the relative clause in which lines B and C are situated. Line D, therefore, evidently stands independently of the preceding two lines. The subject of its first verb, יַעֲשֶׂה, is 3rd person masculine singular which is best taken as agreeing with וְהָיָה at the beginning of the A-line (as, for example, in NIV NASB REB). The subject of וְהָיָה, 'he', refers to the man who delights in and meditates on God's law (v. 2). The man who esteems the divine law in this way will also prosper in everything he does.[8] The fronting of the phrase וְכֹל אֲשֶׁר־יַעֲשֶׂה presents little difficulty. It has been remarked even in the earliest word-order studies in Hebrew that phrases containing the quantifier כֹל ('all') are frequently placed in the clause-initial position.[9] The reason for this can now be identified as pragmatic marking. The adjoining of the quantifier to the subject, object, or prepositional phrase serves to highlight the degree or extent of the entity in question. Here the stress is on the 'everything', '*Everything* he does prospers', not just some things. We may compare this

---

7 See 3.4.2 (g) and 4.2.2 (a).
8 It makes little difference to the present analysis whether the rendering 'He prospers in whatever he does' (cf. NIV NRSV) or 'Everything he does prospers' (cf. NKJV NJB) is adopted. The Hebrew could be read in both ways. See the discussion by Delitzsch, in Keil and Delitzsch, *Commentary on the Old Testament*, vol. 5, 'Psalms', p. 86.
9 E.g., F. I. Andersen, *The Sentence in Biblical Hebrew* (Paris/New York: Mouton Publishers, 1974), pp. 43–44.

Application: Standard and Difficult Texts

with precisely the same markedness of כֹּל אֲשֶׁר in other similar sentences, such as:[10]

כָּל־אֲשֶׁר יַחְפֹּץ יַעֲשֶׂה: (Eccl. 8:3)
He does everything he pleases.

אֶל־כָּל־אֲשֶׁר יִפְנֶה יַשְׂכִּיל: (Prov. 17:8)
Wherever he turns, he prospers.

Having accounted for the constituent order in these four cola, we may now represent the verse using the method of diagramming described earlier in chapter 2:

```
┌─HEAD¹ ──┬── HEAD ─────────────── וְהָיָה כְּעֵץ שָׁתוּל עַל־פַּלְגֵי מָיִם
│         └── Subord ─┬── HEAD ─── אֲשֶׁר פִּרְיוֹ יִתֵּן בְּעִתּוֹ
│                     └── Parallel ── וְעָלֵהוּ לֹא־יִבּוֹל
└─HEAD² ────────────────────────── וְכֹל אֲשֶׁר־יַעֲשֶׂה יַצְלִיחַ
```

Verse 4. As the basic structure of this verse consists of two noun-clauses, it therefore falls outside the scope of the present study. However, we point out the fact that the verb appearing in the relative clause of the B-line occurs in regular VS order.

Verse 5. This verse contains a typical instance of synonymous parallelism.[11] The A-line follows the basic constituent order. In the B-line the verb is gapped, as frequently occurs in such parallel constructions. To compensate for the loss of the verb the B-line retains the balance through the lengthening of the M element.[12] The NP governed by the preposition –בְּ, corresponding to the single word בַּמִּשְׁפָּט in the parallelism, now consists of the construct chain עֲדַת צַדִּיקִים.

Verse 6. The A-line consists of a participial clause. The fronting of the NP[Su] in the B-line of the bicolon is clearly indicative of a contrastive relationship with the A-line. There the psalmist speaks of God knowing דֶּרֶךְ צַדִּיקִים ('the way of the righteous'). The verb 'know' here has the sense of 'protect' or 'guard'.[13] Harman comments, 'The way of the righteous is overseen constantly by the LORD, whereas the way of the ungodly has no future. It is going to perish utterly'.[14] This verse, Harman continues, 'sums up the contrast' between the righteous and the wicked

---

10 Many more examples of clause-initial phrases containing כָּל־אֲשֶׁר could be adduced, e.g., Leviticus 6:11; 11:32; Numbers 19:16; 1 Samuel 2:14; 9:6; 14:47; 2 Kings 10:19; 18:7; Psalm 135:6; Isaiah 19:17; 46:10; Joel 3:5.
11 Craigie, *Psalms 1–50*, p. 61.
12 Cf. the 'ballast variant', described in 2.2.2 (a).
13 See Craigie, *Psalms 1–50*, p. 58; also *NIDOTTE*, vol. 2, p. 412.
14 Harman, *Psalms*, p. 73.

with which the whole psalm is concerned. Many English versions (e.g., NRSV NIV REB) and commentaries (e.g., Terrien, Craigie, Delitzsch) join the two cola with the contrastive conjunction 'but'. What we have in this verse, therefore, is that which has been traditionally designated antithetical parallelism,[15] but which in the context of this study has been redefined in terms of a marked contrastive construction. We are thus not looking at a poetically motivated defamiliar reordering of constituents, but an order which is strictly pragmatically determined.[16]

In conclusion, the labelling of the various clauses contained in this psalm would be as follows:

v. 1 Nom/CAN//DEF//DEF   v. 4 Nom/Nom
v. 2 Nom//MKD   v. 5 CAN//Gap
v. 3 CAN/MKD//MKD/MKD   v. 6 Pctp/MKD

A comparative quantification of colon types appearing in each of the chapters discussed will be included in tabular form in the concluding section below (9.1.6). The relative frequency of the various colon-types in Psalm 1 may be tabulated as:

Chapter	Verbal Clauses	CAN	MKD	DEF
Ps. 1	11	4	5	2

9.1.2 Psalm 103

1a	בָּרֲכִי נַפְשִׁי אֶת־יְהוָה Bless YHWH, O my soul,	V [Voc] O
1b	וְכָל־קְרָבַי אֶת־שֵׁם קָדְשׁוֹ׃ and all that is in me [bless] his holy name.	w-[Voc] O
2a	בָּרֲכִי נַפְשִׁי אֶת־יְהוָה Bless YHWH, O my soul,	V [Voc] O
2b	וְאַל־תִּשְׁכְּחִי כָּל־גְּמוּלָיו׃ and do not forget all his benefits –	w-V^{Ng} O
3a	הַסֹּלֵחַ לְכָל־עֲוֺנֵכִי who forgives all your iniquities,	V^{Pt} O

---

15 Craigie, *Psalms 1–50*, p. 59.
16 See the discussion of antithetical parallelisms and contrast in 6.4.

Application: Standard and Difficult Texts

3b	הָרֹפֵא לְכָל־תַּחֲלֻאָיְכִי׃ who heals all your diseases,	V^{Pt} O
4a	הַגּוֹאֵל מִשַּׁחַת חַיָּיְכִי who redeems your life from the pit,	V^{Pt} M O
4b	הַמְעַטְּרֵכִי חֶסֶד וְרַחֲמִים׃ who crowns you with steadfast love and compassion,	V^{Pt}-o O w-O
5a	הַמַּשְׂבִּיעַ בַּטּוֹב עֶדְיֵךְ who satisfies you with good things as long as you live	V^{Pt} M M
5b	תִּתְחַדֵּשׁ כַּנֶּשֶׁר נְעוּרָיְכִי׃ so that your youth is renewed like the eagle.	V M S
6a	עֹשֵׂה צְדָקוֹת יְהוָה YHWH executes righteousness	V^{Pt} O S
6b	וּמִשְׁפָּטִים לְכָל־עֲשׁוּקִים׃ and justice for all the oppressed.	w-O M
7a	יוֹדִיעַ דְּרָכָיו לְמֹשֶׁה He made known his ways to Moses,	V O M
7b	לִבְנֵי יִשְׂרָאֵל עֲלִילוֹתָיו׃ his deeds to the Israelites.	M O
8a	רַחוּם וְחַנּוּן יְהוָה YHWH is compassionate and gracious,	Comp w-Comp S
8b	אֶרֶךְ אַפַּיִם וְרַב־חָסֶד׃ slow to anger, abounding in steadfast love.	Comp w-Comp
9a	לֹא־לָנֶצַח יָרִיב He will not always contend,	M^{Ng} V
9b	וְלֹא לְעוֹלָם יִטּוֹר׃ nor will he remain angry for ever.	w-M^{Ng} V
10a	לֹא כַחֲטָאֵינוּ עָשָׂה לָנוּ He does not deal with us according to our sins,	M^{Ng} V M
10b	וְלֹא כַעֲוֺנֹתֵינוּ גָּמַל עָלֵינוּ׃ nor does he repay us according to our iniquities.	w-M^{Ng} V M
11a	כִּי כִגְבֹהַּ שָׁמַיִם עַל־הָאָרֶץ For as high as the heavens are above the earth,	C M(Inf S M)
11b	גָּבַר חַסְדּוֹ עַל־יְרֵאָיו׃ so great is his steadfast love for those who fear him;	V S M
12a	כִּרְחֹק מִזְרָח מִמַּעֲרָב as far as the east is from the west	M(Inf S M)

12b	הִרְחִיק מִמֶּנּוּ אֶת־פְּשָׁעֵינוּ׃ so far has he removed our transgressions from us.	V M O
13a	כְּרַחֵם אָב עַל־בָּנִים As a father has compassion on his children,	M(Inf S M)
13b	רִחַם יְהוָה עַל־יְרֵאָיו׃ so does YHWH have compassion on those who fear him;	V S M
14a	כִּי־הוּא יָדַע יִצְרֵנוּ for he knows our frame,	C-S^{Pn} V O
14b	זָכוּר כִּי־עָפָר אֲנָחְנוּ׃ he remembers that we are dust.	Comp C Comp S
15a	אֱנוֹשׁ כֶּחָצִיר יָמָיו As for man, his days are like grass,	N Comp S
15b	כְּצִיץ הַשָּׂדֶה כֵּן יָצִיץ׃ like the flower of the field thus he flourishes;	M M V
16a	כִּי רוּחַ עָבְרָה־בּוֹ וְאֵינֶנּוּ for the wind blows over it and it is no more,	C S V-M w-E^{Ng}
16b	וְלֹא־יַכִּירֶנּוּ עוֹד מְקוֹמוֹ׃ and its place knows it no longer.	w-V^{Ng}-o M S
17a	וְחֶסֶד יְהוָה מֵעוֹלָם וְעַד־עוֹלָם עַל־יְרֵאָיו But the steadfast love of YHWH is from everlasting to everlasting, to those who fear him,	w-S Comp M
17b	וְצִדְקָתוֹ לִבְנֵי בָנִים׃ and his righteousness with their children's children,	w-S M
18a	לְשֹׁמְרֵי בְרִיתוֹ with those who keep his covenant,	w-M
18b	וּלְזֹכְרֵי פִקֻּדָיו לַעֲשׂוֹתָם׃ and who remember to perform his precepts.	w-M Inf-o
19a	יְהוָה בַּשָּׁמַיִם הֵכִין כִּסְאוֹ YHWH has established his throne in heaven,	S M V O
19b	וּמַלְכוּתוֹ בַּכֹּל מָשָׁלָה׃ and his kingdom rules over all.	w-S M V
20a	בָּרֲכוּ יְהוָה מַלְאָכָיו Bless YHWH, his angels,	V O [Voc]
20b	גִּבֹּרֵי כֹחַ עֹשֵׂי דְבָרוֹ you mighty ones who carry out his word,	[Voc]
20c	לִשְׁמֹעַ בְּקוֹל דְּבָרוֹ׃ who obey his word.	Inf O

21a	בָּרְכוּ יְהוָה כָּל־צְבָאָיו Bless YHWH, all his hosts,	V O [Voc]
21b	מְשָׁרְתָיו עֹשֵׂי רְצוֹנוֹ׃ you servants who do his will.	[Voc]
22a	בָּרְכוּ יְהוָה כָּל־מַעֲשָׂיו Bless YHWH, all his works,	V O [Voc]
22b	בְּכָל־מְקֹמוֹת מֶמְשַׁלְתּוֹ everywhere in his dominion.	M
22c	בָּרְכִי נַפְשִׁי אֶת־יְהוָה׃ Bless YHWH, O my soul.	V [Voc] O

Verses 1-6. Non-canonical constituent order is totally absent from these opening lines. Each finite verb in the first two verses is placed at the beginning of its clause and is a 2nd person feminine form, since the psalmist is addressing his own soul (נֶפֶשׁ), as an obviously active topic from his perspective. These, therefore, have predicate focus. 5b is slightly different in that it is an attribute of the soul being addressed, but the information structure remains the same. The other clauses contain masculine participles speaking of various divine activities.

Verse 7. These two cola form a parallelism with the pattern abc//cb. The A-line is perfectly canonical, being a comment on an active topic (God), that is, having predicate-focus structure. The B-line exhibits both gapping of the verb and reordering of constituents. This verse would be designated CAN//Gap.

Verse 8. This bicolon consists of two noun-clauses.

Verse 9. Another parallelism. This instance shows close correspondence at both the semantic and syntactic level, each clause having the same constituent structure as well as order. We note the location of the M element in the initial position. In the explanation of this, we are helped by information-structure analysis. Applying the presupposition-focus articulation to the basic form of these clauses it can be seen that the verbal idea, that of anger, forms the presuppositional component of the clause. The psalmist takes it for granted that God, on occasion, will express his anger against the sins of his people. Such is inevitable in view of the prevalence of human sin. Yet when this is so God tempers his wrath.[17] The fact that the divine anger does not last for ever,[18] is the central message, or focus, of the verse, marked through the

---

17 Cf. Kidner, *Psalms 73–150*, p. 366.
18 Cf. NJB: 'his indignation does not last for ever, nor his resentment remain for all time'. Cf. the comment of S. H. Leupold, 'this means that, whereas the Lord would have a legitimate cause for striving with Israel, He does not carry this

fronting of the relevant constituent. The same focus structure of the A-line carries over into the B, in compliance with the constraint. The colon arrangement of the verse would therefore be MKD//MKD.

In this instance it would be helpful to illustrate how the marked focus structure would differ from the same constituents in unmarked order. The basic 'not V for ever' has three allo-clauses[19] in Biblical Hebrew.[20] These are (reading from right to left):

(1) לֹא V לְעוֹלָם
(2) לְעוֹלָם לֹא V
(3) לֹא לְעוֹלָם V

Sequence (1) is canonical, that is, pragmatically unmarked. There are two alternate ways that it could be understood: (a) 'X will never Y', or (b) 'X will not Y for ever', where X denotes the subject and Y the verbal action. The difference between these two is that in the first case the statement is saying that the agent concerned will not at any time perform the action, while the second implies that the action is already in progress, but that the agent will not perform it for ever. The remaining two allo-sentences are similar in that they both display markedness, yet different in that in (2) it is the verb that is negated, and in (3) the durative PP לְעוֹלָם. It is essential to appreciate the different function of the negation in each case. In (2) it is only the PP that is marked, while in (3) the marked component includes both the PP and the negative. This difference establishes each of these allo-clauses with its own particular focus and presupposition:

(2) לְעוֹלָם לֹא V 'For ever X will not Y'
(3) לֹא לְעוֹלָם V 'Not for ever will X Y'

The presupposition of (2) is that 'X will not Y', and its focus 'for ever'.

The presupposition of (3) is that 'X will Y', and its focus 'not for ever'.

We observe that (2) can only indicate sentence (a) in the previous paragraph, and (3) can only have the sense of sentence (b). Therefore, whereas the unmarked word order could be interpreted in either way, the marked forms can only be one or the other. This information may be tabulated and exemplified in the following manner:

---

through to the bitter end', *Exposition of the Psalms* (Welwyn, Herts: Evangelical Press, 1977), p. 718.

19 For the meaning of this term, see 3.3.3.

20 In this example לְעוֹלָם ('for ever') could be replaced by synonymous phrases, such as לָנֶצַח, etc. Also the alternative negative forms אַל and בַּל might occur in the place of לֹא.

Application: Standard and Difficult Texts

	Allo-form 1: Unmarked	Allo-form 2: Marked	Allo-form 3: Marked
a) X will never Y	לֹא V לְעוֹלָם	לְעוֹלָם לֹא V	
b) X will not Y for ever	לֹא V לְעוֹלָם		V לֹא לְעוֹלָם

Examples	a) X will never Y	b) X will not Y for ever
Allo-form 1 (CAN)	Is. 14:40 לֹא־יִקָּרֵא לְעוֹלָם זֶרַע מְרֵעִים	Jer. 3:12 לֹא אֶטּוֹר לְעוֹלָם:
Allo-form 2 (MKD)	Prov. 10:30 צַדִּיק לְעוֹלָם בַּל־יִמּוֹט	
Allo-form 3 (MKD)		Is. 57:16 כִּי לֹא לְעוֹלָם אָרִיב

Verse 10. This verse presents another parallelism, and also another clear instance of MKD//MKD. With respect to its focus structure it closely matches verse 9. It is presupposed that God will deal with his people in some respect. What is in focus is that such treatment will not be as their sins deserve. When taken alongside the previous verse, this seems to express the similar idea of God's gentle dealings with his people, though this time with reference to the past as that former verse looked to the future.[21]

Verse 11. The A-line contains the protasis of a comparative construction. The B-line contains the apodosis in the form of a canonical verbal clause, making a comment on the active topic of God's steadfast love (cf. v. 4b).

Verses 12 and 13 both consist of comparative sentences each following the same basic structure as verse 11.

Verse 14. Nothing in this verse requires comment apart from the use of the independent 3rd person pronoun הוּא. The appearance of this assigns markedness to the subject of the verb. The reason why this should be so is usually determined by the context. Here the verb with which it is joined is יָדַע ('know'). It is frequently the case, not just in poetry but in other genres also, that this particular verb is found together with the subject pronoun.[22] Since there are no other obvious indications in the context why this subject should be marked, what we are looking at here is probably an instance of

---

[21] The *qatal* verb forms are taken as past by the LXX NASB NKJV REB NLT NCV. Allen, *Psalms 101–150*, p. 17, translates as 'has not treated us … nor has he dealt with us …'.

[22] Other examples in the data include: Psalms 40:10; 69:20; 139:2 142:4; Job 11:11.

the grammatical encoding of an 'evidential', a non-pragmatic phenomenon mentioned earlier.[23] NASB is the only English version consulted that sees some particular markedness in the pronoun, translating it as 'he himself'. All other versions simply have the non-focused 'he'.

Verse 15. Two parallel cola containing comparisons in the form of noun-clauses.

Verse 16. First, mention is made of the wind passing over the grass, with which man was compared in verse 15. This is then followed by two effects that follow that – 'it is no more' (וְאֵינֶנּוּ), and 'its place knows it no longer' (וְלֹא־יַכִּירֶנּוּ עוֹד מְקוֹמוֹ). There can therefore be seen to be some semantic overlap between the final word of line A and the meaning of line B, but as the major part of the first line concerns the passing over of the wind itself rather than its effects, there is strictly no parallelism, either in form or in overall meaning, between the two cola. The one departure from the basic constituent order is that the opening clause places the subject in the preverbal position. Such a sentence-focus SV-clause after the connector כִּי ('for') is common in explanatory clauses, where the topic span is typically only the length of the clause.[24] This is so in both narrative as well as elsewhere in poetry, as the following examples demonstrate:

כִּי תַרְדֵּמַת יְהוָה נָפְלָה עֲלֵיהֶם (1 Sam. 26:12)
for the deep sleep of YHWH had fallen upon them.

כִּי יְהוָה שְׁלָחַנִי עַד־בֵּית־אֵל (2 Kgs 2:2)
for YHWH has sent me as far as Bethel

כִּי יְהוָה יִסְמְכֵנִי (Ps. 3:6)
for YHWH sustained me

כִּי פִּי יְהוָה דִּבֵּר׃ (Is. 40:5)
for the mouth of YHWH has spoken

In verse 14 under discussion the reference to the wind is evidently offering an explanation of the way in which man is like grass, as declared in verse 13. The word order of this clause, we conclude, can be taken as marked. In this case the clause has sentence-focus in that it reports an event to account for a fact stated in the discourse. This 'event-reporting' function, as was noted,[25] is one of the major uses of the SV constituent order in Biblical Hebrew.

Verses 17–18. These contain no verbal clauses.

Verse 19. The word order in both cola departs significantly from canon-

---

23 For 'evidentials', see 4.4.
24 Independent sentence-focus propositions of this kind were discussed in 3.4.1 (c).
25 See 3.4.1 (c). On the use of sentence-focus clauses to provide explanation, see Shimasaki, *Focus Structure*, p. 158.

ical order. There are two preverbal elements in the A-line and also in B. Semantically there is a close enough correspondence of meaning (both relating to the rule of God) to classify the unit as a parallelism.[26] How are we to understand S M V O // S M V order? No contextual factors appear to be present which would allow us to attribute the fronting of the two constituents to pragmatic marking. An explanation in such terms is therefore ruled out. This leads us to look to the other motivation for non-canonical word order, that is, poetic defamiliarisation. In this case there occurs not just a reordering of the B-line, but of both lines. Such a feature, we observed in the previous chapter, functions at the larger level of discourse, indicating either textual boundaries or peak. Here in verse 19 the fact that there is a major division of the psalm is beyond doubt. All the English versions make a new section of the psalm at this point and do so upon good grounds. The psalm commences with a series of imperatives, using the verb בָּרֲכִי, with participial clauses giving the reasons for blessing God (vv. 1–5). The central section (vv. 6–18) is what Allen calls 'a communal hymn of praise, describing Yahweh's revelation of himself to Israel'.[27] The final section (vv. 19–22) returns to the בָּרֲכוּ imperatives of the opening, being 'an imperatival hymn, a summons to all Yahweh's creatures and subjects to praise him as King and Lord'.[28] Other commentators agree in identifying these closing verses as a distinct unit.[29] The particular form of the bicolon of verse 19 can therefore be identified as a boundary-marking device of the form DEF//DEF.

Verses 20–22. After the highly defamiliarised verse 19, marking the opening of a new section, the remaining verses in the psalm contain perfectly regular word order, the verbs being 2nd person imperatives similar to the opening of the psalm (vv. 1–2).

The relative frequency of the various colon-types in this psalm is:

Chapter	Verbal Clauses	CAN	MKD	DEF
Ps. 103	22	14	6	2

---

26 It should be noted, however, that whether this is accepted or not in this particular case in no way affects the conclusions that are drawn from the word order.
27 Allen, *Psalms 101–150*, p. 19. We also note that the first and last sections are couched in the 2nd person but in the middle section the psalmist speaks of 'us' (vv. 10, 12, 14).
28 *Ibid.*
29 E.g., Kraus, *Psalms 60–150*, p. 293; Anderson, *Psalms*, vol. 2, pp. 716-17; and others listed in 8.2.1 (b).

9.1.3 Job 12

2a	אָמְנָם כִּי אַתֶּם־עָם Truly you are the people,	M C S^{Pn}-Comp
2b	וְעִמָּכֶם תָּמוּת חָכְמָה: and wisdom will die with you.	w-M V S
3a	גַּם־לִי לֵבָב כְּמוֹכֶם But I have understanding as well as you;	P-Comp S M
3b	לֹא־נֹפֵל אָנֹכִי מִכֶּם I am not inferior to you.	V^{Pt-Ng} S^{Pn} M
3c	וְאֶת־מִי־אֵין כְּמוֹ־אֵלֶּה: And who does not know such things as these?	w-Q-E^{Ng} Comp
4a	שְׂחֹק לְרֵעֵהוּ אֶהְיֶה I am a laughingstock to my friends;	Comp M V
4b	קֹרֵא לֶאֱלוֹהַּ וַיַּעֲנֵהוּ I who called upon God and he answered me,	V^{Pt} M w-V-o
4c	שְׂחוֹק צַדִּיק תָּמִים: I am a laughingstock, though righteous and blameless.	Comp S Comp
5a	לַפִּיד בּוּז לְעַשְׁתּוּת שַׁאֲנָן Those at ease have contempt for misfortune, (?)	?
5b	נָכוֹן לְמוֹעֲדֵי רָגֶל: but it is ready for those whose feet are unstable.	Comp M
6a	יִשְׁלָיוּ אֹהָלִים לְשֹׁדְדִים The tents of plunderers lie at ease,	V S
6b	וּבַטֻּחוֹת לְמַרְגִּיזֵי אֵל and those who provoke God are secure,	w-S Comp
6c	לַאֲשֶׁר הֵבִיא אֱלוֹהַּ בְּיָדוֹ: who carry their god in their hands.	Comp(R V O M)
7a	וְאוּלָם שְׁאַל־נָא בְהֵמוֹת וְתֹרֶךָּ But ask the animals, and they will teach you,	w-M V-P IO w-V-o
7b	וְעוֹף הַשָּׁמַיִם וְיַגֶּד־לָךְ: or the birds of the air, and they will tell you;	w-O w-V IO
8a	אוֹ שִׂיחַ לָאָרֶץ וְתֹרֶךָּ or speak to the earth, and it will teach you,	C V IO w-V-o
8b	וִיסַפְּרוּ לְךָ דְּגֵי הַיָּם: or let the fish of the sea tell you.	w-V IO S

Application: Standard and Difficult Texts

9a	מִי לֹא־יָדַע בְּכָל־אֵלֶּה Which among all these does not know	Q V^{Ng} M
9b	כִּי יַד־יְהוָה עָשְׂתָה זֹּאת׃ that the hand of YHWH has done this,	C S V O
10a	אֲשֶׁר בְּיָדוֹ נֶפֶשׁ כָּל־חָי who has the life of every creature in his hand,	R Comp S
10b	וְרוּחַ כָּל־בְּשַׂר־אִישׁ׃ and the breath of all mankind?	w-S
11a	הֲלֹא־אֹזֶן מִלִּין תִּבְחָן Does not the ear test words,	Q^{Ng}-S O V
11b	וְחֵךְ אֹכֶל יִטְעַם־לוֹ׃ as the palate tastes food?	w-S O V-M
12a	בִּישִׁישִׁים חָכְמָה Is there not wisdom among the aged,	Comp S
12b	וְאֹרֶךְ יָמִים תְּבוּנָה׃ and does not long life give understanding?	w-Comp S
13a	עִמּוֹ חָכְמָה וּגְבוּרָה To him belong wisdom and greatness,	Comp S w-S
13b	לוֹ עֵצָה וּתְבוּנָה׃ counsel and understanding are his.	Comp S w-S
14a	הֵן יַהֲרוֹס וְלֹא יִבָּנֶה If he tears down, it cannot be rebuilt,	H V w-V^{Ng}
14b	יִסְגֹּר עַל־אִישׁ וְלֹא יִפָּתֵחַ׃ if he shuts someone in, he cannot be released.	V M w-V^{Ng}
15a	הֵן יַעְצֹר בַּמַּיִם וְיִבָשׁוּ If he holds back the waters, there is drought;	H V M w-V
15b	וִישַׁלְּחֵם וְיַהַפְכוּ אָרֶץ׃ if he lets them loose, they overwhelm the earth.	w-V w-V O
16a	עִמּוֹ עֹז וְתוּשִׁיָּה To him belong strength and success;	Comp S w-S
16b	לוֹ שֹׁגֵג וּמַשְׁגֶּה׃ deceived and deceiver are his.	Comp S w-S
17a	מוֹלִיךְ יוֹעֲצִים שׁוֹלָל He leads away counsellors plundered,	V^{Pt} O Comp
17b	וְשֹׁפְטִים יְהוֹלֵל׃ and makes fools of judges.	w-O V

18a	מוּסַר מְלָכִים פִּתֵּחַ He removes the chains[30] put on by kings,	O V
18b	וַיֶּאְסֹר אֵזוֹר בְּמָתְנֵיהֶם: and binds a girdle around their waist.	w-V O M
19a	מוֹלִיךְ כֹּהֲנִים שׁוֹלָל He leads away priests plundered,	V^{Pt} O Comp
19b	וְאֵתָנִים יְסַלֵּף: and overthrows the mighty.	w-O V
20a	מֵסִיר שָׂפָה לְנֶאֱמָנִים He removes the speech of the faithful,	V^{Pt} O M
20b	וְטַעַם זְקֵנִים יִקָּח: and takes away the discernment of elders.	w-O V
21a	שׁוֹפֵךְ בּוּז עַל־נְדִיבִים He pours contempt upon nobles,	V^{Pt} O M
21b	וּמְזִיחַ אֲפִיקִים רִפָּה: and loosens the belt of the strong.	w-O V
22a	מְגַלֶּה עֲמֻקוֹת מִנִּי־חֹשֶׁךְ He reveals deep things from the darkness,	V^{Pt} O M
22b	וַיֹּצֵא לָאוֹר צַלְמָוֶת: and brings deep darkness into the light.	w-V M O
23a	מַשְׂגִּיא לַגּוֹיִם וַיְאַבְּדֵם He makes nations great, and destroys them;	V^{Pt} O w-V-o
23b	שֹׁטֵחַ לַגּוֹיִם וַיַּנְחֵם: he enlarges nations, and leads them away.	V^{Pt} O w-V-o
24a	מֵסִיר לֵב רָאשֵׁי עַם־הָאָרֶץ He removes the understanding of the leaders of the earth,	V^{Pt} O
24b	וַיַּתְעֵם בְּתֹהוּ לֹא־דָרֶךְ: and makes them wander in a wasteland with no roads.	w-V-o M Comp^{Ng}
25a	יְמַשְׁשׁוּ־חֹשֶׁךְ וְלֹא־אוֹר They grope in the dark without light,	V-O w-Comp^{Ng}
25b	וַיַּתְעֵם כַּשִּׁכּוֹר: and he makes them wander like drunkards.	w-V-o M

---

30 Here reading the pointing מוֹסֵר ('bond, chain'), instead of מוּסַר ('correction'), as is done by the majority of translations and commentators. Note the discussion by Dhorme, *Commentary on the Book of Job*, p. 176; Hartley, *The Book of Job*, p. 211, fn. 5.

Application: Standard and Difficult Texts 211

Verse 2. The poem opens with a bicolon consisting of a noun-clause followed by a verbal clause ordered as M V S. There is nothing in the relationship between the two lines to warrant taking them as a parallelism.[31] The preverbal element of the B-line (וְעִמָּכֶם) requires some explanation. First we note two proposed readings of the text which would entirely change the character of the clause in question: (1) Clines brings to notice the suggestion put forward by others that the word appearing as the verb תָּמוּת should in fact be read as the noun תּוּמַּת, meaning 'completeness' or 'perfection'.[32] This is how the word was understood in the Greek versions of Aquila (τελειώματα σοφίας) and Symmachus (ἡ τελειότης τῆς σοφίας). If this were so, then the whole clause would be verbless, having the structure Comp S. (2) Another proposal is that the second line be construed as a relative clause.[33] This would make the position of וְעִמָּכֶם more readily explainable, as this would not be an unnatural place for the relativizer had it been present, אֲשֶׁר עִמָּכֶם תָּמוּת חָכְמָה, 'with whom wisdom will die'. However, taking the MT in the commonly accepted way, is there any discernible pragmatic reason for the fronting of וְעִמָּכֶם? It does, in fact, make good sense to interpret the markedness of this phrase in terms of restrictive focus.[34] Hartley's commentary points in this direction when he writes that Job's friends 'think themselves to be *the only* people with whom wisdom resides'[35] (italics added). Surely this exclusiveness is implicit in Job's remark. Dhorme suggests that 'Job addresses his friends ironically as representatives of popular opinion. All the wisdom of the people is concentrated in them. If they die, wisdom dies with them'.[36] In other words, there is no wisdom to be found outside of these three men. Such a restrictive sense for the fronted element in 2b is perfectly suited to the context. Moreover, the markedness of וְעִמָּכֶם is in harmony with the information structure of the preceding noun-clause אַתֶּם־עָם. There the pronominal element is initial, just as the initial וְעִמָּכֶם also carries the pronominal reference. Again, we see that this first clause may be taken as restrictive, '*You* [alone] are the people'. It is of interest that Jerome added *soli* at this point in his translation – *ergo vos estis soli homines* (Vulg), 'Therefore you alone are the men'.

Verse 3. This verse consists of three non-verbal clauses.

---

31 Cf. Reyburn, *Handbook on the Book of Job*, p. 231, 'this line is not parallel with the first line'.
32 Clines, *Job 1–20*, p. 279.
33 See Hartley, *The Book of Job*, p. 205, fn. 1.
34 See 3.4.2 (d); 4.2.1 (c) and (d).
35 Hartley, *The Book of Job*, pp. 205-6; cf. S. R. Driver and G. B. Gray, *A Critical and Exegetical Commentary on the Book of Job* (Edinburgh: T. & T. Clark, 1986 [1921]), p. 112, 'Job ironically concedes that the three friends are the only living ... embodiment of wisdom'.
36 Dhorme, *Commentary on the Book of Job,* p. 168.

Verse 4. The first colon is verbal, though the verb is הָיָה, 'to be'. This means that the clause contains a complement, here the phrase שְׂחֹק לְרֵעֵהוּ, rather than a direct object. The initial position of the complement in this line is matched by the initial placement of שְׂחוֹק in 4c. Clearly the fact of Job's being an object of laughter[37] is the prominent information in the speaker's mind. This is deduced from both the repetition of the word שְׂחוֹק and its initial position.[38]

Verse 5. Reyburn rightly says 'the Hebrew of verse 5 is far from clear'.[39] He then adds 'numerous changes have been proposed but little agreement reached'. The truth of this statement is reflected in the various commentaries. For our purposes, however, the complexities of this verse do not need to be unravelled here, for though much is uncertain about this verse, it is evident that the whole of 5ab is totally verbless and therefore not immediately relevant to the present topic of study.

Verse 6. A verbal clause in the A-line is conjoined with a semantically parallel noun-clause, itself followed expanded by a relative construction consisting of another verbal clause. The two verbs in 6a and 6c are both clause-initial.

Verse 7. The adversative וְאוּלָם frequently occurs at the head of the clause, especially in the book of Job (cf. 5:8; 11:5; 13:3; 14:18, etc.). The word order of 7a is therefore unremarkable. 7b forms a parallel line to 7a. First Job tells his friend(s) to consult the animals for instruction, and then the birds. These are all predicate-focus clauses. First, through the imperative, Job addresses his friends, who are obviously active topical participants in the discourse. Then, having introduced the animals and birds through the direct object phrases, these become topical subject phrases for the verbs of the second clauses. The whole is framed in topic-comment articulation.[40] The only feature of note is the gapping of the verb in the B-line, but the phrase וְעוֹף הַשָּׁמַיִם is evidently the direct object of the same verb (שְׁאַל) occurring in the A-line. We see then, gapping aside, that the whole bicolon is completely canonical.

Verse 8. The connector אוֹ indicates that this is a continuation of the

---

37 *Ibid.*, p. 169. Dhorme claims that 'The presence of אֶהְיֶה compels us to translate: "A laughingstock to his friend am I, I who invoke Eloah and whom he answers"'. Hartley, *The Book of Job*, p. 207, suggests that the use of אֶהְיֶה 'underscores the change that has taken place in Job's situation'.

38 Alternatively, in the light of Hartley's comments, *The Book of Job*, p. 207, it would be possible to interpret the fronting of this element as an instance of replacing focus. Job himself here echoes the description of himself in chapter 1 as a blameless and righteous man. 'But now', says Hartley, 'he who was accorded the highest honor has become a laughingstock'. The reputation he once had has now been replaced by another.

39 Reyburn, *Handbook on the Book of Job*, p. 233.

40 See 3.3.

Application: Standard and Difficult Texts

previous verse. Syntactically 8a mirrors 7a, and, like that earlier colon, the order of constituents is unmarked. 8b is a regular verbal clause. Since Job's discourse has now turned (v. 7) to the elements of God's creation, the 'earth' and 'fish of the sea' are accessible topics,[41] and so the clauses show predicate focus.

Verse 9. The interrogative clause of 9a is canonically ordered, referring back deictically ('among all these') to the topics of the foregoing context. This is not the case with the next line. 9b contains a complement clause[42] of the order SV that expresses the contents of the verb 'know' in 9a. The sequence SV is explicable in terms of information structure. Where the complement clause after a verb of knowing is reporting an event in which the topic is not currently active from the speaker's viewpoint, the sentence-focus structure (SV) is commonly employed. This is so in narrative:

וְהוּא לֹא יָדַע כִּי יְהוָה סָר מֵעָלָיו (Judg. 16:20)
and he did not know that YHWH had left him

וַיֵּדְעוּ כִּי אֲרוֹן יְהוָה בָּא אֶל־הַמַּחֲנֶה (1 Sam. 4:6)
for they knew that the ark of YHWH had entered the camp

Examples of the same structure are also to be found in poetic texts:

נִבְהָל לַהוֹן אִישׁ רַע עָיִן וְלֹא־יֵדַע כִּי־חֶסֶר יְבֹאֶנּוּ׃ (Prov. 28:22)
The miser hastens to become rich and does not know that poverty will come upon him

וְיָשִׂימוּ וְיַשְׂכִּילוּ יַחְדָּו כִּי יַד־יְהוָה עָשְׂתָה זֹּאת (Is. 41:20)
that they may consider and understand as well, that the hand of YHWH has done this

All these clauses introduced by כִּי are event-reporting. The significant thing about the last example from Isaiah 41 is that verse 20c contains verbatim the same words as in Job, כִּי יַד־יְהוָה עָשְׂתָה זֹּאת, and, like the clause in Job, is a complement clause presenting the knowledge content following verbs of perception.[43] We may therefore satisfactorily account for the order of Job 12:9b as a genuine instance of markedness and not poetic variation.

Verse 10. A verbless bicolon.

Verse 11. The word order of these two lines is highly irregular. Both cola display the same SOV sequence. Are these two pragmatically marked clauses in parallelism, or is the whole unit defamiliarised? First we observe that the verse has the ring of a proverb. Clines describes it as a 'self-evident

---

41 See 3.3.1.
42 For this term, see Van der Merwe (et al.), *Biblical Hebrew Reference Grammar*, p. 65.
43 Of additional interest is the fact that the Isaiah version forms the A-line of a parallelism in which the B-line also exhibits SV word order (וּקְדוֹשׁ יִשְׂרָאֵל בְּרָאָהּ, 'and the Holy One of Israel created it'), in agreement with the constraint on markedness in parallelisms.

truth, cast in proverbial form',[44] while Gordis refers to it as a 'conventional proverb'.[45] By means of this saying the speaker's intention is evidently to draw a comparison. Just as the palate tastes food and can distinguish the good from the bad, so the ear weighs up what it hears and can determine truth from error.[46] Yet, as is common in Hebrew proverbial style, grammatically the two halves are simply co-ordinated. No actual comparative particle is used,[47] but the syntax of two cola creates a parallelism. Secondly, examining the context of this saying does not reveal any obvious reason for marked word order, especially to account for *two* fronted constituents. If each half of the verse had been SV it could have been attributed to its proverbial form, but doubly marked proverbial parallelisms are virtually non-existent in the book of Proverbs.[48] For this reason the verse is probably to be interpreted as two defamiliarised cola, that is, DEF//DEF, thus marking the whole unit as having a role at the larger discourse level. There is little to warrant taking verse 11 as a boundary, but the particular highly defamiliar ordering might be due to peak. At least one scholar has discerned this function on the part of this verse. Reyburn claims that 'The proverb serves as a sarcastic climax to verses 7–10'.[49] Through this saying Job is implicitly rebuking his friends. In verses 7–10 Job had emphasised that even the animals would know it was the hand of God that was against him. The irrational beasts were wise enough to recognise that, but his friends did not. Yet they were the ones with the 'ear' to 'test words' (v. 11), not the animals, but they failed to use their judgement wisely. In support of the irregular form of this verse as an indication of peak is its similarity with Job 4:17.[50] That verse also has a similar DEF//DEF arrangement. Also like this verse it is expressed in the form of a rhetorical question, a feature which in

---

44   Clines, *Job 1–20*, p. 295. Reyburn, *Handbook on the Book of Job*, p. 238, terms it a 'proverb', and Pope, *Job*, p. 92, says it 'may be a proverbial saying'.
45   Gordis, *The Book of Job*, p. 138.
46   Cf. Hartley, *The Book of Job*, p. 210.
47   Similar constructions occur in Job 5:7 and 11:12.
48   There is only one exception – Proverbs 26:27, having the structure SMV//SMV (כֹּרֶה־שַּׁחַת בָּהּ יִפֹּל וְגֹלֵל אֶבֶן אֵלָיו תָּשׁוּב), 'A man who digs a pit will fall into it; and if a man rolls a stone, it will roll back on him.'). Nevertheless in this case an argument might be put forward for the second fronted element in each line, placing the focus upon falling into the very pit which he himself had dug (not any other pit), in order to highlight what Murphy calls the aspect of 'poetic justice' (*Proverbs*, p. 202) conveyed by the saying. Cf. the very closely related Ecclesiastes 10:8, חֹפֵר גּוּמָּץ בּוֹ יִפּוֹל ('He who digs a pit will fall into it'). It is also worth drawing attention to the fact that in Proverbs 26:27 the LXX does not front the second NP of the A-line, but reads ἐμπεσεῖται εἰς αὐτόν, that is, יִפֹּל בָּהּ ('he will fall into it').
49   Reyburn, *Handbook on the Book of Job*, p. 238.
50   Discussed in 8.2.1 (b).

itself may have a 'highlighting function'.[51] Further still, both 4:17 and 12:11 have this important fact in common – they are both quoted later in the speeches of the book of Job. 4:17, a key verse in the whole book, is quoted by various speakers in 9:2; 15:14; and 25:4. 12:11 is later quoted by Elihu in 34:3 (with slight variations). This fact in itself should be sufficient to establish the prominent nature of the verse in question. Therefore, with reasonable grounds, we classify its deviation from canonical word order as a notable instance of poetic defamiliarisation for climactic effect.

Verses 12-13. These verses contain no verbal clauses.

Verses 14-15. In these four balanced cola (see overpage) there are no less than eight verbs, but the whole is canonically structured, commenting upon God as an active topic. All O and M elements occur in the postverbal position.

Verse 16. Another verbless bicolon (cf. v. 13).

Verse 17. This verse consists of two parallel cola.[52] They contain the same essential semantic components, each having to do with the way in which, says Hartley, 'God is able to outwit human wisdom that resides in counselors and judges'.[53] At the syntactic level the two clauses differ in that the first contains a participle and the second a finite verb. It has been remarked before that a *yiqtol* in the B-line is not infreqeuently used to parallel a participle in the A-line. With the parallel line comes the typically inverted word order, OV, seen in the same environment on numerous previous occasions. The word order, therefore, is defamiliar.

Verse 18. We observe here an arrangement of the two cola which is contrary to the norm. Unlike the standard form of parallelism, which may display reordering of constituents in the B-line, here a non-canonical A-line (OV) is followed by a parallel line in seemingly canonical order (VO). This is unusual and should alert us to the presence of something happening in the discourse that would warrant such a deviation from what is commonly seen in parallelisms. First, a pragmatic function for the fronted element of the A-line is ruled out. Nothing in the context suggests any pragmatic presupposition to explain why this direct object should be fronted, yet not that of the B-line. It has been shown on several occasions that if such markedness were present in the first line of a parallelism, then the same marked word order would reappear in the second. The order of constituents, therefore, is best interpreted as a matter of poetic defamiliarisation, not markedness. This defamiliar ordering of the A-line does have the effect, however, of distinguishing the whole parallelism from more common poetic structures and having therefore some special text-level function. To determine what this function is, the whole context needs to be considered. Verse 18 forms part of

---

51   See chapter 8, fn. 25.
52   Cf. Clines, *Job 1–20*, p. 300.
53   Hartley, *The Book of Job*, p. 214.

the larger discourse unit commencing at verse 13 (as in NIV NRSV ESV NKJV REB).⁵⁴ Within this larger section, several smaller units may be delineated on the basis of the repetitions of structurally related cola.⁵⁵ The first sub-section is verses 13–16, which displays a definite inverted parallel structure in its arrangement:⁵⁶

13	עִמּוֹ חָכְמָה וּגְבוּרָה לוֹ עֵצָה וּתְבוּנָה׃	noun-clause	A
14	הֵן יַהֲרוֹס וְלֹא יִבָּנֶה יִסְגֹּר עַל־אִישׁ וְלֹא יִפָּתֵחַ׃	verbal clause	B
15	הֵן יַעְצֹר בַּמַּיִם וְיִבָשׁוּ וִישַׁלְּחֵם וְיַהַפְכוּ אָרֶץ׃	verbal clause	B'
16	עִמּוֹ עֹז וְתוּשִׁיָּה לוֹ שֹׁגֵג וּמַשְׁגֶּה׃	noun-clause	A'

The two outer lines (A and A') are identically constructed around the PPs עִמּוֹ and לוֹ, each with two accompanying nominal constituents. Both central verses (B and B') consist of four verbal clauses, the first in each case being made up of the particle הֵן plus a *yiqtol* verb. In view of the inner structural coherence of 13–16, verse 17 must mark the beginning of the next sub-section, consisting of verses 17–19. This also clearly shows an inverted structure, though this time with only one central unit:

17	מוֹלִיךְ יוֹעֲצִים שׁוֹלָל וְשֹׁפְטִים יְהוֹלֵל׃	pctp // verb	A
18	מוּסַר מְלָכִים פִּתֵּחַ וַיֶּאְסֹר אֵזוֹר בְּמָתְנֵיהֶם׃	verb // verb	B
19	מוֹלִיךְ כֹּהֲנִים שׁוֹלָל וְאֵתָנִים יְסַלֵּף׃	pctp // verb	A'

Again we observe the identical structure of the two outer members (A and A'). Each begins with the same participle מוֹלִיךְ, and ends with a *yiqtol* verb form preceded by its direct object.⁵⁷ The four NP[DO]s all belong to the same semantic domain, that is, people of high status. From this layout of the text we notice that the verse under discussion forms the central element in this ABA arrangement. This is significant in that scholars of Biblical Hebrew poetry recognise the centre of such ABA (and larger) patterns to be

---

54 Cf. Driver and Gray, *Job*, pp. 111–12, where vv. 13–25 are identified as a single major section.
55 This is what Wendland would call 'distant parallelism', *Analyzing the Psalms*, ch. 4.
56 This analysis of vv. 13–16 is accepted by N. C. Habel, *The Book of Job*, OTL (London: SCM Press, 1985), p. 217.
57 Commentators agree that verse 19 is modelled upon verse 17, e.g., Dhorme, *Commentary on the Book of Job*, p. 177; Pope, *Job*, p. 93.

a position of peak.[58] The function of DEF//CAN and similar irregular arrangements has previously been noted as occurring in units indicating a point of salience, or peak, in the discourse. In the sub-section we are dealing with (vv. 17–19) the principal theme is that of God's superior power over various human potentates, and the greatest in rank of those mentioned is the 'king' of the middle verse (v. 18). Even *the king*, we might say, could be overcome by God and restrained.[59] Therefore as this parallelism forms the central and most salient point of the three verses in question, the DEF//CAN order here is entirely appropriate.

Following this sub-section of verses 17–19 the chapter continues with another clearly delineated unit in verses 20–25. Here are a series of bicola in which the first colon of each is headed by a participle. The first (v. 20a) and last (v. 24a) of these participles are both מֵסִיר. The chapter is then concluded with a verse reverting to a finite verb form accompanied by a shift in subject from 3rd person singular to 3rd person plural (v. 25).

Verse 19. This verse, as just mentioned, is obviously based upon verse 17, though this time speaking of priests and the mighty. Syntactically it has an identical structure to that of the earlier verse, and the same inversion in the B-line. This again is to be explained as due to its location in a parallel line, where defamiliarisation of word order is admissible.

Verses 20–21. The syntactic construction and order of components in these two verses matches exactly that of verses 17 and 19 examined above. As with those parallelisms, the B-line in each of these exhibits defamiliar word order (OV).

Verse 22. The A-line continues the same pattern as seen in verses 20–21, that is a participle with adjoining OM. Again the B-line contains a finite verb, though in this case its form and position have both changed. It is, or at least has been vocalised[60] as, a *wayyiqtol* form appearing in the usual clause-initial position, since 'he', God, is the active topic.

Verse 23. Here there is a change in the composition of each colon from the foregoing series of cola. Instead of a participle clause making up the A-line and a finite verbal clause the B-line, each colon in this verse has a participial clause followed by one that is verbal. The two lines form a close parallelism with nothing noteworthy as concerns the word order.

Verse 24. With regards to its general structure this verse repeats that of verse 22. As in that verse, nothing out of the ordinary occurs with respect to the ordering of its constituents.

Verse 25. The chapter concludes with two verbal clauses each having its

---

58 As noted in the analysis of the similarly structured Isaiah 59:7 in 8.2.1 (a).
59 Cf. the comments of Alden, *Job*, p. 154.
60 Though there is no discernible difference in tense or aspect from the foregoing participle.

verb in the canonical initial position. These clauses both have predicate focus. The first comments upon those people introduced in the object phrase of 24b, and so they are now topics available for commenting upon. The second comments upon God, who is already an active topic.

The relative frequency of the various colon-types in this chapter is:

Chapter	Verbal Clauses	CAN	MKD	DEF
Job 12	36	26	3	7

9.1.4 Song of Songs 1

2a	יִשָּׁקֵנִי מִנְּשִׁיקוֹת פִּיהוּ Let him kiss me with the kisses of his mouth,	V-o M
2b	כִּי־טוֹבִים דֹּדֶיךָ מִיָּיִן: for your love is better than wine.	C-Comp S M
3a	לְרֵיחַ שְׁמָנֶיךָ טוֹבִים Your oils smell sweet,	M S Comp
3b	שֶׁמֶן תּוּרַק שְׁמֶךָ your name is [like] ointment poured out.	Comp(S [R] V) S
3c	עַל־כֵּן עֲלָמוֹת אֲהֵבוּךָ: Therefore the maidens love you.	C S V-o
4a	מָשְׁכֵנִי אַחֲרֶיךָ נָּרוּצָה Draw me after you. Let us run!	V-o M V
4b	הֱבִיאַנִי הַמֶּלֶךְ חֲדָרָיו The king brought me into his chambers.	V-o S M
4c	נָגִילָה וְנִשְׂמְחָה בָּךְ We will rejoice and be glad in you,	V w-V M
4d	נַזְכִּירָה דֹדֶיךָ מִיַּיִן we will extol your love more than wine.	V O M
4e	מֵישָׁרִים אֲהֵבוּךָ: Rightly do they love you.	M V
5a	שְׁחוֹרָה אֲנִי וְנָאוָה בְּנוֹת יְרוּשָׁלִָם I am dark, but lovely, O daughters of Jerusalem,	Comp S^{Pn} w-Comp [Voc]
5b	כְּאָהֳלֵי קֵדָר כִּירִיעוֹת שְׁלֹמֹה: like the tents of Kedar, like the curtains of Solomon.	M M

Application: Standard and Difficult Texts

6a	אַל־תִּרְאוּנִי שֶׁאֲנִי שְׁחַרְחֹרֶת Do not look upon me because I am black;	V^{Ng}-o C-S^{Pn} Comp
6b	שֶׁשֱּׁזָפַתְנִי הַשָּׁמֶשׁ because the sun has burnt me.	C-V-o S
6c	בְּנֵי אִמִּי נִחֲרוּ־בִי My mother's sons were angry with me.	S V-M
6d	שָׂמֻנִי נֹטֵרָה אֶת־הַכְּרָמִים They made me look after the vineyards.	V-o O
6e	כַּרְמִי שֶׁלִּי לֹא נָטָרְתִּי׃ I did not look after my own vineyard.	O V^{Ng}
7a	הַגִּידָה לִּי שֶׁאָהֲבָה נַפְשִׁי Tell me, he whom my soul loves,	V IO [Voc]
7b	אֵיכָה תִרְעֶה where do you graze [your sheep]?	Q V
7c	אֵיכָה תַּרְבִּיץ בַּצָּהֳרָיִם Where do you rest [your flock] at midday?	Q V M
7d	שַׁלָּמָה אֶהְיֶה כְּעֹטְיָה עַל עֶדְרֵי חֲבֵרֶיךָ׃ Why should I be as a veiled woman by the flocks of your friends?	Q V Comp M
8a	אִם־לֹא תֵדְעִי לָךְ הַיָּפָה בַּנָּשִׁים If you do not know, most beautiful among women,	C-V^{Ng} M [Voc]
8b	צְאִי־לָךְ בְּעִקְבֵי הַצֹּאן follow the tracks of the sheep,	V-M M
8c	וּרְעִי אֶת־גְּדִיֹּתַיִךְ עַל מִשְׁכְּנוֹת הָרֹעִים׃ and graze your kids by the shepherds' tents.	w-V O M
9	לְסֻסָתִי בְּרִכְבֵי פַרְעֹה דִּמִּיתִיךְ רַעְיָתִי׃ I liken you to a mare among Pharaoh's chariots, my love.	M V-o [Voc]
10a	נָאווּ לְחָיַיִךְ בַּתֹּרִים Your cheeks are lovely with ornaments,	V S M
10b	צַוָּארֵךְ בַּחֲרוּזִים׃ your neck with strings of jewels.	S M
11	תּוֹרֵי זָהָב נַעֲשֶׂה־לָּךְ עִם נְקֻדּוֹת הַכָּסֶף׃ We will make you rings of gold, studded with silver.	O V-M M
12a	עַד־שֶׁהַמֶּלֶךְ בִּמְסִבּוֹ While the king was at his table,	C-S Comp

12b	נִרְדִּי נָתַן רֵיחוֹ׃ my nard gives its scent.	S V O
13a	צְרוֹר הַמֹּר דּוֹדִי לִי My love is a bundle of myrrh to me,	Comp S M
13b	בֵּין שָׁדַי יָלִין׃ he spends the night between my breasts.	M V
14	אֶשְׁכֹּל הַכֹּפֶר דּוֹדִי לִי בְּכַרְמֵי עֵין גֶּדִי׃ My love is a cluster of henna blossoms to me in the vineyards of Engedi.	Comp S M M
15a	הִנָּךְ יָפָה רַעְיָתִי How beautiful you are, my beloved.	H-s Comp [Voc]
15b	הִנָּךְ יָפָה How beautiful you are!	H-s Comp
15c	עֵינַיִךְ יוֹנִים׃ Your eyes are [like] doves.	S Comp
16a	הִנְּךָ יָפֶה דוֹדִי How beautiful you are, my love,	H-s Comp [Voc]
16b	אַף נָעִים and so pleasant!	P Comp
16c	אַף־עַרְשֵׂנוּ רַעֲנָנָה׃ Our couch is green.	P-S Comp
17a	קֹרוֹת בָּתֵּינוּ אֲרָזִים The beams of our house are cedar trees,	S Comp
17b	[רַהִיטֵנוּ] בְּרוֹתִים׃ its rafters are cypress trees.	S Comp

Verse 2. The song opens with a canonical verbal clause. The woman speaking is evidently addressing a presupposed lover. The second line is a noun-clause.

Verse 3. After the initial noun-clause comes the words שֶׁמֶן תּוּרַק שְׁמֶךָ.[61] The basic structure is: Complement + Subject. The complement itself consists, on the level of the surface structure, of S V. However, these two components do not form a verbal clause, but a head noun governing a relative clause, S [R] V. This is an instance of an implicit relativizer,[62] where the relative clause appears alongside the governing noun by means of

---

61 On the lack of gender concord between these two components, see Longman III, *Song of Songs*, p. 90, fn. 17.
62 See later in this chapter, 9.2.3.

Application: Standard and Difficult Texts 221

simple parataxis.⁶³ Such a construction is frequently found in Hebrew poetry (e.g., Gen. 49:27, בִּנְיָמִין זְאֵב יִטְרָף, 'Benjamin is a wolf that rends'; Is. 40:20, עֵץ לֹא־יִרְקַב, 'a tree that does not rot'). Secondly in this verse there is a colon (3c) containing a verbal clause with a fronted subject. The agents performing the verbal action, 'the maidens', are not active topics in the preceding discourse. We suggest that the focus structure of the clause, S V, properly fits the description of sentence focus, of the kind that has previously been classed as 'event-reporting'. Earlier in this chapter (commenting on Ps. 103:16) a similar use of the sentence-focus structure was seen functioning as an explanation (with כִּי). But here in verse 3 it functions as a consequence (with עַל־כֵּן), relating to neither of the two active topics in the discourse, the woman speaking and her lover. Identical SV-clauses following עַל־כֵּן occur in Job 6:3; Psalm 45:18; Isaiah 13:7; 24:6; and Jeremiah 20:11. In each case the S constituent denotes a non-active topic.

Verse 4a. Some ambiguity exists concerning this first clause. Syntactically it may be divided as either V-o M / V, as NRSV NASB REB TEV NJB NLT NCV, or V-o / M V, as AV ASV NKJV. If we follow the majority of versions, the word order is completely canonical. But if we give credence to the more traditional versions, the word order of the second clause requires some explanation. These latter translations, in keeping with their high regard for the traditional text of both testaments, seem to have been influenced by the Masoretic accentuation. Shown with the accents the text appears as:

מָשְׁכֵנִי אַחֲרֶיךָ נָּרוּצָה

Evidently, from the use of the *ṭipḥā* accent with מָשְׁכֵנִי, the Masoretes decided that the first word should stand alone, and grouped the second two words together – 'Draw me. We will run after you'. Delitzsch here, noting the accents, decides to adhere to the Masoretic division.⁶⁴ The more recent commentators (Gordis, Pope, Murphy, and Longman III), agreeing with the modern translations, have chosen to ignore the Hebrew punctuation in this respect. There seems little to favour the traditional division. Delitzsch claims that the verb מָשַׁךְ needs no preposition since the idea of direction, towards the one drawing, is implicit within the meaning of the verb. He argues, therefore, that אַחֲרֶיךָ is more appropriate with the verb רוּץ, 'run', in which no direction is implied. This, however, does not square with the facts, for in Job 21:33 מָשַׁךְ does in fact occur with אַחֲרֵי.⁶⁵ Also against the traditional view, is that to construe אַחֲרֶיךָ with נָּרוּצָה ('we will run') is to place it in the marked focus position, and there is nothing discernible in the

---

63 'Parataxis' is the term used by Williams, *Hebrew Syntax*, §540. Waltke and O'Connor prefer to call it an 'asyndetic relative clause', *Biblical Hebrew Syntax*, p. 338.
64 Delitzsch, *Commentary on the Old Testament*, vol. 6, p. 22.
65 וְאַחֲרָיו כָּל־אָדָם יִמְשׁוֹךְ, 'and all men will draw after him'.

context that would demand such focus upon this particular constituent. At best it might be interpreted as restrictive focus,⁶⁶ implying that they would run after this man and none other. But there is nothing in the surrounding context to suggest that there is any other to make such a restriction necessary. In addition to this, the participant reference is perfectly clear should מָשְׁכֵנִי אַחֲרֶיךָ be taken together, but unclear if the text is divided as אַחֲרֶיךָ נָּרוּצָה. In the former, the woman is saying, 'Draw me after you. Let us run [together]'. There are only two participants to be identified, the woman and the man, the central characters of the discourse. However, the latter interpretation of the syntax requires the introduction of a third participant. 'Draw me', the woman says to the man, but 'we will run after you', now cannot include the man himself within the first person plural. To introduce another, or others, at this point interrupts the flow of the verse, which continues by saying, 'The king brought me into his chambers', again speaking only of the man and the woman.⁶⁷ In the light of the foregoing it would seem that the majority of versions and commentators are right in conjoining אַחֲרֶיךָ with מָשְׁכֵנִי.⁶⁸ The whole line is therefore perfectly canonical with respect to its constituent order.

Verse 4bcd. These three verbal clauses all follow the canonical word order, since they comment upon active topics.

Verse 4e. Once again, there is some ambiguity concerning the syntax of this clause. The difficulty concerns the term מֵישָׁרִים. A number of earlier versions, no doubt from the form of the suffix, took this to be a plural noun, meaning 'the upright'. This is so in Vulg, Syr, Targ, and the Greek versions of Aquila, Symmachus, and Theodotion (though not LXX⁶⁹). This ancient reading of the text found its way into the AV ('the upright'). Yet against this is the fact that the word begins with the prefix מ־. This would not be expected were it the masculine plural noun, 'the upright', which elsewhere invariably appears in the form יְשָׁרִים. The more natural way to take the form מֵישָׁרִים is as an adverbial.⁷⁰ It is found used adverbially in Biblical

---

66 See 3.4.2 (d) and 4.2.1 (c)–(d).
67 It might be thought that 'we' referred to the woman and the daughters of Jerusalem (of v. 5). But it should be noted that nowhere else in the entire Song does the woman group herself with these others using the pronoun 'we'. When on the woman's lips 'we' has reference to herself and her lover (7:12–13). We note too that the 'we' of 1:4cd is generally interpreted as a statement of the other women (as NJKV REB NLT CEV; cf. the comments of Longman III, *Song of Songs*, p. 94).
68 J. Callow's article, 'Units and Flow in the Song of Songs 1:2–2:7', in R. D. Bergen (ed.), *Biblical Hebrew and Discourse Linguistics* (Dallas, Texas: SIL, 1994), written from a modern linguistic perspective, concurs with this conclusion (see p. 478).
69 This version translates the word by the singular abstract noun εὐθύτης, 'uprightness'.
70 For the unlikely proposal that it means 'new wine', see M. H. Pope, *Song of Songs*, AB (New York: Doubleday, 1977), p. 305, though Pope himself accepts the adverbial sense, 'rightly', pp. 291, 305.

Hebrew both with and without the preposition –בְּ (e.g., Pss. 9:9; 58:2; Prov. 23:31; Is. 33:15). This particular usage without –בְּ is described by Murphy as 'an abstract adverbial accusative'.[71] With this the majority of translators and commentators agree. So having established the syntax of the clause to be MV, rather than SV, how is the fronting of the adverbial element to be interpreted? Since the clause does not occur in an environment in which reasons for poetic defamiliarisation might take place, the order must be taken as strictly pragmatic markedness. The clause is saying, 'Rightly do they love you'.[72] From the point of view of information structure it is unquestionable that the verb contains presupposed information. The previous verse (v. 3) had ended with the declaration עַל־כֵּן עֲלָמוֹת אֲהֵבוּךָ ('therefore the maidens love you'). That these also loved the woman's lover is not the point to be communicated here in verse 4e. Rather the speaker places the adverb 'rightly' in marked focus to indicate that these previously known affections for the man whom she also loved was justified. The colon expresses not simply the idea that he is loved, but more exactly the fact that he is worthy to be loved.

Verse 5. The whole of this verse is made up of neatly balanced noun-clauses and noun-phrases.

Verse 6. The first two cola contain canonical verbal clauses. The next colon (6c) shows SV word order. The reason for this is the introduction of new participants into the discourse, the brothers of the woman ('the sons of my mother').[73] What these brothers did was to make their sister look after the vineyards, expressed in a regular verbal clause (6d), which is then followed by the non-canonical OV^{Ng} in the final colon (6e). The fronting of the NP[DO] (כַּרְמִי שֶׁלִּי) is due to the contrastive relationship with הַכְּרָמִים of the previous colon.[74] She had attended the vineyards, *but* not her own. Many English versions (NASB NRSV ESV NKJV REB) add the conjunction 'but' to connect the two clauses.[75]

Verses 7–8. There is no departure from the basic constituent order in the seven verbal clauses making up these verses. This takes the form of an exchange between the man and the woman, the two principal topics in the discourse. Hence predicate-focus clauses are used.

Verse 9. This line has a fronted PP. The contents of this phrase is the object of comparison. The man likens his beloved to a mare among

---

71 Murphy, *The Song of Songs*, p. 126.
72 It is not certain who is speaking these words. Most probably it is the woman, as NKJV NLT CEV and Longman III (*Song of Songs*, p. 90). Others take it as the daughters of Jerusalem.
73 For sentence-focus clauses used for the presentation of new topics, see 3.3.3 (c).
74 On contrastive focus, see 3.4.2 (a) and 4.2.2 (c).
75 As Longman III, *Song of Songs*, p. 95.

Pharaoh's chariots.[76] Elsewhere the verb דִּמָּה is found with the comparative phrase following, for example:

Psalm 102:7

I am like a desert owl.   דָּמִיתִי לִקְאַת מִדְבָּר

Other instances of this constituent order with דִּמָּה even occur within the Song itself (2:17; 7:8). The placing of לְסֻסָתִי בְּרִכְבֵי פַרְעֹה in the clause-initial position here at the beginning of verse 9 could be identified as a marked focus structure. On the other hand, since this verse opens a new section of the discourse,[77] where the male protagonist speaks for the first time, it could also be construed as a boundary-marking device, indicating the onset of a new unit.[78] This is one place where without the aid of prosodic evidence the nature of the word-order variation may be explained in terms of either pragmatic markedness or poetic defamiliarisation. In view of the general tendency throughout the Song to place the comparative phrase after the object being compared, the latter of the two options seems the more probable.

Verse 10. We note here a typical poetic parallelism. The A-line contains unmarked word order, while the verb has been gapped in the B-line: VSM//SM. The topics are accessible in that they are visible parts of the woman's anatomy.

Verse 11. This verse consists of a single verbal clause. The NP[DO] is located before the verb. The fronted element relates to the subject of jewellery, as has just been mentioned in the previous verse: 'Your cheeks are lovely with ornaments, your neck with strings of jewels'. Verse 10 speaks of the items that already adorn the woman. Verse 11 now presents new jewellery that will be made to enhance her beauty even further. Although it cannot be stated dogmatically, the fronting of the direct object may be interpreted as due to expanding (or 'additive') focus.[79] Here is another item to be added to the woman's ornaments just mentioned. Significantly, this sense of 'adding' more jewellery is that given to the first part of the verse by NJPS, 'We will add wreaths of gold'.

Verse 12. A nominal circumstantial clause makes up the first line of this verse, followed by an SVO clause in the second line. The subject, נִרְדִּי ('nard'), is brought into the discourse as the sentence topic only at this point, existing as the topic solely for this particular clause, and then immediately ceases to play a role. These features give the line the

---

76 On the use of singular 'mare' with plural 'chariots', see the comments of Pope, *Song of Songs*, p. 337.
77 Commentaries and versions are unanimous on this point.
78 Note also the use of the vocative in this verse, suggesting the beginning of a new thematic unit. Cf. 8.2.1 (a).
79 See 3.4.2 (e), 4.2.1 (a) and (b).

appearance of a typical event-reporting clause, in which the NP[Su] is invariably placed in the preverbal position.

Verse 13. The A-line of this bicolon is verbless. The B-line has the order MV. As this is ostensibly not a parallelism, this particular ordering of sentence constituents is not merely poetic variation. From the perspective of information structure there is good reason why the M element, בֵּין שָׁדַי ('between my breasts'), should occupy the clause-initial position. The adjoining verb, יָלִין ('he spends the night'), contains presupposed information, since the woman's lover must spend the night somewhere. By placing בֵּין שָׁדַי in the marked focus position the fact is being highlighted, not that the man spent the night somewhere, but the *place* where he spent it, in the intimate embrace of his beloved.[80] The clause therefore has argument focus.

Verses 14–17. These final verses consist wholly of a series of noun-clauses.

The relative frequency of the various colon-types in this chapter is:

Chapter	Verbal Clauses	CAN	MKD	DEF
Song 1	26	18	8	0

9.1.5 Numbers 23:7–10

7a	מִן־אֲרָם יַנְחֵנִי[81] בָלָק From Aram Balak brought me,	M V-o S
7b	מֶלֶךְ־מוֹאָב מֵהַרְרֵי־קֶדֶם the king of Moab from the eastern mountains.	S M
7c	לְכָה אָרָה־לִּי יַעֲקֹב 'Come curse Jacob for me,	V V-M O
7d	וּלְכָה זֹעֲמָה יִשְׂרָאֵל׃ and come, denounce Israel'.	w-V V O
8a	מָה אֶקֹּב לֹא קַבֹּה אֵל How can I curse whom God has not cursed?	Q V [R] V^{Ng} S
8b	וּמָה אֶזְעֹם לֹא זָעַם יְהוָה׃ How can I denounce whom YHWH has not denounced?	w-Q V [R] V^{Ng} S

---

80 Cf. Pope, *Song of Songs*, p. 351, 'the author wishes ... to put in relief the constant presence of the groom and the intimacy of the relation which unites him to the bride'.
81 The prefix form of the verb is probably to be taken as a preterite, cf. Williams, *Hebrew Syntax*, §§176–77.

9a	כִּי־מֵרֹאשׁ צֻרִים אֶרְאֶנּוּ	C-M V-o
	From the rocky heights I see him,	
9b	וּמִגְּבָעוֹת אֲשׁוּרֶנּוּ	w-M V-o
	and from the hills I behold him.	
9c	הֶן־עָם לְבָדָד יִשְׁכֹּן	H-S [R] M V
	Behold, a people [that] dwells alone,	
9d	וּבַגּוֹיִם לֹא יִתְחַשָּׁב׃	w-M V^{Ng}
	and not reckoning itself among the nations!	
10a	מִי מָנָה עֲפַר יַעֲקֹב	Q V O
	Who can count the dust of Jacob,	
10b	וּמִסְפָּר אֶת־רֹבַע יִשְׂרָאֵל	w-V? O
	or number the fourth part of Israel?	
10c	תָּמֹת נַפְשִׁי מוֹת יְשָׁרִים	V S M
	Let me die the death of the upright,	
10d	וּתְהִי אַחֲרִיתִי כָּמֹהוּ׃	w-V S Comp
	and may my end be like his!	

Verse 7. This, the first of the Balaam oracles, opens with an unusually composed parallelism of the form M V-o S // S M (7ab). The fact that the position of the initial M element of the A-line is not matched by the corresponding M of the B-line, in accordance with the constraint regarding markedness in parallelism, suggests that in 7a we have a defamiliarised colon. In the B-line the verb has been gapped, while the sentence fragment[82] contains nominal constituents parallel to those of line A, though in inverted order. The whole parallelism may therefore be labelled DEF//Gap. As noted in chapter 8, only four bicola of this form exist in the entire corpus.[83] Of the other three, two were obvious instances of aperture (Pss. 33:6; 72:1), while the third (Ps. 121:6) might signal either closure or climax, or possibly both. Since this bicolon in Numbers 23:7 commences the oracle in question, we attribute its extraordinary character to its discourse-onset function.

The latter half of verse 7 contains two closely matching parallel lines with predicate focus, having the basic form VVO//VVO. Here Balaam himself, as an obviously active topic, is being addressed by the king.

Verse 8 also consists of two parallel cola with identical syntactic composition and constituent order. In each colon the main clause and the implicit relative clause[84] are both verb-initial. As regards the topics, Balaam

---

82 For this term, see 2.2.2 (a).
83 See 8.2.1 (c).
84 We note that the LXX employs relative pronouns in both lines: τί ἀράσωμαι ὃν μὴ καταρᾶται κύριος ἢ τί καταράσωμαι ὃν μὴ καταρᾶται ὁ θεός.

is active and God is inferable, so both are available for comment through these predicate-focus clauses.

Verse 9. Here the first two cola produce a balanced M V-o // M V-o parallelism (9ab). Adherence to the constraint is to be observed in the fronting of the M constituent in both the head-line and its parallel, that is, it creates a MKD//MKD unit. From the context the focus structure of each clause is best interpreted as argument focus. The fact that Balaam was looking at the people of Israel when he uttered these words is a contextual presupposition (as in 22:41, 'Balak took Balaam and brought him up to Bamoth-baal; and from there he could see part of the people of Israel'; cf. 23:13; 24:2). So the focal information is that it was from the top of a high place that the prophet saw them. Several commentators are of the opinion that, since this is poetry, the meaning is figurative rather than literal. Ashley states that, 'As in much poetry, the image is more than physical; Balaam is speaking of his current elevated state where he not only physically sees Israel but spiritually sees them as well'.[85] This agrees with the emphasis on spiritual vision in 24:4 and 16. So through this argument-focus construction the prophet is identifying not so much the place *from* which, but the manner *in* which, he was able to perceive Israel.

Line 9c is notably non-canonical, HSMV. There are two ways in which the syntax here may be construed. First, it might be taken as a single clause having two preverbal elements, in which case the markedness of each would have to be accounted for. Secondly, the four Hebrew words might be divided into two clauses, the first a noun-clause, to which is adjoined an implicit relative clause (as used in v.8 above), that is, HS[R]MV. In this latter case, there is still a marked verbal clause requiring explanation, but now with only one fronted element. This latter understanding of the syntax is that followed by most of the English versions (NIV NASB REB NJB NJPS TEV NLT NCV).[86] Gross, we note, does not include Numbers 23:9 in his extensive treatment of doubly-marked clauses in Hebrew poetry.[87] Most probably, then, there is just a single marked element in the colon, which is, לְבָדָד, 'alone'. In this verbal clause, now consisting of לְבָדָד יִשְׁכֹּן (lit., 'alone he will dwell'), it is not difficult to see that the verb יִשְׁכֹּן presents only presupposed information. It is assumed that the people of Israel 'will dwell' somewhere or somehow. The fronted adverbial conveys the focused

---

85 Ashley, *The Book of Numbers*, p. 471; cf. G. J. Wenham, *Numbers*, TOTC (Leicester: Inter-Varsity Press, 1981), p. 173, 'Through the Spirit Balaam is able to appreciate Israel's peculiar character'. According to Abraham ibn Ezra (Rabbinic Bible on Numbers 23:8), Balaam saw these things not visually but 'in his wisdom' (ראה בחכמתו).

86 Those translations which render as 'a people dwelling/living alone' (NKJV NRSV) may also be construing the Hebrew text in the same way.

87 Gross, *Doppelt besetztes Vorfeld*.

information that it will be 'alone' that they shall dwell. We conclude then that this verbal clause has argument-focus structure.

In the final colon (9d) there is another marked clause, וּבַגּוֹיִם לֹא יִתְחַשָּׁב. Although perhaps not an obvious parallel when each component is considered separately, the overall meaning is certainly related to the latter clause of 9c. Syntactically also both clauses consist of MV. These reasons are sufficient to justify us taking 9d as a parallel line with לְבָדָד יִשְׁכֹּן, a fact with which Ashley also would concur.[88] If the parallelism obtains, then the sentence information structure must be identical in both lines. If לְבָדָד יִשְׁכֹּן were interpreted as an argument-focus clause, then the clause וּבַגּוֹיִם לֹא יִתְחַשָּׁב needs to be similarly interpreted. This would mean that the verb denotes that which is presuppositional. Indeed, this can be seen to be the case. The concept of 'reckoning oneself', as signified by the Hithpael form יִתְחַשָּׁב, is a mental activity which can be assumed. The Hebrews must have some opinion of themselves.[89] The focus of the utterance tells us that they would not reckon themselves as being 'among the nations' in general. Balaam here shows his appreciation of the religious and moral separateness of Israel as the chosen people of God.

Verse 10 begins with what appears to be a synonymous parallelism. The MT וּמִסְפָּר ('and the number') is in fact a NP, making 10b a verbless clause. However, here we adopt the reading of the Samaritan Pentateuch, מִי סָפַר, that is, 'Who can number', which also underlies the LXX rendering (τίς ἐξαριθμήσεται).[90] This results in a closely matching parallelism, QVO//QVO, having no marked elements needing interpretation.

The latter part of verse 10 (cd) consists of two perfectly canonical verb-initial clauses in a parallel relationship. Balaam is here speaking of himself and thus the verbal clauses have predicate focus.

To conclude our brief analysis of this oracle we observe the regularity of its parallel formations.[91] Verses 8–10 consist of two CAN//CAN bicola, followed by two MKD//MKD, and then another two CAN//CAN, the whole unit being composed of synonymous parallelisms. It is only the unit-initial DEF//Gap bicolon which is radically different.

The relative frequency of the various colon-types in this oracle is:

---

88 Ashley, *The Book of Numbers*, p. 471, refers to '*not considering itself among the nations*' as a 'parallel' to the previous line.
89 The same also holds true if the verb be considered passive (as NASB NJB NJPS). Those of other nations must have some estimation of Israel (as did Balak and Balaam).
90 This reading is also followed by Ashley (*The Book of Numbers*, p. 468, fn. 8), and NRSV NIV NASB NKJV ESV REB NJB.
91 Cf. Kugel, *The Idea of Biblical Poetry*, p. 114, who describes the style of the Balaam oracles as 'terse consistent parallelism'.

Application: Standard and Difficult Texts   229

Chapter	Verbal Clauses	CAN	MKD	DEF
Num. 23	17	12	4	1

9.1.6 Conclusions

Approximately 170 clauses of Biblical Hebrew poetry have been covered in these selected passages, with a more detailed analysis of some 112 verbal clauses in context. The information obtained from these latter regarding their word order can be tabulated as follows:

Chapter	Verbal Clauses	CAN	MKD	DEF
Ps. 1	11	4	5	2
Ps. 103	22	14	6	2
Job 12	36	26	3	7
Song 1	26	18	8	0
Num. 23	17	12	4	1
TOTAL	112	74	26	12

The relative proportions of the three colon types are:

        CAN (74):   66.1%

        MKD (26):   23.2%

        DEF (12):   10.7%

This makes a joint total of 33.9% for the two non-canonical forms. In the original statistical analysis of 1,200 poetic verbal clauses (Appendix 1) the equivalent proportions of canonical and non-canonical clauses were:

        CAN: 66.0%

        Non-CAN: 34.0%

As regards the overall division between canonical and non-canonical constituent order these sets of figures match extremely closely. In both samples canonical verbal clauses number around 66.0%, while non-canonical (i.e., the total MKD and DEF) 34.0%. This shows the truly representative character of the poetic passages that have been analysed with respect to the proportion of unmarked clauses.

When the non-canonical clauses analysed in the texts of the first part of this chapter are further broken down into the categories of pragmatic markedness and defamiliar ordering, then some unevenness is noticeable. Job 12 showed a relatively large number of defamiliar clauses, while Song 1 had none at all. As the figures stand, the passages chosen for analysis displayed defamiliarisation in 10.7% of verbal clauses. If the non-use of defamiliarisation in Song 1 were not to be included in this calculation, then this would make the average proportion of defamiliar clauses amount to 14.0% of the total number of verbal clauses. Possibly we are to conclude that the degree of defamiliarisation of word order reflects the stylistic preferences of the author.

The foregoing analysis of the various poetic passages allows us to state the following by way of conclusion:

1. Rarely is there any difficulty in distinguishing defamiliarised word order from that which is pragmatically marked. The various factors that together serve to disambiguate the two are: (a) the environment in the which colon occurs, that is, the B-line of a parallelism, text-boundary, or peak, (b) the presence or absence of pragmatic connotations which require an explanation of word order with reference to topicality or focality, (c) the presence of a focus particle, and (d) the extent of the variation, that is to say, the more divergent the word order is the more likely it is to be the product of defamiliarisation. Guided by these, the reader or listener would be able to recognise defamiliar patterns as distinct from pragmatically marked constructions.

2. In instances of pragmatic markedness the context usually provides the grounds for such markedness, such as new topic, contrast, replacing focus, specifying focus, and other categories of focus. On a few occasions the particular function of the markedness is not immediately obvious, but more than one option might present itself.

3. This study of various extended poetic texts has confirmed the initial statistical analysis (Appendix 1) that non-canonical word order in poetic verbal clauses extends to 34% of the total number of such clauses. The fact is that approximately 66% of all verbal clauses in poetry manifest the usual verb-initial sequence. This in itself shows that freeness of word order in poetry is restrained. Total freedom is unknown, but only allowable given certain conditions, as specified previously in the earlier chapters of this work.

4. A minor point, but one worthy of note, is the fact that modern biblical commentaries on the poetic books of the Hebrew Scriptures generally fail to comment on variation in word order. The majority of commentators whose works were consulted offered no explanation at all of these features of the text.

5. Finally, this extended application has served both to clarify and verify the solution to word-order variation proposed in this study. It is to be expected in all such studies that a few instances will exist which are not so

Application: Standard and Difficult Texts 231

clear-cut as the others, but in the overwhelming majority of cases the analysis has produced satisfying results.

9.2 Potential Difficulties

We now turn to consider various obstacles that may present themselves in the attempted application of the theory being advanced. In 9.3 we shall consider a number of texts containing a higher proportion of word-order variation, or where no apparent reason for the variation presents itself. Before examining such problematic passages, however, there remain difficulties of another kind which first need to be discussed. Occasionally, what appears to be a non-canonical verbal clause on the surface may in fact not be so at all. What seems to be a departure from the usual constituent order may, when other factors are taken into consideration, be found to be otherwise. Also, it is sometimes the case that a particular unaccounted for instance of divergent constituent order may be seen in a different light when certain causes affecting word order, to be discussed below, are identified.

Here are listed and illustrated a number of diverse factors which may: (a) have the effect of making the constituent order of a clause appear to be other than what it actually is, or (b) affect a change in the linguistic context resulting in a new, or at least an alternative, assessment of the word order:[92]

9.2.1 Incorrect Verse Division

Psalm 107:2–3

Let the redeemed of YHWH say,	יֹאמְרוּ גְּאוּלֵי יְהוָה	A
who he redeemed from the hand of the adversary,	אֲשֶׁר גְּאָלָם מִיַּד־צָר:	B
and gathered from the lands,	וּמֵאֲרָצוֹת קִבְּצָם	C
from the east and from the west,	מִמִּזְרָח וּמִמַּעֲרָב	D
from the north and from the south …	מִצָּפוֹן וּמִיָּם:	E

Verse 2 (AB) ends with the clause אֲשֶׁר גְּאָלָם מִיַּד־צָר. Reading on into verse 3a (C) we see that B, although forming the latter part of a verse according to the traditional versification, is nevertheless the A-line of a synonymous parallelism. Verse 3a begins with the words וּמֵאֲרָצוֹת קִבְּצָם, having the order MV. Both lines contain perfective verb-forms with 3rd person plural object suffixes, accompanied by phrases with the preposition –מִ. Both verbs in this particular context have reference to the deliverance of Israel from the Gentile nations. Clearly then, C constitutes the B-line of a parallel bicolon, which is obscured by the placement of the verse division between the two cola. The non-canonical word order of 3a, therefore, is not

---

92 Certain of these have already been touched upon in previous analysis.

due to pragmatic marking but poetic inversion, i.e., it is a colon of the type DEF forming the secondary line in a CAN//DEF parallelism having the syntactic structure: (R) V-o M // w-M V-o.

9.2.2 Incorrect Syntactic Analysis

As an incorrect understanding of syntax is probably the most prevalent cause for a mistaken analysis of word order, we will examine two different examples.

Where two (or more) preverbal elements appear, it is sometimes the case that they comprise a separate noun-clause, which is then followed by a verbal clause. Consider the following example:

Psalm 49:13

Man in splendour cannot abide.	וְאָדָם בִּיקָר בַּל־יָלִין
He is like the beasts that perish.	נִמְשַׁל כַּבְּהֵמוֹת נִדְמוּ:

The Hebrew text of the first line looks like a single clause, containing the constituent order SMV^{Ng}. It is, however, probably to be analysed as S Comp / V^{Ng}, that is, as two clauses. The evidence for such a construal of the syntax in this particular case is simply the fact that in verse 21 of the same psalm the whole of verse 13 reappears as a refrain,[93] but there the MT reads:

אָדָם בִּיקָר וְלֹא יָבִין נִמְשַׁל כַּבְּהֵמוֹת נִדְמוּ:

The placing of the *wāw* in וְלֹא יָבִין shows that the author intended the first half of the verse to be understood as two separate clauses. In both places the sense could be taken as, 'Man is in a state of splendour, yet does not abide/understand'.

Another possible instance of two preverbal elements which should be explained as a separate clause appears in:

Psalm 106:7

Our fathers in Egypt	אֲבוֹתֵינוּ בְמִצְרַיִם
they did not understand your wonders,	לֹא־הִשְׂכִּילוּ נִפְלְאוֹתֶיךָ
they did not remember your great steadfast love.	לֹא זָכְרוּ אֶת־רֹב חֲסָדֶיךָ

To all appearances the opening words אֲבוֹתֵינוּ בְמִצְרַיִם read as the grammatical subject of the following verbs with an adjoining locative PP, resulting in SMVO for the first sentence. This is how it is translated in a significant number of versions (e.g., NASB REB NJB NLT TEV). Yet there is an alternative way of reading the text. אֲבוֹתֵינוּ בְמִצְרַיִם might stand independently of the verbal clauses and form a separate nominal construction. It is

---

93 Cf. Kidner, *Psalms 1–72*, p. 185; though the refrain appears with the variant reading יָבִין / יָלִין. In the LXX both of these are translated by συνῆκεν ('understand'), reading יָבִין in both places.

noteworthy that the punctuation of the MT suggests such a division:

אֲבוֹתֵינוּ בְמִצְרַיִם ׀ לֹא־הִשְׂכִּילוּ נִפְלְאוֹתֶיךָ

The accent on the PP is that known as *ʾāzlā ləḡarmēh*, a disjunctive accent in the poetic books,[94] invariably accompanied by the following vertical stroke known as *pāsēq*. Evidently the Jewish scribes did not feel that the verse should be read as SMV. It is possible that the opening words be read as a nominal temporal clause, i.e., a setting,[95] with the meaning 'When our fathers were in Egypt'. This is precisely how the Hebrew text has been translated in the NIV: 'When our fathers were in Egypt, they gave no thought to your miracles; they did not remember your many kindnesses'. The CEV does the same. Taken in this way, the whole verse now appears in perfectly canonical word order.

9.2.3 Implicit Relativizer

The omission of the relative pronoun is commonplace in Hebrew poetry.[96] Usually when this takes place, it is readily detected, but sometimes the implicitness of the relativizer may be overlooked by the unwary reader. The following is an obvious case in point:

Psalm 52:9

Behold the man [who] did not make God his refuge.   הִנֵּה הַגֶּבֶר לֹא יָשִׂים אֱלֹהִים מָעוּזּוֹ

On the surface this looks to be a SVO clause. Nevertheless, grammatically the words לֹא יָשִׂים אֱלֹהִים מָעוּזּוֹ are not the predicate of the subject הַגֶּבֶר, but a descriptive relative clause for which הַגֶּבֶר is the head noun. We note the actual addition of the relative pronoun ὅς in the LXX:

ἰδοὺ ἄνθρωπος ὃς οὐκ ἔθετο τὸν θεὸν βοηθὸν αὐτοῦ
Behold the man *who* did not make God his help

All the major English translations include a relative pronoun in this verse.

Sometimes the supposition of an implicit relativizer may be one possible way of reanalysing a problematic text, as in:

Psalm 4:9

I will both lie down and sleep in peace;   בְּשָׁלוֹם יַחְדָּו אֶשְׁכְּבָה וְאִישָׁן
for you alone, YHWH,   כִּי־אַתָּה יְהוָה לְבָדָד לָבֶטַח תּוֹשִׁיבֵנִי׃
make me lie down in safety.

---

94 Gesenius, *Hebrew Grammar*, §15h.
95 See 3.5.
96 Waltke and O'Connor, *Biblical Hebrew Syntax*, p. 338; cf. Watson, *Classical Hebrew Poetry*, p. 54.

The final clause here possesses no less than three fronted elements, besides a vocative: C S^Pn [Voc] M M V-o. As this is the last verse of the psalm it is possible that this is a highly defamiliar closing strategy, of the kind proposed in chapter 8.[97] But it also might be the case that the long chain of preverbal elements should be broken up by the supposition of a relative clause. If a relative pronoun were understood preceding לָבֶ֫טַח, it offers a very good sense to the whole, 'For it is you alone, YHWH, *who* makes me lie down in safety'. This relative construction appears in the texts of REB and NJB.[98] If this were the original reading then only a single focused element (לָבֶ֫טַח) would remain in a MV-clause.

The possible omission of the relativizer, therefore, is one factor that the reader needs to be alerted to for the correct interpretation of word order in poetry.[99]

9.2.4 Unrecognised Embedded Parallelism

Sometimes the presence of an embedded parallelism may be overlooked. Taken alone, the words וְנַפְשִׁי נִבְהֲלָה מְאֹד in Psalm 6:4a, might be interpreted as a marked SV-clause. However, once the whole context is considered, this is seen not to be the case.

Psalm 6:3–4

Be gracious to me, O YHWH,	חָנֵּ֥נִי יְהוָה֮	A
for I am languishing;	כִּ֤י אֻמְלַ֫ל אָ֥נִי	B
heal me, O YHWH,	רְפָאֵ֥נִי יְהוָ֑ה	C
for my bones are troubled,	כִּ֖י נִבְהֲל֣וּ עֲצָמָֽי׃	D
and my soul is greatly troubled.	וְנַפְשִׁי נִבְהֲלָה מְאֹד	E
But you, O YHWH – how long?	[וְאַתָּה] יְהוָ֗ה עַד־מָתָֽי׃	F

From this layout of the text it can be seen that lines A and C correspond, both being an imperatival clause addressing YHWH. To each of these two clauses is adjoined a כי clause giving the reason for the psalmist's call for help. In the first case, the line is a single verbless clause (B), while in the second case it is a fully formed bicolon of two parallel lines (DE). The unit ends with a verbless clause (F) which does not form part of the above

---

97 See 8.3.

98 Craigie, *Psalms 1–50*, p. 77, advocates the rendering, 'for you alone are the Lord; you make me dwell in safety'. This also divides up the three preverbal constituents, though in a different manner.

99 Note that in Appendix 2, an implicit relativizer has been indicated by [R]. Some texts are ambivalent and do not allow complete certainty regarding the presence or absence of a relative clause (e.g., Ps. 7:7d).

Application: Standard and Difficult Texts

structure,[100] other than as a separate conclusion to the whole. Thus the lines A–E create a distinct five-part unit, comprising the basic parallelism AB//CD, and then the embedded CAN//DEF parallelism D//E in the latter part of the larger parallel structure. This latter may be shown as:

```
┌── HEAD¹ ─────────────────── רְפָאֵנִי יְהוָה (CAN)
└── HEAD² ──┬── HEAD ──── כִּי נִבְהֲלוּ עֲצָמָי (CAN)
            └── Parallel ── וְנַפְשִׁי נִבְהֲלָה מְאֹד (DEF)
```

Again we note that the traditional verse division has been placed within this unit, obscuring the parallel relationship of D and E.

9.2.5 Unrecognised Extended Parallelism

On occasions an extended parallelism may go undetected and confuse the character of colon types. This is often due to the interruption of a verse division, as in the following example:

Psalm 145:1–2

I will extol you, my God and King,	אֲרוֹמִמְךָ אֱלוֹהַי הַמֶּלֶךְ	A
and I will bless your name forever and ever.	וַאֲבָרְכָה שִׁמְךָ לְעוֹלָם וָעֶד:	B
Every day I will bless you,	בְּכָל־יוֹם אֲבָרְכֶךָּ	C
and I will praise your name forever and ever.	וַאֲהַלְלָה שִׁמְךָ לְעוֹלָם וָעֶד:	D

Verse 1 is made up of two cola (A and B) which are both CAN, V-o [Voc] and VOM. In verse 2 the first colon (C) consists of MV, and the second (D) VOM. This latter is CAN, while the former, being non-canonical in form, could either be MKD or DEF. An anomaly exists in the fact that the M constituent of line D, לְעוֹלָם וָעֶד, corresponding semantically, as well as syntactically, to the M of line C, בְּכָל־יוֹם, does not occupy the same clause-initial position as required by the constraint.[101] This would seem to suggest that the parallelism C//D is one of those exceptional constructions used to denote some special discourse function. Yet there is no real justification for assigning such a function to verse 2. Most English versions and commentaries fix the opening section of the psalm as verses 1–3 (e.g., NRSV NKJV ESV TEV NLT NCV CEV, Terrien, Allen, Kidner), so verse 2 cannot delineate a textual boundary. Nor is there, regarding its content relative to that of the preceding and ensuing verses, any obvious reason to consider it as marking peak. It does not, therefore, appear to be an independent DEF//CAN or MKD//CAN bicolon in specific distribution. A

---

100 It is evident that line E relates more closely to D than to F.
101 See 7.2.

better explanation is obtained when verses 1–2 are reanalysed as a single introductory colon followed by an extended parallelism:

1a	ארוֹמִמְךָ אֱלוֹהַי הַמֶּלֶךְ	CAN	
1b	וַאֲבָרְכָה שִׁמְךָ לְעוֹלָם וָעֶד׃	CAN	A
2a	בְּכָל־יוֹם אֲבָרֲכֶךָּ	DEF	B
3b	וַאֲהַלְלָה שִׁמְךָ לְעוֹלָם וָעֶד׃	CAN	A'

Displayed like this we are better able to observe the inner coherence of the three-part structure. Lines A and A' both commence with a 1st person singular *yiqtol* verb-form conjoined with ־וְ and suffixed by ־ָה. The NP[DO]s appearing in these two outer lines are identical (שִׁמְךָ), as are the modifying PPs (לְעוֹלָם וָעֶד). The only actual difference between A and A' lies in the verbal roots, which are still semantically related. This leaves the central MV element to be identified as a defamiliar colon, as is frequently found in parallel B-lines. The CAN//DEF//CAN pattern, we note, is common in extended parallelisms (cf. Pss 21:10; 56:2; 94:23). Seen in this way the apparent difficulty is removed and the whole structure conforms perfectly to the norms of parallelistic construction.

Psalm 36:7–8

Your righteousness is like
the mighty mountains,
your justice is like the great deep.
Man and beast you save, O YHWH.
How precious is your steadfast love, O God!
And the sons of men take refuge in the shadow
of your wings.

צִדְקָתְךָ כְּהַרְרֵי־אֵל
מִשְׁפָּטֶךָ תְּהוֹם רַבָּה
אָדָם־וּבְהֵמָה תוֹשִׁיעַ יְהוָה׃
מַה־יָּקָר חַסְדְּךָ אֱלֹהִים
וּבְנֵי אָדָם בְּצֵל כְּנָפֶיךָ יֶחֱסָיוּן׃

Verse 7 begins with two noun-clauses in parallel. These present no problem in themselves. The remaining lines consist of:
7c O w-O V [Voc]
8a Q Comp S [Voc]
8b w-S M V
Most English translations follow the traditional division of the MT as, for example, the NRSV (English vv. 6–8):

> [6] Your righteousness is like the mighty mountains,
> your judgments are like the great deep;
> you save humans and animals alike, O LORD.
> [7] How precious is your steadfast love, O God!

All people may take refuge in the shadow of your wings.
⁸ They feast on the abundance of your house,
and you give them drink from the river of your delights.

Here verse 7c is joined with the preceding noun-clause parallelism. However, the content of 7c does not fit well with 7ab. But then when we look at what follows, it cannot be said that 8a obviously belongs in a couplet with 8b. The unevenness would seem to be resolved by attaching 7c to 8ab to produce a tricolon of the form ABA', as follows:

7c	אָדָם־וּבְהֵמָה תוֹשִׁיעַ יְהוָה׃	MKD	A
8a	מַה־יָּקָר חַסְדְּךָ אֱלֹהִים	Nom	B
8b	וּבְנֵי אָדָם בְּצֵל כְּנָפֶיךָ יֶחֱסָיוּן׃	MKD	A'

This is in fact the division of the text adopted by Craigie.[102] As can be seen, this makes the marked colon of A to be matched by that of the marked colon A'. In these two clauses both marked elements include the noun אָדָם ('man'). The verb phrases in each case relate semantically, 7c speaking of God 'saving' or 'preserving' (cf. NIV) man and beast, while 8b concerns men finding 'protection' (cf. TEV) under the shadow of his wings. The fronted NP in each clause could be explained in terms of specification, while the central noun-clause exclaims the general truth of the quality of God's steadfast love. An alternative way of dividing up the text makes an even closer parallel between A and A'. Some versions and commentators understand אֱלֹהִים at the end of 8a to in fact begin 8b, no doubt due to the awkwardness of the *wāw* attached to וּבְנֵי אָדָם. This would result in the compound NP אֱלֹהִים וּבְנֵי אָדָם (lit., 'gods and sons of man') corresponding to the similar construction אָדָם־וּבְהֵמָה ('man and beast') in 7c. Whereas the NP of 7c speaks of man and animals, that of 8b would now speak of those of high and low status. Several English versions interpret the text in this way: 'Both high and low among men' (NIV); 'Gods and people' (TEV); 'Gods and frail mortals' (REB). Finally on this text, we note that the identification of a parallel relationship between 7c and 8b removes the need to attempt an explanation of the preverbal phrase בְּצֵל כְּנָפֶיךָ in pragmatic terms, which would not seem warranted by the context. Now that 8b is seen as a parallel line it allows for the possibility of defamiliar word order following the placement of the marked constituent in the clause-initial position 7c in adherence to the constraint. In the SMV of 8b, therefore, both pragmatic marking and defamiliarisation

---

102 Craigie, *Psalms 1–50*, p. 289.

are to be observed, the possible co-occurrence of which has previously been affirmed.[103]

9.2.6 Textual Variant

Psalm 116:6

YHWH protects the simple,	שֹׁמֵר פְּתָאיִם יְהוָֹה
when I was brought low, he saved me.	דַּלּוֹתִי וְלִי יְהוֹשִׁיעַ׃

In this non-parallel bicolon the A-line consists of a participle clause V^{Pt} O S, while the B-line contains two verbal clauses, V w-M V, one canonical and one apparently marked. Why the latter should place the prepositional object לִי in the clause-initial position is uncertain. There does not appear to be anything in the context that warrants this element being in focus. Restrictive focus would be technically possible, but not supported by contextual considerations. Ancient translations with a tendency to adhere to the Hebrew word order reflect an unmarked clause: καὶ ἔσωσέν με (LXX, 'and he saved me'); cf. *et liberavit me* (Vulg). Possibly, therefore, the original Hebrew text may have had the order VM.

The following text presents an altogether different situation:

Psalm 34:18

They cry out, and YHWH hears,	צָעֲקוּ וַיהוָה שָׁמֵעַ
and delivers them from all their troubles.	וּמִכָּל־צָרוֹתָם הִצִּילָם׃

Here the first 3rd person plural verb (צָעֲקוּ) lacks an explicit subject. Normally in such circumstances the preceding context would be expected to provide the inferred participant. In this case, however, the preceding verse concerns those described as 'evil-doers' (עֹשֵׂי רָע). To take such as the implicit referent in verse 18 is utterly inappropriate to the rest of the verse. It is obvious that whoever is being spoken of, God favours such people, for the B-line declares that he delivers them from their troubles. In the theological context of the Hebrew Scriptures the prayer of the wicked is an abomination to God (cf. Prov. 15:8, 29, 21:7; 28:9). The text presented by some of the early versions offers a smoother reading, e.g., ἐκέκραξαν οἱ δίκαιοι (LXX, 'the righteous cried out'); *clamaverunt iusti* (Vulg).[104] By the inclusion of the NP[Su] 'the righteous', the difficulty is overcome. These versions may not necessarily have been translating from a better Hebrew text, but it is possible that they have inserted something that dropped out in its early transmission. Accepting this revised reading, the constituent order of the A-line would be V S w-S V. It is now easier to appreciate the reason for the fronting of the divine name in the second clause, וַיהוָה שָׁמֵעַ. With

---

103 See 7.3.
104 According to the critical apparatus of BHS the missing subject also appears in the Targum.

Application: Standard and Difficult Texts 239

the inclusion of the preceding subject phrase we are able to detect the presence of a parallel topic structure,[105] that is, 'The righteous cry out, and God hears'. We note the closely related verse earlier in the same psalm, זֶה עָנִי קָרָא וַיהוָה שָׁמֵעַ וּמִכָּל־צָרוֹתָיו הוֹשִׁיעוֹ ('This poor man calls out, and YHWH hears, and he delivers him from all his troubles', v. 7).[106] Here the A-line contains two clauses of the order S V w-S V. Like contrastive constructions[107] it is also possible that both subject phrases in this parallel construction may be placed in the marked position.

Each of the above situations creates a potential difficulty, but when certain other grammatical, rhetorical, and textual factors are taken into consideration, they are seen to present no real obstacles to the proposed solution regarding word order.

9.3 Difficult Texts

As stated at the beginning of the chapter, in some passages of Biblical Hebrew poetry the degree of word-order variation is much more extensive than others. Having earlier considered a selection of texts showing an average degree of such variation, we now come to present an analysis of a number of texts which show a much greater divergence from the basic constituent order. Even in such cases, we argue, when each departure from the canonical order is carefully studied in context, both at the inter-clausal and at the broader discourse level, the theory we have put forth may still be consistently applied.

9.3.1 Psalm 44:2–9

In the space of just eight verses[108] we count no less than thirteen departures from the usual verb-initial word order. Out of nineteen VPs only six place the verb first. Such a high percentage requires a closer investigation.

2a	אֱלֹהִים בְּאָזְנֵינוּ שָׁמַעְנוּ O God, with our ears we have heard,	[Voc] M V
2b	אֲבוֹתֵינוּ סִפְּרוּ־לָנוּ our fathers have told us	S V-IO

---

105 For this category of markedness, see 3.4.2 (b).
106 The *qatal* verbs are translated as a general present by TEV and NJB in both verse 7 and 18. Most English versions render the *qatal* in verse 18 in the same way.
107 Cf. 4.2.2 (c).
108 These verses form a separate unit, having the character of a 'victory hymn', within the psalm. See Craigie, *Psalms 1–50*, p. 333.

2c	פֹּעַל פָּעַלְתָּ בִימֵיהֶם בִּימֵי קֶדֶם: the work you did in their days, in the days of old.	O[R] V M M
3a	אַתָּה יָדְךָ גּוֹיִם הוֹרַשְׁתָּ [With?] your hand you drove out the nations,	S^{Pn} S? O V
3b	וַתִּטָּעֵם and planted them;	w-V-o
3c	תָּרַע לְאֻמִּים you crushed the peoples	V O
3d	וַתְּשַׁלְּחֵם: and spread them abroad.	w-V-o
4a	כִּי לֹא בְחַרְבָּם יָרְשׁוּ אָרֶץ It was not by their sword that they possessed the land,	C M^{Ng} V O
4b	וּזְרוֹעָם לֹא־הוֹשִׁיעָה לָּמוֹ nor did their arm give them victory;	w-S V^{Ng} IO
4c	כִּי־יְמִינְךָ וּזְרוֹעֲךָ וְאוֹר פָּנֶיךָ but your right hand, and your arm, and the light of your presence,	C-S w-S w-S
4d	כִּי רְצִיתָם: for you were pleased with them.	C V-o
5a	אַתָּה־הוּא מַלְכִּי אֱלֹהִים You are my King, O God;	S^{Pn}Comp[Voc]
5b	צַוֵּה יְשׁוּעוֹת יַעֲקֹב: command victories for Jacob.	V O
6a	בְּךָ צָרֵינוּ נְנַגֵּחַ Through you we will push back our adversaries;	M O V
6b	בְּשִׁמְךָ נָבוּס קָמֵינוּ: through your name we will trample those who rise up against us.	M V O
7a	כִּי לֹא בְקַשְׁתִּי אֶבְטָח For I will not trust in my bow,	C M^{Ng} V
7b	וְחַרְבִּי לֹא תוֹשִׁיעֵנִי: Nor will my sword save me.	w-S V^{Ng}-o
8a	כִּי הוֹשַׁעְתָּנוּ מִצָּרֵינוּ But you have saved us from our adversaries,	C V-o M
8b	וּמְשַׂנְאֵינוּ הֱבִישׁוֹתָ: And you have put to shame those who hate us.	w-O V

Application: Standard and Difficult Texts

9a	בֵּאלֹהִים הִלַּלְנוּ כָל־הַיּוֹם In God we boast continually;	M V M
9b	וְשִׁמְךָ לְעוֹלָם נוֹדֶה סֶלָה׃ and we will praise your name for ever. [*Selah*]	w-O M V

The opening verse (2a–c) commences with a non-parallelism (2ab) consisting of two pragmatically marked clauses, MV and SV respectively. The fronting of בְּאָזְנֵינוּ has been recognised as a focus structure in a number of English versions, having the sense 'with our *own* ears' (TEV and NLT, italics added), or 'for ourselves' (REB NJB). Interpreted this way the clause has predicate focus, with this prepositional phrase being the dominant focal element within the broader focal domain.[109] 2b contains a typical event-reporting clause.[110] This fills out the content of what they had heard. Syntactically it extends into the next clause (2c), having the overall form: S V IO O [R] V M M. The apparent OV order of 2c is explicable with reference to an implicit relativizer [R].[111] Its presence was made explicit by the translators of the LXX, ἔργον ὃ εἰργάσω (cf. NASB, 'the work that you did').

Verse 3 consists of four clauses making two closely parallel lines. The initial element, אַתָּה יָדְךָ (lit., 'you your hand') is problematic. How does this fit into the syntax of the rest of 3a? Possibly the difficulty is caused by a corrupt text. Neither the LXX nor Syriac include anything equivalent to אַתָּה. The majority of English translations take the phrase as a verbal modifier, 'by/with your hand'.[112] While this agrees well with the fact that the grammatical subject of the verb is 'you', referring to God, the absence of a preposition was noted by the LXX as unusual and the phrase was therefore rendered as the subject of the clause with the accompanying verb changed to 3rd person instead of 2nd, ἡ χείρ σου ἔθνη ἐξωλέθρευσεν ('your hand destroyed the nations'). Yet a third possibility is found in the NJB, REB, and the commentaries of Kraus and Dahood.[113] Following a proposal found in the footnotes of the BHS, these place the division between verses 2 and 3 after אַתָּה יָדְךָ rather than before, making these the concluding words of 2c. Taken with the final phrase בִּימֵי קֶדֶם this now

---

109 For dominant focal element, see 3.4.1 (a).
110 It is noteworthy that the almost identical Psalm 78:3b, וַאֲבוֹתֵינוּ סִפְּרוּ־לָנוּ, shows the same SV word order.
111 See 9.2.3 above.
112 As also Craigie, *Psalms 1–50*, p. 330, who, following the LXX and Syr versions, omits the Pn אַתָּה altogether.
113 Kraus, *Psalms 1–59*, p. 443–44; cf. M. Dahood, *Psalms I, 1–50*, AB (New York: Doubleday, 1966), pp. 263, 265. Kraus translates as: 'the work that you finished in their times in remote antiquity – "you, with your own hand"!', and comments 'אַתָּה יָדְךָ is to be taken with v. 1b [English text]; only through this arrangement is the parallelism rounded off properly'.

results in an inverted parallel line:

פֹּעַל פָּעַלְתָּ בִימֵיהֶם // בִּימֵי קֶדֶם אַתָּה יָדְךָ

NJB gives the following '... the deeds you did in their days, in days of old, by your hand,' taking אַתָּה יָדְךָ as a final appositional nominal phrase. REB renders this as, '... what deeds you did in their time, all your hand accomplished in days of old', supposing that the verb has been gapped in the B-line. Whichever translation is preferred, we would endorse a construal of the Hebrew text along these lines, placing אַתָּה יָדְךָ within verse 2.

Having separated אַתָּה יָדְךָ the remainder of verse 3 presents us with a nicely balanced four-clause parallelism:

You drove out the nations and planted them;	גּוֹיִם הוֹרַשְׁתָּ וַתִּטָּעֵם
you crushed the peoples and spread them abroad.	תָּרַע לְאֻמִּים וַתְּשַׁלְּחֵם

There is a close correspondence between the two lines, both semantically and syntactically. A variation occurs, however, in the constituent order, the first line being O V w-V-o, the second V O w-V-o. Verb and object appear in a different order in the two lines, גּוֹיִם הוֹרַשְׁתָּ and תָּרַע לְאֻמִּים. What is noteworthy about this is that it is the non-canonical arrangement which is positioned in the first line. This goes against the typical variation displayed by parallel lines where it is the B-line that varies. This characterises this unit as DEF//CAN, that is, an unusual form of parallelism whereby the whole bicolon is marked for rhetorical effect. In this case, as shall be argued below, the rare pattern O V [V] // V O [V] found here has a definite climactic function within the larger poetic unit in which it occurs.

The word order exhibited by 4a, C M^{Ng} V O, can be readily explained as an instance of marked focus, the prepositional phrase לֹא בְחַרְבָּם, 'not by your sword', being in the fronted position. In verse 4 the psalmist declares that the people of Israel did not take possession of the land of the nations by their own fighting ability, but (כִּי) it was the hand of God that gave them the victory (4c). This is a classic example of replacing focus.[114] In Biblical Hebrew the focus structure 'not [לֹא] X ... but [כִּי] Y ...' is often used, and the element being replaced and/or the one replacing it are commonly located in the marked position.[115] Line 4b forms a parallelism with 4a and therefore exhibits the same marked word order, according to the constraint, though this time it is the grammatical subject, וּזְרוֹעָם, which occupies the fronted position, being the constituent which corresponds semantically with the marked constituent of the A-line. It can be seen, therefore, that there is

---

114 See 3.4.2 (c) and 4.2.2 (b).
115 Cf. the examples of replacing focus from non-poetic genre using 'not [לֹא] ... but [כִּי]...' in Genesis 23:29; Deuteronomy 5:3; 1 Samuel 8:7; 2 Samuel 21:2.

Application: Standard and Difficult Texts 243

nothing in the analysis of verse 4 which is not in full agreement with what has been proposed in the preceding chapters.

Verse 5 contains no marked verbal clause that requires comment. Regarding the structure of the psalm, however, we note that the major English versions make this verse the beginning of a new section. The change of orientation to the supplicant speaking in the 1st person singular,[116] the use of the vocative, and perhaps the occurrence of the nominal clause[117] all lend support to this.

Verse 6 is complex. The order is MOV//MVO. At first sight it is not easy to determine what factors are involved that influence the word order. Taking the initial constituents of the two lines, בְּךָ and בְּשִׁמְךָ, to begin, we see that they correspond at both the syntactic and semantic levels – both being PPs with the preposition –בְּ, relating to God by means of 2nd person pronominal suffixes. The fact that this modifying (M) element occurs first in both A-line and B-line of the parallelism strongly suggests pragmatic markedness. What could require these constituents to be marked? It is surely in keeping with the whole context of verses 2–9 to make salient the fact that it is *only through God* that the Israelites were able to do the things described here. It was to underscore this fact that the psalmist employed the replacing focus structure in verse 4 discussed above. And this is exactly the focus that the NLT assigns to the verse in question, 'Only by your power can we push back our enemies; only in your name can we trample our foes'.[118]

Having assigned a focus function to the two initial constituents of verse 6, the arrangement of the rest of the verse remains to be explained. The final two constituents of each line form an OV//VO pattern:

צָרֵינוּ נְנַגֵּחַ ... ... we will push back our adversaries;

נָבוּס קָמֵינוּ ... ... we will trample down those who rise up against us.

The same arrangement of constituents was met before in verse 3, though there without the addition of a marked element in the first position of each line. We note a close similarity between verse 3 and verse 6 under discussion as regards the place they occupy in their respective sections of the poem. There is an obvious correspondence to be observed between the two sections 2a–4d and 5a–8b.[119] Both of these have the following basic structure:

---

116 Cf. A. Antturi, 'The Hebrew Verb in Poetic Context: Psalm 44' (A paper presented at the University of Leiden, March 1994), p. 4.
117 See Wendland, *Analyzing the Psalms*, p. 112.
118 Most of the major English versions simply keep 'Through you' and 'In your name' in the clause-initial positions.
119 This correspondence is evident from Antturi's lay-out of the psalm, 'The Hebrew Verb in Poetic Context: Psalm 44', p. 4.

General introduction – vv. 2, 5
Defeat of enemies – vv. 3, 6
Supporting unit 1 (כִּי) – vv. 4ab, 7
Supporting unit 2 (כִּי) – vv. 4cd, 8

Each of the two opening verses (v. 2 and v. 5) is general in its scope. The first refers to the 'work' (פֹּעַל) God had done in the days of the fathers; the second refers to 'victories' (יְשׁוּעוֹת) that God would command for Jacob. The second sub-section of each deals (v. 3 and v. 6) more specifically with the conquests that God had granted or would grant[120] to his people. The opposition in the first instance is expressed through the parallel-pair לְאֻמִּים/גּוֹיִם ('nations'/'peoples') and in the second קָמֵינוּ/צָרֵינוּ ('adversaries'/'those who rise against us'). In the first of these it is God who is the direct agent of these events, while in the second it is the Israelites acting in God's strength. The third sub-sections (v. 4ab and v. 7), both introduced by כִּי, show matching items of lexis – the noun 'sword', וְחַרְבִּי/בְחַרְבָּם, and the verb 'deliver', תּוֹשִׁיעֵנִי/הוֹשִׁיעָה. In addition, both these units also contain marked structures indicating replacing focus. The fourth and final sub-sections (v. 4cd and v. 8) both highlight God (addressed in the 3rd person) as the source of victory, each ending with a short line of two stresses.[121]

The point to be noted from the above structural analysis is that the two OV//VO parallelisms (v. 3 and v. 6) correspond, and each could be argued to be the most salient bicolon within its section. Neither is introductory, nor supporting, as those units which follow headed by כִּי. The use of this particle at the beginning of verses 4 and 7 strongly suggests that these verses play a supporting or amplifying role to 3 and 6.[122] By this we mean that these latter two verses each contain the primary statement of the whole unit in which they occur, to each of which is appended a sub-section giving additional information to fill out that statement. Both verses 3 and 6 speak of victory over Israel's enemies, either past or prospective, and then 4 (with respect to 3) and 7–8 (with respect to 6), through replacing focus constructions, ascribe the reason for that victory to God and not to the strength or weaponry of the Israelites.

---

120 Note the basic difference in temporal reference between the two sections. The first is looking at the conquest of the land as a basis for confidence that God would lead his people to future victories. Cf. Craigie, *Psalms 1–50*, p. 333, 'it was the essence of the Hebrew faith that the past could always be appropriated for the present, that the people in faith could look in the present moment for the continuation of those mighty acts of God in the past which had been so pregnant with future implications'.

121 Several of these parallels were noted by Antturi, 'The Hebrew Verb in Poetic Context: Psalm 44', pp. 16–17.

122 On the use of the particle כִּי for introducing such supporting information, see Van der Merwe (et al.), *Biblical Hebrew Reference Grammar*, p. 302c.

Significantly, Antturi recognises verse 3 as 'the central piece', or peak unit, of this section, though for different reasons.[123] He sees the tense-shifting (the interchange of *qatal* and *yiqtol* verb forms – here הוֹרַשְׁתָּ and תְּרַע) exhibited in the parallelism as an indicator of what he calls 'hyperbole', claiming that 'it creates a sense of a total destruction of the nations'. We agree with his conclusion, only we would ascribe the hyperbolic effect to the defamiliar colon pattern OV//VO, rather than to the presence of tense-shifting. It is of note that the two object noun phrases, גּוֹיִם and לְאֻמִּים, occupy the outer limits of the parallelism. This feature is surely more expressive of totality (i.e., from one end to another) than a simple change of verb forms.[124] The placing of the relevant elements at either extreme produces the required effect in a similar way to the rhetorical device of merismus,[125] though here in Psalm 44 it is purely the syntactic positioning that creates the sense of totality while merismus operates primarily on a semantic level.

The conclusion of the foregoing analysis is that the basic OV//VO pattern in verses 3 and 6 of this psalm marks peak. In the latter verse there is the added complication that the defamiliar pattern is preceded by pragmatic markedness in the M constituent in the first position of both lines. So in verse 6 we identify the existence of both pragmatic and defamiliar word-order variation, though, it should be noted, not with respect to the same constituents. The repetition of the fronted M in the same clause-initial position marks it as having pragmatic import. The unusual inversion in the remainder of the verse shows its defamiliarised nature. If this is a correct analysis, then it is another instance where both pragmatic and defamiliarised ordering appear within the confines of a single unit,[126] yet not without distinguishable characteristics.

Finally in this psalm we come to the MVM//OMV parallelism in verse 9. Surprisingly perhaps, we immediately come to another construction of similar form to that of verse 6. Again we find two corresponding constituents, בֵּאלֹהִים ('in God') and וְשִׁמְךָ ('and your name'), at the head of each parallel line. Syntactically they differ, one a PP the other a NP[DO], though semantically they are closely related, both speaking of God. These we interpret as marked focus. This fits well with the overall import of verses 2–9. It has been stressed that the victory comes from God, and so the section closes with God as the object of Israel's boast. It should also be

---

123 Antturi, 'The Hebrew Verb in Poetic Context: Psalm 44', p. 15.
124 Cf. Berlin, *Dynamics of Biblical Parallelism*, p. 145, note 14.
125 Merimus does sometimes make use of word order as was seen, for example, in the placing of 'day' and 'night' at the outer limits of Psalm 121:6, discussed in 8.2.1 (c).
126 Cf. 7.3. The only other examples of this unusual ordering with both markedness and defamiliarisation in the A-line are Proverbs 2:22 (SMV//SVM) and 4:25 (SMV//SVM), both dealt with in ch. 8.

pointed out that elsewhere in the book of Psalms the verb הִלֵּל, when accompanied by a PP (with בְ־) referring to God, mostly occurs with the PP in the fronted position – Psalms 34:3; 56:5, 11; 63:12.[127] In view of this, it is reasonable to suppose an interpretation of the sequence בֵּאלֹהִים הִלַּלְנוּ in terms of marked focus. The particular manner of focus in question could be that of restriction,[128] that is, 'in God only'. Alternatively, the lack of any focus particle equally allows for the possibility of selective focus,[129] meaning that out of a range of different potential objects the psalmist chooses to boast in God.

In our detailed analysis of Psalm 44:2–9 we have accounted for non-canonical word order that is both pragmatically and poetically motivated. Although this passage displays much more variation than is usual in Biblical Hebrew poetry, every instance of variation may be plausibly explained with reference to one of the two possible motivating factors.

9.3.2 Isaiah 42:1–4

This is the first of the so-called Servant Songs found in the latter part of the book attributed to Isaiah. In this passage of twelve cola, seven contain some irregularity pertaining to word order.

1a	הֵן עַבְדִּי אֶתְמָךְ־בּוֹ Here is my servant, whom I uphold,	H Comp [R] V-M
1b	בְּחִירִי רָצְתָה נַפְשִׁי my chosen one, in whom my soul delights.	Comp [R] V S
1c	נָתַתִּי רוּחִי עָלָיו I have put my Spirit upon him;	V O M
1d	מִשְׁפָּט לַגּוֹיִם יוֹצִיא׃ he will bring forth justice to the nations.	O M V
2a	לֹא יִצְעַק וְלֹא יִשָּׂא He will not cry out or lift up his voice,	V^{Ng} w-V^{Ng}
2b	וְלֹא־יַשְׁמִיעַ בַּחוּץ קוֹלוֹ׃ or make it heard in the street.	V^{Ng} M O
3a	קָנֶה רָצוּץ לֹא יִשְׁבּוֹר A bruised reed he will not break,	O V^{Ng}
3b	וּפִשְׁתָּה כֵהָה לֹא יְכַבֶּנָּה and a smouldering wick he will not quench;	w-N V^{Ng}-o

---

127 Only in Psalm 105:3 does the PP follow the verb.
128 See 3.4.2(d) and 4.2.1(d)
129 See 3.4.2(f).

3c	לֶאֱמֶת יוֹצִיא מִשְׁפָּט׃ with truth he will bring forth justice.	M V O
4a	לֹא יִכְהֶה וְלֹא יָרוּץ He will not falter or be crushed	V^{Ng} w-V^{Ng}
4b	עַד־יָשִׂים בָּאָרֶץ מִשְׁפָּט until he has established justice in the earth;	C-V M O
4c	וּלְתוֹרָתוֹ אִיִּים יְיַחֵילוּ׃ פ and the coastlands wait for his law.	w-M S V

At first glance one may believe the opening two cola of verse 1 to contain two non-canonical clauses (1ab). However, this is not so. These two opening lines each contain an implicit relative clause. Once this is realised it can be seen that the verbs do in fact occupy the initial position within their respective relative clauses. The English versions, almost without exception, add the relative pronoun in their translations.[130]

Lines 1cd consist of first a canonical clause, followed by one that is OMV. A poetic bicolon constructed of VOM//OMV would make a typical CAN//DEF parallelism, only here the relationship between the A-line and its B-line can hardly be described as synonymous. Each colon seems semantically quite independent, the latter being the consequence of the former. Therefore, the order of constituents in 1d has to be explained in some other way. This, we propose, is in terms of its structural function. To define this further we need to wait until the remaining verses have been analysed, especially verse 4. Following that, we will return to examine the form and function of line 1d.

Verse 2 contains a series of three negated verbal clauses (2ab), all of which are verb-initial. These are topic-comment, predicate-focus clauses speaking of the Servant introduced in the first verse.

In verse 3 we have three more instances of non-canonical word order. Firstly in 3ab we find a MKD//MKD parallelism where the first of the clauses consists of NP[DO] V^{Ng} matched by an extraposed structure in the B-line. This parallel bicolon is followed by another marked colon, though this time with a fronted PP, לֶאֱמֶת. That these fronted elements are genuinely marked is suggested by contextual considerations. Some manner of contrast is to be discerned between the negative statements of lines 3ab and the positive assertion of line 3c. The prophet first relates what the Servant's *modus operandi* will not be, and then what it will be. This is precisely how

---

130 Note CEV renders quite differently, 'Here is my servant! I have made him strong. He is my chosen one; I am pleased with him'. This translation breaks each colon into two separate clauses, first a noun-clause, then a verbal clause. From the viewpoint of word order it amounts to the same as if an implicit relativizer were supposed since the verbal clauses would also both be verb-initial.

several of the commentaries interpret the verse. This servant, they tell us, will not be as other potentates, maintaining their rule by oppression and violence. On the contrary, he will deal gently[131] with his subjects and administer true justice.[132] Pragmatically this relationship between the negative and positive is that defined as replacing focus. Among the versions this is how the LXX understood it, actually connecting the two parts with ἀλλα, the Greek replacing focus particle (ἀλλὰ εἰς ἀλήθειαν ἐξοίσει κρίσιν, 'but he will bring forth judgment to truth'). With this we may compare the CEV's rendering: 'He won't break off a bent reed or put out a dying flame, but he will make sure that justice is done'. We propose, therefore, that the clause-initial position of לֶאֱמֶת may be accounted for in terms of this replacing focus relationship. As regards the fronting of the two object phrases in the preceding clause, we note that this is not necessitated by the pragmatic relationship with line 3c. Rather, we would suggest that the marking of these two parallel lines be attributed to the focus of specification[133] in that each of the two lines presents a particular category of those who will not suffer at the hands of this Servant.

Verse 4 consists of three lines, the third of which (4c) displays non-canonical order. There is no obvious parallel relationship between any of the three lines. In fact this seems to be excluded by the grammatical relations between them. Line 4a contains two negative verb phrases followed by the subordinated 'until' clause in 4b. Line 4c then follows with its own separate main clause. The punctuation of most English versions separates line 4c from 4b (e.g., NRSV NIV TEV). There is no reason why 4c could not be considered as a separate monocolon, following the bicolon 4ab. Whichever way it is divided matters little in that monocola and tricola share similar discourse functions.[134] Several features of this verse point us in the direction of a concluding unit. The rare colon types, i.e., monocola and tricola, as mentioned previously, often function in this capacity. Manuscripts of the MT also make a division after this verse. Virtually all

---

131 Ibn Ezra understands verse 3ab as implying לא הכריח, 'he does not use force'; Friendländer, *The Commentary of Ibn Ezra on Isaiah*, p. 70 (Hebrew section).
132 This is the interpretation adopted by Oswalt, *The Book of Isaiah 40–66*, p. 111; Young, *Isaiah*, vol. 3, pp. 113–14; and J. A. Alexander, *Commentary on the Prophecies of Isaiah* (Grand Rapids, Michigan: Zondervan, 1976 [1846-47]), vol. 2, pp. 133–34. The latter explains (p. 134), 'This construction, by presenting an antithesis between the true and false way of bringing forth judgment to the Gentiles, is much to be preferred to those constructions which explain the phrase as simply meaning *in truth* (*i.e.,* truly), or *in permanence* (*i.e.,* surely), or *unto truth* (*i.e.,* so as to establish and secure it). All these may be suggested as accessory ideas; but the main idea seems to be the one first stated, namely, that the end in question is to be accomplished not by clamour, not by violence, but by the truth'.
133 See 3.4.2 (g) and 4.2.2 (a).
134 Cf. 2.1.3.

the English versions and commentaries consulted agree that with this verse the opening section of the chapter ends. The unusual constituent order (MSV) of 4c, therefore, is probably to be considered as DEF, a special colon type performing the function of marking closure. The overall structure of verse 4 would be CAN/CAN/DEF.

Finally on this passage, we come again to the question of 1d, a clause consisting of OMV. The possibility of it being the defamiliar B-line of a parallelism was rejected. The two remaining alternatives are that it is either actually marked, or it is DEF, but with a larger discourse function. Of these two, the evidence would seem to favour the latter. OMV would be doubly marked and a highly unusual sequence from the point of view of pragmatic concerns, in addition to which, the context does not offer anything that intimates the presence of any such pragmatic connotations. A discourse-functional use of DEF would therefore seem to be the most likely explanation of its irregular form. Once the rhetorical structure of verses 1–4 is appreciated, then it can be seen that a function of this kind for 1d becomes at least plausible. The chiastic arrangement of these verses has been observed by a number of scholars.[135] While their respective analyses do not harmonise in every detail there is broad agreement between them. Verses 1–4 may be displayed as follows:

1a	Here is my servant, whom I uphold,	Introduction
1b	my chosen one, in whom my soul delights;	of Servant
1c	I have put my spirit upon him.	
1d	He will bring forth justice to the nations.	A
2a	He will not cry out or lift up his voice,	B
2b	or make it heard in the street.	
3a	A bruised reed he will not break,	C
3b	and a smouldering wick he will not quench;	
3c	with truth he will bring forth justice.	
4a	He will not falter or be crushed	B'
4b	until he has established justice in the earth;	
4c	and the coastlands wait for his law.	A'

---

135 E.g., Rosenbaum, *Word-Order Variation in Isaiah 40–55*, p. 203; Motyer, *The Prophecy of Isaiah*, p. 319; K. E. Bailey, '"Inverted Parallelisms" and "Encased Parables" in Isaiah and their Significance for OT and NT Translation and Interpretation', in L. J. de Regt, J. de Waard and J. P. Fokkelman (eds.), *Literary Structure and Rhetorical Strategies in the Hebrew Bible* (Winona Lake, Indiana: Eisenbrauns, 1996), p. 25.

Viewing the text in this way serves to highlight the focal function of the central tricolon C. It also reveals the possibility of a disjuncture between 1c and 1d. In the former, we note, God is still speaking in the 1st person, while from 1d onwards the principal subject is 'he', the Servant. Rosenbaum in fact divides verse 1 after this fashion.[136] Taking 1a–c as a sub-unit, it now shows better inner coherence in that the whole concerns the divine election and qualification of the Servant. The ensuing verses (1d–4c) then go on to describe the ministry of this Servant. It is at this point (1d) that the inverted pattern begins. First to be noted is the neat balancing of the structure. Dividing verse 1 as described now leaves from 1d to 4c an inverted sequence of: monocolon–bicolon–tricolon–bicolon–monocolon. The pattern now opens and closes with a line consisting of a single colon,[137] and it is precisely these two that exhibit the highly non-canonical word order, OMV and MSV respectively. Moreover, these two lines are related semantically: 'He will bring forth justice to the nations', and 'and the coastlands wait for his law'. These two could almost be taken as being in parallelism with each other, having the poetic word-pairs תּוֹרָה/מִשְׁפָּט ('justice'/'law'; cf. Is. 51:4; Ps. 89:31), and אִיִּים/גּוֹיִם ('nations'/'isles'; cf. Is. 40:15; Jer. 31:10). Rosenbaum defines these two lines as an 'inclusio', bracketing the whole structure.[138] For our purposes, we assign to both the discourse function of boundary-marker, that is 1d is DEF marking aperture, and 4c DEF marking closure.

9.3.3 Isaiah 60:1-3

Verses 1–3, an oracle of the glorification of Zion, are widely recognised as a separate sub-section of the chapter.[139] These verses contain a considerable degree of word-order variation, which we shall now undertake to explain.

1a	קוּמִי אוֹרִי כִּי בָא אוֹרֵךְ Arise, shine; for your light has come,	V V C V S
1b	וּכְבוֹד יְהוָה עָלַיִךְ זָרָח׃ and the glory of YHWH has risen upon you.	w-S M V
2a	כִּי־הִנֵּה הַחֹשֶׁךְ יְכַסֶּה־אֶרֶץ For behold darkness shall cover the earth,	C-H S V-O
2b	וַעֲרָפֶל לְאֻמִּים and thick darkness the peoples;	w-S O

---

136 Rosenbaum, *Word-Order Variation in Isaiah 40–55*, p. 203.
137 On the structural function of monocola, see Watson, *Classical Hebrew Poetry*, pp. 169–71.
138 Rosenbaum, *Word-Order Variation in Isaiah 40–55*, p. 203.
139 Cf. Motyer, *The Prophecy of Isaiah*, pp. 493–94.

2c	וְעָלַיִךְ יִזְרַח יְהוָה [but] YHWH will arise upon you,	w-M V S
2d	וּכְבוֹדוֹ עָלַיִךְ יֵרָאֶה׃ and his glory will appear over you.	w-S M V
3a	וְהָלְכוּ גוֹיִם לְאוֹרֵךְ Nations shall come to your light,	w-V S M
3b	וּמְלָכִים לְנֹגַהּ זַרְחֵךְ׃ and kings to the brightness of your dawn.	w-S M

After the opening line only one perfectly canonical clause (3a) appears among the remaining seven cola. In two instances (2b and 3b) the irregularity is due to the gapping of the verb, which is admissible since these both comprise the B-lines of synonymous parallelisms, where gapping is a common enough phenomenon. This leaves five non-canonical clauses to be accounted for with reference to the two operative factors of pragmatic marking and poetic defamiliarisation.

Line 1b is not difficult to account for, since its contents form a close semantic parallelism with the preceding clause: 'for your light has come // and the glory of YHWH has risen upon you'. This is a CAN//DEF parallelism, producing a chiastic VP NP[Su] // NP[Su] VP arrangement.

Line 2a is clearly a marked SV-clause, to which 2b is a parallel colon, though with a gapped verb.[140] We note that the focal element הַחֹשֶׁךְ of 2a, the base-line of this parallelism, is matched by the initial וַעֲרָפֶל of 2b in adherence to the constraint. In this context the SV structure is probably to be taken as sentence focus, since the unit states an event independent of the surrounding clauses.[141] The bicolon 2ab concerns darkness covering the Gentiles, while every other colon in the section relates to the light of the divine glory shining upon Israel. The particle הִנֵּה ('behold') serves to draw attention to the whole of this utterance.[142]

Then follows the problematic unit 2cd. Together these two cola evidently create a parallelism, yet there is some difficulty in interpreting the significance of the word order, MVS//SMV. It would be easy to take the clause-initial וְעָלַיִךְ as marked for contrast with the foregoing parallelism pertaining to darkness. Its sense would be 'but upon you'. This is, in fact,

---

140 For gapping in MKD//MKD parallelisms, see 7.2.6.
141 On the independence of sentence-focus clauses, see 3.4.1 (c).
142 Cf. C. M. Follingstad, '*Hinneh* and Focus Function', *JOTT 7.3* (1995), p. 22, '*Hinnēh* draws attention to a proposition indicating it is important or salient in the given context'; cf. D. Slager, 'The Use of "Behold" in the Old Testament', *OPTAT 3.1* (1989), p. 50, '*hinnēh* ... raises the relative prominence of the information after it, so that the information has an impact on the reader/listener'.

how several English versions interpret it (e.g., NRSV NIV NKJV). However, to do so poses a problem in that if וְעָלַיִךְ is fronted due to the presence of a contrast, then we would expect the same for עָלַיִךְ in the second line of the parallelism. Not to place the corresponding element in the marked position violates the constraint. The result would be a MKD//DEF parallelism. It is not impossible that this should be included among those unusual parallelisms with special discourse functions, yet what would its function be here? Certainly not boundary. Peak would also seem unreasonable in that the contents of 2cd overlap to a large degree with 1ab, so it would be unjustifiable to take one as prominent and not the other. All this may suggest that the order of constituents found in 2cd requires some other explanation. First one has to appreciate the overall structure of the passage. Several writers have recognised that Isaiah 60:1-3 presents a neatly balanced chiastic pattern (see below).[143]

There is a close inverted parallelism, more apparent in the Hebrew text than in the English, between various key phrases in the passage. Interestingly the single construct NP וּכְבוֹד יְהוָה has been divided into two NPs in the second half of the structure.[144] Yet even though separated (in 2c) they still remain adjoining each other and in the inverted order, a fact which intimates that this chiastic patterning of the passage is a careful and deliberate construction.

1a	Arise and shine,	Summons
1b	for **your light** [אוֹרֵךְ] has **come** [בָא]	A B
1c	and **the glory of YHWH** [וּכְבוֹד יְהוָה] has **risen upon you** [עָלַיִךְ זָרָח].	C (1+2) D
2a	For behold **darkness** shall cover the **earth**,	E
2b	and **thick darkness** the **peoples**;	E'
2c	[but] **upon you will arise** [וְעָלַיִךְ יִזְרַח] **YHWH** [יְהוָה],	D' C' (1)
2d	and **his glory** [וּכְבוֹדוֹ] will appear over you.	C' (2)
3a	Nations shall **come** [וְהָלְכוּ] to **your light** [לְאוֹרֵךְ],	B' A'
3b	and kings to the brightness of your dawn.	

---

143 Breck, *The Shape of Biblical Language*, p. 37; K. E. Bailey, *Poet and Peasant* (Grand Rapids, Michigan: Eerdmans, 1983), p. 58.
144 Cf. Alexander, *The Prophecies of Isaiah*, vol. 2, p. 380, 'Jehovah and his glory, which are jointly said to rise in the preceding verse, are here divided between two parallel members, and the rising predicated of the first alone'.

How does this chiastic arrangement help in determining the nature of the colon type in 2cd? Viewed in this way not only does the prominence (being both structurally central and marked by the particle הִנֵּה) and independence of 2ab become more apparent,[145] but it throws into relief the correspondences between the units immediately preceding and following this central unit. In order to solve the puzzle of the word order in 2cd it is proposed that one need look no further than the fact that it is a parallel to 1bc, that is, both a structural, as well as a semantic, parallel. The particular form of cola 2c and 2d has to be interpreted within this framework. We argue, therefore, that 2cd are in fact two DEF cola continuing from the CAN//DEF cola in 1bc. Together these four cola make an obvious extended parallelism:[146]

CAN	for your light has come,
DEF	and the glory of YHWH has risen upon you.
	For behold darkness shall cover the earth,
	and thick darkness the peoples;
DEF	and YHWH will arise upon you,
DEF	and his glory will appear over you.

Note that within each of the three DEF cola the phrase עָלַיִךְ occurs, and in a different position within the clause in each case (third word, first, and second), which is a typical expression of defamiliarisation. This extended parallelism, however, has the added feature that an interruption (2ab) breaks it up into two halves.[147] We would also contend that the purpose of the *wāw* at the beginning of 2c is intended to connect 2cd with the first half of the parallelism in 1bc, rather than to contrast it with 2ab.[148] Not all commentators are of the opinion that the clause-initial וְעָלַיִךְ ('and upon you') in 2c indicates a contrast. Alexander translates the *wāw* simply as 'and'.[149] So, bringing our analysis to its conclusion, we propose the following colon types for Isaiah 60:1–3:

---

145 Breck, *The Shape of Biblical Language*, p. 37, claims that 'The center of the oracle serves as an antithetical pivot'.
146 Wendland deals at some length with the possibility of parallelism not occurring in consecutive cola, but at a distance; *Analyzing the Psalms*, p. 101.
147 Other instances occur in Hebrew poetry where, in an ABA' structure, the central member differs both syntactically and semantically from the outer two units, which are in parallel with each other. See, for example, the analysis of Psalm 36:7–8 earlier in this chapter, and Isaiah 59:6c–7d in 8.2.1 (a).
148 A similar use of the *wāw* was observed in Psalm 1:3d. See 9.1.1 above.
149 Alexander, *The Prophecies of Isaiah*, vol. 2, p. 380.

1a	V V	CAN
1bc	C V S // w-S M V	CAN//DEF
2ab	C-H S V-O // w-S O	MKD//Gap
2cd	w-M V S // w-S M V	DEF//DEF
3ab	w-V S M // w-S M	CAN//Gap

9.4 Summary

In this chapter we firstly analysed several extended poetic texts, such as were typical in the degree and character of the word-order variation they displayed. Then diverse potential causes of confusion in analysing the constituent order of Hebrew verse were investigated. Lastly, we considered poetic passages in which the non-canonical word-order variation was of a greater proportion relative to unmarked clauses, and/or of a more complex nature.

The first section of this chapter has illustrated how our theory may be applied with satisfactory results to larger sections of poetry. The latter two sections have been important in that they have demonstrated that, what at first might be thought to be counter-examples to our claims, have not proved to be so. Upon thorough analysis these were found to have some explanation, either in respect of markedness or defamiliarisation, which was in harmony with the propositions that have been advanced.

CHAPTER 10

Alternative Approaches: Rosenbaum and Gross

Having argued for a particular approach to word order in Biblical Hebrew poetry, some comment must now be made respecting those two other works, mentioned in chapter 1, which offer some treatment of word-order variation in the poetry of the Old Testament. The chief of these is Michael Rosenbaum's *Word-Order Variation in Isaiah 40–55: A Functional Perspective* (1997). Of less importance, since its scope is much more limited, is the volume of Walter Gross entitled *Doppelt besetztes Vorfeld* (2001). It is our aim here to highlight certain of the shortcomings of these two approaches in comparison with that which has been advocated in the foregoing chapters, and to demonstrate from the study of a number of texts how the application of the present study produces more satisfactory results than those of these two previous attempts. To compare the present work with that of these two scholars is to further test the validity of the former.[1]

10.1 General Observations

Before looking at specific weaknesses in the aforementioned works, there are criticisms of a more general nature that may be levelled against both.

(1) Linguistically, both scholars employ a more traditional functional grammatical model. Neither of them apply to the problem of word order the more refined theory of information structure as developed by Lambrecht.[2] By ignoring this they denied themselves the invaluable insights that the theory offers regarding the pragmatic component of language. Consequently they were unaware of certain possible focus structures which might assist in the explanation of specific texts. An appreciation of the three categories of sentence focus, predicate focus and argument focus would have facilitated greater understanding of the word order in many instances. The functional approach used by both scholars did not enable them to see SV-clauses, for instance, in terms of sentence-focus structure, and this is a reasonably

---

1 We use the word 'further' as an initial testing of the present approach was undertaken in the previous chapter in connection with the various problematic passages examined there.
2 Even though Lambrecht's *Information Structure and Sentence Form* had already been published. See 3.3 above.

common marked clause-type in Biblical Hebrew.

(2) Neither scholar presents a clear overall theory to the problem of word-order variation, as has been attempted here. No objective means is proposed of differentiating between variation which is purely poetic and that which is pragmatically marked. Rosenbaum assumes that both kinds of variation exist, but fails to define how we may know which is which. Gross is of the opinion that both may exist in a single sequence of constituents at one and the same time.

(3) No integrated analysis is offered of the various colon-types together with their relative frequency and distribution. As a result, the fact that specific colon arrangements may function to mark significant junctures in the text is undetected.

(4) Each scholar has severely restricted himself in the area of research. With regard to Rosenbaum, it is the amount of the data covered. The conclusions he arrives at regarding Hebrew poetry are based solely upon an examination of sixteen chapters of Isaiah. Gross, on the other hand, while he includes all the poetic books in the Old Testament plus that poetry embedded within narrative texts, only deals with clauses that possess two marked elements. Single preverbal constituents do not fall within the scope of his analysis. In no way, therefore, can either of these studies justifiably be claimed as an extensive study of the problem of word order in the poetic genre.

It is not our intention to diminish the contributions made by each of these scholars to what is a relatively fresh field of research. Despite the above comments, we would not deny that in many instances the interpretations given by Rosenbaum and Gross on individual poetic texts are valid and helpful. Now, however, we look at a sample selection of places where we would contend that the application of the approach presented here would result in a better understanding of the texts in question.

10.2 Rosenbaum's *Word-Order Variation in Isaiah 40–55*

Rosenbaum endeavours to explain word-order variation in these sections of Isaiah through the application of what is essentially the functional model of Simon Dik, modified by the findings of recent studies in discourse analysis.[3]

The author develops the functional grammatical idea that special positions are held by those constituents having certain pragmatic functions, such as topic and focus, and also those that he terms setting and theme.

---

3 See Rosenbaum, *Word-Order Variation in Isaiah 40–55*, pp. 9–20. Though leaning heavily upon Dik, Rosenbaum also makes use of insights from Halliday and others of the Prague School of Linguistics.

Taking VSO as the basic constituent order for Biblical Hebrew,[4] he then outlines the special positions for the language of verbal clauses in Isaiah 40–55. In keeping with the functional model he also proposes rules which describe the placement of constituents in their relative places within the functional pattern.[5]

Besides the general observations made earlier, one further weakness in Rosenbaum's work is his inadequate analysis of parallelism and its bearing on word-order variation. His treatment in this area is superficial and never fully engages with the complexities involved. He fails to explore the various relationships that adhere between the individual cola of poetic couplets (and larger units of tricola and tetracola), whether parallel or not.

We present here a number of examples which will serve to demonstrate how the inadequacy of the linguistic model employed by Rosenbaum can result in faulty or implausible analysis. At the same time we offer an alternative interpretation based upon the theory and application laid out in the preceding chapters of the present work.

10.2.1 Examples Relating to Pragmatic Factors

First we consider word order that he interprets as marked topic:

Isaiah 41:16

You will winnow them, and the wind shall carry them away,	תִּזְרֵם וְרוּחַ תִּשָּׂאֵם	A
and a whirlwind will scatter them;	וּסְעָרָה תָּפִיץ אוֹתָם	B
and you shall rejoice in YHWH,	וְאַתָּה תָּגִיל בַּיהוָה	C
and glory in the Holy One of Israel.	בִּקְדוֹשׁ יִשְׂרָאֵל תִּתְהַלָּל׃	D

For connection we cite verse 15 where God encourages Israel with the words, 'Behold, I will make you into a new threshing sledge with sharp teeth; you shall thresh the mountains and crush them, and make the hills like chaff'. Rosenbaum cites verse 16 as an illustration of an independent Pn[Su], וְאַתָּה in colon C, being employed for 'Resuming a Topic'.[6] He comments, 'In Is 41.15b–16, we see a Given Topic "You" (=Israel/Jacob) which is interrupted by a Sub-Topic "wind/storm" (subsumed under the agricultural metaphor)'. He then goes on to claim[7] that the 'wind/storm' is introduced by 'placing it in the initial P_1 position. (This is also important to avoid confusing the Subjects of the verbs because formally the 2 m sg and 3

---

4   *Ibid.*, p. 21.
5   *Ibid.*, pp. 23–24.
6   *Ibid.*, p. 32. By 'resumed topic' he means the re-entrance of a topic into the discourse after it has not been referred to for a certain time (*ibid.*, p. 28).
7   *Ibid.*, p. 33.

f sg prefix conjugations are identical.) Likewise, when the Speaker resumes the primary Topic (You) ... he places a pronoun in the initial P₁ position to avoid confusion with the Sub-Topic (wind/storm) which precedes and the Resumed Topic (You)'.

Rosenbaum here consistently interprets the three preverbal subjects appearing in this verse as being marked for topic – the first two indicating the introduction of sub-topics, the third a resumed major topic. We would take issue with his interpretation in all three cases. The main topic in this context, Rosenbaum rightly says, is Israel, here addressed by God in the 2nd person singular. The referent Israel is encoded in colon A by means of the subject prefix of the verb תִּזְרֵם. This continues the same topic from 15cd. Following this initial clause in 16a, consisting of a single word, comes an embedded parallelism: וְרוּחַ תִּשָּׂאֵם // וּסְעָרָה תָּפִיץ אוֹתָם, having the order SV-o // SVO. The parallelism is both semantic and syntactic. Rosenbaum's linguistic model does not allow him the possibility of considering that the contents of this parallelism might be event-reporting. For him the fronting of a subject is expressive of topicality. Yet numerous cases exist elsewhere in Hebrew poetry of sub-topics introduced postverbally in canonical VS order (e.g., Ex. 15:8, אָמַר אוֹיֵב; Ps. 40:4, יִרְאוּ רַבִּים), a fact which weighs against Rosenbaum's interpretation. The SV word order *may* be an indication of a newly introduced topic,[8] but this is just one of its several functions. The existence of event-reporting SV-clauses in poetry, as well as in narrative, is well attested, as has been seen. Second Isaiah, the corpus forming the basis of Rosenbaum's research, contains a good number of such event-reporting clauses (e.g., 43:27; 51:3; 54:10; 55:12), and that, we propose, is what is contained in 41:16ab. It is an independent utterance, characteristic of the sentence-focus clause,[9] in the form of a parallel bicolon concerning the judgment brought by the 'wind/whirlwind', after which the same 2nd person singular topic continues. Here in lines AB we have a good example of a marked SV//SV parallelism,[10] adhering to the constraint applicable to markedness in parallelisms.

Coming now to the pronoun וְאַתָּה heading line C, we note from other texts that a resumed major topic does not require such a marked introduction back into the discourse (e.g., Ps. 104:13; Is. 17:13). However, one factor in favour of Rosenbaum's interpretation is the fact that if the pronoun did not appear this might lead to some confusion between the verbal prefix ־תּ indicating 3rd person feminine singular on the verbs תִּשָּׂאֵם and תָּפִיץ and the prefix ־תּ being 2nd person masculine singular on the

---

8   Rosenbaum's interpretation of SV as topic in Isaiah 44:11, 13 is correct (*ibid.*, pp. 37–38).
9   See 3.3.3 (c).
10 See 7.2.1 (a).

Alternative Approaches 259

verb in line C.[11] If this is the reason for the occurrence of וְאַתָּה, then its inclusion is to disambiguate topics in a context where the verbal prefixes are of themselves insufficient, rather than being an example of the normal way in which topics are resumed. Yet we still do not find Rosenbaum's account satisfactory. A better explanation for the occurrence of וְאַתָּה lies in a comparison of lines AB with CD. The variously encoded objects of AB refer back to the 'mountains' and 'hills' of verse 15cd, which in themselves are figures depicting Israel's enemies (as introduced at the onset of this section, v. 11).[12] These had formerly contended against Israel (v. 12c), and had been an object of fear on the part of God's people (v. 14a). But now God would rise up in their defence. These former foes 'will become as nothing and perish' (v. 11d). God says to Israel, 'Though you search for your enemies, you will not find them. Those who wage war against you will be as nothing at all' (v. 12 NIV). Through divine judgment the enemies would completely disappear from the scene. The agricultural metaphors in verses 15–16 of threshing, winnowing and scattering by the wind[13] are expressive of the same truth. Then in verse 16d comes a statement in quite a different tone: 'And you shall rejoice in YHWH, and glory in the Holy One of Israel'. Reading these words in their immediate context the contrast between the bright future of Israel and the fate of her enemies as just portrayed is unmistakable; '... a whirlwind will scatter them [אוֹתָם]; but *you* [וְאַתָּה] will rejoice in YHWH' is clearly the sense intended. This contrastive relationship between the referents of the two clauses is explicitly conveyed in a number of English versions: 'but you' (NIV NASB NJPS); 'whereas you' (NJB),[14] as well as in the translations offered by both Oswalt, 'But you, you will rejoice in the Lord', and Watts, 'But you shall rejoice in Yahweh'.[15] The use of the independent pronoun to indicate contrasting active topic was noted earlier.[16]

Here is a second example, in which Rosenbaum seeks to explain the preverbal subject in terms of sub-topic.

---

11 Rosenbaum, *Word-Order Variation in Isaiah 40–55*, p. 33.
12 Watts interprets as 'the powers of the earth including Babylon' (*Isaiah 34–66*, p. 107) and Delitzsch, 'a figurative expression for proud and mighty foes' (in Keil and Delitzsch, *Commentary on the Old Testament*, vol. 7, 'Isaiah', p. 165); ibn Ezra takes the mountains as a figurative expression for the Babylonians (Friedländer, *The Commentary of Ibn Ezra on Isaiah*, p. 183). An interpretation of these metaphors along these lines is better than that of 'seemingly insurmountable obstacles' (Motyer, *The Prophecy of Isaiah*, p. 313). It is worth remarking that the Targum actually renders 'mountains' and 'hills' by 'peoples' and 'kingdoms' (Watts, *Isaiah 34–66*, p. 100).
13 The scattering by the wind was part of the winnowing process; cf. J. D. Douglas, *New Bible Dictionary* (Leicester: Inter-Varsity Press, 1982), pp. 19–20.
14 Cf. LXX, σὺ δέ.
15 Oswalt, *The Book of Isaiah 40–66*, p. 88; Watts, *Isaiah 34–66*, p. 98. Alexander, *The Prophecies of Isaiah*, vol. 2, p. 124, also supports the contrast.
16 See examples with pronouns in 4.2.2 (c).

Isaiah 44:9ab
Those who fashion an image, all of them are nothing,   יֹצְרֵי־פֶסֶל כֻּלָּם תֹּהוּ
and their desired things shall not profit.   וַחֲמוּדֵיהֶם בַּל־יוֹעִילוּ

We analyse the constituent order as: NP[Ext] S Comp // S V^{Ng} / Comp S V^{Ng} / V^{Ng} C V. Regarding the opening NP, יֹצְרֵי־פֶסֶל, there is no doubt that this is to be identified as the main topic, as Rosenbaum says, 'being initially extraposed then resumed with a pronominal element –*ām* in the verbless clause' (i.e., כֻּלָּם תֹּהוּ).[17] One of the functions of extraposition is, without doubt, the presentation of a new main topic into the discourse.[18] The difficulty respecting word order lies in the following colon, C: וַחֲמוּדֵיהֶם בַּל־יוֹעִילוּ. Rosenbaum refers to the NP וַחֲמוּדֵיהֶם as 'Sub-Topic', which is introduced by placing it in 'the initial P_1 position'.[19] Thus, as with 41:16 considered above, he associates fronting with the topicality function, specifically here the introduction of a sub-topic.

Yet there is an alternative explanation of the SV word order at this point. Taking וַחֲמוּדֵיהֶם to begin, from what has been argued previously in this work we would not define this NP[Su] as a sub-topic. Included in the NP is the possessive pronominal suffix ־הֶם 'their', having anaphoric reference to יֹצְרֵי־פֶסֶל at the head of line A. This fact establishes וַחֲמוּדֵיהֶם, not as a newly activated sub-topic, but rather as an entity belonging to the topical frame[20] evoked by the compound NP יֹצְרֵי־פֶסֶל. There is a twofold relationship between the two NPs, first the coreferentiality of יֹצְרֵי ('Those who fashion') and the 3rd person plural suffix ־הֶם ('their') which is demanded by the context, and secondly the coreferentiality of the noun phrases פֶסֶל and וַחֲמוּדֵיהֶם. In other words, the NP[Su] commencing line B only refers to something pertaining to the NP[Su] of the previous line. This is not a newly introduced sub-topic, but one that is unquestionably contextually inferable. Furthermore, we note that commentators and versions support the fact that by the expression 'desired things' the idols themselves are intended.[21] At a topical level, therefore, everything expressed by וַחֲמוּדֵיהֶם is inferable from יֹצְרֵי־פֶסֶל.

An important factor which Rosenbaum overlooks is that the bicolon contained in 9ab forms a parallelism, both at the semantic and syntactic levels. This is clearly brought out in the rendering of TEV, 'All those who make idols are worthless, and the gods they prize so highly are useless'.[22]

---

17 Rosenbaum, *Word-Order Variation in Isaiah 40–55*, p. 36.
18 See Kahn, *Studies in Semitic Syntax*, pp. 79–81.
19 Rosenbaum, *Word-Order Variation in Isaiah 40–55*, p. 37.
20 See 3.4.1 (a), example (2), and fn. 66.
21 E.g., Motyer, *The Prophecy of Isaiah*, p. 346; Delitzsch, 'Isaiah', p. 207; TEV and NLT; implicit in NJB.
22 Cf. NCV, 'Some people make idols, but they are worth nothing. People treasure them, but they are useless'.

Alternative Approaches

There is a close correspondence between the two subjects and between the two predications. Recalling the principles governing the B-lines of parallelisms, i.e., that marked word order in the A-line will be preserved in B, we observe that the markedness of line A in 44:9, itself signalling the presentation of a new topic ('Those who fashion idols'), is reduplicated in the sentence-focus clause of the B-line.[23] That is to say, the word order of line B is not due to the fact that SV presents an independent sub-topic, as Rosenbaum would judge, but, since the B-line of a parallelism having a marked A-line takes its form from that A-line, the SV order is an outworking of the parallelistic relation that adheres between the two cola. Consequently, the motivating dynamic which accounts for SV in 44:9b is the repetition of the focus structure of the A-line, not the presentation of a sub-topic.

Isaiah 48:13

| Indeed my hand has founded the earth, | אַף־יָדִי יָסְדָה אֶרֶץ |
| and my right hand has stretched out the heavens. | וִימִינִי טִפְּחָה שָׁמָיִם |

Here Rosenbaum again accounts for the SV order as another example of sub-topic, which is introduced, he says, 'by placing the Sub-Topic constituent in the initial P₁ position'.[24] At this point Rosenbaum makes the error of overlooking the presence of אַף. The occurrence of such a particle is important to consider in that it may have some bearing on the word order of the following clause. It has been shown that אַף is in fact a *focus* particle[25] which may serve to place the following topical referent in focus. When the sentence exhibits SV(O) order then there are two possible interpretations of the text. Where S is a previously inactive topic the whole clause is the focus (i.e., having sentence focus). But when the S constituent indicates an already active or semi-active topic, then the focus is upon S only.[26] The NP[Su] יָדִי, 'my hand', falls into this latter category. In the preceding verse (v. 12) God declares, 'Listen to me, Jacob; Israel, whom I have called: I am he; I am the first and I am the last'. The introduction of יָדִי is evidently not introducing some new topic, but is implicit in the currently active topic 'I' (= God), that is, the 'hand' of God is information accessible from the foregoing mention of God himself. So verse 13 is an emphatic affirmation[27] of the basic tenet of

---

23 Even though a noun-cause the pragmatic marking of A is beyond question in view of the presence of the extraposed NP. It has previously been noted that the two different forms of markedness, i.e., extraposition and fronting, are to be found in a parallel relationship (7.2.5). Though the pragmatic marking may differ with respect to form, the markedness is nevertheless present in both lines, thus complying with the constraint.
24 Rosenbaum, *Word-Order Variation in Isaiah 40–55*, p. 36.
25 3.4.2 (e) and 4.2.1 (b); cf. Van der Merwe (et al.), *A Biblical Hebrew Reference Grammar*, pp. 312–13.
26 See the discussion of focus particles in 3.4.2 and 4.2.1.
27 On this particular use of אַף for confirming the truth of a statement, see Van der Merwe (et al.), *A Biblical Hebrew Reference Grammar*, p. 313.

Israel's faith that it is Yahweh who is the one who created the earth and the heavens.

Considering the overall context in which this verse appears we may identify the particular category of focus in question as replacing. In this chapter God contends with those who worship idols. Certain divine abilities are implicitly claimed for the idols, particularly that of declaring the future, which the Lord refutes (v. 5 and v. 14). And so too in verses 12–13, seen in the same light, attributes of Yahweh are affirmed, which the idols entirely lack, that is, his eternal being (v. 12), and the power to create (v. 13). It is Yahweh, and not they (as the idolaters might argue), who alone possesses these things.[28] From the perspective of information structure verse 13 shows argument focus, since the creation of heaven and earth is presupposed due to the obvious fact of their existence.

The focal import of אַף־יָדִי is recognised by many English versions. Of especial note is the NLT, which utilises a cleft-sentence construction to bring out the presence of the focus: 'It was my hand that laid the foundations of the earth'.[29]

The foregoing is a good illustration of the shortcomings of Rosenbaum's approach. We have shown that he has mistaken an initial NP indicating marked focus for the introduction of a new sub-topic. This is one of several places where he confuses the two pragmatic functions. His treatment of this verse also illustrates the insufficient place given to focus particles in the whole of his treatment. Here אַף was ignored completely. In his entire thirty-five page chapter on focus, of the several focus particles as listed by Van der Merwe[30] and Heimerdinger,[31] only אָכֵן and גַּם are mentioned,[32] and these only in passing.

In this next example of Rosenbaum's analysis he identifies the pragmatic function of focus.

Isaiah 49:14–15

And Zion said,	וַתֹּאמֶר צִיּוֹן	A
'YHWH has forsaken me,	עֲזָבַנִי יְהוָה	B
and my Lord has forgotten me.	וַאדֹנָי שְׁכֵחָנִי׃	C
Can a woman forget her nursing child,	הֲתִשְׁכַּח אִשָּׁה עוּלָהּ	D
and not have compassion on the son of her womb?	מֵרַחֵם בֶּן־בִּטְנָהּ	E
Though they may forget,	גַּם־אֵלֶּה תִשְׁכַּחְנָה	F
yet I will not forget you'.	וְאָנֹכִי לֹא אֶשְׁכָּחֵךְ׃	G

---

28 Cf. the similar argument in Jeremiah 10:6–13.
29 NASB NKJV NIV NCV NJPS also show awareness of the presence of focus; cf. Watts, *Isaiah 34–66*, p. 174.
30 Van der Merwe (et al.), *A Biblical Hebrew Reference Grammar*, pp. 311–17.
31 Heimerdinger, *Topic, Focus and Foreground*, p. 170.
32 For אָכֵן, Rosenbaum, *Word-Order Variation in Isaiah 40–55*, pp. 82–83; and for גַּם, pp. 91–92. The former overlaps with אַף in the sense of certainty. See 3.4.2 (d).

Alternative Approaches 263

There are two fronted elements in these verses to which Rosenbaum assigns the focus function. Firstly, he defines גַּם־אֵלֶּה (F) as 'Expanding Focus'.[33] Secondly, he calls וְאָנֹכִי (G) 'an example of *Replacing Focus*'.[34] He adds, 'Isaiah 49.15b [our line G] is a Replacing Focus, replacing Zion's mistaken pragmatic information (49.14) that Yahweh has forgotten/ abandoned her, with the correct information that Yahweh has not in fact forgotten/abandoned Zion; moreover, unlike a mother who may abandon her child (49.15b), Yahweh will never forget Zion'.[35] But Rosenbaum does not stop there. He sees in this final colon (G) an example of what he terms '*Multiple Focusing*'. He explains, 'We have just seen that v 15b contains a Replacing Focus in contrast to v 14. Additionally, it is a *Restricting Focus* in contrast to v 15a (above) since Yahweh, unlike mothers, is not a member of the category of those who forget/abandon their children. Finally, it is *Comparing Focus* in contrast to v 15b '.[36]

We may quickly dismiss Rosenbaum's interpretation of גַּם־אֵלֶּה as 'Even these'. It is common knowledge that Hebrew particles may have not just one function, but several. That גַּם may be a focus particle denoting expanding focus has been frequently observed, yet it may also function as a conjunction introducing a hypotactic clause.[37] The use of גַּם in concessive clauses, where it would be given the sense of 'although' or 'even though', is well documented.[38] The LXX (εἰ δὲ καί) and several English versions (e.g., NIV, 'Though she may forget') have translated 15c in terms of concession.[39] Such an interpretation of גַּם־אֵלֶּה holds more merit than Rosenbaum's expanding focus. It is noteworthy that although Rosenbaum identifies it as expanding he offers nothing whatsoever in explanation of what is being expanded upon.[40]

As far as the second instance of pragmatically marked word order that Rosenbaum deals with in this passage is concerned, וְאָנֹכִי לֹא אֶשְׁכָּחֵךְ, it must be said that his conclusions are highly debatable. Here he manages to find replacing, restricting, and comparing focus, all in the one marked element! This is overloading the text, and making far too complicated what in essence is reasonably simple. Putting the concessive clause together with its main clause, there can be seen to exist a *contrasting* relationship between the topics of the two clauses: 'Though *these* [referring back to the nursing mother of the previous line, v. 15ab] may forget, yet *I* [God] will

---

33 Rosenbaum, *Word-Order Variation in Isaiah 40–55*, p. 92.
34 *Ibid.*
35 *Ibid.*, p. 93.
36 *Ibid.*
37 Traditionally termed 'subordinate' clause.
38 E.g., Gesenius, *Hebrew Grammar*, §160*b*; Williams, *Hebrew Syntax*, §382.
39 Watts, *Isaiah 34–66*, p. 185, also notes this as concessive.
40 Rosenbaum, *Word-Order Variation in Isaiah 40–55*, pp. 91–92.

never forget you'. The two Pn[Su]s thus indicate contrastive topics. By this means Yahweh is affirming the fact that he had not forsaken his people as some were claiming (v. 14).[41]

The contrastive sense of וְאָנֹכִי was well discerned by the translators of the LXX: ἀλλ' ἐγὼ οὐκ ἐπιλήσομαί σου ('but I will not forget you'). A number of English versions also include an adversative particle, either 'but' (NASB NLT), or 'yet' (NJKV NRSV).[42]

10.2.2 Examples Relating to Poetic Factors

We will here examine certain passages in which Rosenbaum identifies variation in word order for purely poetic, rather than pragmatic, reasons.

Isaiah 51:3

| Joy and happiness will be found in her, | שָׂשׂוֹן וְשִׂמְחָה יִמָּצֵא בָהּ |
| thanksgiving and the sound of singing. | תּוֹדָה וְקוֹל זִמְרָה: |

Rosenbaum cites this text as an example of what is commonly known in Hebrew poetic manuals as 'pivot'.[43] This construction consists of an A-line in which the final term (or terms) serves also as the beginning of the B-line. In other words, says Rosenbaum, 'it serves as a kind of "pivot" upon which the A and B lines revolve'.[44] He continues, 'In order to achieve this pattern, with the pivoted term(s) in the final position of the A line, an abnormal word-order will result'.[45] Before going any further we need to make a correction to this statement. It is more accurate to say 'an abnormal word-order *may* result'. In his treatment of the pivotal pattern Watson includes several examples in which there is nothing irregular about the word order, such as Psalm 57:10 and Isaiah 28:24.[46] That minor inaccuracy aside, we need to examine how apposite it is to offer the above text, Isaiah 51:3, as an illustration of 'abnormal' word order created by a pivotal pattern. The bicolon consists of: $S^1 S^2$ V M // $S^1 S^2$. The structure, a verbal clause with two NP[Su]s followed by two appositional NPs, certainly fits the criterion of a pivot. The central V M, יִמָּצֵא בָהּ, is evidently required for a complete sense in both cola. Yet we cannot therefore conclude that the pivot has resulted in this SV word order. The particular word order seen here allows for a pivot pattern to be made with the clause-final VP (יִמָּצֵא בָהּ) as the pivotal element, but the pivot itself is not the cause of the marked word order.

---

41 The speech of this verse contains an event-reporting SV//SV parallelism.
42 Cf. Motyer, *The Prophecy of Isaiah*, p. 394, who translates as, 'But as for me …'
43 Rosenbaum, *Word-Order Variation in Isaiah 40–55*, p. 184. Cf. Watson, *Classical Hebrew Poetry*, pp. 214–21.
44 Rosenbaum, *Word-Order Variation in Isaiah 40–55*, p. 184.
45 *Ibid.*, p. 184.
46 E.g., Watson, *Classical Hebrew Poetry*, pp. 216, and 219.

Rather the SV order of שָׂשׂוֹן וְשִׂמְחָה יִמָּצֵא בָהּ is due to the fact that it is has sentence focus.[47] A future event is being foretold, yet the referents indicated by the grammatical subjects performing these events do not become topical in the discourse. It is, therefore, a future event-reporting clause. In confirmation of this analysis is the occurrence of identical SV-clauses in very similar passages of Second Isaiah foretelling the future joy at the redemption of God's people:

(51:11) שָׂשׂוֹן וְשִׂמְחָה יַשִּׂיגוּן

Joy and happiness will overtake them. [SSV]

(55:12) הֶהָרִים וְהַגְּבָעוֹת יִפְצְחוּ לִפְנֵיכֶם רִנָּה וְכָל־עֲצֵי הַשָּׂדֶה יִמְחֲאוּ־כָף

The mountains and the hills shall break forth before you into singing, [SSVMO]
and all the trees of the field shall clap their hands. [SVO]

We conclude that Rosenbaum is mistaken in his analysis. The variant word order does not exist in order to achieve this pattern. The pivotal pattern results from the word order, not the word order from the pivotal pattern. What we are looking at in Isaiah 51:3 is pragmatic word order, not poetic; and yet the author has utilised the pragmatically marked order to produce a recognised aesthetic feature of Biblical Hebrew poetry in which the central element does double duty. Rosenbaum is incorrect therefore to include this verse as an illustration of poetically motivated ordering.

Isaiah 46:4

Even to your old age, I am he,   וְעַד־זִקְנָה אֲנִי הוּא
and even to grey hairs I will carry you.   וְעַד־שֵׂיבָה אֲנִי אֶסְבֹּל

This text is cited by Rosenbaum as an example of gapping in the A-line,[48] that is, backward gapping,[49] where an element of the second line is necessary for completing the meaning of the first. Rosenbaum comments, 'Such A line gapping is highly defamiliarizing because the A line could be understood, initially, by the Addressee as a nominal sentence, until the B line arrives with the gapped element prompting the Addressee to pause and reanalyze the syntax of both lines'.[50] In this particular text, Rosenbaum claims, the gapped element which the B-line provides is אֲנִי אֶסְבֹּל, 'I will carry'. He further states, 'the placement of the complementary element ʾesbōl at the end of the B line results in a defamiliar word-order'.[51]

There are two points of debate raised by the construction that Rosenbaum places upon this text. Firstly, is the presence of the element

---

47 See 4.2.3 (a).
48 Rosenbaum, *Word-Order Variation in Isaiah 40–55*, pp. 161–62.
49 See above 2.2.2 (a).
50 Rosenbaum, *Word-Order Variation in Isaiah 40–55*, p. 162.
51 *Ibid.*, p. 188.

אֲנִי אֶסְבֹּל in line B really a case of retrograde gapping? And secondly, does the position of אֲנִי אֶסְבֹּל in the clause-final position constitute an authentic instance of 'defamiliar word-order'?

Concerning the former question, it can readily be seen that אֲנִי הוּא in line A can stand independently. 'I am he' may compose a syntactically complete verbless clause. Moreover, the same words אֲנִי הוּא occur as a clause in its own right in 41:4; 43:10, 13; and 48:12, and indeed is a prominent characteristic in the style of Second Isaiah.[52] God wishes Israel to know that 'I am he' (41:4); he declares to them that even 'from ancient days I am he' (43:13 NIV). So it cannot convincingly be argued that 'Even to your old age, I am he' is an incomplete or elliptical statement, as Rosenbaum proposes. This verse well complements the past time reference of 43:13 by affirming the constancy of God in the future. The renderings of the NJB, 'Until your old age I shall be the same', and NJPS, 'Till you grow old, I will still be the same', capture the sense intended. The commentators also interpret it this way.[53] In fact there is little support to be found for Rosenbaum's particular construal of the text. Perhaps his translation of אֲנִי הוּא as 'I alone'[54] reflects his lack of appreciation of the significance of this phrase. Elsewhere in Second Isaiah the word לְבַדִּי is used to express this idea (e.g., 44:24; 49:21).

Regarding the position in which אֲנִי אֶסְבֹּל is placed, if we apply the principles discussed in chapter 7 relating to the B-lines of parallelisms,[55] we find that the order of וְעַד־שֵׂיבָה אֲנִי אֶסְבֹּל, M S V, is determined by the A-line with which it is coupled. In both A- and B-lines the PPs, which are synonymous terms, are fronted. The reason for this fronting can be understood when the whole of verses 3–4 are read:

> [3] Listen to me, house of Jacob,
> and all the remnant of the house of Israel,
> who have been upheld by me from birth,
> who have been carried from the womb.
> [4] Even to your old age, I am he,
> and even to grey hairs I will carry you.
> I have made you, and I will bear you;
> I will carry you, and will deliver you.

---

52 It is interesting to note that the two cases (43:25; 51:12) in Second Isaiah where 'I am he' is not independent, but introduces a participial clause, 'I am he who ...', the pronoun is אָנֹכִי, and not אֲנִי. 52:6 is ambiguous.
53 Oswalt (*The Book of Isaiah 40–66*, p. 227) translates literally as 'I am he', still taking it as an independent verbless clause, as does Watts (*Isaiah 34–66*, p. 164) 'I am the one'. Motyer, *The Prophecy of Isaiah*, p. 369; Alexander, *The Prophecies of Isaiah*, vol. 2, p. 192; Young, *The Book of Isaiah*, vol. 3, p. 222, are all in substantial agreement.
54 Rosenbaum, *Word-Order Variation in Isaiah 40–55*, p. 161.
55 See 7.2.1 (c).

In verse 3cd God reminds Israel that he had sustained them from their very beginnings. This he expresses by means of the parallelism:

הָעֲמֻסִים מִנִּי־בֶטֶן // הַנְּשֻׂאִים מִנִּי־רָחַם:

Each half of the parallelism ends with a PP, מִנִּי־בֶטֶן and מִנִּי־רָחַם, both literally meaning 'from the womb'. Coming to verse 4 it is evident that the two clause-initial PPs וְעַד־זִקְנָה and וְעַד־שֵׂיבָה stand in a focus relationship to the foregoing. Many English versions recognise this, rendering the *wāw* as 'Even' (e.g., NIV NASB NKJV NRSV),[56] as has been done in our translation above, and indeed as Rosenbaum himself translates.[57] It is not just from birth that God has sustained Israel, but he will do the same even to their old age.[58] This is a clear case of expanding focus, in the sense of contra-expectation.[59]

We conclude, therefore, that the position in which the VP אֲנִי אֶסְבֹּל finds itself is not due to the defamiliarisation of the language at this point. Rather the word order of verse 4b is explicable with respect to the pragmatics of the whole verse. The PP of verse 4a stands in an expanding relationship to the previous verse, and verse 4b, being a synonymous (and partially syntactic) parallelism, mirrors the pragmatic structuring of the A-line. The key then to the word order of 46:4 then is the function of the PP וְעַד־שֵׂיבָה, and not the VP אֲנִי אֶסְבֹּל.[60] The ordering is pragmatic, not poetic.[61]

10.2.3 Conclusions

Having examined the application of Rosenbaum's approach we have demonstrated that it is a long way from being a full and satisfactory account of variation in Biblical Hebrew poetic word order, even within those chapters from Isaiah which form the basis of his study. The limitations of his linguistic method, and also no doubt of the extent of his data, have resulted in incorrect or questionable results. The alternative interpretations of word order that have been proposed to those of Rosenbaum have demonstrated that the theory put forward in the present work contributes to a better understanding of the pragmatic marking in the poetic line and its differentiation from what is merely poetic.

---

56 Cf. Watts, *Isaiah 34–66*, p. 164.

57 Rosenbaum, *Word-Order Variation in Isaiah 40–55*, p. 161.

58 Cf. C. Franke, *Isaiah 46, 47, and 48: A New Literary-Critical Reading* (Winona Lake, Indiana: Eisenbrauns, 1994), p. 38, 'The totality of Yahweh's deliverance of his people is expressed by these two extremes of birth/old age'.

59 See 3.4.2 (e) and 4.2.1 (a) and (b).

60 We make no attempt here to account for the presence of the Pn[Su] אֲנִי, other than the fact that this also parallels the identical element in the A-line in the same position.

61 Another questionable example of backwards gapping is to be found in Rosenbaum's treatment of Isaiah 40:15 (*Word-Order Variation in Isaiah 40–55*, p. 162).

Not wishing to end this section on an entirely negative note, we should add that if the observations made above leave one with the impression that Rosenbaum's analysis is always faulty, then we have done him an injustice. This is not the case. We have highlighted some of the weaknesses in his work, but there is much that is helpful in his study. Some of his insights into the interpretation of specific texts have been taken into consideration in this study.[62]

10.3 Gross' *Doppelt besetztes Vorfeld*

Brief mention has been made previously to the 2001 publication of Walter Gross on doubly marked clauses in Biblical Hebrew poetry. Gross, together with other scholars mentioned earlier,[63] has a strong tendency to account for all word-order variation in terms of pragmatic marking, although in his particular case he does seem to believe that the pragmatics can, at least upon occasion, be subordinated to what he calls 'ornamental' factors.[64] Yet even in such instances he would affirm that the pragmatic significance of the constituent order is not entirely absent.[65] Gross does not offer a way of distinguishing between the two, but merely says that both may be present in certain situations, that is, when a rhetorical pattern is created by the sequence of words.

Before studying specific instances of Gross's analysis, a few observations are in order upon his work as a whole. Firstly, Gross is well aware that the structures he is investigating are far more abundant in Hebrew poetry than in prose. Of these clauses with two preverbal constituents he notes 698 occurrences in the former genre, with only 135 in the latter.[66] Yet for such a disparity he offers no explanation. Gross sees no essential distinction between doubly marked sentences whether they occur in prose, in poetry with full pragmatic import, or in poetry with ornamental function. To him they are all a form of clause that is pragmatically structured according to the syntactic patterns admissible in ancient Hebrew.[67] His approach would not seem to allow for the possibility of a genuine poetic freedom with regard to word order which is entirely independent of pragmatic concerns.

---

62 E.g., his division of אֲנִי יָדַי נָטוּ שָׁמַיִם, in Isaiah 45:12 into two separate clauses. This has not been included among the unusual colon arrangements in chapter 8 since we accept Rosenbaum's analysis, *Word-Order Variation in Isaiah 40–55*, p. 48. We also accept his comments on 'Setting' (*ibid.*, pp. 41–44; cf. our section 3.5).
63 Buth and Shimasaki, see comments in 5.2.
64 By this term Gross does not mean exactly the same as defamiliarisation (see below).
65 E.g., *Doppelt besetztes Vorfeld*, pp. 122, 305.
66 *Ibid.*, p. 305.
67 *Ibid.*

Secondly, when Gross encounters certain of the unusual colon patterns discussed earlier in the present work,[68] he proposes an altogether different interpretation of them, one, we suggest, that is less convincing, since he does not undertake any large scale analysis of colon-types. For example, in his discussion of chiasmus, he makes the observation that inverted parallel lines of the pattern V___//___V occur much more commonly than ___V//V___.[69] The latter he appropriately describes as a 'rare' form.[70] With respect to these less frequent patterns, Gross describes the two verbs as being 'in contact-position',[71] the implication being that this is in some way significant, but in which way this is so he fails to define. In fact it is the other more frequent pattern, V___//___V, to which Gross more explicitly assigns the special significance. Speaking of such chiastic forms, he says, 'As a rule the sentence with doubly filled prefield forms the second half of the chiasmus, so that the verbs are at the outer positions, thus drawing special attention to themselves'.[72] Gross's position is confusing in that he seems to want to attribute a special effect to both the outer and the inner positions. Furthermore, he offers no explanation as to why one of these arrangements is much more common than the other. The position we maintain here is that the reason V___//___V is more often found is that the A-line is canonical, i.e., verb-initial, while the B-line is defamiliarised, allowing for the verb to occur either medially or finally, both of which are frequently seen in the data. This is the common CAN//DEF parallelism which has previously been noted many times in the present study. The reverse form, however, which has the canonical order in the B-line, ___V//V___, is, according to our findings, a special colon arrangement, DEF//CAN, which functions as a bounding or climactic device. It ought to be pointed out in passing that the two examples of this rare form which Gross notes in this section of his book, that is, Isaiah 31:9 and Hosea 10:6, are both instances of closure,[73] a factor excluded from his investigation.

---

68 See chapter 8.

69 *Ibid.*, pp. 90–91.

70 *Ibid.*, pp. 91, 104 ('selten').

71 *Ibid.*, p. 91 ('in Kontaktstellung').

72 *Ibid.*, p. 90 ('In der Regel bildet der Satz mit doppelt gefülltem Vorfeld die zweite Hälfte des Chiasmus, so daß die Verben an den Außenpositionen stehen und so wohl besondere Aufmerksamkeit erregen').

73 Neither of these texts falls within the corpus of data that we have selected as the basis of our research, yet both add support to our findings. That Isaiah 31:9 signals a closure is evident from the fact that it closes speech and ends the chapter (excepting the final נְאֻם־יְהוָה speech formula). Hosea 10:6 is taken as marking the end of a section in NRSV ESV NKJV CEV and also more significantly in Wendland's detailed discourse-based investigation of boundaries in Hosea (*The Discourse Analysis of Hebrew Prophetic Literature*, p. 163).

Since Gross makes no allowance for the possibility of a sequence of clause constituents that is purely an expression of poetic licence, then all the preverbal elements in his data are necessarily assigned some pragmatic functions, even though in certain instances he claims these may be secondary to poetic concerns. Poetic defamiliarisation, in its own right, is nowhere acknowledged.

10.3.1 Examples

In the following texts we illustrate how an appreciation of defamiliar colon types would lead to different conclusions from those arrived at by Gross.

Isaiah 49:26

I will make your oppressors eat their own flesh,	וְהַאֲכַלְתִּי אֶת־מוֹנַיִךְ אֶת־בְּשָׂרָם
and they shall be drunk with their own blood	וְכֶעָסִיס דָּמָם יִשְׁכָּרוּן
as with sweet wine.	

Here the colon structure is VOO//MOV. Gross attempts to assign full pragmatic weight to the two preverbal components וְכֶעָסִיס דָּמָם in the second line. He speaks of 'the stronger focusing of the entire prefield',[74] suggesting that both elements are pragmatically marked. In his discussion of comparative phrases, such as וְכֶעָסִיס, in MSV-clauses, Gross consistently interprets their initial position as an indication of focus[75] regardless of other rhetorical or discourse-functional factors as considered in this present work. In the four examples he analyses the focusing of the comparative element is certainly true of Isaiah 29:16 (contra-expectation) and Proverbs 11:28 (a contrast), but in the present example and Psalm 5:13 there is nothing contextual that infers a pragmatic interpretation. The form of these two latter is better attributed to defamiliarisation. In the case of Isaiah 49:26b it can be seen to make up the B-line of two parallel lines. Despite his acknowledgement of a semantic correspondence between the verbs 'give to eat' and 'get drunk', and the use of the word pair 'flesh' and 'blood',[76] Gross does not attribute any further significance to the fact that the deviation from the basic unmarked constituent order that he endeavours to explain is in the second line of a parallelism.[77] It has been our contention

---

74 Gross, *Doppelt besetztes Vorfeld*, p. 75 ('Um dieser starken Fokussierung des gesamten Vorfeldes').
75 *Ibid.*, pp. 74–76.
76 *Ibid.*
77 The bicolon is taken implicitly as a parallelism by both Watts (*Isaiah 34–66*, p. 193) and Motyer (*The Prophecy of Isaiah*, p. 396). Watts sees the metaphors of both lines ('devour their own flesh' and 'be drunk from their own blood') as expressing the same idea, i.e., being reduced to their last extremity. Certainly 'flesh' and 'blood', and the idea of eating and drinking are found elsewhere in parallelism (e.g., Ps. 50:13).

Alternative Approaches

that this is in fact the principal environment in which free variation of word order may take place in Hebrew poetry,[78] and one need look no further than this poetic motivation to account for the non-canonical sequence in this case. The remaining example, from Psalm 5:13, although the second member of a bicolon, is not a member of a parallelism. It is nevertheless to be taken as a special DEF colon as discussed in chapter 8. This example, listed in that chapter,[79] is an instance of a defamiliar clause with a particular discourse function, here marking closure, since it is with this colon that the psalm in question ends.

Proverbs 1:22

How long, simple ones, will you love simplicity?	עַד־מָתַי פְּתָיִם תְּאֵהֲבוּ פֶתִי	A
How long will mockers delight in their mocking,	וְלֵצִים לָצוֹן חָמְדוּ לָהֶם	B
and fools hate knowledge?	וּכְסִילִים יִשְׂנְאוּ־דָעַת׃	C

The three cola present in this verse consist of Q[Voc]VO, SOVM, and SVO respectively. Gross encounters a difficulty in the arrangement of these lines. Since the first is expressed in the 2nd person and the others in the 3rd person, Gross prefers to separate the first line from the remaining two.[80] He also doubts whether the second line could be a continuation of the interrogation in the first as he feels that the *qatal* verb form would not suitably follow a *yiqtol*. Having thus separated 22bc from 22a, he then proceeds to interpret the SOVM sequence in B in terms of focus. He suggests that the whole sentence be taken as focused,[81] that is, focused with respect to all its constituents. The particular manner of focus, however, is rather vaguely defined. This is not surprising seeing that the verse lacks any contextual justification for the presence of focus. An alternative would be to see all the cola as forming a three-part extended parallelism.[82] Without doubt the verbs of each clause ('love', 'delight', and 'hate') all fall within the same semantic domain, as Gross himself remarks, as do the NPs 'simple ones', 'mockers' and 'fools'. The phenomenon of 'tense-shifting' in parallelism has previously been mentioned, and may be called upon to account for the *yiqtol-qatal-yiqtol* sequence.[83] Many of the major English versions take the verse as such a parallelism. Some of these (TEV NLT NCV CEV) even transpose the 3rd person of 22bc to match the 2nd person of the first line, though unnecessarily so since Biblical Hebrew poetry allows for a shift in

---

78 See 5.3.
79 See 8.3.
80 Gross, *Doppelt besetztes Vorfeld*, p. 125.
81 *Ibid.* ('der ganze Satz sei fokussiert').
82 On extended parallelism, see 2.2.2 (c).
83 In such tense-shifting it is the first verb that determines the tense, aspect, and modality of the following verbs. See 5.7.4.

person between two parallel lines.[84] Viewed as a three-colon parallelism, the reordering of B and C, i.e., the secondary lines, may be now explained in terms of defamiliarisation. The overall arrangement of cola would be CAN//DEF//DEF, a common enough pattern in the data (e.g., Ps. 1:1).[85]

Psalm 65:13

| The pastures of the wilderness overflow, | יִרְעֲפוּ נְאוֹת מִדְבָּר |
| the hills gird themselves with rejoicing. | וְגִיל גְּבָעוֹת תַּחְגֹּרְנָה: |

In this bicolon the constituent order is VS//OSV. Each of the preverbal constituents in the second line, וְגִיל גְּבָעוֹת, Gross attempts to account for with reference to focus. Once more the explanation he offers, despite his bold claim that the presence of focus is indisputable, remains doubtful. He writes, 'The focusing of the P1 direct object in 13b is indisputable. Under the condition that the P2 subject "hills" displays correspondence focus in relation to the different types of terrain mentioned in 13a, 14a and 14b, then clause 13b has two peaks'.[86] Here P1 and P2 refer to the first and second positions in the 'Vorfeld', or preverbal domain. Gross evidently interprets the clause as doubly marked, though it is far from clear from his words why each of the two preverbal elements should in fact be focused. As in the previous examples, he sees no relevance with regard to word order in the presence of a parallelism. That the unit is actually a parallel bicolon is apparent, supported by the occurrence of the identical construct chain נְאוֹת מִדְבָּר ('the pastures of the wilderness') found in parallelism with הֶהָרִים ('the mountains', a virtual synonym of גְּבָעוֹת) in Jeremiah 9:9.[87] Again it is simply by recourse to the poetic reordering allowable within the confines of parallel secondary lines that we account for the unusual constituent order in 13b. The particular order of words, we argue, is not to be explained with reference to focus, as Gross unconvincingly attempts.

---

84 E.g., Psalm 104:13. See Berlin, *Dynamics of Biblical Parallelism*, pp. 40–41.
85 While there is nothing to require that two defamiliar lines be balanced in all elements, with respect to the two cola SOVM and SVO (22bc), Gross (*Doppelt besetztes Vorfeld*, p. 125) may well be correct when he suggests that the position of לְצִיּוֹן was motivated by a desire to bring it into contact with the etymologically related לֵצִים.
86 Gross, *Doppelt besetztes Vorfeld*, p. 127 ('Die Fokussierung des P1=dirObj in 13b ist unbestritten; unter der Voraussetzung daß sein P2=Subj: „Hügel" Korrespondenzfokus bezüglich der in 13a.14ab genannten Landschaft-seinheiten trägt, ist der Satz 13b doppelgipflig'). Gross' notion of correspondence focus is simply a matter of two or more elements in a passage which 'correspond' with each other. In the context of Psalm 65 under discussion it would include 'pastures' (13a), 'meadows' (14a), and 'valleys' (14b).
87 'Take up weeping and wailing for the mountains, and a lamentation for the pastures of the wilderness' (NRSV).

Psalm 72:1
O God, give your justice to the king,
and your righteousness to the king's son.

אֱלֹהִים מִשְׁפָּטֶיךָ לְמֶלֶךְ תֵּן
וְצִדְקָתְךָ לְבֶן־מֶלֶךְ׃

In this final example the constituent order is [Voc]OMV//OM. Gross comments on the rarity of the sequence of the first line, with the imperative verb in the final position.[88] Regarding the presence of two preverbal constituents in 1a he concludes that the first line is probably doubly marked,[89] arguing that the order signifies that the direct object receives greater linguistic emphasis[90] than the indirect. Gross looks to the reappearance of the nouns צֶדֶק and מִשְׁפָּט in verse 2 to support the possible fact of their focality in verse 1, but his reasons for the focusing in this particular context are again not clearly indicated. The alternative proposal that we offer is that Psalm 72:1 consists of a boundary-marking DEF//Gap parallelism, of which several examples, including this one, were noted in chapter 8.[91] The verse in question, of course, is that which opens the psalm.

10.3.2 Conclusions

This selection of texts treated by Gross lead us to conclude that the theory he employs to account for marked word order in Hebrew poetry is not totally adequate. The recognition of defamiliarised constituent reordering in certain specifiable contexts is an indispensable component in any attempt to explain variations in word order within the poetic clause. Only when this is appreciated is the reader prevented from seeing various pragmatic nuances in the text that the poet himself did not intend, of the kind that is an unfortunate characteristic of much of the analysis undertaken by Gross.

10.4 Summary

This chapter has demonstrated the deficiencies in the recent work of Rosenbaum and Gross in the area of word order in Biblical Hebrew poetry. The studies of both scholars have been shown to be lacking in a number of respects – the linguistic tools utilised, their general approach, and the resultant questionable analysis of particular texts. Neither advances an all-embracing theory to account for word-order variation in Biblical Hebrew poetry both in its pragmatic and non-pragmatic dimensions. We would contend, therefore, for the greater usefulness of the theory that has earlier been proposed for the interpretation of poetic word order.

---

88 Gross, *Doppelt besetztes Vorfeld*, p. 216.
89 *Ibid.* ('Doppelgipfligkeit erscheint daher wahrscheinlich').
90 *Ibid.* ('größerer sprachlicher Nachdruck').
91 See 8.2.1 (c).

CHAPTER 11

Conclusions

In this final chapter we give a brief summary of the findings of the foregoing study and present diagrammatically the conclusions regarding the various colon-types. Several areas are then noted in which further investigation might prove profitable.

11.1 Summary of Findings

A number of facts have been established relating to the word order of the verbal clause in Biblical Hebrew poetry. Here the principal findings are summarised, with references to the relevant chapter:

1. The same varieties of marked ordering caused by pragmatic factors found in Biblical Hebrew narrative are also to be found in poetry, in precisely the same form, both with and without focus particles. In this respect the fact that the genre is poetry does not cause any changes (Ch. 4).

2. It is primarily within the B-line of synonymous parallelisms that word-order variation as a purely stylistic or rhetorical device, i.e., poetic defamiliarisation, is admissible (Ch. 5).

3. Such variation is an optional not obligatory feature, and chiefly occurs where the A-line of the parallelism is canonical, that is, unmarked (Ch. 5).

4. Where the A-line of a parallelism is marked, the B-line is equally marked. Only a small number of classifiable exceptions exist to this rule, i.e., where the initial position is occupied by phrases of setting or by pronominal forms (Ch. 7).

5. The traditional label 'antithetical parallelism' is used to describe two-line constructions which are in fact strictly pragmatic in their relationship rather than rhetorical. The parallel features observed in these pairs are no more than is required for a contrast to exist (Ch. 6).

6. Gapping of clause constituents mostly occurs in the B-line of synonymous parallelisms (Ch. 2).

7. Where the A-line of a parallelism is unmarked, gapping may occur of any constituent from the B-line (Ch. 2).

8. Where the A-line is marked, gapping does not generally occur of the corresponding fronted constituent(s) (Ch. 7).

9. Any departure from the norms described in points 2, 3, 4, 6 and 8

above is a deliberate literary device which serves to set apart that particular unit as performing some higher text-level function, i.e., aperture, closure, or climax (Ch. 8).

10. The use of defamiliar word order is not uniform. Some poetic texts display a much more prominent use of non-canonical clauses than others. Certain apparent non-canonical forms, however, are in fact not concluded to be so when other factors are considered (Ch. 9).

11. The studies of Rosenbaum and Gross, while making some contrib.-ution to the field of study, fail to provide a satisfactory general theory that is able to account for the diverse kinds of word-order variation that is found in the poetry of the Old Testament (Ch. 10).

11.2 Relative Frequency of Colon-Types

With regard to all verbal clauses in Biblical Hebrew poetry, we have proposed a three-way classification that distinguishes between those non-canonical clauses which are genuinely pragmatically structured, and those whose variation is motivated purely by poetic defamiliarisation:

	1. Canonical clauses	CAN
All verbal clauses	2. Non-canonical clauses	a. MKD
		b. DEF

As regards Hebrew narrative, the relative proportion of canonical and non-canonical clauses was seen to be 85.5% to 14.5% respectively.[1] In such cases the non-canonical component is to be interpreted only in terms of pragmatic markedness.[2] In poetry, however, non-canonical verbal clauses are further subdivided into those which are marked and those which are defamiliar, according to whether the motivation for their deviant word order is either pragmatic or poetic. It is possible to further break down the analysis of the defamiliar clauses depending on the nature of the defamiliarisation involved. There is that reordering occurring in the common environment of parallel B-lines which relates at the intra-clausal level to a foregoing canonical A-line. Then there is that defamiliarisation of word order, appearing in a limited environment, which functions at the extra-clausal level to denote some special juncture in the discourse.

---

1   See Appendix 1.
2   This is not to deny that clauses of a poetic character may occur within a narrative book, but, generally speaking, these are readily distinguished from the surrounding narrative in which they are embedded. In the song of Lamech (Gen. 4:23-24), for example, several of the features discussed in this work are observed, such as parallelism, gapping, and compliance with the marked word order constraint in parallel lines.

Displayed on the following page are the relative proportions of the colon-types in Biblical Hebrew poetry, as compared with narrative clauses (shown in *Figure 1*).[3] The basic division is shown of all poetic verbal clauses into 66.0% canonical and 34.0% non-canonical (*Figure 2a*), a noticeably larger degree of variation than in narrative, though the basic verb-initial clause remains the dominant pattern, as previously noted. In 25.6% of the non-canonical clauses the word order may be ascribed to pragmatic marking, while in the remaining 8.4% the underlying influence is poetic defamiliarisation (*Figure 2b*). These latter are further divided, according to the environment in which they occur. The majority (7.0% of the total number of verbal clauses, and 83.9% of all defamiliar clauses) are found in the common environment of parallel B-lines. The remaining small proportion (1.4% of verbal clauses, and 16.1% of defamiliar clauses) appear in the limited environment, where they perform specific discourse functions (*Figure 2c*). These latter two are distinguished in the chart by the labels DEF and DEF' respectively.

Pragmatically marked clauses, we observe, account for 25.6% of all verbal clauses in Hebrew poetry. Marked, as distinct from defamiliar, word order is consequently seen to be more extensive in poetic discourse than in narrative (14.5%). But why, it may legitimately be asked, should this be the case? To answer this question would require a major separate study. There is one factor, however, that probably contributes at least in some measure to this discrepancy between the two genres, and that is the lack of linearity in poetic discourse. By this we mean that the text is not organised along the lines of its chronological development as is apparent in the case of narrative. In poetry the movement from one episode to another on the basis of spatial or temporal shifts, prominent in prose, is hardly to be found.[4] Instead the organisation is thematic or even spontaneous, as the expression of praise to God. Such being the case, marked clauses presenting new topics may be expected to occur more frequently. It is evident, moreover, that certain categories of focus appear with greater regularity in poetry than in prose. This is true, for instance, of contrast, especially in those texts which are more didactic in nature, such as the wisdom psalms and proverbs. Psalm 1, for example, consisting of only six verses, has three instances of contrast.[5] In addition, much poetry takes the form of a monologue (by the psalmist or God), or a dialogue (between the psalmist and God, or the psalmist and his people). It is arguable that this communicative situation gives rise to more occasions in which marked focus constructions can be suitably employed than in prose.[6]

---

3 Note that the relative sizes of the segments in the diagrams are only approximate.
4 The paucity of temporal and spatial orienters in poetry was noted in 3.5
5 See 9.1.1.
6 For this reason, a comparison of poetry with direct speech in narrative might be fairer, rather than with narrative per se.

Narrative   *Figure 1*

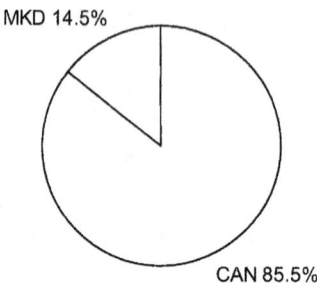

Poetry   *Figure 2a*

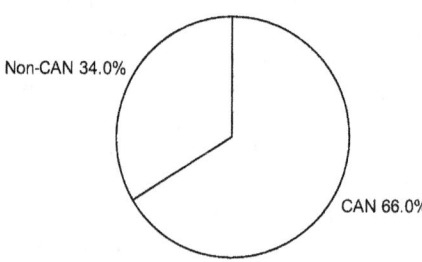

Figure 2b   *Figure 2c*

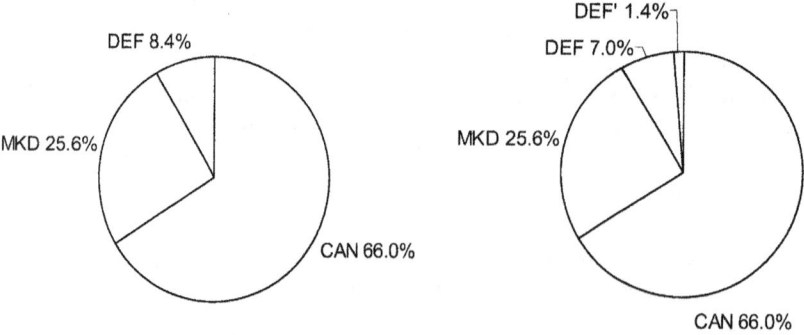

11.3 For Further Study

Since the present work has of necessity had to impose certain boundaries upon the breadth of its research, it is worth identifying a number of areas in which further inquiry would be desirable. These include:

1. How the focus structure of poetic verbal clauses relates to noun-clauses. The same principles disclosed in this work cannot readily be applied to clauses without verbs. For example, in Comp S // Comp S the clause-initial complement cannot be said to be marked in the same way as a preverbal constituent in a verbal clause, since we find that the inverted sequence Comp S // S Comp occurs twice as often as the symmetrical ordering. From this we conclude that the initial element in a noun-clause would appear not to abide by the same constraint which determines that fronted constituents of verbal clauses will occupy the same position in parallel lines.

2. How the focus structure of poetic verbal clauses relates to participle-clauses. Here the subject phrase most often precedes the participle, yet it would seem that any O or M elements that are placed before the participle are marked after the same fashion as in verbal clauses.

3. How the focus structure of poetic verbal clauses relates to infinitive-clauses. What distinction is to be maintained between subordinate clauses consisting of an infinitive construct with affixed preposition when they are located before the main clause and after the main clause? Is this a matter of focus, or something of a different nature?

4. The significance of postverbal word order. Though the clause may be verb-initial, is there any pragmatic difference say between VMS and VSM order?[7]

5. Whether the insights of the foregoing study can be employed in such matters as dating the various strata of Biblical Hebrew poetry, or ascribing a certain style to individual authors. During the course of this study the fact that the use of defamiliar cola is not uniform has been remarked upon. The Song of Solomon, for example, has only a single instance of a defamiliar verbal clause.[8] Further research might reveal that particular writers employed defamiliarisation to varying degrees and in diverse ways.

---

[7] As claimed, for example, by Bandstra, 'Word Order and Emphasis in Biblical Hebrew Narrative', pp. 117–19; and Lode, 'Postverbal Word Order in Biblical Hebrew: Parts 1 and 2.

[8] It is perhaps also significant that a considerable number of psalms or chapters containing rare parallel formations (as described in chapter 8) have more than one. All the following have two instances: Psalms 5, 29, 37, 38, 73, 89, 90, 91, 92, 102, Proverbs 2 and 3. Proverbs 4 has three (see charts in chapter 8 for references). These special parallel forms are noticeably used less frequently in the second book of Psalms (42–72) than in the other four books of that corpus. These facts point to preference on the part of the author in question.

6. An exploration of any potential factors which might determine defamiliarised word order. These are the causes of variations of a strictly non-pragmatic nature. The study of sound, rhythm and balance might produce identifiable causes which influence defamiliar ordering.

7. Whether the findings of this research have any bearing upon the debate concerning the basic unmarked word order of Biblical Hebrew. The constraint regarding markedness in parallel lines provides an indirect argument against those theories which argue that Biblical Hebrew was not actually VSO in its basic constituent order. SVO is sometimes proposed as an alternative unmarked order. The data shows that, like other marked forms such as OV and MV, SV must reproduce the order SV in parallel lines. It is only the verb-initial clauses where this does not apply. This therefore places SV-clauses in the same category, i.e., pragmatically marked, as OV- and MV-clauses, while verb-initial clauses stand out as being free from this particular constraint.

11.4 Concluding Remarks

To end we may say that the foregoing work has proposed a new paradigm for word-order studies in Biblical Hebrew poetry. All poetic cola containing verbal clauses may be categorised by means of form (constituent order), context (pragmatic information), and environment/distribution (A-/B-line of parallelism/place in discourse), into a three-way division of that which is canonical (CAN), marked (MKD), or defamiliarised (DEF). Only once the colon-type is correctly identified may variation in word order then be accurately interpreted.

Bibliography

Alden, R. L., *Job: An Exegetical and Theological Exposition of Holy Scripture* (Nashville, Tennessee: Broadman & Holman, 1993).
Alexander, J. A., *Commentary on the Prophecies of Isaiah*, 2 volumes in 1 (Grand Rapids, Michigan: Zondervan, 1976 [1846–47]).
Allen, L. C., *Psalms 101–150*, Word Biblical Commentary (Waco, Texas: Word Books, 1983).
Alter, R., *The Art of Biblical Poetry* (Edinburgh: T. & T. Clark, 1990 [1985]).
Andersen, F. I., *The Sentence in Biblical Hebrew* (Paris/New York: Mouton, 1974).
– *Job: An Introduction and Commentary*, Tyndale Old Testament Commentary (Leicester: Inter-Varsity Press, 1976).
Anderson, A. A., *The Book of Psalms*, 2 volumes, New Century Bible (London: Oliphants, 1972).
Antturi, A., 'The Hebrew Verb in Poetic Context: Psalm 44' (A paper presented at the University of Leiden, March 1994).
Asher, R. E. (ed.), *The Encyclopedia of Language and Linguistics* (Oxford: Pergamon Press, 1994).
Ashley, T. R., *The Book of Numbers*, New International Commentary of the Old Testament (Grand Rapids, Michigan: Eerdmans, 1993).
Bailey, K. E., *Poet and Peasant and Through Peasant Eyes* (Grand Rapids, Michigan: Eerdmans, 1983).
– '"Inverted Parallelisms" and "Encased Parables" in Isaiah and their Significance for OT and NT Translation and Interpretation', in L. J. de Regt, J. de Waard and J. P. Fokkelman (eds.), *Literary Structure and Rhetorical Strategies in the Hebrew Bible* (Winona Lake, Indiana: Eisenbrauns, 1996), pp. 14–30.
Baker, J. and E. W. Nicholson, *The Commentary of Rabbi David Kimhi on Psalms CXX–CL* (Cambridge: Cambridge University Press, 1973).
Baltzer, K., *Deutero-Isaiah: A Commentary on Isaiah 40–55*, Hermeneia (Minneapolis, Indiana: Fortress Press, 2001).
Bandstra, B. L., 'Word Order and Emphasis in Biblical Hebrew Narrative: Syntactic Observations on Genesis 22 from a Discourse Perspective', in W. R. Bodine (ed.), *Linguistics and Biblical Hebrew* (Winona Lake, Indiana: Eisenbrauns, 1992), pp. 109–23.
Barr, J., 'Line-Forms in Hebrew Poetry' (Review article), *JSS 23* (1978), pp. 228–44.
Beekman, J. and J. Callow, *Translating the Word of* God (Grand Rapids, Michigan: Zondervan, 1974).
Bergen, R. D. (ed.), *Biblical Hebrew and Discourse Linguistics* (Dallas, Texas: SIL, 1994).
Berlin, A., *The Dynamics of Biblical Parallelism* (Bloomington, Indiana: Indiana

University Press, 1985).
Bodine, W. R. (ed.), *Linguistics and Biblical Hebrew* (Winona Lake, Indiana: Eisenbrauns, 1992).
– (ed.), *Discourse Analysis of Biblical Literature: What it is and what it offers*, Semeia Studies (Atlanta, Georgia: Scholars Press, 1995).
Boling, R. G., '"Synonymous" Parallelism in the Psalms', *JSS 5* (1960), pp. 221–49.
Bolkestein, A. M., C. de Groot and J. L. Mackenzie (eds.), *Syntax and Pragmatics in Functional Grammar* (Dordrecht: Foris Publications, 1985).
Bosch, P. and R. van der Sandt, *Focus: Linguistic, Cognitive and Computational Perspectives* (Cambridge: Cambridge University Press, 1999).
Bratcher, R. G. and W. D. Reyburn, *A Handbook on Psalms*, UBS Handbook Series (New York: United Bible Societies, 1993).
Breck, J., *The Shape of Biblical Language: Chiasmus in the Scriptures and Beyond* (New York: St. Vladimir's Seminary Press, 1994).
Bright, W. (ed.), *International Encyclopedia of Linguistics* (New York: Oxford University Press, 1992).
Brown, G. and G. Yule, *Discourse Analysis* (Cambridge: Cambridge University Press, 1983).
Budd, P. J., *Numbers*, Word Biblical Commentary (Waco, Texas: Word Books, 1984).
Buth, R., 'Hebrew Poetic Tenses and the Magnificat', *JSNT 21* (1984), pp. 67–83.
– 'The Taxonomy and Function of Hebrew Tense-Shifting in the Psalms', *START 15* (1986), pp. 26–32.
– 'The Hebrew Verb in Current Discussions, *JOTT 5* (1992), pp. 91–105.
– 'Topic and Focus in Hebrew Poetry: Psalm 51', in J. J. Hwang Shin and W. R. Merrifield (eds.), *Language in Contest: Essays for Robert E. Longacre* (Arlington, Texas: SIL and The University of Texas, 1992), pp. 83–96.
– 'Functional Grammar, Hebrew and Aramaic: An Integrated, Textlinguistic Approach to Syntax', in W. R. Bodine (ed.), *Discourse Analysis of Biblical Literature: What it is and what it offers* (Atlanta, Georgia: Scholars Press, 1995), pp. 77–102.
– 'Word Order in the Verbless Clause', in C. Miller (ed.), *The Verbless Clause in Biblical Hebrew: Linguistic Approaches* (Winona Lake, Indiana: Eisebrauns, 1999), pp. 79–108.
Callow, J., 'Units and Flow in the Song of Songs 1:2–2:6', in R. D. Bergen (ed.), *Biblical Hebrew and Discourse Linguistics* (Dallas, Texas: SIL, 1994), pp. 462–88.
Carr, G. L., *The Song of Solomon*, Tyndale Old Testament Commentaries (Leicester: Inter-Varsity Press, 1984).
Ceresko, A. R., 'The Function of Chiasmus in Hebrew Poetry', *CBQ 40* (1978), pp. 1–10.
Chafe, W. L., 'Language and Memory', *Language 49* (1973), pp. 261–81.
Clines, D. J. A., *Job 1–20*, Word Biblical Commentary (Dallas, Texas: Word Books, 1989).
Clines, D. J. A. (ed.), *The Dictionary of Classical Hebrew* (Sheffield: Sheffield Academic Press, 1993–[publication ongoing]).
Cloete, W. T. W., 'Some Recent Research on Old Testament Verse: Progress, Problems and Possibilities', *JNSL 17* (1991), pp. 189–204.
Collins, T., *Line-Forms in Hebrew Poetry: A Grammatical Approach to the Stylistic Study of the Hebrew Prophets* (Rome: Biblical Institute Press, 1978).

Craigie, P. C., *Psalms 1–50*, Word Biblical Commentary (Waco, Texas: Word Books, 1983).
Dahood, M., *Psalms I, 1–50*, The Anchor Bible (New York: Doubleday, 1966).
– *Psalms II, 51–100*, The Anchor Bible (New York: Doubleday, 1968).
– *Psalms III, 101–150*, The Anchor Bible (New York: Doubleday, 1970).
Dawson, D. A., *Text-Linguistics and Biblical Hebrew*, JSOT Supplement Series (Sheffield: Sheffield Academic Press, 1994).
de Regt, L. J, J. de Waard, and J. P. Fokkelman (eds.), *Literary Structure and Rhetorical Strategies in the Hebrew Bible* (Winona Lake, Indiana: Eisenbrauns, 1996).
de Regt, L. J., 'Hebrew Syntactical Inversions and their Literary Equivalence in Robert Alter's Translation of Genesis', *BT 54.1* (2003), pp. 111–21.
Dhorme, E., *A Commentary on the Book of Job* (Nashville, Tennessee: Thomas Nelson, 1984).
Dik, S. C., *Functional Grammar* (Dordrecht: Foris Publications, 1981).
– *The Theory of Functional Grammar*, Part 1: The Structure of the Clause (Dordrecht: Foris Publications, 1989).
– *The Theory of Functional Grammar*, Part 2: Complex and Derived Constructions (Berlin: Mouton de Gruyter, 1997).
Dooley, R. A. and S. H. Levinsohn. *Analyzing Discourse: A Manual of Basic Concepts* (Dallas, Texas: SIL, 2001).
Dorsey, D. A., *The Literary Structure of the Old Testament* (Grand Rapids, Michigan: Baker Books, 1999).
Douglas, J. D. (ed.), *New Bible Dictionary* (Leicester: Inter-Varsity Press, 1982).
Downing, P. and M. Noonan (eds.), *Word Order in Discourse*, Typological Studies in Language 30 (Amsterdam/Philadelphia: John Benjamin, 1995).
Driver, S. R. and G. B. Gray, *A Critical and Exegetical Commentary on the Book of Job* (Edinburgh: T. & T. Clark, 1986 [1921]).
Dryer, M. S. 'Focus, pragmatic presupposition, and activated propositions', *Journal of Pragmatics 26* (1996), pp. 475–523.
Eisemann, M., *Job: A New Translation with a Commentary Anthologized from Talmudic, Midrashic, and Rabbinic Sources* (New York: Mesorah Publications, 1994).
Estes, D. J., *Hear, My Son: Teaching and Learning in Proverbs 1–9*, New Studies in Biblical Theology 4 (London: Apollos, 1997).
Fabb, N., *Linguistics and Literature: Language in the Verbal Arts of the World* (Oxford: Blackwell, 1997).
Finch, R. G. and G. H. Box, *The Longer Commentary of R. David Kimhi on the First Book of Psalms* (London: Society for Promoting Christian Knowledge, 1919).
Floor, S. J., 'Poetic Fronting in a Wisdom Poetry Text: The Information Structure of Proverbs 7', *JNSL 31.1* (2005), pp. 23–58.
Fokkelman, J. P., *Reading Biblical Poetry, An Introductory Guide* (Louisville, Kentucky: Westminster John Knox Press, 2001).
Follingstad, C. M., '*Hinneh* and Focus Function', *JOTT 7.3* (1995), pp. 1–25.
– *Deictic Viewpoint in Biblical Hebrew Text: A Syntagmatic and Paradigmatic Analysis of the Particle* כי (Dallas, Texas: SIL, 2001).
– 'Additive Strengthening and Restrictive Elimination in Identical and Parallel Contexts: a Relevance-Theory Account of the Two "Alsos" and the Two "Onlys" in Biblical

Hebrew' (A paper presented at a Biblical Hebrew discourse workshop, held by SIL, at Horsleys Green, UK, November 2002).
Fox, M. V., *Proverbs 1-9: A New Translation with Introduction and Commentary*, The Anchor Bible (New York: Doubleday, 2000).
Franke, C., *Isaiah 46, 47, and 48: A New Literary-Critical Reading* (Winona Lake, Indiana: Eisenbrauns, 1994).
Friedländer, M., *The Commentary of Ibn Ezra on Isaiah* (New York: Philipp Feldheim, 1873).
Garrett, D. A., *Proverbs, Ecclesiastes, Song of Songs: An Exegetical and Theological Exposition of Holy Scripture*, New American Commentary (Nashville, Tennessee: Broadman, 1993).
Geller, S. A., *Parallelism in Early Biblical Poetry* (Missoula, Montana: Scholars Press, 1979).
- 'Theory and Method in the Study of Biblical Poetry', *JQR 73.1* (1982), pp. 65-77.
- 'Cleft Sentences with Pleonastic Pronoun: A Syntactic Construction of Biblical Hebrew and Some of its Literary Uses', *JANES 20* (1991), pp. 15-33.
Gerstenberger, E. S., *The Forms of the Old Testament Literature*, vol. 14, Psalms, Part 1 (Grand Rapids, Michigan: Eerdmans, 1988).
Gesenius, W., *Gesenius' Hebrew Grammar*, translated by A. E. Cowley (Oxford: Clarendon Press, 1910).
Givón, T., 'The Drift from VSO to SVO in Biblical Hebrew: The Pragmatics of Tense-Aspect, in C. N. Li (ed.), *Mechanisms of Syntactic Change* (Austin, Texas: University of Texas Press, 1977), pp. 181-254.
Gordis, R., *The Song of Songs and Lamentations* (New York: Ktav, 1974).
- *The Book of Job: Commentary, New Translation and Special Studies* (New York: Jewish Theological Seminary of America, 1978).
Gray, G. B., *The Forms of Hebrew Poetry* (New York: Ktav, 1972 [1915]).
Greenberg, J. H., *Universals of Human Language*, vol. 4: Syntax (Stanford, California: Stanford University Press, 1978).
Greenstein, E. L., 'How does Parallelism Mean?', in S. A. Geller, E. L. Greenstein, and A. Berlin, *A Sense of Text: The Art of Language in the Study of Biblical Literature*, *JQRSupp* (Winona Lake, Indiana: Eisenbrauns, 1982), pp. 41-70.
Grogan, G., *Prayer, Praise and Prophecy* (Fearn, Scotland: Christian Focus Publications, 2001).
Groom, S. A., *Linguistic Analysis of Biblical Hebrew* (Carlisle, Cumbria: Paternoster, 2003).
Gross, W., 'Zur syntaktischen Struktur des Vorfelds im hebräishen Verbalsatz', *ZAH 7* (1994), pp. 203-14.
- *Die Satzteilfolge im Verbalsatz alttestamentlicher Prosa: Untersucht an den Büchern Dtn, Ri und 2Kön*. Forschungen zum Alten Testament 17 (Tübingen: J. C. B. Mohr, 1996).
- 'Is there Really a Compound Nominal Clause in Biblical Hebrew?' in C. Miller (ed.), *The Verbless Clause in Biblical Hebrew: Linguistic Approaches* (Winona Lake, Indiana: Eisebrauns, 1999), pp. 19-49.
- *Doppelt besetztes Vorfeld: Syntaktische, pragmatische und übersetzungs-technische Studien zum althebräischen Verbalsatz* (Berlin: de Gruyter, 2001).
Habel, N. C., *The Book of Job: A Commentary*, Old Testament Library (London: SCM

Press, 1985).
Halivni, D. W., *Peshat and Derash: Plain and Applied Meaning in Rabbinic Exegesis* (New York: Oxford University Press, 1991).
Harman, A., *Psalms*, A Mentor Commentary (Fearn, Scotland: Christian Focus Publications, 1998).
Harold, B. B., 'Subject-Verb Word Order and the Function of Early Position' in P. Downing and M. Noonan (eds.), *Word Order in Discourse* (Amsterdam/ Philadelphia: John Benjamin, 1995), pp. 137–61.
Harris, R. L., G. L. Archer and B. K. Waltke (eds.), *Theological Wordbook of the Old Testament*, 2 volumes (Chicago: Moody Press, 1980).
Hartley, J. E., *The Book of Job*, New International Commentary on the Old Testament (Grand Rapids, Michigan: Eerdmans, 1988).
Heimerdinger, J-M., *Topic, Focus and Foreground in Ancient Hebrew Narratives*, JSOT Supplement Series (Sheffield: Sheffield Academic Press, 1999).
Holladay, W. L., 'Hebrew Verse Structure Revisited (I)', *JBL 118* (1999), pp. 19–32.
– 'Hebrew Verse Structure Revisited (II)', *JBL 118* (1999), pp. 401–16.
Honeyman, A. M., 'Merismus in Biblical Hebrew', *JBL 71* (1952), pp. 11–18.
Jakobson, R., *Language in Literature* (Cambridge, Massachusetts: Harvard University Press, 1987).
Joüon, P. and T. Muraoka, *A Grammar of Biblical Hebrew*, 2 volumes (Rome: Biblical Institute Press, 1991).
Jungraithmayr, H. and W. W. Müller (eds.), *Proceedings of the Fourth International Hamito-Semitic Congress*, Current Issues in Linguistic Theory 44 (Amsterdam: John Benjamin, 1987).
Keil C. F. and F. Delitzsch, *Commentary on the Old Testament*, 10 volumes (Grand Rapids, Michigan: Eerdmans, 1986 [1877]).
Khan, G., *Studies in Semitic Syntax* (Oxford: Oxford University Press, 1989).
Kidner, D., *Proverbs*, Tyndale Old Testament Commentaries (London: Inter-Varsity Press, 1964).
– *Psalms 1–72*, Tyndale Old Testament Commentaries (Leicester: Inter-Varsity Press, 1973).
– *Psalms 73–150*, Tyndale Old Testament Commentaries (Leicester: Inter-Varsity Press, 1975).
König, E., *The Meaning of Focus Particles: A Comparative Perspective* (London: Routledge, 1991).
Korpel, M. C. A. and J. C. de Moor, 'Fundamentals of Ugaritic and Hebrew Poetry', in W. van der Meer and J. C. de Moor (eds.), *The Structural Analysis of Biblical and Canaanite Poetry*, JSOT Supplement Series 74 (Sheffield: Sheffield Academic Press, 1988), pp. 1–61.
Krašovec, J., 'Merism – Polar Expression in Biblical Hebrew', *Biblica 64* (1983), pp. 231–39.
Kraus, H-J., *Psalms 1–59, A Commentary* (Minneapolis: Augsburg, 1988).
– *Psalms 60–150, A Commentary* (Minneapolis: Augsburg, 1989).
Kugel, J. L., *The Idea of Biblical Poetry* (New Haven: Yale University Press, 1981).
Lambrecht, K., *Information Structure and Sentence Form: Topic, focus and the mental representations of discourse referents*, Cambridge Studies in Linguistics 71 (Cambridge: Cambridge University Press, 1994).

Leupold, H. C., *Exposition of the Psalms* (Welwyn, Herts: Evangelical Press, 1977).
Levinsohn, S. H., 'Unmarked and Marked Instances of Topicalisation in Hebrew', Work papers of the Summer Institute of Linguistics, University of North Dakota, vol. 34 (1990), pp. 21–33.
– 'NP References to Active Participants and Story Development in Ancient Hebrew', Work papers of the Summer Institute of Linguistics, University of North Dakota, vol. 44 (2000), {http://www.und.nodak/edu/dept/linguistics/ wp/2000.htm}.
– 'Review of Jean-Marc Heimerdinger's *Topic, Focus and Foreground in Ancient Hebrew Narrative*', *JOTT 14* (2002), pp. 126–47.
– 'Analysis of Narrative Texts' (SIL, 2003), {https://mail.jaars.org/~bt/narr.zip}.
Lode, L., 'Postverbal Word Order in Biblical Hebrew: Structure and Function', *Semitics 9* (1984), pp. 113–64.
– 'Postverbal Word Order in Biblical Hebrew: Structure and Function: Part Two', *Semitics 10* (1989), pp. 24–38.
Longacre, R. E., *The Grammar of Discourse* (New York: Plenum Press, 1983).
– *Joseph: A Story of Divine Providence. A Text Theoretical and Textlinguistic Analysis of Genesis 37 and 39–48* (Winona Lake, Indiana: Eisenbrauns, 1989).
– 'Left Shifts in Strongly VSO Languages', in P. Downing and M. Noonan (eds.), *Word Order in Discourse* (Amsterdam/Philadelphia: John Benjamin, 1995), pp. 331–54.
Longman III, T., 'Biblical Poetry', in L. Ryken and T. Longman III (eds.), *A Complete Literary Guide to the Bible* (Grand Rapids, Michigan: Zondervan, 1993), pp. 80–91.
– *Song of Songs*, New International Commentary of the Old Testament (Grand Rapids, Michigan: Eerdmans, 2001).
Martin, J. D., *Davidson's Introductory Hebrew Grammar* (Edinburgh: T. & T. Clark, 1993).
Matejka, L. and K. Pomorska (eds.), *Readings in Russian Poetics: Formalist and Structuralist Views* (Cambridge, Massachusetts: MIT Press, 1971).
McConville, J. G., *Deuteronomy*, Apollos Old Testament Commentary (Leicester: Inter-Varsity Press, 2002).
McKane, W., *Proverbs*. Old Testament Library (London: SCM Press, 1970).
Merrill, E. H., *Deuteronomy: An Exegetical and Theological Exposition of Holy Scripture*, New American Commentary (Nashville, Tennessee: Broadman & Holman, 1994).
Miller, C. L., 'Introducing Direct Discourse in Biblical Hebrew Narrative', in R. D. Bergen, *Biblical Hebrew and Discourse Linguistics* (Dallas, Texas: SIL, 1994), pp. 199–241.
– (ed.), *The Verbless Clause in Biblical Hebrew: Linguistic Approaches* (Winona Lake, Indiana: Eisebrauns, 1999).
– 'A Linguistic Approach to Ellipsis in Biblical Poetry', *BBR 13.2* (2003), pp. 251–70.
Miller, P. D., 'Synonymous-Sequential Parallelism in the Psalms', *Biblica 61* (1980), pp. 256–60.
Motyer, J. A., *The Prophecy of Isaiah* (Leicester: Inter-Varsity Press, 1993).
Muraoka, T., *Emphatic Words and Structures in Biblical Hebrew* (Leiden: Brill, 1985).
Murphy, R. E., *The Song of Songs*, Hermeneia (Minneapolis, Indiana: Fortress Press, 1990).
– *Proverbs*, Word Biblical Commentary (Nashville, Tennessee: Nelson, 1998).
Myhill, J., 'Non-Emphatic Fronting in Biblical Hebrew', *Theoretical Linguistics 21*

(1995), pp. 93–144.
Niccacci, A., *The Syntax of the Verb in Classical Hebrew Prose* (Sheffield: Sheffield Academic Press, 1990).
— 'Analysing Biblical Hebrew Poetry', *JSOT 74* (1997), pp. 77–93.
O'Connor, M., *Hebrew Verse Structure* (Winona Lake, Indiana: Eisenbrauns, [1980] 1997).
Oswalt, J. N., *The Book of Isaiah Chapters 40–66*, New International Commentary of the Old Testament (Grand Rapids, Michigan: Eerdmans, 1998).
Payne, D., 'Verb Initial Languages and Information Order', in P. Downing and M. Noonan (eds.), *Word Order in Discourse* (Amsterdam/Philadelphia: John Benjamin, 1995), pp. 449–85.
Payne, G., 'Functional Sentence Perspective: Theme in Biblical Hebrew', *Scandinavian Journal of the Old Testament 1* (1991), pp. 62–82.
Payne, T. E., *Describing Morphosyntax* (Cambridge: Cambridge University Press, 1997).
Pope, M. H., *Job: A New Translation with Introduction and Commentary*, The Anchor Bible (New York: Doubleday, 1973).
— *Song of Songs: A New Translation with Introduction and Commentary*, The Anchor Bible (New York: Doubleday, 1977).
Reyburn, W. D., *A Handbook on the Book of Job*, UBS Handbook Series (New York: United Bible Societies, 1992).
Rosenbaum, M., *Word-Order Variation in Isaiah 40–55: A Functional Perspective*, Studia Semitica Neerlandica (Assen, The Netherlands: Van Gorcum, 1997).
Rowley, H. H., *Job*, The Century Bible (London: Nelson, 1970).
Sappan, R., *The Typical Features of the Syntax of Biblical Poetry in its Classical Period* (Jerusalem: Kiryat-Sefer, 1981).
Schökel, L. A., *A Manual of Hebrew Poetics* (Rome: Editrice Pontificio Istituto Biblico, 1988).
Segert, S., 'Phonological and Syntactic Structuring Principles in Northwest Semitic Verse Systems', in H. Jungraithmayr and W. W. Müller (eds.), *Proceedings of the Fourth International Hamito-Semitic Congress*, Current Issues in Linguistic Theory 44 (Amsterdam: John Benjamin, 1987), pp. 543–57.
Seybold, K., *Introducing the Psalms* (T. & T. Clark: Edinburgh, 1990).
Shimasaki, K., *Focus Structure in Biblical Hebrew* (Bethesda, Maryland: CDL Press, 2002).
Siewierska, A., *Functional Grammar* (London: Routledge, 1991).
Slager, D., 'The Use of "Behold" in the OT', *OPTAT 3.1* (1989), pp. 50–79.
Steele, S., 'Word Order Variation', in J. H. Greenberg (ed.), *Universals of Human Language*, vol. 4: Syntax (Stanford, California: Stanford University Press, 1978), pp. 587–623.
Talstra, E., 'Reading Biblical Hebrew Poetry – Linguistic Structure or Rhetorical Device?', *JNSL 25.2* (1999), pp. 101–26.
Tate, M. E., *Psalms 51–100*, Word Biblical Commentary (Dallas, Texas: Word Books, 1990).
Terrien, S., *The Psalms: Strophic Structure and Theological Commentary*, Eerdmans Critical Commentary (Grand Rapids, Michigan: Eerdmans, 2003).
Van Deemter, K., 'Contrastive Stress, Contrariety, and Focus', in P. Bosch and R. van

der Sandt (eds.), *Focus: Linguistic, Cognitive and Computational Perspectives* (Cambridge: Cambridge University Press, 1999), pp. 3–17.
Van der Meer, W. and J. C. de Moor (eds.), *The Structural Analysis of Biblical and Canaanite Poetry*, JSOT Supplement Series 74 (Sheffield: Sheffield Academic Press, 1988).
Van der Merwe, C. H. J., J. A. Naudé, and J. H. Kroeze, *A Biblical Hebrew Reference Grammar* (Sheffield: Sheffield Academic Press, 1999).
Van der Merwe, C. H. J., 'The Function of Word Order in Old Hebrew – with Special Reference to Cases where a Syntagmeme Precedes a Verb in Joshua', *JNSL 17* (1991), pp. 129–44.
– 'Reconsidering Biblical Hebrew Temporal Expressions', *ZAH 10.1* (1997), pp. 42–62.
– 'Explaining Fronting in Biblical Hebrew', *JNSL 25.2* (1999), pp. 173–86.
– 'Review of J.-M. Heimerdinger, *Topic, Focus and Foreground in Ancient Hebrew Narrative*', *Biblica 81* (2000), pp. 574–78.
Van Dijk, T. A., *Macrostructures: An Interdisciplinary Study of Global Structures in Discourse, Interaction and Cognition* (Hillsdale, New Jersey: Lawrence Erlbaum Associates, 1980).
VanGemeren, W. A. (ed.), *New International Dictionary of Old Testament Theology and Exegesis*, 5 volumes (Carlisle, Cumbria: Paternoster, 1997).
Van Peer, W., 'Foregrounding' in R. E Asher (ed.), *Encyclopedia of Language and Linguistics*, vol. 3 (Oxford: Pergaman Press, 1994), pp. 1272–75.
Van Valin Jr., R. D. and R. J. LaPolla, *Syntax, Structure, Meaning and Function* (Cambridge: Cambridge University Press, 1997).
Walkte, B. K. and M. P. O'Connor, *An Introduction to Biblical Hebrew Syntax* (Winona Lake, Indiana: Eisenbrauns, 1990).
Walkte, B. K., *The Book of Proverbs Chapters 1–15*, New International Commentary on the Old Testament (Grand Rapids, Michigan: Eerdmans, 2004).
Watson, W. G. E., 'Chiastic Patterns in Biblical Hebrew Poetry', in J. W. Welch (ed.), *Chiasmus in Antiquity* (Hildersheim: Gerstenberg, 1981), pp. 118–68.
– *Classical Hebrew Poetry*, JSOT Supplement Series (Sheffield: Sheffield Academic Press, 1986).
Watts, J. D. W., *Isaiah 34–66*, Word Biblical Commentary (Waco, Texas: Word Books, 1987).
Welch, J. W. (ed.), *Chiasmus in Antiquity* (Hildersheim: Gerstenberg, 1981).
Wendland, E. R. (ed.), *Discourse Perspectives on the Hebrew Poetry of the Scriptures* (New York: United Bible Societies, 1994).
– *The Discourse Analysis of Hebrew Prophetic Literature* (Lampeter, Wales: Edwin Mellen Press, 1995).
– *Analyzing the Psalms* (Dallas, Texas: SIL, 1998).
Wenham, G. J., *Numbers*, Tyndale Old Testament Commentary (Leicester: Inter-Varsity Press, 1981).
– *Genesis 1–15*, Word Biblical Commentary (Waco, Texas: Word Books, 1987).
Whybray, R. N., *Proverbs*, New Century Bible Commentary (London: Marshall Pickering, 1994).
Wierzbicka, A., 'Semantic Primitives' in W. Bright (ed.), *International Encyclopedia of Linguistics*, vol. 3 (New York: Oxford University Press, 1992), pp. 402–3.
– *Semantics, Primes and Universals* (Oxford: Oxford University Press, 1996).

Williams, R. J., *Hebrew Syntax: An Outline* (Toronto: University of Toronto Press, 1976).
Willis, J. T., 'The Juxtaposition of Synonymous and Chiastic Parallelism in Tricola in Old Testament Hebrew Psalm Poetry', *VT 29* (1979), pp. 465–80.
Winther-Nielsen, N., *A Functional Discourse Grammar of Joshua: A Computer-Assisted Rhetorical Structure Analysis*, Coniectanea Biblica, Old Testament Series (Stockholm: Almqvist and Wiksell International, 1995).
Young, E. J., *The Book of Isaiah*, 3 volumes (Grand Rapids, Michigan: Eerdmans, 2000 [1969]).
Zevit, Z., 'Roman Jakobson, Psycholinguistics, and Biblical Poetry', *JBL 109* (1990), pp. 385–401.
– *The Anterior Construction in Classical Hebrew*, Society of Biblical Literature Monograph Series (Atlanta, Georgia: SBL, 1998).
Zogbo, L. and E. R. Wendland, *Hebrew Poetry in the Bible: A Guide for Understanding and Translating* (New York: United Bible Societies, 2000).
Zuck, R., *Job*, Everyman's Bible Commentary (Chicago: Moody Press, 1978).

APPENDIX 1

Statistical Comparison of Word Order in Biblical Hebrew Prose and Poetry

A total of approximately 1,200 verbal clauses were examined, taken from various poetic sections of the Hebrew Bible. They were divided into two categories: those containing canonical, i.e., V S (O) (M) word order, and those containing non-canonical word order. The results were as follows:

Chapters	Canonical VPs	Non-canonical VPs
Psalms 1–12	192 [66.9 %]	95 [33.1 %]
Psalms 96–99	61 [75.3 %]	20 [24.7 %]
Psalms 142–143	35 [68.6 %]	16 [31.4 %]
Isaiah 61–66[1]	181 [62.0 %]	111 [38.0 %]
Proverbs 5–7	87 [68.0 %]	41 [32.0 %]
Job 3–10	265 [65.6 %]	139 [34.4 %]
TOTAL: **1,243**	821 [66.0 %]	422 [34.0 %]

A similar number of verbal clauses were then analysed, drawn from a selection of chapters from narrative books. The following results were obtained:

Chapters	Canonical VPs	Non-canonical VPs
Genesis 11–14	183 [85.5 %]	31 [14.5 %]
Exodus 1–2	142 [94.0 %]	9 [6.0 %]
Joshua 1–3	170 [83.8 %]	33 [16.2 %]
1 Samuel 5–7	162 [89.0 %]	20 [11.0 %]
1 Kings 1–3	360 [82.0 %]	80 [18.0 %]
TOTAL: **1,190**	**1,017** [85.5 %]	173 [14.5 %]

From these figures we observe a far larger degree of word order variation in poetic texts as compared with narrative: 85.5 % of verbal clauses in narrative adhere to the canonical word order, but only 66.0 % in poetry.

---

[1] This does not include Isaiah 66:18–21, which is commonly considered to be prose.

APPENDIX 2

The Database

This appendix contains charts recording the constituent order for each clause in the following portions of Hebrew poetry:

(a) Psalms 1–150 (d) Proverbs 1–9
(b) Isaiah 40–66 (e) Song of Songs 1–8
(c) Job 3–14   (f) Numbers 23–24 (oracles of Balaam)

To facilitate use of the charts the accompanying notes have been provided. These offer explanation of certain details of the notation system employed and highlight other significant features.

Notes
(1) A complete list of the linguistic notations used is given at the beginning of the book.
(2) Labels describing colon-types are placed in the right-hand column. Cola consisting of a single clause are separated from each other by a backslash /.
(3) The relationship of parallelism between units is indicated by a double backslash //. These units are most frequently cola, though occasionally shorter or longer units are found in parallel relationship.
(4) Where a poetic colon contains more than one grammatical clause, two colon labels are joined by a hyphen, as for example CAN-Nom.
(5) The demarcation of individual colon boundaries is admittedly sometimes uncertain and on occasion the position in which it has been placed is somewhat arbitrary. That is to say, the labelling CAN-Nom might equally be perceived by some as CAN/Nom. Either way the question has no bearing upon the constituent order. On the whole colon boundaries have been located according to the logical segmentation of the text and on the basis of colon length.
(6) Where two or more canonical clauses appear in a colon, a superscript numeral indicates the number of verbal clauses. For example, MKD^2 denotes a colon containing two marked verbal clauses, CAN^3 one containing three canonical clauses.
(7) V^{Ng} denotes a negated verb (e.g., בַּל־נָמוֹטוּ), M^{Ng} a negated modifier (e.g., אַל־בְּאַפְּךָ), Q^{Ng} a negated interrogative (הֲלֹא), etc.
(8) When a verbal clause is contained within a relative clause this is shown by a superscript R as in CAN^R or MKD^R. A relativizer that is only implicit is shown as $CAN^{[R]}$.

(9) In cases where a colon contains two or more verbal clauses, one of which is located in a relative clause, both a numeral and superscript R appear. The position of R relative to the numeral shows which of the two clauses comes first. For example, CAN^{2R} means that the colon consists of two canonical clauses the second of which appears in a relative clause.

(10) A modifying phrase which is constructed of an infinitive with a preposition is indicated by M followed by brackets showing the composition of the infinitival clause, as in M(Inf O M). Similarly, a subject or object phrase which itself is composed of a relative clause will employ brackets, such as O(R V).

(11) In certain instances gapping may alternatively be analysed as apposition. For instance, a bicolon may have an A-line composed of V S O and a B-line having a long O phrase paralleling the O element of the A-line. In such a case the double gapping of both verb and subject might possibly be said to have taken place. In the data presented here, however, an analysis in terms of apposition is preferred. So, for example, the above bicolon will be labelled CAN/Nom. The label Gap has been reserved for those parallelisms in which a minimum of two parallel elements remain in the B-line, as in V S O//S O, which is designated CAN//Gap.

(12) Generally speaking an active participle is indicated by V^{Pt}, while one that is passive is entered as Comp (a complement).

(13) An infinitive absolute is not indicated as Inf nor is it MKD when it is adjoined to a finite verb as an intensifier of the verbal idea. When it is used independently in the place of a main verb it appears as Inf.

(14) In a small number of instances the negative existential particle E is left implicit, while the negative לֹא still appears. Such cases are entered in the data as $[E]^{Ng}$.

(15) כֹּה אָמַר יְהוָה is a fixed formula of speech introduction, in which the initial element is considered to have the role of an M constituent. The colon is labelled in the data as CAN.

(16) Sentence-initial כִּי, like כֹּה in the previous point, is not regarded as rendering the colon marked.

(17) נְאֻם־יְהוָה is simply entered as a Comp (complement), on the basis that it means: '[This is] an oracle of the LORD'.

(18) A single square bracket] means that the words that it closes belong to the preceding verse and not to the following.

(19) The presence of *maqqep̄* in the Masoretic Text, though not directly related to the matter of word order, is indicated in the data by a hyphen (e.g., V-M).

(20) A question mark (?) in the chart means that either the text or its syntactic construction is not certain.

Appendix 2

Ref.	(a) Psalms 1–150 Constituent Order		Colon-Type
Ps. 1			
1ab	Comp S R V^{Ng} M //		Nom-CAN^R//
1cd	w-M V^{Ng} // w-M V^{Ng}		DEF//DEF
2	C Comp S // w-M V M w-M		Nom//MKD
3a	w-V Comp /		CAN/
3bc	R O V M // w-S V^{Ng} /		MKD^R//MKD/
3d	w-O(R V) V		CAN^R-MKD
4	Comp^{Ng} S / C-Comp R V-o S		Nom/Nom-CAN^R
5	C V^{Ng} S M // w-S M		CAN//Gap
6	C-V^{Pt} S O / w-S V		Ptcp/MKD
Ps. 2			
1	Q V S // w-S V-O		CAN//DEF
2	V S // w-S V-M / M w-M		CAN//DEF/Nom
3	V O // w-V M O		CAN//CAN
4	S V // S V-M		MKD//MKD
5	C V M M // w-M V-o		CAN//DEF
6	w-S^{Pn} V O / M		MKD/Nom
7ab	V M / S V M		CAN/MKD
7cd	Comp S^{Pn} // S^{Pn} M V-o		Nom//MKD
8	V M w-V O O // w-O O		CAN^2//Gap
9	V-o M // M V-o		CAN//DEF
10	w-M [Voc] V // V [Voc]		CAN//CAN
11	V O M / w-V M		CAN/CAN
12a-c	V-O / C-V / w-V M		CAN/CAN/CAN
12de	C-V M S / Comp S		CAN/Nom
Ps. 3			
2	[Voc] Q-V S // S V^{Pt} M		CAN//Ptcp
3	S V^{Pt} M / E^{Ng} S Comp M	Selah	Pctp/Nom
4	w-S^{Pn} [Voc] Comp / Comp		Nom/Nom
5	M M V / w-V-o M	Selah	DEF/CAN
6	S^{Pn} V w-V / V / C S V-o		MKD-CAN/CAN/MKD
7	V^{Ng} M / R M V M		CAN/MKD^R
8ab	V [Voc] // V-o [Voc]		CAN//CAN
8cd	C-V O O // O V		CAN//DEF
9	Comp S / Comp S	Selah	Nom/Nom
Ps. 4			
2	M(Inf) V-o [Voc] / M V M / V-o w-V O		CAN/CAN/CAN^2
3	[Voc] Q S Comp / V O // V O	Selah	Nom/CAN//CAN
4	w-V C-V S O M / S V M(Inf) M		CAN^2/MKD
5	V w-V^{Ng} / V M M w-V	Selah	CAN^2/CAN^2
6	V O / w-V M		CAN/CAN
7	S V^{Pt} / Q-V-o O / V-M O [Voc]		Ptcp/CAN/CAN
8	V O M / C S w-S V		CAN/MKD
9	M V w-V / C-S^{Pn} [Voc] M M V-o		MKD-CAN/DEF?
Ps. 5			
2	O V [Voc] // V O		DEF//CAN
3	V M [Voc] / C-M V		CAN/MKD
4	[Voc] M V O // M V-M w-V		MKD//MKD-CAN
5	C Comp^{Ng} S^{Pn} // V^{Ng}-o S		Nom//CAN
6	V^{Ng} S M // V O		CAN//CAN
7	V O // O O V S		CAN//DEF
8	w-S^{Pn} M V O // V M M		DEF//CAN
9	[Voc] V-o M M / V M O		CAN//CAN
10	C E^{Ng} Comp S // S Comp // Comp S // M V		Nom//Nom//Nom//DEF
11	V-o [Voc] / V M / M V-o / C-V M		CAN/CAN//DEF/CAN
12ab	w-V S // M V		CAN//DEF
12cd	V M / w-V M S		CAN/CAN
13	C-S^{Pn} V O [Voc] / M M V-o		MKD/DEF
Ps. 6			
2	[Voc] M^{Ng} V-o // w-M^{Ng} V-o		MKD//MKD
3	V-o [Voc] C Comp S // V-o [Voc] C V S //		CAN/Nom//CAN//CAN//
4	w-S V M / w-S^{Pn} [Voc] Q		DEF/Nom

5	V [Voc] V O / V-o M	CAN²/CAN
6	C E^Ng Comp S // M Q V-O	Nom//MKD
7	V M / V M O // M O V	CAN/CAN//DEF
8	V M S // V M	CAN//CAN
9	V M [Voc] / C-V S O	CAN/CAN
10	V S O // S O V	CAN//DEF
11	V w-V M S / V V M	CAN²//CAN²
Ps. 7		
2	[Voc] M V / V-o M // w-V-o	MKD/CAN//CAN
3	C-V M O / V^Pt w-E^Ng S^Pt	CAN/Ptcp-Nom
4	[Voc] C-V O // C-E-S Comp	CAN//Nom
5	C-V O O // w-V O M	CAN//CAN
6	V S O w-V / w-V M O // w-O M V Selah	CAN²/CAN//DEF
7ab	V [Voc] M // V M	CAN//CAN
7cd	w-V [Voc] / O V	CAN/MKD
8	w-S V-o / w-M M V	MKD/DEF
9	S V O / V-o [Voc] M w-M	MKD/CAN
10	V-M S / w-V O / w-V^Pt O w-O S	CAN/CAN/Ptcp
11	S Comp / V^Pt O	Nom/Ptcp
12	S Comp / S V^Pt O	Nom/Ptcp
13	C-V^Ng / O V // O V w-V-o	CAN/MKD//MKD-CAN
14	w-M V O // O M V	DEF/DEF
15	H V-O // w-V O // w-V O	CAN//CAN//CAN
16	O V w-V-o // w-V M [R] V	MKD/CAN²ᴿ
17	V S M // w-M S V	CAN//DEF
18	V O M // w-V O	CAN//CAN
Ps. 8		
2	[Voc] Q-Comp S M / C Inf S M	Nom/Inf
3	M V O M / Inf O w-O	MKD/Inf
4	C-V O O / O w-O R V	CAN/Nom(CANᴿ)
5	Q-S C-V-o // w-S C V-o	Nom-CAN//Nom-CAN
6	w-V-o M // w-O w-O V-o	CAN//DEF
7	V-o M / O V M	CAN/MKD
8	O w-O / w-P O	Nom/Nom
9	O / w-O V^Pt O	Nom/Nom
10	[Voc] Q-Comp S M	Nom
Ps. 9		
2	V O M / V O	CAN/CAN
3	V w-V M / V O [Voc]	CAN²/CAN
4	M(Inf S M) / V w-V M	Inf/CAN²
5	C-V O w-O / V M V^Pt O	CAN/CAN-Ptcp
6	V O V O / O V M	CAN²/MKD
7	S V Comp M / w-O V V S	MKD/MKD-CAN
8	w-S M V / V M O	MKD/CAN
9	w-S^Pn V-O M // V O M	MKD//CAN
10	w-V S Comp M // Comp M	CAN//Gap
11	w-V M S / C V^Ng O [Voc]	CAN/CAN
12	V M V^Pt / V M O	CAN-Ptcp/CAN
13	C-S^Pt O V / V^Ng O	DEF/CAN
14	V-o [Voc] / V O M [Voc]	CAN/CAN
15	C V O M // V M	CAN//CAN
16	V S M [R] V // M-R V V S	CAN²ᴿ//Nom-CANᴿ²
17	V S M [R] V / M V S Selah	CAN²⁽ᴿ⁾/MKD
18	V S M / S	CAN/Nom
19	C M^Ng V S // S V M	DEF//DEF
20	V [Voc] / V^Ng S / V S M	CAN/CAN/CAN
21	V [Voc] O M / V S / Comp S Selah	CAN/CAN/Nom
Ps. 10		
1	Q [Voc] V M // V M M	CAN//CAN
2	M V O / V M R V	MKD/CAN²ᴿ
3	C-V S M / w-S V / w-V O	CAN//MKD/CAN
4	S M V^Ng / E^Ng S Comp	MKD/Nom
5	V S M / Comp S M / N V M	CAN/Nom/MKD
6	V M / V^Ng / M Comp^Ng	CAN/CAN/Nom

Appendix 2 297

7	M S V w-M // Comp S w-S	DEF//Nom
8	V M // M V O // S M V	CAN//DEF//DEF
9	V M M // V Inf O / V O M	CAN//CAN/CAN
10	w-V V / w-V M S	CAN^2/CAN
11	V M V S / V O // V^{Ng} M	CAN^2/CAN//CAN
12	V [Voc] // [Voc] V O / V^{Ng} O	CAN//CAN/CAN
13	Q V S O // V M V^{Ng}	CAN//CAN^2
14ab	V C-S^{Pn} O w-O / V Inf M	CAN/CAN
14cd	M V S / M? S^{Pn} V Comp	MKD/MKD
15	V O / V-O V^{Ng}	CAN/CAN^2
16	S Comp M / V S M	Nom/CAN
17	O V [Voc] / V O // V O	MKD/CAN//CAN
18	Inf O w-O / V^{Ng} M / Inf S M	Inf/CAN/Inf
Ps. 11		
1	M V / Q V M / V M [Voc]	MKD/CAN/CAN
2	C H S V O / V O M / Inf M O	MKD/CAN/Inf
3	C S V / N Q-V	MKD/MKD
4ab	S Comp // N Comp S	Nom//Nom
4cd	S V // S V O	MKD//MKD
5	S O V / w-O w-O V S	MKD/MKD
6	V M O w-O / w-S Comp	CAN/Nom
7	C-Comp S O V / S V O	Nom-MKD/MKD
Ps. 12		
2	V [Voc] C-V S // C-V S M	CAN^2//CAN
3	O V S M // M? M V	MKD//MKD
4	V S O / O(S V^{Pt} O)	CAN/Nom
5	C V M V / S Comp / Q Comp M	CAN-MKD/Nom/Nom
6	M M / M V V S / V M [R] V M	Nom/CAN^2/CAN^2
7	S Comp / Comp M / Comp M	Nom/Nom/Nom
8	S^{Pn}-[Voc] V-o / V-o M M	MKD/CAN
9	M S V / M(Inf S M)	DEF/Inf
Ps. 13		
2	Q [Voc] V-o M // Q V O M	Nom-CAN//CAN
3	Q V O M // O M M / Q V S M	CAN//Gap/CAN
4	V V-o [Voc] / V O C-V O	CAN^2/CAN^2
5	C-V S V-o // S V C V	CAN^2//DEF-CAN
6ab	w-S^{Pn} M V / V S M	MKD/CAN
6cd	V M / C V M	CAN/CAN
Ps. 14		
1ab	V S M / E^{Ng} S	CAN/Nom
1cd	V V O / E^{Ng} S^{Pt}	CAN^2/Nom
2	S M V M / Inf Q-E S^{Pt} /V^{Pt} O	DEF/Inf/Ptcp
3	S V M V / E^{Ng} S^{Pt} / E^{Ng} P-S	MKD^2/ Nom/Nom
4	Q^{Ng} V S^{Pt} / V^{Pt} O [C] V O / O V^{Ng}	CAN/Pctp-CAN/MKD
5	M V O / C-S Comp	CAN/Nom
6	O V / C S Comp	MKD/Nom
7ab	Q V M O / M(Inf S O)/	CAN/Inf/
7cd	V S // V S	CAN//CAN
Ps. 15		
1	[Voc] Q-V M // Q-V M	CAN//CAN
2	V^{Pt} M // w-V^{Pt} O / w-V^{Pt} O M	Ptpc//Ptcp/Ptcp
3	V^{Ng} M / V^{Ng} M O // w-O V^{Ng} M	CAN/CAN//DEF
4	V^{Pt} M S / w-O V / V Inf w-V^{Ng}	Pctp/MKD/CAN^2
5	O V^{Ng} M // O M V^{Ng} / S^{Pt} V^{Ng} M	MKD//MKD/MKD
Ps. 16		
1	V-o [Voc] / C-V M	CAN/CAN
2	V M / Comp S^{Pn} / S E^{Ng} M?	CAN/Nom/Nom
3	N? R Comp S / Comp	Nom/Nom
4ab	V S [R] O V	CAN-MKD^R
4cd	V^{Ng} O M // w-V^{Ng} O M	CAN//CAN
5	S Comp // S^{Pn} V O	Nom//MKD
6	S V-M M // P-S Comp?	MKD//Nom
7	V O R V-o / P-M V-o S	CAN^{2R}/MKD
8	V O M M / C M V^{Ng}	CAN/MKD

9	C V S // w-V S / P-S V M	CAN//CAN/MKD
10	C V^{Ng} O M // V^{Ng} O Inf O	CAN//CAN
11	V-o O / S Comp // S Comp M	CAN/Nom//Nom
Ps. 17		
1	V [Voc] O // V O // V O / M	CAN//CAN//CAN/Nom
2	M S V // S V O	DEF//DEF
3	V O V M / V-o V^{Ng} / V V^{Ng}-S	CAN^2/CAN^2/CAN^2
4	N? M? / S^{Pn} V M	Nom/MKD
5	V S M // V^{Ng} S	CAN//CAN
6ab	S^{Pn}-V-o / C-V-o [Voc]	MKD/CAN
6cd	V-O M // V O	CAN//CAN
7	V O [Voc(V^{Pt} O / M M)]	CAN-Ptcp/Nom
8	V-o M // M V-o	CAN//DEF
9	M(S R V-o / S [R] V M	Nom-CAN^R//CAN^R
10	O V / S V M	MKD/MKD
11	V-o M V-o / O V Inf M	CAN^2/MKD
12	S Comp V Inf // w-S V^{Pt} M	Nom-CAN//Ptcp
13	V [Voc] V O V-o / V O M M	CAN^3/CAN
14ab	M [Voc] // M	Nom//Nom
14c-e	w-M? V O V S / V O M	MKD?-CAN/CAN
15	S^{Pn} M V O / V M(Inf) O?	MKD/CAN
Ps. 18		
2	V [Voc]	CAN
3a	S Comp w-Comp w-Comp /	Nom/
3b-d	S Comp V M / Comp w-Comp Comp	Nom-CAN/Nom
4	Comp V O / w-M V	MKD/MKD
5	V-o S // w-S V-o //	CAN//DEF//
6	S V-o // V-o S	DEF//CAN
7ab	M V O // w-M V	CAN//DEF
7cd	V M O // w-S M V M	CAN//DEF
8	w-V w-V S // w-S V / w-V C-V M	CAN^2//DEF/CAN^2
9	V S M // w-S-M V // S V M	CAN//DEF//DEF
10	w-V O w-V / S Comp	CAN^2/Nom
11	w-V M w-V // w-V M	CAN^2//CAN
12	V O O M / O O	CAN/Nom
13	M S V / S w-S	MKD/Nom
14	w-V M S // w-S V O / O w-O	CAN//DEF/Nom
15	w-V O w-V-o // w-O w-V-o	CAN^2//Gap-CAN
16	w-V S // w-V S / M [Voc] // M	CAN//CAN/Nom//Nom
17	V M V-o / V-o M	CAN^2/CAN
18	V-o M / w-M C-V M	CAN/Nom-CAN
19	V-o M / w-V-S Comp M	CAN/CAN
20	w-V-o M / V-o C V M	CAN/CAN^2
21	V-o S M // M V M	CAN//DEF
22	C-V O // w-V^{Ng} M	CAN//CAN
23	C S Comp M // w-O V^{Ng} M	Nom//DEF
24	w-V Comp M // w-V M	CAN//CAN
25	w-V-S M M / M M	CAN/Nom
26	M V // M V	MKD//MKD
27	M V / w-M V	MKD/MKD
28	C-S^{Pn} O V / w-O V	MKD/MKD
29	C-S^{Pn} V O // S V O	MKD//MKD
30	C M V O // w-M V O	MKD//MKD
31	N Comp S / S Comp / Comp S M	Nom/Nom/Nom
32	C Q Comp M // w-Q Comp M	Nom//Nom
33	S V^{Pt}-o O / w-V O O	Ptcp/CAN
34	V^{Pt} O M // w-M V-o	Ptcp//DEF
35	V^{Pt} O M / w-V O S	Ptcp/CAN
36	w-V M O / w-S V-o // w-S V-o	CAN/MKD//MKD
37	V O M // w-V^{Ng} S	CAN//CAN
38	V O w-V-o / w-V^{Ng} M(Inf)	CAN^2/CAN
39	V-o w-V^{Ng} Inf // V M	CAN^2//CAN
40	w-V-o O M / V O M	CAN/CAN
41	w-O V M O // w-N V-o	MKD//MKD

Appendix 2

42	V w-E^{Ng} S // M w-V^{Ng}-o	CAN-Nom//Gap-Nom
43	w-V-o M M // M V-o	CAN//DEF
44	V-o M / V-o M / S [R] V^{Ng} V-o	CAN/CAN/MKD-CAN$^{[R]}$
45	M V M / S V-M //	MKD/MKD//
46	S V / V M	MKD/CAN
47	Comp S / w-Comp S / w-V S	Nom/Nom/CAN
48	S V^{Pt} O M / w-V O M	Ptcp/CAN
49	V^{Pt}-o M // C M V-o // M V-o	Ptcp//DEF//DEF
50	C V-o M [Voc] // w-M V	CAN//DEF
51	V^{Pt} O // w-V^{Pt} O M / M M	Ptcp//Ptpc/Nom
Ps. 19		
2	S V^{Pt} O // w-O V^{Pt} S	Ptcp//Ptcp
3	M V O // w-M V-O	MKD//MKD
4	E^{Ng} S w-E^{Ng} S // V^{Pt-Ng} S	Nom^2//Ptcp
5	M V S // w-M S / M V-O M	MKD//Gap/MKD
6	w-S^{Pn} M V^{Pt} M / V M Inf O	Ptcp/CAN
7	Comp S // w-S Comp / w-S V^{Pt} M	Nom//Nom/Ptcp
8ab	S Comp / V^{Pt} O	Nom/Ptcp
8cd	S V^{Pt} / V^{Pt} O	Ptcp/Ptcp
9ab	S Comp / V^{Pt} O	Nom/Ptcp
9cd	S Comp / V^{Pt} O	Nom/Ptcp
10ab	S Comp / V^{Pt} M	Nom/Ptcp
10cd	S Comp / V M	Nom/CAN
11	V^{Pt} M w-M / w-M w-M	Ptcp/Nom
12	P-S V^{Pt} M / Comp(Inf) S	Ptcp/Inf
13	O Q-V / M V-o	MKD/MKD
14ab	P M V O / V^{Ng}-M	MKD/CAN
14cd	C V / w-V M	CAN/CAN
15	V M S / w-S M / [Voc]	CAN/Nom/Nom
Ps. 20		
2	V-o S M / V-o S	CAN/CAN
3	V-O M // w-M V-o	CAN//DEF
4	V O // w-O V Selah	CAN//DEF
5	V-M M // w-O V	CAN//DEF
6	V M // w-M V / V S O	CAN//DEF/CAN
7ab	M V / C V S O	CAN/CAN
7cd	V-o M / M	CAN/Nom
8	S^{Pn} M S^{Pn} M / w-S^{Pn} M V	Gap^2/MKD
9	S^{Pn} V w-V / w-S^{Pn} V w-V	MKD/MKD
10	[Voc] V O / V-o M(Inf)	CAN/CAN
Ps. 21		
2	[Voc] M V-S // w-M Q V M	MKD//MKD
3	O V M // w-O V^{Ng} M Selah	MKD//MKD
4	C V-o O // V M O	CAN//CAN
5	O V M V M / O M	MKD-CAN/Nom
6	Comp S M / O w-O V M	Nom/MKD
7	C-V-o O M / V-o M M	CAN/CAN
8	C-S V^{Pt} M // w-M V^{Ng}	Ptcp//DEF
9	V S M // S V O	CAN//DEF
10	V-o M / M [Voc] / S M V-o / w-V-o S	CAN/Nom/MKD/CAN
11	O M V / w-O M	MKD//Gap
12	C-V M O // V M V^{Ng}	CAN//CAN^2
13	C V-o O / M V M	CAN/MKD
14	V [Voc] M / V w-V O	CAN/CAN^2
Ps. 22		
2	[Voc] Q V-o / Comp M M	CAN/Nom
3	[Voc] V M w-V^{Ng} // w-M w-Ng S Comp	CAN^2//Gap-Nom
4	S^{Pn} Comp / V^{Pt} O	Nom/Ptcp
5	M V S / V w-V-o	MKD/CAN^2
6	M V w-V // M V w-V^{Ng}	MKD//MKD-CAN
7ab	w-S^{Pn} Comp / w-Comp^{Ng}	Nom/Nom
7cd	Comp // w-Comp	Nom//Nom
8	S V M / V M // V O	MKD/CAN//CAN
9	V M V-o / V-o C V M	CAN^2/CAN^2

10	C-S^{Pn} Comp M // V^{Pt} M	Nom//Ptcp
11	M V M // M Comp S^{Pn}	MKD//Nom
12	V^{Ng} M / C-S Comp // C-E^{Ng} S^{Pt}	CAN/Nom//Nom
13	V-o S // S V-o	CAN//DEF
14	V M S / S V^{Pt} w-V^{Pt}	CAN/$Ptcp^2$
15	M V / w-V S / V S Comp / V M	MKD/CAN/CAN/CAN
16	V M S / w-S V^{Pt} O / w-M V-o	CAN/Ptcp/MKD
17	C V-o S // S V-o / V? O w-O	CAN//DEF/CAN
18	V O / S^{Pn} V V-M	CAN/MKD-CAN
19	V O M // w-M V O	CAN//DEF
20	w-S^{Pn} [Voc] V^{Ng} / [Voc] M V	MKD/MKD
21	V M O // M O	CAN//Gap
22	V-o M // w-M V-o	CAN//DEF
23	V O M // M V-o	CAN//DEF
24	[Voc] V-o // [Voc] V-o // w-V M [Voc]	CAN/CAN//CAN
25ab	C V^{Ng} / w-V^{Ng} O	CAN/CAN
25c-e	w-V^{Ng} O M / w-M(Inf) V	CAN/Inf-MKD
26	Comp S M / O V M	Nom/MKD
27	V S w-V / V O S / V S M	CAN^2/CAN/CAN
28	V w-V M S // w-V M S	CAN^2//CAN
29	C Comp S // w-V^{Pt} M	Nom//Ptcp
30	V w-V S // M V S / w-O V^{Ng}	CAN^2//DEF/MKD
31	S V-o / V M M	MKD/CAN
32	V w-V O / M C V	CAN^2/Nom-CAN
Ps. 23		
1	S Comp V^{Ng}	Nom-CAN
2	M V-o // M V-o	MKD//MKD
3	O V / V-o M M	MKD/CAN
4	C-V M / V^{Ng} O / C-S^{Pn} Comp / N S^{Pn} V-o	CAN/CAN/Nom/MKD
5	V M O / M / V M O / S Comp	CAN/Nom/CAN/Nom
6	P S w-S V-o / M / w-V M / M	MKD/Nom/CAN/Nom
Ps. 24		
1	Comp S w-S // S w-S	Nom//Nom
2	C-S^{Pn} M V-o // w-M V-o	MKD//MKD
3	Q V M // w-Q V M	CAN//CAN
4ab	Comp // w-Comp	Nom//Nom
4cd	R V^{Ng} M O // w-V^{Ng} M	CAN^R//CAN
5	V O M // w-O M	CAN//Gap
6	S^{Pn} Comp // V^{Pt} [Voc] Selah	Nom/Pctp
7	V [Voc] O // w-V [Voc] / w-V S	CAN//CAN/CAN
8	Q Comp / Comp // Comp	Nom/Nom//Nom
9	V [Voc] O // w-V [Voc] / w-V S	CAN//CAN/CAN
10	Q Comp / N / S^{Pn} Comp Selah	Nom/Nom/Nom
Ps. 25		
1	M [Voc] O V	DEF
2	[Voc] M V V^{Ng} / V^{Ng} S M	MKD-CAN/CAN
3	P S V^{Ng} / V S	MKD/CAN
4	O [Voc] V-o // w-O V-o	MKD//MKD
5	V-o M w-V-o / C-S^{Pn} Comp / O V M	CAN^2/Nom/MKD
6	V-O [Voc] w-O / C Comp S^{Pn}	CAN/Nom
7	O w-O V^{Ng} / M V-O-S^{Pn} / M [Voc]	MKD/MKD/Nom
8	Comp w-Comp S / C V O M	Nom/CAN
9	V O M // w-V O O	CAN//CAN
10	S Comp w-Comp / M(V^{Pt} O w-O)	Nom/Ptcp
11	M [Voc] / w-V O C Comp-S^{Pn}	Nom/CAN-Nom
12	Q Comp / V-o M [R] V	Nom/$CAN^{2[R]}$
13	S M V // w-S V O	MKD//MKD
14	S Comp // w-S Comp	Nom/Nom
15	S M Comp / C S^{Pn}-V M O	Nom/MKD
16	V M w-V-o / C Comp w-Comp S^{Pn}	CAN/Nom
17	O V / M V-o	MKD/MKD
18	V O w-O / w-V O	CAN/CAN
19	V-O C-V / w-O V-o	CAN^2/MKD
20	V O w-V-o / V^{Ng} C-V M	CAN^2/CAN^2

Appendix 2

21	S w-S V-o / C V-o	MKD/CAN
22	V [Voc] O / M	CAN/Nom
Ps. 26		
1ab	V-o [Voc] / C-S^{Pn} M V	CAN/MKD
1cd	w-M V / V^{Ng}	MKD/CAN
2	V-o [Voc] w-V-o // V O w-O	CAN^2//CAN
3	C-S Comp / w-V M	Nom/CAN
4	V^{Ng} M // w-M V^{Ng}	CAN//DEF
5	V O // w-M V^{Ng}	CAN//DEF
6	V M O // w-V O [Voc]	CAN/CAN
7	Inf M // w-Inf O	Inf//Inf
8	[Voc] V O // w-O	CAN//Nom
9	V^{Ng} M S // w-M S	CAN//Gap
10	R-Comp S // w-S V O	Nom//DEF
11	w-S^{Pn} M V / V-o w-V-o	MKD/CAN^2
12	S V M / M V O	MKD/MKD
Ps. 27		
1	S Comp w-Comp S / Q V // S Comp / Q V	Nom/CAN//Nom/CAN
2	M(Inf M S Inf O) / N S^{Pn} V w-V	Inf/MKD-CAN
3ab	C-V M S / V^{Ng} S //	CAN/CAN//
3cd	C V M S / M S^{Pn} V^{Pt}	CAN/Ptcp
4ab	O V M / O V	MKD/MKD
4c-e	Inf M M / Inf M / w-Inf M	Inf/Inf/Inf
5	C V-o M M // V-o M // M V-o	CAN//CAN//DEF
6	w-M V S / M M / w-V M O / V w-V M	CAN/Nom/CAN/CAN^2
7	V-[Voc] // O V / w-V-o w-V-o	CAN//DEF?/CAN^2
8	M V S / V O / O [Voc] V	MKD/CAN/MKD
9ab	V^{Ng} O M // V^{Ng} M O	CAN//CAN
9c-e	Comp V / V^{Ng}-o w-V^{Ng}-o [Voc]	Nom/CAN^2
10	C S w-S V-o / S V-o	MKD/MKD
11	V-o [Voc] O // w-V-o M / M	CAN/CAN/Nom
12	V^{Ng}-o M / C V M S / w-V O	CAN/CAN/CAN
13	C V / Inf M M	CAN//Inf
14	V M / V w-V S / w-V M	CAN/CAN^2/CAN
Ps. 28		
1ab	M [Voc] V / [Voc] V^{Ng} M	MKD/CAN
1cd	C-V M / w-V M	CAN/CAN
2	V O M(Inf M) / M(Inf M)	CAN/Inf
3	V^{Ng}-o M / w-M / V^{Pt} O M / w-O M	CAN/Nom/Ptcp/Nom
4	V-M M w-M // M V M // V O M	CAN/DEF//CAN
5	C V^{Ng} M / w-M / V-o w-V^{Ng}-o	CAN/Nom/CAN^2
6	Comp S / C-V O	Nom/CAN
7a-c	S Comp w-Comp / M V S w-V	Nom/CAN^2
7de	w-V S // w-M V-o	CAN//DEF
8	S Comp // w-Comp S	Nom//Nom
9	V O // w-V O / w-V-o w-V-o M	CAN//CAN/CAN^2
Ps. 29		
1	V M [Voc] // V M O w-O //	CAN//CAN//
2	V M O / V M M	CAN/CAN
3	S Comp / S V / S Comp	Nom/MKD/Nom
4	S Comp // S Comp	Nom//Nom
5	S V^{Pt} O // w-V S O	Ptcp//CAN
6	w-V-o M // O w-O M	CAN//Gap
7	S V^{Pt} O	Ptcp
8	S V O // V S O //	MKD//DEF//
9	S V O / w-V O / w-M S V^{Pt} O	MKD/CAN/Ptcp
10	S M V / w-V S M	DEF//CAN
11	S O M V // S V O M	DEF//DEF
Ps. 30		
2	V-o [Voc] C V-o / w-V^{Ng} O M	CAN^2/CAN
3	[Voc] V M / w-V-o	CAN/CAN
4	[Voc] V M O // V-o M	CAN//CAN
5	V M [Voc] // w-V M	CAN//CAN
6ab	C S Comp? / S Comp?	Nom/Nom

6cd	M V S // w-M S	MKD//Gap
7	w-S^{Pn} V M / V^{Ng} M	MKD/CAN
8	[Voc] M V M / V O V Comp	MKD/CAN^2
9	M [Voc] V // w-M V	MKD//MKD
10ab	Q-S Comp / M(Inf M)	Nom/Inf
10cd	Q-V-o S // Q-V O	CAN//CAN
11	V-[Voc] w-V-o / [Voc] V Comp M	CAN^2/Nom
12	V O M / V O // w-V-o O	CAN/CAN//CAN
13	C V-o S w-V^{Ng} / [Voc] M V-o	CAN^2/DEF
Ps. 31		
2	M [Voc] V / V^{Ng} M / M V-o	MKD/CAN/MKD
3ab	V M O / M V	CAN/MKD
3cd	V M Comp // Comp Inf-o	CAN//Gap
4	C-Comp w-Comp S^{Pn} / w-M V-o w-V-o	Nom/MKD-CAN
5	V-o M R V M / C-S^{Pn} Comp	CAN^{2R}/Nom
6	M V O / V O [Voc]	MKD/CAN
7	V O / w-S^{Pn} M V	CAN/MKD
8	V w-V M / C V O / V M	CAN^2/CAN/CAN
9	w-V^{Ng}-o M / V M O	CAN/CAN
10	V-o [Voc] C S Comp / V M S / S w-S	CAN-Nom/CAN-Nom
11ab	C V M S // w-S M /	CAN//Gap
11cd	V M S / w-S V	CAN//DEF
12	M V Comp // w-M M // Comp M / S^{Pt} V M	MKD//Gap//Gap/MKD
13	V M // V Comp	CAN//CAN
14ab	C V O / S Comp	CAN/Nom
14cd	M(Inf M M) / Inf O V	Inf/MKD
15	w-S^{Pn} M V [Voc] / V Comp S^{Pn}	MKD/CAN
16	Comp S V-o / M w-M	Nom-CAN/Nom
17	V O M / V-o M	CAN/CAN
18	[Voc] V^{Ng} C V-o / V S V M	CAN^2/CAN^2
19	V S / V^{Pt} M O M w-M	CAN/Ptcp
20	Q Comp-S / R V M // [R] V M M	Nom/CAN^R//CAN$^{[R]}$
21	V-o M M // V-o M M	CAN//CAN
22	Comp S / C V O M M	Nom/CAN
23	w-S^{Pn} V M / V M / M V O M(Inf)	MKD/CAN/CAN
24	V O [Voc] / O V^{Pt} S / w-V^{Pt} M O	CAN/Ptcp/Ptcp
25	V w-V O / [Voc]	CAN^2/Nom
Ps. 32		
1	Comp S // S	Nom//Nom
2	Comp S [R] V^{Ng} S M O / w-E^{Ng} Comp S	Nom-CAN/Nom
3	C-V V S / M(Inf M)	CAN^2/Inf
4	C M w-M V M S / V S M Selah	MKD/CAN
5ab	O V-o // w-O V^{Ng}	MKD//MKD
5c-e	V V M M / w-S^{Pn} V O Selah	CAN^2/MKD
6	C V S M / M / M / M V^{Ng}	CAN/Nom/Nom/MKD
7	S^{Pn} Comp M / M V-o // M V-o Selah	Nom/MKD//MKD
8	V-o w-V-o M R V / V M M	CAN^{3R}/CAN
9	V^{Ng} M / M E^{Ng} S / Comp S Inf / V^{Ng} M	CAN/Nom/Nom/CAN
10	S Comp / w-N S V-o	Nom/MKD
11	V M w-V [Voc] // w-V [Voc]	CAN^2//CAN
Ps. 33		
1	V [Voc] M / M S Comp	CAN/Nom
2	V M M // M V-M	CAN//DEF
3	V-M O / V Inf M	CAN/CAN
4	C-Comp S // w-S Comp	Nom//Nom
5	V^{Pt} O w-O / O V S	Ptcp/MKD
6	M S V // M S	DEF//Gap
7	V^{Pt} M O // V^{Pt} M O	Ptcp//Ptcp
8	V M S // M V S	CAN//DEF
9	C S^{Pn} V w-V // S^{Pn} V w-V	MKD-CAN//MKD-CAN
10	S V O // V O	MKD//CAN
11	S M V // S M	MKD//Gap
12	Comp S R-S Comp // O [R] V M M	Nom^2//Nom-CAN^R
13	M V S / V O //	MKD/CAN//

Appendix 2

14	M V / M	MKD/Nom
15	V^{Pt} M O / V^{Pt} M	Ptcp/Ptcp
16	Ng-S V^{Pt} M // S V^{Ng} M	Ptcp//CAN
17	Comp S M // w-M V^{Ng}	Nom//DEF
18	H S Comp / Comp	Nom/Nom
19	Inf M O // w-Inf-o M	Inf//Inf
20	C-M V S // C M V	MKD//MKD
21	V-S [Voc] Comp / C V M	CAN/CAN
Ps. 34		
2	V O M // M S Comp	CAN//Nom
3	M V S / V S w-V	MKD/CAN^2
4	V O M // w-V O M	CAN//CAN
5	V O w-V / w-M w-V	CAN^2/MKD
6	V M w-V // w-S V^{Ng}	CAN^2//DEF
7	S V w-S V / w-M V-o	MKD^2/MKD
8	V^{Pt} S / M w-V-o	Ptcp/CAN
9	V w-V C Comp S / Comp S [R] V M	CAN^2-Nom/Nom/CAN^R
10	V O [Voc] / C-E^{Ng} S Comp	CAN/Nom
11	S w-S V / w-S^{Pt} V^{Ng} O	MKD/MKD
12	V-[Voc] V-M / O V-o	CAN^2/MKD
13	Q-S V^{Pt} O // S V^{Pt} O Inf O	Ptcp//Ptcp
14	V O M // w-O M(Inf O)	CAN//Gap
15	V M w-V O // V O w-V-o	CAN^2//CAN^2
16	S Comp // w-S Comp	Nom//Nom
17	S Comp / Inf M O	Nom/Inf
18	V w-S V / w-M V-o	CAN-MKD/MKD
19	Comp S M / w-O V	Nom//MKD
20	Comp S / w-M V-o S	Nom/MKD
21	V^{Pt} O / S V^{Ng}	Ptcp/MKD
22	V O S // w-S V	CAN//DEF
23	V^{Pt} S O / w-V^{Ng} S^{Pt}	Ptcp/CAN
Ps. 35		
1	V [Voc] O // V O	CAN//CAN
2	V O w-O / w-V M	CAN/CAN
3	w-V O w-O / M / V M / Comp S^{Pn}	CAN/Nom/CAN/Nom
4	V w-V / S^{Pt} // V M w-V / S^{Pt}	CAN^2/Nom//CAN^2/Nom
5	V Comp / w-S^{Pt} V	CAN/Ptcp
6	V S Comp w-Comp / w-S V^{Pt}-o	CAN/Ptcp
7	C-M V M O // M V M	MKD//MKD
8	V-o S [R] V^{Ng} // S R V V-o // M V M	CAN^{2R}//DEF//DEF
9	w-S V M // V M	MKD//CAN
10ab	S V / [Voc] Q Comp /	MKD/Nom/
10cd	V^{Pt} O M // w-O O M	Ptcp//Nom
11	V S / R V^{Ng} V-o	CAN/MKD-CAN^R
12	V-o O M / S Comp	CAN/Nom
13	w-S^{Pn} M S Comp // V M O // w-S M V	Nom//CAN//DEF
14	M M V // M M(V^{Pt}) V	MKD//MKD
15a-c	w-M V w-V / V M S /	MKD-CAN/CAN/
15d-f	w-V^{Ng} / V w-V^{Ng}	CAN/CAN^2
16	M / Inf M O	Nom/Inf
17	[Voc] Q V / V O M // M O	CAN/CAN//Gap
18	V-o M // M V-o	CAN//DEF
19	V^{Ng}-M S // S M V-O	CAN//DEF
20	C Ng O V / w-M O V	MKD/MKD
21	w-V M O / V [Exc Exc] V S	CAN/CAN^2
22	V [Voc] V^{Ng} // [Voc] V^{Ng} M	CAN^2//CAN
23	V w-V M / [Voc] Comp?	CAN^2//Nom
24	V-o M [Voc] / w-V^{Ng}-M	CAN/CAN
25	V^{Ng} M [Exc] Comp // V^{Ng} V-o	CAN//CAN^2
26	V w-V M / S^{Pt} // V O w-O / S^{Pt}	CAN^2/Nom//CAN/Nom
27	V w-V S / w-V M / V S	CAN^2/CAN/CAN
28	w-S V O // M O	MKD//Gap
Ps. 36		
2	S M Comp / E^{Ng} S Comp	Nom/Nom

3	C-V M M / Inf O Inf	CAN/Inf
4	S Comp w-Comp / V Inf Inf	Nom/CAN
5	O V M / V M / O V^{Ng}	MKD//DEF//MKD
6	[Voc] Comp S // S Comp	Nom//Nom
7ab	S Comp // S Comp	Nom//Nom
7c	O w-O V [Voc] //	MKD//
8	Q-Comp S [Voc]? // w-S M V	Nom//MKD
9	V M // w-O V-o	CAN//DEF
10	C-Comp S / M V O	Nom/MKD
11	V O M // w-O M	CAN//Gap
12	V^{Ng}-o S // w-S V^{Ng}-o	CAN//DEF
13	M V S / V w-V Inf	CAN/CAN^2
Ps. 37		
1	V^{Ng} M // V^{Ng} M	CAN//CAN
2	C M M V // w-M V	MKD//MKD
3	V M w-V O / V O w-V O	CAN^2/CAN^2
4	w-V M / w-V M O	CAN/CAN
5	V M O // w-V M w-S^{Pt} V	CAN//CAN-MKD
6	w-S M O // w-O M	CAN//Gap
7	V M w-V M / V^{Ng} M / M	CAN^2/CAN/Nom
8	V M w-V O / V^{Ng} P-Inf	CAN^2/CAN
9	C-S V / w-N S^{Ph} V-O	MKD/MKD
10	w-M w-E^{Ng} S / w-V M w-E^{Ng}	Nom/CAN-Nom
11	w-S V-O / w-V M	MKD/CAN
12	V^{Pt} S M // w-V^{Pt} M O	Ptcp//Ptcp
13	S V-M / C-V C-V S	MKD/CAN^2
14ab	O V S // w-V O	DEF//CAN
14cd	Inf O w-O // Inf O	Inf//Inf
15	S V M // w-S V	MKD//MKD
16	Comp S M / M	Nom/Nom
17	C S V / w-V^{Pt} O S	MKD/Ptcp
18	V^{Pt} S O // w-S M V	Ptcp//DEF
19	V^{Ng} M // w-M V	CAN//DEF
20	C S V / w-S Comp / V M V	MKD/Nom/CAN^2
21	V^{Pt} S w-V^{Ng} / w-S V^{Pt} w-V^{Pt}	Ptcp-CAN/Ptcp^2
22	C S^{Pt} V O / w-S^{Pt} V	MKD/MKD
23	M S V // w-O V	DEF//DEF
24	C-V V^{Ng} / C-S V^{Pt} O	CAN^2/Ptcp
25	Comp V P-V / w-V^{Ng} O w-O	MKD-CAN/CAN
26	M V^{Pt} w-V^{Pt} / w-S Comp	Ptcp^2/Nom
27	V M w-V-O / w-V M	CAN^2/CAN
28	C S V^{Pt} O / w-V^{Ng} O / M V / w-S V	Ptcp/CAN/MKD/MKD
29	S V-O // w-V M M	MKD/CAN
30	S V O // w-S V O	MKD//MKD
31	S Comp / V^{Ng} S	Nom/CAN
32	V^{Pt} S M / w-V^{Pt} Inf-o	Ptcp/Ptcp
33	S V^{Ng}-o M / w-V^{Ng} M(Inf)	MKD/CAN
34	V M w-V O / w-V-o Inf O / M(Inf S) V	CAN^2/CAN/CAN
35	V O / w-V^{Pt} M	CAN/Ptcp
36	w-V w-H E^{Ng} / w-V-o w-V^{Ng}	CAN-Nom/CAN^2
37	V-O // w-V O / C-S Comp	CAN//CAN/Nom
38	w-S V M // S V	MKD//MKD
39	w-S Comp / Comp M	Nom/Nom
40	w-V-o S w-V-o // V-o M w-V-o / C-V O	CAN^2//CAN^2/CAN
Ps. 38		
2	[Voc] M^{Ng} V-o // w-M V-o	MKD//MKD
3	C-S V M // w-V M S	DEF//CAN
4	E^{Ng}-S Comp M // E^{Ng}-S Comp M	Nom//Nom
5	C S V O / M V M	MKD/MKD
6	V V S / M	CAN^2/Nom
7	V V M // M V^{Pt} V	CAN//DEF
8	C S V M / w-E^{Ng} S M	MKD/Nom
9	V w-V M / V M	CAN^2/CAN
10	[Voc] Comp S // w-S M V^{Ng}	Nom//DEF

11	S V // V S / w-N P-S^{Pn} E^{Ng} Comp	DEF//CAN/Nom
12	S w-S M V // w-S M V	MKD//MKD
13	w-V S^{Pt} // w-S^{Pt} V O // w-O M V	CAN//DEF//DEF
14	w-S^{Pn} M V^{Ng} // w-M V^{Ng}-O	MKD?//MKD?
15	w-V Comp // w-E^{Ng} Comp S	CAN//Nom
16	C-M [Voc] V / S^{Pn} V [Voc]	MKD/MKD
17	C-V C-V-M // M(Inf S) M V	CAN^2/CAN
18	C-S^{Pn} Comp / w-S Comp M	Nom/Nom
19	C-O V // V M	DEF//CAN
20	w-S V // w-V S^{Pt} //	MKD//DEF//
21	S(V^{Pt} O M) / V-o M	Ptcp/MKD
22	V^{Ng}-o [Voc] // [Voc] V^{Ng} M	CAN//CAN
23	V M [Voc]	CAN
Ps. 39		
2	V V O M M / V M M M	CAN^2/CAN
3	V Comp V M / w-S V	CAN^2/MKD
4	V-S M // M V-S / V M	CAN//DEF/CAN
5	V-o [Voc] O w-O // V Q-Comp S^{Pn}	CAN//CAN-Nom
6	H O V O // w-S Comp M / P Comp S V^{Pt} Selah	MKD//Nom/Ptcp
7	P-M V-S // P-O V / V w-V^{Ng} Q V-o	MKD//MKD/CAN^3
8	w-M Q-V [Voc] / N Comp S^{Pn}	CAN/Nom
9	M V-o / O V^{Ng}-o	MKD/MKD
10	V V^{Ng}-O / C S^{Pn} V	CAN^2/MKD
11	V M O / M S^{Pn} V	CAN/MKD?
12	M V O / w-V M O / P Comp S Selah	MKD/CAN/Nom
13a-c	V-O [Voc] // w-O V // M V^{Ng}	CAN//DEF//DEF
13de	C Comp S^{Pn} M // Comp M	Nom//Nom
14	V M w-V / C V w-E^{Ng}	CAN^2/CAN-Nom
Ps. 40		
2	Inf V O / w-V M w-V O	CAN/CAN^2
3ab	w-V-o M / M /	CAN/Nom/
3cd	w-V M O // V O	CAN//CAN
4ab	w-V M O // O M	CAN//Nom
4cd	V S w-V / w-V M	CAN^2/CAN
5	Comp S R-V O O / w-V^{Ng} M	CAN^R/CAN
6ab	O V S^{Pn} [Voc] O / w-O M	MKD/Nom
6cd	Inf^{Ng} M / w-V V M(Inf)	Inf/CAN^2
7	O w-O V^{Ng} // O V M // O w-O V^{Ng}	MKD//MKD//MKD
8	C V H-V / M Comp M	CAN^2/Nom
9	Inf-O [Voc] V / w-S Comp	MKD/Nom
10	V O M / H O V^{Ng} / [Voc] S^{Pn} V	CAN/MKD/MKD
11	O V^{Ng} M // O w-O V // V^{Ng} O w-O M	MKD//MKD//DEF
12	S^{Pn} [Voc] V^{Ng} O M / S w-S M V-o	MKD/MKD
13	C V-M S / V-o S w-V^{Ng} Inf / V M / w-S V-o	CAN/CAN^2/CAN/MKD
14	V [Voc] Inf-o // [Voc] M V	CAN//DEF
15	V w-V M S^{Pt} Inf-o // V M w-V S	CAN^2//CAN^2
16	V M / V^{Pt} M Exc Exc	CAN/Ptcp
17	V w-V M S^{Pt} / V M V S	CAN^2/CAN^2
18ab	S^{Pn} Comp w-Comp / S V M	Nom/MKD
18cd	Comp w-Comp S^{Pn} / [Voc] V^{Ng}	Nom/CAN
Ps. 41		
2	Comp S^{Pt} M / M V-o S	Nom/CAN
3	S V-o w-V-o V M / w-V^{Ng}-o M	MKD-CAN^2/CAN
4	S V-o M / O V M	MKD/MKD
5	S^{Pn}-V [Voc] V-o / V O C-V M	MKD-CAN/CAN^2
6	S V O M / Q V w-V S	MKD/CAN^2
7	w-C-V Inf M V / S V-O M / V M V	CAN^2/MKD/CAN^2
8	M M V S^{Pt} // M V O M	MKD//MKD
9	S V M / w-R V V^{Ng} Inf	MKD/CAN^{R2}
10	P-S / R-V M V^{Pt} O / V M O	Nom/CAN^R/MKD
11	w-S^{Pn} [Voc] V-o w-V-o / w-V M	MKD-CAN/CAN
12	M V C-V M / C V^{Ng} S M	MKD-CAN/CAN
13	w-S^{Pn} M V M / w-V-o M M	MKD/CAN
14	Comp S M w-M / Exc w-Exc	Nom/Nom

Ps. 42		
2	M(S V M) / M S V M [Voc]	MKD/MKD
3	V S M M / Q V w-V O?	CAN/CAN²
4	V-M S Comp M w-M / M(Inf M M) Q S	CAN/Inf-Nom
5a-c	O V w-V M O / C V M /	MKD-CAN/CAN/
5de	V M / M Comp	CAN/Nom
6	Q-V [Voc] / w-V M / V M / C-M V-o O	CAN/CAN/CAN/MKD
7	M S V / C V-o M w-M	DEF/CAN
8	S V^Pt M / S w-S M V	Ptcp/MKD
9	M V S O / w-M S Comp S	MKD/Nom
10	V M Q V-o / Q-V^Pt V M	CAN²/MKD
11	M M V-o S / M(Inf M M) Q S	MKD/Inf-Nom
12	Q-V [Voc] / w-Q-V M / V M / C-M V-o O	CAN/CAN/CAN/MKD
Ps. 43		
1	V-o [Voc] / w-V O M // M V-o	CAN/CAN//DEF
2	C-S^Pn [Voc] / Q V-o / Q-V^Pt V M	Nom/CAN/MKD
3	V-O w-O S^Pn V-o / V-o M w-M	CAN-MKD/CAN
4	w-V M M / w-V-o M [Voc]	CAN/CAN
5	Q-V [Voc] / w-Q-V M / V M / C-M V-o O	CAN/CAN/CAN/MKD
Ps. 44		
2ab	[Voc] M V / S V-M	MKD/MKD
2cd	O [R] V M M	Nom-CAN^[R]
3	S^Pn S? O V w-V-o // V O w-V-o	DEF-CAN//CAN²
4ab	C M^Ng V O // w-S V^Ng M	MKD//MKD
4cd	C-S w-S w-S / C V-o	Nom/CAN
5	S^Pn Comp [Voc] / V O	Nom/CAN
6	M O V // M V O	MKD//MKD
7	C M^Ng V // w-S V^Ng-o	MKD//MKD
8	C V-o M // w-O V	CAN//DEF
9	M V M // w-O M V Selah	MKD//MKD
10	P-V w-V-o / w-V^Ng M	CAN²/CAN
11	V-o M M // w-S V M	CAN//DEF
12	V-o M // w-M V-o	CAN//DEF
13	V-O M // w-V^Ng M	CAN//CAN
14	V-o O M // O w-O M	CAN//Gap
15	V-o O M // O M	CAN//Gap
16	M S Comp // w-S? V-o	Nom//DEF
17	M // M	Nom//Nom
18	S V-o w-V^Ng-o / w-V^Ng M	MKD-CAN/CAN
19	V^Ng M S // w-V S M	CAN//CAN
20	C V-o M / w-V M M	CAN/CAN
21	C-V O / w-V O M	CAN/CAN
22	Q^Ng S V-O / C-S^Pn V^Pt O	MKD/Ptcp
23	C-M V M / V M	MKD/CAN
24	V Q V [Voc] // V V^Ng M	CAN²//CAN²
25	Q-O V / V O w-O	MKD/CAN²
26	C V M S // V M S	CAN//CAN
27	V M / w-V-o M	CAN/CAN
Ps. 45		
2	V S M / V^Pt S^Pn O M / S Comp	CAN/Ptcp/Nom
3	V M / V S M / C V-o S M	CAN/CAN/CAN
4	V-O M [Voc] / M w-M	CAN/Nom
5	w-M V V M w-M / w-V-o O S	MKD-CAN/CAN
6	S Comp / S M V / M	Nom/MKD/Nom
7	S [Voc] Comp // Comp S	Nom//Nom
8	V O // w-V O / C V-o S M M	CAN/CAN/CAN
9	S Comp w-Comp / M S V-o	Nom/MKD
10	S Comp / V S M M	Nom/CAN
11	V -[Voc] w-V w-V O / w-V O w-O	CAN³/CAN
12	w-V S O / C-S^Pn Comp w-V M	CAN/Nom-CAN
13	w-S Comp ? / O V S	Nom?/MKD
14	Comp S M / Comp S	Nom/Nom
15	M V M / S Comp S V^Pt M	MKD/Nom-Ptcp
16	V M w-M / V M	CAN/CAN

Appendix 2 307

17	Comp V S / V-o M M		MKD/CAN
18	V O M / C S V-o M		CAN/MKD
Ps. 46			
2	S M Comp w-Comp // Comp V^{Pt} M		Nom//Nom-CAN^R
3	C V^{Ng} M(Inf S) // w-M(Inf S M)		CAN-Inf//Inf
4	V V S / V-S M	*Selah*	CAN^2/CAN
5	N S V O / O		MKD/Nom
6	S Comp V^{Ng} / V-o S M		Nom-CAN/CAN
7	V S // V S // V M / V S		CAN//CAN/CAN^2
8	S Comp // Comp S	*Selah*	Nom//Nom
9	V-V O / R-V O M		CAN^2/CAN^R
10	V^{Pt} O M / O V // V O // O V M		Ptcp/MKD//DEF//MKD
11	V w-V / C-S^{Pn} Comp / V M // V M		CAN^2/Nom/CAN//CAN
12	S Comp // Comp S	*Selah*	Nom//Nom
Ps. 47			
2	[Voc] V-O // V M M		CAN//CAN
3	C-S Comp / Comp M		Nom/Nom
4	V O M // w-O M		CAN//Gap
5	V-M O / O R-V	*Selah*	CAN/CAN^R
6	V S M // S M		CAN//Gap
7	V O V // V M V		CAN^2//CAN^2
8	C Comp S / V M		Nom/CAN
9	V S M // S V M		CAN//DEF
10	S V / S / C Comp S / M V		MKD/Nom/Nom/MKD
Ps. 48			
2	Comp S w-Comp M / M M		Nom/Nom
3	Comp Comp S / S Comp Comp		Nom^2/Nom^2
4	S Comp / V M		Nom/CAN
5	C-H S V / V M		MKD/CAN
6	S^{Pn} V M V / V V		MKD^2/CAN^2
7	S V-o M // S M		MKD//Gap
8	M / V O		Nom/MKD
9	C V M V / M M / S V-o M	*Selah*	CAN-MKD/Nom/MKD
10	V [Voc] O / M		CAN/Nom
11	Comp [Voc] Comp S M / O V S		Nom^2/MKD
12	V S // V S / M		CAN//CAN/Nom
13	V O w-V-o / V O		CAN^2/CAN
14	V O M / V O / C V M		CAN/CAN/CAN
15	C S^{Pn} Comp M / S^{Pn} V-o M		Nom/MKD
Ps. 49			
2	V-O [Voc] // V [Voc]		CAN//CAN
3	[Voc] // [Voc]		Nom//Nom
4	S V O // w-S O		MKD//Gap
5	V M O // V M O		CAN//CAN
6	Q V M / S V-o		CAN/MKD
7	V^{Pt} M // w-M V		Ptcp//DEF
8	C? Inf^{Ng} V S // V^{Ng} M O		CAN?//CAN
9	w-V S / w-V M		CAN/CAN
10	w-V-M M / V^{Ng} O		CAN/CAN
11	C V S V // M S w-S V / w-V M O		CAN-MKD//MKD/CAN
12	S Comp M // Comp M / V M M		Nom//Nom/CAN
13	w-S M V^{Ng} / V M [R] V		MKD?/CAN^{2R}
14	S^{Pn} Comp / w-N? M V	*Selah*	Nom/MKD?
15ab	M M V / S V-o /		MKD/MKD/
15c-e	w-V M S M / w-S Comp? / w-S Comp M		CAN/Nom?/Nom
16	P-S V O M / C V-o	*Selah*	MKD/CAN
17	V^{Ng} C-V S // C-V O		CAN^2//CAN
18	C M^{Ng} V O / V^{Ng}M S		MKD/CAN
19	C-O M V / w-V-o C-V M		MKD/CAN^2
20	V M / M V^{Ng}-O		CAN/MKD
21	S Comp w-V^{Ng} / V M [R] V		Nom-CAN/ CAN^{2R}
Ps. 50			
1	S S S V w-V-O / M M		MKD-CAN/Nom
2	M S V		MKD

3	V S w-V^{Ng} / S-M V // w-M V M	CAN^2/MKD//MKD
4	V M M / w-M Inf O	CAN/Nom
5	V-M O / O(V^{Pt} O M)	CAN/Ptcp
6	w-V S O / C-S Comp Selah	CAN/Nom
7	V [Voc] w-V / [Voc] w-V M / Comp S^{Pn}	CAN^2//CAN/Nom
8	M^{Ng} V-o / w-S Comp M	MKD/Nom
9	V M O // M O	CAN//Gap
10	C-Comp S / S	Nom//Nom
11	V O // w-S Comp	CAN//Nom
12	C-V V^{Ng} M / C-Comp S w-S	CAN^2/Nom
13	Q-V O // w-O V	CAN//DEF
14	V M O // w-V M O	CAN//CAN
15	w-V-o M / V-o w-V-o	CAN/CAN^2
16	w-M V S / Q Inf O / w-V O M	MKD/Inf/CAN
17	w-S^{Pn} V O // w-V O M	MKD//CAN
18	C-V O w-V M // w-Comp S	CAN^2//Nom
19	O V M // w-S? V M	MKD//MKD
20	V M V // M V-o	CAN-MKD//MKD
21	O V w-V / V Inf-V Comp / V-o w-V M	MKD-CAN/CAN^2/CAN^2
22	V-P O [Voc] / C-V w-V^{Pt-Ng}	CAN/CAN-Ptcp
23	S^{Pt} V-o w-V O / V-o M	MKD-CAN/CAN
Ps. 51		
3	V-o [Voc] M // M V O	CAN//DEF
4	V V-o M // w-M V-o	CAN^2//DEF
5	C-O S^{Pn} V // w-S Comp M	MKD//Nom
6ab	M M V // w-O V /	MKD//MKD/
6cd	C V M // V M	CAN//CAN
7	H-M V // w-M V-o S	MKD//MKD
8	H-O V M // w-M? O V-o	MKD//MKD
9	V-o M w-V // V-o w-M V-o	CAN^2//CAN-MKD
10	V-o O w-O // V S [R] V	CAN//CAN$^{2[R]}$
11	V O M // w-O V	CAN//DEF
12	O V-M [Voc] // w-O V M	MKD//MKD
13	V^{Ng}-o M // w-O V^{Ng} M	CAN//DEF
14	V M O // w-M V-o	CAN//DEF
15	V O O // w-S M V	CAN//DEF
16	V-o M [Voc] / V S O	CAN/CAN
17	[Voc] O V / w-S V O	MKD/MKD
18	C V^{Ng} O w-V-o // O V^{Ng}	CAN^2//DEF
19	S Comp // O [Voc] V^{Ng}	Nom//DEF
20	V M O // V O	CAN//CAN
21	C V O O w-O // C V M O	CAN//CAN
Ps. 52		
3	Q-V M [Voc] // [Voc]? M	CAN//Gap?
4	O V S / M V^{Pt} O	MKD/Ptcp
5	V O M // O M(Inf O) Selah	CAN//Gap
6	V O [Voc]	CAN
7	P-S V-o M / V-o w-V-o M // w-V-o M Selah	MKD/CAN^2//CAN
8	w-V S w-V / w-M V	CAN^2/MKD
9ab	H S [R] V^{Ng} O O /	Nom-CAN$^{[R]}$/
9cd	w-V M // V M	CAN//CAN
10	w-S^{Pn} Comp M / V M M	Nom/CAN
11	V-o M C V / w-V O C-Comp M	CAN^2/CAN-Nom
Ps. 53		
2	V S M / E^{Ng} S / V w-V O / E^{Ng} S^{Pt}	CAN/Nom/CAN^2/Nom
3	S M V M / Inf Q-E S V^{Pt} O	DEF/Inf-Ptcp
4	S V M V / E^{Ng} S^{Pt} E^{Ng} P-S	MKD^2/ Nom^2
5	Q^{Ng} V S^{Pt} / V^{Pt} O [C] V O / O V^{Ng}	CAN/Ptcp-CAN/MKD
6	M V-O V^{Ng} S / C-S V O / V C-S V-o	CAN^2/MKD/CAN-MKD
7ab	Q V M O / M(Inf S O) /	CAN/Inf/
7cd	V S // V S	CAN//CAN
Ps. 54		
3	[Voc] M V-o // w-M V-o	MKD//MKD
4	[Voc] V O // V M	CAN//CAN

Appendix 2

5	C S V O // w-S V O / V^{Ng} O M	Selah	MKD//MKD/CAN
6	H S V^{Pt} M // S Comp		Ptcp//Nom
7	V O M / M V-o		CAN/MKD
8	M V-M / V O [Voc] C-Comp		MKD/CAN-Nom
9	C M V-o / w-M V S		MKD/MKD
Ps. 55			
2	V [Voc] O // w-V^{Ng} M		CAN//CAN
3	V M w-V-o / V M w-V /		CAN^2/CAN^2/
4	M M / C-V M O // w-M V-o		Nom/CAN//DEF
5	S V M // w-S V M //		MKD//MKD//
6	S w-S V M // w-V-o S		MKD//DEF
7	w-V Q-V-M O M / V w-V		CAN^2/CAN^2
8	H V Inf / V M	Selah	CAN/CAN
9	V OM / M M		CAN/Nom
10	V [Voc] V O / C-V O w-O M		CAN^2/CAN
11	M w-M V-o M / w-S w-S Comp		MKD/Nom
12	S Comp // w-V^{Ng} M S w-S		Nom//CAN
13a-c	C Ng-S [R] V-o w-V //		Nom-CAN$^{[R]2}$//
13d-f	Ng-S [R] M V w-V M		Nom-CAN$^{[R]2}$
14	w-S^{Pn} Comp M / Comp w-Comp		Nom/Nom^2
15	R M V O / M V M		MKD^R/MKD
16	V? S M / V M M / C-S Comp M		CAN?/CAN/Nom
17	S^{Pn} M V / w-S V-o		MKD/MKD
18	M w-M w-M V w-V / w-V O		MKD-CAN/CAN
19	V M O M / C-M? V Comp		CAN/MKD
20a-c	V S w-V-o / w-V^{Pt} M	Selah	CAN^2/CAN
20de	R E^{Ng} S M / w-V^{Ng} O		Nom/CAN
21	V O M / V O		CAN/CAN
22	V S w-Comp-S // V S M w-S^{Pn} Comp		CAN-Nom//CAN-Nom
23	V M O / w-S^{Pn} V-o / V^{Ng} M O M		CAN/MKD/CAN
24	w-S^{Pn} [Voc] V-o M / S V^{Ng} O /		MKD/MKD/
25	w-S^{Pn} V M		MKD
Ps. 56			
2	V-o [Voc] C V-o S / M S^{Pt} V-o		CAN^2/MKD
3	V S M / C-S V^{Pt} M M		CAN/Ptcp
4	M [R] V / S^{Pn} M V		CAN$^{[R]}$/MKD
5	M [R] V O / M V V^{Ng} / Q V S M		CAN$^{[R]}$/MKD-CAN/CAN
6	M O V // M S Comp		DEF//Nom
7	V V S^{Pn} // O V / C V O		CAN^2//DEF/CAN
8	M V-M // M O V		MKD//MKD
9	O V S^{Pn} / V O M / Q^{Ng} Comp		MKD/CAN/Nom
10	C V S M C V / O-V C-S Comp		CAN^5/MKD-Nom
11	M V O // M V O		MKD//MKD
12	M V V^{Ng} / Q-V S M		MKD-CAN/CAN
13	Comp [Voc] S / V O M		Nom/CAN
14	C V O M / Q^{Ng} S Comp / Inf M M		CAN/Nom/Inf
Ps. 57			
2	V-o [Voc] V-o / C M V S // M V / C V S		CAN^2/MKD//MKD/CAN
3	V M / M(V^{Pt} M)		CAN/Nom
4a-c	V O w-V-o / V O	Selah	CAN^2/CAN
4d	V S O w-O		CAN
5ab	S M V / V^{Pt} O /		MKD/Ptcp/
5cd	S Comp w-Comp // w-S Comp		Nom//Nom
6	V M [Voc] / Comp S		CAN/Nom
7	O V M / V S / V M O / V M	Selah	MKD/CAN/CAN/CAN
8	Comp S [Voc] // Comp S / V // w-V		Nom//Nom/CAN//CAN
9	V [Voc] // V [Voc] / V O		CAN//CAN/CAN
10	V-o M [Voc] // V-o M		CAN//CAN
11	C-Comp M S // M S		Nom//Gap
12	V M [Voc] // Comp S		CAN//Nom
Ps. 58			
2	Q-M [Voc]? O V // M V O		MKD//MKD
3	P-M O V // M O V		MKD//MKD
4	V S M // V M S		CAN//CAN

5	S-Comp M // M(S [R] V O)	Nom//Nom-CAN[R]
6	R V[Ng] M / V[Pt] O	CAN[R]/Ptcp
7	[Voc] V-O M // O V [Voc]	CAN//DEF
8	V M [R] V-M // V O C V	CAN[2(R)]//CAN[2]
9	C S [R] V V // S [R] V[Ng] O	CAN[(R) 2]//CAN[(R)]
10	C V S O / Comp Comp V-o	CAN/Nom-CAN
11	V S C-V O / O V M	CAN[2]/MKD
12	w-V S P-S Comp // P E-S V[Pt] M	CAN-Nom//Ptcp
Ps. 59		
2	V-o M [Voc] // M V-o	CAN//DEF
3	V-o M // w-M V-o /	CAN//DEF
4ab	C H V M // V M S /	CAN//CAN/
4c	Comp[Ng] w-Comp[Ng] [Voc]	Nom
5	M V w-V / V Inf-o w-V	MKD-CAN/CAN[2]
6	w-S[Pn] [Voc] / V Inf O / V[Ng] O Selah	Nom/MKD/CAN
7	V M V M / w-V O	CAN[2]/CAN
8	H V M / S Comp / C-Q V[Pt]	CAN/Nom/Ptcp
9	S[Pn] [Voc] V-M // V M	MKD//CAN
10	[Voc]? M V / C-S Comp	MKD/Nom
11	S V-o // S V-o M	MKD//MKD
12	V[Ng]-o C-V S / V-o M w-V-o [Voc]	CAN[2]/CAN[2]
13	S Comp S Comp / w-V M / w-M w-M [R] V	Nom[2]/CAN/Nom-CAN[R]
14	V M V M w-E[Ng] / w-V C-S V[Pt] M M Selah	CAN[2]-Nom/CAN-Ptcp
15	w-V M V M / w-V O	CAN[2]/CAN
16	S[Pn] V Inf / C V[Ng] w-V	MKD/CAN[2]
17	w-S[Pn] V O / w-V M O / C-V Comp M / w-Comp M	MKD/CAN/CAN/Nom
18	[Voc] M V / C-S Comp Comp	MKD/Nom
Ps. 60		
3	[Voc] V-o V-o / V V M	CAN[2]/CAN[2]
4	V O V-o / V O C-V	CAN[2]/CAN[2]
5	V O O // V-o O	CAN//CAN
6	V M O Inf / M Selah	CAN/Nom
7	C V S / V M w-V-o	CAN/CAN[2]
8	S V M / V V O // w-O V	MKD/CAN[2]//DEF
9ab	Comp S // w-Comp S /	Nom//Nom/
9cd	w-S Comp // S Comp //	Nom//Nom//
10	S Comp] M V O // M V	Nom]MKD//MKD
11	Q V-o O // Q V-o M	CAN//CAN
12	Q-S[Pn] [Voc] V-o / w-V[Ng] [Voc] M	MKD/CAN
13	V-M O M / w-Comp S	CAN/Nom
14	M V-O / w-S[Pn] V O	MKD/MKD
Ps. 61		
2	V [Voc] O // V O	CAN//CAN
3	M M V / M(Inf S) / M [R] V M V-o	MKD/Inf/CAN[R]-MKD
4	C-V Comp M / Comp M	CAN//Nom
5	V M // V M Selah	CAN//CAN
6	C-S[Pn] [Voc] V M / V O	MKD/CAN
7	O M V // S Comp	MKD//Nom
8	V M M / O w-O V V-o	CAN/MKD-CAN
9	M V O M / Inf O M	CAN/Inf
Ps. 62		
2	P M Comp S / Comp S	Nom/Nom
3	P-S[Pn] Comp w-Comp / Comp V[Ng] M	Nom/Nom-CAN
4	Q V M / V S / M M	CAN/CAN/Nom
5	P M V Inf / V O / M V w-M V Selah	MKD/CAN/MKD[2]
6	P M Comp S / C-Comp S	Nom/Nom
7	P-S[Pn] Comp w-Comp / Comp V[Ng]	Nom/Nom-CAN
8	Comp S w-S / Comp? S Comp	Nom/Nom
9	V M M [Voc] // V-M O / S Comp-M Selah	CAN//CAN/Nom
10ab	P Comp S // Comp S	Nom//Nom
10cd	M Inf / S[Pn] Comp M	Inf/Nom
11ab	V[Ng] M // w-M V[Ng] /	CAN//DEF/
11cd	S C-V / V[Ng] O	MKD/CAN
12	M V S // M-O V / C S Comp	MKD//MKD-Nom

Appendix 2   311

13	w-Comp-[Voc] S / C-S^{Pn} V M M	Nom/MKD
Ps. 63		
2ab	[Voc] Comp S^{Pn} V-o /	Nom-CAN/
2c-e	V M S // V M S / M M	CAN//CAN/Nom
3	C M V-o / Inf O w-O	CAN/Inf
4	C-Comp S M / S V-o	Nom/MKD
5	C V-o M / M V O	CAN/MKD
6	M V S / M V-S	MKD/MKD
7	C-V-o M // M V-M	CAN//DEF
8	C-V Comp M // w-M V	CAN//DEF
9	V S M // M V S	CAN//DEF
10	w-S^{Pn} [R] M V O / V M	MKD$^{[R]}$?/CAN
11	V-o M / Comp V	CAN/MKD
12	w-S V M / V S^{Pt} / C V S	MKD/CAN/CAN
Ps. 64		
2	V-[Voc] O M / M V O //	CAN/MKD//
3	V-o M // M	DEF//Gap
4	R V M O / V O O	CAN^R/CAN
5	Inf M O / M V-o w-V^{Ng}	Inf/CAN^2
6	V-M O / V Inf O / V Q V-M	CAN/CAN/CAN^2
7	V-O V O / w-S w-S Comp	CAN^2/Nom
8	w-V-o S O / M V S	CAN/CAN
9	w-V-o M M? / V S^{Pt}	CAN/CAN
10	w-V S w-V O // w-O V	CAN^2//DEF
11	V S M w-V M // w-V S	CAN^2//CAN
Ps. 65		
2	M Comp S [Voc] M // w-M V-S //	Nom//MKD//
3	[Voc] M S V	MKD
4	S V M / N S^{Pn} V-o	MKD/MKD
5	Comp [R] V w-V V O / V M M	CAN$^{[R]}$/CAN
6	O M V-o [Voc] / [Voc]	MKD/Nom
7	V^{Pt} O M / V^{Pt} M	Ptcp/Ptcp
8	V^{Pt} O / O w-O	Ptcp/Nom
9	w-V S M // O w-O V	CAN//DEF
10a-c	V O w-V-o / M V-o	CAN^2/CAN
10d-f	S Comp M / V O C-M V-o	Nom/CAN^2
11ab	O Inf // Inf O //	Inf//Inf//
11cd	M V-o // O V	MKD//MKD
12	V O // w-S V O	CAN//DEF
13	V S // w-O S V	CAN//DEF
14	V S O // w-S V-O / V P-V	CAN//DEF/CAN^2
Ps. 66		
1	V M [Voc]	CAN
2	V O // V O O	CAN//CAN
3	V M Q-Comp S / M V M S	CAN-Ptcp/MKD
4	S V M // w-V M // V O Selah	MKD//CAN//CAN
5	V w-V O / Comp S M	CAN^2/Ptcp
6	V O M / M V M / M V-M	CAN/CAN/CAN
7	V^{Pt} M M / S M V / S^{Pt} V^{Ng} M Selah	Ptcp/MKD/MKD
8	V [Voc] O // w-V O	CAN//CAN
9	V^{Pt} O M / w-V^{Ng} M O	Ptcp/CAN
10	C-V-o [Voc] // V-o M	CAN//CAN
11	V-o M // V O M	CAN//CAN
12	V O M / V-M w-M / w-V-o M	CAN/CAN/CAN
13	V O M // V M O	CAN//CAN
14	R-V S // V-S M	CAN^R//CAN
15	O V-M // M O V M / O M Selah	MKD//MKD/Nom
16	V-V w-V [Voc] / R V M	CAN^3/CAN^R
17	M M-V / w-V M	MKD/CAN
18	O C-V M / V^{Ng} S	MKD/CAN
19	M V S // V M	CAN//CAN
20	Comp S / R V^{Ng} O w-O M	Nom/CAN^R
Ps. 67		
2	S V-o w-V-o / V O M Selah	MKD-CAN/CAN

3	Inf M O // M O		Inf//Gap
4	V-o S [Voc] // V-o S		CAN//CAN
5	V w-V S / C-V O M // O M V-o	Selah	CAN²/CAN//DEF
6	V-o S [Voc] // V-o S		CAN//CAN
7	S V O / V-o S		MKD/CAN
8	V-o S / w-V O S		CAN/CAN
Ps. 68			
2	V S V S // w-V S M		CAN²//CAN
3	M(Inf S) V // M(Inf S M) V S M		MKD//MKD
4	w-S V V M // w-V M		MKD-CAN/CAN
5a-c	V M // V O // V M		CAN//CAN//CAN
5de	Comp S w-V M		Nom-CAN
6	Comp w-Comp / S M		Nom/Nom
7	S V^{Pt} O M // V^{Pt} O M / P S V O		Ptcp//Ptcp/MKD
8	[Voc] M(Inf) M // M(Inf) M	Selah	Inf//Inf
9	S V // P-S V M // S M		MKD//MKD//Gap
10	O V [Voc] / N w-V S^{Pn} V-o		MKD/CAN-MKD
11	S V-M / V M M [Voc]		MKD/CAN
12	S V-O / S^{Pt} Comp		MKD/Nom
13	S V V / w-S V O		MKD-CAN/MKD
14	C-V M / S V^{Pt} M // w-S M		CAN/Ptcp//Gap
15	M(Inf S O M) / V M		Inf/CAN
16	Comp S // Comp S		Nom//Nom
17	Q V [Voc] O / [R] V M(Inf) / P-S V M		CAN/CAN$^{[R]}$/MKD
18	S Comp Comp / S V? O M		Nom/MKD?
19	V M V O / V O M / w-P M Inf S		CAN²/CAN/Nom-Inf
20	Comp S M / V-M S	Selah	Nom/CAN
21	S M Comp // w-Comp M S		Nom//Nom
22	P-S V O / O / V^{Pt} M		MKD/Nom/Ptcp
23	V S M V // V M		CAN-DEF//CAN
24	C V S M / N Comp S		CAN/Nom
25	V O [Voc] / O M		CAN/Nom
26	V S Comp S / M		CAN-Nom/Nom
27	M V O / O Comp		MKD/Nom
28	Comp S V^{Pt}-o / S S S		Nom-Ptcp/Nom
29	V [Voc] O / V [Voc] R V M		CAN/CAN^{2R}
30	M M] / M V S O		Nom]/MKD
31a-c	V O / O M / V^{Pt} M		CAN/Nom/Ptcp
31d	V O [R] O V		CAN-MKD$^{[R]}$
32	V S M // S V O M		CAN//DEF
33	[Voc] V M // V O	Selah	CAN//CAN
34	M(V^{Pt} M) / H V M		Ptcp/CAN
35	V O M Comp S // S Comp		CAN-Nom//Nom
36ab	Comp S M / N S^{Pn} V^{Pt} O w-O M		Ptcp/Ptcp
36c	Comp S		Nom
Ps. 69			
2	V-o [Voc] / C V S M		CAN/CAN
3ab	V M w-E^{Ng} S /		CAN-Nom/
3cd	V M // w-S V-o		CAN//DEF
4	V M(Inf) V S / V S V^{Pt} M		CAN²/CAN-Ptcp
5	V M S^{Pt} M / V S^{Pt} Comp M / R V^{Ng} C V		CAN/CAN-Nom/CAN^{R2}
6	[Voc] S^{Pn} V M // w-S M V^{Ng}		MKD//DEF
7	V^{Ng} M S^{Pt} [Voc] // V^{Ng} M S^{Pt} [Voc]		CAN-Nom//CAN-Nom
8	C-M V O // w-V S O		MKD//CAN
9	Comp V M // w-Comp M		MKD//Gap
10	C-S V-o / w-S V M		MKD/MKD
11	w-V M M / w-V Comp M		CAN/CAN
12	w-V O O / w-V M Comp		CAN/CAN
13	V M S^{Pt} / w-Comp		CAN/Nom
14	w-S^{Pn} S-Comp [Voc] M / [Voc] M V-o M		Nom/MKD
15	V-o M w-V^{Ng} / V M w-M		CAN²/CAN
16	V^{Ng}-o S // w-V^{Ng}-o S / w-V^{Ng}-M S O		CAN//CAN/CAN
17	V-o [Voc] C-Comp S / M V M		CAN-Nom/MKD
18	w-V^{Ng} O M / C-Comp-M / V V-o		CAN/Nom/CAN²

Appendix 2

19	V M V-o // M V-o	CAN²//DEF
20	S^Pn V O w-O w-O / Comp S	MKD/Nom
21ab	S V O w-V /	MKD-CAN/
21c-f	w-V M w-E^Ng // w-M w-V^Ng	CAN-Nom//Gap-CAN
22	w-V M O // w-M V-o O	CAN//DEF
23	V-S M M // w-M M	CAN/Gap
24	V S M(Inf) // w-O M V	CAN//DEF
25	V-M O // w-S V-o	CAN//DEF
26	V-S Comp // Comp V^Ng S^Pt	CAN//DEF
27	C-S^Pn R-V V // w-M V	MKD-CAN^R//MKD
28	V-O M // w-V^Ng M	CAN//CAN
29	V M // w-M V^Ng	CAN//DEF
30	w-S^Pn Comp w-V^Pt / S [Voc] V-o	Nom-Ptcp/MKD
31	V O M // w-V-o M	CAN//CAN
32	w-V M M / Comp	CAN/Nom
33	V S V / [Voc] w-V S	CAN²/CAN
34	C-V^Pt M S // w-O V^Ng	Ptcp//DEF
35	V-o S w-S / S w-S	CAN/Nom
36	C S V O // w-V O / w-V M w-V-o	MKD//CAN/CAN^R
37	S V-o // w-S^Pt V-M	MKD//MKD
Ps. 70		
2	[Voc] Inf-o // [Voc] Inf-o V	Gap//DEF
3	V w-V S^Pt // V M w-V S	CAN²//CAN²
4	V M / V^Pt Exc Exc	CAN/Ptcp
5	V w-V M S // w-V M (V S) S	CAN²//CAN(CAN)
6ab	w-S^Pn Comp w-Comp / [Voc] V-M	Nom/CAN
6cd	Comp w-Comp S^Pn / [Voc] V^Ng	Nom/CAN
Ps. 71		
1	M-[Voc] V / V^Ng M	MKD/CAN
2	M V-o w-V-o / V-M O w-V-o	MKD-CAN/CAN²
3	V M Comp Inf? M / V Inf-o / C-Comp w-Comp S^Pn	CAN/CAN/Nom
4	[Voc] V-o M / M	CAN/Nom
5	C-S^Pn Comp[Voc] / [Voc] Comp M	Nom/Nom
6	M V M / M S^Pn Comp / Comp S M	MKD/Nom/Nom
7	Comp V M / w-S^Pn Comp	MKD/Nom
8	V S O / M O	CAN/Nom
9	V^Ng-o M // M(Inf S) V^Ng-o	CAN//DEF
10	C-V S M // w-S^Pt V M	CAN//DEF
11	Inf S V-o / V w-V-o / C-E^Ng S^Pt	Inf-MKD/CAN²/Nom
12	[Voc] V M // [Voc] M V	CAN//CAN
13	V V S^Pt // V O w-O S^Pt	CAN²//CAN
14	w-S^Pn M V / V M	MKD/CAN
15	S V O / M O / C V^Ng O	MKD/Nom/CAN
16	V M // V O M	CAN//CAN
17	[Voc] V-o M / w-M V O	CAN/MKD
18a	w-P M [Voc] V^Ng /	CAN/
18b-d	C-V O M // M(S [R] V) O	CAN//Gap-CAN^[R]
19	w-S [Voc] Comp / R-V O / [Voc] Q Comp	Nom/CAN^R/Nom
20	R V-o O / V V-o / M V V-o	CAN^R/CAN/MKD
21	V O / w-V V-o	CAN/CAN
22	P-S^Pn V-o M O [Voc] // V M M [Voc]	MKD//CAN
23	V S C V-M // w-S R V	CAN²/Nom-CAN^R
24	P-S M V O / C-V C-V S^Pt	MKD/CAN²
Ps. 72		
1	[Voc] O M V // w-O M	DEF//Gap
2	V O M // w-O M	CAN//Gap
3	V S O M // w-S M	CAN//Gap
4	V O // V O / w-V O	CAN//CAN/CAN
5	V-o M / w-M M	CAN/Nom
6	V M M / M	CAN/Nom
7	V-M S // w-S M	CAN//Gap
8	w-V M M / w-M M	CAN//Gap
9	M V S // w-S O V	CAN//DEF
10	S O V // S O V	MKD//MKD

11	w-V-M S // S V-o	CAN//DEF
12	C-V O V^{Pt} / w-O w-O(w-E^{Ng}-S^{Pt} M)	CAN/Nom^2
13	V M // w-O V	CAN//DEF
14	M w-M V O / w-V S M	MKD/CAN
15	w-V w-V-M M / w-V M M // M V-o	CAN^2/CAN//DEF
16ab	V S Comp // M V /	CAN//DEF/
16cd	Comp S / w-V M M	Nom/CAN
17ab	V S Comp // M V S /	CAN//DEF/
17cd	w-V M // S V-o	CAN//DEF
18	Comp S // V^{Pt} O M	Nom/Ptcp
19ab	w-Comp S M / w-V S O	Nom/CAN
19cd	Exc w-Exc	Nom-Nom
Ps. 73		
1	P-Comp M S / M	Nom/Nom
2	w-S^{Pn} M V S // M V S	MKD//MKD
3	C-V M // O V	CAN//DEF
4	C E^{Ng} S Comp / w-Comp S	Nom/Nom
5	Comp E^{Ng} // w-M V^{Ng}	Nom//MKD
6	C Comp S // V-O O M	Nom//CAN
7	V M S / V S	CAN/CAN
8	V w-V M // O M V	CAN//DEF
9	V M O // w-S V M	CAN//DEF
10	C V S M / w-S V M	CAN/MKD
11	w-V Q V-S // w-E S Comp	CAN^2//Nom
12	H-S^{Pn} Comp / Comp V-O	Nom/Nom-CAN
13	P-M V M // w-V M O	MKD//DEF
14	w-V Comp M // w-Comp M	CAN//Gap
15	C-V V M / H O V	CAN^2/MKD
16	w-V Inf O / Comp S^{Pn} M	CAN/Nom
17	C-V M / V M	CAN/CAN
18	P M V M // V M	MKD//DEF
19	Q V Comp M / V V M	CAN/CAN^2
20	M M(Inf) // [Voc] M(Inf) O V	Inf//Inf-MKD
21	C V S // w-S V	CAN//DEF
22	w-S^{Pn} Comp w-V^{Ng} // Comp V M	Nom-CAN//DEF
23	w-S^{Pn} M Comp / V M	Nom/CAN
24	M V-o / w-C M V-o	MKD/MKD
25	Q-Comp M // w-M V^{Ng} M	Nom//MKD
26	V S w-S / Comp w-Comp S M	CAN/Nom
27	C-H S V // V O M	DEF//CAN
28	w-S^{Pn} S M-Comp / V M O / Inf O	Nom/CAN/Inf
Ps. 74		
1	Q [Voc] V M / V S M	CAN/CAN
2	V O [R] M / V O / O R V M	CAN$^{2[R]}$/CAN/Nom-CAN^R
3	V O M / O-V S M	CAN/MKD
4	V S M / V O O	CAN/CAN
5	V M(V^{Pt} M / M O)	CAN/Nom
6	w-M O M / w-M V	Nom/MKD
7	V M O // M V O	CAN//DEF
8	V M V M / V O M	CAN^2/CAN
9	O V^{Ng} E^{Ng}-M S / w-Comp^{Ng} S(V^{Pt} O)	MKD-Nom/Nom-Ptcp
10	Q V [Voc] S // V S O M	CAN//CAN
11	Q V O w-O // M V	CAN//DEF
12	S Comp M / V^{Pt} O M	Nom/Ptcp
13	S^{Pn} V M O // V O M	MKD//CAN
14	S^{Pn} V O // V-o O M	MKD//CAN
15	S^{Pn} V O w-O // S^{Pn} V O	MKD//MKD
16	Comp S P-Comp S / S^{Pn} V O w-O	Nom^2/MKD
17	S^{Pn} V O // N S^{Pn} V-o	MKD//MKD
18	V-O S V [Voc] // w-S V O	CAN-MKD//MKD
19	V^{Ng} M O // O V^{Ng} M	CAN//DEF
20	V M / C V S O	CAN/CAN
21	V^{Ng} S V^{Pt} / S w-S V O	CAN/MKD
22	V [Voc] V O / V O M M	CAN^2/CAN

Appendix 2 315

23	V^{Ng} O / S V^{Pt} M	CAN/Ptcp
Ps. 75		
2	V M [Voc] / V w-Comp S / V O	CAN/CAN-Nom/CAN
3	C V O / S^{Pn} M V	CAN/MKD
4	V^{Pt} S w-S / S^{Pn} V O Selah	Ptcp/MKD
5	V M V^{Ng} // M V^{Ng} O	CAN^2//Gap-CAN
6	V^{Ng} M O // V M	CAN//CAN
7	C Ng Comp w-Comp / w-Ng Comp S	Nom/Nom
8	C-S V^{Pt} / O V w-O V	Ptcp/MKD^2
9a-c	C S Comp / w-S V Comp M /	Nom/MKD-Nom/
9d-f	w-V M / P-O V V S	CAN/MKD-CAN
10	w-S^{Pn} V M // V M	MKD//CAN
11	w-O V / V S	DEF/CAN
Ps. 76		
2	V M S // M Comp S	CAN//Nom
3	w-V Comp S // w-S Comp	CAN//Gap
4	M V O / O w-O w-O Selah	CAN?/Nom
5	V^{Pt} S^{Pn} Comp M	Ptcp-Nom
6	V S V O / w-V S O	CAN^2/CAN
7	M [Voc] / V^{Pt} w-S w-S	Nom/Ptcp
8	S^{Pn} Comp S^{Pn} / w-Q-V M M	Nom/CAN
9	M V O / S V w-V	MKD/MKD-CAN
10	M(Inf M S) / Inf O Selah	Inf/Inf
11	C-S V-o / O V	MKD/MKD
12	V w-V M / S V O M	CAN^2/MKD
13	V O / Comp M	CAN/Ptcp
Ps. 77		
2	S Comp w-V // S Comp w-V M	Nom-CAN?//Nom-CAN?
3	M O V / S M V w-V^{Ng} / V Inf S	MKD/MKD-CAN/CAN
4	V O w-V // V w-V S Selah	CAN^2//CAN^2
5	V O / V w-V^{Ng}	CAN/CAN^2
6	V O / O	CAN/Nom
7	V O M / M V w-V S	CAN/MKD-CAN
8	Q-M V S / w-V^{Ng} Inf M	MKD/CAN
9	Q-V M S // V S M	CAN//CAN
10	Q-V Inf S // C-V M O Selah	CAN//CAN
11	w-V Comp S^{Pn} / Comp	CAN-Nom/Nom
12	V O // C-V M O	CAN//CAN
13	w-V M // w-M V	CAN//DEF
14	[Voc] Comp S / Q-Comp M	Nom/Nom
15	S^{Pn} Comp V^{Pt} O / V M O	Nom/CAN
16	V M O / O w-O Selah	CAN/Nom
17	V-o S [Voc] // V-o S V / P V S	CAN//CAN^2/CAN
18	V O S // O V S // P-S V	CAN//DEF//DEF?
19	S Comp // V S O / V w-V S	Nom/CAN/CAN^2
20	Comp S // w-S Comp / w-S V^{Ng}	Nom//Nom/MKD
21	V M O / M	CAN/Nom
Ps. 78		
1	V [Voc] O // V O M	CAN//CAN
2	V M O // V O M	CAN//CAN
3	R V w-V-o / w-S V-M	CAN^{R2}/MKD
4	V^{Ng} M / M V^{Pt} O / w-O w-O R V	CAN/Ptcp/Nom-CAN^R
5ab	w-V O M // w-O V M /	CAN//DEF/
5cd	R V O / Inf-o M	CAN^R/Inf
6	C V S S [R] V / V w-V M	CAN-Nom-CAN$^{[R]}$/CAN^2
7	w-V M O / w-V^{Ng} O / w-O V	CAN/CAN/MKD
8ab	w-V^{Ng} Comp Comp /	CAN-Nom/
8cd	S [R] V^{Ng} O / w-V^{Ng} M S	Nom-CAN$^{[R]}$/CAN
9	S(V^{Pt} V^{Pt}-O) V M	MKD
10	V^{Ng} O // w-M V Inf	CAN//DEF
11	w-V O / w-O R V-o	CAN/Nom-CAN^R
12	M V O / M M	MKD/Nom
13	V O w-V-o / w-V-O M	CAN^2/CAN
14	w-V-o M M / w-M M	CAN/Nom

15	V O M / w-V M	CAN/CAN
16	w-V O M // w-V M O	CAN//CAN
17	w-V M Inf-M // Inf O M	CAN-Inf//Inf
18	w-V-O M / Inf-O M	CAN/Inf
19	w-V M V / Q-V S Inf O M	CAN^2/CAN
20a-c	C V-O w-V S // w-S V /	CAN^2//CAN/
20de	Q-P-O V Inf // C-V O M	MKD//DEF
21	C V S w-V / w-S V M // w-P-S V M	CAN^2/MKD//MKD
22	C V^{Ng} M // w-V^{Ng} M	CAN//CAN
23	w-V O M // w-O V	CAN//DEF
24	w-V M O Inf // w-O V M	CAN//DEF
25	O V S // O V M M	MKD//MKD
26	V O M // w-V M O	CAN//CAN
27	w-V M M O // w-M O	CAN//Gap
28	w-V M / M	CAN/Nom
29	w-V w-V M // w-O V M	CAN^2//DEF
30	V^{Ng} M // M S Comp	CAN//Nom
31	w-S V M / w-V M // w-O V	MKD/CAN//DEF
32	M V-M / w-V^{Ng} M	MKD/CAN
33	w-V-M O // w-O M	CAN//Gap
34	C-V-o w-V-o / w-V w-V-O	CAN^2/CAN^2
35	w-V C-S Comp // w-S Comp	CAN-Nom//Nom
36	w-V-o M // w-M V-M	CAN//DEF
37	w-S V^{Ng} M / w-V^{Ng} M	MKD/CAN
38a-c	w-S^{Pn} Comp / V O w-V^{Ng} /	Nom/CAN^2/
38de	w-V Inf O // w-V^{Ng} O	CAN//CAN
39	w-V C-Comp S^{Pn} / S V^{Pt} w-V^{Ng}	CAN-Nom/Ptcp-CAN
40	Q V-o M // V-o M	CAN//CAN
41	w-V w-V O // w-O V	CAN^2//DEF
42	V^{Ng} O / O R-V-o M	CAN/Nom-CAN^R
43	R-V M O // w-O M	CAN^R//Gap
44	w-V M O // w-O V^{Ng}	CAN//DEF
45	V M O w-V-o // w-S w-V-o	CAN^2//DEF
46	w-V M O // w-O M	CAN//Gap
47	V M O // w-O M	CAN//Gap
48	w-V M O // w-O M	CAN//Gap
49	V-M O / O w-O w-O / O	CAN/Nom/Nom
50	V O M / V^{Ng} M O / w-O M V	CAN/CAN/MKD
51	w-V O M // O M	CAN//Gap
52	w-V M O // w-V-o M M	CAN//CAN
53	w-V-o M w-V^{Ng} / w-O V S	CAN^2/MKD
54	w-V-o M / M [R]? V S	CAN/Nom-$CAN^{[R]}$
55	w-V M O / w-V-o M O / w-V M O	CAN/CAN/CAN
56	w-V w-V O // w-O V^{Ng}	CAN^2//DEF
57	w-V w-V M // V M	CAN^2//CAN
58	w-V-o M // w-M w-V-o	CAN//DEF
59	V S w-V / w-V M M	CAN^2/CAN
60	w-V O / O [R] V M	CAN/Nom-$CAN^{[R]}$
61	w-V M O // w-O M	CAN//Gap
62	w-V M O // w-M V	CAN//DEF
63	O V-S / w-S V^{Ng} //	MKD/MKD//
64	S M V / w-S V^{Ng}	MKD/MKD
65	w-V M S / M(V^{Pt} M)	CAN/Ptcp
66	w-V-O M // O V M	CAN/MKD
67	w-V M // w-M V^{Ng}	CAN//DEF
68	w-V O / O R V	CAN/Nom-CAN^R
69	w-V M O / M [R] V-o M	CAN/Nom-$CAN^{[R]}$
70	w-V M / w-V-o M	CAN/CAN
71	M V-o Inf M / w-M	MKD-Inf/Nom
72	w-V-o M // w-M V-o	CAN//DEF
Ps. 79		
1	[Voc] V S M // V O // V O M	CAN//CAN//CAN
2	V O O M // O M	CAN/Gap
3	V O M M / w-E^{Ng} S^{Pt}	CAN/Nom

Appendix 2

4	V Comp M // Comp w-Comp M	CAN//Gap
5	Q [Voc] V M // V M S	Nom-CAN//CAN
6a-c	V O M R V^{Ng}-o //	CAN-Nom-CAN^R//
6de	w-M R M V^{Ng}	Nom-MKD^R
7	C V O // w-O V	CAN//DEF
8	V^{Ng}-M O / V V-o S / C V M	CAN/CAN^2/CAN
9	V-o [Voc] M // w-V-o w-V M M	CAN//CAN^2
10	Q V S Q S / V M M S	CAN-Nom/CAN
11	V M S / M V O	CAN/MKD
12	w-V M O M / O R V-o [Voc]	CAN/Nom-CAN^R
13	w-S^{Pn} (S w-S) / V M M // M V O	Nom/MKD//DEF
Ps. 80		
2	[Voc] V / V^{Pt} M O / [Voc] V /	CAN/Ptcp/CAN/
3	M] V O / w-V M M	Nom]CAN/CAN
4	[Voc] V-o / w-V O w-V	CAN/CAN^2
5	[Voc] / Q V M	Nom/CAN
6	V-o O // w-V-o M	CAN//CAN
7	V-o O M // w-S V-M	CAN//DEF
8	[Voc] V-o / w-V O w-V	CAN/CAN^2
9	O M V / V O w-V-o	DEF/CAN^2
10	V M / w-V O w-V-O	CAN/CAN^2
11	V S M // w-M S	CAN//Gap
12	V O M // w-M O	CAN//Gap
13	Q V O / w-V-o S	CAN/CAN
14	V-o S M // w-S V-o	CAN//DEF
15	[Voc] V-P / V M w-V / w-V O	CAN/CAN^2/CAN
16	w-O R-V S // w-M [R] V M	Nom-CAN^R//Nom-CAN$^{[R]}$
17	Comp M Comp / M V	Nom^2/MKD
18	V-S Comp / Comp(S [R] V M)	CAN/Nom-CAN$^{[R]}$
19	w-V^{Ng} M / V-o w-M V	CAN/CAN-MKD
20	[Voc] V-o / V O w-V	CAN/CAN^2
Ps. 81		
2	V M // V M	CAN//CAN
3	V-O w-V-O / M M	CAN^2/Nom
4	V M O / M M	CAN/Nom
5	C Comp M S^{Pn} // Comp M	Nom//Nom
6	O M V-o / M(Inf M) / O [R] V^{Ng} V	MKD/Inf/CAN$^{[R]}$-MKD
7	V M O // S M V	CAN//DEF
8	M V w-V-o / V-o M / V-o M Selah	CAN^2/CAN/CAN
9	V [Voc] w-V M /[Voc] C-V-M	CAN^2/CAN
10	V^{Ng} Comp S // w-V^{Ng} M	CAN//CAN
11	S^{Pn} Comp V^{Pt}-o M / V-O w-V-o	Nom-Ptcp/CAN^2
12	w-V^{Ng} S M // w-S V^{Ng} M	CAN//DEF
13	w-V-o M / V M	CAN/CAN
14	C S V^{Pt} M // S M V	Ptcp//DEF
15	M O V // w-M V O	MKD//MKD
16	S V-M / w-V S Comp	MKD/CAN
17	w-V-o M // w-M V-o	CAN//DEF
Ps. 82		
1	S V^{Pt} M // M V	Ptcp//DEF
2	Q V-O // w-O V Selah	CAN//DEF
3	V-O w-O // O w-O V	CAN//DEF
4	V-O w-O // M V	CAN//DEF
5	V^{Ng} w-V^{Ng} M V / V S	CAN^2-MKD/CAN
6	S^{Pn}-V Comp S^{Pn} // w-Comp S^{Pn}	MKD-Nom//Nom
7	M M V // w-M V	MKD//MKD
8	V [Voc] V O / C-S^{Pn} V M	CAN^2/MKD
Ps. 83		
2	[Voc] Ng S Comp? // V^{Ng} w-V^{Ng} [Voc]	Nom//CAN^2
3	C-H S V // w-S V O	MKD//MKD
4	M V O // w-V M	DEF//CAN
5	V V w-V-o M / w-V^{Ng} S M	CAN^3/CAN
6	C V M // M O V	CAN//DEF
7	S w-S // S w-S	Nom//Nom

8	S w-S w-S // S M	Nom//Nom
9	P-S V M / V Comp M Selah	MKD/CAN
10	V-M M / M M M	CAN/Nom
11	V M / V Comp M	CAN/CAN
12	V-o O M w-M // w-M w-M O	CAN//Gap
13	R V V M / O	CAN^{R2}/Nom
14	[Voc] V-o M // M M	CAN//Nom
15	M(S V O) // M(S V O)	MKD//MKD
16	M V-o M // w-M V-o	CAN//DEF
17	V O O / w-V O [Voc]	CAN/CAN
18	V w-V M // w-V w-V	CAN^2//CAN^2
19	w-V C-S^{Pn} (S Comp) M / Comp M	CAN-Nom/Nom
Ps. 84		
2	Q-Comp S / [Voc]	Nom/Nom
3	V w-P V S M // S w-S V M	CAN^2//DEF
4ab	P-S V O // w-S O M	MKD//Gap
4cd	R-V O M [Voc] / [Voc] w-[Voc]	CAN^R/Nom
5	Comp S^{Pl} / M V-o Selah	Nom/MKD
6	Comp S [R] S-M Comp / S Comp	Nom^2/Nom
7	V^{Pt} M O V-o / P-O V S	Ptcp-MKD/MKD
8	V M M / V M M	CAN/CAN
9	[Voc] V O // V [Voc] Selah	CAN//CAN
10	O V [Voc] // V O	DEF//CAN
11	C Comp-S M M / V Inf M / M	Nom/CAN/Nom
12	C Comp w-Comp S / O w-O V S / V^{Ng}-O M	Nom/MKD/CAN
13	[Voc] / Comp S V^{Pt} M	Nom/Nom
Ps. 85		
2	V [Voc] O // V O	CAN//CAN
3	V O // V O Selah	CAN//CAN
4	V O // V M	CAN//CAN
5	V-o [Voc] // w-V O M	CAN//CAN
6	Q-M V-M // V O M	DEF//CAN
7	Q^{Ng}-S^{Pn} V V-o / w-S V-M	MKD-CAN/MKD
8	V-o [Voc] O // w-O V-M	CAN//DEF
9	V Q-V S / C V O M w-M / w-V^{Ng} M	CAN^2/CAN/CAN
10	P Comp M S / Inf S M	Nom/Inf
11	S-w-S V // S w-S V	MKD//MKD
12	S M V // w-S M V	MKD//MKD
13	P-S V O // w-S V O	MKD//MKD
14	S M V / w-V M O	DEF/CAN
Ps. 86		
1	V-[Voc] O V-o / C-Comp w-Comp S^{Pn}	CAN^2/Nom
2ab	V O C Comp S^{Pn} //	CAN-Nom//
2c-e	V O (S^{Pn} Comp) V^{Pt} M	CAN(Nom)-Ptcp
3	V-o [Voc] / C M V M	CAN/MKD
4	V O / C M [Voc] O V	CAN/MKD
5	C-S^{Pn} [Voc] Comp w-Comp / w-Comp M	Nom/Nom
6	V [Voc] O // w-V M	CAN//CAN
7	M V-o / C V-o	CAN/CAN
8	E^{Ng}-M M [Voc] // w-E^{Ng} M	Nom//Nom
9	S R V V / w-V M [Voc] / w-V M	MKD-CAN^R/CAN/CAN
10	C-Comp S^{Pn} w-V^{Pt} O / S^{Pn} Comp M	Nom-Ptcp/Nom
11	V-o [Voc] O V M / V S M	CAN^2/CAN
12	V-o [Voc] M // w-V O M	CAN//CAN
13	C-S Comp M / w-V O M	Nom/CAN
14	[Voc] S V-M // w-S V M / w-V^{Ng} M	MKD//MKD/CAN
15	w-S^{Pn} [Voc] Comp / Comp w-Comp	Nom/Nom
16	V M w-V-o V-O M / w-V O	CAN^3/CAN
17	V-M O M / w-V S w-V / C-S^{Pn} [Voc] V-o w-V-o	CAN/CAN^2/MKD-CAN
Ps. 87		
1	S Comp	Nom
2	V^{Pt} S O / M	Ptcp/Nom
3	S V^{Pt} M / [Voc] Selah	Ptcp/Nom
4	V O w-O M / H S w-S M / S V-M	CAN/Nom/MKD

Appendix 2 319

5	w-M V S w-S V-M / w-S^{Pn} V-o S		MKD^2/MKD
6	S V M / S V-M	*Selah*	MKD/MKD
7	w-S M? / S Comp		Nom?/Nom
Ps. 88			
2	[Voc] / M-[R]-V M M		Nom/CAN$^{[R]}$
3	V M S // V-O M		CAN//CAN
4	C-V M S // w-S M V		CAN//DEF
5	V M // V Comp		CAN//CAN
6	M Comp M Comp / R V^{Ng}-o M / w-S^{Pn} M V		Nom^2/CAN^R/MKD
7	V-o M / M M		CAN/Nom
8	M V S / w-M V	*Selah*	MKD/MKD
9	V O M / V-o O M / Comp w-V^{Ng}		CAN/CAN/Nom-CAN
10	S V M / V-o [Voc] M / V M O		MKD/CAN/CAN
11	Q-M V-O // C-S V V-o	*Selah*	MKD//MKD-CAN
12	Q-V M S // S M		CAN//Gap
13	Q-V M S // w-S M		CAN//Gap
14	w-S^{Pn} M [Voc] V / w-M S V-o		MKD/MKD
15	Q [Voc] V O // V O M		CAN//CAN
16	Comp S^{Pn} w-V^{Pt} M / V O V		Nom-Ptcp/CAN^2
17	M V S // S V-o		MKD//DEF
18	V-o M M // V M M		CAN//DEF
19	V M O w-O / S Comp		CAN/Nom
Ps. 89			
2	O M V // M V O M		DEF//DEF
3	C-V M S V O // N V O M		CAN-DEF//DEF
4	V O M // V M		CAN//CAN
5	M V O // V M O	*Selah*	DEF//CAN
6	w-V S O [Voc] / P-O M		CAN/Nom
7	C Q V M // V M M		CAN//CAN
8	S Comp M // Comp M		Ptcp//Ptcp
9	[Voc] Q-M Comp [Voc] / w-S Comp		Nom/Nom
10	S^{Pn} V^{Pt} M / M S^{Pn} V-o		Ptcp/MKD
11	S^{Pn} V M O / M V O		MKD/MKD
12	Comp S P-Comp S / N S^{Pn} V-o //		Nom^2/MKD//
13	N S^{Pn} V-o / S w-S M V		MKD/MKD?
14	Comp S M // V S // V S		Nom//CAN//CAN
15	S w-S Comp // S w-S V O		Nom//MKD
16	Comp S(V^{Pt} O) /[Voc] M V		Nom-Ptcp/MKD
17	M V M // w-M V		MKD//MKD
18	C-Comp S^{Pn} / w-M V S		Nom/MKD
19	C Comp S // w-Comp S		Nom//Nom
20	C V-M M / w-V V O M // V O M		CAN/CAN^2//CAN
21	V O / M V-o		CAN//MKD
22	R S V M // P-S V-o		MKD^R//MKD
23	V^{Ng} S M // w-S V^{Ng}-o		CAN//DEF
24	w-V M O // w-O V		CAN//DEF
25	S w-S Comp / w-M V S		Nom/MKD
26	w-V M O // w-M O		CAN//Gap
27	S^{Pn} V-o Comp S^{Pn} / w-Comp		MKD-Nom/Nom
28	P-S^{Pn} O V-o / O M		MKD/Nom
29	M V-M O / w-S V^{Pt} M		MKD/Ptcp
30	w-V M O // w-S Comp		CAN//Nom
31	C-V S O // w-O V^{Ng} //		CAN//DEF//
32	C-O V // w-O V^{Ng}		DEF//DEF
33	w-V M O // w-M O		CAN//Gap
34	w-O V^{Ng} M // w-V^{Ng} M //		MKD//DEF//
35	V^{Ng} O // w-O V^{Ng}		DEF//MKD
36	O V M / C-M V		MKD/MKD
37	S M V // w-S Comp M		MKD/Nom
38	M V M / Comp	*Selah*	MKD/Nom
39	w-S^{Pn} V w-V / V M		MKD-CAN/CAN
40	V O // V M O		CAN//CAN
41	V O // V O O		CAN//CAN
42	V-o S^{Pt} // V Comp M		CAN//CAN

43	V O // V O		CAN//CAN
44	P-V O // w-V^{Ng}-o M		CAN//CAN
45	V O // w-O M V		CAN//DEF
46	V O / V M O	Selah	CAN/CAN
47	Q [Voc] V M // V M S		Nom-CAN//CAN
48	V-S^{Pn} Q-Comp / M V O		CAN-Nom/MKD
49	Q V w-V^{Ng}-O // V O M	Selah	CAN^2//CAN
50	Q Comp [Voc] / V M M		Nom/CAN
51	V [Voc] O / Inf M O		CAN/Inf
52	R V S [Voc] // R V O		CAN^R//CAN^R
53	Comp S M / Exc w-Exc		Nom/Nom^2
Ps. 90			
1	[Voc] Comp S^{Pn} V M M		MKD
2	C S V // w-V S w-S / M S^{Pn} Comp		DEF//CAN/Nom
3	V O M / w-V V [Voc]		CAN/CAN^2
4	C S M Comp C V / w-Comp		Nom-CAN/Nom
5	V-o Comp V / M Comp [R] V		CAN-MKD/Nom-CAN$^{[R]}$
6	M V w-V // M V w-V		MKD-CAN//MKD-CAN
7	C-V M // w-M V		CAN//DEF
8	V O M // O M		CAN//Gap
9	C S V M // V O M		DEF//CAN
10	S M Comp / w-C M Comp / w-S Comp / C-V M w-V		Nom/Nom/Nom/CAN^2
11	Q-V^{Pt} O / w-Comp S		Ptcp/Nom
12	Inf O M V / w-V O		Inf-MKD/CAN
13	V [Voc] Q / w-V M		CAN-Nom/CAN
14	V-o M O / w-V w-V M		CAN/CAN^2
15	V-o M [R] V-o // M [R] V O		CAN-CAN$^{[R]}$//CAN-CAN$^{[R]}$
16	V M S // w-S M		CAN//Gap
17	w-V S M / w-O V M // w-O V		CAN/MKD//MKD
Ps. 91			
1	V^{Pt} M S // M V		Ptcp//DEF
2	V M Comp w-Comp / Comp [R] V M		CAN-Nom/Nom-CAN$^{[R]}$
3	C S^{Pn} V-o M / M		MKD/Nom
4	M V M // w-M V / Comp w-Comp S		MKD//MKD/Nom
5	V^{Ng} M / M [R] V M //		CAN/Nom-CAN$^{[R]}$//
6	M [R] M V // M [R] V M		Nom-DEF//Nom-CAN$^{[R]}$
7	V M S // w-S M / M V^{Ng}		CAN//Gap/MKD
8	P M V / w-O V		MKD/MKD
9	C-S^{Pn} [Voc] Comp / O V O		Nom/MKD
10	V^{Ng} M S // w-S V^{Ng} M		CAN//DEF
11	C O V-M / Inf-o M		MKD/Inf
12	M V-o / C-V M O		MKD/CAN
13	M V // V O w-O		DEF//CAN
14	C M V w-V-o / V-o C-V O		MKD-CAN/CAN^2
15	V-o w-V-o Comp-S^{Pn} M / V-o w-V-o		CAN^2-Nom/CAN^2
16	O V-o // w-V-o M		DEF//CAN
Ps. 92			
2	Comp Inf O // Inf O [Voc]		Nom-Inf//Inf
3	Inf M O // w-O M		Inf//Gap
4	M w-M / M M		Nom/Nom
5	C V-o [Voc] M // M V		CAN//DEF
6	Q-V S [Voc] // M V S		CAN//DEF
7	S V^{Ng} // w-S V^{Ng} O		MKD//MKD
8	M(Inf S M) // w-V S^{Pt} / Inf-o M		Inf//CAN/Inf
9	w-S^{Pn} Comp M [Voc]		Nom
10	C H S [Voc] // C-H S V // V S		Gap//MKD//DEF
11	w-V M O // V M		CAN//CAN
12	w-V S M // M V S		CAN//DEF
13	S M V // M V		DEF//DEF
14	Comp M // M V		Nom//MKD
15	M V M / Comp w-Comp V		CAN/MKD
16	Inf C-Comp S / Comp w-[E]^{Ng} M		Inf-Nom/Nom^2
Ps. 93			
1a	S V /		MKD/

Appendix 2

1b-d	O V // V S // O V	MKD//DEF//MKD
1ef	P-V O V^{Ng}	CAN^2
2	V^{Pt} S M / Comp S^{Pn}	Nom/Nom
3	V S [Voc] // V S O // V S O	CAN//CAN//CAN
4	M / Comp M S	Nom/Nom
5	S V M / M V-S / [Voc] M	MKD/MKD/Nom
Ps. 94		
1	[Voc] [Voc] // [Voc] V	Gap//CAN
2	V [Voc] / V O M	CAN/CAN
3	Q S [Voc] // Q S V	Gap//MKD
4	V V O / V S^{Pt}	CAN^2/CAN
5	O [Voc] V // w-O V	MKD//MKD
6	O w-O V // w-O V	MKD//MKD
7	w-V V^{Ng}-S // w-V^{Ng} S	CAN^2//CAN
8	V [Voc] // w-[Voc] Q V	CAN//CAN
9	Q-S^{Pt} Q-V^{Ng} // C-S^{Pt} Q-V^{Ng} //	MKD//MKD//
10	Q-S^{Pt} Q-V^{Ng} / S^{Pt}	MKD/Ptcp
11	S V^{Pt} O / C-S^{Pn} Comp	Ptcp/Nom
12	Comp S R-V-o S // w-M V-o	Nom-CAN//DEF
13	Inf M M / C V M S	Inf/CAN
14	C V^{Ng} S O // w-O V^{Ng}	CAN//DEF
15	C-M V S / w-Comp S	MKD/Nom
16	Q-V M M // Q-V M M	CAN//CAN
17	C S Comp M / M V M S	Nom/CAN
18	C-V V S / S [Voc] V-o	CAN^2/MKD
19	M(Inf S) M / S V O	Inf/MKD
20	Q-V-o S / V^{Pt} O M	CAN/Ptcp
21	V M // w-O V	CAN//DEF
22	w-V S M Comp / w-S Comp	CAN//Gap
23	w-V M O // w-M V-o // V-o S	CAN//DEF//CAN
Ps. 95		
1	V V M // V M	CAN^2//CAN
2	V O M // M V M	CAN//DEF
3	C Comp S // w-Comp M	Nom//Nom
4	R Comp S // w-S Comp	Nom//Nom
5	R-Comp S w-S^{Pn} V-o // w-O [R] S V	Nom-MKD//Nom-MKD$^{[R]}$
6	V M w-V // V M	CAN^2//CAN
7ab	C S^{Pn} Comp / w-S^{Pn} Comp w-Comp	Nom/Nom
7c	M C-M V /	MKD/
8	V^{Ng} O M /M M	CAN/Nom
9	C V-o S / V-o P-V O	CAN/CAN^2
10	M V M / w-V Comp S / w-S^{Pn} V^{Ng} O	MKD/CAN-Nom/MKD
11	C-V M / C-V M	CAN/CAN
Ps. 96		
1	V M O // V M [Voc]	CAN//CAN
2	V M // V O / V M O	CAN//CAN/CAN
3	V M O // M O	CAN//Gap
4	C Comp S w-Comp M / Comp S^{Pn} M	Nom/Nom
5	C S Comp / w-S O V	Nom/MKD
6	S w-S Comp // S w-S Comp	Nom//Nom
7	V M [Voc] // V M O w-O	CAN//CAN
8	V M O / V-o w-V M	CAN/CAN^2
9	V M M / V M [Voc]	CAN/CAN
10	V M S V / P-V S V^{Ng} / V O M	CAN-MKD/CAN^2/CAN
11	V S // w-V S // V S w-S //	CAN//CAN//CAN//
12	V S w-S / C V S	CAN/CAN
13a-c	M C V^{Pt} / C V^{Pt} Inf O /	Nom-Ptcp/Ptcp/
13de	V-O M // w-O M	CAN//Gap
Ps. 97		
1	S V V S // V S	MKD-CAN//CAN
2	S w-S Comp // S w-S Comp	Nom//Nom
3	S M V / w-V M	MKD/CAN
4	V S O / V w-V S	CAN/CAN^2
5	S M V M / M	MKD/Nom

6	V S O // w-V S O	CAN//CAN
7	V S V^{Pt} M / V-M [Voc]	CAN-Ptcp/CAN
8	V w-V S // w-V S / M [Voc]	CAN^2//CAN-Nom
9	C-S^{Pn} [Voc] Comp M // M V M	Nom//CAN
10	[Voc] V O / V^{Pt} O // M V-o	CAN/Ptcp//DEF
11	S Comp M // w-M S	Nom//Nom
12	V [Voc] M // w-V M	CAN//CAN
Ps. 98		
1	V M O / C-O V / V-M S w-S	CAN/MKD/CAN
2	V S O // M V O	CAN//DEF
3	V O w-O M / V S O	CAN/CAN
4	V M [Voc] / V w-V w-V	CAN/CAN^3
5	V M M / M w-M //	CAN/Nom//
6	M w-M V M	DEF
7	V S w-S // S w-S //	CAN//Gap//
8	S V-O // M S V	DEF//DEF
9ab	M / C-V Inf O /	Nom/CAN/
9cd	V O M // w-O M	CAN//Gap
Ps. 99		
1	S V V S // V^{Pt} M V S	MKD-CAN//Ptcp-CAN
2	S M Comp // w-V^{Pt} S^{Pn} M	Nom//Ptcp
3	V O / w-Comp S^{Pn}	CAN/Nom
4ab	Comp S O V /	Nom-MKD
4cd	S^{Pn} V O // O w-O M S^{Pn} V	MKD//MKD
5	V O // w-V M Comp S^{Pn}	CAN//CAN-Nom
6ab	S w-S Comp // w-S Comp /	Nom//Nom/
6cd	V^{Pt} M w-S^{Pn} V-o	Ptcp-CAN
7	M V M / V O // w-O V-M	CAN/CAN//DEF
8	[Voc] S^{Pn} V-o / Comp V M / w-V^{Pt} M	MKD/MKD/Ptcp
9	V O // w-V M / Comp S^{Pn}	CAN//CAN/Nom
Ps. 100		
1	V M [Voc]	CAN
2	V O M // V M M	CAN//CAN
3a-c	V C-N S^{Pn} Comp / S^{Pn} V-o /	CAN-Nom/CAN/
3de	Comp S^{Pn} / Comp w-Comp	Nom/Nom
4ab	V O M // O M /	CAN//Gap/
4cd	V M // V O	CAN//CAN
5	C-Comp S Comp S // w-Comp S	Nom^2//Nom
Ps. 101		
1	O w-O V // M [Voc] V	MKD//MKD
2	V M / Q V M / V M M	CAN/CAN/CAN
3	V^{Ng} M O // O V / V^{Ng} M	CAN//DEF/CAN
4	S V M // O V^{Ng}	MKD//MKD
5	N O^{Pn} V // N O^{Pn} V^{Ng}	MKD//MKD
6	S Comp Inf M / N S^{Pn} V-o	Nom-Inf/MKD
7	V^{Ng} M S^{Pt} S^{Pt} // V^{Ng} M	CAN//CAN
8	M V O / Inf M O	MKD/Inf
Ps. 102		
2	[Voc] V O // w-S M V	CAN//DEF
3	V^{Ng} O M M / V-M O / C [R] V V V-o	CAN/CAN/CAN$^{[R]3}$
4	C-V M S // w-S M V	CAN//DEF
5	V-M w-V S / C-V M(Inf O)	CAN^2/CAN
6	M / V S M	Nom/CAN
7	V M // V Comp	CAN//CAN
8	V w-V Comp / V^{Pt} M	CAN^2/Ptcp
9	M V-o S // S M V	DEF//DEF
10	C-O M V // w-O M V	MKD//MKD
11	M / C V-o w-V-o	Nom/CAN^2
12	S M Comp / w-S^{Pn} M V	Nom/MKD
13	w-S^{Pn} [Voc] M V // w-S Comp	MKD//Nom
14ab	S^{Pn} V V O /	MKD-CAN/
14cd	C-S Comp // C-V S	Nom//CAN
15	C-V S O // w-O V	CAN//DEF
16	w-V S O // w-S O	CAN//Gap

Appendix 2

17	C-V S O / V M	CAN/CAN
18	V M // w-V^{Ng} O	CAN//CAN
19	V S M / w-S V-O	CAN/MKD
20	C-V M // S M M V	CAN//DEF
21	Inf O // Inf O	Inf//Inf
22	Inf M O // w-O M	Inf//Gap
23	M(Inf S M) / w-S Inf O	Inf/Inf
24	V M O // V O	CAN//CAN
25	V [Voc] V^{Ng}-o M / Comp S	CAN^2/Nom
26	M O V // w-Comp S	DEF//Nom
27	S^{Pn} V w-S^{Pn} V / w-S M V // M V w-V	MKD^2/MKD//MKD
28	w-S^{Pn} Comp / w-S V^{Ng}	Nom/MKD
29	S V // w-S M V	MKD//MKD
Ps. 103		
1	V [Voc] O // w-[Voc] O	CAN//CAN
2	V [Voc] O // w-V^{Ng} O	CAN//CAN
3	V^{Pt} O // V^{Pt} O	Ptcp//Ptcp
4	V^{Pt} M O // V^{Pt}-o O w-O	Ptcp//Ptcp
5	V^{Pt} M M / V M S	Ptcp/CAN
6	V^{Pt} O S / w-O M	Ptcp/Nom
7	V O M // M O	CAN//Gap
8	Comp w-Comp S // Comp w-Comp	Nom//Nom
9	M^{Ng} V // w-M^{Ng} V	MKD//MKD
10	M^{Ng} V M // w-M^{Ng} V M	MKD//MKD
11	C M(Inf S M) / V S M	Inf/CAN
12	M(Inf S M) / V M O	Inf/CAN
13	M(Inf S M) / V S M	Inf/CAN
14	C-S^{Pn} V O // Comp C-Comp S	MKD//Ptcp-Nom
15	N Comp S // M M V	Nom//CAN
16	C S V-M w-E^{Ng} / w-V^{Ng}-o M S	MKD-Nom/CAN
17	w-S Comp M // w-S M	Nom//Nom
18	w-M // w-M Inf-o	Ptcp//Pctp
19	S M V O // w-S M V	DEF//DEF
20	V O [Voc] // [Voc] / Inf M	CAN//[Voc]/Inf
21	V O [Voc] // [Voc]	CAN//[Voc]
22ab	V O [Voc] / M	CAN/Nom
22c	V [Voc] O	CAN
Ps. 104		
1	V [Voc] O / [Voc] V M / O w-O V	CAN/CAN/MKD
2	V^{Pt}-O M // V^{Pt} O M	Ptcp//Ptcp
3	V^{Pt} M O // V^{Pt}-O O // V^{Pt} M	Ptcp//Ptcp//Ptcp
4	V^{Pt} O O // O O	Ptcp//Gap
5	V-O M / V^{Ng} M	CAN/CAN
6	N M V-o / M V-S	MKD/MKD
7	M V / M V	MKD/MKD
8ab	V S // V S /	CAN//CAN/
8cd	M R V M	Nom-CAN^R
9	O-V V^{Ng} / V^{Ng} Inf O	MKD-CAN/CAN
10	V^{Pt} O M // M V	Ptcp//DEF
11	V O // V S O	CAN//CAN
12	M S V // M V-O	DEF//DEF
13	V^{Pt} O M // M V S	Ptcp//DEF
14	V^{Pt} O M // w-O M / Inf O M	Ptcp//Gap/Inf
15a-c	w-S [R] V O / Inf O M //	Nom-CAN$^{[R]}$/Inf//
15de	w-S [R] O V	Nom-DEF$^{[R]}$?
16	V S / S R V	CAN/Nom-CAN^R
17	R-M S V // N Comp S	MKD^R//Nom
18	S Comp // S Comp M	Nom//Nom
19	V O M // S V O	CAN//DEF
20	V-O w-V Comp / M-V S	CAN^2/MKD
21	S V^{Pt} M / w-Inf M O	Ptcp/Inf
22	V S V / w-M V	CAN^2/MKD
23	V S M / w-M M	CAN/Nom
24	Q-V S [Voc] / O M V / V S O	CAN/MKD/CAN

25	S^{Pn} Comp w-Comp / Comp-S w-E^{Ng} S / S M	Nom/Nom²/Nom
26	M S V / S-R V Inf-M	MKD/Nom-CAN^R
27	S M V / Inf O M	MKD/Inf
28	V M V // V S V O	CAN²//CAN²
29	V O V // V O V / w-M V	CAN²//CAN²/MKD
30	V O V / w-V O	CAN²/CAN
31	V S Comp / V S M	CAN/CAN
32	V^{Pt} M w-V // V M w-V	Ptcp-CAN//CAN²
33	V M M // V M M	CAN//CAN
34	V M S / S^{Pn} V M	CAN/MKD
35ab	V S M / w-S M E^{Ng}	CAN/Nom
35cd	V [Voc] O / V-O	CAN/CAN
Ps. 105		
1	V M // V M / V M O	CAN//CAN/CAN
2	V-M // V-M / V M	CAN//CAN/CAN
3	V M / V S	CAN/CAN
4	V O w-O // V O M	CAN//CAN
5	V O R-V / O w-O	CAN^{2R}/Nom
6	[Voc] // [Voc]	Nom//Nom
7	S^{Pn} Comp / Comp S	Nom/Nom
8	V M O / O [R] V M	CAN/Nom-CAN$^{[R]}$
9	R V M / w-O M	CAN^R/Nom
10	w-V-o M M // M M	CAN//Gap
11	Inf M V O / O	Inf-MKD/Nom
12	M(Inf Comp / Comp w-Comp M)	Inf-Nom/Nom
13	w-V M M // M M	CAN//Gap
14	V^{Ng} O Inf-o / w-V M O	CAN/CAN
15	V^{Ng} M // w-M V^{Ng}	CAN//DEF
16	w-V O M // O V	CAN//DEF
17	V M O // M V S	CAN//DEF?
18	V M O // M V S	CAN//DEF
19	M (Inf S) / S V-o	Inf/MKD
20	V S w-V-o // S w-V-o	CAN²//Gap-CAN
21	V-o O M / w-O M	CAN//Gap
22	Inf O M / w-O V	Inf//DEF
23	w-V S O // w-S V M	CAN//DEF
24	w-V O M // w-V-o M	CAN//CAN
25	V O Inf O // Inf O	CAN-Inf//Inf
26	V O / O R-V M	CAN/Nom-CAN^R
27	V-M O // w-O M	CAN//Gap
28	V O w-V / w-V^{Ng} O	CAN²/CAN
29	V O M / w-V O	CAN/CAN
30	V S O / M	CAN/Nom
31	V w-V S / S M	CAN²/Nom
32	V O O / O M	CAN/Nom
33	w-V O w-O // w-V O	CAN//CAN
34	V w-V S / w-S w-E^{Ng} S	CAN²/Nom²
35	w-V O M // w-V O	CAN//CAN
36	w-V O M / O M	CAN/Nom
37	w-V-o M w-M / w-E^{Ng} Comp S^{Pt}	CAN/Nom
38	V S M(Inf) / C-V S M	CAN/CAN
39	V O M // w-S Inf O	CAN//Nom-Inf
40	V w-V O // w-O V-o	CAN²//DEF
41	V O w-V S / V M M	CAN²/CAN
42	C-V O / O	CAN/Nom
43	w-V O M // M O	CAN//Gap
44	w-V M O // w-O V	CAN//DEF
45ab	C V O // w-O V	CAN//DEF
45c	V-O	CAN
Ps. 106		
1a	V-O	CAN
1b-d	V M C-Comp / C Comp S	CAN-Nom/Nom
2	Q V O // V O	CAN//CAN
3	Comp S(V^{Pt} O // V^{Pt} O M)	Nom-Ptcp//Ptcp

Appendix 2 325

4	V-o [Voc] M // V-o M	CAN//CAN
5	Inf M // Inf M // Inf M	Inf//Inf//Inf
6	V M / V V	CAN/CAN^2
7	S M V^{Ng} O // V^{Ng} O / w-V M M	Nom?-CAN//CAN/CAN
8	w-V-o M / Inf O	CAN/Inf
9	w-V M w-V / w-V-o M M	CAN^2/CAN
10	w-V-o M // w-V-o M	CAN//CAN
11	w-V-S O / S V^{Ng}	CAN/MKD
12	w-V M // V O	CAN//CAN
13	V V O // V^{Ng} M	CAN^2//CAN
14	w-V O M // w-V-O M	CAN//CAN
15	w-V M O / w-V O M	CAN/CAN
16	w-V M M / M	CAN/Nom
17	V-S w-V O // w-V M	CAN^2//CAN
18	w-V-S M // S V O	CAN//DEF
19	V-O M // w-V M	CAN//CAN
20	w-V O / M	CAN/Nom
21	V O / V^{Pt} O M //	CAN/Ptcp//
22	O M // O M	Gap//Gap
23	w-V Inf-o / C S V M M / Inf O M(Inf)	CAN/MKD/Inf
24	w-V M / V^{Ng} M	CAN/CAN
25	w-V M / V^{Ng} M	CAN/CAN
26	w-V O M / Inf O M //	CAN/Inf//
27	w-Inf O M // w-Inf-o M	Inf//Inf
28	w-V M / w-V O	CAN/CAN
29	w-V M / w-V-M S	CAN/CAN
30	w-V S w-V / w-V S	CAN^2/CAN
31	w-V M M / M M	CAN/Nom
32	w-V M / w-V M M	CAN/CAN
33	C-V O / w-V M	CAN/CAN
34	V^{Ng} O / R V S M	CAN/CAN^R
35	w-V M / w-V O	CAN/CAN
36	w-V O / w-V M Comp	CAN/CAN
37	w-V O / w-O M	CAN/Nom
38	w-V O / w-O R V M / w-V S M	CAN/Nom-CAN^R/CAN
39	w-V M // w-V M	CAN//CAN
40	w-V-S M // w-V O	CAN//CAN
41	w-V-o M // w-V M S	CAN//CAN
42	w-V-o S // w-V M	CAN//CAN
43	M V-o / w-S^{Pn} V M / w-V M	MKD/MKD/CAN
44	w-V M M / M(Inf O)	CAN/Inf
45	w-V M O // w-V M	CAN//CAN
46	w-V O M / M	CAN/Nom
47ab	V-o [Voc] / w-V-o M /	CAN/CAN/
47cd	Inf M // Inf M	Inf//Inf
48a-c	Comp-S M w-M / V S Exc	Nom/CAN-Nom
48d	V-O	CAN
Ps. 107		
1	V M C-Comp / C Comp S	CAN-Nom/Nom
2	V S / R V-o M //	CAN/CAN^R//
3	w-M V-o / M w-M // M w-M	DEF/Nom//Nom
4	V M M / O V^{Ng}	CAN/MKD
5	Comp w-Comp / S M V	Nom/MKD
6	w-V M M / M w-V-o	CAN/MKD
7	w-V-o M / Inf M	CAN/Inf
8	V M O / w-O M	CAN/Nom
9	C-V O // w-O V-O	CAN//DEF
10	Comp^{Pt} // Comp	Ptcp//Nom
11	C-V O // w-O V	CAN//DEF
12	w-V M S / V w-E^{Ng} S^{Pt}	CAN/CAN-Nom
13	w-V M M / M V-o	CAN/MKD
14	V-o M w-M // w-O V	CAN//DEF
15	V M O / w-O M	CAN/Nom
16	C-V O // w-O V	CAN//DEF

17	Comp M // w-M V	Nom//DEF
18	O V S / w-V M	MKD/CAN
19	w-V M M / M V-o	CAN/MKD
20	V O w-V-o / w-V M	CAN^2/CAN
21	V M O / w-O M	CAN/Nom
22	w-V O // w-V O M	CAN//CAN
23	Comp^{Pt} M / Comp^{Pt} M	Ptcp/Ptcp
24	S^{Pn} V O / w-O M	MKD/Nom
25	w-V w-V O / w-V O	CAN^2/CAN
26	V O V O / S M V	CAN^2/MKD
27	V w-V M / w-S V	CAN/MKD?
28	w-V M M / w-M V-o	CAN/MKD
29	V O M // w-V S	CAN//CAN
30	w-V C-V / w-V-o M	CAN^2/CAN
31	V M O / w-O M	CAN/Nom
32	w-V-o M // w-M V-o	CAN//DEF
33	V O M // w-O M //	CAN//Gap//
34	O M / M	Gap/Nom
35	V O M // w-O M	CAN//Gap
36	w-V M O / w-V O	CAN/CAN
37	w-V O w-V O / w-V O	CAN^2/CAN
38	w-V-o w-V M / w-S V^{Ng}	CAN^2/MKD
39	w-V w-V / M	CAN^2/Nom
40	V^{Pt} O M / w-V-o M	Ptcp/CAN
41	w-V O M / w-V M O	CAN/CAN
42	V O w-V / w-S V O	CAN^2/MKD
43	Q-Comp w-V-O // w-V O	Nom-CAN//CAN
Ps. 108		
2	Comp S [Voc] / V w-V P-M	Nom/CAN^2
3	V [Voc] / V O	CAN/CAN
4	V-o M [Voc] // w-V-o M	CAN//CAN
5	C-Comp M S // w-M S	Nom//Nom
6	V M [Voc] // w-Comp S	CAN//Nom
7	C V S / V M w-V-o	CAN/CAN^2
8	S V M / V V O // w-O V	MKD/CAN^2//DEF
9	Comp S // Comp S // w-S Comp // S Comp //	Nom//Nom//Nom//Nom//
10	S Comp / M V O // M V	Nom/MKD//MKD
11	Q V-o M // Q V-o M	CAN//CAN
12	Q^{Ng}-[Voc] V-o // w-V^{Ng} [Voc] M	CAN//CAN
13	V-M O M / w-Comp S	CAN/Nom
14	M V-O / w-S^{Pn} V O	MKD/MKD
Ps. 109		
1	[Voc] V^{Ng}	CAN
2	C S w-S M V // V M M //	MKD//DEF//
3	w-M? V-o / w-V-o M	MKD/CAN
4	M V-o / w-S^{Pn} Comp	MKD/Nom
5	w-V M O M // w-O M	CAN//Gap
6	V M O // w-S V M	CAN//DEF
7	M(Inf) V Comp // w-S V Comp	Inf-CAN//DEF
8	V-S Comp // O V S	CAN//DEF
9	V-S Comp // w-S Comp	CAN//Nom
10	Inf V S w-V / w-V M	CAN^2/CAN
11	V S O // w-V S O	CAN//CAN
12	V^{Ng}-M S^{Pt} // w-V^{Ng} S^{Pt}	CAN//CAN
13	V-S Comp // M V S	CAN//DEF
14	V S M // w-S V^{Ng}	CAN//DEF
15	V Comp M // w-V M O	CAN//CAN
16	C V^{Ng} Inf O / w-V O w-O / w-O Inf	CAN/CAN/Inf
17	w-V O w-V-o // w-V^{Ng} M w-V M	CAN^2//CAN^2
18	w-V O M / w-V M M // w-M M	CAN/CAN//Gap
19	V-M Comp [R] V // w-M [R] M V-o	CAN$^{2[R]}$//Gap-CAN$^{[R]}$
20	S^{Pn} Comp M // w-V^{Pt} O M	Nom//Gap-Ptcp
21	w-S^{Pn} [Voc] V-M M / C Comp S V-o	MKD/Nom-CAN
22	C-Comp w-Comp S^{Pn} / w-S V M	Nom/MKD

Appendix 2   327

23	M V / V M	MKD?/CAN
24	S V M // w-S V M	CAN//CAN
25	w-S^{Pn} V Comp M / V-o V O	MKD/CAN^2
26	V-o [Voc] // V-o M	CAN//CAN
27	w-V C-Comp S^{Pn} / S^{Pn} [Voc] V-o	CAN-Nom/MKD
28	V-S^{Pn} w-S^{Pn} V / V w-V / w-S V	CAN-MKD/CAN^2/MKD
29	V S O // w-V M O	CAN//CAN
30	V O M M // w-M V-o	CAN//DEF
31	C-V M / Inf M	CAN/Inf
Ps. 110		
1	Comp M V M / C-V O O M	Nom-CAN/CAN
2	O V S M / V M	MKD/CAN
3	S Comp M / M M / Comp S	Nom/Nom/Nom
4	V S w-V^{Ng} / S^{Pn}-Comp M M	CAN^2/Nom
5	S Comp / V M O	Nom/CAN
6	V M V^{Pt} O / V O M	CAN-Ptcp/CAN
7	M V / C V O	MKD/CAN
Ps. 111		
1a	V O	CAN
1bc	V O M / M w-M	CAN/Nom
2	Comp S / Comp M	Nom/Nom
3	Comp w-Comp S / w-S V^{Pt} M	Nom/Ptcp
4	O V M / Comp w-Comp S	MKD/Nom
5	O V M / V M O	MKD/CAN
6	O V M / Inf M O	MKD/Inf
7	S Comp w-Comp // V^{Pt} S	Nom//Ptcp
8	Comp M // Comp M	Nom//Nom
9	O V M // V-M O / Comp w-Comp S	DEF//CAN/Nom
10	Comp S / Comp M / S V^{Pt} M	Nom/Nom/Ptcp
Ps. 112		
1a	V O	CAN
1b-d	Comp-S [R] V O / M V M	Nom-CAN$^{[R]}$/MKD
2	Comp V S / S V	MKD/MKD
3	S-w-S Comp / w-S V^{Pt} M	Nom/Ptcp
4	V M S M / Comp w-Comp w-Comp	CAN/Nom
5	Comp-S V^{Pt} w-V^{Pt} / V O M	Nom/CAN
6	C-M V^{Ng} // Comp V S	MKD//MKD
7	M V^{Ng} / Comp S Comp	MKD/Nom
8	Comp S V^{Ng} / C-V M	Nom-CAN/CAN
9	V V M / S V^{Pt} M // S V M	CAN^2/Ptcp//MKD
10ab	S V w-V /	MKD-CAN/
10c-e	O V w-V / S V	MKD-CAN/MKD
Ps. 113		
1a	V O	CAN
1bc	V [Voc] // V O	CAN//CAN
2	V S Comp / M w-M	CAN/Nom
3	M M / Comp S	Nom/Nom
4	V^{Pt} M S // Comp S	Ptcp//Nom
5	Q Comp / V^{Pt} Inf	Nom/Ptcp
6	V^{Pt} Inf / M w-M	Ptcp/Nom
7	V^{Pt} M O // M V O	Ptcp//DEF
8	Inf M / M	Inf/Nom
9ab	V^{Pt} O / O	Ptcp/Nom
9c	V-O	CAN
Ps. 114		
1	M(Inf S M // S M)	Inf//Gap
2	V S Comp / S Comp	CAN//Gap
3	S V w-V // S V M	MKD-CAN//MKD
4	S V M // S M	MKD//Gap
5	Q-M [Voc] C V // [Voc] V M	Nom-CAN//CAN
6	S V M // S M	MKD//Gap
7	M V [Voc] / M	MKD/Nom
8	V^{Pt} O O // O M	Ptcp//Gap

Ps. 115		
1	M^{Ng} [Voc] M^{Ng}/C-M V O / M M	Nom/MKD/Nom
2	Q V S / Q-P S	CAN/Nom
3	w-S Comp / O(R-V) V	Nom/CAN^R- MKD
4	S Comp w-Comp / Comp	Nom/Nom
5	S-Comp w-V^{Ng} // S Comp w-V^{Ng} //	Nom-CAN//Nom-CAN//
6	S Comp w-V^{Ng} // S Comp w-V^{Ng} //	Nom-CAN//Nom-CAN//
7ab	S w-V^{Ng} //	Nom-CAN//
7c-e	S w-V^{Ng} / V^{Ng} M	Nom-CAN/CAN
8	Comp V S / S^{Pt}	MKD/Ptcp
9	[Voc] V M / Comp w-Comp S^{Pn} //	CAN/Nom//
10	[Voc] V M / Comp w-Comp S^{Pn} //	CAN/Nom//
11	[Voc] V M / Comp w-Comp S^{Pn}	CAN/Nom
12ab	S V-o V /	MKD-CAN/
12cd	V O // V O //	CAN//CAN//
13	V O / O	CAN/Nom
14	V S M / M w-M	CAN/Nom
15	Comp S^{Pn} M / V^{Pt} O w-O	Nom/Ptcp
16	S Comp / w-O V M	Nom/MKD
17	Ng S V-O // w-Ng S	MKD//Gap
18ab	w-S^{Pn} V O / M w-M	MKD/Nom
18c	V-O	CAN
Ps. 116		
1	V C-V S O	CAN-CAN
2	C-V O M / w-M V	CAN/MKD
3	V-o S // w-S V-o / O w-O V	CAN//DEF/MKD?
4	w-M V / P [Voc] V O	MKD/CAN
5	Comp S w-Comp // w-S V^{Pt}	Nom//Ptcp
6	V^{Pt} O S / V w-M V	Ptcp/CAN-MKD
7	V [Voc] M / C-S V M	CAN/MKD
8	C V O M // O M // O M	CAN//Gap//Gap
9	V M / M	CAN/Nom
10	V C V / S^{Pn} V M	CAN^2/MKD
11	S^{Pn} V M / S V^{Pt}	MKD/Ptcp
12	Q-V M / M	CAN/Nom
13	O V / w-M V	MKD/MKD
14	O M V / M	MKD/MKD
15	Comp M / S	Nom
16	P [Voc] C-S^{Pn} Comp / S^{Pn} Comp / V O	Nom/Nom/CAN
17	M-V O / w-M V	MKD/MKD
18	O M V / M /	MKD/Nom/
19ab	M / M [Voc]	Nom/Nom
19c	V-O	CAN
Ps. 117		
1	V O [Voc] // V-o [Voc]	CAN//CAN
2ab	C V M S / w-S Comp	CAN/Nom
2c	V-O	CAN
Ps. 118		
1	V M C-Comp / C Comp S	CAN-Nom//Nom
2	V-P S / C Comp S //	CAN/Nom//
3	V-P S / C Comp S //	CAN/Nom//
4	V-P S / C Comp S	CAN/Nom
5	M V O / V-o M S	MKD/CAN
6	S Comp V^{Ng} / Q-V M S	Nom-CAN/CAN
7	S Comp M / w-S^{Pn} V M	Nom/MKD
8	Comp Inf M / M(Inf M)	Nom-Inf/Inf
9	Comp Inf M / M(Inf M)	Nom-Inf/Inf
10	S V-o / M P V-o	MKD/MKD?
11	V-o P-V-o / M P V-o	CAN^2/MKD?
12	V-o M V M / M P V-o	CAN^2/MKD?
13	Inf V-o Inf / w-S V-o	CAN/MKD
14	Comp w-Comp S / w-V-M Comp	Nom/CAN
15	S Comp / S V^{Pt} O //	Nom/Ptcp//
16	S V^{Pt} // S V^{Pt} O	Ptcp//Ptcp

Appendix 2   329

17	V^{Ng} C-V / w-V O	CAN^2/CAN
18	Inf V-o S / w-M V^{Ng}-o	CAN/MKD
19	V-M O / V-M V O	CAN/CAN^2
20	S^{Pn} Comp / S V M	Nom/MKD
21	V-o C V-o / w-V-M Comp	CAN^2/CAN
22	S([R] V S) / V Comp	$CAN^{[R]}$/MKD
23	Comp V S^{Pn} / S^{Pn} Comp M	MKD/Nom
24	S^{Pn}-Comp [R] V S / V w-V M	Nom-$CAN^{[R]}$ /CAN^2
25	P [Voc] V P // P [Voc] V P	CAN//CAN
26	Comp S^{Pt} / V-o M	Nom/CAN
27	Comp S w-V M / V-O M / M	Nom-CAN/CAN/Nom
28	Comp S^{Pn} w-V-o // Comp V-o	Nom-CAN//Nom-CAN
29	V M C-Comp / C Comp S	CAN-Nom//Nom
Ps. 119		
1	Comp S / V^{Pt} M	Nom/Ptcp
2	Comp S^{Pt} / M V-o	Nom/MKD
3	P V^{Ng} O / M V	CAN/MKD
4	S^{Pn} V O / Inf M	MKD/Inf
5	P V S / Inf O	CAN/Inf
6	C V^{Ng} / M(Inf M)	CAN/Inf
7	V-o M / M(Inf O)	CAN/Inf
8	O V / V^{Ng}-o M	MKD/CAN
9	Q V-S O / Inf O	CAN/Inf
10	M V-o / V^{Ng}-o M	MKD/CAN
11	M V O / C V^{Ng}-M	MKD/CAN
12	Comp S^{Pt} [Voc] / V-o O	Nom/CAN
13	M V / O	MKD/Nom
14	M V / M	MKD/Nom
15	M V / w-V O	MKD/CAN
16	M V / V^{Ng} O	MKD/CAN
17	V M V / w-V O	CAN^2/CAN
18	V-O w-V / O M	CAN^2/Nom
19	Comp S^{Pn} M / V^{Ng} M O	Nom/CAN
20	V S M / M M	CAN/Nom
21	V O / V^{Pt} M	CAN/Ptcp
22	V M O w-O / C O V	CAN/MKD
23	P V S M V / S V M	CAN-MKD/MKD
24	P-S Comp / Comp	Nom/Nom
25	V M S / V-o M	CAN/CAN
26	O V w-V-o / V-o O	MKD-CAN/CAN
27	O V-o / w-V M	MKD/CAN
28	V S M / V-o M	CAN/CAN
29	O V M / w-O V-o	MKD/MKD
30	O V // O V	MKD//MKD
31	V M / [Voc] V^{Ng}-o	CAN/CAN
32	O V / C V O	MKD/CAN
33	V-o [Voc] O / w-V-o M	CAN/CAN
34	V-o w-V O / w-V-o M	CAN^2/CAN
35	V-o M / C-M V	CAN/MKD
36	V-O M / w-M^{Ng}	CAN/Nom
37	V O M(Inf O) / M V-o	CAN/MKD
38	V M O / R M	CAN/Nom
39	V O R V / C S Comp	CAN^{2R}/Nom
40	H V M / M V-o	CAN/MKD
41	w-V-o S [Voc] // S M	CAN//Gap
42	w-V O O / C-V M	CAN/CAN
43	w-V^{Ng} M O M / C M V	CAN/MKD
44	w-V O M / M	CAN/Nom
45	w-V M / C O V	CAN/MKD
46	w-V M M / w-V^{Ng}	CAN/CAN
47	w-V M / R V	CAN/Nom^R
48	w-V-O M R V / w-V M	CAN^{2R}/CAN
49	V-O M / C V-o	CAN/CAN
50	S^{Pn} Comp M / C S V-o	Nom/MKD

51	S V-o M / M V^{Ng}	MKD/MKD
52	V O M / [Voc] w-V	CAN/CAN
53	S V-o M / V^{Pt}	MKD/Ptcp
54	Comp V-M S / M	MKD?/Nom
55	V M O [Voc] / w-V O	CAN/CAN
56	S^{Pn} V-M / C O V	MKD/MKD
57	Comp S / V Inf O	Nom/CAN
58	V O M / V-o M	CAN/CAN
59	V O / w-V O M	CAN/CAN
60	V w-V^{Ng} / Inf O	CAN^2/Inf
61	S V-o / O V^{Ng}	MKD/MKD
62	M V Inf O / M	MKD/Nom
63	Comp S^{Pn} M(V-o) / w-M	Nom-CAN^R/Nom
64	O [Voc] V S / O V-o	MKD/MKD
65	O V M / [Voc] M	MKD/Nom
66	O w-O V / C M V	MKD/MKD
67	C V S^{Pn} V^{Pt} / w-M O V	CAN-Ptcp/MKD
68	Comp S^{Pn} w-V^{Pt} / V-o O	Nom-Ptcp/CAN
69	V M M S / S^{Pn} M V O	CAN/MKD
70	V M S / S^{Pn} O V	CAN/MKD
71	Comp M C-V / C V O	Nom-CAN/CAN
72	Comp M S /M	Nom/Nom
73	S V-o w-V-o / V-o w-V O	MKD-CAN/CAN^2
74	S^{Pt} V-o w-V / C M V	MKD-CAN/MKD
75	V [Voc] C Comp S / w-M V-o	CAN-Nom/MKD
76	V-P S Inf-o / M M	CAN-Inf/Nom
77	V-o S w-V / C-S Comp	CAN^2/Nom
78	V S C-M V-o / S^{Pn} V M	CAN-MKD/MKD
79	V M S^{Pt} / w-S^{Pt}?	CAN/Nom?
80	V-S Comp M / C V^{Ng}	CAN/CAN
81	V M S / M V	CAN/CAN
82	V S M / Inf Q V-o	CAN/Inf-CAN
83	C-V Comp M / O V^{Ng}	CAN/MKD
84	Q-S / Q V M O	Nom/CAN
85	V-M S O / R Comp^{Ng}	CAN/Nom
86	S Comp / M V-o V-o	Nom/MKD-CAN
87	M V-o M / w-S^{Pn} V^{Ng} O	CAN/MKD
88	M V-o / w-V O	MKD/CAN
89	Comp [Voc] S / V^{Pt} M	Nom/Ptcp
90	Comp S / V O w-V	Nom/CAN^2
91	M? V M / C S Comp	MKD/Nom
92	C S Comp / C V M	Nom/CAN
93	M V^{Ng} O / C M V-o	MKD/MKD
94	Comp S^{Pn} V-o / C O V	Nom-CAN/MKD
95	M V S Inf-o / O V	MKD/MKD
96	M V O / Comp S M	MKD/Nom
97	Q-V O / M S^{Pn} Comp	CAN/Nom
98	M V-o S / C M S^{Pn}-Comp	MKD/Nom
99	M V / C S Comp M	MKD/Nom
100	M V / C O V	MKD/MKD
101	M V O / C V O	MKD/CAN
102	M V^{Ng} / C-S^{Pn} V-o	MKD/MKD
103	Q-V M S / M M	CAN/Nom
104	M V / C V O	MKD/CAN
105	Comp-M S // w-Comp M	Nom//Nom
106	V w-V / Inf O	CAN^2/Inf
107	V M / [Voc] V-o M	CAN/CAN
108	O V-P [Voc] / w-O V-o	MKD/MKD
109	S Comp M / w-O V^{Ng}	Nom/MKD
110	V S O M / w-O V^{Ng}	CAN/MKD
111	V O M / C-Comp S^{Pn}	CAN/Nom
112	V O Inf O / M	CAN/Nom
113	O V / w-O V	MKD/MKD
114	Comp w-Comp S^{Pn} / M V	Nom/MKD

Appendix 2 331

115	V-M [Voc] / w-V O	CAN/CAN
116	V-o M w-V / w-V^{Ng}-o M	CAN^2/CAN
117	V-o w-V / w-V M M	CAN^2/CAN
118	V O / C-Comp S	CAN/Nom
119	M V O / C V O	MKD/CAN
120	V M S / w-M V	CAN/MKD
121	V O w-O / V^{Ng}-o M	CAN/CAN
122	V O M / V^{Ng}-o S	CAN/CAN
123	S V M / w-M	CAN/Nom
124	V M M / w-O V-o	CAN/MKD
125	Comp-S^{Pn} V-o / w-V O	Nom-CAN/CAN
126	Comp? M / V O	Nom/CAN
127	C V O / M w-M	CAN/Nom
128	C O V / O V	MKD/MKD
129	Comp S / C V-o S	Nom/CAN
130	S V / V^{Pt} O	MKD/Ptcp
131	O-V w-V / C M V	MKD-CAN/MKD
132	V-M w-V-o / M M	CAN^2/Nom
133	O V M / w-V^{Ng}-M S	MKD/CAN
134	V-o M / w-V O	CAN/CAN
135	O V M / w-V-o O	MKD/CAN
136	S? V O? / C V^{Ng} O	MKD/CAN
137	Comp S^{Pn} [Voc] / w-Comp S	Nom/Nom
138	V M O / w-M	CAN/Nom
139	V-o S / C-V O S	CAN/CAN
140	Comp S M / w-S V-o	Nom/MKD
141	Comp S^{Pn} w-V^{Pt} / O V^{Ng}	Nom-Ptcp/MKD
142	S Comp M / w-S Comp	Nom/Nom
143	S w-S V-o / S Comp	MKD/Nom
144	S Comp M / V-o w-V	Nom/CAN^2
145	V M V-o [Voc] / O V	CAN^2/MKD
146	V-o V-o / w-V O	CAN^2/CAN
147	V M w-V / M V	CAN^2/MKD
148	V S O / Inf M	CAN/Inf
149	O V M / [Voc] M V-o	MKD/MKD
150	V S^{Pt} / M V	CAN/MKD
151	Comp S^{Pn} [Voc] / w-S Comp	Nom/Nom
152	M V M / C M V-o	MKD/MKD
153	V-O w-V-o / C-O V^{Ng}	CAN^2/MKD
154	V O w-V-o / M V-o	CAN^2/MKD
155	Comp M S / C-O V^{Ng}	Nom/MKD
156	S Comp [Voc] / M V-o	Nom/MKD
157	Comp S^{Pt} w-S / M V^{Ng}	Nom/MKD
158	V O w-V / C O V^{Ng}	CAN^2/MKD
159	V C-O V / [Voc] M V-o	CAN-MKD/MKD
160	S Comp / w-Comp S	Nom/Nom
161	S V-o M / w-M V S	MKD/MKD
162	V^{Pt} S^{Pn} M / M(V^{Pt} O)	Ptcp/Ptcp
163	O V w-V / O V	MKD-CAN/MKD
164	M V / M	MKD/Nom
165	Comp M / w-E^{Ng}-Comp S	Nom/Nom
166	V M [Voc] / w-O V	CAN/MKD
167	V S O / w-V-o M	CAN/CAN
168	V O w-O / C S Comp	CAN/Nom
169	V S M [Voc] / M V-o	CAN/MKD
170	V S M / M V-o	CAN/MKD
171	V S O / C V-o O	CAN/CAN
172	V S O / C S Comp	CAN/Nom
173	V-S Comp / C O V	CAN-Inf/MKD
174	V M [Voc] / w-S Comp	CAN/Nom
175	V-S w-V-o / w-S V-o	CAN^2/MKD
176	V M V O / C O V^{Ng}	CAN^2/MKD
Ps. 120		
1	M M V / w-V-o	DEF/CAN

2	[Voc] V O M / M	CAN/Nom
3	Q-V M / w-Q V M [Voc]	CAN/CAN
4	Comp / M	Nom/Nom
5	Exc-M C V O // V M	Nom-CAN//CAN
6	M V-M S / M(V^{Pt} O)	CAN/Ptcp
7	S^{Pn}-Comp w-C V / S^{Pn} Comp	Nom-CAN/Nom
Ps. 121		
1	V O M / Q V S	CAN/CAN
2	S Comp / V^{Pt} O w-O	Nom/Ptcp
3	V^{Ng} Inf O / V^{Ng} S^{Pt}	CAN/CAN
4	H V^{Ng} w-V^{Ng} / S^{Pt}	CAN^2/Ptcp
5	S V^{Pt} / S Comp M	Ptcp/Nom
6	M S V^{Ng}-o // w-S M	DEF//Gap
7	S V-o M / V O	MKD/CAN
8	S V-O w-O / M w-M	MKD/Nom
Ps. 122		
1	V M(V^{Pt} M) / O V	CAN/MKD
2	Comp V S / M [Voc]	MKD/Nom
3	S Comp / M R V-M M	Nom/Nom-CAN^R
4	M V S S Comp / Inf M	CAN/Inf
5	C M V S M // S M	CAN//Gap
6	V O / V S^{Pt}	CAN/CAN
7	V-S Comp // S Comp	CAN//Gap
8	M / V-P S Comp	Nom/MKD-Nom
9	M / V O M	Nom/MKD
Ps. 123		
1	M V O / [Voc]	MKD/Nom
2	H M(S Comp) // M(S Comp) / M S Comp / C-V-o	Nom//Nom/Nom/CAN
3	V-o [Voc] V-o / C-M V O	CAN^2/MKD
4	M V-M S O / O	CAN/Nom
Ps. 124		
1	C S R-V M / V-P S	Nom-CAN^R/CAN
2	C S R-V M / M(Inf M S)	Nom-CAN^R/Inf
3	C Comp V-o / M(Inf S M)	MKD/Inf
4	C S V-o // S V M	MKD//MKD
5	C V M / S	CAN
6	Comp S / R-V^{Ng}-o O M	Nom/CAN^R
7	S M V M / S V^{Pt} w-S^{Pn} V	MKD/Ptcp-MKD
8	S Comp / V^{Pt} O w-O	Nom/Ptcp
Ps. 125		
1	S^{Pt} Comp / V^{Ng} M V	Nom/CAN-MKD
2	N S Comp / w-S Comp M / M	Nom/Nom/Nom
3	C V^{Ng} S M / C V^{Ng} S M	CAN/CAN
4	V [Voc] M / w-M M	CAN/Nom
5a	w-N V-o S M	MKD
5b	S Comp	Nom
Ps. 126		
1	M(Inf S O) / V Comp	Inf/CAN
2ab	C V O S // w-S O	CAN//Gap
2cd	C V M / V S Inf M	CAN/CAN
3	V S Inf M / V Comp	CAN/CAN
4	V [Voc] O / M	CAN/Nom
5	S(V^{Pt} M) / M V	Ptcp/MKD
6ab	Inf V w-Inf / V^{Pt} O	CAN/Ptcp
6cd	Inf-V M / V^{Pt} O	CAN/Ptcp
Ps. 127		
1	C-S V^{Ng} O / M V S^{Pt} // C-S V^{Ng} -O / M V S^{Pt}	MKD/MKD//MKD/MKD
2	Comp M V^{Pt} V^{Pt} / V^{Pt} O / M V M O	Nom-$Ptcp^2$/Ptcp/CAN
3	H S Comp // S Comp	Nom//Nom
4	M / Comp S	Nom/Nom
5	Comp S R V O M / V^{Ng} C-V M M	Nom-CAN^R / CAN^2
Ps. 128		
1	Comp S^{Pt} / V^{Pt} M	Nom/Ptcp
2	O C V / Comp w-Comp M	MKD/Nom

Appendix 2   333

	3	S Comp M // S Comp M	Nom//Nom
	4	H C-M V S	CAN
	5	V-o S M / w-V M M	CAN/CAN
	6	w-V-O M / S Comp	CAN/Nom
Ps. 129			
	1	M V-o M / V-P S	CAN/CAN
	2	M V-o M / P V^{Ng} M	CAN/CAN
	3	M V S^{Pt} / V M	CAN/CAN
	4	S Comp / V O	Nom/CAN
	5	V w-V M / S^{Pt}	CAN^2/Nom
	6	V Comp / R-C V V	CAN/CAN^2
	7	R-V^{Ng} O S^{Pt} // w-O S^{Pt}	CAN//Gap
	8	w-V^{Ng} S^{Pt} / S Comp / V O M	CAN/Nom/CAN
Ps. 130			
	1	M V-o[Voc]	CAN
	2	[Voc] V M // V S Comp M	CAN//CAN
	3	C-O V-S / [Voc] Q V	MKD/CAN
	4	C-Comp S / C V	Nom/CAN
	5	V O // V S // w-M V	CAN//CAN//DEF
	6	S Comp / M M	Nom/Nom^2
	7	V S M / C-Comp S / w-Comp M S	CAN/Nom/Nom
	8	w-S^{Pn} V O / M	MKD/Nom
Ps. 131			
	1	[Voc] V^{Ng} S // w-V^{Ng} S / w-V^{Ng}M w-M M	CAN//CAN/CAN
	2	C-V^{Ng} w-V O / M // Comp M S	CAN/Nom//Nom
	3	V S M / M	CAN/Nom
Ps. 132			
	1	V-[Voc] M / O	CAN/Nom
	2	C V M // V M	CAN//CAN
	3	C-V M // C-V M	CAN//CAN
	4	C-V O M // M O	CAN//Gap
	5	C-V O M // O M	CAN//Gap
	6	H V-o M // V-o M	CAN//CAN
	7	V M // V M	CAN//CAN
	8	V [Voc] M / S^{Pn} w-S	CAN/Nom
	9	S V-O // w-S V	MKD//MKD
	10	M / V^{Ng} O	Nom/CAN
	11	V-S M O / V^{Ng} M / M V M	CAN/CAN/MKD
	12	C-V S O // w-O R V-o / P-S M V M	CAN//Nom-CAN^R/MKD
	13	C-V S M / V-o M	CAN/CAN
	14	S-Comp M / M V C V-o	Nom/MKD-CAN
	15	O Inf V // O V O //	MKD//MKD//
	16	w-O V O // w-S Inf V	MKD//MKD
	17	M V O M // V O M	CAN//CAN
	18	O V O / w-M V S	MKD/MKD
Ps. 133			
	1	H Q-Comp w-Q-Comp / Inf S M	Nom^2/Inf
	2ab	M M / V^{Pt} M /	Nom/Ptcp/
	2c	R-V^{Pt} M //	Ptcp//
	3	M R-V^{Pt} M / C M V S O / O M	Ptcp/MKD/Nom
Ps. 134			
	1	H V O [Voc] / V^{Pt} M M	CAN/Ptcp
	2	V-O M / w-V O	CAN/CAN
	3	V S M / V^{Pt} O w-O	CAN/Ptcp
Ps. 135			
	1a	V O	CAN
	1bc	V O // V [Voc]	CAN//CAN
	2	R-V^{Pt} M / M	Ptcp/Nom
	3	V-O C-Comp S // V M C Comp	CAN-Nom//CAN-Nom
	4	C-O V M S // O M	MKD//Gap
	5	C S^{Pn} V C-Comp S // w-S M	MKD-Nom//Nom
	6	O R-V S V M w-M / M w-M	MKD-CAN^R/Nom
	7	V^{Pt} O M // O M V // V^{Pt}-O M	Ptcp//DEF//Ptcp
	8	R-V O / M	CAN^R/Nom

9	V O w-O M / M w-M	CAN/Nom
10	R-V O // w-V O	CAN^R//CAN
11	M // w-M // w-M	Nom//Nom//Nom
12	w-V O O / O M	CAN/Nom
13	[Voc] S Comp // [Voc] S Comp	Nom//Nom
14	C-V S O // w-M V	CAN//DEF
15	S Comp w-Comp / Comp	Nom/Nom
16	S-Comp w-V^{Ng} // S Comp w-V^{Ng} //	Nom-CAN//Nom-CAN//
17	S Comp w-V^{Ng} / P E^{Ng} S M	Nom-CAN/Nom
18	Comp V S^{Pt} / S^{Pt}	MKD/Nom
19	[Voc] V O // [Voc] V O //	CAN//CAN//
20	[Voc] V O // [Voc] V O	CAN//CAN
21	Comp S M / V^{Pt} O / V-O	Nom/Ptcp/CAN
Ps. 136		
1	V M C-Comp / C Comp S	CAN-Nom/Nom
2	V M / C Comp S	CAN/Nom
3	V M / C Comp S	CAN/Nom
4	M(V^{Pt} O M) / C Comp S	Ptcp/Nom
5	M(V^{Pt} O M) / C Comp S	Ptcp/Nom
6	M(V^{Pt} O M) / C Comp S	Ptcp/Nom
7	M(V^{Pt} O) / C Comp S	Ptcp/Nom
8	O M / C Comp S	Nom/Nom
9	O w-O M / C Comp S	Nom/Nom
10	M(V^{Pt} O M) / C Comp S	Ptcp/Nom
11	w-V O M / C Comp S	CAN/Nom
12	M w-M / C Comp S	Nom/Nom
13	M(V^{Pt} O M) / C Comp S	Ptcp/Nom
14	w-V O M / C Comp S	CAN/Nom
15	w-V O w-O M / C Comp S	CAN/Nom
16	M(V^{Pt} O M) / C Comp S	Ptcp/Nom
17	M(V^{Pt} O) / C Comp S	Ptcp/Nom
18	w-V O / C Comp S	CAN/Nom
19	M / C Comp S	Nom/Nom
20	w-M / C Comp S	Nom/Nom
21	w-V O M / C Comp S	CAN/Nom
22	O M / C Comp S	Nom/Nom
23	R-M(Inf) V M / C Comp S	CAN/Nom
24	w-V-o M / C Comp S	CAN/Nom
25	M(V^{Pt} O M) / C Comp S	Ptcp/Nom
26	V M / C Comp S	CAN/Nom
Ps. 137		
1	M M V P-V / M(Inf O)	CAN^2/Inf
2	M / V O	Nom/CAN
3	C M V-o S^{Pt} O / w-S^{Pt} O / V M M	CAN//Gap/CAN
4	Q V O / M	CAN/Nom
5	C-V [Voc] / V S	CAN/CAN
6	V-S M / C V^{Ng}-o / C V^{Ng} O M	CAN/CAN/CAN
7ab	V [Voc] M / M /	CAN/Nom
7c-f	V^{Pt} V V / M	Ptcp-CAN^2/Nom
8ab	[Voc] Comp R-V-M /	Nom-CAN^R/
8cd	O R-V M //	Nom-CAN^R/
9	Comp R-V w-V / O M	Nom-CAN^{R2}/Nom
Ps. 138		
1	V-o M // M V-o	CAN//DEF
2	V M / w-V O M w-M / C-V M O	CAN/CAN/CAN
3	C V w-V-o / V-o M	CAN^2/CAN
4	V-o [Voc] S / C-V O	CAN/CAN
5	w-V M / C Comp S	CAN/Nom
6	C-V^{Pt} S w-O V / w-O M V	Ptcp-MKD/MKD
7	C-V M V-o / M V O / w-V-o S	CAN^2/MKD/CAN
8	S V M / [Voc] S Comp / O V^{Ng}	MKD/Nom/MKD
Ps. 139		
1	[Voc] V-o w-V	CAN^2
2	S^{Pn} V O w-O // V M M	MKD//CAN

Appendix 2 335

3	O w-O V // w-O V	MKD//MKD
4	C E^{Ng} S Comp / H [Voc] V O	Nom/CAN
5	M w-M V-o / w-V M O	MKD/CAN
6	Comp S M / Comp V^{Ng} M	Nom/Nom-CAN
7	Q V M // w-Q M V	CAN//DEF
8	C-V M Comp S^{Pn} // V M H-s	CAN-Nom//CAN-Nom
9	V M // V M /	CAN//CAN/
10	P-M S V-o // w-V-o S	DEF//CAN
11	w-V P-S V-o // w-S Comp M	CAN-MKD//Nom
12	P-S V^{Ng} M // w-S M V / S Comp	MKD//MKD/Nom
13	C-S^{Pn} V O // V-o M	MKD//CAN
14	V-o C M V / Comp S / w-S V^{Pt} M	CAN-MKD/Nom/Ptcp
15	V^{Ng} S M C-V M // V M	CAN^2//CAN
16	O V S / w-M S V / S [R] V / w-Ng S	MKD/MKD/CAN$^{[R]}$/Nom
17	w-M Q-V S [Voc] // Q V S	MKD//CAN
18	V-o M V / V w-M-s Comp	CAN-MKD/CAN-Nom
19	C-V [Voc] O / w-[Voc] V M	CAN/CAN
20	R V-o M // V M S	CAN^R//CAN
21	Q^{Ng}-O [Voc] V // w-O V	MKD//MKD
22	M V-o / Comp V M	MKD/MKD
23	V-o [Voc] w-V O // V-o w-V O	CAN-CAN//CAN-CAN
24	w-V C-S-Comp / w-V-o M	CAN-Nom/CAN
Ps. 140		
2	V-o [Voc] M // M V-o	CAN//DEF
3	R V O M / M V O	CAN^R/MKD
4	V O M / S Comp *Selah*	CAN/Nom
5	V-o [Voc] M // M V-o / R V Inf O	CAN//DEF/CAN^R
6	V-S O M w-O // V O M // O V-M *Selah*	CAN//CAN//DEF
7	V M Comp S^{Pn} / V [Voc] O	CAN-Nom//CAN
8	[Voc] [Voc] / V M M	Nom/CAN
9	V^{Ng} [Voc] O / O V V *Selah*	CAN/MKD-CAN
10	N / S V-o	Nom/MKD
11	V M S M / V-o M V^{Ng}	CAN/CAN^2
12	S V^{Ng} M // N S V-o M	MKD//MKD
13	V C-V S O / O	CAN^2/Nom
14	P S V M // V S M	MKD//DEF
Ps. 141		
1	[Voc] V-o V M / V O M(Inf M)	CAN^2/CAN
2	V S Comp M // S Comp	CAN//Gap
3	V [Voc] O M // V M	CAN//CAN
4	V^{Ng}-O M / Inf O M M / w-V^{Ng} M	CAN/Inf/CAN
5a-d	V-o S Comp // w-V-o Comp /	CAN-Nom//CAN-Nom
5ef	V^{Ng} S / C-M w-S Comp	CAN/Nom
6	V M S / w-V O C V	CAN/CAN^2
7	C V^{Pt} w-V^{Pt} M / V S M	Ptcp^2/CAN
8	C Comp [Voc] S / M V V^{Ng} O	Nom/MKD-CAN
9	V-o M [R] V M / w-M	CAN$^{2[R]}$/Nom
10	V M S / M S^{Pn} C-V	CAN/Nom-CAN
Ps. 142		
2	M M V // M M V	DEF//DEF
3	V M O // O M V	CAN//DEF
4ab	M(Inf M S) / w-S^{Pn} V O	Inf//MKD
4c-e	M-R V / V O M	Nom-CAN^R/CAN
5a-c	V O w-V / w-E^{Ng}-Comp S /	CAN^2/Nom
5de	V S M / E^{Ng} S^{Pt} M	CAN/Nom
6	V M[Voc] / V S^{Pn} Comp / Comp M	CAN/CAN-Nom/Nom
7	V M C-V M // V-o M C V M	CAN^2//CAN^2
8	V M O Inf O / M V S C V M	CAN-Inf/MKD-CAN
Ps. 143		
1	V O // V M / M V-o M	CAN//CAN/MKD
2	w-V^{Ng} M M / C V^{Ng} M S	CAN/CAN
3	C V S O / V M O / V-o M M	CAN/CAN/CAN
4	w-V M S / M V S	CAN//DEF
5	V O M / V M // M V	CAN/CAN//DEF

6	V O M / S Comp M	*Selah*	CAN/Nom
7	V V-o [Voc] / V S / V^{Ng} O M / w-V M		CAN^2/CAN/CAN/CAN
8	V-o M O / C-M V / V-o O-R V / C-M V O		CAN/MKD/CAN^{2R}/MKD
9	V-o M [Voc] / M V		CAN/MKD
10	V-o Inf O / C-S^{Pn} Comp / S V-o M		CAN/Nom/MKD
11	M [Voc] V-o // M V M O //		MKD//MKD//
12	w-M V O // w-V O / C S^{Pn} Comp		MKD//DEF-Nom
Ps. 144			
1	Comp S / V^{Pt} O M // O M		Nom/Ptcp//Gap
2ab	Comp w-Comp // Comp w-Comp-M /		Nom//Nom/
2c-e	Comp w-M V / V^{Pt} O M		Nom-CAN/Ptcp
3	[Voc] Q-S w-V-o // S w-V-o		Nom-CAN//Nom-CAN
4	S M V // S Comp		MKD//Nom
5	[Voc] V-O w-V // V M w-V		CAN^2//CAN^2
6	V O w-V-o // V O w-V-o		CAN^2//CAN^2
7	V O M V-o // w-V-o M / M		CAN^2/CAN/Nom
8	R S V-O // w-S Comp		Nom-CAN^R/Nom
9	[Voc] O V M // M V-M		MKD//MKD
10	V^{Pt} O M // V^{Pt} O M		Ptcp//Ptcp
11	V-o w-V-o M / R S V-O / w-S Comp		CAN^2/Nom-CAN^R/Nom
12	C S Comp M // S Comp Comp		Nom//Nom-Nom
13	S V^{Pt} M M // S V^{Pt} M		Ptcp//Ptcp
14	S Comp / E^{Ng} S w-E^{Ng} S // w-E^{Ng} S Comp		Nom-Nom^2//Nom
15	Comp S R-Comp M // Comp S R-S Comp		Nom-Nom//Nom-Nom
Ps. 145			
1	V-o [Voc] / w-V O M //		CAN/CAN//
2	M V-o // w-V-o O M		DEF//CAN
3	Comp S w-Comp M / Comp E^{Ng} S		Nom^2/Nom?/Nom
4	S M V O // w-O V		DEF//DEF
5	O / w-O V //		Nom/MKD//
6	w-O V // w-N V-o //		MKD//MKD//
7	O V // w-O V		MKD//MKD
8	Comp w-Comp S / Comp w-Comp		Nom^2//Nom^2
9	Comp-S M // w-S Comp		Nom//Nom
10	V-o [Voc] S // w-S V-o		CAN//DEF
11	O V // w-O V		MKD//MKD
12	Inf M O / w-O		Inf/Nom
13	S Comp // w-S Comp		Nom//Nom
14	V^{Pt} S M // w-V^{Pt} M		Ptcp//Ptcp
15	S M V / w-S^{Pn} V^{Pt}-M O M		MKD/Ptcp
16	V^{Pt} O / w-V^{Pt} M O		Ptcp/Ptcp
17	Comp S M // w-Comp M		Nom//Nom
18	Comp S M / M(S R V-o M)		Nom/Nom-CAN^R
19	O V // w-O V w-V-o		MKD//MKD-CAN
20	V^{Pt} S O // w-O V		Ptcp//DEF
21	O V-S / w-V S O M		MKD/CAN
Ps. 146			
1a	V-O		CAN
1b	V [Voc] O		CAN
2	V O M // V M M		CAN//CAN
3	V^{Ng} M / M R-E^{Ng} Comp S		CAN/Nom
4	V S V M / M V S		CAN^2/CAN
5	Comp R-S Comp // S Comp		Nom//Nom
6	V^{Pt} O w-O / O w-O / V^{Pt} O M		Ptcp/Nom/Ptcp
7	V^{Pt} O M // V^{Pt} O M // S V^{Pt} O		Ptcp//Ptcp//Ptcp
8	S V^{Pt} O // S V^{Pt} O // S V^{Pt} O		Ptcp//Ptcp//Ptcp
9	S V^{Pt} O // O w-O V / w-O V		Ptcp//DEF/MKD
10ab	V S M // S [Voc] M		CAN//Gap
10c	V-O		CAN
Ps. 147			
1a	V-O		CAN
1bc	C-Comp S O // C-Comp S		Nom//Nom
2	V^{Pt} O S // O V		Ptcp//DEF
3	V^{Pt} O // w-V^{Pt} O		Ptcp//Ptcp

Appendix 2

4	V^{Pt} O M // M O V	Ptcp//DEF
5	Comp S w-Comp / Comp E^{Ng} S	Nom^2/Nom
6	V^{Pt} O S // V^{Pt} O M	Ptcp//Ptcp
7	V M M // V M M	CAN//CAN
8	V^{Pt} O M // V^{Pt} M O // V^{Pt} O O	Ptcp//Ptcp//Ptcp
9	V^{Pt} M O / M R V	Ptcp/Nom-CAN^R
10	M^{Ng} V // M^{Ng} V	MKD//MKD
11	V^{Pt} S O / O M	Ptcp/Ptcp
12	V [Voc] O // V O [Voc]	CAN//CAN
13	C-V O // V O M	CAN//CAN
14	V^{Pl}-O O // O V-o	Ptcp/DEF
15	V^{Pt} O M / M V S	Ptcp/MKD
16	V^{Pt} O M // O M V	Ptcp/DEF
17	V^{Pt} O M / M Q V	Ptcp/MKD
18	V O w-V-o // V O V S	CAN^2//CAN^2
19	V^{Pt} O M // O w-O M	Ptcp//Gap
20ab	V^{Ng} M M / w-N V^{Ng}-o	CAN/MKD
20c	V-O	CAN
Ps. 148		
1a	V-O	CAN
1bc	V O M // V-o M	CAN//CAN
2	V-o [Voc] // V-o [Voc]	CAN//CAN
3	V-o [Voc] // V-o [Voc]	CAN//CAN
4	V-o [Voc] / w-[Voc]	CAN/Nom
5	V O / C S^{Pn} V w-V	CAN/MKD-CAN
6	w-V-o M / O-V w-V^{Ng}	CAN/MKD-CAN
7	V O M / [Voc] /	CAN/Nom/
8	[Voc] / [Voc]	Nom/Nom
9	[Voc] / [Voc]	Nom/Nom
10	[Voc] / [Voc]	Nom/Nom
11	[Voc] / [Voc]	Nom/Nom
12	[Voc] / [Voc]	Nom/Nom
13	V O / C-V^{Pt} S M / S Comp	CAN/Ptcp/Nom
14	w-V O M // O M / M / V-O	CAN//Gap/Nom/CAN
Ps. 149		
1a	V-O	CAN
1b-d	V M O // O M	CAN//Gap
2	V S M // S V M	CAN//DEF
3	V O M // M V M	CAN//DEF
4	C-V^{Pt} S M / V O M	Ptcp/CAN
5	V S M / V M	CAN/CAN
6	S Comp // w-S Comp	Nom//Nom
7	Inf O M // O M	Inf//Gap
8	Inf O M // w-O M	Inf//Gap
9ab	Inf M O / Comp S^{Pn} M	Inf/Nom
9c	V-O	CAN
Ps. 150		
1a	V-O	CAN
1bc	V O M // V-o M	CAN//CAN
2	V-o M // V-o M	CAN//CAN
3	V-o M // V-o M w-M	CAN//CAN
4	V-o M w-M // V-o M w-M	CAN//CAN
5	V-o M // V-o M //	CAN//CAN
6a	S V O	MKD
6b	V-O	CAN

	(b) Isaiah 40–66	
Ref.	Constituent Order	Colon-Type
Is. 40		
1	V V O / V S	CAN^2/CAN
2ab	V M / w-V M	CAN/CAN
2cd	C V S / C V S	CAN/CAN
2ef	C V M O / M	CAN/Nom

338   Appendix 2

3	S V^{Pt} / M V O // V M O M	Ptcp/DEF//CAN
4ab	S V // w-S w-S V	MKD//MKD
4cd	w-V S Comp // w-S Comp	CAN//Gap
5	w-V S / w-V S M / C S V	CAN/CAN/MKD
6a-d	S V^{Pt} V / w-V Q V	Ptcp-CAN/CAN^2
6ef	S Comp // w-S Comp	Nom//Nom
7ab	V S // V S	CAN//CAN
7cd	C S V M / M Comp S	MKD/Nom
8	V S // V S / w-S V M	CAN//CAN//MKD
9ab	M V-M[Voc] / V M O [Voc]	CAN//CAN
9c-f	V V^{Ng} / V M H Comp	CAN^2/CAN-Nom
10ab	H S M V / w-S V^{Pt} M	DEF/Ptcp
10cd	H S Comp // w-S Comp	Nom//Nom
11	M V // M V O // w-M V // O V	MKD//MKD//MKD//MKD
12ab	Q-V M O // w-O M V	CAN//DEF
12c-e	w-V M O // w-V M O // w-O M	CAN//CAN//Gap
13	Q-V O // w-S O V-o	CAN//DEF
14	Q V w-V-o // w-V-o M // w-V-o O // w-O V-o	CAN^2//CAN//CAN//DEF
15	H S Comp // w-M V // H S M V	Nom//DEF//DEF
16	w-Comp E^{Ng} S // w-S E^{Ng} Comp	Nom//Nom
17	S Comp M // M w-M V-M	Nom//DEF
18	w-Q V O // w-Q V M	CAN//CAN
19	O V S / w-S^{Pt} M V-o / w-O V^{Pt}	MKD/MKD/Ptcp
20ab	S^{Pt} O [R] V V / O V-M /	MKD-CAN^R/MKD/
20cd	Inf O [R] V^{Ng}	Inf-CAN$^{[R]}$
21	Q-V^{Ng} // Q^{Ng} V // Q-V^{Ng} M // Q^{Ng} V M	CAN//CAN//CAN//CAN
22ab	V^{Pt} M / w-S Comp	Ptcp/Nom
22cd	V^{Pt} M O // w-V-o M	Ptcp//CAN
23	V^{Pt} O M / O M V	Ptcp//DEF
24a-c	P V^{Ng} // P V^{Ng} // P V^{Ng} M S	CAN//CAN//CAN
24de	w-P-V M w-V // w-S M V-o	CAN^2//DEF
25	w-Q V-o w-V / V S	CAN^2/CAN
26a-c	V-M O / w-V Q-V O	CAN/CAN^2
26de	V^{Pt} M O // M M V	Ptcp//DEF
26fg	M w-M / S V^{Ng}	Nom/MKD
27ab	Q V [Voc] // w-V [Voc] /	CAN//CAN/
27cd	V S M // w-M S V	CAN//DEF
28ab	Q-V^{Ng} // C-V^{Ng}	CAN//CAN
28cd	Comp S / V^{Pt} O	Nom/Ptcp
28ef	V^{Ng} w-V^{Ng} / E^{Ng} S Comp	CAN^2/Nom
29	V^{Pt} M O // w-M O V	Ptcp//DEF
30	w-V S w-V // w-S Inf V	CAN^2//DEF
31ab	w-S^{Pt} V O / V M M	MKD/CAN
31cd	V w-V^{Ng} // V w-V^{Ng}	CAN^2//CAN^2
Is. 41		
1ab	V M [Voc] // w-S V O?	CAN//DEF?
1cd	V C V // M M V	CAN^2//DEF
2ab	Q V M O / V-o M	CAN/CAN
2cd	V M O // w-O V	CAN//DEF
2ef	V M M // M M	CAN//Gap
3	V-o V M // O M V^{Ng}	CAN^2/MKD
4ab	Q V w-V / V^{Pt} O M	CAN^2/Ptcp
4cd	S^{Pn} S Comp // w-M S^{Pn}-Comp	Nom//Nom
5	V S w-V // S V V w-V	CAN^2//DEF-CAN^2
6	S O V // w-M V V	MKD//MKD-CAN
7ab	w-V S O // S^{Pt} O^{Pt}	CAN//Gap
7cd	V^{Pt} M Comp S^{Pn} / w-V-o M V^{Ng}	Ptcp-Nom/CAN^2
8	w-S^{Pn} [Voc] // [Voc (R V-o)] // [Voc]	Nom//Nom-CAN^R//Nom
9ab	R V-o M // w-M V-o	CAN^R//DEF
9c-f	w-V M Comp-S^{Pn} / V-o w-V^{Ng}	CAN-Nom/CAN^2
10a-d	V^{Ng} C Comp-S^{Pn} // V^{Ng} C-S^{Pn} Comp	CAN-Nom//CAN-Nom
10e-g	V-o P-V-o // P-V-o M	CAN^2//CAN
11	H V w-V / S^{Pt} // V Comp w-V / S	CAN^2/Nom//CAN^2/Nom
12	V-o w-V^{Ng}-o / O / V Comp w-Comp S	CAN^2/Nom/CAN

Appendix 2 339

13ab	C S^{Pn} Comp / V^{Pt} O	Nom/Ptcp
13c-e	V^{Pt} M V^{Ng} / S^{Pn} V-o	Ptcp-CAN/MKD
14ab	V^{Ng} [Voc] / [Voc]	CAN/Nom
14c-e	S^{Pn} V-o Comp / w-Comp S	MKD-Nom/Nom
15ab	H V-o M / Comp	CAN/Nom
15c-e	V O w-V // w-O M V	CAN^2//DEF
16a-c	V-o w-S V-o // w-S V O	CAN-MKD//MKD
16de	w- S^{Pn} V M // M V	MKD//DEF
17a-c	S w-S V^{Pt} O w-E^{Ng} // S M V	Ptcp-Nom//DEF
17de	S^{Pn} S V-o // S V^{Ng}-o	MKD//MKD
18ab	V M O // w-M O	CAN//Gap
18cd	V O M // w-O M	CAN//Gap
19	V M O / O w-O w-O // V M O / O w-O M	CAN/Nom//CAN/Nom
20a-d	C V w-V // w-V w-V M	CAN^2//CAN^2
20ef	C S V O // w-S V-o	MKD//MKD
21	V O V S // V O V S	CAN^2//CAN^2
22a-d	V w-V M O(R V) // O (Q S) V	CAN^{3R}//DEF-Nom
22e-g	w-V O w-V O // C O V-o	CAN^2//DEF
23a-c	V O M / w-V O w-V C Comp S^{Pn}	CAN/CAN-Nom
23d-g	P-V w-V / w-V w-V M	CAN^2//CAN^2
24	H S^{Pn} Comp // w-S Comp / Comp S(R V M)	Nom//Nom/Nom-CAN^R
25a-c	V M w-V // M V M	CAN^2//DEF
25de	w-V O M // w-M V-O	CAN//DEF
26a-c	Q-V M w-V // w-M w-V O	CAN^2//DEF
26d-f	P E^{Ng}-S^{Pt} // P E^{Ng} S^{Pt} // P E^{Ng}-S^{Pt}	Nom//Nom/Nom
27	M M H H-s // w-M O V	Nom^2//DEF
28	w-V w-E^{Ng} S // w-M w-E^{Ng} S / w-V-o w-V O	CAN-Nom//Nom^2/CAN^2
29	H S Comp // Comp S / Comp w-Comp S	Nom//Nom//Nom
Is. 42		
1a-d	H Comp [R] V-M // Comp [R] V S	Nom-CAN$^{[R]}$//Nom-CAN$^{[R]}$
1ef	V O M / O M V	CAN/DEF
2	V^{Ng} w-V^{Ng} // w-V^{Ng}M O	CAN^2//CAN
3	O V^{Ng} // w-N V^{Ng}-o / M V O	MKD//MKD/MKD
4	V^{Ng} w-V^{Ng} // C-V M O // w-M S V	CAN^2/CAN//DEF
5a-d	M-V S / V^{Pt} O w-V^{Pt}-o // V^{Pt} O w-O	CAN/Ptcp^2//Ptcp
5ef	V^{Pt} O M M // w-O M	Ptcp//Gap
6ab	S^{Pn} S V-o M / w-V M	MKD/CAN
6c-e	w-V-o w-V-o / M M	CAN^2/Nom
7	Inf O // Inf M O // M O	Inf//Inf//Gap
8	S^{Pn} Comp S^{Pn} Comp / w-O M V^{Ng} // O M	Nom^2/MKD//Gap
9	N H-V // w-O S^{Pn} V^{Pt} / C V V O	MKD//Ptcp/CAN^2
10ab	V M O // O M	CAN//Gap
10cd	[Voc] // [Voc]	Nom//Nom
11a-c	V S w-S / S [R] V S	CAN/Nom-CAN^R
11de	V S // M V	CAN//DEF
12	V M O // w-O M V	CAN//DEF
13ab	S M V // M V O	DEF//DEF
13cd	V C-V // M V	CAN//DEF
14ab	V M // V V	CAN//CAN^2
14cd	M V / V w-V M	MKD/CAN^2
15	V O w-O // w-O M // w-V O M // w-O V	CAN//DEF//CAN//DEF
16a-d	w-V O M [R] V^{Ng} // M [R] V^{Ng} V-o	CAN$^{2[R]}$// CAN$^{[R]}$-DEF
16ef	V O M // w-O M	CAN//Gap
16g-i	S^{Pn} Comp [R] V-o / w-V^{Ng}-o	Nom-CAN^R/CAN
17	V M V M / S^{Pt} / V^{Pt} M / S^{Pn} Comp	CAN^2/Ptcp/Ptcp/Nom
18	[Voc] V // w-[Voc] V Inf	CAN//CAN
19ab	Q Comp C-S // w-Comp M [R] V	Nom//Nom-CAN$^{[R]}$
19cd	Q Comp M // w-Comp M	Nom//Nom
20	V? O w-V^{Ng} // Inf O w-V^{Ng}	CAN^{27}/ Inf-CAN
21	S V M / V O w-V	MKD/CAN^2
22a-c	w-S^{Pn} Comp w-Comp / Inf M S // w-M V	Nom/Inf//DEF
22d-h	V Comp w-E^{Ng} S // Comp w-E^{Ng} S^{Pt} V	CAN-Nom//Nom^2-CAN
23	Q V O // V w-V M	CAN//CAN^2
24ab	Q-V M O // w-O M	CAN//Gap

24cd	Q^{Ng} Comp R V M	Nom-CAN^R
24ef	w-V^{Ng} M Inf // w-V^{Ng} M	CAN//CAN
25ab	w-V M O / w-O	CAN/Nom
25c-f	w-V-o M w-V^{Ng} // w-V-M w-V^{Ng} M	CAN^2//CAN^2
Is. 43		
1a-c	w-M M-V S / V^{Pt}-o [Voc] // w-V^{Pt}-o [Voc]	CAN/Ptcp//Ptcp
1d-g	V^{Ng} C V-o / V-o M Comp-S^{Pn}	CAN^2/CAN-Nom
2a-d	C-V M Comp-S^{Pn} // w-M V^{Ng}-o //	CAN-Nom//Gap-CAN//
2e-g	C-V M V^{Ng} // w-S V^{Ng}-M	CAN^2//DEF
3ab	C-S^{Pn} Comp // Comp Comp	Nom//Nom
3cd	V O O // O w-O M	CAN//Gap
4a-c	C V M // V w-S^{Pn} V-o	CAN//CAN-MKD
4de	w-V O M // w-O M	CAN//Gap
5ab	V^{Ng} C Comp-S^{Pn}	CAN-Nom
5cd	M V O // w-M V-o	MKD//MKD
6a-d	V M V // w-M V^{Ng}	CAN^2//Gap-CAN
6ef	V O M // w-O M /	CAN//Gap/
7	O] w-M V-o / V-o P-V-o	Nom]MKD/CAN^2
8	V O w-S E // w-O w-S Comp	CAN-Nom//Gap-Nom
9ab	S V M // w-V S	DEF//CAN
9cd	Q V O // w-O V-o	CAN//DEF
9e-h	V O w-V // w-V w-V O	CAN^2//CAN^2
10a-d	S^{Pn} Comp Comp / w-Comp R V	Nom^2/Nom-CAN^R
10e-h	C V w-V M / w-V C-S^{Pn} Comp	CAN^2/CAN-Nom
10ij	M V^{Ng} S // w-M V^{Ng}	MKD/MKD
11	S^{Pn} S^{Pn} Comp / w-E^{Ng} Comp S^{Pt}	Nom/Nom
12a-d	S^{Pn} V w-V w-V / w-E^{Ng} Comp S	MKD-CAN^2/Nom
12e-g	w-S^{Pn} Comp Comp / w-S^{Pn}-Comp	Nom^2/Nom
13	P-M S^{Pn} Comp / w-E^{Ng} Comp S^{Pt} / V w-Q V-o	Nom/Nom/CAN^2
14ab	M-V S / Comp	CAN/Nom
14c-e	M V M / w-V O / w-O M	MKD/CAN/Nom
15	S^{Pn} Comp / V^{Pt} O Comp	Nom/Ptcp-Nom
16	M V S / V^{Pt} M O // w-M O	CAN/Ptcp//Gap
17ab	V^{Pt} O w-O / O w-O M	Ptcp/Nom
17c-f	V V^{Ng} // V M V	CAN^2//CAN-MKD
18	V^{Ng} O // w-O V^{Ng}	CAN//DEF
19a-c	H-s V^{Pt} O / M V Q-V^{Ng}-o	Ptcp/CAN^2
19de	P V M O // M O	CAN//Gap
20ab	V-o S / S w-S	CAN/Nom
20c-e	C-V M O // O M / Inf O	CAN//Gap-Inf
21	O-R V M / O V	Nom-CAN^R/MKD
22	w-O^{Ng} V [Voc] / C-V M [Voc]	MKD/CAN
23ab	V^{Ng} M O O // w-M V^{Ng}-o //	CAN//DEF//
23cd	V^{Ng}-o M // w-V^{Ng}-o M //	CAN//CAN//
24ab	V^{Ng} M M // w-O V^{Ng}-o //	CAN//DEF//
24cd	P V-o M // V-o M	CAN//CAN
25	S^{Pn} S^{Pn} Comp / V^{Pt} O M // w-O V^{Ng}	Nom/Ptcp/DEF
26	V-o V M / V S^{Pn} C V	CAN^2/CAN^2
27	S V // w-S V M	MKD//MKD
28	w-V O / w-V M O // w-O M	CAN/CAN//Gap
Is. 44		
1	w-M V [Voc] // w-[Voc([R] V M)]	CAN//Gap-CAN$^{[R]}$
2a-d	M-V S V^{Pt}-o / w-V^{Pt}-o M V-o	CAN-Ptcp/Ptcp-CAN
2e-g	V^{Ng} [Voc] // w-[Voc([R] V M)]	CAN//Gap-CAN$^{[R]}$
3ab	C V-O M // w-O M	CAN//Gap
3cd	V O M // w-O M	CAN//Gap
4	w-V M / M M	CAN//Nom
5a-c	S^{Pn} V Comp S^{Pn} // w-S^{Pn} V M //	MKD-Nom//MKD//
5d-f	w-S^{Pn} V M Comp // w-M V	MKD-Nom//MKD
6a-c	M-V S Comp / w-Comp Comp /	CAN-Nom/Nom/
6d-f	S^{Pn} Comp // w-S^{Pn} Comp / w-Comp E^{Ng} S	Nom//Nom/Nom
7a-d	w-Q-Comp V / w-V-o w-V-o M /	Nom-CAN/CAN^2/
7e-h	M(Inf O) / w-O w-O(R V) V M	Inf/Nom-CAN^R-MKD
8ab	V^{Ng} // w-V^{Ng} /	CAN//CAN/

Appendix 2 341

8c-e	Q^{Ng}-M V-o w-V / w-S^{Pn} Comp /	MKD-CAN/Nom/
8f-h	Q-E S Comp // E^{Ng} S V^{Ng}	Nom//Nom-CAN
9	N S Comp / w-S V / N S^{Pn} V^{Ng} / w-V^{Ng} C V	Nom/MKD/MKD/CAN^2
10	Q-V O // w-O V Inf^{Ng}	CAN//CAN-Inf
11ab	H S V / w-N S^{Pn} Comp	MKD/Nom
11c-f	V S w-V / V V M	CAN^2/CAN^2
12a-c	S O? / w-V M // w-M V-o //	Nom/CAN//DEF//
12d-h	w-V-o M / P-V w-E^{Ng} S / V^{Ng} O w-V	CAN/CAN-Nom/CAN^2
13a-d	S V O // V-o M // V-o M // w-M V-o	MKD//CAN//CAN//DEF
13e-g	w-V-o M / M Inf M	CAN/Nom-Inf
14ab	V?-M O // w-V O w-O	CAN?//CAN
14cd	V-M M // V O w-S V	CAN//CAN-MKD
15a-d	w-V M Inf / w-V M w-V /	CAN-Inf/CAN^2/
15e-j	P-V w-V O // P-V-O w-V // V-o O w-V-M	CAN^2/CAN^2//CAN^2
16ab	O V M // M O V /	MKD//MKD/
16c-h	V O w-V / P-V w-V Exc / V V O	CAN^2/CAN^2/CAN^2
17a-c	w-O M V M / V-M w-V /	MKD/CAN^2/
17d-g	w-V M w-V / V-o C Comp S^{Pn}	CAN^2/CAN-Nom
18a-d	V^{Ng} w-V^{Ng} / C V M(Inf) S //	CAN^2/CAN-Inf/
18ef	M(Inf) S	Gap-Inf
19a-d	w-V^{Ng} M / w-$[E]^{Ng}$ S w-$[E]^{Ng}$ S Inf	CAN/Nom//Nom-Inf
19e-h	O V M / w-P V M O / V O w-V	MKD/CAN/CAN^2
19ij	w-O M V / M V	MKD/MKD
20a-c	V^{Pt} O / S [R] V V-o /	Ptcp/MKD-CAN$^{[R]}$/
20d-f	w-V^{Ng} O / w-V^{Ng} Q^{Ng} Comp M	CAN/CAN-Nom
21a-c	V-O[Voc] / w-[Voc] C Comp-S^{Pn}	CAN/Nom^2
21d-f	V-o Comp-M S^{Pn} / [Voc] V^{Ng}-o	CAN-Nom/CAN
22	V M O / w-M O / V M C V-o	CAN/Gap/CAN^2
23a-c	V [Voc] C-V S // V [Voc] //	CAN^2//CAN//
23de	V [Voc] O / [Voc] /	CAN/Nom/
23fg	C-V S O // w-M V	CAN//DEF
24a-c	M-V S V^{Pt}-o / V^{Pt}-o M /	CAN-Ptcp/Ptcp/
24de	S^{Pn} Comp V^{Pt} O /	Nom-Ptcp/
24f-h	V^{Pt} O M // V^{Pt} O M Q-Comp	Ptcp//Ptcp-Nom
25ab	V^{Pt} O // w-O V //	Ptcp//DEF//
25cd	V^{Pt} O M // w-O V	Ptcp//DEF
26ab	V^{Pt} O // w-O V	Ptcp//DEF
26c-e	V^{Pt} M V //	Ptcp-CAN//
26f-h	w-M V // w-O V	Gap-CAN//DEF
27	V^{Pt} M V // w-O V	Ptcp-CAN//DEF
28a-c	V^{Pt} M Comp // w-O V	Ptcp-Nom//DEF
28d-f	w-Inf M V // w-S V	Inf-CAN//DEF
Is. 45		
1a-c	M-V S M / M R-V M	CAN/Nom-CAN^R
1de	Inf-M O // w-O V	Inf//DEF
1fg	Inf M O // w-S V^{Ng}	Inf//DEF
2	S^{Pn} M V w-O V // O V M // w-O V	MKD/MKD//MKD//MKD
3ab	w-V M O / w-O	CAN/Nom
3c-f	C V C S^{Pn}-Comp / V^{Pt} M Comp	CAN-Nom/Ptcp-Nom
4ab	M // w-M	Nom//Nom
4c-e	w-V M M // V-o w-V^{Ng}-o	CAN//CAN^2
5	S^{Pn} Comp w-E^{Ng} M // Comp E^{Ng} S / V-o w-V^{Ng}-o	Nom^2//Nom/CAN^2
6ab	C V M w-M / C-E^{Ng} Comp /	CAN/Nom/
6cd	S^{Pn} Comp w-E^{Ng} M	Nom^2
7	V^{Pt} O w-V^{Pt} O // V^{Pt} O w-V^{Pt} O / S^{Pn} Comp V^{Pt} O	Ptcp^2//Ptcp^2/Nom-Ptcp
8ab	V [Voc] M // w-S V-O //	CAN//DEF//
8c-f	V-S w-V O // w-O V M / S^{Pn} S V-o	CAN^2//DEF/MKD
9ab	Exc V^{Pt} M / Comp M	Ptcp/Nom
9c-f	Q-V S M Q-V // w-N E^{Ng}-S Comp	CAN^2//Gap-Nom
10	Exc V^{Pt} M Q-V // w-M Q-V	Ptcp-CAN//Gap-CAN
11	M-V S w-V^{Pt}-o / O V-o M // w-M V-o	CAN-Ptcp/MKD//MKD
12ab	S^{Pn} V O // w-O M V	MKD//DEF?
12cd	S^{Pn} S V O // w-O V	MKD//DEF?
13ab	S^{Pn} V-o M // w-O V	MKD//DEF?

13cd	S^{Pn}-V O // w-O V	MKD//DEF
13ef	M^{Ng} w-M^{Ng} / V S	Nom/CAN
14a-c	M V S / S w-S / w-S /	CAN/Nom/Nom/
14d-g	M V w-Comp V / M V M V /	MKD^2/MKD^2/
14hi	w-M V // M V	MKD//MKD
14j-l	P Comp S / w-E^{Ng} M E^{Ng} S	Nom/Nom^2
15	M S^{Pn} Comp / [Voc]	Nom/Nom
16	V w-P-V S M // V M S	CAN^2//CAN
17	S V M / M / V^{Ng} w-V^{Ng} / M	MKD/Nom/CAN^2/Nom
18a-c	C M V-S / V^{Pt} O S^{Pn} Comp /	CAN/Ptcp-Nom/
18d-f	V^{Pt} O w-V^{Pt}-o / S^{Pn} V-o /	$Ptcp^2$/MKD/
18g-k	O^{Ng} V-o / Inf V-o / S^{Pn} Comp w-E^{Ng} S	MKD/Inf-MKD/Nom^2
19a-d	M^{Ng} V / M / V^{Ng} M / M V-o	MKD/Nom/Can/MKD
19ef	S^{Pn} S V^{Pt} O // V^{Pt} M	Ptcp//Ptcp
20a-d	V w-V V M / [Voc]	CAN^3/Nom
20e-h	V^{Ng} S(V^{Pt} O) / w-S(V^{Pt} M [R] V^{Ng})	CAN-Ptcp//Ptcp-$CAN^{[R]}$
21a-c	V w-V / P V M /	CAN^2/CAN/
21de	Q V O M // M V-o	CAN//DEF
21f	Q^{Ng} S^{Pn} Comp /	Nom/
21g-j	w-E^{Ng}-M S Comp // Comp w-V^{Pt} / E^{Ng} Comp	Nom//Nom-Ptcp/Nom
22	V-M w-V / [Voc] / C S^{Pn}-Comp w-E^{Ng} M	CAN^2/Nom/Nom^2
23a-c	M V / V M M S / w-V^{Ng}	MKD/CAN/CAN
23de	C-M V S // V S	MKD//CAN
24ab	P Comp M V S w-S	Nom-MKD
24c-e	M V w-V / S^{Pt} //	MKD-CAN/Nom//
25	M V w-V / S	MKD-CAN/Nom
Is. 46		
1ab	V S // V^{Pt} S	CAN//Ptcp
1c-e	V S Comp w-Comp / S Comp Comp M	CAN/Nom^2
2	V V M / V^{Ng} Inf O / w-S M V	CAN^2/CAN/MKD?
3ab	V M [Voc] // [Voc]	CAN/Nom
3cd	Comp M // Comp M	Nom//Nom
4ab	w-M S^{Pn} Comp // w-M S^{Pn} V	Nom//MKD
4c-f	S^{Pn} V w-S^{Pn} V // w-S^{Pn} V w-V	MKD^2//MKD-CAN
5	Q V-o w-V // w-V-o w-V	CAN^2//CAN^2
6ab	V^{Pt} O M // w-O M V	Ptcp//DEF
6c-f	V O w-V-o O // V P-V	CAN^2//CAN^2
7a-e	V-o M V-o / w-V-o M w-V / M V^{Ng}	CAN^2/CAN^2/MKD
7f-h	P-V M V^{Ng} / M V^{Ng}-o	CAN^2/MKD
8	V-O w-V // V [Voc] M	CAN^2/CAN
9	V O M / C S^{Pn} Comp w-E^{Ng} M // Comp w-E^{Ng} M	CAN/Nom^2//Nom^2
10a-c	V^{Pt} M O // w-M O(R V^{Ng})	Ptcp//Nom-CAN^R
10de	V^{Pt} S V // w-O V	Ptcp-MKD//MKD
11ab	V^{Pt} M O // M O	Ptcp//Gap
11c-f	P-V P-V-o // V P-V-o	CAN^2/CAN^2
12	V M [Voc] / Comp M	CAN/Nom
13a-c	V O V^{Ng} // w-S V^{Ng}	CAN^2//DEF
13de	w-V M O // M O	CAN//Gap
Is. 47		
1a-d	V w-V M [Voc] // V-M E^{Ng} S [Voc]	CAN^2//CAN-Nom
1e-g	C V^{Ng} V-M / Comp w-Comp	CAN^2/Nom
2	V O w-V O / V O-V-o V-O V O	CAN^2/CAN^4
3ab	V S // P V S /	CAN//CAN/
3cd	O V / w-V^{Ng} O	MKD/CAN
4	N Comp S / Comp	Nom/Nom
5a-c	V M w-V M / [Voc] /	CAN^2/Nom/
5de	C V^{Ng} V-M / Comp	CAN/Nom
6	V M V O / w-V-o M / V^{Ng} M O / M V O M	CAN^2/CAN/CAN/MKD
7ab	w-V M V Comp /	CAN-MKD/
7cd	C V^{Ng} O M // V^{Ng} O	CAN//CAN
8a-d	w-M V-O [Voc] / V^{Pt} M / V^{Pt} M / S^{Pn} w-E^{Ng} M /	CAN/Ptcp/Ptcp/Nom/
8ef	V^{Ng} Comp // w-V^{Ng} O	CAN//CAN
9ab	w-V M S // M M	CAN/Nom/
9c-e	S w-S / M V M / M M	Nom/MKD/Nom

Appendix 2   343

10a-c	w-V M / V E^{Ng} S^{Pt} /	CAN/CAN-Nom/
10d-f	N S V-o / w-V M / S^{Pn} w-E^{Ng} M	MKD/CAN/Nom
11ab	w-V M S / V^{Ng} O //	CAN/CAN//
11cd	w-V M S / V^{Ng} Inf-o //	CAN/CAN//
11ef	w-V M M S / V^{Ng}	CAN/CAN
12a-c	V-P M w-M / R V M /	CAN-Nom/CAN^R/
12de	C V Inf // C V	CAN//CAN
13a-c	V M / V-P / w-V-o S^{Pt} /	CAN/CAN/CAN/
13d-f	V^{Pt} M // V^{Pt} M / R V M	Ptcp/Ptcp/CAN^R
14a-d	H V Comp S V-o / V^{Ng} O M /	CAN-MKD/CAN-Nom/
14ef	E^{Ng}-S Comp / S Comp M	Nom/Nom
15	M V-M R V / S^{Pt} M / S M V / E^{Ng} S^{Pt}	CAN^{2R}/Nom/MKD/Nom
Is. 48		
1a-c	V-O [Voc] / V^{Pt} M // w-M V /	CAN/Ptcp//DEF/
1de	V^{Pt} M // w-M V /	Ptcp//DEF/
1fg	M^{Ng} // w-M^{Ng}	Nom//Nom
2	C-M V // w-M V / Comp S	MKD//MKD/Nom
3	O M V / w-M V w-V-o / M V w-V	DEF/MKD-CAN/MKD-CAN
4ab	M(Inf) C Comp S^{Pn} /	Inf-Nom/
4cd	Comp S // w-S Comp	Nom//Nom
5a-c	w-V M M // C V V-o /	CAN//CAN^2/
5d-f	C-V S V-o // w-S w-S V-o	CAN-MKD//MKD
6a-c	V V O / w-S^{Pn} V^{Ng} /	CAN^2/MKD/
6d-f	V-o O M / w-O w-V^{Ng}-o	CAN/Nom-CAN
7ab	M V w-M^{Ng} //	CAN-Nom//
7c-f	w-M w-V^{Ng}-o / C-V H V-o	Nom-CAN/CAN^2
8a-c	P V^{Ng} // P V^{Ng} // P M V^{Ng} S /	CAN//CAN//CAN/
8d-f	C V Inf V / w-Comp V M	CAN^2/MKD
9	M V O // w-M V-M / M(Inf-o)^{Ng}	MKD//MKD/Inf
10	H V-o w-M^{Ng} // V-o M	CAN-Nom//CAN
11	M M V / C Q V // w-O M V^{Ng}	MKD/CAN//DEF
12ab	V M[Voc] / w-[Voc] /	CAN/CAN/
12c-e	S^{Pn}-Comp S^{Pn} Comp / P S^{Pn} Comp	Nom^2/Nom
13ab	P-S V O // w-S V O /	MKD//MKD/
13cd	V^{Pt} S^{Pn} M / V M	Ptcp/CAN
14a-c	V [Voc] w-V / Q V O /	CAN^2/CAN/
14d-f	S V-o V O M / w-M?	MKD-CAN/Nom
15	S^{Pn} S^{Pn} V P-V / V-o w-V O	MKD-CAN/CAN^2
16a-c	V M V-O / M^{Ng} M V /	CAN^2/MKD/
16d-f	M(Inf) Comp S^{Pn} / w-M S V-o w-O	Inf-Nom/MKD
17ab	M-V S / Comp /	CAN/Nom/
17c-f	S^{Pn} Comp / V^{Pt}-o Inf // V^{Pt}-o M([R] V)	Nom/Ptcp//Ptcp-CAN$^{[R]}$
18	C V M / w-V Comp S // w-S Comp	CAN/CAN//Gap
19	w-V Comp S / w-S Comp / V^{Ng} w-V^{Ng} S M	CAN//Gap/CAN^2
20a-c	V M // V M / M V /	CAN//CAN/MKD/
20d-g	V O / V-o M / V V S O	CAN/CAN/CAN^2
21ab	w-V^{Ng} M V-o /	CAN-MKD/
21c-e	O M V M // w-V-O w-V S	DEF//CAN^2
22	E^{Ng} S V S M	Nom-CAN
Is. 49		
1ab	V [Voc] M // w-V [Voc] M /	CAN//CAN/
1cd	S M V-o // M V O	MKD//MKD
2	w-V O M / M V-o // w-V-o M / M V-o	CAN-MKD//CAN-MKD
3	w-V M Comp-S^{Pn} / Comp R-M V	CAN-Nom/Nom-MKD^R
4a-c	w-S^{Pn} V M V // M O V	MKD-MKD//MKD
4de	M S Comp // w-S Comp	Nom//Nom
5ab	w-M V S / V^{Pt}-o M M /	CAN/Ptcp/
5cd	Inf O M // w-S M V	Inf//DEF
5ef	w-V M / w-S V Comp	CAN/MKD
6	w-V V M(Inf M S) / Inf O // w-O Inf / V-o M / Inf S M	CAN^2-Inf/Inf//Inf/CAN/Inf
7a-c	M V S / V^{Pt} O w-Comp /	CAN/Ptcp-Nom/
7d-f	Inf-O M(V^{Pt} O) / M /	Inf-Ptcp/Nom/
7g-i	S V w-V // S w-V /	MKD//Gap-CAN/
7j-m	M R V^{Pt} // Comp w-V-o	Nom-Ptcp^R//Nom-CAN

8a-c	M V S / M V-o // w-M V-o	CAN/MKD//MKD
8d-g	w-V-o w-V-o M / Inf O / Inf O	CAN^2/Inf/Inf
9a-d	Inf M V // M V	Inf-CAN//Gap-CAN
9ef	M V // w-Comp S	MKD//Nom
10a-c	w-V^{Ng} w-V^{Ng} / w-V^{Ng}-o S w-S	CAN^2/CAN
10de	C-S^{Pt} V-o / w-M V-o	MKD/MKD
11	w-V O M // w-S V	CAN//DEF
12	H-S M V // w-H-S M w-M // w-S M	MKD//Gap//Gap
13a-c	V [Voc] // w-V [Voc] // V [Voc] O /	CAN//CAN//CAN/
13de	C-V S M // w-O V	CAN//DEF
14	w-V S V-o S // w-S V-o	CAN^2//DEF
15	Q-V S O / M(Inf O) / P-S V / w-S^{Pn} V^{Ng}-o	CAN/Inf/MKD/MKD
16	H M V-o / S Comp M	MKD/Nom
17	V S O? / w-S M V	CAN/MKD?
18a-f	V-M O w-V / S V V-M / Comp-S^{Pn} Comp /	CAN^2/MKD-CAN/Nom^2/
18gh	C S M V // w-V-o M	DEF//CAN
19	C S w-S / w-S / C M V M / w-V S^{Pt}	Nom/Nom/CAN/CAN
20	M V M S / Comp-M S / V-M w-V	CAN/Nom/CAN^2
21ab	w-V M / Q V-M O	CAN/CAN/
21cd	w-S^{Pn} Comp w-Comp / Comp w-Comp /	Nom/Nom/
21e-g	w-O Q V / H S^{Pn} V M / N Q S^{Pn}	MKD/MKD/Nom
22a-c	M-V S / H V M O // w-M V O /	CAN/CAN//DEF/
22de	w-V O M // w-S M V	CAN//DEF
23ab	w-V S Comp // w-S Comp	CAN//Gap
23cd	M V M // w-O V	MKD//MKD
23ef	w-V C-S^{Pn} Comp / R V^{Ng} S^{Pt}	CAN-Nom/CAN^R
24	Q-V M S // w-C-S V	CAN//DEF
25a-c	C-M V S / P-S V // w-S V /	CAN/MKD//MKD/
25de	w-M S^{Pn} V // w-M S^{Pn} V	MKD/MKD
26ab	w-V O O // w-M O V /	CAN//DEF/
26c-e	w-V S / C S^{Pn} Comp Comp // w-Comp Comp	CAN/Nom//Nom
Is. 50		
1a-c	M V S / Q S / R V-o /	CAN/Nom/CAN^R/
1de	C Q M / R-V O M /	Nom/CAN^R/
1fg	H M V // w-M V S	MKD//MKD
2a-d	Q V w-E^{Ng} S // V w-E^{Ng} S^{Pt}	CAN-Nom//CAN-Nom
2e-g	Q-Inf V S M // w-C-E^{Ng}-Comp S Inf	CAN-//Nom-Inf
2hi	H M V O / V O O /	MKD?/CAN
2j-l	V S M(E^{Ng} S) // w-V M	CAN-Nom//CAN
3	V O O / w-O V O	CAN//DEF
4a-d	S V M O / Inf Inf O M / V M M /	CAN-Nom/Inf/CAN/
4ef	V M O / Inf M	CAN/Inf
5	S V-M O / w-S^{Pn} V^{Ng} / M V^{Ng}	MKD/MKD/MKD
6	O V M // w-O M / O V^{Ng} / M w-M	MKD//Gap//MKD/Nom
7	w-S V-M / C V^{Ng} / C V O M / w-V C V^{Ng}	MKD/CAN/CAN/CAN^2
8	Comp S^{Pt} Q-V M / V M // Q-Comp / V M	Nom-CAN/CAN//Nom/CAN
9ab	H S V-M / Q V-o	MKD/CAN
9cd	H S M V // S V-o	MKD//MKD
10a-d	Q Comp / V^{Pt} M / R V M / E^{Ng} S Comp /	Nom/Ptcp/CAN^R/Nom/
10ef	V M // w-V M	CAN//CAN
11ab	H [Voc] / [Voc] /	Nom/Nom/
11cd	V M / w-M [R] V	CAN/Nom-CAN$^{[R]}$
11ef	M V-S Comp / M V	MKD/MKD
Is. 51		
1ab	V M [Voc] / [Voc] /	CAN/Nom/
1c-f	V M [R] V // w-M [R] V	CAN$^{2[R]}$//Gap-CAN$^{[R]}$
2a-c	V M Comp // w-M [R] V-o /	CAN//Gap-CAN$^{[R]}$
2d-f	C-M V-o / w-V-o w-V-o /	MKD/CAN^2
3ab	C-V S O // V O /	CAN//CAN/
3cd	w-V O M // w-O M /	CAN//Gap/
3ef	S w-S V M / S w-S	MKD/Nom
4ab	V M[Voc] // w-[Voc] M V	CAN//DEF
4cd	C S M V // w-S M V	MKD//MKD
5a-c	Comp S V S / w-S O V //	Nom-CAN/DEF//

Appendix 2 345

5de	M S V // w-M V	DEF//DEF
6ab	V M O // w-V M M /	CAN//CAN/
6c-e	C-S M V // w-S M V // w-S M V	MKD//MKD//MKD
6fg	w-S M V // w-S V^{Ng}	MKD//MKD
7ab	V M [Voc] / [Voc] /	CAN/Nom/
7cd	V^{Ng} O // w-M V^{Ng}	CAN//DEF
8ab	C M V-o S // w-M V-o S	MKD//MKD
8cd	w-S M V // w-S M	MKD//Gap
9a-f	V V V-O / [Voc] / V M / M	CAN^3/Nom/CAN/Nom
9gh	Q^{Ng} S^{Pn}-S^{Pn} V^{Pt} O // V^{Pt} O //	Ptcp//Ptcp//
10ab	Q^{Ng} S^{Pn}-S^{Pn} V^{Pt} O // O /	Ptcp//Nom/
10cd	V^{Pt} O / O Inf S	Ptcp/Nom
11ab	w-S V / w-V O M	MKD/CAN/
11c-e	w-S Comp // O w-O V // V S w-S	Nom/DEF//CAN
12ab	S^{Pn} S^{Pn} Comp (S^{Pn} V^{Pt}-o) /	Nom-Ptcp/
12c-e	Q-Comp w-V M([R] V) //	Nom-$CAN^{2[R]}$//
12f-h	w-M([R] M V)	Gap-Nom-$MKD^{[R]}$
13a-c	w-V O / V^{Pt} O // w-V^{Pt} O /	CAN/Ptcp//Ptcp/
13d-g	w-V M M / M / C V Inf / w-Q S	CAN/Nom/CAN/Nom
14	V S Inf / w-V^{Ng} M / w-V^{Ng} O	CAN/CAN/CAN
15	w-S^{Pn} Comp / V^{Pt} O w-V S / Comp S	Nom/Ptcp-CAN/Nom
16ab	w-V O M // w-M V-o /	CAN//DEF/
16c-f	Inf O // w-Inf O / w-Inf M Comp-S^{Pn}	Inf//Inf/Inf-Nom
17a-c	V V / V [Voc] /	CAN^2//CAN/
17d-f	R V M O // O V V	CAN^R/DEF-CAN
18a-c	E^{Ng} S^{Pt} M / M [R] V //	Nom/Nom-$CAN^{[R]}$//
18d-f	w-E^{Ng} S^{Pt} M / M [R] V	Nom/Nom-$CAN^{[R]}$
19	S V-o / Q V M / S w-S w-S w-S / Q V-o	MKD/CAN/Nom/CAN
20	S V / V M M / V^{Pt} M / M	MKD/CAN/Ptcp/Nom
21	C V-P O [Voc] / [Voc]	CAN/Nom
22ab	M-V S / w-S [R] V O /	CAN/Nom-$CAN^{[R]}$/
22cd	H V M O // O V^{Ng} Inf-o M	CAN//DEF
23a-d	w-V-o M / R-V M / V w-V /	CAN/CAN^R/CAN^2/
23ef	w-V M O // w-M M	CAN//Gap
Is. 52		
1a-e	V V / V O [Voc] // V O / [Voc] /	CAN^2/CAN//CAN/Nom/
1fg	C V^{Ng} V-M M / S w-S	CAN/Nom
2	V M V [Voc] // V O [Voc]	CAN^2//CAN
3	C-M V S / M V // w-M^{Ng} V	CAN/MKD//MKD
4	C M V S / M V-S M Inf M // w-S M V	CAN/MKD-Inf//MKD
5a-e	w-M Q-Comp M Comp / C-V S M / S^{Pt} V Comp /	Nom^2/CAN/MKD-Nom/
5f	w-M M S V^{Pt}	Ptcp
6	C V S O / C M / C-S^{Pn} Comp (S^{Pn} V^{Pt}) H-s	CAN/Gap?/Ptcp-Nom
7a-c	Q-V M S^{Pt} / V^{Pt} O // V^{Pt} O //	CAN/Ptcp//Ptcp//
7d-f	V^{Pt} O / V^{Pt} M / V S	Ptcp/Ptcp/CAN
8a-c	Comp? V O // M V /	Nom-CAN//DEF/
8de	C M V / M(Inf S O)	MKD/Inf
9a-c	V V M / [Voc] /	CAN^2/Nom/
9de	C-V S O // V O	CAN//CAN
10	V S O / M / w-V S / O	CAN/Nom/CAN/Nom
11	V V V M / O V^{Ng} / V M V / [Voc]	CAN^3/MKD/CAN^2/Nom
12ab	C M^{Ng} S // w-M V^{Ng} /	MKD//MKD/
12cd	C-V^{Pt} M S // w- V^{Pt}-o S	Ptcp//Ptcp
13	H V S / V w-V w-V M	CAN/CAN^3
14	C V M S / M-Comp M S // w-S M	CAN/Nom//Nom
15ab	M V O / M V S O /	CAN/MKD/
15c-f	C O(R V^{Ng} M) V // w-O(R V^{Ng} M) V	MKD-CAN^R//MKD-CAN^R
Is. 53		
1	Q V O // w-S Q V	CAN//DEF
2ab	w-V M M // w-M M	CAN//Gap
2c-e	$[E]^{Ng}$ S Comp w-$[E]^{Ng}$ S w-V-o //	Nom^2-CAN//
2fg	w-$[E]^{Ng}$ S w-V-o	Nom-CAN
3a-d	V^{Pt} w-Comp / Comp w-Comp /	Ptcp-Nom/Nom^2/
3e-g	w-Comp / V^{Pt} w-V^{Ng}-o	Nom/Ptcp-CAN

4ab	M O S^{Pn} V // w-N V-o	MKD//MKD
4c-e	w-S^{Pn} V-o Comp / Comp w-Comp	MKD-Nom/Nom^2
5ab	w-S^{Pn} Comp M // Comp M /	Nom//Nom/
5cd	S Comp // w-M V-M	Nom//MKD
6ab	S M V // S M V	MKD//MKD
6cd	w-S V M / O	MKD/Nom
7a-c	V w-S^{Pn} V / w-V^{Ng}-O	CAN-MKD/CAN
7de	w-M M V // w-M M V / w-V^{Ng} O	MKD//MKD/CAN
8ab	M w-M V / w-O Q V	MKD/MKD
8cd	C V M // M Comp M	CAN//Nom
9ab	w-V M O // w-O M /	CAN//DEF/
9cd	M^{Ng} V // w-$[E]^{Ng}$ S Comp	MKD//Nom
10a-c	w-S V Inf-o V / C-V O O	MKD-CAN/CAN
10d-f	V O V O / w-S M V	CAN^2/MKD
11	M V V / M V S M / w-O S^{Pn} V	MKD-CAN/MKD/MKD
12ab	C V-M M // w-M V O /	CAN//DEF/
12cd	C V M O // w-O V	CAN//DEF
12ef	w-S^{Pn} O V / w-M V	MKD/MKD
Is. 54		
1a-c	V [Voc ([R] V^{Ng})] //	CAN-Nom-CAN$^{[R]}$//
1d-f	V O w-V [Voc ([R] V^{Ng})]	CAN^2-Nom-CAN$^{[R]}$
1gh	C Comp S M / V S	Nom/CAN
2ab	V O // w-O V	CAN//DEF
2cd	V^{Ng} V O // w-O V	CAN^2//DEF
3	C-M w-M V / w-S O V // w-O V	MKD/DEF//DEF
4	V^{Ng} C-V^{Ng} // w-V^{Ng} C V^{Ng} / C O V // w-O V^{Ng}-M	CAN^2//CAN^2/MKD//MKD
5	C Comp S^{Pt} / Comp S / w-Comp S^{Pt} / Comp V	Nom/Nom/Nom/MKD
6	C-M V-o S / w-M C V V S	MKD/CAN^2
7	M V-o / w-M V-o	MKD/MKD
8	M V O M M / w-M V-o / V S	MKD/MKD/CAN
9a-c	C-Comp S M / C V / M(Inf S M M)	Nom/CAN/Inf
9d-f	M V M(Inf M) // w-M(Inf-M)	CAN-Inf//Inf
10ab	C S V // w-S V /	MKD//MKD/
10c-e	w-S M V^{Ng} // w-S V^{Ng} / V S	MKD//MKD/CAN
11	[Voc] [Voc] [Voc] / H S^{Pn} V^{Pt} M O // w-V-o M	Nom^3/Ptcp//CAN
12	w-V O O // w-O M // w-O M	CAN//Gap//Gap
13	w-S Comp / w-Comp S	Nom/Nom
14	M V / V M C-V^{Ng} // w-M C V^{Ng} M	MKD/CAN^2//Gap-CAN
15	H Inf V / E^{Ng} Comp / Q-V M / M V	CAN/Nom/CAN/MKD
16	H S^{Pn} V O / V^{Pt} M O // w-V^{Pt} O M / w-S^{Pn} V O Inf	MKD/Ptcp/Ptcp/MKD
17a-d	S([R] V M) V^{Ng} // w-O([R] V-M M) V	MKD-CAN$^{[R]}$//MKD-CAN$^{[R]}$
17e-g	S Comp / w-Comp M Comp	Nom/Nom^2
Is. 55		
1ab	Exc [Voc] V M // w-[Voc] V	CAN//CAN
1c-g	V w-V / w-V V M / w-M O w-O	CAN^2/CAN^2/Nom
2ab	Q V-O M // w-O M	CAN//Gap
2cd	V Inf M w-V-O / w-V M S	CAN^2/CAN
3a-d	V O w-V M // V w-V S	CAN^2//CAN^2
3ef	w-V M O / O	CAN/Nom
4	H O M V-o // O w-O M	MKD//Gap
5a-d	H O([R] V^{Ng}) V // S([R] V^{Ng}) M V /	MKD-CAN$^{[R]}$//MKD-CAN/
5e-g	M / w-M C V-o	Nom/Nom-CAN
6	V O M(Inf) // V M(Inf Comp)	CAN-Inf//CAN-Inf
7ab	V S O // w-S O /	CAN//Gap/
7c-f	w-V M w-V-o // w-M C-V Inf	CAN^2//Gap-CAN
8	C Ng S Comp // w-Ng S Comp / Comp	Nom//Nom/Nom
9	C-V S M / M V S M // w-S M	CAN/CAN//Gap
10a-c	C C V S / w-S M / w-M V^{Ng}	CAN/Nom/CAN
10d-f	C-V O / w-V-o w-V-o /	CAN/CAN^2/
10gh	w-V O M / w-O M	CAN//Gap
11a-c	M V S R V M / V^{Ng} M M	CAN^{2R}/CAN
11d-g	C-V O(R V) // w-V O(R V-o)	CAN^{2R}//CAN^{2R}
12ab	C-M V // w-M V	MKD//MKD
12cd	S w-S V M O // w-S V-O	MKD//MKD

Appendix 2 347

13ab	M V S // M V S	MKD//MKD
13c-e	w-V M Comp / M [R] V^{Ng}	CAN/Nom-CAN$^{[R]}$
Is. 56		
1a-c	M V S / V O // w-V O	CAN/CAN//CAN
1d-g	C-Comp S Inf // w-S Inf	Nom-Inf//Gap-Inf
2a-d	Comp S [R] V-O // w-S [R] V M	Nom-CAN$^{[R]}$//Gap-CAN$^{[R]}$
2e-h	V^{Pt} O M(Inf-o) // w-V^{Pt} O M(Inf O)	Ptcp-Inf//Ptcp-Inf
3a-c	w-V^{Ng} S / V^{Pt} M Inf /	CAN/Ptcp-Inf/
3d-f	Inf V-o S M / w-V^{Ng} S / H S^{Pn} Comp	CAN/CAN/Nom
4a-c	C-M V S / M R V O /	CAN/Nom-CAN^R/
4d-f	w-V M(R V) // w-V^{Pt} M /	CAN^{2R}//Ptcp/
5ab	w-V M M M O w-O / Comp M w-M	CAN/Nom
5cd	O V-M / R V^{Ng}	MKD/CAN^R
6a-d	w-S V^{Pt} M / Inf-o w-Inf O / Inf M M	Ptcp/Inf^2/Inf
6e-g	S-V^{Pt} O M(Inf O) // w-V^{Pt} M /	Ptcp-Inf//Ptcp/
7ab	w-V-o M // w-V-o M	CAN//CAN
7cd	S w-S Comp M / C S Comp V M	Nom/MKD
8	Comp / V^{Pt} O / M V M M	Nom/Ptcp/CAN
9	[Voc] V Inf / [Voc]	CAN/Nom
10a-d	S^{Pt} Comp M / V^{Ng} / S Comp / V^{Ng} Inf /	Nom/CAN/Nom/CAN/
10e-g	V^{Pt} V^{Pt} / V^{Pt} Inf	Ptcp^2/Ptcp
11a-d	w-S Comp / V^{Ng} O / w-S^{Pn} Comp / V^{Ng} Inf /	Nom/CAN/Nom/CAN/
11fg	S M V / S M M	MKD/Nom
12a-c	V V-O // w-V O /	CAN^2//CAN/
12de	w-V Comp S / Comp M	CAN/Nom
Is. 57		
1a-c	S V / w-E^{Ng} S V^{Pt} M //	MKD/Nom-Ptcp//
1d-f	w-S V^{Pt} / M(E^{Ng} S^{Pt}) / C-M V S	Ptcp/Nom/MKD
2	V M / V M / S^{Pt}	CAN/CAN/Nom
3	w-S^{Pn} V-M / [Voc] / [Voc]	MKD/Nom/Nom
4a-c	Q V / Q V S // V O	CAN/CAN//CAN
4de	Q^{Ng}-S^{Pn} Comp / Comp	Nom/Nom
5	V^{Pt} M / M // V^{Pt} M / M	Ptcp/Nom//Ptcp/Nom
6ab	Comp S / S^{Pn} S^{Pn} Comp /	Nom/Nom/
6c-e	P-M V O // V O / Q-M V	MKD//CAN/MKD
7	M V O / P-M V Inf O	MKD/MKD
8a-c	w-M V O / C M V w-V /	MKD/MKD-CAN/
8d-f	V O / w-V-M M /	CAN/CAN^2/
8gh	V O / O V	CAN/MKD
9ab	w-V M M / w-V O	CAN/CAN
9cd	w-V O M / w-V M	CAN//CAN
10a-c	M V / V^{Ng} Comp	MKD/CAN-Nom
10de	O V / C V^{Ng}	MKD/CAN
11a-c	Q V w-V / C V /	CAN^2/CAN/
11de	w-O V^{Ng} // V^{Ng} M	MKD//CAN
11fg	Q^{Ng} S^{Pn} V^{Pt} M? / w-O V^{Ng}	Ptcp/MKD
12	S^{Pn} V O w-O / w-V^{Ng}-o	MKD/CAN
13a-c	M(Inf) V-o S / w-O V-S V-S	CAN/MKD-CAN
13de	w-S^{Pt} V-O // w-V O	MKD/CAN
14	w-V V-V V-O / V O M	CAN^4/CAN
15a-c	C M V S^{Pt} w-S^{Pt} / V^{Pt} M w-S Comp /	CAN/Ptcp-Nom/
15de	O w-O V / w-O w-O /	MKD/Nom/
15fg	Inf O // w-Inf O	Inf//Inf
16ab	C M^{Ng} V // w-M^{Ng} V /	MKD//MKD/
16c-e	C-S M V // w-O [R] S^{Pn} V	MKD//Nom-MKD$^{[R]}$
17	M V / w-V-o Inf w-V / w-V Comp M	MKD/CAN^2/CAN
18	O V w-V-o w-V-o / w-V O M w-M	MKD-CAN^2/CAN
19	V^{Pt} O / Exc Exc M w-M / V S w-V-o	Ptcp/Nom/CAN^2
20	w-S Comp / C Inf V^{Ng} / w-V S O w-O	Nom/CAN/CAN
21	E^{Ng} S V S Comp	Nom-CAN
Is. 58		
1a-c	V M V^{Ng} // M V O	CAN^2//CAN
1de	w-V M O // w-M O	CAN//Gap
2ab	w-O M V / w-O V	MKD/MKD

2c-e	M-S R-O V / w-O V^{Ng}	Nom-MKD^R/MKD
2fg	V-o O // O V	CAN//DEF
3a-d	Q V w-V^{Ng} // V O w-V^{Ng}	CAN^2//CAN^2
3ef	H M V-O // w-O V //	MKD//DEF//
4	H M w-M V / w-Inf M / V^{Ng} M / Inf M O	MKD/Inf/CAN/Inf
5a-c	Q-M V S [R] V-o / Comp	MKD-CAN$^{[R]}$/Nom
5de	Q-Inf M O // w-O w-O V	Inf//DEF
5fg	Q-M V-O / w-O M	MKD/Nom
6ab	Q^{Ng} S^{Pn} Comp [R] V-o /	Nom-CAN$^{[R]}$/
6c-f	Inf O // Inf O // w-Inf O Comp // w-O V	Inf//Inf//Inf//DEF
7ab	Q^{Ng} Inf M O // w-O V M	Inf//DEF
7c-e	C-V O w-V-o // w-M V^{Ng}	CAN^2/DEF
8	C V M S // w-S M V // w-V M S // S V-o	CAN//DEF//CAN//DEF
9a-e	C V w-S V // V w-V H-s	CAN-MKD//CAN^2-Nom
9fg	C-V M O / O w-O /	CAN/Nom/
10ab	w-V M O // w-O V /	CAN//DEF/
10cd	w-V M S // w-S M	CAN//Gap
11a-c	w-V-o S M // w-V M O // w-O V	CAN//CAN//DEF
11d-f	w-V Comp / w-Comp R V^{Ng} S	CAN/Nom-CAN^R
12ab	w-V M O // O V	CAN//DEF
12cd	w-V M Comp / Comp	CAN/Nom
13ab	C-V M O // Inf O M	CAN//Inf
13cd	w-V M Comp // w-M Comp	CAN//Nom
13e-h	w-V-o M(Inf O) // M(Inf O) // w-Inf O	CAN-Inf//Inf//Inf
14	C V M / w-V-o M / w-V-o O / C S V	CAN/CAN/CAN/MKD
Is. 59		
1	H V^{Ng} S M(Inf) // w-V^{Ng} S M(Inf)	CAN//CAN
2	C-S V V^{Pt} M M // w-S V O M M(Inf)	MKD//MKD
3	C S V M // w-S M // S V-O // S O V	MKD//Gap//MKD//MKD
4ab	E^{Ng} S^{Pt} M // w-E^{Ng} S^{Pt} M	Nom//Nom
4cd	Inf M // w-Inf-O /	Inf//Inf/
4ef	Inf O // w-Inf O /	Inf//Inf/
5ab	O V // w-O V //	MKD//MKD//
5cd	S^{Pt} V // w-S^{Pt} V O //	MKD//MKD//
6ab	S V^{Ng} Comp // w-V^{Ng} M /	MKD//DEF/
6cd	S Comp // w-S Comp	Nom//Nom
7ab	S M V // w-V Inf O	DEF//CAN
7cd	S Comp // S w-S Comp	Nom//Nom
8ab	O V^{Ng} / w-E^{Ng} S Comp	MKD/Nom
8cd	O V M / S^{Pt} V^{Ng} O	MKD/MKD
9ab	C V S M // w-V^{Ng}-o S	CAN//CAN
9c-f	V M w-H-S // M M V	CAN-Nom//Gap-MKD
10ab	V M O // w-M V	CAN//DEF
10cd	V M M / M M	CAN/Nom
11ab	V M S // w-M Inf V	CAN//DEF
11c-f	V M w-E^{Ng} // M V M	CAN-Nom//Gap-CAN
12ab	C-V S M // w-S V M	CAN//DEF
12cd	C-S Comp // w-N V-o	Nom//MKD
13a-c	Inf w-Inf M // w-Inf M //	Inf^2//Inf//
13de	Inf O w-O // Inf w-Inf M O	Inf//Inf
14ab	w-V M S // w-S M V	CAN//DEF
14cd	C-V M S // w-S V^{Ng} Inf	CAN//DEF
15ab	w-V S Comp / w-S^{Pt} V^{Pt}	CAN/Ptcp
15cd	w-V S w-V M / C-E^{Ng} S	CAN^2/Nom
16a-d	w-V C-E^{Ng} S // w-V C E^{Ng} S^{Pt}	CAN-Nom//CAN-Nom
16ef	w-V M S // N S^{Pn} V-o	CAN//DEF
17ab	w-V O M // w-O M	CAN/Nom
17cd	w-V O O // w-V M O	CAN//CAN
18	M M? V / O M // O M / M O V	MKD/Nom//Nom/DEF
19ab	w-V M O // w-M O	CAN//Gap
19cd	C-V M S / S V M	CAN/MKD
20	w-V M S^{Pt} // w-M M / Comp	CAN/Nom/Nom
21ab	w-S^{Pn} S Comp M / V S /	Nom/CAN/
21c-e	S(R Comp / w-S R V M) /	Nom/Nom-CAN^R/

Appendix 2 349

21f-i	V^{Ng} M / w-M w-M / V S / M	MKD/Nom/CAN/Nom
Is. 60		
1	V V C V S // w-S M V	CAN^3//DEF
2ab	C-H S V-O // w-S O	MKD//Gap
2cd	w-M V S // w-S M V	DEF//DEF
3	V S M // w-S M	CAN//Gap
4a-d	V-M O w-V / S V V-M /	CAN^2/MKD-CAN/
4ef	S M V // w-S M V	MKD//MKD
5a-d	C V w-V / w-V w-V S /	CAN^2/CAN^2/
5ef	C-V M S // S V M	CAN//DEF
6ab	S V-o / S /	MKD/Nom/
6c-e	S M V / O w-O V // w-O V	MKD/MKD//MKD
7ab	S V M // S V-o /	MKD//MKD/
7cd	V M O // w-O V	CAN//DEF
8	Q-S [R] M V / w-M M	Nom-MKD/Nom
9a-d	C-M S V / w-S Comp / Inf O M / S w-S Comp /	MKD/Nom/Inf/Nom/
9e-g	M / w-M C V-o	Nom/Nom-CAN
10ab	w-V S O // w-S V-o /	CAN//DEF/
10cd	C M V-o / w-M V-o	MKD/MKD
11ab	w-V O M // M w-M V^{Ng} /	CAN//DEF/
11cd	Inf M O / w-O	Inf/Nom
12	C-S w-S(R V^{Ng}-o) V // w-S Inf V	CAN^R-MKD//MKD
13ab	S M V / S S w-S M /	MKD/Nom/
13cd	Inf O // w-O V	Inf//DEF
14ab	w-V M M S // w-V M S S^{Pt} /	CAN//CAN/
14cd	w-V M Comp / Comp	CAN/Nom
15	M(Inf Comp / w-Comp w-E^{Ng} S^{Pt}) / w-V-o M / M	Inf/Nom^2/CAN/Nom
16ab	w-V O // w-O V	CAN//DEF
16c-e	w-V C S^{Pn} Comp Comp // w-Comp Comp	CAN-Nom//Nom
17a-d	M V O // w-M V O // w-M O // w-M O	MKD//MKD//Gap//Gap
17ef	w-V O O // w-O O	CAN//Gap
18ab	V^{Ng} M S M // S w-S M	CAN//Gap
18cd	w-V Comp O // w-O Comp	CAN//Gap
19ab	V^{Ng}-M M S Comp M // w-M S V^{Ng} M /	CAN//DEF/
19cd	w-V-M S Comp // w-S Comp	CAN//Gap
20ab	V^{Ng}-M S // w-S V^{Ng} /	CAN//DEF/
20cd	C S V-M Comp / w-V S	MKD/CAN
21a-d	w-S Comp / M V O / Comp / Comp Inf	Nom/MKD/Nom/Nom
22ab	S V Comp // w-S Comp	MKD/Gap
22c	S^{Pn} S M V-o	MKD?
Is. 61		
1ab	S Comp / C V S O	Nom/CAN/
1c-g	Inf O V-o // Inf O // Inf M O // w-M O //	Inf-CAN//Inf//Inf//Gap//
2	Inf O M // w-O M // Inf O //	Inf//Gap//Inf//
3a-d	Inf M // Inf M O M // O M // O M	Inf//Inf//Gap//Gap
3e-g	w-V M Comp / Comp Inf	CAN/Nom-Inf
4	w-V O // O V // w-V O / O	CAN//DEF//CAN/Nom
5	w-V S w-V O // w-S Comp w-Comp	CAN//CAN
6ab	w-S^{Pn} Comp V // Comp V M	MKD//MKD
6cd	O V // w-M V	MKD//MKD
7ab	C Comp S / M V M	Nom/MKD
7cd	C M O V / S V Comp	DEF/MKD
8ab	C S S^{Pn} S V^{Pt} O // V^{Pt} O M	Ptcp//Ptcp
8cd	w-V O M // w-O V M	CAN//DEF
9ab	w-V M S // w-S M	CAN//Gap
9c-e	S^{Pt} V-o / C S^{Pn} Comp [R] V S	MKD/Nom-$CAN^{[R]}$
10ab	Inf V M // V S M /	CAN//CAN/
10cd	C V-o O // O V-o /	CAN//DEF/
10ef	M-S V O // w-M-S V O	MKD//MKD
11ab	C M-S V O // w-M-S O V /	MKD//MKD/
11cd	M S V O / w-O M	MKD/Nom
Is. 62		
1ab	M V^{Ng} // w-M V^{Ng} /	MKD//MKD/
1cd	C-V M S // w-S M V	CAN//DEF

Appendix 2

2ab	w-V S O // w-S O	CAN//Gap
2cd	w-V M Comp / R S V-o	CAN/MKD^R
3	w-V Comp M // w-Comp M	CAN//Gap
4ab	V^{Ng} M M Comp // w-M V^{Ng} M Comp	CAN//DEF
4cd	C M V Comp // w-M Comp	MKD//Gap
4ef	C-V S M // w-S V	CAN//DEF
5ab	C-M(Inf S M) / V-o S //	Inf-MKD//
5cd	w-M M / V M S	Nom-MKD
6	M [Voc] V O / M w-M M V^{Ng} / [Voc] V^{Ng} M	MKD/MKD/CAN
7	w-V^{Ng} O M C-V / w-C-V O O M	CAN^2/CAN
8ab	V S M // w-M /	CAN/Nom/
8c-e	C-V O M O M // w-C-V S O R V M	CAN//CAN^{2R}
9	C S^{Pt} V-o / w-V O / w-S^{Pt} V-o M	MKD/CAN/MKD
10a-c	V V M / V O /	CAN^2/CAN
10d-g	V V O / V M / V O M	CAN^2/CAN/CAN
11a-c	H S V M / V M / H S V /	MKD/CAN/MKD/
11de	H S Comp // w-S Comp	Nom//Nom
12ab	w-V M Comp / Comp	CAN/Nom
12cd	w-M V Comp / Comp(S [R] V^{Ng})	MKD/Nom-CAN$^{[R]}$
Is. 63		
1ab	Q-S^{Pn} V^{Pt} M / M M /	Ptcp/Nom/
1cd	S^{Pn} Comp M / V^{Pt} M /	Nom/Ptcp/
1ef	Comp V^{Pt} M / Comp Inf	Nom-Ptcp/Nom-Inf
2	Q S Comp / w-S Comp	Nom//Nom
3ab	O V M / w-M E^{Ng} S Comp /	MKD/Nom/
3cd	w-V-o M // w-V-o M /	CAN//CAN/
3ef	w-V S M // w-O V	CAN//DEF
4	C S Comp // w-S V	Nom//Nom
5a-d	w-V w-E^{Ng} S^{Pt} // w-V w-E^{Ng} S^{Pt}	CAN-Nom//CAN-Nom
5ef	w-V M S / w-N S^{Pn} V-o	CAN/MKD
6	w-V O M // w-V-o M / w-V M O	CAN//CAN/CAN
7ab	O V O /	MKD-Nom/
7c-e	M(O R-V-o S) / w-M M /	Nom-CAN^R/Nom/
7fg	R-V-o M / w-M	CAN^R/Nom
8ab	w-V P-Comp S^{Pn} //	CAN-Nom//
8c-e	Comp [R] V^{Ng} / w-V M Comp	Nom-CAN$^{[R]}$/CAN
9ab	M Comp S / w-S V-o	Nom/MKD
9c-e	M w-M S^{Pn} V-o / w-V-o w-V-o M	MKD/CAN^2
10	w-S^{Pn} V w-V O / w-V M M / S^{Pn} V-M	MKD-CAN/MKD
11ab	w-V O / O O	CAN/Nom
11cd	Q V^{Pt}-o M M? // Q V^{Pt} M O /	Ptcp//Ptcp/
12	V^{Pt} M O M // V^{Pt} O M / Inf M O /	Ptcp//Ptcp-Inf/
13	V M / M M V^{Ng}	CAN/MKD
14	M-S M V / S V-o / M V O / Inf M O	MKD/MKD/CAN/Inf
15ab	V M // w-V M	CAN//CAN
15c-e	Q S w-S / S w-S M? / V^{Ng}	Nom/Nom/CAN
16a-c	C-S^{Pn} Comp / C S V^{Ng}-o // w-S V^{Ng}-o /	Nom/MKD//MKD
16d-f	S^{Pn} Comp / Comp Comp S	Nom/Nom^2
17ab	Q V^{Ng} S M // V O M	CAN//CAN
17cd	V M / M	CAN/Nom
18	M V S / S V O	MKD/MKD
19a-c	V Comp V^{Ng} M / V^{Ng} S M	CAN^2/CAN
19d-f	C-V O V / M S V	CAN^2/DEF?
Is. 64		
1ab	M(Inf S O) // O V-S	Inf//MKD
1cd	Inf O M / M S V	Inf/DEF?
2	M(Inf O [R] V) / V M S V	Inf-CAN$^{[R]}$/CAN-DEF?
3	w-M V^{Ng} V^{Ng} / S V^{Ng} O M / [R] V M	MKD-CAN/MKD/CAN$^{[R]}$
4a-c	V O w-V^{Pt} O // M V-o	CAN-Ptcp//DEF
4d-g	H-S^{Pn} V w-V / Comp M w-V	MKD-CAN/Nom-CAN
5ab	w-V Comp S // w-Comp S /	CAN//Nom/
5cd	w-V M S // w-S M V-o	CAN//DEF
6ab	w-E^{Ng} S^{Pt} M // V^{Pt} Inf M /	Nom//Ptcp/
6cd	C-V O M / w-V-o M	CAN/CAN

Appendix 2 351

7a	w-M [Voc] Comp S^{Pn} /	Nom/
7b-d	S^{Pn} Comp w-S^{Pn} Comp / w-Comp S	Nom^2/Nom
8ab	V^{Ng} [Voc] M // w-M^{Ng} V O	CAN//DEF
8cd	H V-P Comp S	CAN-Nom
9	S V Comp / S Comp V // S Comp	MKD/MKD//Gap
10	S(R V-o S) V Comp // w-S V Comp	CAN^R-MKD//MKD
11	Q-M V [Voc] // V w-V-o M	CAN//CAN^2
Is. 65		
1a-d	V M(V^{Ng}) // V M(V^{Ng}-o) /	CAN^2//CAN^2/
1e-g	V H-s H-s /	CAN-Nom^2/
1hi	M [R] V^{Ng} M	Nom-$CAN^{[R]}$
2	V S M M / V^{Pt} M M	CAN/Ptcp
3	S V^{Pt} O M M / V^{Pt} M // w-V^{Pt} M /	Ptcp/Ptcp//Ptcp/
4ab	V^{Pt} M // w-M V /	Ptcp//DEF/
4cd	V^{Pt} O // w-S Comp	Ptcp//Nom
5a-c	V^{Pt} V M // V^{Ng}-M C V-o /	Ptcp-CAN//CAN^2/
5de	S^{Pn} Comp M / Comp	Nom/Nom
6	H Comp M / V^{Ng} C-V / w-V M	Nom/CAN^2/CAN
7ab	O w-O M / V S]	Nom-CAN]
7c-e	R V M // M V-o / w-V O M	CAN//DEF/CAN
8ab	M V S / C V S M /	CAN/CAN/
8c-g	w-V V^{Ng}-o / C S Comp / M V M / Inf^{Ng} O	CAN^2/Nom/CAN/Inf
9ab	w-V M O // w-M O /	CAN/Gap/
9cd	w-V-o S // w-S V-M	CAN//DEF
10	w-V S Comp // S Comp / M(R V-o)	CAN//Gap/Nom-CAN^R
11ab	w-S^{Pn} V^{Pt} / V^{Pt} O /	Ptcp/Ptcp/
11cd	V^{Pt} M // w-V^{Pt} M O	Ptcp//Ptcp
12ab	w-V O M // w-S M V /	CAN//DEF/
12cd	C V w-V^{Ng} // V w-V^{Ng}	CAN//CAN/
12e-g	w-V O M // w-O(R V^{Ng}) V	CAN//DEF-CAN^R
13a	C M-V S /	CAN/
13bc	H S V / w-S^{Pn} V //	MKD/MKD//
13de	H S V / w-S^{Pn} V //	MKD/MKD//
13fg	H S V / w-S^{Pn} V //	MKD/MKD//
14	H S V M / w-S^{Pn} V M // w-M V	MKD/MKD//DEF
15	w-V O M M / w-V-o S / w-M V O	CAN/CAN/MKD
16ab	R S^{Pt} V M // w-S^{Pt} V M /	MKD//MKD/
16cd	C V S // w-C V M	CAN//CAN
17ab	C-H-s V^{Pt} O / w-O /	Ptcp/Nom/
17cd	w-V^{Ng} S // w-V^{Ng} M	CAN//CAN
18a-c	C-V w-V M / R S^{Pn} V^{Pt} /	CAN^2/MKD^R/
18de	C H-s V^{Pt} O Comp // w-O Comp	Ptcp//Gap
19ab	w-V M // w-V M /	CAN//CAN/
19cd	w-V^{Ng} M M S / w-S	CAN/Nom
20a-c	V^{Ng} M M S / w-S R V^{Ng} O /	CAN/Nom-CAN^R/
20de	C S Comp V // w-S^{Pt} Comp V	MKD//MKD
21	w-V O w-V // w-V O w-V O	CAN^2//CAN^2
22a-d	V^{Ng} w-S V / V^{Ng} w-S V /	CAN-MKD//CAN-MKD/
22ef	C-Comp S / w-O V S	Nom/MKD
23ab	V^{Ng} M // w-V^{Ng} M /	CAN//CAN/
23cd	C Comp S^{Pn} / w-S Comp	Nom/Nom
24	w-V C-V w-S^{Pn} V // M S^{Pn} V^{Pt} w-S^{Pn} V	CAN^2-MKD//Ptcp-MKD
25a-c	S w-S V M // w-S M V-O // N Comp S /	MKD//MKD//Nom
25d-f	V^{Ng} w-V^{Ng} M / V S	CAN^2/CAN
Is. 66		
1a-c	M V S / S Comp // w-S Comp /	CAN/Nom//Nom/
1de	Q S R V-M // Q S	Nom-CAN-M//Nom
2a-c	w-O S V // w-V S Comp /	DEF//CAN-Nom/
2de	w-M V / M w-M w-M	MKD/Nom
3a-d	S^{Pt} Comp // S^{Pt} Comp // S^{Pt} Comp // S^{Pt} Comp /	Nom//Nom//Nom//Nom/
3ef	P-S^{Pn} V O / w-M S V	MKD//DEF
4ab	P-S^{Pn} V M // w-O V M /	MKD//DEF/
4cd	C V E^{Ng} S^{Pt} / V w-V^{Ng}	CAN-Nom/CAN^2
4e-g	w-V O M / w-M(R V^{Ng}) V	CAN//DEF-CAN^R

352   *Appendix 2*

Ref.	Constituent Order	Colon-Type
5a-d	V M [Voc] / V S $V^{Pt}V^{Pt}$ M /	CAN/CAN-Ptcp²/
5e-g	V S w-V M / w-S^{Pn} V	CAN²/MKD
6ab	S Comp // S Comp /	Nom//Nom/
6cd	Comp V^{Pt} O M	Nom-Ptcp
7	C V V // C V S M w-V O	CAN²//CAN²
8ab	Q-V M // Q V M /	CAN//CAN
8c-f	Q-V S M // C-V S M / C-V P-V S O	CAN//CAN/CAN²
9a-c	Q-S^{Pn} V w-V^{Ng} / V S //	MKD-CAN/CAN//
9d-f	C-$S^{Pn}V^{Pt}$ w-V / V S /	Ptcp-CAN/CAN
10	V M // w-V M [Voc] // V M O [Voc]	CAN/CAN//CAN
11	C V w-V M // C V w-V M	CAN²//CAN²
12a-c	C-M V S / H-s V^{Pt}-M M O // w-M O	CAN/Ptcp//Gap
12d-f	w-V M V // w-M V	CAN-MKD//MKD
13	M-S R S V-o / M S^{Pn} V-o / w-M V	Nom-MKD^R/MKD/MKD
14a-c	w-V w-V S // w-S M V	CAN²//DEF
14de	w-V S M // w-S M	CAN//DEF
15ab	C-H S M V // M S /	DEF//Nom/
15cd	Inf M O // w-O M	Inf//Gap
16	C M S V^{Pt} / w-M O / w-V S	Ptcp/Nom/CAN
17	S^{Pt} w-S^{Pt} M M / V^{Pt} O w-O w-O / M V Comp	Nom/Ptcp/MKD-Nom
18-21	[Prose?]	—
22ab	C C S w-S / R S V^{Pt} /	Nom/Ptcp^R/
22c-e	V^{Pt} M Comp / M V S w-S	Ptcp-Nom/CAN
23	w-V M M / w-M M / V S Inf M / V S	CAN/Nom/CAN/CAN
24	w-V w-V M / C S V^{Ng} // w-S V^{Ng} / w-V Comp M	CAN²/MKD//MKD/CAN

	(c) Job 3–14	
Ref.	Constituent Order	Colon-Type
Job 3		
3	V S [R] V M // w-S [R] V / V S	CAN$^{2[R]}$//Gap-CAN$^{[R]}$ /CAN
4	S V Comp / V^{Ng}-o S M // w-V^{Ng} M S	MKD/CAN//CAN
5	V-o S w-S // V-M S // V-o S	CAN//CAN//CAN
6	N V-o S / V^{Ng} M // M V^{Ng}	MKD/CAN//CAN
7	H S V Comp // V^{Ng} S M	MKD/CAN
8	V-o S / S^{Pt}	CAN/Ptcp
9	V S / V-M w-E^{Ng} // w-V M	CAN/CAN-Nom//CAN
10	C V^{Ng} O / w-V O M	CAN/CAN
11	Q M^{Ng} V // M V w-V	MKD//MKD
12	Q V-o S // w-Q-S C V	CAN//Nom-CAN
13	C-M V w-V // V C V M /	CAN²//CAN²/
14	M / V^{Pt} O	Nom/Ptcp
15	C M / V^{Pt} O M	Nom/Ptcp
16	C M V^{Ng} // M [R] V^{Ng} O	MKD//Gap-CAN$^{[R]}$
17	M S V O // w-M V S //	MKD//DEF//
18	M S V / V^{Ng} O	MKD/CAN
19	N Comp S^{Pn} / S Comp	Nom/Nom
20	Q V M O // w-O M	CAN//Gap
21	V^{Pt} M w-E^{Ng} / w-V-o M	Ptcp-Nom/CAN
22	V^{Pt} M / V C V-O	Ptcp/CAN²
23	M R-S Comp / w-V S M	Nom/CAN
24	C M-S V // w-V M S	DEF//CAN
25	C O [R] V w-V // w-S V M	MKD-CAN$^{[R]}$//MKD
26	V^{Ng} // w-V^{Ng} // w-V^{Ng} / w-V S	CAN//CAN//CAN/CAN
Job 4		
2	Q-V O M V / w-Inf M Q V	CAN²/Inf-MKD
3	H V O // w-O V //	CAN//DEF//
4	O V S // w-O V	DEF//DEF
5	C M V M w-V / V M w-V	CAN²//CAN²
6	Q^{Ng} S Comp // Comp S	Nom//Nom
7	V-P / w-Q S^{Pn} Comp V // w-Q S V	CAN/MKD//MKD
8	C V / S^{Pt} w-S^{Pt} V-o	CAN/MKD
9	M V // w-M V	MKD//MKD
10	S w-S / w-S V	Nom/MKD

Appendix 2 353

11	S V^{Pt} M // w-S V	Ptcp//MKD
12	w-M S V // w-V S O M	DEF//CAN
13	M M // M(Inf S M)	Nom//Inf
14	S V-o w-S // w-O V	MKD//MKD
15	w-S M V / V S	MKD/CAN
16	V w-V^{Ng} O / S Comp / O w-O V	CAN^2/Nom/MKD
17	Q-S M V // C M V S	DEF//DEF
18	H M V^{Ng} // w-M V O	MKD//MKD
19	C S^{Pt} R-Comp S / V-o M	Nom^2/CAN
20	M V / M M V	MKD/MKD
21	Q^{Ng}-V S M / V w-M^{Ng}	CAN/CAN
Job 5		
1	V-P Q-E S^{Pt} / w-Q V	CAN-Nom/CAN
2	C-O V-S // w-O V S	MKD/MKD
3	S^{Pn}-V O V^{Pt} / w-V O M	MKD/CAN
4	V S M / w-V M w-E^{Ng} S^{Pt}	CAN/CAN-Nom
5	R O S V / w-M V-o / w-V S O	MKD^R/MKD/CAN
6	C V^{Ng} M S // w-M V^{Ng} S	CAN//DEF
7	C-S M V / w-S V Inf	MKD/MKD
8	M S^{Pn} V M // w-M V O	MKD//DEF
9	V^{Pt} O w-E^{Ng} S // O-E^{Ng} S	Ptcp-Nom//Gap-Nom
10	V^{Pt} O M // w-V^{Pt} O M	Ptcp//Ptcp
11	Inf O M // w-S V M	Inf//DEF
12	V^{Pt} O / w-V^{Ng} S O	Ptcp/CAN
13	V^{Pt} O M // w-O V	Ptcp//DEF
14	M V-O // w-M V M	MKD//MKD
15	w-V M M / w-M O	CAN/Nom
16	w-V Comp S / w-S V O	CAN/MKD
17	H Comp S [R] V-o S // w-O V^{Ng}	Nom-CAN$^{[R]}$/DEF
18	C S^{Pn} V w-V // V w-S V	MKD-CAN//CAN-MKD
19	M V-o // w-M V^{Ng} M S	MKD//MKD
20	M V-o M // w-M M //	MKD//Gap//
21	M V // w-V^{Ng} M C V //	MKD//DEF-CAN//
22	M w-M V // w-M V^{Ng}	MKD//MKD
23	C-Comp S // w-S V-M	Nom//MKD
24	w-V C-Comp S / w-V O w-V^{Ng}	CAN-Nom/CAN^2
25	w-V C-Comp S // w-S Comp	CAN-Nom//Nom
26	V M M / M(Inf S M)	CAN/Inf
27	H-N V-o Comp-S^{Pn} / V-o w-S^{Pn} V-M	MKD-Nom/CAN-MKD
Job 6		
2	C Inf V S // w-S M V-M	CAN//DEF
3	C-M V / C S V	MKD/MKD
4	C S Comp / R O V^{Pt} S / S V-o	Nom/Nom-Ptcp^R/MKD
5	Q-V-S M // C V-S M	CAN//CAN
6	Q-V S M // C-E-S Comp	CAN//Nom
7	V Inf S / S^{Pn} Comp	CAN-Inf/Nom
8	Q-V V S // w-O V S	CAN//DEF
9	w-V S w-V-o // V O w-V-o	CAN^2/CAN^2
10	w-V M S / w-V M [R] V^{Ng} / C-V^{Ng} O	CAN/CAN$^{2[R]}$/CAN
11	Q-S C-V // w-Q-S C-V O	Nom-CAN//Nom-CAN
12	C-Comp S // C-S Comp	Nom//Nom
13	Q-C E^{Ng} S Comp // w-S V M	Nom//DEF
14	Comp M S / w-O V	Nom/MKD
15	S V M / M [R] V	MKD/Nom-CAN$^{[R]}$
16	V^{Pt} M // M V-S	Ptcp//DEF
17	M [R] V V // M V M	CAN$^{[R]2}$//MKD
18	V S O / V M w-V	CAN/CAN^2
19	V S // S V-M	CAN//DEF
20	V C-V / V M w-V	CAN^2/CAN^2
21	C-M V Comp / V O w-V	CAN/CAN^2
22	Q-C-V V M // w-M V M	CAN^2//DEF
23	w-V-o M // w-M V-o	CAN//DEF
24	V-o w-S^{Pn} V / w-Q-V V M	CAN-MKD/CAN^2

25	Q-V S / w-Q-V Inf M	CAN/CAN
26	Q-Inf O V / w-Comp S^{Pt}	Inf-MKD/Nom
27	P-M V // w-V M	MKD//DEF
28	w-M V V-M / w-M C-V	CAN^2/MKD
29	V-P V^{Ng} S / w-V M S-Comp	CAN^2/CAN-Nom
30	Q-E-Comp S // C-S V^{Ng} O	Nom//DEF
Job 7		
1	Q^{Ng}-S Comp M // w-Comp S	Nom//Nom
2	C M(S [R] V-O) // w-M(S [R] V O)	Nom-$CAN^{[R]}$//Nom-$CAN^{[R]}$
3	M V M O // w-O V-M	CAN//DEF
4	C-V w-V / Q V w-V-S / w-V M M	CAN^2/CAN^2/CAN
5	V S M w-M // S V w-V	CAN//DEF
6	S V M / w-V M	MKD/CAN
7	V C-Comp S / V^{Ng} S Inf O	CAN-Nom/CAN-Inf
8	V^{Ng}-o S / S Comp w-E^{Ng}-s	CAN/Nom^2
9	V S w-V / M $S^{Pt} V^{Ng}$	CAN^2/MKD
10	V^{Ng} M M // w-V^{Ng}-o M S	CAN//CAN
11	P-$S^{Pn} V^{Ng}$ O / V M // V M	MKD/CAN//CAN
12	Q-Comp S^{Pn} C-Comp / C-V M O	Nom^2/CAN
13	C-V V-o S // V M S	CAN^2//CAN
14	w-V-o M // w-M V-o	CAN//DEF
15	w-V O S / O M	CAN/Nom
16	V M^{Ng} V / V M C-Comp S	CAN-MKD/CAN-Nom
17	Q-S C V-o // w-C V M O	Nom-CAN//CAN
18	w-V-o M // M V-o	CAN//DEF
19	Q V^{Ng} M // V^{Ng}-o C-Inf O	CAN//CAN-Inf
20	V Q V [Voc] / Q V-o M M / w-V M Comp	CAN^2/CAN/CAN
21ab	w-Q V^{Ng} O // w-V O /	CAN//CAN/
21c-e	C-M M V / w-V-o w-E^{Ng}-s	MKD/CAN-Nom
Job 8		
2	Q V-O // w-Comp S	CAN//Nom
3	Q-S V O // w-C-S V-O	MKD//MKD
4	C-S V-M / w-V-o M	MKD/CAN
5	C-S^{Pn} V M // w-M V	MKD//DEF
6	C-Comp w-Comp S^{Pn} / C-M V M / w-V O	Nom^2/CAN/CAN
7	w-V S Comp / w-S V M	CAN/MKD
8	C-V-P M / w-V M	CAN/CAN
9	C-Comp S^{Pn} w-V^{Ng} / C Comp S M	Nom-CAN/Nom
10	Q^{Ng}-S^{Pn} V-o V M // w-M V O	MKD-CAN//CAN
11	Q-V-S M // V-S M	CAN//CAN
12	M V^{Ng} // w-M V	MKD//MKD
13	Comp S / w-S V	Nom/MKD
14	R-V S // w-Comp S	CAN^R//Nom
15	V M w-V^{Ng} // V M w-V^{Ng}	CAN^2//CAN^2
16	Comp S^{Pn} M // w-M S V //	Nom//MKD//
17	M S V // O V	MKD//MKD
18	C-V-o M / w-V M V^{Ng}-o	CAN/CAN^2
19	H-S^{Pn} Comp / w-M S V	Nom/DEF
20	H-S V^{Ng}-O // w-V^{Ng} M	MKD//CAN
21	C-V M O // w-O M	CAN//Gap
22	S^{Pn} V-O / w-S E^{Ng}	MKD/Nom
Job 9		
2	M V C-Comp / w-Q-V S M	CAN-Nom/CAN
3	C-V Inf M / V^{Ng}-o M M	CAN/CAN
4	Comp w-Comp / Q-V M w-V	Nom^2/CAN^2
5	V^{Pt} O w-V^{Ng} / R V-o M	CAN^2/CAN^R
6	V^{Pt} O M // w-S V	Ptcp//DEF
7	V^{Pt} M w-V^{Ng} // w-M V	Ptcp-CAN//DEF
8	V^{Pt} O M // w-V^{Pt} M	Ptcp//Ptcp
9	V^{Pt}-O O / w-O w-O	Ptcp/Nom
10	V^{Pt} O C-E^{Ng} S // w-O C-E^{Ng} S	Ptcp-Nom//Gap-Nom
11	H V M w-V^{Ng} // w-V w-V^{Ng} M	CAN^2//CAN^2
12	H V Q V-o // Q-V M Q-V	CAN^2//CAN^2

Appendix 2   355

13	S V^{Ng} O / M V S^{Pt}	MKD/MKD
14	C-S^{Pn} V-o // V O M	MKD//CAN
15	C-V V^{Ng} / M V	CAN^2/MKD
16	C-V w-V-o / V^{Ng} C-V O	CAN^2/CAN^2
17	C-M V-o / w-V O M	MKD/CAN
18	V^{Ng}-o Inf O / C V-o M	CAN-Inf/CAN
19	C-M Comp H / w-C-M Q V-o	Nom^2/Nom-CAN
20	C-V S V-o // Comp S^{Pn} w-V-o	CAN-MKD//Nom-CAN
21	Comp S^{Pn} V^{Ng} O // V O	Nom-CAN//CAN
22	Comp S^{Pn} C V / O w-O S^{Pn} V	Nom-CAN/Ptcp
23	C-S V M / M V	MKD/MKD
24	S V M / O V / C-Ng P Q-S^{Pn}	MKD/MKD/Nom^2
25	w-S V M / V V^{Ng} O	MKD/CAN^2
26	V M / M-S V M	CAN/MKD
27	C-Inf V O / V O w-V	Inf-CAN/CAN^2
28	V O / V C-V^{Ng}-o	CAN/CAN^2
29	S^{Pn} V / Q-M V	MKD/MKD
30	C-V M // w-V M O	CAN//CAN
31	C M V-o / w-V-o S	MKD/CAN
32	C-Comp^{Ng}-M w-V-o / V M M	Nom-CAN/CAN
33	E^{Ng}-Comp S^{Pt} / V O M	Nom/CAN
34	V M O // w-S V^{Ng}-o	CAN//DEF
35	V w-V^{Ng}-o / C-Comp^{Ng} S^{Pn} M	CAN^2/Nom
Job 10		
1	V S M / V M O // V M	CAN^2//CAN
2	V M V^{Ng}-o / V-o Q-V-o	CAN^2/CAN^2
3	Q-Comp M C-V // C-V O / w-M V	Nom-CAN//CAN/MKD
4	Q-S Comp // C-M(Inf S) V	Nom//Inf-MKD
5	Q-Comp S // C-S Comp	Nom//Nom
6	C-V M // w-M V	CAN//DEF
7	M C-V^{Ng} / w-E^{Ng} Comp S^{Pt}	Nom-CAN/Nom
8	S V-o w-V-o / M M w-V-o	MKD-CAN/Nom-CAN
9	V-P C-M V-o / w-M V-o	CAN-MKD/MKD
10	Q^{Ng} M V-o // w-M V-o	MKD//MKD
11	O w-O V-o // w-M V-o	MKD//MKD
12	O w-O V M // w-S V O	MKD//MKD
13	w-O V M / V C-S^{Pn} Comp	MKD/CAN-Nom
14	C-V w-V-o / w-M V^{Ng}-o	CAN^2/MKD
15a-d	C-V Exc M / w-V V^{Ng} O /	CAN-Nom/CAN^2/
15ef	Comp w-V O	Nom-CAN
16	w-V M V-o / w-V V-M	CAN^2/CAN
17	V O M // w-V O M / S w-S Comp	CAN//CAN/Nom
18	w-Q M V-o / V w-S V^{Ng}-o	MKD/CAN-MKD
19	C V^{Ng} V / M M V	CAN^2/MKD
20	Q^{Ng}-Comp S w-V / w-V M w-V M	Nom-CAN/CAN^2
21	C V w-V^{Ng} / M	CAN^2/Nom
22	Comp M / Comp Comp^{Ng} / w-V M	Nom/Nom^2/CAN
Job 11		
2	Q-S V^{Ng} // w-C-S V //	MKD//MKD//
3	S M V / w-V w-E^{Ng} S^{Pt}	MKD/CAN-Nom
4	w-V Comp S // w-Comp V M	CAN-Nom//MKD
5	w-M Q-V S Inf // w-V O M	CAN-Inf//CAN
6	w-V-M O / C-S Comp / w-V C-V M S M	CAN/Nom/CAN^2
7	Q-O V // C-M V	MKD//MKD
8	Comp Q-V // Comp M Q-V	Nom-CAN//Nom-CAN
9	Comp M S // w-Comp M	Nom//Nom
10	C-V w-V / w-V w-Q V-o	CAN^2/CAN^2
11	C-S^{Pn} V O / w-V-O w-V^{Ng}	MKD/CAN^2
12	w-S V / w-S Comp V	MKD/DEF
13	C-S^{Pn} V O / w-V M O	MKD/CAN
14	C-S Comp V-o // w-V^{Ng} M S	Nom-CAN//CAN
15	C-C V O M // w-V Comp w-V^{Ng}	CAN/CAN^2
16	C-S^{Pn} O V / M [R] V V	MKD/CAN$^{[R]}$-MKD

17	w-M V S // V? Comp V	MKD/CAN-MKD
18	w-V C-E S / w-V M V	CAN-Nom/CAN-MKD
19	w-V w-E^{Ng} S^{Pt} / w-V O S	CAN-Nom/CAN
20	w-S V / w-S V M / w-S Comp	MKD/MKD/Nom
Job 12		
2	M C S^{Pn}-Comp / w-M V S	Nom/MKD
3	P-Comp S M / V^{Pt-Ng} S^{Pn} M / w-Q-E^{Ng} Comp	Nom/Ptcp/Nom
4	Comp M V / V^{Pt} M w-V-o / Comp S	MKD/Ptcp-CAN/Nom
5	Comp? S? / Comp M	Nom/Nom
6	V S // w-S Comp / M(R V O M)	CAN//Nom/Nom-CAN^R
7	w-M V-P IO w-V-o // w-O V-M //	CAN^2//Gap-CAN//
8	C V w-V-o // w-V M S	Gap-CAN//CAN
9	Q V^{Ng} M / C S V O	CAN/CAN
10	R Comp S / w-S	Nom^R/Nom
11	Q^{Ng}-S O V // w-S O V-M	DEF//DEF
12	Comp S // w-Comp S	Nom//Nom
13	Comp S w-S // Comp S w-S	Nom//Nom
14	H V w-V^{Ng} // V M w-V^{Ng}	CAN^2//CAN^2
15	H V M w-V // w-V-o w-V O	CAN^2//CAN^2
16	Comp S w-S // Comp S^{Pt} w-S^{Pt}	Nom//Nom
17	V^{Pt} O Comp // w-O V //	Ptcp//DEF//
18	O V // w-V O M	DEF//CAN
19	V^{Pt} O Comp // w-O V //	Ptcp//DEF//
20	V^{Pt} O M // w-O V //	Ptcp//DEF//
21	V^{Pt} O M // w-O V //	Ptcp//DEF//
22	V^{Pt} O M // w-V M O //	Ptcp//CAN//
23	V^{Pt} O w-V-o // V^{Pt} O w-V-o //	Ptcp-CAN//Ptcp-CAN//
24	V^{Pt} O // w-V-O Comp^{Ng}	Ptcp-CAN
25	V-M w-Comp^{Ng} / w-V-o M	CAN/CAN
Job 13		
1	H-O V S / V S w-V M	MKD/CAN^2
2	M V P-S^{Pn} / V^{Pt-Ng} S^{Pn} M	CAN/Ptcp
3	M S^{Pt} M V // w-Inf M V	MKD//MKD
4	w-M S^{Pn} Comp // Comp S	Nom//Nom
5	Q-V Inf V / w-V M Comp	CAN^2/CAN
6	V-P O // w-O V	CAN//DEF
7	Q-M V O // w-M V O	MKD//MKD
8	Q-O V // C-M V	MKD//MKD
9	Q-Comp C-V O / C-M(Inf M) V M	Nom-CAN/Inf-MKD
10	Inf V O / C-M O V	CAN/MKD
11	Q^{Ng} S V O // w-S V M	MKD//MKD
12	S Comp // Comp S	Nom//Nom
13	V M w-V-S^{Pn} / w-V M S	CAN^2/CAN
14	Q V O M // w-O V M	CAN//DEF
15	H V-o M? V / P-O M V	CAN-MKD/MKD
16	P-S^{Pn}-M Comp / C Ng M S V	Nom/DEF
17	V Inf O // w-S Comp	CAN//Nom
18	H-P V O / V C S^{Pn}-V	CAN/CAN-MKD
19	Q-S^{Pn} [R] V M / C-M V w-V	Nom-CAN$^{[R]}$/CAN^2
20	P-O V^{Ng} M / C M V^{Ng}	MKD/MKD
21	S M V // w-S V^{Ng}-o	MKD//MKD
22	w-V w-S^{Pn} V / C-V w-V-o	CAN-MKD/CAN^2
23	Q Comp S w-S / O w-O V-o	Nom/MKD
24	Q-O V / w-V-o M M	MKD/CAN
25	O V // w-O V	MKD//MKD
26	C-V M O / w-V-o O	CAN/CAN
27	w-V M O // w-V O // M V	CAN//CAN//DEF
28	w-S^{Pn} M V / M(O [R] V-o S)	MKD/Nom-CAN$^{[R]}$
Job 14		
1	S Comp / Comp w-Comp	Nom/Nom^2
2	M V w-V / w-V M w-V^{Ng}	MKD-CAN/CAN-MKD
3	P-M V O // w-O V M M	MKD//MKD
4	Q V O M / [E]^{Ng} S	CAN/Nom

Appendix 2

Appendix 2 357

5	C Comp S // S Comp / O V w-V^{Ng}	Nom//Nom/MKD-CAN
6	V M w-V / C-V M O	CAN^2/CAN
7	C E Comp S / C-V w-M V / w-S V^{Ng}	Nom/CAN^2/MKD
8	C-V M S // w-M V S	CAN//DEF
9	M V / w-V O M	MKD/CAN
10	w-S V w-V // w-V S w-E-S	MKD-CAN//DEF-Nom
11	V-S M // w-S V w-V	CAN//DEF-CAN
12	S V w-V^{Ng} / C-E^{Ng} S / V^{Ng} w-V^{Ng} M	MKD-CAN/Nom/CAN^2
13	Q V M V-o / V-o C-Inf S /	CAN-MKD/CAN-Inf/
13	V M O w-V-o	CAN^2
14	C-V S Q-V / M V / C-Inf S	CAN^2/MKD/Inf
15	V w-S^{Pn} V-o / M V	CAN-MKD/MKD
16	C-M O V / V^{Ng} M	MKD/CAN
17	Comp S / w-V M	Nom/CAN
18	w-M S^{Pt} V // w-S V M //	MKD//MKD//
19	O V S // V-S O // w-O V	MKD//DEF/MKD
20	V-o M w-V / V^{Pt} O w-V-o	CAN^2/Ptcp-CAN
21	V S w-V^{Ng} // w-V w-V^{Ng} M	CAN^2//CAN^2
22	P-S M V // w-S M V	MKD//MKD

	(d) Proverbs 1–9	
Ref.	Constituent Order	Colon-Type
Prov. 1		
2	Inf O w-O // Inf O //	Inf//Inf//
3	Inf O / O w-O w-O	Inf/Nom
4	Inf M O / M O w-O	Inf//Gap
5	V S w-V O // w-S O V	CAN^2//DEF
6	Inf O w-O / O w-O	Inf/Nom
7	S Comp / O w-O S V	Nom/DEF
8	V [Voc] O // w-V^{Ng} O	CAN//CAN
9	C Comp S^{Pn} M // w-Comp M	Nom//Nom
10	[Voc] C-V S V^{Ng}	CAN^2
11	C-V / V M V M // V M M	CAN/CAN^2//CAN
12	V-o M M // w-M M	CAN//Gap
13	O V / V O M	MKD/CAN
14	O V M / S V Comp	MKD/MKD
15	[Voc] V^{Ng} M M // V O M	CAN//CAN
16	C S M V // w-V Inf-M	DEF//CAN
17	C-M V^{Pt} S / M	Ptcp/Nom
18	w-S^{Pn} M V // V M	MKD//CAN
19	Comp S // O V	Nom//MKD
20	S M V // M V O //	MKD//MKD//
21	M V // M M O V	MKD//MKD
22	Q [Voc] V O // w-S O V M // w-S V-O	CAN//DEF//DEF
23	V M / H V M O // V O M	CAN/CAN//CAN
24	C V w-V // V O w-E S^{Pt}	CAN^2//CAN-Nom
25	w-V O // w-O V^{Ng}	CAN//DEF
26	P-S^{Pn} M V // V M(Inf S) //	MKD//DEF//
27	M(Inf M S) // w-S M V // M(Inf M S w-S)	Inf// MKD//Inf
28	C V-o w-V^{Ng} // V-o w-V^{Ng}-o	CAN^2//CAN^2
29	C-V O // w-O V^{Ng}	CAN//DEF
30	V^{Ng} O // V O	CAN//CAN
31	w-V M // w-M V	CAN//DEF
32	C S V-o // w-S V-o	MKD//MKD
33	S^{Pt} V-M // Comp M	MKD//Nom
Prov. 2		
1	[Voc] C-V O // w-O V M	CAN//DEF
2	Inf M O // V O M	Inf//CAN
3	C M V // M V O	MKD//MKD
4	C-V-o M // w-M V-o	CAN//DEF
5	C V O // w-O V	CAN//DEF
6	C-S V O // Comp S w-S	MKD//Nom
7	w-V M O / Comp M	CAN/Nom

8	Inf O // w-O V	Inf//DEF
9	C V O w-O / w-O O	CAN/ Nom
10	C-V S M // w-S M V	CAN//DEF
11	S V M // S V-o	MKD//MKD
12	Inf-o M / M(V^{Pt} O)	Inf/Ptcp
13	V^{Pt} O / Inf M	Ptcp/Inf
14	V^{Pt} Inf O // V M	Ptcp//CAN
15	R S Comp // w-Comp M	Nom//Ptcp
16	Inf-o M / M [R] O V	Inf/Nom-MKD$^{[R]}$
17	V^{Pt} O // w-O V	Ptcp//DEF
18	C V M S // w-M S	CAN//Gap
19	S^{Pt} V^{Ng} // w-V^{Ng} O	DEF//CAN
20	C V M // w-O V	CAN//DEF
21	C-S V-O // w-S V M	MKD//MKD
22	w-S M V // w-S V M	MKD//MKD
Prov. 3		
1	[Voc] O V^{Ng} // w-O V S	MKD//MKD
2	C O w-O / w-O V M	Nom/MKD
3	S w-S V^{Ng}-o / V-o M // V-o M	MKD/CAN//CAN
4	w-V O w-O / M	CAN/Nom
5	V M M / w-M V^{Ng}	CAN/MKD
6	M V-o / w-S^{Pn} V O	MKD/MKD
7	V^{Ng} Comp M / V O w-V M	CAN/CAN^2
8	Comp V M // w-Comp M	MKD//Gap
9	V O M // w-M	CAN/Nom
10	w-V S M // w-M S V	CAN//DEF
11	O [Voc] V^{Ng} // w-V^{Ng} M	DEF//CAN
12	C O(R V S) V // w-C-S O [R] V	MKD-CAN^R//Nom-MKD
13	Comp S [R] V O // w-S V O	Nom-CAN$^{[R]}$//DEF
14	C Comp S M // w-M S	Nom//Gap
15	Comp S^{Pn} M / S V^{Ng}-M	Nom/MKD
16	S Comp // Comp S w-S	Nom//Nom
17	S Comp // w-S Comp //	Nom//Nom
18	Comp S^{Pn} M(V^{Pt} M) // S^{Pt} V^{Pt}	Nom-Ptcp//Ptcp
19	S M V-O // V O M	DEF//CAN
20	M S V // w-S V-O	DEF//DEF
21	[Voc] V^{Ng} M // V O w-O	CAN//CAN
22	w-V Comp M // w-Comp M	CAN//Gap
23	C V M O // w-S V^{Ng}	CAN//DEF
24	C-V V^{Ng} // w-V w-V S	CAN^2//CAN^2
25	V^{Ng} M M / w-M C V	CAN/Nom-CAN
26	C-S V Comp / w-V O M	MKD/CAN
27	V^{Ng}-O M / M(Inf M Inf)	CAN/Inf
28	V^{Ng} M V w-V / w-M V w-E Comp	CAN^3/MKD-Nom
29	V^{Ng} M O / w-S^{Pn}-V^{Pt} M M	CAN/Ptcp
30	V^{Ng} M M / C-V^{Ng}-o O	CAN/CAN
31	V^{Ng} M / w-V^{Ng} M	CAN/CAN
32	C Comp S / w-Comp S	Nom/Nom
33	S Comp / w-O V	Nom/MKD
34	M S^{Pn}-V // w-M V-O	MKD/MKD
35	O S V / w-O? V^{Pt} M?	DEF/Ptcp
Prov. 4		
1	V [Voc] O // w-V Inf O	CAN//CAN
2	C O V M / O V^{Ng}	MKD/MKD
3	C-Comp V M // Comp w-Comp M	MKD//Gap
4	w-V-o w-V M / V-O S // V O w-V	CAN^2/CAN//CAN^2
5	V O // V O / V^{Ng} w-V^{Ng} M	CAN//CAN/CAN^2
6	V^{Ng}-o w-V-o // V-o w-V-o	CAN^2//CAN^2
7	Comp V O / w-M V O	Nom-CAN/MKD
8	V-o w-V-o // V-o C V-o	CAN^2//CAN^2
9	V M O // O V-o	CAN//DEF
10	V [Voc] w-V O / w-V M S	CAN^2/CAN
11	M V-o // V-o M	DEF//CAN
12	M(Inf) V^{Ng} S // w-C-V V^{Ng}	Inf-CAN//CAN^2

Appendix 2 359

13	V M V^{Ng} // V-o C-S^{Pn} Comp	CAN^2//CAN-Nom
14	M V^{Ng} // w-V^{Ng} M	DEF//CAN
15	V-o V^{Ng}-M // V M w-V	CAN^2//CAN^2
16	C V^{Ng} C-V^{Ng} // w-V S C-V^{Ng}	CAN^2//CAN^2
17	C V O // w-O V	CAN//DEF
18	w-S Comp / V^{Pt} w-V^{Pt} M	Nom/Ptcp
19	S Comp / V^{Ng} Q V	Nom/CAN^2
20	[Voc] M V // M V-O	MKD//MKD
21	V^{Ng} M // V-o M	CAN//CAN
22	C-Comp S^{Pn} M // w-M Comp	Nom//Nom
23	M V O / C-Comp S	MKD/Nom
24	V M O // w-O V M	CAN//DEF
25	S M V // w-S V M	MKD//MKD
26	V O // w-S V	CAN//DEF
27	V^{Ng}-O w-O / V O M	CAN/CAN
Prov. 5		
1	[Voc] M V // M V-O	MKD//MKD
2	Inf O // w-O S V	Inf//DEF
3	C O V S // w-Comp M S	MKD//Nom
4	w-S Comp M // Comp M	Nom//Nom
5	S V^{Pt} M // O S V	Ptcp//DEF
6	O C-V / V S V^{Ng}	MKD/CAN^2
7	w-M [Voc] V-M // w-V^{Ng} M	CAN//CAN
8	V M O // w-V^{Ng} M	CAN//CAN
9	C-V M O // w-O M	CAN//Gap
10	C-V S O // w-S Comp	CAN//Nom
11	w-V M / M(Inf S w-S)	CAN/Inf
12	w-V Q V O // w-O V S	CAN^2//DEF
13	V^{Ng} M // w-M V^{Ng} O	CAN//DEF
14	M V Comp / M	CAN/Nom
15	V-O M // w-O M	CAN//Gap
16	V S M // M S	CAN//Gap
17	V-Comp M / w-E^{Ng} Comp M	CAN/Nom
18	V-S Comp / w-V M	CAN/CAN
19	Comp w-Comp / S V-o M // M V M	Nom/MKD//MKD
20	w-Q V [Voc] M // w-V O	CAN//CAN
21	C Comp S // w-O V^{Pt}	Nom//Ptcp
22	S V-o O // w-M V	MKD//MKD
23	S^{Pn} V M(E^{Ng} S) // w-M V	MKD//DEF
Prov. 6		
1	[Voc] C-V M // V M O	CAN//CAN
2	V M // V M	CAN//CAN
3	V O M [Voc] / w-V C V M / V V w-V O	CAN/CAN^2/CAN^3
4	V^{Ng} O M // w-O M	CAN//Gap
5	V M M // w-M M	CAN//Gap
6	V-M [Voc] / V O w-V	CAN/CAN^2
7	R E^{Ng} S-Comp / S^{Pt} w-S^{Pt}	Nom/Nom
8	V M O // V M O	MKD//MKD
9	Q [Voc] V // Q V M	CAN//CAN
10	Comp? Comp? / Comp? Inf	Nom^2/Nom
11	w-V M S // w-S M	CAN//Gap
12	S S / V^{Pt} M	Nom/Ptcp
13	V^{Pt} M // V^{Pt} M // V^{Pt} M	Ptcp//Ptcp//Ptcp
14	S Comp V^{Pt} O M // O V	Nom-Ptcp//DEF
15	C M V S // M V w-E^{Ng} S^{Pt}	MKD//MKD-Nom
16	O? V S // w-S Comp	MKD//Nom
17	S S / w-S	Nom/Nom
18	S V^{Pt} O / S V^{Pt} Inf M	Ptcp/Ptcp-Inf
19	V O S / V^{Pt} O M	CAN?/Ptcp
20	V [Voc] O // w-V^{Ng} O	CAN//CAN
21	V-o M M // V-o M	CAN//CAN
22	M(Inf) V O // M(Inf) V O // V S^{Pn} V-o	CAN/CAN//CAN-MKD
23	C Comp S // w-S Comp / w-Comp S	Nom//Nom/Nom
24	Inf-o M / M	Inf/Nom

25	V^{Ng} O M // w-V^{Ng}-o M	CAN//CAN
26	C Comp? S? / w-S O V	Nom/MKD
27	Q-V S O M / w-S V^{Ng}	CAN/MKD
28	C-V S M / w-S V^{Ng}	CAN/MKD
29	Comp S^{Pt} / V^{Ng} S^{Pt}	Nom/CAN
30	V^{Ng} O C V / Inf O C V	CAN^2/Inf-CAN
31	w-V V M / O V	CAN^2/MKD
32	S^{Pt} Comp / N S^{Pn} V-o	Nom/MKD
33	O w-O V // w-S V^{Ng}	MKD//MKD
34	C-S Comp / w-V^{Ng} M	Nom/CAN
35	V^{Ng} O // w-V^{Ng} C V-O	CAN//CAN^2
Prov. 7		
1	[Voc] V O // w-O V M	CAN//DEF
2	V O w-V / w-O M	CAN^2/Nom
3	V-o M // V-o M	CAN//CAN
4	V M Comp S^{Pn} // w- Comp M V	CAN-Nom//DEF
5	Inf-o M // M [R] O V	Inf/Nom-$CAN^{[R]}$
6	C M / M V	Nom/MKD
7	w-V M // V M / O	Can//CAN/Nom
8	V^{Pt} M M / w-O V	Ptcp/MKD?
9	M M // M w-M	Nom//Nom
10	w-H S Comp / Comp w-Comp	Nom/Nom^2
11	V^{Pt} S w-V^{Pt} / M V^{Ng} S	$Ptcp^2$/MKD
12	M M / w-M V	Nom/MKD
13	w-V-o M w-V-o M / V O w-V M	CAN^2/CAN^2
14	S Comp / M V O	Nom/CAN
15	C V Inf-o / Inf-o O w-V-o	CAN/Inf-CAN
16	M V O / M	MKD/Nom
17	V O M / M w-M	CAN/Nom
18	V V O M // V M	CAN^2//CAN
19	C E^{Ng} S Comp / V M M	Nom/CAN
20	O V M / M V O	MKD/MKD
21	V-o M // w-M V-o	CAN//DEF
22	V^{Pt} M M / M(S M V) // M M	Ptcp/MKD//Nom
23	C V S M / M(Inf S M) / w-V^{Ng} C-Comp S^{Pn}	CAN/Inf/CAN/Nom
24	w-M [Voc] V-M // w-V M	CAN//CAN
25	V^{Ng} M S // V^{Ng} M	CAN//CAN
26	C-O V / w-Comp S	MKD/Nom
27	Comp S / V^{Pt} M	Nom/Ptcp
Prov. 8		
1	Q^{Ng}-S V / w-S V O	MKD//MKD
2	M M / M V //	Nom/MKD//
3	M M / M V	Nom/MKD
4	M [Voc] V // S Comp ?	DEF//Nom
5	V [Voc] O // w-[Voc] V O	CAN//CAN
6	V C-O V // w-S Comp	CAN-MKD//Nom
7	C-O V S // w-Comp S	MKD//Nom
8	Comp S // E^{Ng} Comp S w-S	Nom/Nom
9	S Comp M // w-Comp M	Nom//Nom
10	V-O w-O^{Ng} / w-O M	CAN-Nom//Gap
11	C-Comp S M / S V^{Ng}-M	Nom/MKD
12	S^{Pn}-S V O // w-O V	MKD//DEF
13	S Comp / O w-O w-O V	Nom/MKD
14	Comp-S w-S // S^{Pn} Comp Comp S	Nom/Nom^2
15	M S V // w-S V O //	MKD//MKD//
16	M S V // w-S S	MKD/Nom
17	S^{Pn} O V / w-S V-o	MKD/MKD
18	S w-S Comp / S w-S	Nom/Nom
19	Comp S M w-M // w-S M	Nom//Gap
20	M V / M	MKD/Nom
21	Inf O O // w-O V	Inf//DEF
22	S V-o Comp / Comp	MKD/Nom
23	M V / M M	MKD/Nom
24	M(E^{Ng} S) V / M(E^{Ng} S)	MKD/Nom

Appendix 2

25	C S V // M V	MKD//MKD
26	C-V^{Ng} O w-O / w-O	CAN/Nom
27	M(Inf O) Comp S^{Pn} / M(Inf O M) //	Inf-Nom/Inf//
28	M(Inf O M) // M(Inf O) //	Inf//Inf//
29	M(Inf M O) / w-S V^{Ng}-O / M(Inf O)	Inf/MKD/Inf
30	w-V M Comp / w-V Comp M / V^{Pt} M M	CAN/CAN/Ptcp
31	V^{Pt} M // w-S Comp	Ptcp//Nom
32	w-M [Voc] V-M // Comp [R] O V	CAN/Nom-MKD[R]
33	V O // w-V w-V^{Ng}	CAN//CAN^2
34	Comp S V^{Pt} M / Inf M M // Inf O	Nom-Ptcp/Inf//Inf
35	C S^{Pt} V O / w-V O M	MKD/CAN
36	w-S^{Pt} V^{Pt} O / S^{Pt} V O	MKD/MKD
Prov. 9		
1	S V O // V O	MKD//CAN
2	V O // V O // P V O	CAN//CAN//CAN
3	V O // V M	CAN//CAN
4	S(Q-Comp) V M // N V M	MKD//MKD
5	V V M // w-V M [R] V	CAN^2//CAN$^{2[R]}$
6	V O w-V / w-V M	CAN^2/CAN
7	S^{Pt} V^{Pt} M O // w-S^{Pt} M O	Ptcp//Gap
8	V^{Ng} O C-V-o // V M w-V-o	CAN^2//CAN^2
9	V M w-V-M // V M w-V O	CAN^2//CAN^2
10	S Comp // w-S Comp	Nom//Nom
11	C-M V S // w-V M S	MKD//CAN
12	C-V V M / w-V M V	CAN^2/CAN-MKD?
13	S V^{Pt} // Comp w-V^{Ng} Q	Ptcp//Nom-CAN
14	w-V M / M M	CAN/Nom
15	Inf M / V^{Pt} O	Inf/Ptcp
16	S(Q-Comp) V M // w-N w-V M	MKD//MKD
17	S V // w-S V	MKD//MKD
18	w-V^{Ng} C-S Comp / Comp S	CAN-Nom/Nom

	(e) Song of Songs 1–8	
Ref.	Constituent Order	Colon-Type
Song 1		
2	V-o M / C-Comp S M	CAN/Nom
3	M S Comp / Comp(S [R] V) S / C S V-o	Nom/Nom-CAN[R]/MKD
4ab	V-o M V / V-o S M	CAN^2/CAN
4c-e	V w-V M / V O M / M V	CAN^2/CAN/MKD
5ab	Comp S^{Pn} w-Comp / [Voc] /	Nom/Nom/
5cd	M // M	Nom//Nom
6a-c	V^{Ng}-o C-S^{Pn} Comp // C-V-o S	CAN-Nom//CAN
6d-f	S V-M / V-o O / O V^{ng}	MKD/CAN/MKD
7	V M [Voc] / Q V // Q V M / Q V Comp M	CAN/CAN//CAN/CAN
8	C-V^{Ng} M / [Voc] / V-M M / w-V O M	CAN/Nom/CAN/CAN
9	M / V-o [Voc]	MKD/Nom
10	V S M // S M	CAN//Gap
11	O V-M / M	MKD/Nom
12	C-S Comp / S V O	Nom/MKD
13	Comp S M / M V	Nom/MKD
14	Comp S M / M	Nom/Nom
15	H-s Comp [Voc] // H-s Comp / S Comp	Nom//Nom/Nom
16	H-s Comp [Voc] / P Comp / P-S Comp	Nom/Nom/Nom
17	S Comp // S Comp	Nom//Nom
Song 2		
1	S^{Pn} Comp // Comp	Nom//Nom
2	M M / Comp S M //	Nom/Nom//
3ab	M M / Comp S M	Nom/Nom
3c-e	M V w-V / w-S Comp M	MKD-CAN/Nom
4	V-o M / w-S M Comp	CAN/Nom
5	V-o M // V-o M / C-Comp S^{Pn}	CAN//CAN/Nom
6	S Comp // w-S V-o	Nom/MKD
7ab	V O [Voc] / M C M /	CAN/Nom/

7cd	C-V w-C-V O / C-V	CAN^2/CAN
8ab	Comp H-S^{Pn}V^{Pt} /	Nom-Ptcp/
8cd	V^{Pt} M // V^{Pt} M	Ptcp//Ptcp
9ab	V^{Pt} S M C M / H-S^{Pn} V^{Pt} M /	Ptcp/Ptcp/
9cd	V^{Pt} M // V^{Pt} M	Ptcp//Ptcp
10	V S w-V M / V M [Voc] w-V-M	CAN^2/CAN^2
11	C-H S V // S V V M //	MKD//MKD-CAN//
12	S V M // S V // w-S V M //	MKD//MKD//MKD//
13	S V O // w-S V O / V M [Voc] w-V-M	MKD//MKD/CAN^2
14a-d	[Voc] M // M / V-o O // V-o O	Nom//Nom/CAN//CAN
14ef	C-S Comp // w-S Comp	Nom//Nom
15	V-M O / Comp V^{Pt} O / w-S Comp	CAN/Ptcp/Nom
16	S Comp // w-S^{Pn} Comp / V^{Pt} M	Nom//Nom/Ptcp
17	C-V S / w-V S / V V-M [Voc] M / C M M	CAN/CAN/CAN^2/Nom
Song 3		
1	M V O(R-V S) / V-o w-V^{Ng}-o	MKD-CAN^R/CAN^2
2a-c	V P w-V M / M w-M /	CAN^2/Nom/
2d-g	V O(R-V S) / V-o w-V^{Ng}-o	CAN^{2R}/CAN^2
3	V-o S^{Pt} V^{Pt} M / O(R-V S) V	CAN-Ptcp/MKD-CAN^R
4a-c	C-V M / C-V O(R-V S) /	CAN/CAN^{2R}/
4d-g	V-o w-V^{Ng}-o / C-V-o M / w-M	CAN^2/CAN/Nom
5ab	V O [Voc] / M C M /	CAN/Nom/
5c-e	C-V w-C-V O / C-V	CAN^2/CAN
6	Q S^{Pn} V^{Pt} M / M / Comp / M	Ptcp/Nom/Nom/Nom
7	H Comp / S Comp M / M	Nom/Nom/Nom
8	S Comp / Comp / N S Comp / M	Nom/Nom/Nom/Nom
9	O V M S / M	MKD/Nom
10a-c	O V M // O M // O M //	MKD//Gap//Gap//
10de	S Comp / M	Nom/Nom
11	V w-V [Voc] M / M(R-V-M S M / w-M)	CAN^2/Nom-CAN^R/Nom
Song 4		
1ab	H-s Comp [Voc] // H-s Comp /	Nom//Nom/
1c-e	S Comp M // S Comp / R-V M //	Nom//Nom/CAN^R//
2	S Comp / R-V M / R-S Comp / w-S E^{Ng} M	Nom/CAN^R/Nom^R/Nom
3	Comp S / w-S Comp // Comp S M	Nom//Nom//Nom
4	Comp S / Comp M / S Comp M / S Comp	Nom/Nom/Nom/Nom
5	S Comp / Comp / V^{Pt} M	Nom/Nom/Ptcp
6	C-V S / w-V S / V M M / w-M	CAN/CAN/CAN/Nom
7	S Comp [Voc] // w-S E^{Ng} M	Nom//Nom
8ab	M M [Voc] // M M V /	Gap//DEF/
8c-f	V M / M / M / M	CAN/Nom/Nom/Nom
9	V-o [Voc] / V-o M / M	CAN/CAN/Nom
10	Q-V S [Voc] // Q-V S M // w-S M	CAN//CAN//Gap
11	O V S [Voc] / S w-S Comp / w-S Comp	MKD/Nom/Nom
12	Comp S / Comp Comp	Nom/Nom^2
13	S Comp / M / Comp M	Nom/Nom/Nom
14a-d	Comp w-Comp / Comp w-Comp /	Nom^2/Nom^2/
14e-h	M / Comp w-Comp / M	Nom/Nom^2/Nom
15	Comp Comp / w-Comp M	Nom^2/Nom
16a-d	V [Voc] // w-V [Voc] / V O V S /	CAN//CAN/CAN^2/
16ef	V S M / w-V O	CAN/CAN
Song 5		
1a	V M [Voc] /	CAN/
1b-d	V O M // V O M // V O M	CAN//CAN//CAN
1e-g	V [Voc] // V w-V [Voc]	CAN/CAN^2
2ab	S^{Pn} Comp / w-S V^{Pt} /	Nom/Ptcp/
2c-e	S V^{Pt} / V-M [Voc] / [Voc] /	Ptcp/CAN/Nom/
2fg	C-S V^{Pt}-M // S M	Ptcp//Gap
3	V O Q V-o // V O Q V-o	CAN^2//CAN^2
4	S V O M / w-S V M	MKD/MKD
5ab	V S^{Pn} Inf M /	CAN-Inf/
5c-e	w-S V-O // w-S O / M	MKD//Gap/Nom
6a-c	V S^{Pn} M / w-S V V /	CAN/MKD-CAN/
6d-i	S V M(Inf) / V-o w-V^{Ng}-o // V-o w-V^{Ng}-o	MKD-Inf/CAN^2//CAN^2

Appendix 2 363

7	V-o $S^{Pt}V^{Pt}$ M / V-o V-o / V O M S^{Pt}	CAN-Ptcp/CAN^2/CAN
8	V O [Voc] / C-V O / Q-V M / C-Comp S^{Pn}	CAN/CAN/CAN/Nom
9	Q-S M [Voc] // Q-S M / C-M V-o	Nom//Nom/MKD
10	S Comp w-Comp / Comp M	Nom/Nom
11	S Comp / Comp M	Nom/Nom/Nom
12	S Comp M / V^{Pt} M // V^{Pt} M	Nom/Ptcp//Ptcp
13	S Comp / Comp // S Comp / V^{Pt} O	Nom/Nom//Nom-Ptcp
14	S Comp / Comp M // S Comp / Comp M	Nom/Nom//Nom/Nom
15	S Comp / Comp M // S Comp / Comp M	Nom/Nom//Nom/Nom
16	S Comp / w-S Comp / S^{Pn} Comp w-S^{Pn} Comp / [Voc]	Nom/Nom/Nom^2/Nom
Song 6		
1	Q V S [Voc] // Q V S w-V-o M	CAN//CAN^2
2	S V M M / Inf M w-Inf O	MKD/Inf^2
3	S^{Pn} Comp w-S Comp / V^{Pt} M	Nom^2/Ptcp
4	Comp S^{Pn} [Voc] M // Comp M // Comp M	Nom//Nom//Nom
5ab	V O M / C-S^{Pn} V-o /	CAN/MKD/
5cd	S Comp R-V M //	Nom-CAN^R//
6ab	S Comp R-V M /	Nom-CAN^R/
6cd	C-S Comp / w-S E^{Ng} Comp	Nom/Nom
7	Comp S M	Nom
8	Comp? w-Comp? / w-Comp? E^{Ng} S	Nom^2/Nom^2
9a-c	Comp S^{Pn} N / Comp S^{Pn} M // Comp S^{Pn} M /	Nom/Nom//Nom/
9d-g	V-o S w-V-o // S w-S w-V-o	CAN^2//Gap-CAN
10	Q-S V^{Pt} M / Comp M Comp M / Comp M	Nom-Ptcp/Nom^2/Nom
11ab	M V Inf M /	MKD-Inf/
11c-e	Inf Q-V S // V S	Inf-CAN//CAN
12	V^{Ng} S V-o M	CAN-MKD
Song 7		
1	V V [Voc] V V / w-V-M / Q-V M M	CAN^4/CAN/CAN
2	Q-V S M [Voc] / S Comp Comp	CAN/Nom^2
3	S Comp V^{Ng} S / S Comp Comp	Nom-CAN/Nom^2
4	S Comp Comp	Nom^2
5	S Comp // S Comp M // S Comp V^{Pt} M	Nom//Nom//Nom-Ptcp
6	S M Comp // w-S Comp / S Comp M	Nom//Nom/Nom
7	Q-V w-Q-V / [Voc] M	CAN^2/Nom
8	S V M // w-S M	MKD//Gap
9	V V M V M / w-V-P S Comp // w-S Comp //	CAN^3/CAN//Gap//
10	w-S Comp V^{Pt} M M / V^{Pt} O	Nom-Ptcp/Ptcp
11	S^{Pn} Comp / w-Comp S	Nom/Nom
12	V [Voc] V M // V M	CAN^2//CAN
13	V M V C V S // V S // V S / M V O M	CAN^3//CAN//CAN/CAN
14	S V-O / w-Comp S / Comp P-Comp / [Voc] V M	MKD/Nom/Nom/CAN
Song 8		
1	Q V-o M M / V^{Pt} O / V-o M V-o / P V^{Ng} M	CAN/Ptcp/CAN^2/CAN
2a-d	V-o V-o / M [R] V-o /	CAN^2/Nom-CAN$^{[R]}$/
2ef	V-o M / M	CAN/Nom
3	S Comp // w-S V-o	Nom//MKD
4	V O [Voc] / Q-V w-Q V O / C-V	CAN/CAN^2/CAN
5ab	Q S^{Pn} V^{Pt} M / V^{Pt} M	Ptcp/Ptcp
5c-f	M V-o / M V-o S // M V [R] V-o	MKD/MKD//MKD-CAN$^{[R]}$
6a-d	V-o M M // M M / C-Comp M S // Comp M S /	CAN//Gap/Nom//Nom/
6ef	S Comp / Comp	Nom/Nom
7a-c	S V^{Ng} Inf O // w-S V^{Ng}-o /	MKD-Inf//MKD/
7de	C-V S O M / Inf V M	CAN/CAN
8ab	S Comp / w-S E^{Ng} Comp /	Nom/Nom/
8c-e	Q-V M / M R-V-M	CAN/Nom-CAN^R
9	C-Comp S^{Pn} V M O // w-C-Comp S^{Pn} V M O	Nom-CAN//Nom-CAN
10	S^{Pn} Comp / w-S Comp / C V M Comp	Nom/Nom/CAN
11	S V Comp M / V O M / S V M O	MKD/CAN/MKD
12	S Comp / S Comp [Voc] // w-S Comp	Nom/Nom//Nom
13	[Voc] / S V^{Pt} M / V-o	Nom/Ptcp/CAN
14	V [Voc] / w-V-M M / C M M	CAN/CAN/Nom

Ref.	(f) Numbers 23–24 Constituent Order	Colon-Type
Num. 23	First Oracle	
7ab	M V-o S // S M /	DEF//Gap
7c-f	V V-M O // w-V V O	CAN^2//CAN^2
8	Q V [R] V^{Ng} S // w-Q V [R] V^{Ng} S	CAN$^{2[R]}$//CAN$^{2[R]}$
9ab	C-M V-o // w-M V-o	MKD//MKD
9cd	H-S [R] M V // w-M V^{Ng}	Nom-MKD$^{[R]}$//MKD
10ab	Q V O // w-V? O	CAN//CAN?
10cd	V S O // w-V S Comp	CAN//CAN
	Second Oracle	
18	V [Voc] w-V / V M [Voc]	CAN^2//CAN
19a-d	Comp^{Ng} S w-V // w-Comp w-V /	Nom-CAN//Gap-CAN/
19e-h	Q-S^{Pn} V w-V^{Ng} // w-V w-V^{Ng}-o	MKD-CAN//CAN^2
20	H Inf V / w-V w-V^{Ng}-o	MKD/CAN^2
21ab	V^{Ng} O M // w-V^{Ng} O M	CAN//CAN
21cd	S Comp // w-Comp M	Nom//Nom
22	S V^{Pt}-o M / Comp M	Ptcp/Nom
23ab	C [E]^{Ng} S Comp // w-[E]^{Ng} S Comp	Nom//Nom
23cd	M V M w-M / Q-V S	CAN/CAN
24ab	H-S M V // w-M V /	MKD//MKD
24c-e	V^{Ng} C-V O // w-O V	CAN^2//DEF
Num. 24	Third Oracle	
3	Comp // w-Comp	Nom//Nom
4a-c	Comp(V^{Pt} O // R O V /	Nom-Ptcp//MKD^R/
4de	V^{Pt} w-Comp)	Ptcp-Nom
5	Q-V S [Voc] // S [Voc]	CAN//Gap
6ab	M // M //	Nom//Nom//
6c-e	M(O [R] V S) // M	Nom-CAN$^{[R]}$//Nom
7ab	V-O M / w-S Comp /	CAN/Nom/
7cd	w-V M S // w-V S	CAN//CAN
8ab	S V^{Pt}-o M / Comp M /	Ptcp/Nom/
8c-e	V O Comp / w-O V // w-M V	CAN/MKD//MKD
9a-d	V V M / w-M Q V-o /	CAN^2/Nom-CAN
9ef	S^{Pt} Comp // w-S^{Pt} Comp	Nom//Nom
	Fourth Oracle	
15	Comp // w-Comp	Nom//Nom
16a-c	Comp(V^{Pt} O // V^{Pt} O //	Nom-Ptcp//Ptcp//
16d-f	[R] O V / V^{Pt} w-Comp)	MKD^R/Ptcp-Nom
17a-d	V-o w-M^{Ng} // V-o w-Comp^{Ng} /	CAN-Nom//CAN-Nom/
17ef	V S M // w-V S M	CAN//CAN
17gh	w-V O // w-V O	CAN//CAN
18	w-V S Comp // w-V Comp S / w-S V^{Pt} O	CAN//CAN/Ptcp
19	w-V M / w-V O M	CAN/CAN

Scripture Index

References follow the Hebrew versification

Genesis
3:3 *54–55*
3:13 *79–80*
3:23 *23*
4:2 *128*
6:14 *53*
6:16 *53*
13:17 *62*
14:10 *84–85*
14:21 *43*
17:15 *82–83*
19:2 *50*
22:4 *57*
23:29 *242*
28:13 *62*
29:9 *46*
31:19 *46*
31:32 *58*
34:15 *70–71*
35:12 *62*
37:2–3 *98*
38:22 *54*
39:9 *88*
42:8 *77*
45:8 *88*
45:14 *48*
49:27 *221*

Exodus
2:4 *42*
2:15 *42*
14:4 *49*
15:8 *258*

Leviticus
6:11 *199*
11:32 *199*

Numbers
5:2–3 *72–73*
10:30 *50*
12:6–8 *74*
13:28 *52*
15:36 *72*
19:3 *72*
19:6 *199*
22:41 *227*
23:7–10 *225–29*
23:7 *226*
23:8–10 *228*
23:8 *226–27*
23:9 *135, 227–28*
23:10 *228*
23:13 *227*
23:15 *49*
24:2 *227*
24:4 *227*
24:16 *227*
24:25 *64*
31:13 *72*
32:22 *180*

Deuteronomy
1:37–38 *83–84*
5:3 *89, 242*
7:6 *142*
10:15 *69*
15:17 *52*
28:44 *77*
33:2 *182*

Joshua
6:5 *58*
8:27 *50*
18:5 *44*

Judges
1:1–2 *44*
1:2 *53*
7:2 *50*
16:20 *213*
19:24 *78*
20:48 *65*
21:25 *85–86*

Ruth
1:14 *128*
4:4 *93*

1 Samuel
2:14 *199*
4:1 *48*
4:6 *213*
8:4–6 *45*
8:7 *44, 89, 242*
9:6 *199*
14:26–27 *75–76*
14:47 *199*
15:15 *78*
16:7 *48, 77*
17:28 *93*
18:12 *48*
19:27 *80*
25:21 *51*
26:12 *206*
26:25 *104*

2 Samuel
7:14 *63*
7:15 *63*
9:2 *53*
12:1 *82*
12:9 *88*

12:10 *88*
12:13 *88*
19:25–28 *52*
19:31 *52*
21:2 *242*
22:29 *15*

1 Kings
5:19 *55*
14:11 *81*
16:32–33 *67*
20:35 *46*
22:44 *51*

2 Kings
2:2 *206*
5:13 *160*
10:19 *199*
16:3 *67*
17:8–12 *67*
18:7 *199*
23:19 *67*

1 Chronicles
16:31 *81*

2 Chronicles
12:5 *67–68*
19:8 *65–66*

Job
1:1 *27*
3:3 *83*
3:6 *82–83*
3:24 *163, 168*
4:3–4 *20, 114*
4:9 *134–35*
4:10 *19, 189*
4:11–13 *164–65*
4:11 *17*
4:12 *163, 164*
4:17 *177, 180, 214, 215*
5:7 *214*
5:8 *187, 212*
6:3 *221*
6:27 *184*
8:2–7 *187*

8:5 *186, 187*
8:6 *25*
8:19 *191*
9:2 *180, 215*
9:3 *23*
9:7–8 *85*
10:10–11 *20*
11:5 *212*
11:11 *93, 205*
11:12 *191, 214*
12 *208–18, 229, 230*
12:2 *211*
12:3 *211*
12:4 *212*
12:5 *212*
12:6 *212*
12:7–10 *214*
12:7 *212*
12:8 *212–13*
12:9 *213*
12:10 *213*
12:11 *177, 213–15*
12:12–13 *215*
12:13–25 *216*
12:13–16 *216*
12:14–15 *215*
12:16 *215*
12:17–19 *216, 217*
12:17 *215*
12:18 *169, 215–17*
12:19 *216, 217*
12:20–21 *217*
12:22 *217*
12:23 *217*
12:24 *217, 218*
12:25 *217–18*
13:3 *212*
13:4 *22*
13:11 *133*
13:16 *191*
13:20 *70–71*
13:21 *71*
13:25 *134*
14:3 *69, 138–39*
14:7–9 *185*
14:10 *185*
14:14 *185*

14:18 *212*
14:22 *138*
15:14 *215*
21:33 *181, 221*
25:4 *180, 215*
34:3 *215*
35:11 *126*

Psalms
1 *195–200, 229*
1:1 *196, 272*
1:2 *196–97*
1:3 *197–99, 253*
1:4 *199*
1:5 *199*
1:6 *199–200*
2:4 *133*
2:6–7 *68*
3:5 *190*
3:6 *206*
4:2 *59*
4:6 *91*
4:8 *110*
4:9 *190, 233–34*
5:2 *108, 161*
5:4 *135*
5:8 *161*
5:13 *190, 270, 271*
6:3–4 *234–35*
6:10 *101, 102*
6:11 *13*
7:6 *108*
7:7 *234*
7:8 *190*
7:13 *134*
7:14 *190*
7:17 *108*
9:9 *153, 223*
9:10 *142*
9:13 *190*
9:16 *101*
9:19 *176*
10:7 *182*
12:9 *190*
14:2 *190*
14:5 *152*
14:7 *23*

15:5 *13*	38:16 *92*	68:23 *161*
16:7 *69*	38:17 *170*	69:6 *93, 186*
16:9 *18, 124*	38:19 *169, 170–71*	69:8 *154*
17:1 *20*	38:22 *110*	69:20 *205*
17:2 *176*	39:6 *139*	69:22 *101*
18:5–6 *111, 113*	40:4 *258*	70:2 *188*
18:7 *152*	40:10 *93, 205*	71:11 *79–80*
18:29 *16*	41:5 *87–88, 93*	71:22 *153*
18:30 *135*	41:10 *67*	72:1 *180, 226, 273*
18:50 *122*	42:7 *191*	72:10 *138*
19:2 *27*	44:2–9 *239–46*	73:9 *16*
19:5 *143*	44:2 *241, 242, 244*	73:13 *184*
20:4–6 *96, 110*	44:3 *169, 241–42, 243, 244, 245*	73:18 *184*
20:8 *190*		73:27 *161*
20:9 *77*	44:4 *242–43, 244*	75:11 *191, 192*
21:3 *134*	44:5 *243, 244*	77:2 *176, 177–78*
21:10 *112–13, 236*	44:6 *166, 169, 243–46*	78:3 *241*
24:2 *153*	44:7 *244*	78:20 *65, 184*
25:1 *191*	44:8 *244*	78:71 *18*
26:4–5 *112*	44:9 *151*	79:10 *13, 23*
29:10 *161*	45:18 *221*	79:13 *185, 186*
29:11 *176*	46:10 *146–47*	80:9 *191*
30:13 *191*	47:6 *19*	80:19 *92*
31:7 *91–92*	48:10 *23*	82:6 *93*
32:3–5 *171*	49:13 *232*	82:7 *135*
32:6 *69*	50:13 *270*	83:3–5 *173*
33:2 *92, 100*	50:16 *19*	83:3 *133*
33:6 *180, 226*	50:23 *140–41*	83:4 *169, 173–74*
33:9 *153*	51:3–4 *97–102*	83:9 *64*
33:10 *183*	51:5 *93*	84:4 *140, 142*
33:11 *143–44*	51:6 *87–88*	84:9 *110*
34:3 *246*	52:9 *233*	84:10 *162*
34:7 *239*	53:6 *152*	85:6 *169, 180*
34:18 *238–39*	54:8 *92*	85:13 *140*
35:9 *183*	55:5–6 *149*	85:14 *191*
35:28 *187–88*	56:2 *236*	86:9 *88–89*
36:7–8 *236–38, 253*	56:5 *246*	88:4 *108*
37:9 *84*	56:6 *182*	89:2 *176*
37:14 *161*	57:10 *264*	89:3 *176*
37:15 *133*	58:2 *223*	89:5 *162*
37:22 *77–78*	58:3 *140*	89:16–17 *144–45*
37:23 *176*	58:4 *99, 101, 102, 108*	89:27–28 *68*
37:30 *132*	62:5 *58*	89:30 *62*
38:3 *161*	63:12 *246*	89:31–33 *63*
38:11 *161*	65:13 *272*	89:31–32 *114*
38:12 *138, 170*	65:14 *108, 272*	89:31 *250*
38:14 *170*	66:12 *24*	89:34–35 *147–48*

89:34 *63*
90:2 *162*
90:9 *162*
90:17 *134*
91:8 *69–70*
91:12 *23*
91:13 *162*
91:16 *162*
92:2 *122*
92:10 *189*
92:13 *176*
93:1 *81*
93:3 *190*
94:1 *189*
94:3 *189*
94:23 *147, 236*
96:7 *190*
96:10 *81, 187*
97:1 *81, 187*
99:1 *81*
101:5 *141*
101:6 *141*
102:4 *108*
102:7 *224*
102:9 *176*
102:14 *24*
102:15 *142*
102:20 *101*
102:26 *182*
103 *200–7, 229*
103:1–6 *203*
103:7 *203*
103:8 *203*
103:9 *203–5*
103:10 *205*
103:11 *205*
103:12–13 *205*
103:14 *205–6*
103:15 *206*
103:16 *206, 221*
103:17–18 *206*
103:19 *176, 206–7*
103:20–22 *207*
104:7 *135*
104:12 *177*
104:13 *258, 272*
105:1 *92*

105:3 *246*
105:8–10 *61–62*
105:11 *61, 62, 87*
106:7 *232–33*
106:43 *77*
107:2–3 *231*
109:11 *101*
109:24 *133*
111:9 *162*
114:4 *17*
115:1 *88–89*
115:16 *126–27*
116:6 *238*
116:11 *93*
116:17 *92*
118:18 *7*
119:113 *78*
120:1 *191*
120:2 *18*
121:6 *180, 181, 226, 245*
122:5 *152*
122:6 *12*
125:20 *128*
127:1 *135–36*
132:2–3 *99*
132:15–16 *148*
133:3 *152*
135:4 *142–143*
135:6 *199*
137:3 *152*
138:6 *123*
139:2 *93, 205*
139:10 *58, 152, 169–70*
139:12 *140*
140:14 *184*
141:4 *93, 168*
142:2 *177–78*
142:3 *101, 108, 128*
145:1–2 *235–36*
145:4 *177, 205*
145:6–7 *144–45*
145:11 *133–34*
146:9 *122*
147:2 *117*
147:12 *110*
149:2 *99–100, 104–5, 116*

150:3 *100*

Proverbs
1:5 *121*
1:7 *192*
1:16 *169, 174*
1:22 *271–72*
1:23–24 *99*
2:3 *135*
2:10 *109*
2:11 *133*
2:19 *163*
2:21–22 *165–66*
2:22 *163, 175, 245*
3:1 *166*
3:5 *78*
3:10 *108*
3:11 *163*
3:13 *118*
3:19 *163*
3:20 *177*
3:35 *192*
4:11 *163, 166–68*
4:14 *163, 166–68*
4:17 *168*
4:20 *135*
4:25 *163, 166, 169, 174–76, 245*
5:12–13 *97*
5:12 *109*
5:15 *18, 116–17, 142*
5:23 *186*
6:4 *19*
6:8 *16*
6:26 *121*
6:27–28 *18*
7:4 *108*
8:4 *182*
8:5 *110*
8:12 *185, 186*
8:25 *17*
9:1–2 *20*
9:1 *183*
9:5 *17*
10:1 *78*
10:8 *78*
10:12 *129*

10:21 *78*
10:27 *78*
10:30 *205*
10:31 *78, 132*
10:32 *78*
11:3 *78*
11:27 *78*
11:28 *270*
12:2 *84*
12:17 *78*
12:24 *78*
12:25 *78*
13:6 *78*
13:9 *78*
13:11 *78*
13:16 *78*
13:20 *78*
14:1 *78*
14:11 *78*
14:15 *78*
14:17 *78*
14:33 *88*
15:1 *78*
15:2 *78*
15:5 *78*
15:8 *238*
15:14 *78*
15:18 *78*
15:20 *78*
15:28 *78*
15:29 *238*
15:30 *132*
16:9 *78*
16:28 *132*
17:5 *88*
17:8 *199*
17:20 *132*
17:22 *78*
17:24 *175*
18:7 *151–52*
18:14 *78*
18:15 *132*
18:23 *129*
19:4 *78*
19:5 *132*
19:15 *132*
19:28 *132*

20:32 *132*
21:7 *238*
21:14 *132*
21:28 *78*
23:1 *168*
23:31 *223*
23:33 *132*
25:23 *132*
26:14 *132*
26:27 *214*
26:28 *132*
27:12 *78*
27:18 *132*
27:20 *132*
28:4 *78*
28:5 *78*
28:9 *238*
28:13 *78*
28:18 *78*
28:22 *213*
28:25 *78*
29:3 *78*
29:4 *78*
29:8 *78*
29:10 *78*
29:25 *78*
30:33 *132*

Ecclesiastes
8:3 *199*
10:8 *214*

Song of Songs
1 *218–25, 229, 230*
1:2 *220*
1:3 *220–21*
1:4 *221–23*
1:5 *222, 223*
1:6 *223*
1:7–8 *223*
1:9 *223–24*
1:10 *224*
1:11 *224*
1:12 *224–25*
1:13 *225*
1:14–17 *225*
2:8 *17*

2:10–13 *145, 149*
2:11–13 *20*
2:17 *224*
4:1–7 *188*
4:8 *188*
7:8 *224*
7:12–13 *222*
8:1 *23*
8:11 *82*

Isaiah
1:3 *31*
2:2 *17*
3:17 *102–3*
9:19 *86*
11:7 *150*
11:12 *117*
13:7 *221*
14:40 *205*
16:4 *117*
17:13 *258*
19:12 *102*
19:17 *199*
24:6 *221*
27:12 *117*
28:24 *264*
29:12 *127*
29:16 *270*
31:9 *269*
33:15 *223*
35:1 *165*
35:6 *165*
40:3 *162, 165*
40:5 *206*
40:7 *146*
40:9 *58*
40:10 *178, 191, 192*
40:11 *135*
40:12 *95, 108*
40:15 *190, 250, 267*
40:20 *221*
40:27 *108*
41:1 *75*
41:4 *266*
41:7 *75*
41:15 *17, 24, 257–59*
41:16 *186, 257–60*

41:19 *165*
41:20 *133, 213*
42:1–4 *246–50*
42:1 *191, 247, 249*
42:2 *247, 249*
42:3 *247–48, 249*
42:4 *191, 247, 248–50*
42:12 *108*
42:13 *177, 178, 192*
42:15–16 *96*
42:18 *110*
43:9 *162, 165*
43:10 *266*
43:13 *266*
43:19 *100*
43:20 *100*
43:23–24 *113–14*
43:25 *266*
43:27 *258*
44:5 *148*
44:9 *260–61*
44:11 *258*
44:13 *258*
44:16 *151*
44:17 *89–91*
44:24 *266*
45:2 *134*
45:8 *190*
45:12–13 *150, 186–87*
45:12 *268*
45:14 *89–91*
45:16–17 *76*
45:18 *74–75*
46:3–4 *266*
46:4 *190, 265–67*
46:6 *101*
46:10 *199*
47:15 *86*
48:3 *191*
48:9 *135*
48:12 *266*
48:13 *140, 261–62*
48:21 *162*
49:13 *116*

49:14–15 *262–64*
49:18 *162*
49:21 *266*
49:22 *17, 137–38*
49:25 *138*
49:26 *270–71*
50:6 *146*
50:9 *22*
51:3 *165, 258, 264–65*
51:4 *138, 179, 250*
51:5 *177, 178–79*
51:6 *145, 179*
51:11 *162, 265*
51:12 *266*
54:3 *177*
54:10 *133, 258*
55:12 *258, 265*
56:8 *117*
57:3 *183*
57:6 *154*
57:7 *65–66, 154*
57:11 *153–54*
57:16 *205*
58:8 *108*
59:2–4 *171*
59:2–3 *72–73*
59:5 *134, 171*
59:6–7 *253*
59:6 *171–72*
59:7 *169, 171–73, 174, 217*
59:9 *171*
59:14 *108*
60:1–3 *250–54*
60:1 *251, 252, 253*
60:2 *251–52, 253*
60:3 *252*
60:4 *136–38,*
60:6 *134*
60:7 *133*
60:10 *78*
61:4 *107*
61:7 *191*
61:11 *151*

62:1 *108*
62:2 *23*
62:9 *133*
64:5 *108*
64:9 *151*
65:7 *17*
65:13 *136*
65:14 *186*
65:25 *150–51*
66:2 *162*
66:2–3 *151*
66:3–4 *186–87*
66:8 *17*
66:12 *135*
66:15 *178, 182, 192*

Jeremiah
3:12 *205*
9:9 *272*
10:6–13 *262*
20:11 *221*
31:10 *250*
31:37 *181*

Ezekiel
36:28 *49*

Hosea
10:6 *269*

Joel
3:5 *199*

Obadiah
7 *168*

Jonah
2:9 *92*

Nahum
3:10 *9*

Habakkuk
3:3 *182*

Author Index

Alden, R. L., 164
Alexander, J. A., 117, 248, 252, 253, 259, 266
Allen, L. C., 135, 142, 170, 180, 205, 207, 217, 235
Alter, R., 12, 19, 20
Andersen, F. I., 31, 134, 198
Anderson, A. A., 161, 189, 207
Antturi, A., 243, 244, 245
Ashley, T. R., 73, 227, 228

Bailey, K. E., 249, 252
Baltzer, K., 178, 179
Bandstra, B. L., 4, 7, 28, 279
Barr, J., 9
Beekman, J., 24
Bergen, R. D., 62, 222
Berlin, A., 9, 14, 15, 16, 17, 20, 21, 110, 114, 117, 118, 181, 245, 272
Bodine, W. R., 4, 7
Boling, R. G., 15
Bratcher, R. G., 16
Breck, J., 173, 252, 253
Brown, G., 125
Budd, P. J., 73
Buth, R., 7, 28, 84, 97–102, 104, 106, 118, 119, 125, 197, 268

Callow, J., 24, 222
Carr, G. L., 188
Ceresko, A. R., 173
Chafe, W. L., 56
Clines, D. J. A., 71, 134, 135, 139, 180, 185, 211, 214, 215
Cloete, W. T. W., 11
Collins, T., 7, 9
Craigie, P. C., 3, 6, 78, 85, 91, 132, 140, 143, 144, 161, 164, 170, 171, 183, 196, 199, 200, 234, 237, 239, 241, 244

Dahood, M., 18, 241
Davidson, A. B., 27
Dawson, D. A., 28
Delitzsch, F., 68, 70, 81, 91, 92, 126, 140, 141, 173, 183, 189, 198, 221, 259, 260
de Moor, J. C., 14
de Regt, L. J., 85, 249
Dhorme, E., 3, 71, 126, 139, 210, 211, 212, 216
Dik, S. C., 34, 44, 47, 49, 54, 110, 256
Dooley, R. A., 57
Dorsey, D. A., 172
Downing, P., 4, 53, 54
Driver, S. R., 211, 216
Dryer, M. S., 36

Eisemann, M., 27
Estes, D. J., 121

Fabb, N., 2, 14, 15, 107
Floor, S. J., 102
Fokkelman, J. P., 106, 249
Follingstad, C. M., 51, 67, 171, 251
Fox, M. V., 167
Franke, C., 267

Geller, S. A., 1, 9, 15, 54
Gerstenberger, E. S., 3,
Gesenius, W., 27–28, 31, 106, 139, 160, 233, 263
Givón, T., 42
Gordis, R., 184, 214, 221
Gray, G. B., 14, 211, 216
Greenstein, E. L., 15

Grogan, G., 14
Groom, S. A., 4
Gross, W., 6, 7, 9, 28, 56, 152, 227, 255, 256, 268-73

Habel, N. C., 216
Halivni, D. W., 27
Harman, A., 3, 63, 67, 81, 88, 89, 92, 123, 132, 140, 143, 146, 164, 189, 199
Harold, B. B., 53
Hartley, J. E., 3, 126, 135, 139, 187, 210, 211, 212, 214, 215
Heimerdinger, J.-M., 28, 31, 32, 37, 41, 42, 43, 45, 46, 47, 48, 49, 52, 53, 56, 79, 262
Holladay, W. L., 18, 189
Honeyman, A. M., 181

Jakobson, R., 2, 14, 110, 193
Joüon, P., 4, 31, 56, 57, 86

Ibn Ezra, A., 27, 154, 227, 248, 259

Khan, G., 54, 55, 83, 84, 260
Kidner, D., 12, 19, 81, 124, 129, 134, 140, 142, 143, 146, 168, 181, 183, 186, 189, 203, 232, 235
Kimhi, D., 27
König, E., 47, 52
Korpel, M. C. A., 14
Krašovec, J., 181
Kraus, H-J., 161, 186, 189, 207, 241
Kugel, J. L., 11, 20, 21, 228

Lambrecht, K., 4, 30, 31, 32-41, 42, 43, 45, 46, 48, 49, 56, 59, 102, 104, 125, 156, 255
LaPolla, R. J., 30, 33, 35, 36, 43
Leupold, H. C., 203
Levinsohn, S. H., 28, 30, 43, 56, 57
Lode, L., 7, 279
Longacre, R. E., 4, 28, 193
Longman III, T., 82, 188, 220, 221, 222, 223

Martin, J. D., 28
Matejka, L., 2

McConville, J. G., 69
McKane, W., 175
Merrill, E. H., 77
Miller, C. L., 6, 7, 19, 62, 125
Miller, P. D., 15
Motyer, J. A., 66, 74, 86, 90, 117, 137, 162, 171, 178, 179, 187, 250, 259, 260, 264, 266, 270
Muraoka, T., 4, 7, 28, 31, 56, 57, 86
Murphy, R. E., 78, 82, 116, 118, 121, 167, 168, 174, 175, 188, 214, 216, 223
Myhill, J., 4

Niccacci, A., 1, 6, 128
Noonan, M., 4, 53, 54

O'Connor, M., 4, 9, 11, 18, 19, 28, 70, 75, 170, 171, 177, 221, 233
Oswalt, J. N., 10, 66, 73, 90, 113, 137, 138, 154, 178, 183, 186, 248, 259, 266

Payne, D., 54
Payne, G., 56
Payne, T. E., 29, 47, 52
Pomorska, K., 2
Pope, M. H., 3, 214, 216, 221, 222, 224, 225

Reyburn, W. D., 3, 16, 139, 180, 211, 212, 214
Rosenbaum, M., 9, 10, 34, 47, 49, 56, 57, 58, 190, 249, 250, 255, 256-68

Sappan, R., 1, 3, 106
Schökel, L. A., 18
Segert, S., 13
Seybold, K., 19
Shimasaki, K., 28, 30, 31, 32, 37, 41, 42, 44, 45, 46, 47, 49, 52, 53, 56, 75, 78, 79, 80, 102-4, 106, 125, 127, 206, 268
Shklovsky, V., 2
Siewierska, A., 47
Slager, D., 251
Steele, S., 8
Talstra, E., 6, 9,

Author Index

Tate, M. E., 63, 68, 70, 81, 88, 162, 183, 189
Terrien, S., 161, 162, 173, 189, 235

Van Deemter, K., 127
Van der Meer, W., 14
Van der Merwe, C. H. J., 4, 7, 23, 28, 29, 47, 51, 56, 85, 117, 118, 139, 213, 244, 261, 262
Van Dijk, T. A., 33
Van Valin Jr., R. D., 30, 33, 35, 36, 43

Walkte, B. K., 4, 28, 70, 75, 170, 171, 177, 221, 233
Watson, W. G. E., 1, 2, 3, 11, 13, 17, 18, 108, 109, 110, 114, 126, 127, 128, 129, 145, 164, 169, 181, 233, 250, 264,
Watts, J. D. W., 66, 73, 90, 137, 150, 154, 178, 183, 187, 259, 262, 263, 266, 267, 270

Welch, J. W., 11
Wendland, E. R., 3, 5, 11, 12, 13, 15, 18, 20, 21, 25–26, 106, 145, 148, 164, 168, 169, 172, 173, 216, 243, 253, 269
Wenham, G. J., 80, 84, 128, 227
Whybray, R. N., 174
Wierzbicka, A., 93
Williams, R. J., 4, 221, 225, 263
Willis, J. T., 170
Winther-Nielsen, N., 47

Young, E. J., 66, 75, 86, 90, 91, 137, 138, 165, 171, 183, 248, 266
Yule, G., 125

Zevit, Z., 46, 188, 193
Zogbo, L., 3
Zuck, R., 139, 185

Paternoster Biblical Monographs

(All titles uniform with this volume)
Dates in bold are of projected publication

Joseph Abraham
Eve: Accused or Acquitted?
A Reconsideration of Feminist Readings of the Creation Narrative Texts in Genesis 1–3

Two contrary views dominate contemporary feminist biblical scholarship. One finds in the Bible an unequivocal equality between the sexes from the very creation of humanity, whilst the other sees the biblical text as irredeemably patriarchal and androcentric. Dr Abraham enters into dialogue with both camps as well as introducing his own method of approach. An invaluable tool for any one who is interested in this contemporary debate.

2002 / 0-85364-971-5 / xxiv + 272pp

Octavian D. Baban
Mimesis and Luke's on the Road Encounters in Luke-Acts
Luke's Theology of the Way and its Literary Representation

The book argues on theological and literary (mimetic) grounds that Luke's on-the-road encounters, especially those belonging to the post-Easter period, are part of his complex theology of the Way. Jesus' teaching and that of the apostles is presented by Luke as a challenging answer to the Hellenistic reader's thirst for adventure, good literature, and existential paradigms.

2005 */ 1-84227-253-5 / approx. 374pp*

Paul Barker
The Triumph of Grace in Deuteronomy

This book is a textual and theological analysis of the interaction between the sin and faithlessness of Israel and the grace of Yahweh in response, looking especially at Deuteronomy chapters 1–3, 8–10 and 29–30. The author argues that the grace of Yahweh is determinative for the ongoing relationship between Yahweh and Israel and that Deuteronomy anticipates and fully expects Israel to be faithless.

2004 / 1-84227-226-8 / xxii + 270pp

Jonathan F. Bayes
The Weakness of the Law
God's Law and the Christian in New Testament Perspective

A study of the four New Testament books which refer to the law as weak (Acts, Romans, Galatians, Hebrews) leads to a defence of the third use in the Reformed debate about the law in the life of the believer.

2000 / 0-85364-957-X / xii + 244pp

July 2005

Mark Bonnington
The Antioch Episode of Galatians 2:11-14 in Historical and Cultural Context

The Galatians 2 'incident' in Antioch over table-fellowship suggests significant disagreement between the leading apostles. This book analyses the background to the disagreement by locating the incident within the dynamics of social interaction between Jews and Gentiles. It proposes a new way of understanding the relationship between the individuals and issues involved.

2005 / 1-84227-050-8 / approx. 350pp

David Bostock
A Portrayal of Trust
The Theme of Faith in the Hezekiah Narratives

This study provides detailed and sensitive readings of the Hezekiah narratives (2 Kings 18–20 and Isaiah 36–39) from a theological perspective. It concentrates on the theme of faith, using narrative criticism as its methodology. Attention is paid especially to setting, plot, point of view and characterization within the narratives. A largely positive portrayal of Hezekiah emerges that underlines the importance and relevance of scripture.

2005 / 1-84227-314-0 / approx. 300pp

Mark Bredin
Jesus, Revolutionary of Peace
A Non-violent Christology in the Book of Revelation

This book aims to demonstrate that the figure of Jesus in the Book of Revelation can best be understood as an active non-violent revolutionary.

2003 / 1-84227-153-9 / xviii + 262pp

Robinson Butarbutar
Paul and Conflict Resolution
An Exegetical Study of Paul's Apostolic Paradigm in 1 Corinthians 9

The author sees the apostolic paradigm in 1 Corinthians 9 as part of Paul's unified arguments in 1 Corinthians 8–10 in which he seeks to mediate in the dispute over the issue of food offered to idols. The book also sees its relevance for dispute-resolution today, taking the conflict within the author's church as an example.

2006 / 1-84227-315-9 / approx. 280pp

Daniel J-S Chae
Paul as Apostle to the Gentiles
His Apostolic Self-awareness and its Influence on the Soteriological Argument in Romans

Opposing 'the post-Holocaust interpretation of Romans', Daniel Chae competently demonstrates that Paul argues for the equality of Jew and Gentile in Romans. Chae's fresh exegetical interpretation is academically outstanding and spiritually encouraging.

1997 / 0-85364-829-8 / xiv + 378pp

Luke L. Cheung
The Genre, Composition and Hermeneutics of the Epistle of James

The present work examines the employment of the wisdom genre with a certain compositional structure and the interpretation of the law through the Jesus tradition of the double love command by the author of the Epistle of James to serve his purpose in promoting perfection and warning against doubleness among the eschatologically renewed people of God in the Diaspora.

2003 / 1-84227-062-1 / xvi + 372pp

Youngmo Cho
Spirit and Kingdom in the Writings of Luke and Paul

The relationship between Spirit and Kingdom is a relatively unexplored area in Lukan and Pauline studies. This book offers a fresh perspective of two biblical writers on the subject. It explores the difference between Luke's and Paul's understanding of the Spirit by examining the specific question of the relationship of the concept of the Spirit to the concept of the Kingdom of God in each writer.

2005 / 1-84227-316-7 / approx. 270pp

Andrew C. Clark
Parallel Lives
The Relation of Paul to the Apostles in the Lucan Perspective

This study of the Peter-Paul parallels in Acts argues that their purpose was to emphasize the themes of continuity in salvation history and the unity of the Jewish and Gentile missions. New light is shed on Luke's literary techniques, partly through a comparison with Plutarch.

2001 / 1-84227-035-4 / xviii + 386pp

Andrew D. Clarke
Secular and Christian Leadership in Corinth
A Socio-Historical and Exegetical Study of 1 Corinthians 1–6
This volume is an investigation into the leadership structures and dynamics of first-century Roman Corinth. These are compared with the practice of leadership in the Corinthian Christian community which are reflected in 1 Corinthians 1–6, and contrasted with Paul's own principles of Christian leadership.
2005 / 1-84227-229-2 / 200pp

Stephen Finamore
God, Order and Chaos
René Girard and the Apocalypse
Readers are often disturbed by the images of destruction in the book of Revelation and unsure why they are unleashed after the exaltation of Jesus. This book examines past approaches to these texts and uses René Girard's theories to revive some old ideas and propose some new ones.
2005 / 1-84227-197-0 / approx. 344pp

David G. Firth
Surrendering Retribution in the Psalms
Responses to Violence in the Individual Complaints
In *Surrendering Retribution in the Psalms*, David Firth examines the ways in which the book of Psalms inculcates a model response to violence through the repetition of standard patterns of prayer. Rather than seeking justification for retributive violence, Psalms encourages not only a surrender of the right of retribution to Yahweh, but also sets limits on the retribution that can be sought in imprecations. Arising initially from the author's experience in South Africa, the possibilities of this model to a particular context of violence is then briefly explored.
2005 / 1-84227-337-X / xviii + 154pp

Scott J. Hafemann
Suffering and Ministry in the Spirit
Paul's Defence of His Ministry in II Corinthians 2:14–3:3
Shedding new light on the way Paul defended his apostleship, the author offers a careful, detailed study of 2 Corinthians 2:14–3:3 linked with other key passages throughout 1 and 2 Corinthians. Demonstrating the unity and coherence of Paul's argument in this passage, the author shows that Paul's suffering served as the vehicle for revealing God's power and glory through the Spirit.
2000 / 0-85364-967-7 / xiv + 262pp

Scott J. Hafemann
Paul, Moses and the History of Israel
The Letter/Spirit Contrast and the Argument from Scripture in 2 Corinthians 3
An exegetical study of the call of Moses, the second giving of the Law (Exodus 32–34), the new covenant, and the prophetic understanding of the history of Israel in 2 Corinthians 3. Hafemann's work demonstrates Paul's contextual use of the Old Testament and the essential unity between the Law and the Gospel within the context of the distinctive ministries of Moses and Paul.
2005 / 1-84227-317-5 / xii + 498pp

Douglas S. McComiskey
Lukan Theology in the Light of the Gospel's Literary Structure
Luke's Gospel was purposefully written with theology embedded in its patterned literary structure. A critical analysis of this cyclical structure provides new windows into Luke's interpretation of the individual pericopes comprising the Gospel and illuminates several of his theological interests.
2004 / 1-84227-148-2 / xviii + 388pp

Stephen Motyer
Your Father the Devil?
A New Approach to John and 'The Jews'
Who are 'the Jews' in John's Gospel? Defending John against the charge of antisemitism, Motyer argues that, far from demonising the Jews, the Gospel seeks to present Jesus as 'Good News for Jews' in a late first century setting.
1997 / 0-85364-832-8 / xiv + 260pp

Esther Ng
Reconstructing Christian Origins?
The Feminist Theology of Elizabeth Schüssler Fiorenza: An Evaluation
In a detailed evaluation, the author challenges Elizabeth Schüssler Fiorenza's reconstruction of early Christian origins and her underlying presuppositions. The author also presents her own views on women's roles both then and now.
2002 / 1-84227-055-9 / xxiv + 468pp

July 2005

Robin Parry
Old Testament Story and Christian Ethics
The Rape of Dinah as a Case Study

What is the role of story in ethics and, more particularly, what is the role of Old Testament story in Christian ethics? This book, drawing on the work of contemporary philosophers, argues that narrative is crucial in the ethical shaping of people and, drawing on the work of contemporary Old Testament scholars, that story plays a key role in Old Testament ethics. Parry then argues that when situated in canonical context Old Testament stories can be reappropriated by Christian readers in their own ethical formation. The shocking story of the rape of Dinah and the massacre of the Shechemites provides a fascinating case study for exploring the parameters within which Christian ethical appropriations of Old Testament stories can live.

2004 / 1-84227-210-1 / xx + 350pp

Ian Paul
Power to See the World Anew
The Value of Paul Ricoeur's Hermeneutic of Metaphor in Interpreting the Symbolism of Revelation 12 and 13

This book is a study of the hermeneutics of metaphor of Paul Ricoeur, one of the most important writers on hermeneutics and metaphor of the last century. It sets out the key points of his theory, important criticisms of his work, and how his approach, modified in the light of these criticisms, offers a methodological framework for reading apocalyptic texts.

2006 / 1-84227-056-7 / approx. 350pp

Robert L. Plummer
Paul's Understanding of the Church's Mission
Did the Apostle Paul Expect the Early Christian Communities to Evangelize?

This book engages in a careful study of Paul's letters to determine if the apostle expected the communities to which he wrote to engage in missionary activity. It helpfully summarizes the discussion on this debated issue, judiciously handling contested texts, and provides a way forward in addressing this critical question. While admitting that Paul rarely explicitly commands the communities he founded to evangelize, Plummer amasses significant incidental data to provide a convincing case that Paul did indeed expect his churches to engage in mission activity. Throughout the study, Plummer progressively builds a theological basis for the church's mission that is both distinctively Pauline and compelling.

2006 / 1-84227-333-7 / approx. 324pp

David Powys
'Hell': A Hard Look at a Hard Question
The Fate of the Unrighteous in New Testament Thought
This comprehensive treatment seeks to unlock the original meaning of terms and phrases long thought to support the traditional doctrine of hell. It concludes that there is an alternative—one which is more biblical, and which can positively revive the rationale for Christian mission.

1997 / 0-85364-831-X / xxii + 478pp

Sorin Sabou
Between Horror and Hope
Paul's Metaphorical Language of Death in Romans 6.1-11
This book argues that Paul's metaphorical language of death in Romans 6.1-11 conveys two aspects: horror and hope. The 'horror' aspect is conveyed by the 'crucifixion' language, and the 'hope' aspect by 'burial' language. The life of the Christian believer is understood, as relationship with sin is concerned ('death to sin'), between these two realities: horror and hope.

2005 / 1-84227-322-1 / approx. 224pp

Rosalind Selby
The Comical Doctrine
The Epistemology of New Testament Hermeneutics
This book argues that the gospel breaks through postmodernity's critique of truth and the referential possibilities of textuality with its gift of grace. With a rigorous, philosophical challenge to modernist and postmodernist assumptions, Selby offers an alternative epistemology to all who would still read with faith *and* with academic credibility.

2005 / 1-84227-212-8 / approx. 350pp

Kiwoong Son
Zion Symbolism in Hebrews
Hebrews 12.18-24 as a Hermeneutical Key to the Epistle
This book challenges the general tendency of understanding the Epistle to the Hebrews against a Hellenistic background and suggests that the Epistle should be understood in the light of the Jewish apocalyptic tradition. The author especially argues for the importance of the theological symbolism of Sinai and Zion (Heb. 12:18-24) as it provides the Epistle's theological background as well as the rhetorical basis of the superiority motif of Jesus throughout the Epistle.

2005 / 1-84227-368-X / approx. 280pp

Kevin Walton
Thou Traveller Unknown
The Presence and Absence of God in the Jacob Narrative
The author offers a fresh reading of the story of Jacob in the book of Genesis through the paradox of divine presence and absence. The work also seeks to make a contribution to Pentateuchal studies by bringing together a close reading of the final text with historical critical insights, doing justice to the text's historical depth, final form and canonical status.
2003 / 1-84227-059-1 / xvi + 238pp

George M. Wieland
The Significance of Salvation
A Study of Salvation Language in the Pastoral Epistles
The language and ideas of salvation pervade the three Pastoral Epistles. This study offers a close examination of their soteriological statements. In all three letters the idea of salvation is found to play a vital paraenetic role, but each also exhibits distinctive soteriological emphases. The results challenge common assumptions about the Pastoral Epistles as a corpus.
2005 / 1-84227-257-8 / approx. 324pp

Alistair Wilson
When Will These Things Happen?
A Study of Jesus as Judge in Matthew 21–25
This study seeks to allow Matthew's carefully constructed presentation of Jesus to be given full weight in the modern evaluation of Jesus' eschatology. Careful analysis of the text of Matthew 21–25 reveals Jesus to be standing firmly in the Jewish prophetic and wisdom traditions as he proclaims and enacts imminent judgement on the Jewish authorities then boldly claims the central role in the final and universal judgement.
2004 / 1-84227-146-6 / xxii + 272pp

Lindsay Wilson
Joseph Wise and Otherwise
The Intersection of Covenant and Wisdom in Genesis 37–50
This book offers a careful literary reading of Genesis 37–50 that argues that the Joseph story contains both strong covenant themes and many wisdom-like elements. The connections between the two helps to explore how covenant and wisdom might intersect in an integrated biblical theology.
2004 / 1-84227-140-7 / xvi + 340pp

Stephen I. Wright
The Voice of Jesus
Studies in the Interpretation of Six Gospel Parables
This literary study considers how the 'voice' of Jesus has been heard in different periods of parable interpretation, and how the categories of figure and trope may help us towards a sensitive reading of the parables today.
2000 / 0-85364-975-8 / xiv + 280pp

Paternoster
9 Holdom Avenue,
Bletchley,
Milton Keynes MK1 1QR,
United Kingdom
Web: www.authenticmedia.co.uk/paternoster

Paternoster Theological Monographs
(All titles uniform with this volume)
Dates in bold are of projected publication

Emil Bartos
Deification in Eastern Orthodox Theology
An Evaluation and Critique of the Theology of Dumitru Staniloae

Bartos studies a fundamental yet neglected aspect of Orthodox theology: deification. By examining the doctrines of anthropology, christology, soteriology and ecclesiology as they relate to deification, he provides an important contribution to contemporary dialogue between Eastern and Western theologians.

1999 / 0-85364-956-1 / xii + 370pp

Graham Buxton
The Trinity, Creation and Pastoral Ministry
Imaging the Perichoretic God

In this book the author proposes a three-way conversation between theology, science and pastoral ministry. His approach draws on a Trinitarian understanding of God as a relational being of love, whose life 'spills over' into all created reality, human and non-human. By locating human meaning and purpose within God's 'creation-community' this book offers the possibility of a transforming engagement between those in pastoral ministry and the scientific community.

2005 / 1-84227-369-8 / approx. 380 pp

Iain D. Campbell
Fixing the Indemnity
The Life and Work of George Adam Smith

When Old Testament scholar George Adam Smith (1856–1942) delivered the Lyman Beecher lectures at Yale University in 1899, he confidently declared that 'modern criticism has won its war against traditional theories. It only remains to fix the amount of the indemnity.' In this biography, Iain D. Campbell assesses Smith's critical approach to the Old Testament and evaluates its consequences, showing that Smith's life and work still raises questions about the relationship between biblical scholarship and evangelical faith.

2004 / 1-84227-228-4 / xx + 256pp

Tim Chester
Mission and the Coming of God
Eschatology, the Trinity and Mission in the Theology of Jürgen Moltmann
This book explores the theology and missiology of the influential contemporary theologian, Jürgen Moltmann. It highlights the important contribution Moltmann has made while offering a critique of his thought from an evangelical perspective. In so doing, it touches on pertinent issues for evangelical missiology. The conclusion takes Calvin as a starting point, proposing 'an eschatology of the cross' which offers a critique of the over-realised eschatologies in liberation theology and certain forms of evangelicalism.
2006 / 1-84227-320-5 / approx. 224pp

Sylvia Wilkey Collinson
Making Disciples
The Significance of Jesus' Educational Strategy for Today's Church
This study examines the biblical practice of discipling, formulates a definition, and makes comparisons with modern models of education. A recommendation is made for greater attention to its practice today.
2004 / 1-84227-116-4 / xiv + 278pp

Darrell Cosden
A Theology of Work
Work and the New Creation
Through dialogue with Moltmann, Pope John Paul II and others, this book develops a genitive 'theology of work', presenting a theological definition of work and a model for a theological ethics of work that shows work's nature, value and meaning now and eschatologically. Work is shown to be a transformative activity consisting of three dynamically inter-related dimensions: the instrumental, relational and ontological.
2005 / 1-84227-332-9 / xvi + 208pp

Stephen M. Dunning
The Crisis and the Quest
A Kierkegaardian Reading of Charles Williams
Employing Kierkegaardian categories and analysis, this study investigates both the central crisis in Charles Williams's authorship between hermetism and Christianity (Kierkegaard's Religions A and B), and the quest to resolve this crisis, a quest that ultimately presses the bounds of orthodoxy.
2000 / 0-85364-985-5 / xxiv + 254pp

Keith Ferdinando
The Triumph of Christ in African Perspective
A Study of Demonology and Redemption in the African Context
The book explores the implications of the gospel for traditional African fears of occult aggression. It analyses such traditional approaches to suffering and biblical responses to fears of demonic evil, concluding with an evaluation of African beliefs from the perspective of the gospel.
1999 / 0-85364-830-1 / xviii + 450pp

Andrew Goddard
Living the Word, Resisting the World
The Life and Thought of Jacques Ellul
This work offers a definitive study of both the life and thought of the French Reformed thinker Jacques Ellul (1912-1994). It will prove an indispensable resource for those interested in this influential theologian and sociologist and for Christian ethics and political thought generally.
2002 / 1-84227-053-2 / xxiv + 378pp

David Hilborn
The Words of our Lips
Language-Use in Free Church Worship
Studies of liturgical language have tended to focus on the written canons of Roman Catholic and Anglican communities. By contrast, David Hilborn analyses the more extemporary approach of English Nonconformity. Drawing on recent developments in linguistic pragmatics, he explores similarities and differences between 'fixed' and 'free' worship, and argues for the interdependence of each.
***2006** / 0-85364-977-4 / approx. 350pp*

Roger Hitching
The Church and Deaf People
A Study of Identity, Communication and Relationships with Special Reference to the Ecclesiology of Jürgen Moltmann
In *The Church and Deaf People* Roger Hitching sensitively examines the history and present experience of deaf people and finds similarities between aspects of sign language and Moltmann's theological method that 'open up' new ways of understanding theological concepts.
2003 / 1-84227-222-5 / xxii + 236pp

July 2005

John G. Kelly
One God, One People
The Differentiated Unity of the People of God in the Theology of Jürgen Moltmann

The author expounds and critiques Moltmann's doctrine of God and highlights the systematic connections between it and Moltmann's influential discussion of Israel. He then proposes a fresh approach to Jewish–Christian relations building on Moltmann's work using insights from Habermas and Rawls.

2005 / 0-85346-969-3 / approx. 350pp

Mark F.W. Lovatt
Confronting the Will-to-Power
A Reconsideration of the Theology of Reinhold Niebuhr

Confronting the Will-to-Power is an analysis of the theology of Reinhold Niebuhr, arguing that his work is an attempt to identify, and provide a practical theological answer to, the existence and nature of human evil.

2001 / 1-84227-054-0 / xviii + 216pp

Neil B. MacDonald
Karl Barth and the Strange New World within the Bible
Barth, Wittgenstein, and the Metadilemmas of the Enlightenment

Barth's discovery of the strange new world within the Bible is examined in the context of Kant, Hume, Overbeck, and, most importantly, Wittgenstein. MacDonald covers some fundamental issues in theology today: epistemology, the final form of the text and biblical truth-claims.

2000 / 0-85364-970-7 / xxvi + 374pp

Keith A. Mascord
Alvin Plantinga and Christian Apologetics

This book draws together the contributions of the philosopher Alvin Plantinga to the major contemporary challenges to Christian belief, highlighting in particular his ground-breaking work in epistemology and the problem of evil. Plantinga's theory that both theistic and Christian belief is warrantedly basic is explored and critiqued, and an assessment offered as to the significance of his work for apologetic theory and practice.

2005 / 1-84227-256-X / approx. 304pp

Gillian McCulloch
The Deconstruction of Dualism in Theology
With Reference to Ecofeminist Theology and New Age Spirituality
This book challenges eco-theological anti-dualism in Christian theology, arguing that dualism has a twofold function in Christian religious discourse. Firstly, it enables us to express the discontinuities and divisions that are part of the process of reality. Secondly, dualistic language allows us to express the mysteries of divine transcendence/immanence and the survival of the soul without collapsing into monism and materialism, both of which are problematic for Christian epistemology.
2002 / 1-84227-044-3 / xii + 282pp

Leslie McCurdy
Attributes and Atonement
The Holy Love of God in the Theology of P.T. Forsyth
Attributes and Atonement is an intriguing full-length study of P.T. Forsyth's doctrine of the cross as it relates particularly to God's holy love. It includes an unparalleled bibliography of both primary and secondary material relating to Forsyth.
1999 / 0-85364-833-6 / xiv + 328pp

Nozomu Miyahira
Towards a Theology of the Concord of God
A Japanese Perspective on the Trinity
This book introduces a new Japanese theology and a unique Trinitarian formula based on the Japanese intellectual climate: three betweennesses and one concord. It also presents a new interpretation of the Trinity, a co-subordinationism, which is in line with orthodox Trinitarianism; each single person of the Trinity is eternally and equally subordinate (or serviceable) to the other persons, so that they retain the mutual dynamic equality.
2000 / 0-85364-863-8 / xiv + 256pp

Eddy José Muskus
The Origins and Early Development of Liberation Theology in Latin America
With Particular Reference to Gustavo Gutiérrez
This work challenges the fundamental premise of Liberation Theology, 'opting for the poor', and its claim that Christ is found in them. It also argues that Liberation Theology emerged as a direct result of the failure of the Roman Catholic Church in Latin America.
2002 / 0-85364-974-X / xiv + 296pp

Jim Purves
The Triune God and the Charismatic Movement
A Critical Appraisal from a Scottish Perspective

All emotion and no theology? Or a fundamental challenge to reappraise and realign our trinitarian theology in the light of Christian experience? This study of charismatic renewal as it found expression within Scotland at the end of the twentieth century evaluates the use of Patristic, Reformed and contemporary models of the Trinity in explaining the workings of the Holy Spirit.

2004 / 1-84227-321-3 / xxiv + 246pp

Anna Robbins
Methods in the Madness
Diversity in Twentieth-Century Christian Social Ethics

The author compares the ethical methods of Walter Rauschenbusch, Reinhold Niebuhr and others. She argues that unless Christians are clear about the ways that theology and philosophy are expressed practically they may lose the ability to discuss social ethics across contexts, let alone reach effective agreements.

2004 / 1-84227-211-X / xx + 294pp

Ed Rybarczyk
Beyond Salvation
Eastern Orthodoxy and Classical Pentecostalism on Becoming Like Christ

At first glance eastern Orthodoxy and classical Pentecostalism seem quite distinct. This ground-breaking study shows they share much in common, especially as it concerns the experiential elements of following Christ. Both traditions assert that authentic Christianity transcends the wooden categories of modernism.

2004 / 1-84227-144-X / xii + 356pp

Signe Sandsmark
Is World View Neutral Education Possible and Desirable?
A Christian Response to Liberal Arguments
(Published jointly with The Stapleford Centre)

This book discusses reasons for belief in world view neutrality, and argues that 'neutral' education will have a hidden, but strong world view influence. It discusses the place for Christian education in the common school.

2000 / 0-85364-973-1 / xiv + 182pp

Hazel Sherman
Reading Zechariah
The Allegorical Tradition of Biblical Interpretation through the Commentary of Didymus the Blind and Theodore of Mopsuestia
A close reading of the commentary on Zechariah by Didymus the Blind alongside that of Theodore of Mopsuestia suggests that popular categorising of Antiochene and Alexandrian biblical exegesis as 'historical' or 'allegorical' is inadequate and misleading.
2005 / 1-84227-213-6 / approx. 280pp

Andrew Sloane
On Being a Christian in the Academy
Nicholas Wolterstorff and the Practice of Christian Scholarship
An exposition and critical appraisal of Nicholas Wolterstorff's epistemology in the light of the philosophy of science, and an application of his thought to the practice of Christian scholarship.
2003 / 1-84227-058-3 / xvi + 274pp

Damon W.K. So
Jesus' Revelation of His Father
A Narrative-Conceptual Study of the Trinity with Special Reference to Karl Barth
This book explores the trinitarian dynamics in the context of Jesus' revelation of his Father in his earthly ministry with references to key passages in Matthew's Gospel. It develops from the exegeses of these passages a non-linear concept of revelation which links Jesus' communion with his Father to his revelatory words and actions through a nuanced understanding of the Holy Spirit, with references to K. Barth, G.W.H. Lampe, J.D.G. Dunn and E. Irving.
2005 / 1-84227-323-X / approx. 380pp

Daniel Strange
The Possibility of Salvation Among the Unevangelised
An Analysis of Inclusivism in Recent Evangelical Theology
For evangelical theologians the 'fate of the unevangelised' impinges upon fundamental tenets of evangelical identity. The position known as 'inclusivism', defined by the belief that the unevangelised can be ontologically saved by Christ whilst being epistemologically unaware of him, has been defended most vigorously by the Canadian evangelical Clark H. Pinnock. Through a detailed analysis and critique of Pinnock's work, this book examines a cluster of issues surrounding the unevangelised and its implications for christology, soteriology and the doctrine of revelation.
2002 / 1-84227-047-8 / xviii + 362pp

Scott Swain
God According to the Gospel
Biblical Narrative and the Identity of God in the Theology of Robert W. Jenson
Robert W. Jenson is one of the leading voices in contemporary Trinitarian theology. His boldest contribution in this area concerns his use of biblical narrative both to ground and explicate the Christian doctrine of God. *God According to the Gospel* critically examines Jenson's proposal and suggests an alternative way of reading the biblical portrayal of the triune God.
2006 / 1-84227-258-6 / approx. 180pp

Justyn Terry
The Justifying Judgement of God
A Reassessment of the Place of Judgement in the Saving Work of Christ
The argument of this book is that judgement, understood as the whole process of bringing justice, is the primary metaphor of atonement, with others, such as victory, redemption and sacrifice, subordinate to it. Judgement also provides the proper context for understanding penal substitution and the call to repentance, baptism, eucharist and holiness.
2005 / 1-84227-370-1 / approx. 274 pp

Graham Tomlin
The Power of the Cross
Theology and the Death of Christ in Paul, Luther and Pascal
This book explores the theology of the cross in St Paul, Luther and Pascal. It offers new perspectives on the theology of each, and some implications for the nature of power, apologetics, theology and church life in a postmodern context.
1999 / 0-85364-984-7 / xiv + 344pp

Adonis Vidu
Postliberal Theological Method
A Critical Study
The postliberal theology of Hans Frei, George Lindbeck, Ronald Thiemann, John Milbank and others is one of the more influential contemporary options. This book focuses on several aspects pertaining to its theological method, specifically its understanding of background, hermeneutics, epistemic justification, ontology, the nature of doctrine and, finally, Christological method.
2005 / 1-84227-395-7 / approx. 324pp

Graham J. Watts
Revelation and the Spirit
A Comparative Study of the Relationship between the Doctrine of Revelation and Pneumatology in the Theology of Eberhard Jüngel and of Wolfhart Pannenberg
The relationship between revelation and pneumatology is relatively unexplored. This approach offers a fresh angle on two important twentieth century theologians and raises pneumatological questions which are theologically crucial and relevant to mission in a postmodern culture.
2005 / 1-84227-104-0 / xxii + 232pp

Nigel G. Wright
Disavowing Constantine
Mission, Church and the Social Order in the Theologies of John Howard Yoder and Jürgen Moltmann
This book is a timely restatement of a radical theology of church and state in the Anabaptist and Baptist tradition. Dr Wright constructs his argument in dialogue and debate with Yoder and Moltmann, major contributors to a free church perspective.
2000 / 0-85364-978-2 / xvi + 252pp

Paternoster
9 Holdom Avenue,
Bletchley,
Milton Keynes MK1 1QR,
United Kingdom
Web: www.authenticmedia.co.uk/paternoster

www.ingramcontent.com/pod-product-compliance
Lightning Source LLC
Chambersburg PA
CBHW052129010526
44113CB00034B/1044